WAYNESBURG COLLEGE LIBRARY
WAYNESBURG, PA.

364.148　　　　　　　　　　　　　　　　R486h
Ribton-Turner, Charles James
A history of vagrants and vagrancy
100881

MAR 1 '74

DISCARDED

A HISTORY OF

VAGRANTS AND VAGRANCY

AND

BEGGARS AND BEGGING

PATTERSON SMITH REPRINT SERIES IN
CRIMINOLOGY, LAW ENFORCEMENT, AND SOCIAL PROBLEMS
A listing of publications in the SERIES *will be found at rear of volume*

Publication No. 138: Patterson Smith Reprint Series in
Criminology, Law Enforcement, and Social Problems

A HISTORY OF
VAGRANTS AND VAGRANCY
AND
BEGGARS AND BEGGING

BY

C. J. RIBTON-TURNER

ILLUSTRATED

MONTCLAIR, NEW JERSEY
PATTERSON SMITH
1972

First published 1887 by Chapman & Hall Ltd.
Reprinted 1972 by arrangement
by Patterson Smith Publishing Corporation
Montclair, New Jersey 07042

Library of Congress Cataloging in Publication Data
Ribton-Turner, Charles James.
    A history of vagrants and vagrancy, and beggars and begging.

    (Patterson Smith reprint series in criminology, law enforcement, and social problems. Publication no. 138)
    Reprint of the 1887 ed.
    "Law texts cited": p.
    1. Tramps—Gt. Brit.—History. 2. Begging—Gt. Brit.—History. 3. Vagrancy—Gt. Brit.—History. I. Title.
HV4546.R6 1972   364.14′8′0942   75-129315
ISBN 0-87585-138-X

This book is printed on
permanent/durable paper

Dedicated

TO

THE EARL OF LICHFIELD

UNDER WHOSE KIND AUSPICES

THE STUDIES

WHICH HAVE RESULTED IN THE PRESENT WORK

WERE FIRST UNDERTAKEN.

PREFACE.

"De mendico male meretur qui ei dat quod edit aut quod bibat,
 Nam et illud quod dat perdit et illi producit vitam ad miseriam."
                              PLAUTUS (*Trinummus*, Act II. Sc. 2).

"He deserves ill of a beggar who gives him to eat or to drink,
 For he both loses that which he gives and prolongs for the other a life of misery."

IN the course of collecting materials for a history of vagrancy and begging I have become conscious of the magnitude of the subject I have undertaken, and that to describe fully from the earliest period the condition of the outcasts of society involves an account of the social and political struggles of the lower classes to emancipate themselves. To trace out, in fact, the vicissitudes of the servile classes from the time they are servile by inheritance or by destiny, until they become free members of society, and leave only a remnant who are servile or abject from choice, and whose history becomes a record of hypocrisy, humbug, and habitual idleness.

I have endeavoured, during a long period of research, to gather together all the most noteworthy particulars regarding the homeless wanderer, and the beggar and vagabond, derivable from the laws, from historical records, and from the most trustworthy contemporaries or commentators of the periods I have attempted to illustrate.

To bring the work within as moderate a compass as possible, consistently with the requirements of the subject, has necessitated the omission of much that would otherwise have extended it considerably, on numerous interesting and relevant collateral issues, both social and political, many of which, happily, have already been treated by abler pens than mine, and those that remain are not likely to slumber long in the face of the vivid interest now manifested in all questions affecting the poorer classes. Such as it is, the work is now brought to a conclusion.

The pleasantest part of my task, however, yet remains, and that is to endeavour to express my gratitude to the numerous friends and correspondents who have given me valuable aid towards the accomplishment of my work. Those only who have engaged in similar pursuits can estimate the time and research often requisite to verify a few facts or dates which occupy a space wholly incommensurate with the amount of labour they have entailed. Hence it arises that my obligations are frequently very great for what appears upon the surface to be a very small amount of assistance.

To the courteous kindness of VISCOUNT LYONS, H.M.'s Ambassador at Paris, I am indebted for much valuable information regarding France. To that of EARL GRANVILLE and of LORD EDMOND FITZMAURICE for the graphic reports on vagrancy and mendicity in Germany and Austria-Hungary, of MR. C. S. SCOTT and MR. VICTOR DRUMMOND. To that of MR. C. I. ELTON, Q.C., M.P., for the revision of the translation of the ancient laws of England; and here I may observe parenthetically that an English rendering of the perplexing jargon in which our oldest statutes are couched, and which by courtesy is termed Latin, is much to be desired, as well as a revision of the already existing translation of our Norman-French laws. To SIR EDGAR MACCULLOCH, Bailiff of Guernsey, and my friend DR. EDWIN PEARS, of Constantinople, I am wholly indebted for the accounts of vagrancy and mendicity in Guernsey and Turkey respectively. To MR. HUGH OWEN, of the English Local Government Board, and to MR. W. D. WODSWORTH, of the Irish Local Government Board, I owe much valuable official matter. To Sir W. L. DRINKWATER, first Deemster of the Isle of Man, I am under obligations for information regarding the laws of the island. SIR GEORGE BERTRAM, Bailiff of Jersey, has been kind enough to revise the translation of the laws of that island. CAPTAIN MONRO, Inspector of Constabulary in Scotland, LIEUT.-COLONEL PAUL, Chief Constable of the Isle of Man, and GENERAL WRAY, Lieut.-Governor of Jersey, have each furnished me with valuable information regarding the existing condition of vagrancy and mendicity in their respective localities.

PREFACE.

Mr. CULLINAN, of the Irish Secretary's Office, has been good enough to supply the repeals of numerous Irish statutes.

Mr. SCARGILL-BIRD and Mr. OVEREND have each helped me with information from the Record Office. To Mr. DOUGLAS, the Master of the Marylebone Workhouse, I owe many interesting details. Mr. BEDFORD, of the Marylebone Union, and Mr. VALLANCE, of the Whitechapel Union, have each aided me with serviceable information.

Mr. EGERTON PHILLIMORE has been kind enough to revise the translation of the Welsh laws. Mr. SHERIFF SPENS, of Glasgow, has kindly answered queries regarding the Scotch laws. To my friend the REV. M. S. A. WALROND I owe many useful pieces of information, and my friend Mr. OSBORN WALFORD has assisted me with suggestions which have lightened many of my researches.

In more general terms I have to express my obligations to COLONEL SIR E. Y. HENDERSON, late Chief Commissioner of the Metropolitan Police; to MR. C. S. LOCH, of the Charity Organisation Society; MR. W. H. FORBES, of Balliol College, Oxford; MR. COSTEKER, of the Reformatory and Industrial Schools Department; MR. W. M. HENNESSY, of the Irish Record Office; MR. GOMM, of the Mendicity Society; and to the following Chief Constables of counties who have also kindly assisted me:—

MR. A. PORTER, of Roxburghshire; CAPTAIN RUSSELL, of the West Riding of Yorkshire; ADMIRAL CHRISTIAN, of Gloucestershire; CAPTAIN AMYATT, of Dorsetshire; COLONEL BLANDY, of Berkshire. The following officers of Trades Unions have also favoured me with information:—MR. JOSEPH ARCH, MR. JOHN BURNETT, MR. WILLIAM HANCOCK, MR. PETER SHORROCKS, and MR. EDWARD WOODS.

MR. JOHN MURRAY has kindly given me permission to make extracts from Borrow's valuable work on the Gypsies.

To those correspondents, several hundreds in number, who have favoured me with answers to isolated inquiries, I would offer publicly, as I have already done privately, my hearty acknowledgments for their kindness.

C. J. R.-T.

BRIEF SYNOPSIS OF

CONTENTS.

CHAPTER I.
368—1066.

The early denizens of England—The Attacotti—Condition of bond slaves under the Anglo-Saxons—The laws of Hlothære and Eadric regarding the entertainment of strangers—The chapman—Laws of King Ine—Fugitive ceorls—Laws of King Wihtræd—Wandering monks—Ordinances of Archbishop Ecgbert—Ecclesiastical alms and relief to travellers—Hospitality of the Anglo-Saxons—Laws of Edward the Elder and Æthelstan—Lordless men—Penalties on those who harboured other people's dependents—Laws of Edmund—Cnut and the poor—Laws against foreign slave-dealing—The harbourage of strangers—Laws of Edward the Confessor—Causes of vagrancy during the period—Fall of the Anglo-Saxon rule 1

CHAPTER II.
1066—1272.

Results of the Norman Conquest—Condition of bond slaves—Laws of William the Conqueror—Incentives to nomadic life under William II.—Laws of Henry I.—The 'Wargus' or Social Outcast—Foreign vagabonds in England—Condition of the lower classes—The troubles of the reign of King Stephen and their consequences—Action of the clergy—Accession of Henry II.—Incursions of the Welsh and Scotch—The assizes of Clarendon and Northampton—Law of 1180—The foreign slave-trade—Condition of vagabondage under Richard I.—The forest laws and their effects—Social effects of the reign of Henry III.—Causes of vagrancy during the period 18

CHAPTER III.
1272—1509.

Accession of Edward I.—Ordinance against bards and vagabonds in Wales—Condition of the Welsh border—Laws against robbers and strangers in towns—Regulations respecting highways—Vagabondism in the City of London—Social state of the country under Edward II.—Sir Gosseline Denville and his band—Laws of Edward III. against

CONTENTS.

pardon for felony—The Welsh westour or unbidden guest—The black death and the statute of labourers—Prohibition on almsgiving to beggars—Prevalence of beggars on the highways—Lepers and their clack dish—Results of the attempt to regulate wages—Proclamations against vagrants in London—Staf-strikers and sturdy rogues—William Langland's description of the peasant and the beggar—Richard II. and refractory villeins—The rebellion of Wat Tiler—Measures against vagabondism—Attempts to regulate wages and their result—Provision for the impotent poor—Begging scholars of the Universities—Social state of the country—Laws of Henry IV. against Welsh vagabonds—Laws of Henry V. against Irishmen in England—Laws of Henry VI. against Irish robbers and murderers in England—The rebellion of Jack Cade—Laws of Henry VII. against beggars and vagabonds 34

CHAPTER IV.
1509—1558.

Accession of Henry VIII.—Mummers and disguised persons to be treated as vagabonds—Begging in 1521—The Court infested with beggars—The supplication for beggars—Laws against the gypsies and vagabonds and beggars—Professors of physiognomy and palmistry, and other "crafty" sciences—Forms of licence for begging—Proclamations against beggars—Excessive pasture a cause of poverty—Law against Welsh commorthas—Further legislation against vagabonds and beggars—Whipping vagrants—"The hye way to the Spyttel house"—The effects of the suppression of monasteries—Strolling players and ballad singers—Manumission of bondmen—Condition of vagabondage at the commencement of the reign of Edward VI.—Legislation under Edward VI.—Sir John Cheke on vagabondage—Proclamation against players—Further legislation—The relief of the poor—Law against tinkers and pedlars—Proclamations against vagabonds and players—Regulation of the Borders—The reign of Mary—Legislation against gypsies—Proclamation against vagabonds —Laws for the relief of the poor 70

CHAPTER V.
1558—1603.

Accession of Elizabeth—Legislation against vagabonds—Attempts to settle the rate of wages—General night search for vagabonds, beggars, and gypsies—Action of the City of London—Orders by the Lord Mayor and Aldermen—Returns of vagrants apprehended—Renewed legislation—Licences to beg—Sir Thomas More on Irish and Welsh vagabondage—The privileges of John Dutton and his heirs—Causes of the legislation against stage-players and bearwards—Beggars at Bath and Buxton—Renewed search for vagabonds—Final manumission of bond-slaves—Repression of vagrancy in the City—Internal management of Houses of Correction—Number of rogues and vagabonds—Repressive measures in the City—Treatment of vagrants at the house of a great nobleman —Proclamations against vagrants—Further legislation—Small tenements and beggars—Observance of fish days enjoined as a means of preventing idleness—State of vagabondism in 1596—Further legislation for the relief of the poor and repression of vagrancy—The Border laws—Begging soldiers and mariners 100

CONTENTS. xiii

CHAPTER VI.
1603—1660.

PAGE

Accession of James I.—Proclamation against vagabonds and order for their deportation—Legislation against vagrants—Plague infected persons treated as vagabonds—Stanleye's remedy for beggars and robbers—Estimated number of idle vagrants—The whipping of vagrants—Proclamation against overcrowding—Legislation of 1609-10—Deportation of vagrants to Virginia—Action of the City of London—Issue of copper farthings or tokens—Levy of vagrants as soldiers for the war in the Palatinate—Reign of Charles I.—Irish vagabonds—Commission of 1630 for putting in execution the laws for the relief of the poor and the suppression of vagrancy—Beggars in the City—Legislation by the Long Parliament—Acts against Players—Prynne's *Histrio-Mastix*—Proclamations in the City—Law of 1656 132

CHAPTER VII.
1660—1713.

Accession of Charles II.—Disbandment of the army—The law of settlement—Speech of the King regarding beggars—Results of the new law—Captain Graunt on beggars—Sir Matthew Hale on workhouses—Proclamations against vagrants and beggars and persons carrying combustible matters—Pretended lunatics—Alterations of the law of settlement under James II. and William III.—Highwaymen—The poor receiving relief to wear badges—Bandying about of the poor—Mr. John Cary on the wholesome effect of workhouses—Demoralising results of passing beggars home—Estimate of the dependent classes—Depravity of beggar children—Legislation under Anne—Consolidation of the laws against vagrants and beggars in 1713 162

CHAPTER VIII.
1713—1760.

Accession of George I.—Inquiry by the House of Commons into the expenditure on the poor in London in 1715—Metropolitan mendicity in 1716—Legislation against idlers under 21, and persons deserting their wives or families—End-gatherers treated as vagabonds—Mr. Joshua Gee on the employment of the poor—Condition of workhouses—State of mendicity and crime, 1719—1734—Enactments against players and their origin—Special legislation against beggars in the city of Bath—Committee of 1735 on the poor—Legislation of 1739-40, 1743-4, and 1751-2 against vagabonds—Expulsion of vagrants from towns—Mendicity in London in 1753 183

CHAPTER IX.
1760—1820.

Accession of George III.—Persons damaging underwood, destroying quicksets, or taking bark treated as vagabonds—Report of the Committee of 1775 on vagrancy—Condition of workhouses and legislation regarding them—Persons having a criminal intent, poachers, and unlicensed dealers in lottery tickets deemed vagabonds—Abuses of the system of passing vagrants—Permission to soldiers, sailors, &c., to beg—Mendicity in London in 1796—Legislation regarding the removal of the poor—Alarming increase of vagrancy in 1814—Report of a Committee of the House of Commons—Estimate of beggars in the metropolis and their average receipts—Encouragement of idleness and vice—Common lodging-houses—Twopenny post beggars—Knocker beggars—Movable beggars—Public-houses depending for support on beggars—Impostures practised—Depravity of beggars—Irish vagrants in London—Their idleness and gains as beggars 204

CHAPTER X.

1820—1837.

Accession of George IV.—Report of the Select Committee of 1821 on vagrancy—Review of previous legislation—Abuses tolerated and frauds practised—Cozenage and fraud connected with the system of conveyance by pass—Number of vagrants passed from 1807 to 1820—Vagrant Act of 1822—The existing Vagrant Act and the additions made to it—Irish and Scotch vagrants in England, and the cost of their removal.—The Poor Law Amendment Act of 1834—Abuses connected with the removal of vagrants 228

CHAPTER XI.

1837—1848.

Accession of Victoria—Circulars of the Poor Law Commissioners—Report of 1839 by the Constabulary Commissioners relative to vagrancy—Number of vagrants, begging-letter writers, and bearers of begging letters—Habits of vagrants—The three sorts of cant—Style of living amongst tramps—Vagrancy and juvenile delinquency—Naked beggars—Ring droppers—Pretended rag sellers—Quack doctors—Umbrella menders—Turnpike sailors—Act to provide asylums for the homeless poor—Report of the Committee of 1846 on the non-establishment of these asylums—Increase of vagrancy owing to the inducements held out to agricultural labourers to migrate to large and populous towns—Irish vagrants—Increase of vagrancy brought about by night refuges—Profitable character of these asylums—Revelations of "A. B."—General conduct of vagrants—Their lawless character—The Irish famine and consequent influx of poor Irish into England . . . 243

CHAPTER XII.

1848—1854.

Reports of the Poor Law Inspectors in 1848 on the existing condition of vagrancy—Character and conduct of vagrants—Immense increase of vagrancy and its causes—Description of the Irish poor in England—Effect of sending Irish vagrants home—Intercommunication amongst vagrants—Gaol a favourite resort of the vagrant—Concealment of property by tramps—Social demoralisation produced by vagrancy—Poor Law accommodation for vagrants—Report of the Committee of 1854 on the removal of the Irish and Scotch poor from England—Decrease of vagrancy in Ireland and its causes—Irish paupers sent home from Liverpool—Results of the influx of Irish poor into Liverpool 261

CHAPTER XIII.
1854—1882.

Arguments in favour of establishing industrial schools for vagrant children—Legislation of 1857—Subsequent amendments of the Industrial Schools Acts—Evasion of the maintenance of vagrants by Metropolitan Boards of Guardians—Attempted remedy by the Houseless Poor Act of 1864—Accommodation provided for vagrants—Reports on vagrancy by the Poor Law Inspectors in 1866—Character of tramps and their conduct in the vagrant ward—Estimated proportion of vagrants who devote themselves to idleness, crime, &c.—Average ages of vagrants—Arson by tramps—Systematic communication amongst them—Increase of vagrancy—Legislation of 1871—Vagrant Italian children in England—Committee of 1879 on settlement—Decrease of Irish vagrancy in England and its causes—Further increase of vagrancy and its causes—The Casual Poor Act, 1882 . 284

CHAPTER XIV.
1882—1886.

Modern begging—Its various divisions—Average earnings of beggars—The effect of free night refuges and soup kitchens—The rules of trades unions regarding travelling members—Average improvement of the working classes during the last fifty years—Various systems for the repression of vagrancy in Cumberland, Berks, Dorset, Kent, Hants, &c.—The cause of failure of the Poor Law system—Contempt of the vagrant for the inmate of the workhouse—Increased nomadic habits of the agricultural labourers.—The teachings of history regarding the vagrant—Suggested remedy for vagrancy 311

CHAPTER XV.
SCOTLAND.
968—1885.

The condition of bondmen—Vagrancy in the reigns of Duffe, Kenneth III., and David II.—Legislation under Robert II. against caterans and vagrants—Laws of James I. against sorners and beggars—Laws of James II. against masterful beggars with horses and hounds and feigned fools—Further acts of James III., IV., and V.—Laws of James VI.—The punishment of vagabonds shooting at game—Legislation against vagabondism in the Borders and Highlands—Further laws against vagabonds and beggars and gypsies—Students with weapons to have them confiscated—Masters of Coalheughs empowered to apprehend and employ vagabonds—Innkeepers not to receive masterless men, rebels at the horn, &c.—Charles I.—Complaints of the non-enforcement of the acts against beggars—Correction houses to be established—Enforcement of the laws under the Commonwealth—

xvi   CONTENTS.

Charles II.—Re-enactment of measures against vagabonds—James VII.—Magistrates of Edinburgh to purge the streets of beggars—William III.—Re-enactment of measures against vagrants—Attempts to regulate the rate of wages.—Legislation of 1845, 1862, and 1865—Account of vagrancy from 1815 to 1878.—Condition of vagrancy in 1885 334

CHAPTER XVI.
IRELAND.
450—1701.

The Brehon laws—Legislation in favour of almsgiving and against fugitives—Regulations relating to compulsory hospitality—Social condition of Ireland at the English Conquest—Laws of Edward II. against maintaining idle men and cearns—Laws of Henry VI. against coigny and livery—Laws of Henry VI. and Edward IV. allowing liege men to kill or take notorious thieves—Extortionate practices of the soldiery—Law of Elizabeth against idlers—Laws of Charles I. against rogues, vagabonds, and cosherers—Condition of the country in the reign of William III. 373

CHAPTER XVII.
IRELAND.
1701—1885.

Reign of Anne—Provision for erecting a workhouse in Dublin—Treatment of vagabonds—Act for suppressing tories, robbers, and rapparees—George I.—Act authorising vagrant children to be apprenticed to Protestant housekeepers, &c.—Evil results of the lax punishment of offenders—Acts against idle and disorderly persons in the city of Dublin— Condition of mendicity in 1729—George II.— Act to authorise the transportation of vagabonds, or their compulsory service in the fleet—Act to restrain vagrants labouring under bodily disorders—George III.—Vagrants to be kept apart from children—Condition of vagrancy in 1752—The helpless poor receiving relief to wear badges—News cryers, shoe cleaners, basket carriers from market, &c., without licence deemed vagabonds—Punishment of persons harbouring rogues—Act to authorise the detention of suspicious strangers as vagabonds—Act against unlawful oaths—Reports of the Committees of 1803 and 1828 as to existing provisions for the support of the aged and infirm poor and punishment of vagrants—Act of 1836 against persons deserting their wives or children—Meeting in 1842 on the increase of vagrancy—Act of 1847 for the repression of vagrancy—Reports of the Poor Law Inspectors on the condition of vagrancy in 1856—Number of vagrants relieved in 1870 and 1885 397

CHAPTER XVIII.
WALES.
943—1284.

The Venedotian, Dimetian, and Gwentian Codes and the Anomalous Laws relating to Gwestva dues, harbouring of guests, and description and treatment of bondmen—The fine for an offence against a homeless beggar—Welsh hospitality in the 12th century . . . 429

CONTENTS. xvii

CHAPTER XIX.
THE ISLE OF MAN AND THE CHANNEL ISLANDS.

PAGE

THE ISLE OF MAN, 1422—1885.—Reign of Henry V—No one to leave the island without a licence—All Scots to avoid the land—No man to bring in beggars or vagabonds—Reign of Elizabeth—No alien to pass without a licence—Loitering Irishwomen to be banished—Reign of Charles II.—Poor not to beg out of their parishes—Apprentices to serve for five years—Reign of Victoria—Masters of vessels bringing over paupers to be punished—Condition of mendicity 1879-85 .

JERSEY, 1669—1885.—Letters patent of Charles II. providing for the correction and restraint of vagabonds and beggars—Code of 1771—Provision for the maintenance of the poor—Infirm people to be licensed to beg—Pauper children not to be taken out of the island—Inhabitants not to receive strangers more than one night—Tavern keepers not to tolerate vagabonds—Condition of mendicity in 1885 . .

GUERNSEY, 1534—1885.—1534, penalty for harbouring strangers—1537, poor strangers to be banished—1542, young men and young women to take service—1566, orphans, &c., to be apprenticed—1566, strange servants not to be received—1583, banished criminals to quit the island—1588-9, vagabonds to quit the island—1597, infirm poor to be relieved—1611, begging without a licence forbidden—1684-5, ordinances relating to the poor and mendicants—Condition of mendicity in 1885 440

CHAPTER XX.
THE SECRET JARGON OF THE VAGRANT AND MENDICANT.

First accounts of the cant language in England—Harman's vocabulary, 1567—Constituent elements of the vocabulary—Derivation of the words beggar and rogue—Derivation of cant words from the Welsh, Gaelic, Erse, Manx, Lowland Scotch, Latin, Provincial English, Gypsy, and from foreign languages—Metaphorical terms—Modern cant 466

CHAPTER XXI.
THE MENDICANT OR BEGGING FRIARS.

Vagrant monks in the year 390—Institution of mendicant friars in 1209—John Wicliffe's opinion of them 480

CHAPTER XXII.
THE GYPSIES IN ENGLAND.

Various names by which they are known—Their origin—Arrival in England—Act of 1530-1 against them—Letter from Lord Cromwell to the President of the Marches in 1537—Letter to the Earl of Essex—Act of 1554—Arrest of Gypsies in the reign of Elizabeth—Act of 1562-3 against them—Execution of Gypsies under this Act—Letter of Mr. Hext regarding them in 1596—Subsequent history according to Borrow—Description of the Gypsies in the years 1858-9 . . . 483

CHAPTER XXIII.

SWEDEN, DENMARK, BELGIUM, AND HOLLAND.

SWEDEN.—New Poor Law of 1871 as to beggars and mendicant children— Definition of vagabonds and vagrants—Nature of their punishment— Number of vagabonds in gaols and Houses of Correction and employed on public works in 1876 . . . .
DENMARK.—Punishment of vagrants—Numbers imprisoned for vagrancy from 1871 to 1880 . . . .
BELGIUM, 1808—1870.—Law as to vagrants and beggars—Suppression of free admission to the depôt de mendicité in 1848—New law of 1866 —Population of the depôts de mendicité 1840 to 1870 . . .
HOLLAND.—Present penal laws as to beggars and vagrants—Beggars' institutions 507

CHAPTER XXIV.

FRANCE.

570—1885.

Ordinance of the 2nd Council of Tours—Ordinances of St. Louis—Edict of John in 1350—Rôdeurs de filles under Charles VIII.—Measures of repression under François I.—Edict of Henri II.—Description of the various orders of mendicants—Ordinances of Louis XIII.—Suppression of the Cours des Miracles by Louis XIV.—Action of the National Assembly—Decree of 1809—Depôts de Mendicité—Circulars issued by the Ministry of the Interior to the Préfets in 1864, 1872, 1874, and 1881—Results of the inquiries instituted in consequence of the circular of 1881—The four classes of vagabonds—Steps recommended by the Préfets for the repression of vagabondage—Report of a Special Committee to the National Assembly in 1873—Census of vagabondage—Table of vagabondage 517

CHAPTER XXV.

THE GERMAN EMPIRE.

1497—1885.

Historical introduction—Imperial penal code—Societies for the suppression of mendicity—Absence of official statistics—Increase of vagrancy 1874—1884—Its probable causes—Abnormal demand for labour 1871 —1874—Large number of labourers eventually thrown out of work— Abolition of passes for the interior—Reform of poor laws—Present state of vagrancy not sensibly affected by the state of the labour market—Change for the worse in the present type of vagrants— Reports from country districts—Encouragements to vagabondage— Indiscriminate almsgiving—Alleged negligence of local police— Wayside inns—Statistics from Bavaria, Saxony, and Prussia—Large proportion of juvenile vagrants—Estimate of average number of vagrants in Germany—Proportion of irreclaimable and reclaimable vagabonds—Remedial measures—Vagabondage in Saxe-Coburg and Gotha, Leipzig, Bavaria, and Baden—The description of beggars in the *Liber Vagatorum* edited by Martin Luther in 1528 . 535

CONTENTS. xix

CHAPTER XXVI.
AUSTRIA.

Vagabonds and beggars in Vienna—Municipal and charitable institutions—Municipal workhouse—Police shelter refuge for the homeless—Mendicity Society—Results obtained—Vagrants sent home from Vienna—Vagrants returned to Vienna—Vagrancy in the country—Proposed remedial measures 547

CHAPTER XXVII.
ITALY.
1586—1872.

Law of 1586 regarding vagrants and beggars—Former attempt at repression— The Company of St. Elizabeth, or Beggars' Guild—The "forty hours"—Description of the orders of beggars by Giacinto Nobili in 1627—The tricks of the *Bianti* in Sicily—Their punishment by the Duke of Sessa 553

CHAPTER XXVIII.
RUSSIA, PORTUGAL, AND TURKEY.

RUSSIA.—Low standard of comfort of the Russian peasantry—Mendicity among the urban population and its causes—Committee for the relief of beggars in St. Petersburg—Treatment of beggars in Moscow, Odessa, Finland, Revel and Poland . . . . .
PORTUGAL.—General condition of mendicity . . . . .
TURKEY.—Organisation for the relief of the poor—Professional beggars—Begging dervishes—Incentives to almsgiving—Feigned madmen—Beggars at mosques—Administration of the Imarets and Evcaf—Christian charity in Turkey— Precepts of the Koran regarding charity—Sayings of the prophet regarding almsgiving and charity . 566

CHAPTER XXIX.

EXTRACTS FROM VARIOUS WRITERS ILLUSTRATING THE HABITS AND IMPOSTURES OF THE VAGRANT AND BEGGAR.
1383—1567.

CHAUCER, The Begging Friar and the Pardoner (1383)—FOXE, The Blind Impostor (circa 1430—35)—LYDGATE, The Foolish Penniless Beggar (circa 1430)—SKELTON and the beggar (circa 1490)—SAMUEL ROWLANDS, The Runnagate Race, a History of Rogues from 1450 to 1534—ALEXANDER BARCLAY, Of Foolish Beggars and their Vanities (1508)—DUNBAR, The Excess of Beggars (1509)—HENRY WATSON, Of Beggars and their Vanities (1517)—JAMES V. OF SCOTLAND, The Gaberlunyie Man (circa 1530—40)—SIR DAVID LYNDSAY, The Pardoner (circa 1539)—A Begging Letter in 1542—HUGH LATYMER, On Valiant Beggars (1552)—The Fraternity of Vagabonds (1561)—THOMAS HARMAN, A Caveat or Warning for Common Cursetors (1567) 576

CONTENTS.

CHAPTER XXX.

EXTRACTS FROM VARIOUS WRITERS ILLUSTRATING THE HABITS AND IMPOSTURES OF THE VAGRANT AND BEGGAR.

1610—1700.

SAMUEL ROWLANDS, Slang Beggars' Songs (1610)—SIR THOMAS OVERBURY, A Tinker and a Canting Rogue (1616)—BEN JONSON, The Masque of the Gypsies metamorphosed (1621)—JOHN FLETCHER, The Beggars' Bush (1622)—The Song of the Beggar (1629)—The Cunning Northern Beggar (1635)—RICHARD BROME, A Jovial Crew, or the Merry Beggars (1641)—The Beggars' Chorus in the Jovial Crew (1641)—The Tinker and the Beggar (1661)—RICHARD HEAD, Meriton Latroon, a Complete History of the most Eminent Cheats of both Sexes (1665)—The Jovial Crew or Beggars' Bush (1671)—Supplementary verses to the Jovial Crew, styled the Beggar's Song (1700)—DANIEL DEFOE, The Complete Mendicant (1699) 601

CHAPTER XXXI.

EXTRACTS FROM VARIOUS WRITERS ILLUSTRATING THE HABITS AND IMPOSTURES OF THE VAGRANT AND BEGGAR.

1708—1875.

Memoirs of the right villainous JOHN HALL (1708)—The Lazy Beggar (1731)—G. PARKER, Illustrations of Low Life (1781)—FRANCIS GROSE, Beggars and Vagrant Impostors (1796)—J. T. SMITH, Vagabondiana (1817)—WILLIAM HONE, Anty Brignal and the Begging Quaker (1827)—JOHN BADCOCK, Beggars and Tinkers (1828)—W. A. MILES, Poverty, Mendicity, and Crime (1839)—Letters from GEORGE ATKINS BRINE (1848, 1871, 1875)—CHARLES DICKENS, The Begging Letter Writer and Tramps (1850)—HENRY MAYHEW, London Labour and the London Poor—The Patterer—The Screever—Beggar Streetsellers (1851)—A Blind Impostor (1865)—J. HORNSBY WRIGHT, Confessions of an Old Almsgiver (1871)—A. H. TOULMIN, Rogues and Vagabonds of the Racecourse (1872)—Pseudo Missionaries (1872)— Rich Beggars—Frozen-out Beggars—Beggars' Barns—Gypsy anecdote—Begging Letter Impostures (1874) 625

CHAPTER XXXII.

L'Envoyé 666

STATISTICS 673

SYNOPTICAL TABLE OF LAWS QUOTED, ENGLISH, SCOTCH, IRISH, WELSH, MANX, JERSEYIAN AND GUERNSEYIAN 675

INDEX 703

LIST OF ILLUSTRATIONS.

SIR GOSSELINE DENVILLE AND HIS BAND LISTENING TO THE DOMINICAN MONK . . . . *to face page* 40
STOCKS AT THE WEST RIDING COURT-HOUSE AT BRADFORD . . 48
METOPOSCOPY 76
PHYSIOGNOMY 180
WHIPPING STOCKS AT WALTHAM ABBEY 205
PALMISTRY, OR CHIROMANCY 236
WILLIAM READ 257
A SPURIOUS DOCUMENT 312
STOCKING AND WHIPPING 488
BEGGARS 520
FOOLISH BEGGARS AND THEIR VANITIES 586
THE CUNNING NORTHERN BEGGAR 610
THE SOLDIER AND HIS DOXY; AND THE POET BETWEEN HIS TWO DEBORAHS 632
A CADGERS' RESORT 636
GEORGE ATKINS BRINE; AND WALTER SCOTT 640
POTATO HOOK; INSTRUMENT FOR REMOVING CLOTHES-PINS; THE BULLY TRAMP AND JOLLY TRAMP 654
THE LUBBERLY TRAMP; THE UNWHOLESOME TRAMP; THE ABJECT TRAMP; AND MRS. TRAMP 658
A SPURIOUS DOCUMENT 664
NICOLAS GENINGS, THE BEGGING IMPOSTOR 666

VAGRANTS AND VAGRANCY.

CHAPTER I.

A.D. 368 — 1066.

The early denizens of England—The Attacotti—Condition of bond slaves under the Anglo-Saxons—The laws of Hlothære and Eadric regarding the entertainment of strangers—The chapman—Laws of King Ine—Fugitive ceorls—Laws of King Wihtræd—Wandering monks—Ordinances of Archbishop Ecgbert—Ecclesiastical alms and relief to travellers—Hospitality of the Anglo-Saxons—Laws of Edward the Elder and Æthelstan—Lordless men—Penalties on those who harboured other people's dependents—Laws of Edmund—Cnut and the poor—Laws against foreign slave-dealing—The harbourage of strangers—Laws of Edward the Confessor—Cause of vagrancy during the period—Fall of the Anglo-Saxon rule.

As a necessary prelude to the subject before us, we must in the first instance take a cursory glance at the constituent elements of the population of England during its early history.

Geological investigation has established that in the dim past these islands were inhabited by a race who, so far as research has yet gone, appears to have left no traces either in our language or in our local nomenclature. This race, which was of Iberic or Basque type, was small in stature and dark in complexion. It was conquered and with occasional exceptions, such as the tribe of the Silures, brought into subjection by an invading immigration of Gaels, the earliest race of whom there are any linguistic traces in the country, and whose course from the plains of India to Brita*n*nia*

---

* It would be out of place here to enter into a disquisition on the origin of the name of *Britain*, but a careful study of all the known forms of the word and its permutations induces a very strong belief that it springs from the *Gael*. *Breas tàn*, the "great land." This would be quite in harmony with the statement of *Dion Cassius*, "that it had been a disputed point whether the land was a continent or an island." Independently even of this it was the largest island known to the ancients, and compared with the Scillies or with Ireland it would emphatically be the "Great land."

may be traced in various countries by means of the suffix *tan*,*
the equivalent of the Sanskrit *sthâna*, a country. These invaders
were followed at an interval of time by a race whom we may term
South British, represented by the extinct Cornish language. At
a later period still, probably after the Roman occupation, came
the *Cymry* or Welsh, a third Celtic race, from Denmark (the
Chersonesus *Cimbrica*) and the south of Sweden, about *Cimbris-*
hamn, who, landing in Scotland about the parts adjacent to *Aber-*
deen, forced their way southward through *Cumber*land until, being
encountered by the opposing tide of Anglo-Saxons in the midland
counties of England, they were deflected into Wales and there
dominated or drove out the existing Gaelic and Iberic population.†

"In the age of Alfred we all know that those regions now distributed under the county names of Dorset, Wilts, Somerset,
Devon, were denominated in the Anglo-Saxon language *Weal-*
cynne, the territory or dominion of the "strangers," or Britons, a
designation which clearly shows that though the supreme authority might by arrangement under stress of conquest be in the
hands of the Wessex king, "rex totius Britanniæ," the Britons
occupied the soil and maintained virtual rule.

Even so late as the reign of Athelstan, who died A.D. 940, or
within a hundred and twenty-six years of the Norman Conquest,
Exeter, the ancient capital of the Damnonii (the people of *Dyvn-*
naint), was governed by a compromise between the two races.
The city was divided into two parts, the British part and English
part, and each had equal power in the government of the place."‡

To this may be added the fact that the South British element
probably extended northwards as far as Herefordshire, as in the
twelfth century the *Liber Llandavensis* makes mention of *Llan*
Cerniw, or the Cornish place situated on the river Dour, a tributary

* *Gael, tàn, tàin,* a country, region, territory, land.

† That there must have been a large Gaelic element in Wales at a comparatively recent period is conclusively proved by the discovery of stones bearing
Ogham inscriptions apparently as late as the seventh century in South Wales,
as well as the statement in the *Brut y Tywysogion* that the men of the south
in the year 1020 accepted *Rein a Scot* as their king; and when the King of
Gwynedd made war against him, Rein boldly led on his host *after the man-*
ner of the Scots. Moreover, most of the classical names of the tribes in Britain
are undoubtedly of Gaelic origin, *e.g. Atrebatii* from *Aitreabhach*, an inhabitant; *Cornabii* from *Cornaveagh*, the raven's hill; *Mona* from *Muine*, a brake or
shrubbery.

‡ Nicholas.

of the Wye, which seems to indicate an outlying Cornish settlement there.

The subject people in Anglo-Saxon times were therefore composed of at least three races. The Iberians, who had been subjected by the Gaels, the Gaels themselves, and the South British race.

The earliest reference to vagabondage in the British Isles is to be met with in the Roman History of *Ammianus Marcellinus* under the year 368, when he states, " That at that time the Picts, who were divided into two nations, the Dicalydonas * and the Verturiones,† and likewise the Attacotti, a very warlike people, and the Scots, were all roving over different parts of the country and committing great ravages." These Attacotti are identified by the Irish annalists with the Aitheach-Tuatha, which signifies, according to O'Curry, the rent-paying tribes or people, and they are said to have risen against their lords on account of the exorbitant exactions levied upon them to support their prodigal entertainments, exactions which in later times were known under the name of coshering. Perhaps also their treatment as slaves may, as in later times, have had something to say to the uprising, since *Strabo* informs us that the Britons were in the habit of *exporting slaves* to Gaul, and *Cicero* says that Cæsar could not find an ounce of silver or other spoil *except slaves* in Britain.

Beyond this, prior to the arrival of the Saxons, we have, generally speaking, few authentic records of the social history of Britain, and the history of England during the period of the Saxon domination is itself a mere meagre record of events. Our knowledge of vagrancy in those times can therefore as a rule only be deduced inferentially from an examination of such laws as have been handed down to us, for since it may ordinarily be accepted as an axiom that laws are not made in anticipation of evils which may occur, but to remedy such as are proved to exist, we may safely assume that vagrancy did exist on an extensive scale in Saxon times, and that otherwise we should not find laws dealing with it in the Statute Book. The lowest classes of the population were at that time sunk in bondage, in slavery as absolute as it is possible to conceive, and under which they were liable to

* *Calldainn* is a hazel copse. This tree was formerly held in great estimation in Ireland. Mac Cuill (" son of the hazel "), one of the three last kings of the Tuatha De Danann, was so called because he worshipped the hazel. (*Joyce*.)

† *Fir-tire* (men of the territory) ; a tribe of this name existed in Wicklow.

the uncontrolled tyranny of master or mistress without power of appeal. This population was, as we have already seen, composed of several nationalities and tongues—the Anglo-Saxons proper, themselves divided into numerous dialects and tribes; the races subject to them; and later on, towards the close of the eighth century, the Danes and Norsemen.

Slaves or *theows* were of two classes, those who were so by birth and those who became so as captives in war, or were reduced to slavery through crime, insolvency, gambling, superior legal power, voluntary surrender, or illegal violence. In addition therefore to the causes of discontent naturally arising from the lot which reduced many people to the rank of slaves, there must have been fruitful sources of discord in the enforcement of the differing customs of the half-savage tribes who then inhabited the country.

But the next in rank above the slave, the freedman or *ceorl*, suffered also from disabilities which he must often have desired to shake off. "At the earliest period of Anglo-Saxon history a *freedman* became the "man" of the master who had emancipated him, and had no right of choosing another lord, a disability which, in the opinion of the age, derogated from perfect freedom. Many powerful men therefore, when they freed their slaves, expressly gave them this right. But even in these cases the poor man was constantly robbed of his privilege on the pretence that there were debts due, or fees payable, to the lord's heir or ministers. To such an extent was this carried that, in the tenth century, the freedman had practically lost one of the most important rights that the laws professed to secure to him. Alfred the Great was probably well aware of this fact; for by his will, in which he enfranchised all his dependents, and gave them express liberty to select their future lord, he says, "I, in the name of the living God, bid that no man hinder them, either by demands of fee or any other thing, from choosing as lord whomsoever they will."

Notwithstanding, however, the efforts of Alfred, the poor freeman's right was soon completely lost. In *Domesday Book* the privilege of leaving his land and changing his lord is spoken of as one of the distinguishing marks of the gesithcundman, or demi-noble; and in *Saloman and Saturn* we read, "Lo! a wealthy noble may easily choose for himself, according to his mind, a mild lord, a prince of noble birth; but *a poor man cannot do so.*" *

* Thrupp.

Vagrancy must consequently have been a natural result of such a state of things. The fugitive, with the brand of Cain on him, was a vagrant of necessity, hunted to death like a wolf. The same may almost be said of the slave who served under a hard or cruel taskmaster or taskmistress, for even mistresses in those days sometimes whipped their female slaves to death. Add to this the restless desires of many to change their lot or to see something of the outer world, and we can form some idea of the leading causes of vagrancy.

But the position of the vagrant then was very different to what it is now. There were neither inns nor workhouses to shelter him. Monasteries there were, which could give him casual shelter, but they were far apart, too far in most instances to enable him to cover the distance in a day's journey; there were therefore only two sources of subsistence open to him, private hospitality or plunder.

The primary laws against vagrancy which we should therefore naturally expect to find on the Statute Book would be, if one may so term it, laws of single-barrelled severity against fugitive dependents, and of double-barrelled severity against fugitive dependents who had committed other infractions of the tribal code.

The first of these laws of which we have any record is that of Kings *Hlothære* and *Eadric*, who respectively reigned in Kent from 673 to 685, and from 685 to 686. This law enacts that—

"If a man entertain a stranger for three nights at his own home, a chapman, or any other that has come over the march,* and then feed him with his own food, and he then do harm to any man, let the man bring the other to justice, or do justice for him." †

The host therefore who entertained a stranger did so at the risk of incurring responsibility for any offence he might subsequently commit, but the law is silent both as to the duration of this responsibility and the mode of its enforcement.

The chapman was in Anglo-Saxon times an important personage. He was the general dealer or itinerant shopkeeper; and both for the security of his goods and for the purpose of conveying them must as a rule have had numerous attendants. He could

* Employed to denote not only the whole district occupied by one small community, but more especially those forests and wastes by which the arable was enclosed, and which separated the possessions of one tribe from those of another.
† C. 15.

be an encourager of vagrancy in two ways—by receiving and disposing of the goods of the vagrant plunderer, and by taking the fugitive, whether theow or ceorl, into his train. One of the laws of *Ine*, King of Wessex from 688 to 725, is directed against the first of these forms of delinquency.

" If a chapman traffic up among the people, let him do it before witnesses. If stolen property be attached with a chapman, and he have not bought it before good witnesses, let him prove, according to the 'wite,' * that he was neither privy (to the theft) nor thief; or pay as 'wite' xxxvi shillings." †

This was supplemented in the reign of King Alfred (871—901) by a restrictive measure upon those whom the chapman took in his train.

" It is also directed to chapmen, that they bring the men whom they take up with them before the King's reeve at the folk-mote,‡ and let it be stated how many of them there are; and let them take such men with them as they may be able afterwards to present for justice at the folk-mote; and when they have need of more men up with them on their journey, let them always declare it, as often as their need may be, to the king's reeve, in presence of the 'gemōt.'" §

At the same time it is quite possible that this law may also have been partially framed with a view to restrict the traffic in slaves, because in the famous story of *St. Gregory* and the English slaves who were brought to Rome for sale in the sixth century, *Bede*, who relates it, says that the slaves were brought by the *chapmen* among many other saleable things.

In all ages it has been found that those whose circumstances border on poverty have most sympathy with the poor; and the following law of *King Ine* appears to recognise the fact, as it forbids the ceorl who stood lowest in the ranks of freemen to harbour fugitives, and it shows inferentially that the practice prevailed extensively. This sympathy in many instances probably arose from two causes, sympathy with the oppressed and sympathy of race, as a good many ceorls and a large number of theows were without doubt of Celtic race, and would therefore have a common

---

* Mulct, fine. This was the penalty falling to the king (except in cases of alienation to others) or to the state, for violation of the law.

† C. 25. Of the journeying of chapmen up the country.

‡ A general assembly of the people, whether it was held in a city or town (burg), or consisted of the whole shire.

§ C. 34. Of Chapmen.

bond of antipathy to the Saxon lord. The law also forbids the "gesithman" to take recruits from the vagrant class.

"If a man accuse a 'ceorlish' man of harbouring a fugitive, let him clear himself according to his own 'wēr.' * If he cannot, let him pay for him according to his own 'wēr'; and the 'gesithman' † in like manner according to his 'wēr.'" ‡

The fugitive ceorl next appears as the subject of legislation in the reign of *King Ine*. The punishment which the law inflicted on him was nominally a pecuniary one; and considering that a cow or a sheep was in those days valued at a shilling, the penalty was a severe one, and could only have been paid with the assistance of his friends and kinsfolk.

"If any one go from his lord without leave, or steal himself away into another shire, and he be discovered, let him go where he was before, and pay to his lord LX shillings." §

If the ceorl failed to pay this amercement he became a *wīte-theow* or penal slave, a class condemned to slavery for crime, or from inability to pay the fines incurred for violation of the law. Should he have committed theft before he was degraded to the condition of a *wīte-theow* he was liable to a cruel whipping at the hands of his accuser, and if he fled from his master the penalty was ignominious death.

"If any man be a 'wīte-theow' newly made a 'theow,' and he be accused that he had before thieved ere he was made a 'theow,' then may the accuser have one scourging at him: let him follow him to the scourging according to his value." ‖

"If a 'wīte-theow,' an Englishman,¶ steal himself away, let him be hanged, and nothing paid to his lord. If any one slay him let nothing be paid to his kindred, if they have not redeemed him within twelve months." **

The next law, that of *Wihtrœd*,†† king of Kent from 690 to 725, is directed against wandering monks who appear even at that

* The amount payable to the relations of a murdered man as compensation for killing him, or payable by him to redeem his life when forfeited.
† A military companion or follower of an Anglo-Saxon chief or king. Some of these "gesiths" had land, others had not.
‡ C. 30. In case a "Ceorlish" man harbour a fugitive.
§ C. 39. Of going from his lord without leave.
‖ C. 48. Of wīte-theowmen.
¶ *I.e.* an *Anglo-Saxon*; a *Celt* was denominated a *Wealh*, or foreigner.
** C. 24. Of slaying a "wīte-theow."
†† *King Wihtrœd*, though a legislator, was not a scholar, as we find him about the year 700 affixing his cross to a charter which he granted, to which was added "pro ignorantia literarum."

early period to have gone about in such numbers as to need repressive legislation.

"If a shorn man go wandering about for hospitality, let it be given him once; and, unless he have leave, let it not be that any one entertain him longer." *

The ecclesiastical authorities seem also to have felt called upon to deal with the evil, as *Ecgbert*, who was Archbishop of York from 732 to 767, made the following ordinance:—

"Let not monks remove from place to place, but let them remain in the same obedience which they undertook at the time of their conversion."

These erratic habits on the part of the monks were probably engendered by the fact that for want of churches the priests had in the earliest times been accustomed in the discharge of their office to wander from place to place.

Poor laws there were none at this period; in fact, in point of theory there ought not to have been any in need of public charity, as every person of the lowest rank was by custom supposed to be the dependent of a superior rank. But there must have been ceorls who sank into poverty owing to misfortune, such as accident, famine, cattle murrain, and other causes, and who being unable to find any one in their neighbourhood able to take them into service became in danger of starvation; and again there were probably harsh and cruel masters who discarded their infirm, impotent, or superfluous servants or their children, and left them without subsistence. Being forbidden to wander, these poor people would therefore starve if no source of relief were open to them, and the only source from which they could derive it was the Church. From the time of Archbishop *Theodore* downwards, there seems to have been great need for this provision, judging from the ecclesiastical ordinances which have been handed down to us.

Archbishop *Ecgbert* says: "The priests are to take tithes of the people, and to make a written list of the names of the givers, and according to the authority of the canons they are to divide them in the presence of the men that fear God. The first part they are to take for the adornment of the church; but the second they are in all humility mercifully to distribute with their own hands for the use of the poor and strangers; the third part, however, the priests may reserve for themselves." † "Be thou gentle and

* § 7. † Excerptiones Ecgberti, Arch. Ebor. V.

charitable to the poor, zealous in almsgiving, in attendance at church, and in the giving of tithe to God's church and the poor." *

"The monasteries were open at all times and all seasons for the relief of travellers; extra buildings were provided for their reception, and officers appointed whose duty it was to see that they were liberally entertained, and that they conducted themselves discreetly." †

The duty of hospitality was also strongly inculcated by the Church, as is evident from the following ordinance of *Theodore,* Archbishop of Canterbury from 668 to 690.

"Whosoever doth not receive a sojourner into his house, as his Lord ordaineth and promiseth of the Kingdom of Heaven therefor, where He saith, ' Come ye blessed of my Father, receive the Kingdom,' for such time as he receiveth not sojourners and hath not fulfilled the commands of the gospel, and hath not washed the feet of the poor, nor done alms, so long let him do penance on bread and water, if he amend not." ‡

"The Anglo-Saxon monarchs were famous for their hospitality, particularly at festive seasons. At Christmas, Easter, and Whitsuntide they kept open house for several days, entertaining all comers, high, low, rich, and poor, and the nobles imitated their example."§

King Alfred, we are told by Asser, "bestowed alms and largesses on both natives and foreigners of all countries."

In the reign of *King Edward the Elder* (901—924) the fugitive bondsman again forms the subject of legislation.

"Let no man receive another man's man without his leave whom he before followed, and until he be blameless towards every hand. If any one so do, let him make 'bōt' ‖ my 'oferhyrnes¶." **

The reign of *Æthelstan* (924—940), whose life was, according to *William of Malmesbury,* "in time little—in deeds great," was especially fruitful in legislation.

The first enactment of this reign deals with the lordless man, or

* Confessionale Ecgberti, Arch. Ebor.
† Thrupp.
‡ Liber Penitentialis Theodori Arch. Cantuar. Eccl. XXV. Of rapine and usury, and him who doth not receive sojourners and doth not fulfil the commands of the gospel.
§ Thrupp.
‖ Compensation.
¶ Contempt in the present legal sense of the term; also the penalty attached to such contempt, the various rates of which were fixed according to the party offended.
** C. 10. Of him who receives another man's man without leave.

man without a master, for whom a master must be found and for whose appearance to answer any accusation his kindred must be responsible, otherwise he may be slain wherever he is met with.*

"And we have ordained: respecting those lordless men of whom no law can be got, that the kindred be commanded that they domicile him to folk-right,† and find him a lord in the folk-mote; and if they then will not or cannot produce him at the term, then be he thenceforth a 'flyma,'‡ and let him slay him for a thief who can come at him: and whoever after that shall harbour him, let him pay for him according to his 'wēr,' or by it clear himself." §

The next law deals with the freeman who, having deserted his original settlement, desired to return to it.

"And we have ordained: if any landless man should become a follower in another shire, and again seek his kinsfolk; that he may harbour him on this condition, that he present him to folk-right if he there do any wrong, or make 'bōt' for him. ||

The next four deal with the penalties incurred by those who

---

* The Commonwealth was knit together by the law of the "free borgh." This was a system of mutual surety, and also of mutual espial, for it rendered every man answerable for his neighbour; and consequently compelled him to watch his neighbour's acts with suspicion and jealousy. When blood was shed, the nearest townsmen were attached, and an account was required from them. The township and the hundred might be amerced for the transgressions of those who were within their Pledge. He who refused to appear in court, after lawful summons, broke the compact which bound him to the Commonwealth; he became an outlaw; he had spurned the protection of the social community, and he obtained none; his property was forfeited, he bore a "wolf's head," and he might be slain with impunity. But outlawry could not be pronounced unless by the solemn judgment of the Shire or the Burghmoot, nor until the offender had been oftentimes required to come in, and abide the sentence of the law.

The punishments of the law were rigorous. Occasionally they were mitigated by that yearning to do justice in mercy so often occasioning a painful struggle in the legislator who has subjected himself to duties which he regrets to perform. If the Criminal had taken sanctuary, he might save his life by abjuring the realm; and the white wand, which he bore in his hand whilst he was journeying to the sea-shore, protected him against all further harm. Some lives were saved by the "benefit of clergy," which substituted a severe and painful imprisonment for capital punishment. An appeal, whether of theft or murder, could not be released or pardoned by the king. But the king's justices, even in early times, greatly discouraged this vindictive remedy. They required the utmost nicety in the pleadings: and by allowing the defendant to avail himself of every technical objection which he could raise, the appellor was easily sent out of court.—PALGRAVE.

† The original, unwritten, understood compact, by which every freeman enjoyed his rights as a freeman. The common or customary law of the land.

‡ A runaway, vagabond. § I. c. 2. Of lordless men.

|| I. c. 8. Of landless men.

harbour other people's dependents without the leave of their master :—

"And let no man receive another man's man, without his leave whom he before followed. If any one so do: let him give up the man, and make 'bōt' the king's 'oferhyrnes.' And let no one dismiss his accused man from him before he has done what is right." *

"Let not any one harbour the man of another without the leave of him to whom he owed suit before, neither within nor without the mark. Moreover, let not a lord refuse soke-right † to a free man if he has him rightfully in his keeping." ‡

"And whosoever shall harbour, whether within or without the mark, the man of another who, on his ill-doing, has let him depart and is unable to punish him, let him pay to the king a hundred and twenty shillings, and let the man return to the place whence he came forth and do right to the lord whom he served before." §

"And he who receives another man's man, whom he for his evil conduct turns away from him, and whom he cannot clear of his evil, let him pay for him to him whom he before followed, and give to the king cxx shillings. But if the lord will foredo the man wrongfully; then let him clear himself, if he can, at the folkmote: and if he be innocent, let him seek whatever lord he will, in virtue of that testimony; because I grant that each of them who is innocent may follow such lord as he will. And such reeve as shall neglect this, and will not care about it, let him to pay to the king his 'oferhyrnes,' if any one truly charge it to him, and he cannot exculpate himself. And such reeve as shall take meed-money,‖ and thereby suppress another's right; let him pay the king's 'oferhyrnes,' and also bear the disgrace, so as we have ordained. And if it be a thane who shall so do, be it the like." ¶

This law pretty plainly indicates that the sheriffs frequently accepted bribes for countenancing false accusations against the dependents of the lords.

Next comes a law of *King Edmund* (940—946), which requires the host who knowingly entertains a fugitive offender to bring him to justice or to pay compensation for his misdeeds :—

* I. c. 22. Of him who receives another man's man.
† Privileges or franchises.   ‡ II. c. 4.
§ III. c. 4. Of him who harbours the man of another.
‖ A bribe, hush money.
¶ IV. c. 1. Of him who receives another man's man.

"And I will not that any one harbour the man of another before he be quit in respect of every authority that may claim right from him; and if any maintain or sustain a man to the doing of damage, let him keep him in charge to produce him to make amends, otherwise let him make good what the other ought to make good."*

We now come to the canons enacted under *King Edgar* (958— 975), which probably owe their origin to the energy of *St. Dunstan*, and which again inculcate the duty of almsgiving.

"And we enjoin, that the priests so distribute the people's alms, that they do both give pleasure to God, and accustom the people to alms."

"When a man fasts, then let the dishes that would have been eaten be all distributed to God's poor."

The *Ecclesiastical Institutes* urge the duty of almsgiving more forcibly still.

"It is daily needful for every man, that he give his alms to poor men; but yet when we fast, then ought we to give greater alms than on other days, because the meat and the drink we should then use if we did not fast, we ought to distribute to the poor. †

"A multitude of persons partook of the hospitality of the rich man's mansion who were not worthy to be admitted to his tables. These assembled at meal-times outside the gate of his house, and it was a custom to lay aside a portion of the provisions to be distributed among them, with the fragments from the table. In *Alfric's* homily for the second Sunday after Pentecost, the preacher, after dwelling on the story of Lazarus, who was spurned from the rich man's table, appeals to his Anglo-Saxon audience: "Many Lazaruses ye have now lying at your gates, begging for your superfluity." *Bede* tells us of the good King Oswald, that when he was once sitting at dinner, on Easter-day, with his bishop, having a silver dish full of dainties before him, as they were just ready to bless the bread, the servant whose duty it was to relieve the poor, came in on a sudden, and told the king that a great multitude of needy persons from all parts were sitting in the streets begging some alms of the king. The latter immediately ordered the provisions set before him to be carried to the poor, and the

---

* *Concilium Culintonense*, c 3. Of him who shall harbour the man of another or shall maintain any to another's damage. † XXXVIII.

dish to be cut in pieces and divided among them. In the picture of a Saxon house given in an old manuscript, we find the lord of the household on a sort of throne at the entrance to his hall, presiding over the distribution of his charity. This seat, generally under an arch or canopy, is often represented in the Saxon manuscripts, and the chief or lord seated under it, distributing justice or charity."* Begging was termed *wædl*, and to beg *wædlian*, from which we get the English word *wheedle*, which is an eloquent witness of the coaxing character of the beggar's appeal.

King Cnut (1017—1035), whose laws exhibit a higher degree of social development than those which preceded them, repeated the law against harbouring another man's man in the following terms:—

"And that no one receive any man longer than three nights, unless he shall recommend him whom he before followed; and let no one dismiss his man before he be clear of every suit to which he had been previously cited." †

At the same time an attempt seems to have been made to protect the friendless man from lynch law by the following enactment.

"And if a friendless man ‡ or a comer from afar be so distressed, through want of friends, that he has no ' borh ' § at the ' frum-tihtle ; ' ‖ let him then submit to prison, and there abide, until he go to God's ordeal, and there let him fare as he may. Verily he who dooms a worse doom to the friendless and the comer from afar than to his fellow, injures himself." ¶

It is quite possible that this law may have been intended to serve as a species of conciliation to the fugitive, in order to prevent him from resorting to extreme measures against his pursuers, as he was able to retaliate on them in a formidable manner by setting fire to their homesteads and woods. That the crime of arson had very much increased may be inferred from the fact that whereas in the reign of Æthelstan (I. c. 6), the penalty for this offence was the same as for avenging a thief, viz. cxx shillings, in the reign of *Cnut* it was made " bōtless " ** (c. 65), that is, punishable by death only.

Judged by his decrees, *Cnut* seems to have been solicitous for the welfare of the poor and oppressed. In his epistle to the

---

* Wright. † C. 28. Quod nemo plus triduo accipiatur hospitio.
‡ A murderer, an outlaw, a thief, and a runaway convict slave were considered friendless men and might not be avenged.
§ Surety. ‖ First accusation, first charge.
¶ C. 35. Of friendless men. ** Not pecuniarily recompensable.

English on his departure from Rome, he says, "I now therefore adjure all my bishops and governors throughout my kingdom, by the fidelity they owe to God and to me, to take care that, before I come to England, all dues owing by ancient custom be discharged, that is to say, plough-alms.* . . . If these and such like things are not paid before I come to England, all who shall have offended will incur the penalty of a royal mulct."

Robbery with violence was common enough in Anglo-Saxon times, the prevailing law being the law of the strongest. Three classes of offenders are mentioned in the laws, the first consisting of those who robbed in parties of less than seven, the second of those who numbered more than seven and not more than thirty-five in a "hloth" or troop, and the third those who pillaged in larger numbers, and who formed a "here" or host.† In order to limit the evil, *Cnut* hit upon the device of making every male take a pledge against thieving. "And we will, that every man above twelve years make oath that he will neither be a thief nor cognisant of theft." ‡

Like his predecessors *Ine* and *Ethelred*, he legislated against selling slaves out of the country, especially into heathendom; but the law cannot have been much respected if a passage in *William of Malmesbury* is to be trusted. Speaking of Cnut's sister, the wife of Godwin, Earl of Kent, he says, "It is reported that she was in the habit of purchasing companies of slaves in England, and sending them into Denmark, more especially girls, whose beauty and age rendered them more valuable, that she might accumulate money by this horrid traffic."

We now arrive at the reign of *Edward the Confessor* (1042—1066), when the law regarding the harbourage of strangers becomes much more elaborate, the reason being that many influential landowners frequently fostered wandering criminals to further their own nefarious purposes, and then denied responsibility for their acts on the ground that the offenders were guests and not servants.

"If any entertain a man known or unknown for two nights, he may keep him as a sojourner; and if the man do wrong the host shall suffer no loss for him. But if he to whom the man has done wrong makes complaint to justice in that it was done by the

---

* A penny for every plough, that is, for as much land as a plough could till, to be distributed to the poor : it was payable in fifteen days from Easter.
† Laws of *King Ine*, c. 13.   ‡ C. 21. Of Thieves.

counsel of the host, then the host shall purge himself by oath with
two law-worthy neighbours if he can, both of his counsel and of
the deed. Otherwise he shall make good the loss and the wrong.
But if he shall entertain the man a third night and that man shall
do wrong to any, the host shall bring him to justice as though he
were one of the household; as the English say, *Tuuo nicte
geste the thirdde nicte agen hine.** And if he is unable to
bring him to justice he shall have the term of a month and a
day. And if he is able to find the man, the wrongdoer shall make
good the damage done and the amends, if he can, and (the wite)
for the body, if the wrong was done thereto. And if the wrongdoer cannot make good the damage done, the host who entertained
him shall make good the loss and the forfeit, and if he himself be
suspect of justice he shall purge himself by the judgment of the
hundred or shire." †

Next comes a law which marks an important era in the repression of extorted maintenance. The virtues of hospitality were
sedulously cultivated by the Anglo-Saxons, and strangers were
everywhere welcomed and entertained. But this very virtue
became in course of time a source of abuse. Kings and nobles
strove to convert voluntary hospitality into an obligatory right
to entertain themselves and their followers, and in course of time
this system of free billeting became a burdensome and intolerable
nuisance. Many monasteries in the ninth century claimed and
obtained grants from the king freeing them from this liability or
expressly limiting it in extent, but the first legal recognition of
its illegality occurs in the Libertas Civitatum, c. 2, De Libertate
Civ. Lundon.

"It is also to be known that a man who is of the Court of the
King or of his Barons has no right either by grant or custom to
be entertained in the house of any citizen of London III (days)
except by the favour of his host. But if he make a forcible sojourn
on the host in his house and there be killed by the host, let the
host choose six of his relations and swear with them himself as
the seventh, that he slew the man for the cause aforesaid, and so
he shall remain quit of the slaying of the dead man towards the
king, and the relations and lords of the dead man." The necessity
for this measure was amply proved by the conduct of Eustace,

---

* "Two nights a guest, the third night one's own servant."
† C. 23. Of Strangers.

Count of Boulogne, who had married Goda, the sister of King Edward. On his way home from visiting the King in the year 1051, he and his companions proceeded to Dover. " When they came thither, they resolved to quarter themselves wherever they liked. Then came one of his men, and would lodge at the house of a master of a family against his will; but having wounded the master of the house, he was slain by the other. Then was Eustace quickly upon his horse, and his companions upon theirs; and having gone to the master of the family, they slew him on his own hearth; then going up to the boroughward, they slew both within and without more than twenty men. The townsmen slew nineteen men on the other side, and wounded more, but they knew not how many." *

" In towns the hospitality of the burghers was not always given gratis, for it was a common custom, even among the richer merchants, to make a profit by receiving guests. These letters of lodgings were distinguished from the innkeepers, or *hostelers*, by the title of *herbergeors*, or people who gave harbour to strangers, and in the larger towns they were subjected to municipal regulations. The great barons and knights were in the custom of taking up their lodgings with these herbergeors rather than going to the public hostels; and thus a sort of relationship was formed between particular nobles or kings and particular burghers, on the strength of which the latter adopted the arms of their habitual lodgers as their signs. These herbergeors practised great extortions upon their accidental guests, and they appear to have adopted various artifices to allure them to their houses." †

In Wales this system of enforced hospitality was known by the name of *gwestva*, in Scotland of *sorning*, and in Ireland of *coshering*. In the first case it was not attempted to be put down by legal enactment until the year 1284, in the second until 1385, and in the last until 1310, so that England was in this matter long in advance of its sister territories.

The causes of vagrancy during this period may be thus briefly summed up—want of the means of existence owing to the destruction of property by hostile tribes, impotence from age or infirmity, failure of crops and cattle murrain, slavery and harsh treatment, natural inclination for a nomadic or plundering life, and criminal conduct necessitating flight.

* A. S. Chronicle. † Wright.

That during the Anglo-Saxon period there was no uprising on the part of the lower orders against the system of bondage in which they were held was no doubt due to four principal causes: 1st, to the differences of race and language which existed among them; 2nd, to the internecine warfare which was perpetually being waged; 3rd, to the manumission of large numbers by several kings in order to enable them to carry on their wars, for while a slave was not allowed to carry arms a freeman was bound to do so and to fight for his country; and 4th, to a gradual manumission by purchase.

On the whole, there can be little doubt that the abolition of the Anglo-Saxon rule marked a progressive stage towards a higher and better order of things, and that William of Malmesbury's summary of the social evils which were rife at the time was generally speaking correct.

"The monks mocked the rule of their order by fine vestments, and the use of every kind of food. The nobility, given up to luxury and wantonness, went not to church in the morning after the manner of Christians, but merely, in a careless manner, heard matins and masses from a hurrying priest in their chambers, amid the blandishments of their wives. The commonalty, left unprotected, became a prey to the most powerful, who amassed fortunes, by either seizing on their property, or by selling their persons into foreign countries; although it be an innate quality of this people to be more inclined to revelling than to the accumulation of wealth. There was one custom, repugnant to nature, which they adopted; namely, to sell their female servants, when pregnant by them and after they had satisfied their lust, either to public prostitution, or foreign slavery. Drinking in parties was a universal practice, in which occupation they passed entire nights as well as days. They consumed their whole substance in mean and despicable houses; unlike the Normans and French, who, in noble and splendid mansions, lived with frugality. The vices attendant on drunkenness which enervate the human mind followed; hence it arose that engaging William, more with rashness and precipitate fury than military skill, they doomed themselves and their country to slavery, by one, and that an easy, victory." *

* Book III.

CHAPTER II.

A.D. 1066 — 1272.

Results of the Norman Conquest—Condition of bond slaves—Laws of William the Conqueror—Incentives to nomadic life under William II.—Laws of Henry I.—The "Wargus" or social outcast—Foreign vagabonds in England—Condition of the lower classes—The troubles of the reign of King Stephen and their consequences—Action of the clergy—Accession of Henry II.—Incursions of the Welsh and Scotch—The assizes of Clarendon and Northampton—Law of 1180—The foreign slave trade—Condition of vagabondage under Richard I.—The forest laws and their effects—Social effects of the reign of Henry III.—Causes of vagrancy during the period.

THE social outcome of the Norman Conquest was undoubtedly the temporary though well-merited degradation of the upper and middle classes of England. Though, as we have already seen, the *ceorl* had been gradually sinking in the social scale owing to the progressive efforts of his superiors to confiscate his rights, so that subsequent to the reign of Alfred he had practically lost the greater part of them, on the other hand, the position of the *theow* had improved to a very great degree, partly owing to the social progress of the nation and partly to the exhortations of the leading clergy, the consequence being that wherever he could he was generally allowed to purchase his freedom. This would not generally be difficult of accomplishment for prœdial slaves of a frugal disposition, as they were usually designated to a stated amount of task work, all results of their labour in excess of their tasks being consequently their own property; the condition of serfdom at this period was therefore gradually merging into that of servile tenure. The net conclusion was to bring the status of the *ceorl* and the *theow* to the same level by depressing the one and raising the other, both enjoying a qualified form of freedom, a freedom which was subject to the services and dues which the lord was entitled to exact. Though absolute slavery, that is the power of disposing of the body of the bondman in the open market apart from the property to which his services attached him, appears to have been forbidden by the law, it nevertheless continued to exist as an article of traffic with foreign countries, principally owing to the connivance of the officers who ought to have put a stop to it, and partly possibly owing to the willingness of many to exchange their lot in the hope of bettering it.*

From the period of the Conquest the *ceorl* and the *theow* become the *villanus* or *nativus*, and the first law we meet with under *William the Conqueror* (1066—1087) deals with both classes under one title, that of the *nativus* or born servant or bondman.

" Bondmen shall not go away from their lands, nor make device how they may defraud their lord of the service due to him ; and if any bondman shall so depart, a man shall not harbour him or his goods, but shall cause him to return to his lord with all that is his." †

The next, with regard to the harbouring of guests, is little more than a repetition of the law of King Cnut.

" No man shall harbour a guest beyond the third night unless that man with whom he was before bid the host so to do. Nor shall any one allow his man to depart from him after he has been arraigned." ‡

The Welsh at this period appear to have held great numbers of the English in slavery, as in the year 1081 the Anglo-Saxon Chronicle tells us that " the King led an army into Wales and there freed many hundreds of men." The social condition of the people and the consequent incentives to many to lead a nomadic and plundering life may be judged from the following extract from the same Chronicle.

" A.D. 1087. The King let his land at as high a rate as he possibly could; then came some other person, and bade more than the former one gave, and the king let it to the men that bade him more. Then came the third, and bade yet more, and the king let it to hand to the men that bade him most of all : and he recked

---

* And we forbid that any sell a man out of his country. But if any man wish to make his slave free, let him deliver the slave by his right hand to the sheriff in full County Court : [and] the sheriff ought to quit-claim and release him from the yoke of his slavery and show him roads and gates free, and hand him free weapons, that is, the lance and sword, and thereupon he is made a free man.—III. 15.
† C. 30. Of Bondmen.
‡ C. 48. That none shall harbour a guest beyond three nights.

not how very sinfully the stewards got it of wretched men, nor how many unlawful deeds they did; but the more men spake about right law, the more unlawfully they acted. They erected unjust tolls, and many other unjust things they did, that are difficult to reckon."

"A.D. 1088. In this year was this land much stirred, and filled with great treachery; so that the richest Frenchmen that were in this land would betray their lord the king, and would have his brother Robert king, who was earl in Normandy. . . . . This conspiracy was formed in Lent. As soon as Easter came then went they forth, and harrowed, and burned, and wasted the king's farms; and they despoiled the lands of all the men that were in the king's service."

We now come to the laws of *Henry I.*, supposed to have been promulgated about the year 1101, and which the king put forth in the following terms: "The law of Edward, I restore to ye, with the emendations whereby my father amended it, by the council of his barons." The first of these laws establishes new and more elaborate regulations with regard to the discharge of bondmen or wandering men, who have outstayed the allotted term of irresponsible entertainment.

"No one shall, beyond the space of three days, detain an unknown or wandering man without giving security, nor harbour the man of another without recommendation or a pledge, nor shall any one dismiss his own man without the licence of the Provost* (of his hundred) and the testimony of the neighbours that he is quit in all things wherein he has been accused." †

The next law practically repeats the law of *King Ine* against going from a lord without leave, without, however, defining the amount of the penalty, and must consequently have thrown considerable discretionary power into the hands of the officers of the law, who were almost always flagrantly open to bribery.

"If any man leaves his lord without licence, he shall be fined for the escape, and he shall be compelled to return and to do right in all respects." ‡

The next deals with masterless men, and orders them to be tried where they are known to have offended.

* Sine prelati sui licencia.
† C. 8 § 5. Of the limits of hundreds.
‡ C. 43 § 2. That no one impleaded by the king shall answer in another's suit.

"It is onewise with a vagabond if he have a lord and otherwise if he have not; but if there shall be such and he do wrong anywhere, let him be brought before the judge of that place and dealt with according to his counsel." *

The next practically repeats the law of *King Cnut* regarding friendless men, and in addition imposes upon their accusers the duty of supporting them while in prison.

"If any friendless man or foreigner come to such distress that he has none to befriend him, on the first accusation let him be laid to prison, and there let (his accuser) sustain him till he shall come to the ordeal." †

The next appears to be an attempt to make the man on whose land the wandering man is found responsible for the administration of justice.

"If any vagabond does wrong let justice be sought wherever he is found to be; and by the counsel and licence of him in whose land and jurisdiction he is found, let him be rightly brought to give satisfaction by pledge or oath or sureties. But if he thwarts this altogether, and this by reason of time, place, or other accident, let something of his be retained for in-borg ‡ and let this be done reasonably and with lawful witnesses, lest worse befall; which things must be attended to the more carefully according as the accused appears trustworthy, and has submitted quietly to being charged or detained, and as it is known whether the thing retained is his or not. And all this is renewed with more abundant solemnity when [the question is] as to the slaying of relatives or friends, or corporal or pecuniary damage. And if even he in whose land he shall be found shall deny justice altogether, nevertheless let nothing be done with regard to them unadvisedly, but let it be craved in his jurisdiction, and let the matter be brought before the king or his minister." §

The spoliation of graves was amongst the Anglo-Saxons accounted a very serious offence. Archbishop Theodore, in the latter half of the seventh century, ordered that any person who violated a sepulchre should do seven years' penitence, three of them on bread and water; and the same injunction is repeated by Archbishop Ecgbert. What purpose the ancient resurrectionists could have

* C. 58. Of vagabonds.   † C. 65 § 5. Of the discharge of a thief.
‡ Bail, pledge; consisting in the chattels of a party unable to obtain a personal " borg " or surety.
§ C. 82 § 2. Of men at enmity with each other.

had in view must be a matter of conjecture, but the probability is that it had some connection with charms and incantations. The practice, too, of burying objects of value with the dead must have offered a considerable temptation to sacrilegious thieves. To judge by the severity of the following law * the crime must have become very rife by the commencement of the twelfth century.

"And if any wicked person shall presume contumeliously to dig up or despoil any body placed in the earth, or in a wooden coffin, or in a rock, or under any obelisk † or other structure, let him be accounted a *wargus*.‡

"The terrific 'war-wolf,' or 'loup-garou,' seems to have been originally only the 'wargus,' a wretch banished from his fellow-creatures by the judicial sentence which forbade his nearest kindred, his wife or his child, from affording him the smallest aid. And it is not altogether difficult to understand how the depredations to which such a wretched outcast was incited by his need, or prompted by his ferocity, may have contributed to form the popular notion of this direful visitant. Nor is it less singular that the crime which, amongst the Franks, more particularly drew down this punishment was the spoliation of the corpse. The vengeance of the disembodied spirit may have been considered as concurring in the punishment of the unhappy offender; aided by the imprecations which in the days of Paganism accompanied the sentence thundered forth from the rocky temple—the scene of government, of judgment, and of unholy sacrifice." §

According to the Anglo-Saxon Chronicle foreign vagabonds appear to have been both numerous and audacious at the commencement of this reign.

"A.D. 1102. And in this same year, in the week of the feast of Pentecost, there came thieves, some from Auvergne, some from France, and some from Flanders, and brake into the minster of Peterborough, and therein seized much property in gold and silver, namely, roods, and chalices, and candlesticks."

---

* C. 83 § 5. "That it is lawful for everyone to defend himself in any matter whatsoever except against his lord."

† The original reads "*sub pyramide.*" In Normandy an obelisk is styled a pyramid. The term would also apply to a *dolmen* or *menhir*.

‡ *Wargus*, an outcast, exile, one driven for his crimes from the society of man; from A.S. *wearg*, a wretch, a villain; *wearh*, wicked. O.N. *wargr*, wolf, outlaw; M.G. *wargs*, an accursed man, an evildoer. Hence a man who was declared "*wargus*" was said "*lupinum caput* (wluesheued) *gerere*."

§ Palgrave.

The condition of the lower classes in this reign may be judged from the following extracts.

"A.D. 1117. But Normandy was very much afflicted both by the exactions and by the armies which the King Henry collected against them. This nation also was severely oppressed through the same means, namely, through manifold exactions."

"A.D. 1124. This same year, after St. Andrew's mass, and before Christmas, held Ralph Basset and the king's thanes a wittenmoot in Leicestershire, at Huncothoe, and there hanged more thieves than ever were known before; that is, in a little while, four and forty men altogether; and despoiled six men of their eyes and of their testicles. Many true men said that there were several who suffered very unjustly; but our Lord God Almighty, who seeth and knoweth every secret, seeth also that the wretched people are oppressed with all unrighteousness. First they are bereaved of their property, and then they are slain. Full heavy year was this. The man that had any property was bereaved of it by violent guilds and violent moots. The man that had not was starved with hunger."

During the disturbed reign of King Stephen the troubles of the poor seem to have reached their climax; between the contending parties they were completely crushed, both by being set on by their lords to kill one another and by the exactions not only of their superiors but of marauders of all kinds. The Chronicle gives an eloquently simple and pathetic account of this terrible period.

"A.D. 1137. When the traitors understood that he (King Stephen) was a mild man, and soft and good, and no justice executed, then did they all wonder. They had done him homage, and sworn oaths, but they no truth maintained. They were all forsworn, and forgetful of their troth; for every rich man built his castles, which they held against him: and they filled the land full of castles. They cruelly oppressed the wretched men of the land with castle-works; and when the castles were made, they filled them with devils and evil men. Then took they those whom they supposed to have any goods, both by night and by day, labouring men and women, and threw them into prison for their gold and silver, and inflicted on them unutterable tortures; for never were any martyrs so tortured as they were. Some they hanged up by the feet, and smoked them with foul smoke; and some by the thumbs, or by the head, and hung coats of mail on their feet. They tied knotted strings about their heads, and twisted them till the pain went to the brains. They put them into dungeons wherein were adders, and snakes, and toads; and so destroyed them. Some they placed in a crucet-house; that is, in a chest that was short and narrow, and not deep; wherein they put sharp stones, and so thrust the man therein, that they broke all the limbs. In many of the castles were things loathsome and grim, called 'Sachenteges,'* of which two or three men had enough to bear one. It was thus made: that is, fastened to a beam; and they placed a sharp iron (collar) about the man's throat and neck, so that he could in no direction either sit, or lie, or sleep, but bear all that iron. Many thousands they wore out with hunger. I neither can, nor may I tell all the wounds and all the pains which they inflicted on wretched men in this land. This lasted the 19 winters while Stephen was king; and it grew continually worse and worse. They constantly laid guilds on the towns, and called it 'tenserie;'† and when the wretched men had no more to give, then they plundered and burned all the towns; that well thou mightest go a whole day's journey and never shouldest thou find a man sitting in a town, nor the land tilled. Then was corn dear, and flesh, and cheese, and butter, for none was there in the land. Wretched men starved of hunger. Some had recourse to alms, who were for a while rich men, and some fled out of the land. Never yet was there more wretchedness in the land; nor ever did heathen men worse than they did: for, after a time they spared neither church nor churchyard, but took all the goods that were therein, and then burned the church and all together. Neither did they spare a bishop's land, or an abbot's or a priest's, but plundered both monks and clerks; and every man robbed another who could. If two men, or three, came riding to a town, all the township fled for them; concluding them to be robbers. The bishops and learned men cursed them continually, but the effect thereof was nothing to them; for they were all accursed, and forsworn, and abandoned. To till the ground was to plough the sea: the earth bare no corn, for the land was all laid waste by such deeds; and they said openly, that Christ slept, and his saints.

* *Sacu*, an accusation; *tege*, a drawing out; or *tege*, *teag*, a band, snare.
† *Cens* and *Censerie*, in Norman French, signify taxation and tribute, from *census*, Lat. *C* and *t* are often confounded.—*Ingram*.

Such things and more than we can say, suffered we nineteen winters for our sins."

The clergy managed at length with some measure of success to mitigate this dreadful condition of things, as we are informed by *Roger of Wendover* that in the year 1142 " *William, Bishop of Winchester*, legate of the apostolic see, in the middle of Lent held a council at London, in presence of the king and the other bishops; for no respect or reverence was at this time shown to the Church of God or its ordained ministers by the profligate wretches who plundered the country, but everybody was laid violent hands on, and ransomed or kept in prison, just as they pleased, whether he was clerk or layman. It was therefore decreed that any one who violated a church or churchyard, or laid violent hands on a clerk or other religious person, should be incapable of receiving absolution except from the Pope himself. It was also decreed that ploughs in the fields, and the rustics who worked at them, should be sacred, just as much as if they were in a churchyard. They also excommunicated with lighted candles all who should contravene this decree, and so the rapacity of these human kites was a little checked."

The reign of *Henry II.* opened (A.D. 1138) with a cruel inroad of the Scots into England, intensifying the miseries of the lower orders, as *Ordericus Vitalis* tells us that they "exercised on the people the barbarity natural to their race in the most brutal manner. They spared no one, butchering young and old, all alike." This was followed in A D. 1139-1140 by an incursion of the Welsh, by whom, according to *Ordericus*, " atrocious villainies were perpetrated in all parts. They say that more than ten thousand of these barbarians spread themselves over England, and that having no reverence for religion, they did not even spare the consecrated places, but gave themselves up to pillage, and burning and bloodshed." The firm will of the King, however, soon brought about an abatement in the evils from which the kingdom suffered during the reign of his predecessors, the bands of robbers were broken up, judges were appointed to go their circuits to try offenders, and the castles of the lesser barons were demolished.

Early in 1166 the King held a great assembly or assize, consisting of the archbishops, bishops, abbots, earls, and barons, at Clarendon, near Salisbury, when a number of most important provisions for the repression of crime were drawn up and afterwards furnished to the judges. The Saxon system of frank pledge or mutual security was revived, large powers of search were given to the sheriffs, and strangers were only allowed to be entertained in towns, and only there for a single night, unless sureties for their good behaviour were forthcoming. The following are the leading clauses relating to the vagabond classes:—

"And in cities or boroughs, let no man have or take men into his house, or land, or soke, whom he will not undertake for, that he will bring them before the judges if they be summoned or be within frankpledge."

"And let there be none within city, borough or castle or without, (nor moreover within the Honour of Wallingford),* who shall forbid the sheriffs to enter their land or soke, to take those who shall have been accused, or notoriously reputed to be robbers, or (secret) murderers, or thieves, or receivers of such, or outlawed or accused with regard to the Forest: but (the King) bids them to aid the sheriffs in capturing such men."

"And the Lord King forbids that any waif (*i.e.* vagabond) or unknown ('uncuth') man, be entertained anywhere except in a borough, and there only for one night, unless he or his horse be detained there by sickness so that an essoign † can be shown."

"And if he shall have been there more than one night, let him be taken and held, until his lord come to give surety for him, or until he himself find safe pledges, and in like manner let him be taken who shall have entertained (the waif)."

In the year 1176 another great council or assize was held at Northampton, when the assize of Clarendon was re-enacted and expanded in the shape of instructions to the justices, of whom eighteen were appointed to travel the kingdom, which was divided into six circuits. The provision relating to the entertainment of strangers was in the following terms:—

"It shall be lawful for no one, either in a borough or vill, to entertain in his house for more than one night any stranger for whose forthcoming he shall be unwilling to give security, unless he who is so entertained shall have some reasonable essoign, which the landlord of the house is to shew to his neighbours, and when he departs he is to depart before the neighbours, and in the daytime."

It would seem, however, that this provision was found too

---

* The king was lord paramount of this seignory.
† A valid excuse by reason of sickness or infirmity.

stringent for practical application, as according to *Roger de Hoveden* the following law, which is a re-enactment of the law of *Edward the Confessor* regarding strangers, was promulgated in a code of laws issued in 1180.

"If any person shall entertain a friend or a stranger, which in English is called '*cuth other uncuth*,'* he shall be at liberty to keep him for two nights as a guest; and if he shall be guilty of an offence, the host shall not incur a penalty for the guest. But if any injury shall be committed on any person, and such person shall make a charge before a court of justice against him that by his counsel the offence was committed, then, together with two of his neighbours, lawful men, he shall clear himself by oath of either counselling or abetting the same. And if he shall not do so, he shall make good the loss and pay a penalty. But if he shall be entertained a third night, and shall commit an offence against any person, then the host is to produce him to justice, as though one of his own household, which in English is expressed by *Tuain nichte gest, thridde nicht hawen man.*† And if in such case he shall not be able to produce him to justice, then he shall have the space granted him of a month and a day. And if the offender shall be found, he shall make amends for the injury he has done, and shall make good the same, even with his body, if that shall be adjudged against him. But if the offender shall not be able to make good the injury he has done, then his host shall make it good, and shall pay a fine. And if the justice shall hold him suspected, then he shall clear himself according to the court of the hundred or the shire."‡

In the year 1169, according to *Gervase of Canterbury*, Henry promulgated an edict to the effect that "if any Welshman, cleric or laic, shall come into England, unless he have passports from our lord the King, let him be apprehended and put in prison, and let all Welshmen who are in the schools in England be turned out." This edict, while no doubt primarily directed against the Welsh sympathisers with the rebellious actions of Thomas à Becket, must also have been intended to include those Welsh vagabonds in England who a little more than a century later were made the subject of a special proclamation.

"It will be easily understood that when travelling was beset

---
* "Kith or unkith"; "acquainted or unacquainted."
† Meaning two nights your guest, the third night one of your household.
‡ C. 23. Of entertaining guests.

with so many inconveniences, private hospitality would be looked upon as one of the first of virtues, for people were often obliged to have recourse to it, and it was seldom refused. In the country every man's door was open to the stranger who came from a distance, unless his appearance were suspicious or threatening. In this there was a mutual advantage; for the guest generally brought with him news and information which was highly valued at a time when communication between one place and another was so slow and uncertain. Hence the first questions put to a stranger were, whence he had come, and what news he had brought with him." *

In this reign the foreign slave trade received a thorough check. Upon the invasion of Ireland by the English in the year 1170, a synod of the clergy was convoked at Armagh to consider the matter.

"At length it was unanimously resolved, that it appeared to the synod that the Divine vengeance had brought upon them this severe judgment for the sins of the people, and especially for this, that they had long been wont to purchase natives of England as well from traders as from robbers and pirates, and reduce them to slavery; and that now they also, by reciprocal justice, were reduced to servitude by that very nation. It was therefore decreed by the synod, and proclaimed publicly by universal accord, that all Englishmen throughout the island who were in a state of bondage should be restored to freedom." †

Previously to this *Wulfstan*, Bishop of Worcester, at the time of the Conquest repeatedly preached at Bristol against the practice, and induced the traders there who had distinguished themselves by this abominable traffic to abandon it, and in the year 1092 *Remigius*, Bishop of Lincoln, distinguished himself by a crusade against the practice in that town. English slaves must, however, have been plentiful in Scotland, as *Roger de Hoveden*, writing about the commencement of the thirteenth century, says under the year 1070: "At this period, a countless multitude of Scots, under the command of King Malcolm, passing through Cumberland, and making their way towards the east, fiercely laid waste the whole of Teesdale and its neighbourhood, far and wide. ... But the young men and young women, and whoever besides seemed adapted for toil and labour, were driven away in fetters in

* Wright.   † Giraldus Cambrensis.

front of the enemy, to endure a perpetual exile in captivity as servants and handmaids. . . . In consequence of this, Scotland became filled with men servants and maid servants of English parentage; so much so, *that even at the present day* not only not even the smallest village, but not even the humblest house, is to be found without them."

We now come to the reign of *Richard I.*, when it appears that notwithstanding the efforts made in the previous reign for their suppression, robbery, outrage, and vagabondage in every form again prevailed, for in the year 1195 *Hubert*, Archbishop of Canterbury, as justiciary of the whole of England, found it necessary to send throughout England a form of oath to be taken as follows:—

"That all subjects of the kingdom of England, shall, to the best of their power, keep the peace of their lord the king; that they shall not be thieves or robbers, nor yet harbourers of them, nor shall in any way abet them; and that whenever they shall be able to know of any malefactors of that character, they shall, to the best of their ability, endeavour to take them, and deliver them up to the sheriffs, and they shall on no account be liberated but by our lord the king, or his chief justice; and if they shall not be able to arrest them, they shall give notice of them, whoever they may be, to the bailiffs of our lord the king. When a hue and cry is raised for the pursuit of outlaws, robbers, thieves, or the harbourers of such, all shall join in the pursuit of them to the best of their ability; and if they shall see any one, and it shall be clear that he has not joined in the said pursuit, or that he has, without permission, withdrawn himself therefrom, they shall take such same persons as though they were the offenders, and deliver them to the sheriffs, not to be set at liberty, but by the king, or by his chief justice.

"Also, the knights who are appointed for that purpose, shall make all persons of their respective districts, of the age of fifteen years and upwards, appear before them, and shall make them swear that they will keep the peace of our lord the king, in manner above mentioned, and that they will not be outlaws, robbers, or thieves, nor yet harbourers of them, nor will in any way abet them; and that they will, in manner above stated, make full pursuit of them, and, if they shall take any one in the commission of an offence, will deliver them to the knights placed over them in their respective districts and for that purpose appointed, who shall deliver him into the custody of the sheriff; and in like manner, on a hue and cry being raised for the purpose of pursuing the said offenders, if they shall see any person, or it shall be known to them that any person does not join in the pursuit, or if he shall, without leave, withdraw himself from the pursuit, they shall take him as the offender, and deliver him to the aforesaid knights, for the purpose of being delivered into the custody of the sheriff, as though he were the offender himself; and he shall not be liberated, except by the command of our lord the king, or his chief justice."

"Accordingly, for the purpose of carrying out these orders, select and trustworthy men were sent throughout all the counties of England, who, upon the oaths of trusty men, arrested many in their respective neighbourhoods, and put them in the king's prisons. Many, however, being forewarned thereof, and having bad consciences, left their homes and possessions, and took to flight."*

"The severity of the old forest laws of England has become a byword, and no wonder when we know that with *the Conqueror* a sovereign's paternal care for his subjects was understood to apply to red deer, not to Saxon men; and that accordingly of the two, the lives of the former alone were esteemed of any particular value. But it was not the severity merely that was, after the Conquest, introduced (whether into the spirit or into the letter of the forest laws is immaterial), but also to the vast extent of fresh land then afforested, and to which such laws were for the first time applied, that gave rise to so much opposition and hatred between the Norman conquerors and the Saxon forest inhabitants; and that in particular parts of England infused such continuous vigour into the struggle commenced at the invasion, long after that struggle had ceased elsewhere. The Conqueror is said to have possessed in this country no less than sixty-eight forests, and these even were not enough; so the afforesting process went on, reign after reign, till the awful shadow of Magna Charta began to pass more and more frequently before royal eyes, producing first a check, and then a retreat; disafforesting then began, and the forest laws gradually underwent a mitigating process. But

---

* Roger de Hoveden. This edict is an amplification of the 21st law of *Cnut* against thieves (see p. 14.) Since the enforcement was committed to knights assigned for the purpose, it may be said to be the incipient development of the office of justice of the peace.

this was the work of the nobility of England, and occupied the said nobility a long time first to determine upon, and then to carry out; the people in the interim could not afford to wait, but took the matter to a certain extent into their own hands; free bands roved the woods, laughing at the King's laws, and killing and eating his deer, and living a life of perfect immunity from punishment, partly through bravery and address, and still more through the impenetrable character of the woods, that covered a large portion of the whole country from Trent to the Tyne. Among the more famous of the early leaders of such men were Robin Hood, Adam Bell, Clym of the Clough, and William of Cloudesley, the heroes of many a northern ballad."*

Part of the immunity which the outlaws enjoyed was no doubt owing to the connivance of the officers of the forest, who levied forced contributions from them, and compelled all who feared their displeasure to drink at ale-houses which they kept, this extortionate practice being known as *Scothala* or *Scotteshale*. These exactions were curbed by the Statute of fines levied (27 Ed. I., A.D. 1299), which enacted that, "No Forester or Bedel from henceforth shall make *Scotal*, or gather garb, or oats, or any corn, lamb, or pig, nor shall make any (gathering but) by the sight and upon the (view) of the twelve Rangers, when they shall make their (range)." This was re-affirmed by the 25 Edw. III., Stat. 5, cap. vii. "Moreover it is accorded and stablished, that no Forester, nor Keeper of Forest or chase, nor any other minister, shall make or gather sustenance, nor other gathering of victuals, nor other thing, by colour of their office, against any man's will, within their Bailiwick nor without, but that which is due of old right."

During the tyrannical and disturbed reign of *John* vagabondage flourished, and the only concession which Magna Charta made to the villein was to protect his "wainage" or implements of husbandry from seizure for fines to the King. At the same time the provisions of the Charter for the administration of justice would, when properly carried out, no doubt prevent many from being driven to adopt a roving and plundering life.

The reign of *Henry III.* was even worse than that of *John* in its immediate social effects, vagabondage and robbery being rife owing to the disturbed state of the country, arising from the broils

* C. Knight.

and battles which occurred. The lower orders were not the only offenders, as the Act of Concord, known as the "Award made between the King and his Commons at Kenilworth," in the year 1266 specifies that "Knights and esquires, which were robbers, and among the principal robbers in wars and roads, if they have no lands, but have goods, shall pay for their ransom (the half) of their goods, and shall find sufficient sureties to keep the peace of the King and of the realm from thenceforth." The same instrument enjoins, "Let all men from henceforth keep the peace firmly, and let none commit burning of houses, robberies, nor other outrages against the peace." There must have been plenty of need of it, as *Matthew Paris* tells us that "this year throughout was fruitful, but notorious for the rapacious acts of robbers."

About three months before the death of Alexander II. of Scotland (1249), a meeting was held on the marches of England and Scotland, for ascertaining the laws of those marches, and enforcing their observation. This work was committed to twelve knights of each kingdom. Among other laws the following was unanimously agreed to :—

"That if any vassal or bondsman in Scotland should, with or without his goods, fly into England with the intention of escaping from his lord ; and if within forty-two days after he should be pursued by his lord or his lord's bailiff, the fugitive should be brought back to Scotland, on the oath of the pursuer, without any opposition from the English; the same being understood to hold with regard to fugitives from England. But if the fugitive was not pursued before forty-two days were elapsed, his lord could not recover him, without a brief from the sovereign of the kingdom where he remained : and on his being discovered *there*, after the expiration of forty-two days, his lord might seize him, upon giving his own oath, accompanied by the oath of six others."

We have now arrived at the dawn of a period when the representative power of the people upon the despotic will of the sovereign began to make itself felt, and when law and order were beginning to emerge from oppression and corruption, and we may here therefore appropriately review the condition of vagabondage as it existed from the date of the Conquest.

The evidence shows that the causes of vagrancy were numerous and varied. Some adopted it to escape slavery, some to save themselves from starvation or torture, some were compelled to adopt it through being deprived of the means of existence by the incursions of the Scotch and Welsh, or by those of armed bands of their own countrymen; some were driven to it by the royal and baronial exactions; some by the afforestation of their lands and the harsh forest laws; some were compelled or incited by their superiors to embark with them in a course of robbery and plunder; and some no doubt adopted a nomadic life from the force of evil example or innate love of wandering or plundering.

To set against all these incitements to vagrancy were two social gains, the cessation of the foreign slave trade and the acquisition of freedom from servitude to which villeins became entitled if they had lived unclaimed a year and a day in a town.*

Almsgiving was prevalent, owing to its inculcation by the Church. *William of Malmesbury* says that *Margaret,* sister of *Edgar Atheling* and wife of *Malcolm Canmore,* king of Scotland, was distinguished for almsgiving. "During her whole life, wherever she might be, she had twenty-four persons whom she supplied with meat and clothing. Departing from the Church, she used to feed the poor; first three, then nine, then twenty-four, at last three hundred; herself standing by with the King, and pouring water on their hands." An Anglo-Norman tract states that on the anniversary of *Sir Hugh de Mortimer,* who died at Cleobury in the reign of *King Stephen,* "a hundred poor persons were plentifully fed, each having a loaf and two herrings, because the anniversary happened in Lent. The other charities which he established for himself, each day to beggars and strangers in the hostelry, no man could number them."

Fitzstephen in his description of London in the reign of *Henry II.,* says:—

"I cannot imagine there is any city in which more laudable customs are observed: such as frequenting churches for attendance on divine service, reverencing God's ordinances, keeping festivals, giving alms, maintaining hospitality."

Begging was termed *beogaunt,* and beggars were styled *mendinantz, mendians,* and *weux. Vagrants* were termed *wakerantz* and *wandering, vagarant.*

* "Also if slaves shall have remained unclaimed for a year and a day in our cities, boroughs, walled towns or castles, from that day let them be made free and remain free from the yoke of their slavery for ever."—*Laws of William the Conqueror,* xvi. (De Servis).

CHAPTER III.

1272—1509.

Accession of Edward I.—Ordinance against bards and vagabonds in Wales—Condition of the Welsh border—Laws against robbers and strangers in towns—Regulations respecting highways—Vagabondism in the City of London—Social state of the country under Edward II.—Sir Gosseline Denville and his band—Laws of Edward III. against pardon for felony—The Welsh westour or unbidden guest—The black death and the statute of labourers—Prohibition on almsgiving to beggars—Prevalence of beggars on the highways—Lepers and their clack dish—Results of the attempt to regulate wages—Proclamations against vagrants in London—Staf-strikers and sturdy rogues—Robert Langland's description of the peasant and the beggar—Richard II. and refractory villeins—The rebellion of Wat Tiler—Measures against vagabondism—Attempts to regulate wages and their results—Provision for the impotent poor—Begging scholars of the Universities—Social state of the country—Laws of Henry IV. against Welsh vagabonds—Laws of Henry V. against Irishmen in England—Laws of Henry VI. against Irish robbers and murderers iń England—The rebellion of Jack Cade—Laws of Henry VII. against beggars and vagabonds.

THE reign of Edward I. is memorable for the benefits it conferred on the nation. Corrupt judges were displaced and justices were compelled to swear that they would never accept bribes. The turbulent barons were forced to conform to the law, many new and excellent laws were enacted, and others were improved, which has earned for the King the title of the English Justinian. In this reign, too, free labourers began to exist, as is proved by the fact that in certain cases servile tenants were allowed to provide labourers for their lords instead of working themselves.

The first military expedition of this reign was against the Welsh, which was followed by the subjugation of the principality. After its annexation, the King, in the year 1284, held a parliament at Rhuddlan, where a set of statutes were enacted for the government of the country, one of the articles being an order for inquiry "of them that give lodging to persons unknown more than two nights."* The old Welsh law did not impose any limi-

* 12 Edward I., c. 1.

tation on the time a guest might be entertained, being content with stipulating for guarantees for his good behaviour. It was found necessary to follow up the statutes of Wales with an ordiance "that the Westours,* Bards, Rhymers, and other idlers and vagabonds, who live upon the gifts called Cymmortha,† be not sanctioned or supported in the country, lest by their invectives and lies they lead the people to mischief and burden the common people with their impositions." ‡

"It is to be observed that this really salutary prohibition is directed against the irregular and wandering bards, and not against those who were more orderly; and in the assertion made by Sir John Wynn in the *History of the Gwedir Family*, and repeated by Carte in his *History of England*, that many bards were put to death by this monarch, there does not seem to be a word of truth; for we find many bards of note living at the date of the alleged massacre, A.D. 1294—1300. Similar proclamations were issued by Henry IV., Henry VIII., and Elizabeth; but all concur in making a distinction between the orderly and disorderly bards, censuring the oppressive exactions of the latter, and proving the lower grade of bards to have been a numerous and not very conscientious class of persons." §

* *Welsh, Gwestwr,* an unbidden guest, one who goes about; from *gwest,* a going out, a visit; and *gwr,* a man.
† *Welsh, Cymhorth,* assistance, help, aid, or succour. It is customary for poor people in Wales to brew ale, or to provide any other entertainment, and invite the neighbourhood to partake, when a collection is made on the occasion.
‡ No. V. Ex. Record Carnarv., fol. 81.
§ Stephens.
"The language of the proclamations is strong, explicit, and condemnatory of the lower grade of bards and minstrels; but coming from strangers they may be looked upon as prejudgments. We will borrow a description, from the satire of Taliesin on the bards of Maelgwn Gwynedd :—

> ' Minstrels perverse in their false custom,
> Immoral ditties are their delight,
> Vain and tasteless praise they recite,
> Falsehood at all times do they utter,
> Innocent persons do they ridicule ;
> Married women by their flattery,
> Through mischievous intent, they deceive ;
> The pure white virgins of Mary they corrupt ;
> Those who believe them they bring to shame ;
> They cause uneasiness to moral men,
> As they pass their lives away in vanity ;
> At night they get drunk, they sleep the day,
> In idleness without work they feed themselves.'

The petty bards were called 'Beirdd Yspyddaid,' smell-feast or small-beer poets."—*Myv. Arch.* i. 377.

The condition of the border at the beginning of the reign is thus described.

"At the close of the great baronial contest, the open country on the border of Wales must have presented a fearful picture of desolation, such as we can now with difficulty conceive. Even much of the forests had been destroyed by the effects of war, either cleared away that they might no longer serve as a retreat or place of ambush for crafty enemies, or cut down to furnish wood for the continual repairs of the fortification of castles and towns, destroyed by designing or accidental incendiaries. The woods which remained were long afterwards the haunt of thieves and outlaws, who not only robbed and murdered the passengers on the high roads when they travelled singly or weakly armed, but even at times associated together to attack and plunder the fairs and markets."*

The next act of this reign (the Statute of Winchester, A.D. 1285) shows to what an extent marauders possessed the sympathies of the lower classes as it commences with this recital—

"Forasmuch as from Day to Day, Robberies, Murthers, and Burnings of Houses be more often used than they have been heretofore, and Felons cannot be attainted by the Oath of Jurors, which had rather suffer felonies done to Strangers to pass without pain, than to indite the Offenders, of whom great part be People of the same Country, or at least if the Offenders be of another Country, the Receivers be of places near." It then proceeds in the spirit of the Anglo-Saxon law of the *Frith-borg* to make the hundred responsible for all robberies committed within its limits, and further declares that "for the more Surety of the Country, the King hath commanded that in great Towns, being walled, the gates shall be closed from the Sun-setting until the Sun-rising; and that no man do lodge in Suburbs, nor in any foreign part of the Town, but in the Day-time, nor yet in the Day-time without his Host will answer for him."

"And the Bailiffs of Towns every week, or at the least every Fifteenth Day, shall make Inquiry of all Persons being lodged in the suburbs, or in foreign parts of the Towns; and if they do find any that do lodge or receive in any manner men of whom there is suspicion that they be People against the Peace, the Bailiffs shall do right therein. And the King commandeth, that from henceforth watches be made as it hath been used in times passed, that is to

* Wright.

wit, from the Day of the Ascension unto the Day of St. Michael, in every City by six men at every gate, in every Borough by Twelve Men, in every Town by Six or Four, according to the number of the Inhabitants of the Town, and they shall watch the Town continually all Night, from the Sun-setting unto the Sun-rising. And if any Stranger do pass by them, he shall be arrested until morning; and if no Suspicion be found, he shall go quit; and if they find cause of Suspicion, they shall forthwith deliver him to the Sheriff, and the Sheriff may receive him without Damage, and shall keep him safely, until he be delivered in due manner."

"And Further, It is commanded, That Highways leading from one Market Town to another shall be enlarged, whereas Bushes, Woods, Hedges, or Dykes be, so that there be neither Dyke, Underwood, nor Bush, whereby a man may lurk to do hurt, within two hundred foot of the one side, and two hundred foot on the other side of the way, so that this Statute shall not extend unto Oaks,* nor unto great Trees, so as it be clear underneath. And if by Default of the Lord that will not abate the Dyke, Underwood or Bushes, in the manner aforesaid, any Robberies be done therein, the Lord shall be answerable for the Felony; and if Murther be done the Lord shall make a Fine at the King's Pleasure. And if the Lord be not able to fell the Underwoods, the Country shall aid him therein. And if percase a Park be near to the Highway, it is requisite that the Lord shall minish his Park so that there be a border of two hundred foot near the Highway as before is said, or that he make such a Wall, Dyke, or Hedge, that Offenders may not pass, ne return to do evil."

"And Further, It is commanded, that every Man have in his house Harness for to keep the Peace after the antient assize."

"Execution of the Act is respited until Easter next following, to see whether such Felonies and Robberies do cease." †

A careful study of the Act makes it very evident that armed bands of robbers commanded by people of position must still have been roaming about much as in the previous reigns. The order for cutting the underwood for two hundred feet on each side of the highway shows the favourite method of lurking adopted by the robbers, and the stringent penalties imposed on lords who neglected to cut away the underwood on their property makes it

---

* *Keynss* (chênes). This is translated "Ashes" in the authorised version of the Statutes.

† Stat. Wynton (The Statute of Winchester), 13 Edwardi I., c. 4, A.D. 1285.

appear that many of them must have sheltered or connived at the presence of robbers, taking doubtless for the protection afforded a percentage of the plunder.

Even the City of London was not exempt from vagabondism and ruffianism of the worst type, judged by the following enactment:—

"Whereas many Evils, as Murders, Robberies, and Manslaughters, have been committed heretofore in the City by Night and Day, and People have been beaten and evil entreated, and divers other mischances have befallen against his peace; It is enjoined that none be so hardy to be found going or wandering about the Streets of the City, after Curfew tolled at St. Martin's-le-Grand, with Sword or Buckler, or other Arms for doing Mischief, or whereof evil suspicion might arise; nor in any other manner unless he be a great Man or other lawful person of good repute, or their certain Messenger, having their warrants to go from one to another, with Lanthern in hand. And if any be found going about contrary to the Form aforesaid, unless he have cause to come late into the City, he shall be taken by the keeper of the Peace and be put into the place of confinement appointed for such Offenders; and on the morrow he shall be brought and presented before the Warden, or the Mayor of the City for the Time being, and before the aldermen; and according as they shall find that he offended, and as the custom is, he shall be punished."

"And Whereas such Offenders as aforesaid going about by Night, do commonly resort and have their Meetings and hold their evil talk in Taverns more than elsewhere, and there do seek for shelter, lying in wait, and watching their time to do mischief; it is enjoined that none do keep a Tavern open for wine or ale, after tolling of the aforesaid Curfew; but they shall keep their tavern shut after that hour, and none therein drinking or resorting; neither shall any Man admit others in his House, except in common Taverns, for whom he will not be answerable unto the King's Peace. And if any Taverner be found doing the contrary, the first time he shall be put in pledge by his Tavern drinking cup, or by other good pledge there found, and be amerced forty pence; and if he be found a second time offending, he shall be amerced half a mark; and the third time Ten Shillings; and the fourth time he shall pay the whole penalty double, that is to say Twenty shillings; and the fifth time he shall be forejudged of his Trade for ever." *

* Statuta Civitatis London (Statutes for the City of London), 13 Edwardi I.

These enactments seem to have been put in force by the City authorities, as in the year 1311 we find "John Blome indicted as a common *wagabund* by night for committing batteries and other mischiefs in the ward of Aldersgate and divers other wards. Therefore he was committed to prison. On the Thursday next before the Feast of Easter he was delivered on the surety of William de Suningham and others, who undertook that he should behave himself properly."

Professional fencers, who in 1597-8 were classed as vagabonds, appear long before to have been regarded as disreputable persons, as in the same year, 1311, "Master Roger le Skirmisour* was indicted for keeping a fencing school for divers men, and for enticing thither the sons of respectable persons so as to waste and spend the property of their fathers and mothers upon bad practices, the result being that they themselves became bad men. Therefore he was committed to prison."

The strong measures for the repression of crime and the enforcement of good order enacted in the reign of Edward I. were in a few years unfortunately wholly nullified by the imprudent and weakminded conduct of *Edward II.*, whose foolish predilection for favourites caused him to sanction unpopular exactions. His barons rose against him, and the country was plunged into civil war with all its train of turbulence and criminal license.

Favoured by the lawlessness which prevailed during this reign, robbers riding about in troops were numerous. One of the most noted was Sir Gosseline Denville, of Northallerton in Yorkshire, a knight of old lineage and of considerable property inherited from his father. Having run through his patrimony by riotous living, he and his brother Robert took to public robbery, sparing neither rich nor poor, so that in a little time they became the dread and terror of all travellers in the north of England. Their boldness was such that other robbers when they were in any danger flew to them for succour and protection. The band therefore soon became almost formidable enough to bid defiance to the *posse comitatus* of any sheriff. Near Darlington they robbed two cardinals who came to England for the purpose of arranging a peace between the kingdoms of Scotland and England. They broke open houses in the daytime, taking what money and plate they found, and killing any who opposed them. Monasteries and

* Fencer or fencing master.

nunneries did not escape their outrages, and they stripped the altars in several churches of their plate. On one occasion Sir Gosseline and his gang robbed a Dominican monk named Bernard Sympson, and then for pastime forced him to climb a tree and preach a sermon, in which he succeeded so well that they gave him his liberty and returned him the property of which he had been robbed.

The roads being at length guarded by large parties of horse and foot, Sir Gosseline and his gang, to the number of two hundred, disguised themselves as friars and continued their course of robbery. They did not even spare the King himself, whom they met in a progress to Norwich. The King, taking them to be religious men come to meet him on some petition, stopped with his retinue to hear what they had to say, whereupon Sir Gosseline, approaching his Majesty with a low obeisance, told him that he had not in the least come to talk with his liege about religion, because that was a thing he never thought of any more than himself, but he had come to discourse with him about secular affairs, and required him to lend him and his needy brethren what money he had about him, otherwise they would put him to very hard penance in spite of all the indulgences and absolution he could procure of the Pope. The King finding it vain to resist so large a force with his small following, which did not exceed forty persons, gave what money he had to Sir Gosseline, who then searched the pockets of the noblemen in attendance before he allowed them to proceed.

Enraged at this insult, the King issued a proclamation offering a reward of 1,000 merks for the capture of Sir Gosseline dead or alive, 500 merks for his brother Robert dead or alive, and 100 merks for every one of his accomplices taken alive. The next great exploit of the band was to rob the Bishop of Durham's palace, which they rifled from top to bottom; they then stripped the prelate and his servants stark naked, and bound them hand and foot. Soon after this Sir Gosseline, with his brother and several members of his band, were surrounded at a lone inn in Yorkshire by the sheriff of the county at the head of five or six hundred men. The robbers made a desperate resistance, and killed two hundred men before they were overpowered. They were then conveyed to York, where they were hanged without trial.

Edward II. was succeeded by *Edward III.*, who gave early proof of his energy and strength of will, first by destroying the Queen's

SIR GOSSELINE DENVILLE AND HIS BAND LISTENING TO THE
DOMINICAN MONK (Temp. Edw. II.)

favourite, Mortimer, who had in reality constituted himself Regent of the kingdom, and next by the whole course of his legislation.

One of the first acts of this reign, 2 Edw. III., 1328 (the statute of Northampton), was an effort to control the pardons for felony which were procured by great men, and to prevent the people from riding or going armed to the disturbance of the peace. The recital runs thus:—

"Whereas offenders have been greatly encouraged, because (the) Charters of Pardon have been so easily granted in times past of Manslaughters, Robberies, Felonies, and other Trespasses against the Peace; It is ordained and enacted, that such Charter shall not be granted, but only where the King may do it by his Oath, that is to say, where a Man slayeth another in his own defence, or by misfortune. . . . That no man great or small, of what condition soever he be, except the King's Servants in his presence, and his Ministers in executing of the King's Precepts, or of their office, and such as be in their Company assisting them, and also (upon a Cry for Arms to keep the Peace, and in the same in such places where such Acts happen,) be so hardy to come before the King's Justices, or other of the King's Ministers doing their office, with force and arms, nor bring no force in affray of the peace, nor to go nor ride armed by night nor by day, in Fairs, Markets, nor in the presence of the Justices or other Ministers, nor in no part elsewhere, upon pain to forfeit their Armour to the King, and their Bodies to prison at the King's pleasure."

In spite of this Act, it seems that pardons for crimes were so freely granted by those in authority—principally without doubt in return for bribes—that it became necessary to legislate afresh on the subject in the following still more stringent terms.

"Because divers Charters of Pardon have been granted of Felonies, Robberies, and Manslaughter, against the Form of the Statute lately made at Northampton, containing that no man should have such Charters out of the Parliament, whereby such misdoers have been the more bold to offend; (2) it is enacted That from henceforth the same Statute shall be kept and maintained in all points."*

Robbery and disorder appear, however, to have been still sufficiently rampant to necessitate further legislation, and accordingly in the succeeding year the following enactment was passed.

* 4 Edw. III., c. 13 (1330).

"Whereas in the Statute made at Winchester in the time of King Edward, Grandfather to the King that now is, it is contained, That if any stranger pass by the Country in the Night, of whom any have suspicion, he shall presently be arrested and delivered to the Sheriff, and remain in ward till he be duly delivered: And because there have been divers Manslaughters, Felonies, and Robberies done in Times past, by People that be called Roberdesmen, Wastours, and Draghlacche;* It is accorded that if any may have any evil suspicion of such, be it by day or by night, they shall be incontinently arrested by the Constables of the Towns."†

Two things deserve notice in this statute—the first is that the Welsh westour, or unbidden guest, had evidently made his way into England and given his name to this form of wandering rascality; and second, that the provisions of the statute of Edward I., by which suspicious persons might be arrested in the night time, were now extended to the day time.

At this time "the English counties beyond the Severn were overrun by bands of outlaws. In Gloucestershire they had joined together and elected themselves a chieftain, to whom they gave sovereign power, and in whose name they issued proclamations; and, setting in defiance the King and his laws, they infested equally the sea and the land, capturing and plundering the king's ships on the one element, and murdering and robbing his subjects on the other. In 1347 the King sent a commission to Gloucester to concert means of seeking out the offenders and bringing them to justice." ‡

The year 1348 brought a terrible visitation to the shores of England in the shape of a plague called the Black Death, which originated in the East and ravaged the whole of Europe. This fearful disease broke out violently in the towns where the complete neglect of sanitary precautions common in those days afforded it a firm foothold; from thence it spread to the villages, and ultimately depopulated the country of from one-third to one-half of its inhabitants, according to various estimates. The result was a scarcity of labour, and a danger that a great part of the land would remain untilled. Wages rose as the labourers found that they were practically masters of the situation, in being able to make whatever demands they liked for their services. The number of labourers wandering about to sell their labour in the best market swelled

* Draw-latches. † 5 Edw. III., c. 14 (1331). ‡ Wright.

the ranks of vagrancy, and their idle habits naturally gave birth to other disorders. The number of free labourers had by this time greatly increased, as in the year 1339 the King, as a means of raising money, of which he was very much in want, allowed a number of his bondmen to purchase their manumission, and this example was no doubt followed by members of the nobility who found themselves in similar straits.

To check both the increase of vagrancy and the inordinate augmentation of wages, an instrument was prepared in the year 1349 (23 Edw. III), which is known under the title of "Statutum de Servientibus," or Statute of Labourers; but the Parliament, though called, did not meet in that year on account of the plague. This instrument is recited in the Statute of Labourers (25 Edw. III., stat. 1) as an ordinance of the King and his council, and by 2 Rich. II., stat. 1, c. 8 (1378) it is expressly enacted that this ordinance should be affirmed and held as a statute. The preamble states—

"Because a great part of the people, and especially of workmen and servants, late died of the pestilence, many seeing the necessity of masters and great scarcity of servants, will not serve unless they may receive excessive wages, and some rather willing to beg in idleness than by labour to get their living; We, considering the grievous incommodities which of the lack especially of ploughmen and such labourers may hereafter come, have upon deliberation and treaty with the prelates and nobles, and learned men assisting us, of their mutual consent ordained:"

It then proceeds—

"That every man and woman of our realm of England, of what condition he be, free or bond, able in body, and within the age of threescore years, not living in merchandise, nor exercising any craft, nor having of his own whereof he may live, nor proper land, about whose tillage he may himself occupy, and not serving any other, if he in convenient service (his estate considered) be required to serve, he shall be bounden to serve him which so shall him require; And take only the wages, livery, meed, or salary which were accustomed to be given in the places where he oweth to serve, the xx year of our reign of England, or five or six other common years next before. Provided always, that the lords be preferred before other in their bondmen or their land tenants, so in their service to be retained: so that nevertheless the said lords shall retain no more than be necessary for them; And if any such man or woman, being so required to serve, will not the same do, that proved by two true men before the sheriff or the bailiff, lord, or constable of the town where the same shall happen to be done, he shall anon be taken by them, or any of them, and committed to the next gaol, there to remain under strait keeping, till he find surety to serve in the form aforesaid.

"That if a workman or servant depart from service before the time agreed upon, he shall be imprisoned.

" That the old wages and no more shall be given to servants.

"That if the lord of a town or manor do offend against this statute in any point, he shall forfeit the treble value.

" That if any artificer or workman take more wages than were wont to be paid, he shall be committed to the gaol.

" That victuals shall be sold at reasonable prices.

" Item, because that many valiant * beggars, as long as they may live of begging, do refuse to labour, giving themselves to idleness and vice, and sometime to theft and other abominations; none upon the said pain of imprisonment shall, under the colour of pity or alms, give anything to such, which may labour, or presume to favour them towards their desires, so that thereby they may be compelled to labour for their necessary living.

"That he that taketh more wages than is accustomably given, shall pay the surplusage to the town where he dwelleth, towards a payment to the King of a tenth and fifteenth granted to him."

The necessity for the prohibition regarding almsgiving to valiant beggars was doubtless intended as a corrective to the sedulous inculcation by the Church of the duty of bestowing charity on *all poor persons*. *Richard Rolle*, of Hampole, near Doncaster, a hermit of the order of St. Augustine and a doctor of divinity, who died in this very year, gives us an idea of the ecclesiastical view of the matter in the *Stimulatus Conscientia* or *Pricke of Conscience*.

> " When thou mayst help through wisdom and skill,
> And will not help, but holdest thee still;
> When thou speakest sharply to the poor,
> That some good ask at thy door,
>   Be it without, be it within,
>   Yet it is a venial sin."

* The word "valiant" is here used in the sense of strong in body.

"Loaves at this period were made of a secondary quality of flour, and these were first pared and then cut into thick slices, which were called in French *tranchoirs*, and in English *trenchers*, because they were to be carved upon. The portions of meat were served to the guests on these tranchoirs, and they cut it upon them as they eat it. The gravy, of course, went into the bread, which the guest sometimes, perhaps always at an earlier period, eat after the meat; but in later times, and at the tables of the great, it appears to have been more frequently sent away to the alms-basket, from which the leavings of the table were distributed to the poor at the gate. All the bread used at table seems to have been pared before it was cut, and the parings were thrown into the alms-dish. Walter de Bibblesworth, in the latter part of the thirteenth century, among other directions for the laying out of the table, says, 'Cut the bread which is pared, and let the parings be given to the alms.'"*

"The roads appear to have been infested with beggars of all descriptions, many of whom were cripples, and persons mutilated in the most revolting manner, the result of feudal wantonness and of feudal vengeance. A manuscript of the fourteenth century gives a curious representation of a very deformed cripple, whose means of locomotion is furnished by wooden clogs attached to his hands and knees by straps. The beggar and the cripple, too, were often only robbers in disguise, who waited their opportunity to attack single passengers, or who watched to give notice to comrades of the approach of richer convoys. The mediæval popular stories give abundant instances of robbers and others disguising themselves as beggars and cripples. Blindness also was common among these objects of commiseration in the Middle Ages, often, as in the case of mutilation of other kinds, the result of deliberate violence."†

Every town had its cross, at which engagements, whether of a religious or worldly interest, were entered into. Every churchyard had one whereon to rest the bodies of the deceased, from which the preacher gave his lessons on the mutability of life. At the turning of every public road was placed a cross, for the twofold purposes of rest for the bearers of the pious defunct, and for reminding travellers of the Saviour who died for their salvation. The boundaries of every parish were distinguished by crosses, at which, during the ancient perambulations, the people alter-

* Wright. † *Ib.*

nately prayed and regaled themselves. Crosses in short were multiplied by every means which the ingenuity of man could invent; and the people were thus kept in constant remembrance, both at home and on their journeys, as well as in every transaction of their lives, of the foundation of the Christian faith.

The afflicted poor solicited alms at these crosses by importunate entreaties for Christ's sake ; and hence arose the old saying when a person was urgent or vehement in preferring any petition, that " he begged like a cripple at a cross."

But the favourite mode of attracting attention was by means of the *clack dish*, an alms-basket with a clapper, which lepers were obliged to employ in soliciting charity, standing " afar off," lest their touch should pollute the benevolent. They were a race entirely apart, and in order to participate in divine service they were compelled to gather in the churchyard and hear it through a window called the leper's window, usually found on the north side of the chancel. The dreadful disease from which they suffered was introduced into Europe by the Crusaders, and raged with such virulence during the Middle Ages as to necessitate the establishment of lazar-houses for the reception and isolation of those afflicted with it. One was founded at Southampton in 1173-4. By the commencement of the eighteenth century leprosy was almost extinct in England, though a case was known and reported so late as the year 1809. The leper's clack dish was so productive that other mendicants adopted it, and hence the saying, " I know you as well as the beggar knows his dish." In the " Family of Love," in the year 1608, we find " ' Can you think I get my living by a bell and clack dish ? ' ' How's that ? ' Why, begging, sir.' " And in the " Blind Beggar of Bednall Green " (1659), " ' Tush, man, 'tis he. I know him as well as the Beggar knows his dish.' "

The futility of endeavouring to regulate the rate of wages by ordinance was speedily demonstrated, though not acknowledged, as in the year 1350 it was found necessary to pass an Act (25 Edw. III., stat. 1) dealing further with the same subject, the preamble of which tells its own tale :—

" Whereas late against the malice of servants, which were idle, and not willing to serve after the pestilence, without taking excessive wages, it was ordained by our lord the King, and by assent of the prelates, earls, barons, and others of his council, That such manner of servants, as well men as women, should be bound to serve, receiving salary and wages, accustomed in places where they ought to serve, in the twentieth year of the reign of the King that now is, or five or six years before; and that the same servants refusing to serve in such manner should be punished by imprisonment of their bodies, as in the said statute is more plainly contained; (2) whereupon commissions were made to divers people in every county to enquire and punish all them which offend against the same. (3) And now forasmuch as it is given the King to understand in this present parliament, by the petition of the commonalty, that the said servants having no regard to the said ordinance, but to their ease and singular covetise, do withdraw themselves to serve great men and others, unless they have livery and wages to the double or treble of that they were wont to take the said twentieth year, and before, to the great damage of the great men, and impoverishing of all the said commonalty, whereof the said commonalty prayeth remedy: wherefore in the same parliament, by the assent of the said prelates, earls, barons, and other great men of the same commonalty there assembled, to refrain the malice of the said servants, be ordained and established the things underwritten :—

"That Carters, Ploughmen, Drivers of the plough, Shepherds, Swineherds, Deies,* and all other servants, shall take liveries and wages, accustomed the said Twentieth year, or Four years before, and that they be (allowed) to serve by a whole year, or by other usual terms and not by the Day.

"That the same servants be sworn two times in the year before lords, stewards, bailiffs, and constables of every town, to hold and do these ordinances, and that none of them go out of the town, where he dwelleth in the winter, to serve the summer, if he may serve in the same town, taking as before is said. Saving that the people of the counties of *Stafford, Lancaster,* and *Derby,* and people of *Craven,* and of the marches of *Wales* and *Scotland,* and of other places, may come in time of *August,* and labour in other counties, and safely return, as they were wont to do before this time. And that those which refuse to make such oath, or to perform that they be sworn to, or have taken upon them, shall be put in the stocks by the said lords, stewards, bailiffs, and constables of the towns by three days or more, or sent to the next gaol, there

* Drivers of geese.

to remain till they will justify themselves. And that stocks* be made in every town by such occasion betwixt this and the feast of *Pentecost.*

" That Carpenters, Masons, and Tilers, and other Workmen of Houses, shall not take by the Day for their Work, but in manner as they were wont, that is to say ; a Master Carpenter iii d., and another ii d., a Master free-stone Mason iiii d., and other Masons iii d., and their Servants i d. ob. Tylers iii d., and their Knaves i d. ob., and other Coverers of Fern and Straw iii d., and their Knaves i d. ob. Plasterers and other workers of Mudwalls, and their Knaves, by the same manner, without Meat or Drink, from Easter to Saint Michael ; and from that time less, according to the Rate and Discretion of the Justices.

" That Cordwainers and Shoemakers shall not sell Boots nor Shoes, nor none other thing touching their Mystery, in any other manner than they were wont the said xx. year. Artificers shall be sworn to use their crafts as they did in the said Twentieth year.

" Stewards, bailiffs, and constables of the towns are to be sworn before the justices to certify offenders to the justices, and the justices shall enquire and punish them by fine and ransom to the King and also command them to prison, there to remain till they have found surety, to serve, and take, and do their work, and to sell things vendible as the Act directs, and if any of them come against his oath and be attainted, he is to be imprisoned for forty days, and on a succeeding conviction a quarter of a year, and so on doubling the penalty for each conviction. Those who will sue against servants, workmen, labourers, and artificers for excess of wages received shall have the excess refunded to them, and if none will sue, then it should be levied and delivered to the collectors of the Quinzime, in alleviation of the towns where such excesses were taken.

* The stocks were a very ancient form of correction. They figure in pictures of Anglo-Saxon punishments. The latest instance of their use appears to have been on the 5th of May, 1862, at *Keighley* in Yorkshire, when one Joseph Spence, *alias* " Boxer," was placed in the stocks, Church Green, for gambling, at the beginning of March, in a lane near Exleyhead. A crowd of persons witnessed his punishment, which seems to have been intended as a caution to the numerous persons who then congregated on bypaths and highways for gambling purposes. Three days previously another offender, named Isaac Pickering, was similarly punished for three hours for the same offence. The stocks at *Bradford* were last used on the 26th July 1860, when John Dodgson a labourer of Idle, was placed in them for six hours for drunkenness.

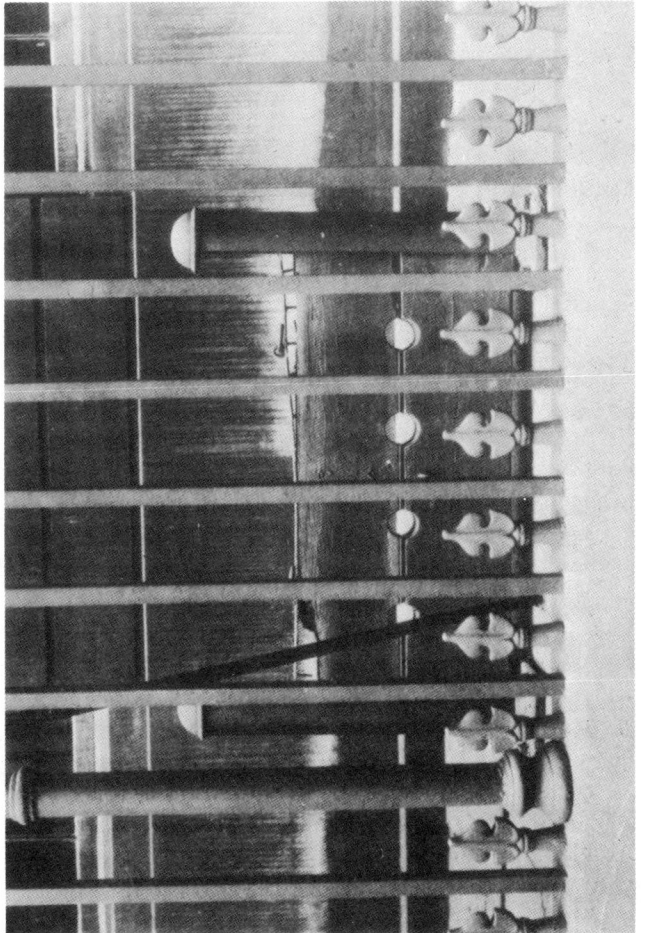

STOCKS AT THE WEST-RIDING COURT-HOUSE AT BRADFORD (YORKS) 1886
From a Photograph specially taken by A. F. & C. Fox, Bradford.

"Sheriffs, constables, bailiffs, gaolers, nor other officers, shall exact anything of the same servants. The forfeitures of servants shall be employed to the aid of dismes and quinzimes granted to the King by the Commons.

"The justices shall hold their sessions four times a year, and at all times needful. Servants which flee from one country to another shall be committed to prison."

The exemption in favour of natives of Stafford, Lancaster, Derby, and Craven, and the Marches of Wales and Scotland, was of course to enable them to assist in getting in the harvest wherever labour was deficient for that purpose. The effect of this statute was, as might have been expected, the very opposite of that intended by its framers. Labourers took to flight from their native counties in order to evade its provisions, and many took refuge in corporate towns in order to obtain their enfranchisement. Strikes and combinations became frequent amongst the artisan class. The enforcement of the law was in fact an impossibility; prices were necessarily enhanced by the dearth of labour, and the imprisonment of large numbers of labourers could only have the effect of increasing the scarcity of labourers. On the one hand, therefore, labourers could not live on the wages formerly paid, and on the other it was futile to attempt to imprison them. The only result of this legislation, consequently, was to embitter the relations between the upper and the lower classes, and to institute a common bond of union amongst the latter.

In 1360-1, by the 34 Edw. III., c. 1, magistrates were appointed for the purpose of exercising jurisdiction over offenders, rioters, and barrators* in the following terms.

"In every county of England shall be assigned, for the keeping of the peace, one lord, and with him three or four of the most worthy in the county, with some learned in the law, and they shall have power to restrain the offenders, rioters, and all other barrators, and to pursue, arrest, take, and chastise them according to their trespass or offence; and to cause them to be imprisoned and duly punished according to the law and customs of the realm, and according to that which to them shall seem best to do by their discretions and good advisement; and also to inform them and to inquire of all those that have been pillors and robbers in the parts beyond the sea, and be now come again, and go wandering, and

* *Barrator*, a promoter of quarrels, originally a cheat, a deceiver.

will not labour as they were wont in times past; and to take and arrest all those that they may find by indictment, or by suspicion, and to put them in prison; and to take of all them that be [not] of good fame, where they shall be found, sufficient surety and mainprise of their good behaviour towards the King and his people, and the other duly to punish; to the intent that the people be not by such rioters or rebels troubled nor endamaged, nor the peace blemished, nor merchants nor others passing by the highways of the realm disturbed, nor put in fear by peril which might happen of such offenders."

With regard to this Act Dr. Stubbs says:—

"After the passing of the Statute of Winchester, the office of conservator of the peace, whose work was to carry out the provisions of that enactment, was filled by election in the Shiremoot. The Act of the 1st Edward III., c. 16, which orders the appointment, in each county, of good men and loyal to guard the peace, connects itself more naturally with the Statute of Winchester, and through it with the *milites assignati* of Henry III. and Richard I., than with the chosen *custodes* of Edward I. These nominated conservators, two or three in number, were commissioned by the 18th Edward III., stat. 2, c. 2, to hear and determine felonies, and by 34 Edward III., c. 1, were regularly empowered to do so. The office thus became a permanent part of the county machinery in the hands of the Justices of the Peace."

In order to meet the continued petitions for the enforcement of the statutes against labourers on the part of the employers, a further statute was passed in this year (34 Edw. III., cc. 10, 11), imposing harsher penalties on the labourers who fled from their employers.

"Of Labourers and Artificers that absent them out of their services in another Town, or another County, the Party shall have the Suit before the Justices, and that the Sheriff take him at the first Day, as is contained in the Statute, if he be found, and do of him Execution as afore is said; and if he return, that he is not found, he shall have an Exigend at the first Day, and the same pursue till he be outlawed, and after the Outlawry a writ of the same Justices shall be sent to every Sheriff of England, that the Party will sue, to take him, and to send him to the Sheriff of the County where he is outlawed; and when he shall be there brought, he shall have there Imprisonment, till he will justify himself, and have made gree to the Party; and nevertheless for the Falsity he shall be burnt in the Forehead, with an Iron made and formed to this Letter F, in token of Falsity,* if the Party grieved the same will sue; but this Pain of Burning shall be put in respite till Saint Michael next ensuing, and then not executed, unless it be by the Advice of the Justices; and the Iron shall abide in the Custody of the Sheriff. And that the Sheriff and every Bailiff of Franchise be attending to the Plaintiff, to put this Ordinance in Execution, upon the Pain aforesaid; And that no Labourer nor Artificer shall take no manner of Wages the festival Days."

"If any Labourer, Servant, or Artificer, absent himself in any City or Borough, and the Party Plaintiff come to the Mayor and Bailiffs, and require Delivery of his Servant, they shall make him Delivery without Delay; and if they refuse to do the same, the Party shall have his Suit against the Mayor and Bailiffs before the Justices of Labourers; and if they be thereof attainted, they shall pay to the King Ten Pounds, and to the Party One hundred Shillings."

In the year 1359 the authorities of the City of London issued the following proclamation against the country labourers who flocked into the city.

"Forasmuch as many men and women, and others, of divers Counties, who might work, to the help of the common people, have betaken themselves from out of their own country to the City of London, and do go about begging there, so as to have their own ease and repose, not wishing to labour or work for their sustenance, to the great damage of such the common people; and also, do waste divers alms, which would otherwise be given to many poor folks, such as lepers, blind, halt, and persons oppressed with old age and divers other maladies, to the destruction of the support of the same: We do therefore command on behalf of our Lord the King, whom may God preserve and bless, that all those who go about begging in the said city, and who are able to labour and work, for the profit of the common people, shall quit the said city between now and Monday next ensuing, and if any such shall be found begging after the day aforesaid, the same shall be taken and put in the stocks on Cornhulle,† for half a day the first time; and the

* En signe de Fauxine.
† These stocks originally stood on the site of the present Mansion House. They were removed in 1282 to make way for a fish and flesh market, which took the name of Stocks Market.

second time he shall be taken, he shall remain in the stocks one whole day; and the third time, he shall be taken, and shall remain in prison for 40 days, and then forswear the said city for ever. And every constable, and the bedel of every ward of the said city, shall be empowered to arrest such manner of folks, and to put them in the stocks in manner aforesaid."*

This was succeeded in the year 1375 by an ordinance against common beggars.

"That no one who by handicraft, or by the labour of his body, can gain his living, shall counterfeit the begging poor, or shall set any one to beg for his living in the said city; on pain of imprisonment, and of being punished according to the ordinance of the Mayor and Aldermen thereon; and that no lazar shall go about in the said city, on the same pain: and that every constable and bedel shall have power to take such persons, and bring them to Cornhulle, and put them in the stocks, there to remain according to the ordinance made thereupon."†

In the year 1363 the King introduced into this country the practice of feeding, clothing, and distributing money to indigent persons on Maundy Thursday; and this practice has since been followed by successive sovereigns, many of whom also, in order to show their humility, washed the feet of those selected as the proper objects of their beneficence.

In the last year of this reign (1376) we find the Commons petitioning the King "that Ribalds‡ and Sturdy Beggars may be banished out of every town," to which the King made answer:

"Touching Ribalds, the Statute of Winchester § and the Declaration of the same, with other Statutes, of Roberdsmen shall be executed: and for such as make themselves Gentlemen and Men of Arms, or archers, if they cannot so prove themselves, let them be driven to their occupation or service, or to the Place, from whence they came."

The Commons further "made great complaints in this year, that masters were obliged to give their servants and labourers great wages, to prevent their running away; and that the encouragement which they received in these evil practices often induced them,

---

* Proclamation made against Vagrants within the City. 33 Edw. III. (A.D. 1359).
† Ordinance as to Poulterers; the Thames, and the Fosses; and Common Beggars. 49 Edw. III. (A.D. 1375).
‡ One of the rabble, a scoundrel, a rascal, ruffian.
§ 13 Edw. I., c. 4.

upon the slightest cause of disgust, to quit their masters: that they wandered thus from country to country; and that many of the runaways turned beggars, and led idle lives in cities and boroughs; although they had sufficient bodily strength to gain a livelihood, if they pleased to work. Many became *staf-strikers*, (cudgel-players, or quarter-staffmen), and wandered in parties of two, three, and four from village to village; but that the greater number turned out *sturdy rogues*, and infested the kingdom with frequent robberies. To remedy those evils, the Commons proposed that no relief should be given to those who were able to work, within boroughs or in the country; that vagrant beggars and staf-strikers should be imprisoned till they consented to return home to work; and that whosoever harboured any runaway servant in his service should be liable to a penalty of £10. It does not appear from the rolls that the King assented to this Bill, but it shows us the early opinions of Parliament on the subject of mendicity."*

Some idea of the height to which the audacity of robbers attained in the later years of this reign may be formed from the fact that in the year 1363 "the King of Cyprus whilst travelling through England was greatly robbed. For this reason King Edward conceded to the London citizens more extensive powers of trial of evildoers and of acquittal of prisoners within the city, the King's justiciaries not being, as they used to be, called in regard to these matters."† There were many causes for these excesses of vagabondism. The freebooting lives which the soldiery led while fighting in France during the numerous wars must have tended materially to unfit them for resuming peaceful pursuits when they returned home. Labour, too, being scarce, owing to the devastation caused by plagues, and the drain upon the population caused by the foreign wars, many labourers naturally took advantage of the condition of things to roam where they pleased and work when they pleased. The King himself, too, set a bad example. He had impoverished his exchequer by his wars and other expenses, and as a result paid no one, and lived at the expense of his subjects during his progresses through the kingdom. Archbishop Islip writes to him, "When men hear of your coming, everybody at once for sheer fear sets about hiding, or eating, or getting rid of their geese and chickens or other possessions, that

* Eden. † Walsingham.

they may not utterly lose them through your arrival." The King left the administration of the kingdom very much in the hands of an unpopular ministry, and after the death of Queen Philippa in 1369 was completely dominated by his mistress, the natural result being popular discontent and disorder.

Robert Langland, who wrote the "Vision of Peers Ploughman" in or about the year 1362, gives some graphic pictures of the peasant and the beggar at this period.

"Confusion to the poor man though he plead for ever. The law is so lordly and dilatory, that without bribes few can gain their ends. Faithful burghers and bondmen she often bringeth to ruin, and reduceth all the commons to care and covetousness."

The condition of the peasant is thus described.

"No man knows, I think, who is worthy to receive: but if we take good heed, the most needy is our neighbour, as prisoners in dungeons, and poor people in cabins, burdened with children, and chief rent to be paid to their lords. What they may save by spinning, they (spenen) spend in house-rent, in milk and in meal to make their cakes, to satisfy their children who cry for food. Themselves also suffer greatly from hunger, and much distress in winter from watching at night, that they may rise to the reel, to rock the cradle, to card, and to comb wool, to mend and wash clothes, to rub and reel yarn, to peel rushes for lights, so that it is pity to read or declare in rhyme the misery that these women who live in poor cottages, and many men besides, endure, both galled in their fingers with frost, and forced to turn the best side outward. Such are ashamed to beg, and would not have it known at their neighbours' houses, what their wants are at noon and evening. But I certainly know, as experience in the world teaches me, what are the wants of others, who have many children and no cattle, and nothing but their own craft to feed and cloath them, with many to depend upon it, and small wages to receive, for, *there* is bread and penny ale taken as a treat, and cold meat and cold fish, instead of baked venison. For such a family on Fridays and fast-days, a farthing's worth of mussels and as many cockles were a feast. True alms it were to help those who have such charges, and to comfort such cottagers, together with the blind and decrepit."

The peasant is recommended to give to the needy wayfarer in preference to the beggar.

"And Peers, if thou be of ability, whoever cries for food at thy gate, divide with him thy bread, thy pottage, and drink, for the love of God. Lend him some of thy loaf, though thou eat the less: and though liars, and drawlatches, and idle loiterers knock, let them wait till the table is cleared, but carry them not a crumb, until all thy poor neighbours have made their (mone) complaint to thee."

Beggars are described as "having no other church than the brewhouse unless they be blind, or ruptured, or sick, begging about the country at other men's buttery hatches or loitering on Fridays and festivals in churches, which is the loller's way of life, filling their bags and stomachs by lies, sitting at night over a hot fire, where they untie their legs, which have been bound up in the daytime, and lying at ease, roasting themselves over the coals, and turning their back to the heat, drinking gallantly and deep, after which they then draw to bed, and rise when they are in the humour. Then they roam abroad and keep a sharp lookout where they may soonest get a breakfast, or a rasher of bacon, money, or victuals, and sometimes both, a loaf, or half a loaf, or a thick piece of cheese, which they carry to their own cabin, and contrive to live in idleness and ease, by the labours of other men. They observe no law, nor marry any woman with whom they have been connected. They beget bastards, who are beggars by nature, and either break the back, or some other bone of their little ones, and go begging with them on false pretences ever after. There are more mis-shapen children among such beggars than among any other men that walk on this earth."

The begging hermits were it appears no better.

"But as to hermits who take up their abode by the highway sides, and in boroughs, among brewers, and beg in churches, whatever holy hermits hate and despise, as wealth, respect of men, and the alms of the rich, these vagabonds and drawlatches, ignorant hermits as they are, covet on the contrary. For they, such loiterers over their ale, are but boys in reading and languages, neither are they holy of life as the old hermits, who formerly dwelt with wild beasts in the woods."

It seems, too, that they expected a reward for their prayers. The pitiful feelings of Peers appear, however, to have been evoked, not without reason, for two classes of beggars—lunatics and pauper residents.

"Yet there are other beggars, who seem to be in health, both men and women, yet want their understanding. Such are lunatic vagrants, and wanderers about, who are more or less mad according to the phases of the moon. These care for no cold, nor reckon aught of heat, and move after the moon, wandering without money, over many wide countries, without understanding, but with no evil intent."

"There is great joy in May among the beasts of the field, and so long as summer lasteth their comfort endureth; and thus there is great merriment among the rich, who have health and plenty, whereas beggars, at Midsummer (when corn begins to grow scarce), sup without bread; yet is winter far worse for them, for they go wet-shod, frost-bitten, and with blains on their fingers, besides being foully rebuked of the rich, so that it is pitiful to hear. O Lord! send a summer of comfort and joy at length to them who have spent all their lives here in want and misery."

Peers is also of opinion that "if Holy Church would also lend its aid, there would be no beggars," that is, no doubt, in inculcating the practice of carefully discriminated charity in lieu of indiscriminate charity, which many regarded as an atonement for sin.

By the commencement of the reign of Richard II. the antagonism between employers and employed had become very much embittered, as may be gathered from the 1 Rich. II., c. 6 (1377).

It recites "that the *villeins* had assembled riotously in considerable bodies, and had, by the advice of certain evil counsellors and abettors, endeavoured to withdraw their services from their *lord*, not only those which they owed to him by tenure of their lands, but likewise the services of their body. That they chiefly attempted to evade these services under colour of certain exemplifications from *Domesday Book*, with relation to the manors or villages in which they lived, and that, by false interpretation of these transcripts, they claimed to be entirely free." The statute therefore enacts "that commissions shall issue under the great seal, upon application of any *lord* (*seigneur*) to inquire into the offences of these refractory villeins; and that they shall be immediately committed to prison without bail or mainprise, if their lords shall so insist." With regard to the exemplifications from Domesday, it is likewise declared "that the offering them in evidence shall not be of any advantage to him who shall so produce them."

Nothing could be more severe than this law, either in its provisions or in its subsequent execution.

The young King had been advised by one part of his council to increase the power of the lower people and to lessen that of the barons, and the King endeavoured to do so by proclamation, but John of Gaunt put himself at the head of the barons, and soon compelled the withdrawal of the proclamation. This merely added fuel to the popular flame. Coupled with the repressive measures adopted to stop the growing freedom of the labourer and to force him back into that serfdom from which he was escaping, as well as to deprive him of the better wages which were legitimately his right, his exasperation reached a point which rendered him ripe to join in a popular outbreak, and that outbreak naturally came on the first opportunity. In the year 1380 a poll-tax was granted to be levied on all persons of adult age except beggars for the purpose of supporting a senseless war in France, and the labourers were thus directly called upon to pay for an expenditure which they had no voice in limiting. To make the matter worse, the necessities of the King forced him to anticipate the proceeds of the tax and to place the collection in the hands of farmers, who naturally exacted it with the greatest rigour. As is well known, a brutal insult offered by one of the collectors to the daughter of a Tiler at Dartford served to give the signal for revolt. The insurrection spread with inconceivable rapidity throughout the kingdom, and its popularity has been attested by the contemporary Latin verses of Gower, which have been thus rendered by Fuller :—

"Tom comes, thereat, when call'd by Wat, and Simm as forward we finde,
Bet calls as quick to Gibb and to Hykk, that neither would tarry behinde.
Gibb, a good whelp of that litter, doth help mad Coll more mischief to do,
And Will he doth vow, the time is come now, he'l joyn with their company too.
Davie complains, whiles Grigg gets the gaines, and Hobb with them doth partake,
Lorkin aloud, in the midst of the croud, conceiveth as deep is his stake.
Hudde doth spoil, whom Judde doth foile, and Tebb lends his helping hand,
But Jack, the mad patch, men and houses doth snatch, and kills all at his command."

The rebels demanded :—

1st. The total abolition of slavery for themselves and their children for ever.

2nd. The reduction of the rent of good land to 4d. per acre.

3rd. The full liberty of buying and selling like other men, in all markets and fairs.

4th. A general pardon for all past offences.

The second of these demands shows that the villeins aspired to become leaseholders. Overawed by the imposing array of the rebels, the King consented to all their demands, and granted them charters of emancipation. But immediately on the dispersion of the peasants after the death of their leader, Wat Tiler, the King and the nobles attacked them at the head of armed bands, and spread death and destruction amongst them, both by the sword and by the pitiless execution of large numbers of them. But although the villeins had failed in their immediate object, they had demonstrated their power in combination, and the landlords, recognising that this power must increase as time rolled on, gradually let their lands on lease, and accepted money payments as a substitute for labour. Moreover, by this means they obtained an income which enabled them to provide for their expenses in attending the Court and for other purposes of luxury or recreation. The labourer may therefore now be considered to be passing from the condition of swelling the outcast rank of vagrancy to the settled rank of resident independence.

Vagabondism was not, however, in any way repressed, as in the year 1383 it was found necessary to pass the following Act (7 Rich. II., c. 5) for the purpose of enforcing the provisions of the 13th Edward I. and the 5th Edward III., cap. 14, and also for supplementing them by conferring unlimited power on the judges for dealing with offenders.

"It is ordained and asserted, That the Statutes made in the Time of King Edward, Grandfather to our Sovereign Lord the King that now is, of Roberdsmen and Drawlatches be firmly holden and kept; moreover it is ordained and asserted, to refrain the malice of divers People, Feitors,* and wandering from Place to Place, running in the Country more abundantly than they were wont in times past, that from henceforth the Justices of Assises in their Sessions, the Justices of Peace, and the Sheriffs in every County shall have power to enquire of all such Vagabonds and Feitors, and of their offences, and upon them to do that the law demandeth; and that as well the Justices and Sheriffs, as the Mayors, Bailiffs, Constables, and other Governors of

* A Norman French word, signifying slothful people; from the French *fait tard*.

Towns and places where such Feitors and Vagabonds shall come, shall from henceforth have power to examine them diligently, and to compel them to find surety of their good bearing, by sufficient mainpernors, of such as be distrainable, if any default be found in such Feitors and Vagabonds; and if they cannot find such surety, they shall be sent to the next gaol, there to abide till the coming of the Justices assigned for the Deliverance of the Gaols, who in such case shall have power to do upon such Feitors and Vagabonds so imprisoned that which to them best shall seem by the law."

This law, however, speedily proved as inefficacious for the purposes for which it was intended as those that preceded it.

We now come to a law which is generally regarded as the commencement of our English poor law, the 12 Rich. II. (1388). It enacts, "That all the Statutes of Artificers, Labourers, Servants, and Victuallers, made as well in the time of our Sovereign Lord the King that now is, as in the Time of his noble Grandfather,* whom God assoil, not repealed, shall be firmly holden and kept." It then ordains, "That Servants going from their service are to carry Letters testimonial from the duly appointed authority of their district. If found wandering without such letters they are ordered to be put in the stocks and kept till they find surety to return to the service or place from whence they came. The penalty for forging such letters is forty days' imprisonment, and any one receiving a servant without them is liable to a penalty to be limited by the Justices of the Peace."

Complaint is then made that " servants and labourers will not serve and labour without outrageous and excessive hire." A rate of wages of servants in husbandry is then decreed, and givers and takers of more than is specified are each to pay a penalty amounting to the value of the excess for a first offence, and double and treble for a second and third offence. Those who "laboured at the plough and cart, or other labour of husbandry," up to the age of twelve years, were not to be put to any mystery or handicraft, and any covenant or bond of apprentice to the contrary was declared to be null. This shows that the agricultural labourers were being drawn to the towns, not only by the attractions of superior wages and better style of living, but also by the freedom they acquired by a residence there of a year and a day. The Act then goes on to recite: "That of every person that goeth begging, and is able

* The 23 and 25 Edw. III.

to serve or labour, it shall be done of him as of him that departeth out of the Hundred and other Places aforesaid without Letter Testimonial, as afore is said, except People of Religion and Hermits having Letters testimonial of their Ordinaries. And that the Beggars impotent to serve shall abide in the Cities and Towns where they be dwelling at the Time of the Proclamation of this Statute; and if the People of Cities or other Towns will not or may not suffice to find them, that then the said beggars shall draw them to other Towns within the Hundreds, Rape or Wapentake, or to the towns where they were born, within Forty Days after the Proclamation made, and there shall continually abide during their lives. And that of all them that go in Pilgrimage as Beggars, and be able to travail, it shall be done as of the said Servants and Labourers, if they have no Letters testimonial of their Pilgrimage under the said seals. And that the Scholars of the Universities that go so begging, have Letters testimonial of their Chancellor upon the same pain."

"They that feign themselves men travelled out of the realm, and there to be imprisoned, shall bring Letters testimonial of the Captains where they were abiding, or of the Mayors or Bailiffs where they arrived, under the same penalties."

"Sheriffs, mayors, bailiffs, and keepers of gaols are ordered to put these enactments in execution under a penalty of 100s."

Here for the first time we have a distinction made between the beggars able to labour and beggars impotent to serve, and it is this distinction which has caused many to regard this Act as the beginning of our poor laws. No express statutory provision is, however, made for the beggars impotent to serve who are now forbidden to wander over the country, but it is evidently hoped that they will be provided for either by the inhabitants of the towns or by the Church.

Poor scholars proceeding to the universities unprovided with the means of subsistence on the way must have been common at this period, as in the *Nigelli Speculum Stultorum*, an Anglo-Latin satirical poem of the twelfth century, we are told that *Burnellus*, who is supposed to be proceeding to study in the celebrated schools in Paris—

> "Hastens with quick body, mind, and foot to his native land,
> But because he was poor and his purse low,
> He often stops his journey to beg."

Regarding the University of Oxford, *Mr. Anstey* says:—

"As to journeys and vacation expenses, the two being closely connected, we would observe that no scholar left Oxford at all, or in rare cases, between October 9th and July 7th at the least; a very large number did not leave the university at all even during the long vacation. Those who did leave probably often walked home, and even begged their way about the country, being, as we find from other sources, quite a nuisance sometimes to the farmer and others at whose doors they sought alms."

Mr. Mullinger thus describes the condition of poor scholars at Cambridge in early times:—

"No scholar was to be rudely repulsed on the score of poverty; if unable to pay for both lodging and tuition he often rendered an equivalent in the shape of very humble services; he waited at table, went on errands, and, if we may trust the authority of the Pseudo-Boethius, was often rewarded by his master's left-off garments. The aids held out by the university were then but few. There were some nine or ten poorly endowed foundations, one or two university exhibitions, and finally the university chest, from which, as a last resource, the hard-pinched student might borrow if he had aught to pledge. The hostel where he resided protected him from positive extortion, but he was still under the necessity of making certain payments towards the expenses. The wealthier class appear to have been under no pecuniary obligations whatever. When therefore a scholar's funds entirely failed him, and his *Sentences* or his *Summulæ*, his Venetian cutlery, and his winter cloak had all found their way into the proctor's hands as security for moneys advanced, he was compelled to have recourse to other means. His academic life was far from being considered to preclude the idea of manual labour. It has been conjectured, by a high authority, that the long vacation was originally designed to allow of members of the universities assisting in the then all-important operation of the ingathering of the harvest. But however this may have been, there was a far more popular method of replenishing an empty purse, a method which the example of the Mendicants had rendered all but universal, and this was no other than begging on the public highways. Among the vices of that rude age parsimony was rarely one, the exercise of charity being in fact regarded as a religious duty. Universal begging implies universal giving. And so it not unfrequently happened that the wealthy merchant, journeying between London and Norwich, or the well-beneficed ecclesiastic or prior of a great house on his way to some monastery in the fen country, would be accosted by some solitary youth with a more intelligent countenance and more educated accent than ordinary, and be plaintively solicited either in English or in Latin, as might best suit the case, for the love of our Lady to assist a distressed votary of learning. In the course of time this easy method of replenishing an empty purse was found to have become far too popular among university students, and it was considered necessary to enact that no scholar should beg in the highways until the Chancellor had satisfied himself of the merits of each individual case and granted a certificate for the purpose."

Scotch scholars were, according to *Dr. Lindsay*, also to be found amongst the mendicant class.

"The University of Oxford itself was accustomed to issue official letters to poor students, allowing them to beg from the townspeople—*literas testimoniales sub sigillo officii ad petendam eleemosynam.* It was almost the only bursary they had to give them, and answered the purpose very well. Begging was a recognised way by which 'clerks' got their living in these days. They repaid their benefactors in prayers. Chaucer's poor clerk

'Busily 'gan for the souls pray
Of them that gave him wherewith to scolay.'"

Besides the young noble and the young Churchman, there must have been many a poor scholar who hurried over the border to swell the ragged hungry crowd, which was one of the most peculiar accompaniments of mediæval university life. How the "poor clerks" could travel as they did from university to university, and how they could live while studying, no one can well tell. Perhaps the Oxford Chancellor's book, with its records of poaching and plundering, highway robbery, and masterful begging, may help to explain the mystery of their lives. Among the crowd there must have been many a Scotchman. They might cross the border as servants to some of those companies of Scottish merchants who were always getting license to trade in England. They might beg or thieve their way alone. They might go in bands, living very much as gipsies do now. At all events, they were to be found in Oxford in the fourteenth century ready to claim their share of the poor's pence on St. Scholastica's Day, and of any other money which the charitable had left for the poor clerks."

The uselessness of trying to fix the rate of wages by Act of Parliament was recognised in the next year (1389-90) by the 13 Rich. II., c. 8, which enacted that justices shall, at certain times, make proclamation *according to the dearth of victuals* how much labourers and handicraftsmen are to take by the day.

In 1392 a more specific provision was made for the impotent poor, as by the 15 Rich. II., c. 6, it was ordained that in every licence of the appropriation of any parish church, "the diocesan shall ordain a convenient sum of money to be distributed yearly of the fruits and profits of the same to the poor parishioners in aid of their living and sustenance for ever."

Froissart says of this reign, " The state generally of all men in England began to murmur and to rise one against another, and ministering of justice was clear stopped up in all courts of England, whereof the valiant men and prelates, who loved rest and peace, and were glad to pay their duties, were greatly abashed; for there rose in the realm companies in divers routs, keeping the fields and highways, so that merchants durst not ride abroad to exercise their merchandise for doubt of robbing; and no man knew to whom to complain to do them right, reason, and justice, which things were right prejudicial and displeasant to the good people of England, for it was contrary to their accustomable usage."

Richard at length wore out the patience of his subjects by his forced loans, oppressive exactions, and other forms of misgovernment, and he was accordingly deposed in favour of his cousin Henry, Duke of Lancaster, who came to the throne as *Henry IV.* in September, 1399.

The first acts of this reign were directed against the turbulence of the Welsh. In March, 1401, an ordinance was published which forbid any collection or "Comortha" to be made in North Wales without the permission of the authorities. It also set forth "that the Minstrels, Bards, Rhymers, and Westours, and other Welsh vagabonds in North Wales, should not henceforth be allowed to overburden the country as hitherto, but that they should be strictly forbidden under penalty of a year's imprisonment." This was further emphasised in the following year by the passing of the 4 Hen. IV., c. 27 (1402), which enacted that—

"To eschew many Diseases and mischiefs, which have happened before this time in the Land of Wales, by many Wasters,* Rhymers, Minstrels and other Vagabonds: It is ordained and stablished, that no Westour,* Rhymer, Minstrel, nor Vagabond, be in any wise sustained in the land of Wales, to make Commorthies or gathering upon the common people there."

Other Acts were also passed to repress the forays of the Welsh, and by the 7 Henry IV., c. 17, the 25 Edward III. and the 12 Richard II. are confirmed, and on account of the scarcity of labourers the apprenticing of their children is forbidden under penalties unless the parents have land or rent of the value of twenty shillings a year. It further directs that "once in the year all the labourers and artificers dwelling in the same leet, shall be sworn to serve and take for their service after the form of the said statutes; and if they refuse that to do, they shall be put in the stocks in the town where they be taken, for three days, without bail or mainprise, till they will make gree, and from thence they shall be sent to gaol."

Up to this time the Welsh appear to have been the only troublesome vagabonds not of English birth against whom it was found necessary to legislate, but in the commencement of the reign of Henry V. those of Irish birth seem to have been sufficiently numerous in England to require special repression, as the 1 Henry V., c. 8 (1413), is directed against Irishmen and Irish clerks mendicant, and orders them to depart the realm.

"For the Quietness and Peace within the Realm of England, and for the increase and enstoring of the Land of Ireland, It is ordained and stablished in this present Parliament, That all Irishmen and begging Irish Clerks, called Chamberdeacons†, be voided out of the Realm, betwixt the Feast of St. Michael next coming, and the Feasts of All Saints next following, upon Pain to lose their Goods, and to be imprisoned at the King's Pleasure; except such as be Graduates in the Schools, and Serjeants and Apprentices of the Law, and such which be Inheritors in England, and religious Persons professed; and except also the Merchants born in Ireland

---

* In the Norman French they are styled *Westours*, which the English version renders "Wasters." *Kelham* gives the meaning of "Westours" as "Wassailers."* The true derivation is *Gwestwr*, see p. 35.

† Toutz Irrois & Clercs Irrois mendinauntz appellez Chaumberdeakyns.

of good name, and their Apprentices now dwelling in England, and them with whom the King will dispense. And that all the Irishmen which have Benefices or offices in the Land of Ireland, shall dwell upon their offices or Benefices for the defence of the Land of Ireland aforesaid."

The disturbed state of Ireland and Wales, the superior wealth of England and the comforts to be obtained in it, were without doubt the causes which brought Irishmen and Welshmen into the country.

By the 2 Henry V., c. 4 (1414), the Statute of 12 Richard II. and all other good Statutes of labourers made and not repealed were ordered to be firmly holden and kept and put in due execution, and large and irresponsible powers were conferred on the justices for purposes of examination and punishment. It appears too by this Act that certain hospitals which had been founded for the reception of impotent men and women, lazars, men out of their wits, and poor women with child, and to nourish, refresh, and relieve other poor people in the same, were for the most part decayed owing to the malversation of their endowments. Inquiry was therefore ordered into these misuses.

In the *Liber Albus* or *White Book of the City of London* about this period we find "Judgment of Pillory upon one who feigned himself a beggar (*i.e.* a proctor or collector of alms by proxy) for the Hospital of Bethlehem."

Henry VI. was only nine months old when he succeeded his father in 1422, and the kingdom during his minority was governed by a Council. One of the first enactments of this reign (1 Hen. VI., c. 3) was an Act against Irishmen in consequence of complaints of the Commons. It runs thus—

"Forasmuch as divers Manslaughters, Murders, Rapes, Robberies, and other Felonies, Riots, Conventicles, and divers other offences now late have been done in divers Counties of England, by People born in Ireland, repairing to the town of Oxenford, and there dwelling under the Jurisdiction of the University of Oxenford, to the great fear of all manner of People dwelling thereabout, as by all the Commons of the same Realm assembled in Parliament it was grievously complained; the King by the Assent aforesaid, and at the Request of the same Commons hath ordained That all people bórn in Ireland shall depart out of the Realm within a month after Proclamation made of this ordinance, upon pain to lose their goods, and to be imprisoned at the King's will, excepting Graduates, Beneficed Clergy, &c., who shall find surety."

The 6 Henry VI., cap. 3 (1427), recites the statutes 12 and 13 Richard II., and then declares that these statutes are not observed —"that is to say, the first statute, because that the punishment in the same is too hard upon the masters of such servants, forasmuch as they shall be destitute of servants if they should not pass (*i.e.* disregard) the ordinance of the statute; and the second statute, because that no pain is limited against him that doeth contrary thereto. It is therefore ordained that justices of the peace and the mayors and bailiffs of cities and towns shall, once in the year in full session, make proclamation how much every servant of husbandry shall take for his service by the year then next following; and further, that they shall make like proclamation at Easter and Michaelmas how much every artificer and workman shall take by the day, and by the week. Every servant, artificer, or workman acting contrary to the proclamation is to forfeit every time the value of his wages, and in default to go to prison for forty days, and is also liable to yield to the party grieved his double damages." So that the employer might first make a contract, and having obtained its fulfilment might sue for damages under it.

In the year 1444 a new scale of wages was established by the 23 Henry VI., c. 12, and servants in husbandry are required to give their masters warning, and to engage with some other master before quitting their present service, otherwise they are to continue to serve their first master for the next year. The wages prescribed for agricultural labourers in this Act are more than double those allowed by the Act of 1388.

In the year 1442 bitter complaints were made by the Commons of the counties of Hereford, Gloucester, and Salop, of "the great oppressions and extortions which the people of Wales and the Marches committed daily on the inhabitants of the said counties, by taking and carrying away their horses, cattle, and other goods and chattels into the Marches," and there retaining them till the persons to whom they belonged ransomed them or compounded for them, and as a consequence in the year 1446-7 all statutes against Welshmen were confirmed by the 25 Henry VI.

In the year 1450 occurred a rebellion similar in many respects to that of the year 1381. An Irishman named John Cade, taking advantage of the discontent of the lower orders, and assuming the name of Mortimer in order to give himself importance, proclaimed that he would procure a remission of taxation and greater liberties for the people. He assembled a large army of the people in Kent, and for nearly six weeks was able to overawe the forces of the Crown. Insurrections also took place in other parts of the country, and thus again demonstrated the power of the lower orders, and the necessity for conciliating them by timely concessions.

In 1461 the turbulent reign of Henry VI. came to an end. Of that of his successor, Edward IV., there is little to be said beyond that the disturbed state of the country favoured vagabondism and robbery. After the peace of Picquigny in 1475, the English soldiers on their return from France plundered their own countrymen to compensate themselves for the loss of booty which they were led to expect they would obtain in France.

The short reign of Richard III. was also a disturbed one, and did not produce any legislation bearing on vagrancy.

In the next reign the first Act against vagabondism is the 11 Henry VII., c. 2 (1495), which commences by reciting, "For asmoche as the Kyngis grace moost entierly desireth amonges all erthly thingis the prosperite and restfulnes of this his land and his subgettis of the same to leve quietly and surefully to the plesure of God and according to his lawes, willing and alweiss of his pitie intending to reduce theym therunto by softer meanes then by such extreme rigour therfor purveied in a Statute made in the tyme of King Richard the second, considering also the great charges that shuld growe to his subgettis for bringing of vagabondes to the Gaoles according to the same Statute and the long abiding of theym therin, wherby by likelehede many of theym shuld lose their lives." It then proceeds to enact that the authorities shall make due search and take all idle vagabonds and suspected persons living suspiciously and set them in the stocks for three days and three nights without other sustenance than bread and water, and then to be commanded to avoid the town, and if they are taken again in the same town they are to be set in the stocks for six days, with the same diet, any person giving them meat or drink while in the stocks or favouring them in their misdoing is to forfeit twelvepence for each offence.

All beggars not able to work are to go to their several places of abode or birth, or to be punished as aforesaid. Clerks of the universities, soldiers, shipmen, or travelling men, are not to be exempt from punishment unless they carry proper certificates. Officers not executing the Act are liable to a fine of twenty pence for each omission. Diminution of punishment is to be made in the case of women great with child, and men and women in extreme sickness.

This statute appears to reflect the character of the King, who always professed to love and seek peace. It differs from the 7 Richard II. in substituting the penalty of the stocks for committal to gaol, and also in imposing a penalty of twenty pence on any officer who neglects to carry out its provisions, and a penalty of twelvepence on the misguided almsgivers who aided and abetted the captured vagrant.

The lawlessness and turbulence which prevailed during the wars of the Roses must have swelled the ranks of vagrancy to a very great extent, and the gaols would therefore have been inadequate for the reception of captured vagrants. Moreover, their conveyance to gaol must have been troublesome and expensive; the rough-and-ready punishment of the stocks was consequently more convenient and more likely to be put in practice.

An Act for regulating the rate of servants' wages (11 Hen. VII., c. 22) was also passed in this year, but was repealed in the following year, possibly on account of wheat having risen to a famine price.

The next Act against vagabonds and beggars is the 19 Hen. VII., c. 12 (1503-4), which commences with a similar recital to the 11 Hen. VII., c. 2, and then proceeds to enact that vagabonds are only to be set in the stocks for one day and one night, with no other sustenance than bread and water, and they are then to go to the place of their birth or where they last lived for three years. If they are again taken in the same town they are to be put in the stocks for three days and three nights with a like diet. Any person giving them meat or drink while in the stocks, or favouring them in their misdoing, or receiving or harbouring them over one night, is to forfeit twelvepence for each offence. Beggars not able to work are to go to the place of their birth or where they last resided for three years, upon pain of being punished as aforesaid; and any harbouring them for more than one night is liable to the same penalties. Clerks of the universities, soldiers, shipmen, and travelling men are not to be exempt unless they carry proper certificates. The penalties on officers neglecting to execute the Act are raised to 3s. 4d. for each offence. Diminution of punishment is to be made in the case of women great with child, men and women in great sickness, and persons being impotent and above seventy years of age. Justices are empowered to make privy searches for offenders four times a year.

The punishments under this Act are, it will be perceived, very much milder than those of the preceding Act, the reason being, no doubt, that its provisions were found too severe to be popular, and therefore the penalties under it were either perfunctorily enforced or not enforced at all. Almsgiving, even of an indiscriminate character, it must be remembered was encouraged by the precepts of the Church, and it must therefore have been difficult at first to convince people that what they had been taught to believe was a religious duty was as regards the law a criminal offence. For a first offence the penalty is reduced to one day and one night in the stocks, instead of three, and for a second offence three instead of six. Impotent beggars are now directed to go to the place of their birth or where they last resided for three years. A penalty of 12d. is imposed on any one succouring them while in the stocks, and, in addition, any one harbouring them more than one night is liable to a similar penalty. So far as length of sojourn goes, this prohibition resembles that in the Assize of Clarendon. The provisions for the diminution of punishment are decidedly humane, and particularly so for such an age.

Justice was well administered during this reign, and vagabondage must have been reduced, both from this cause and from the curtailment of the power of the nobles which Henry systematically carried out. Notwithstanding his love of money, he built and endowed several religious foundations, and was a great almsgiver.

CHAPTER IV.

1509—1558.

Accession of Henry VIII.—Mummers and disguised persons to be treated as vagabonds—Begging in 1519—The court infested with beggars—The supplication for beggars—Laws against the gypsies and vagabonds and beggars — Professors of physiognomy, palmistry, and other "crafty sciences"—Forms of license for begging—Proclamations against beggars—Excessive pasture a cause of poverty—Law against Welsh conmorthas—Further legislation against vagabonds and beggars—Whipping of vagrants—" The hye way to the spyttel house "—The effects of the suppression of monasteries—Strolling players and ballad singers—Social condition of the Scottish border—Manumission of bondmen—Condition of vagabondage at the commencement of the reign of Edward VI.—Legislation under Edward VI.—Sir John Cheke on vagabondage—Proclamation against players — Further legislation — The relief of the poor — Law against tinkers and pedlars—Proclamation against vagabonds and players.—Regulation of the Borders—The reign of Mary — Legislation against gypsies—Proclamation against vagabonds—Laws for the relief of the poor.

WE now come to the reign of Henry VIII., a period memorable for its social and political changes.

The first Act of this reign dealing with vagabonds is the 3 Hen. VIII., c. 9 (1511-12), which is ostensibly directed against mummers or performers in dumb show, whose performances had been popular for a period of nearly three centuries. It is styled " An Act against disguised persons and wearing of visours," and recites that "lately within this realm divers persons have disguised and apparelled them, and covered their faces with visours and other things in such manner that they should not be known, and divers of them in a company together naming themselves mummers have come to the dwelling place of divers men of honour and other substantial persons ; and so departed unknown ; whereupon murders, felony, rape, and other great hurts and inconveniences have aforetime grown and hereafter be like to come by the colour thereof, if the said disorder should continue not reformed."
It then enacts that " the scid mommers or disgysed persones and

every of theym shalbe arrested by eny of the Kings liege people as Suspectes or Vacabundes and be committed to the Kings gaole, Ther to be imprisoned by the space of thre months wythowte bayle or maymprys, and then to make fyne to the Kyng by the discrescion of the Justices by whome they shalbe delyvered owte of prisone."

In the year 1514-15 a renewed attempt was made by the 6 Hen. VIII., c. 3, to regulate the wages of artificers and labourers, which appears to show that the labouring classes were again struggling for an increase, which the masters on the other hand were determined to prevent. The Act, as might be expected, was futile for the purposes for which it was intended, and in the following year it was repealed so far as it affected masons, carpenters, and other artificers in the City of London, probably in consequence of the immense amount of building which was then going on.

Owing to the impetus given to commerce in the reign of Henry VII. and its continuance in the present reign, the wealth of the nation had greatly increased, and was followed by a luxurious style of living, of which the King himself set an example. Careless profusion is a certain progenitor of idleness, and idleness of begging, so that we can easily perceive one great cause of the increase of vagrancy at an early period of this reign.

Harman gives us the following picture of the condition of begging in the year 1521.

"I thought it meéte to confer with a very old man that I was well acquaynted with, whose wyt *and* memory is mervelous for his yeares, beinge about the age of fourescore, what he knewe when he was yonge of these lousey leuterars.* And he shewed me, that when he was yonge he wayted upon a man of much worshyp in Kent, who died immediatly after the last Duke of Buckingham was beheaded :† at his buryall there was such a number of beggers, besides poore housholders dwelling there aboutes, that unneth ‡ they mighte lye or stande aboute the House : then was there prepared for them a great and large barne, and a great fat ox sod § out in Furmenty for them, with bread *and* drinke aboundantly to furnesh out the premisses ; and every person had two pence, for such was the dole. When night approched, *the* pore housholders repaired home to their houses : the other wayfaring bold beggers remained alnight in *the* barne ; and the same barne being serched with light in the night by this old man (and then yonge),

* Idle vagabonds.   † May 17, 1521.   ‡ Scarcely (*A.S.*)   § Boiled.

with others, they tolde seven score persons of men, every of them having his woman, except it were two women that lay alone to gether for some especyall cause. Thus having their makes to make merry withall, the buriall was turned to bousing.* *and* belly chere,† morning to myrth, fasting to feasting, prayer to pastyme *and* pressing of papes, and lamenting to Lechery! "

Beggars even infested the Court itself, as in 1526 a new order was made for the Knight Marshal to see to the exclusion from the Court of " boys and vile persons and punishment of vagabonds and mighty beggars, also of unthrifts and common women. The Lord Steward was at the same time commanded to keep the Court."

In 1529 the famous " Supplicacyon for the Beggers " by Simon Fish was published. It professes to be a complaint on behalf of the impotent poor against the Church of Rome, and opens thus :—

" To The King oure sovereygne lorde,—

"Most lamentably compleyneth theyre wofull mysery unto youre highnes youre poore daily bedemen, the wretched hidous monstres (on whome scarcely for horror any yie dare loke,) the foule, unhappy sorte of lepres, and other sore people, nedy, impotent, blinde, lame, and sike, that live onely by almesse, howe that theyre nombre is daily so sore encreased, that all the almesse of all the weldisposed people of this youre realme is not halfe ynough for to susteine theim, but that for verey constreint they die for hunger. And this most pestilent mischief is comen uppon youre said poore beedmen by the reason that there is, yn the tymes of youre noble predecessours passed, craftily crept ynto this youre realme an other sort (not of impotent, but) of strong, puissaunt, and counterfeit holy, and ydell, beggers and vacabundes whiche syns the tyme of theyre first entre by all the craft and wilinesse of Satan are nowe encreased under your sight, not onely into a great nombre, but also ynto a kingdome. These are (not the herdes, but the ravinous wolves going in herdes clothing, devouring the flocke,) the Bisshoppes, Abbottes, Priours, Deacons, Archedeacons, Suffraganes, Prestes, Monkes, Chanons, Freres, Pardoners, and Somners."

In the succeeding year an Act was passed against the gypsies (22 Hen. VIII., c. 10). This was followed by a most elaborate statute against vagrancy, the 22 Hen. VIII., c 12 (1530-1), which

---

* Drinking.   † Eating.

recites " where in all places throughe out this Realme of Englande, Vacabundes and Beggers have of longe tyme increased & dayly do increase in great & excessyve nombres by the occasyon of ydelnes, mother & rote of all vyces, wherby hath insurged & spronge & dayly insurgethe & spryngeth contynuall theftes murders & other haynous offences & great enormytes to the high displeasure of God the inquyetacon & damage of the Kyngis People & to the marvaylous disturbance of the Comon Weale of this Realme. And whereas many & sondry goode lawes, streyte statutes & ordenances have ben before this time devysed & made as well by the Kyng our Sovreign Lorde as also by divers his most noble progenytours Kyngis of Englande for the most necessary & due reformacion of the premysses, yet that notwythstonding the sayde nombers of vacabundes & beggers be not sene in any partie to be mynysshed, but rather dayly augmentyd & encreased into greate routes and companyes as evydently it dothe & maye appere." It then proceeds to enact that justices of peace in every county shall make diligent search of all aged, poor, and impotent persons which live by alms of charity, and may license them to beg within certain limits ; beggars begging outside these limits are to be set in the stocks for two days and nights with a diet of bread and water only, and sworn without delay to return to their own limits. Beggars without licenses are to be stripped from the middle upwards and whipped, or else at the discretion of the justice or high constable set in the stocks for three days and nights with a diet of bread and water, and they are then to be furnished with a license assigning them a limit within which to beg. All able-bodied persons found begging are to be taken to the nearest market town, or other place most convenient, and there to be tied to the end of a cart naked and be beaten with whips throughout the town till their bodies are bloody, after which they are to return to the place where they were born, or where they last dwelt by the space of three years, being furnished with a pass for the purpose certifying their punishment and limiting the time within which they have to return, and every time they make default in the order they are to be whipped.

If the constables of any town or parish neglect to arrest and punish a beggar, the township or parish is to forfeit for every impotent beggar 3s. 4d., and for every strong beggar 6s. 8d.

All scholars of the universities of Oxford and Cambridge that go about begging not being authorised under the seal of the said universities, all shipmen pretending losses of their ships and goods, are to be punished as able-bodied beggars. All proctors and pardoners, and all other idle persons going about, some of them using divers and subtle crafty and unlawful games and plays, and some of them feigning themselves to have knowledge in physic, physiognomy, palmistry, or other crafty sciences, whereby they bear the people in hand, that they can tell their destinies, diseases, and fortunes, and such other like fantastical imaginations, to the great deceit of the King's subjects, are punishable by whipping for two days together. For a second offence they are to be scourged two days and the third day to be put in the pillory from 9 to 11 o'clock in the forenoon and to have one of their ears cut off; and for a third offence they are to be whipped, put in the pillory, and have their other ear cut off.

Persons giving harbourage, money, or lodging to able-bodied beggars are liable to fines at the discretion of the justices. Any person hindering the execution of the Act or making rescue against any mayor or other person endeavouring to execute it, is liable to forfeit one hundred shillings in addition to imprisonment at the King's will.

Prisoners on their release from prison begging without a license from the gaoler are liable to the same punishment as able-bodied beggars.

The following forms were authorised under the Act:—

License to an Impotent Beggar to beg.

"Kanc ss. Memorand that A. B. of Dale for reasonable consideracõns ys lycensed to begge wythin the Hundred of P.K. and L. in the sayde Countie, yoven under the Seale of that lymytte, Tali die & anno."

Letter to be delivered to a Beggar or Vagabond after he had been whipped.

"Kent ss. J. S. whypped for a vagarant stronge begger at Dale in the sayde Countie, accordyng to the lawe in the xijth daye of July in the xxiij^{ti} yere of Kyng Henry the viij was assigned to passe forthwyth & directly from thens to Sale in the Countye of Midd; where he sayth he was borne, or where he last dwelled by the tyme of iij yeres; and he ys lymytted to be there wythin xiiij dayes next ensuyng at his parell, or wythin such nomber of dayes as to hym shalbe lymytted by the dyscretion of the maker of the sayde letter: In wytnes wherof the seale of the lymytte of the sayde place of his punysshement herunto is sette."

The prohibition regarding the practice of "physiognomy, palmistry, or other crafty sciences," on the part of itinerant professors, affords curious evidence of the ignorance and superstition which prevailed then and for long afterwards; in fact, it can hardly be said to be extinct now.

Physiognomy was a method of prediction founded on an examination of the lineaments, and the colour and appearance of the veins, and was, like palmistry, treated as an abstruse science only to be indulged in by qualified professors. The jealousy with which the common herd of empirics were regarded by the self-elected professors is thus set forth by *Richard Saunders* in "Palmistry, the Secrets thereof disclosed," published in 1664.

"Having thus far asserted the laudable utillity of *Christian Prudent Science*, let me warn my *Reader* of those *Sycophants*, and *Delusive Ignorants*, through whose *Sides* this *pretious Science* is dayly wounded, such *spawn* of *shame*, that impudently make Profession of Art, not onely in several *Countryes*, but lurk in *Obscure corners*, in and about this Famous City, many *Illiterate* peices of *Non-scence* and *Impudence*, of the Female kind, whose Ignorance transcends the Vulgar *Gypsies*, and Impudence sufficient to out face a *Whipping post*, *Ptolomy* in his time complain'd of such, and *Cardan* found a Generation *Quicum* saith he *non sint, videri volunt, lucrique cupiditate artem profitentur, quam vix a limine salutarunt*, such though they were *not*, yet would seem to be *Artists*, and for *Lucres* sake professe it, though they had not *saluted* the thresholds thereof; *Haly* mentions *one* before *His* time, that *Affirmed* when *Cor. Leonis* in such a Year, came to the fifteenth Degree of *Leo*, it would set the *world* on *Flame* through excesse of *Heat*, the consequence of which was, it was the most cruel *cold* and *Sharpest* Winter known before; and *Petrus Aretinus*, mentions such an *Ignoramus* in His time, that Predicted a great *Flood*, or rather a *Deluge* in the month of *February*, 1524; which so frighted the People (notwithstanding the evil Season of the Year) that they *Left* their *Dwellings*, and fled with their *Goods* to the *Mountains*, which when the *Time* came, there was not any *Month* in the *Year* so *Fair* nor more *Serene* weather, no *Rain*, nor *Clouds* threatning the least of *Rain*, which in many ages was not known before. There hath not wanted such *Ideots* in *our* times, frighting the People, and Prognosticating in their Illiterate *Hare-brain'd* Predictions, the *End* of the *World*, which I have not omitted to take notice of, in my *Apollo Anglicanus*, especially for the Year, 1656, &c. But for the *time* to *come*, that our Country may be *undeceiv'd*, I will premise such *Quallifications* as every *able Artist* ought to be indued with, according to the approbation of the best *Learned* and *Judicious*, which will serve as a *Touch stone* to examine every *Professor*, and to discern the *Prudent* from the *Impudent*.

" 1. The first Quallification requisite to constitute an *Artist* is, that he be highly *Ingenious*.

" 2. Is required, a good and strong memory.

" 3. That he be *Prudent, Discreet, Honest,* and of a *Good* and sound judgment.

" 4. That he chiefly value and esteem the *Truth in* and *above* all things.

" 5. That he be a good *Linguist* and *Scholler*.

" 6. That he be a good *Phylosopher*, skil'd in all parts of Phylosophy, viz. *Logick, Physicks, Ethicks,* and *Metaphisiques*.

" 7. That he be well *verst* in the *Stars ;* their *Natures, Motions,* and *Accidents,* viz. be a good *Astronomer*.

" 8. That he be a *Good* and *able Arithmetition*.

" 9. That he be a Diligent *Hearer* and *Observer* of the most Eminent Persons in his time, which hold forth the most Excellent and Admirable Conclusions, drawn down to us by their own Experience, and that he give much *Diligence* to *Reading* those *Books* which have been written by the most *worthy, judicious,* and *Famous* authors upon that Subject.

" 10. That he be assiduously *Diligent* in Studies and Labours wholly intent upon the art.

" 11. That he be sedulously *diligent* in *Collecting, Recording,* and *Observing* all practical experiments.

" 12. It's very requisite that he be furnished with a meet knowledge of *agriculture*, with knowledge Nautical, *Millitary,* and Physical, as also the *Geometrical* and *Geographical* Position, and description of places, *the Habitual Dispositions* and *Manners* of men, of *Regions*, of their Laws, *Religious Customs,* and generally of all things.

" These Quallifications *premised*, will sufficiently *inform* such of the *forfeit* of their *Judgments, Reason,* and *Discretions*, that heed *Babling* Women and *Obscure* Persons, *Seducers,* the very *shame* and *bane* of Science."

I have here added, for the benefit of the studious, divers Effigies of Metoposcopy noted according to most acurate and exact observation, which being as an Epitomy of this whole Doctrine, may delight the Reader: In which he shall do well to consider the lines relating to the Planets, as they are before in the Book noted, viz. the upper line next the hair to Saturn; the second to Jupiter, and so of the rest.

Such a Line of Jupiter, signifies riches, prudence and a good nature.

A circle in the Line of Jupiter, predicts loss of riches.

A line inflex, and so bowing towards the nose, denotes the worst of conditions.

The lines in this manner straight, denote a good wit, most honest, approved, and commendable moralities and conditions, nothing of fraud, or dissimulation; he is too plain and honest to thrive, without a miracle.

This position of the forehead and lines, renders the person to be disposed to divers things, having a various genius, and a flattering, false, unstable fortune.

Such lines signifie riches and good Fortune.

The

The arrogant and charlatanic assumption of pretentious scholarship of this description is contemptuously exposed by *Erasmus* in his "Praise of Folly," written in 1511.*

"But those of them who feel most conscious of their own superior erudition, and regard with peculiar contempt the ignorance of others, are the mathematicians. These men when engaged in scrawling their mysterious geometrical hieroglyphics, their triangles, squares, circles, and so forth, adding to one another in the queerest manner possible, and concocting at last a sort of eccentric looking picture, having the appearance of a kind of labyrinth, with letters of the alphabet dotted about it here and there like soldiers in sentry boxes, first placed in one order and then anon in another, make unsophisticated lookers-on wonder immensely what inscrutable conjurations they are up to. They effectually accomplish one object, at any rate, which they have ever much at heart, that of throwing a plentiful amount of dust into inexperienced people's eyes, and gaining to themselves credit for an intelligence they don't possess!

"To this philosophical brotherhood belong all those who give out that they can foretell future events by observing the positions of the stars. And they predict occurrences of the most prodigious proportions. Talk of the marvels of magic! Why they dwindle to insignificance when compared with the astounding wonders which astrologers declare to us are about to be. Yet—fortunate men—they find gullible people enough in the world to swallow their wildest announcements!"

The principal other "crafty" sciences practised at this time were—*Metoposcopy*, or judging of things to come by the aspect of the forehead; *Æromancy*, or divination by figures in the air; *Alectromancy*, or divination by a cock; *Aruspicy*, by signs appearing in the bowels of sacrificed animals; *Augury*, by the flight or chattering of birds or the voices of animals; *Christallomancy*, by the lots of numbers; *Clidomancy*, by a key; *Corilomancy*, by a forked rod; *Coscinomancy*, by turning a sieve; *Dactilomancy*, by a ring; *Geomancy*, by figures or lines drawn on the earth, or by certain signs appearing in the earthly bodies, as in wood, iron, or polished stones, beryls, or glass; *Hydromancy*, by appearances in the water; *Necromancy*, by using blood and writing or speaking certain verses for the purpose of raising the dead to speak and

* Translated by James Copner, 1878.

teach future things; *Onychomancy*, or *Onymancy*, by the finger-nails of an unpolluted boy; *Pyromancy*, by forms appearing in the fire; *Spatulamancy* (called in Scotland *Slinneanach*), by reading the speal bone or the blade bone of a shoulder of mutton well scraped. The signification of omens, dreams (or *Oneirocracy*) and of moles on the body also formed part of this scientific curriculum.

Immediately upon the passing of the Act a proclamation was issued commanding that—

"If within two days after the publication of the proclamation any are found out of the hundred where they were born, or have resided for three years before and have not demanded a billet to convey them thither, they are to be stripped naked from the privy parts upwards and sharply scourged, old and sick persons, and women with child, alone excepted; after which a billet is to be delivered to them certifying the infliction of the punishment, according to a form annexed, signed by the justices. The vagrant must then lose no time on his way homeward, on pain of a repetition of the punishment."

This was followed by another proclamation specially applying to the Court.

"All vagabonds, mighty beggars, and other idle persons are to leave the court in twenty-four hours. No person is to keep more than his proper number of servants, or have vagabonds resorting to his chamber. No person is to keep hounds or greyhounds, or hunt, without licence; and no one is allowed to keep ferrets."

In 1533-4, the 25 Henry VIII., c. 13, was passed for the purpose of preventing the union of farms and the conversion of arable land into pasture on the ground of encouraging vagabond habits. The Act recites that "dyvers and sundry of the Kynge's subjectes, to whome God of hys goodnes hath disposed greate plentie and abundaunce of moveable substance, nowe of late within fewe yeres have dayly studyed and invented ways and meanes how they myght accumulate and gather together into few handes, as well great multitude of fermes as greate plentie of catall, and in especiall shepe, puttyng suche londes as they can gett to pasture, and not to tyllage, wherby they have not only pulled downe churches and townes, and inhanced the old ratis of the rentis, or els brought it to suche excessyve fines that no poure man is able to meddel with it, but also have raysed and enhaunsed the prises of all manner of corne, cattal, woll, pygges, geese, hennes, chekyns, egges, and suche other, almoste doble above the prices which hath byn accustomed, by reason wherof a mervaylous multitude and nombre of the people of this Realme be not able to provyde meate, drynke, and clothes necessary for theym selfes, theire wyfes, and childern, but be so discoraged with myserye and povertie *that they fall dayly to thefte, robbery, and other inconvenience,* or pitifully dye for hunger and colde." It then proceeds to assert that the chief reason is "the greate profette that comyth of shepe," and orders as a remedy that no man shall keep above two thousand sheep, under the penalty of 3s. 4d. for every one kept above that number. This Act denotes that the woollen manufacture was largely increasing, and it seems curious that the surplus agricultural population should not have been absorbed by the manufacturing towns, and rather points to their inadaptability to new conditions of life.

The next Act we have to notice (26 Henry VIII., c. 6, s. 4) passed in the year 1534, is another direction against " Commorthas " and collections in Wales.

"That no person nor persons from henseforth, without licence of the said comyssioners in writinge, shall within Wales or marches of the same, or in any shires adjoyninge to the same, requiyre procure, gather, or levye any commorthe, bidalle, tenantale, or other colleccon or exaccon of goodes, cattulles, money or any other thinge, under colour of marienge or suffringe of their children, sayenge or synginge their fyrste masses or gospelles of any prestes or clarkes, or for redempcion of any murder or any other felonye, or for any other maner of cause by whatt name or names soever they shalbe callyd."

A printer named *Robert Copland*, in a tract entitled, "The Hye Way to the Spyttelhouse," gives a picture of the state of the poor at this period, in the form of a conversation between himself and the porter of St. Bartholomew's Hospital, which was founded by Rahere in 1102, and re-endowed by Henry VIII. after the dissolution. Speaking of those gathered at the gate of the "spital" seeking admission, *Copland* says, they were people with bag and staff, crooked, lame, and blind, scabby and scurvy, pock eaten both in flesh and skin, lousy and scald, and bald as apes, with scarcely a rag to cover them, breechless, barefooted, all stinking with dirt, with a thousand tatters drabbling to the skirt. Boys, girls, and lazy strong knaves, shivering and distracted, leaning on their staves and crying, "Good master, for your mother's blessing, give us a halfpenny towards our lodging." *The porter* expostulates with them for begging, pointing out that they will be lodged in the hospital. In answer to *Copland, the porter* says they take in all such folk who ask lodging for our Lord's sake, though they refuse certain classes. *Copland* asks if they take in losels,* mighty beggars, and vagabonds, truands,† michers,‡ hedge creepers,§ fylloks,|| and lusks,¶ who during the summer live in ditches and under bushes, loitering and wandering by by-ways from place to place without working, living upon haws and blackberries, and indulging in hedge-breaking, who in winter resort to the town and do nothing but wander up and down. He adds that he marvels since they offer lodging to the poor so many of them are to be found sleeping out under stalls, in porches, and in doorways. *The porter* says that all such folks as *Copland* describes are "michers" that live in "truandise,"** whom they will not admit. The people whom they relieve are those who are unable to labour and have no friends to help them, such as old people, the sick and impotent, poor women in childbed, men suffering from bodily injury, people afflicted with smallpox or pestilence, honest folk fallen into poverty, wayfarers, maimed soldiers, and bedridden people. *Copland* proceeds to say that common beggars are to be met with in all the streets, and that as he walked to St. Paul's Church beggars sat on each side the way. There was "one mighty stubborn slave," who begged for others for the sake of the "five joys of the Virgin," vowing to recite Our Lady's psalter three times in return. An honest serving-man after performing his devotions had compassion on the beggar, and when he was gone the beggar pulled out eleven pence,†† and called to his companions to go to dinner, saying it was an unprofitable day. *The porter* says they do not admit such people, but that they resort to the Barbican, to Turnmill Street, in Houndsditch and behind the Fleet, and twenty places more, where they revel and indulge in drunken debauchery. Some "beggarly churls" to whom they resort are, he says, the maintainers of a great set of "mighty lubbers," and have them in their service some as jour-

---

* Bad worthless fellows. † Miserable beggars.
‡ Petty thieves. § Those who lurked about hedges for the purpose of stealing and spoiling.
|| Wanton girls.
** Wretchedness. ¶ Lusty beggars and thieves.
†† Equivalent to about the same number of shillings in the present day.

neymen and some as apprentices, they go on crutches * to each
market and fair, and to all places to which people repair, and so
dissimulate as false thieving flowches,† with bloody clouts about
their legs, and plaisters on their skin; some counterfeit leprosy,
and others put soap in their mouths to make foam, and fall down
as if they had St. Cornelius's evil." *Copland* asks if any masterless men come to the "spital," such as have served the King
beyond the sea, and who being without means must either beg or
steal. Some of them, he says, are proper men and tall. *The
porter* answers that such men do one bad thing, which is to wear
soldier's clothes and so deceive the people. He says they are
in general vagabonds who will not submit to discipline nor stay
long in any employment, and who will rob their masters. Many
of them live by open begging, going with bag, dish, and staff,
ragged and lousy, and mixing with the "riff raff." These go
from spital to spital prowling, and poaching at every door for
lumps of bread and meat. Others whom the porter terms "Nightingales of Newgate," walk and strut about pretending that they
have suffered shipwreck, or have been in captivity in France and
are penniless. They rob solitary passengers, and do not desire
food or drink, but "very white thread to sew good ale." Other
"rogers" ‡ pretend to be poor scholars of Oxford and Cambridge.

After five years' experience of the Vagrant Act passed in 1530-1,
another Act was passed for the purpose of supplying a deficiency
in the previous Act, namely the relief of the poor. This Act
(27 Hen. VIII., c. 25, 1535-6), commences by reciting that
all beggars are required to repair to the place of their birth, or
where they had last dwelt for three years, and that no provision
is made in the Act 22 Hen. VIII., c. 12, for their employment
or relief, and then enacts that officers of cities, &c., shall receive
and relieve such beggars, and set all sturdy and valiant beggars
to work for their maintenance, parishes are bound to carry out
this provision under a penalty of twenty shillings a month.
Beggars travelling homewards with a pass are at the end of every
ten miles ordered to repair to the constable of the parish, who is to
furnish them with meat and drink for one meal and lodging for
one night only.

* Even before the Conquest cripples used to assemble to solicit charity at
Cripplegate in London, pleading the example of the lame man who begged
alms of St. Peter and St. John at the gate of the temple.
† Big, fat, dirty persons.   ‡ A cant name for a rogue.

The Act then recites that all and every idle person, ruffelers calling themselves serving-men, having no masters, are liable to punishment under 22 Hen. VIII., c. 12. Officers of cities are authorised to direct searches by night for ruffelers, sturdy vagabonds, and valiant beggars, and all persons required are to assist in such searches. Ruffelers, sturdy vagabonds, and valiant beggars offending a second time are not only to be whipped again, but to have the upper part of the gristle of the right ear clean cut off, and then sent back to their place of settlement. Such persons found wandering in idleness after this punishment are adjudged to suffer pains and execution of death as felons.

"Leprous and bedridden creatures" are at liberty to remain in the place where they are, and are not compelled to go to their place of settlement. Children above five and under fourteen found begging or idle may be apprehended and placed in charge of masters of husbandry or other crafts or labours to be taught by the which they may get their livings when they come of age. Clothes being given them to enable them to enter the service. Any above the age of twelve and under sixteen who refuse such service or leave it without reasonable cause, are to be openly whipped with rods at the discretion of the authorities, and sent back to service. Any person refusing to execute the punishment is to be set in the stocks two days with a diet of bread and water.

Officers and churchwardens are ordered to gather alms for the maintenance of impotent and the employment of sturdy beggars, and the Clergy are commanded to exhort people to alms for the purposes of this Act.

No persons are permitted to make any common or open doles, or give any ready money in alms except to be applied to the purposes of this Act under a penalty of 10s.

The authorities are commanded to appoint certain of the poor people to collect broken meats and fragments two or three times a week, to be distributed evenly amongst the poor.

The Act is restricted from applying to persons giving personal alms to parishioners or prisoners. It also provides that "in as moche as Friers Mendiantes have litle or nothing to lyve uppon but onely by the charitie and almes of Christien people," they and those who relieve them are exempted from the provisions of the Act, as also are Alms from Monasteries, Almshouses, Hospitals, or other foundations or brotherhoods, and also alms given to shipwrecked mariners, and casually by the wayside to lame, blind, sick, aged, or impotent people.

This Act it will be observed introduces for the first time some important provisions regarding the poor. It orders that able-bodied vagrants shall be set to work; that all poor except the really helpless, such as lepers and bedridden creatures, shall be sent to their place of settlement, and be maintained on their road there; that the children of beggars are to be taken from them and placed in suitable employment; and that the authorities are to make collections for the purpose of relieving the impotent poor. The previous Act had evidently broken down on the crucial question of relief, as the beggars accustomed to alms and doles must naturally have asked how they were to live, and charitably minded persons would as naturally continue to relieve and foster them.

The following is an example of the punishment of a vagrant under this Act taken from the Harleian MSS.

"How valyant beggers ough to
be punyshed accordinge to Kinge's statute."

"Wm. Payne whipped for a vagraunt strong begger at Chester in the county of the citty of Chester according to the law the xiii day of February in the xxix yere of the reigne of o^r moast dred soveigne Lord H. th'eight was assigned to passe forth w^h and dyrectly from thens to Chippen Warren in the countie of Northampton where he saith he was borne and he is lymittyd to be there w^{t}in xvi dayez then next ensuying at his pell. I witnez wherof the seale of the offyc of the mairaltie of the citie aforseid and place where he was ponysshed herunto is sett."

We now come to a momentous change in the social condition of the country, and which has an important bearing on vagrancy and mendicity. By 27 Hen. VIII., c. 28 (1536), all monasteries and religious houses not possessing more than £200 per annum were suppressed; and by 31 Hen. VIII., c. 13 (1539), all institutions of that nature were dissolved. They amounted to 186 greater and 374 lesser monasteries, in addition to 48 houses of the Knights Templars; making a total of 608. Their income was estimated at £137,000 a year. If we adopt Mr. Froude's estimate that for a penny at this time, " the labourer could buy as much bread, beef, beer, and wine, he could do as much towards finding lodging for himself and his family, as the labourer of the nineteenth century can for a shilling," this sum would be equal to an annual revenue of £1,644,000 in the present day.

The population then was probably about four millions as compared with twenty-six millions in the present day; and as the amount expended on the relief of the poor is now about £9,000,000, if we estimate that one-third of the income of the abbeys ought to have been devoted to the uses of the poor, their *pro ratâ* contribution should have amounted to 2s. 9d. per head of the population, as against 6s. 4d. per head, the amount raised by taxation in the present day. This computation altogether leaves out of account the charity bestowed in connection with churches and special foundations for the relief of the poor.

The monastic establishments had reached the summit of their wealth and luxury, and were in most cases abodes of notorious profligacy. Their suppression cannot therefore have excited much commiseration on the part of the main body of the nation, particularly as the abbeys were generally in the habit of exacting their dues rigorously both from their villeins and the townsmen who held under them.

It may not be here amiss to observe the mode in which the alms of the abbeys were collected and distributed, taking the abbey of Bury St. Edmunds as an example. There the *eleemosynarius*, or almoner, distributed the alms and charitable donations of the convent to pilgrims, travellers, and the poor who assembled at the gate; for which purpose he had an office called the almonry. He also made the distributions on the founder's day, and other obits and anniversaries. He and his servants were to attend at the dinner of the abbot and monks to receive the alms. He was not to collect through the tables; but if anything was handed to him he might take it and devote it to alms. When the convent left the refectory, he could go round the tables, and destine to alms the drink which remained of the charity.

But that this charity was always benevolently bestowed is very questionable, as in a " Poem on the Evil Times of Edward II." we are told—

> " For if there come to an abbey two poor men or three,
> And ask of them help for holy charity,
> Scarcely will any do his errand, either young or old,
> But let him cower there all day in hunger and in cold,
>   and starve.
> Look what love there is to God, whom they say that they serve."

AND BEGGARS AND BEGGING. 85

While the religious houses did good by the relief of the impotent poor, they did an immense amount of harm in encouraging able-bodied beggars to lead a life of idleness and profligacy. The opinion of *Fuller*, the Church historian, on this point a little more than a century later, is pregnant with common sense.

" Some will object, that this their hospitality was but *charity mistaken*, promiscuously entertaining some, who did not need, and moe, who did not deserve it. Yea, these abbeys did but maintain the poor which they made. For, some Vagrants, accounting the Abbey-almes their own *inheritance*, served an *apprentiship*, and afterwards wrought *journey-work* to no other trade than *begging*; all whose children were, by their *father's copie*, made free of the *same company*. Yea, we may observe, that generally such places wherein the great Abbeys were seated (some few excepted, where *cloathing* began, when their *Covent* did end) swarm most with poor people at this day, as if beggary were entailed on them, and that lazinesse not as yet *got out of their flesh*, which so long since was *bred* in their *bones*." *

The immediate result of the dissolution must, however, have been a large increase in the number of vagrants, for it has been calculated that these institutions contained about fifty thousand inmates who led an idle life. Many of these were no doubt soon absorbed in the civil population, but a very great number must have been so much inoculated with indolence and ignorance from the life they had been accustomed to lead, that they would naturally resort to whining mendicity as a means of livelihood. The districts adjacent to the Scottish border at this period were also fostering and propagating vagabondage on an extensive scale.

" The survey of 1542 describes the Redesdale men as living in sheels † during the summer months, and pasturing their cattle in

---

* " There can be no doubt that many of the impotent poor derived support from their charity. But the blind eleemosynary spirit inculcated by the Romish Church is notoriously the cause, not the cure, of beggary and wretchedness. The monastic foundations, scattered in different counties, but by no means at regular distances, and often in sequestered places, could never answer the end of local and limited succour, meted out in just proportion to the demands of poverty. Their gates might indeed be open to those who knocked at them for alms, and came in search of streams that must always be too scanty for a thirsty multitude. Nothing could have a stronger tendency to promote that vagabond mendicity, which unceasing and very severe statutes were enacted to repress."—*Hallam.*

† A hut or residence for those who have the care of sheep.

the grains * and hopes † of the country on the south side of the Coquet, about Wilkwood and Ridlees; or in the waste grounds which sweep along the eastern marshes of North Tynedale. At this time they not only joined the men of Tynedale in acts of rapine and spoil, but often went as guides to the thieves of Scotland, in expeditions to ravage the towns and villages between the Coquet and Wansbeck. To counteract these outrages Sir Cuthbert Ratcliff, with divers of the most wise borderers, devised a watch to be set from sunset to sunrise at all passages and fords 'endalong' all the middle marches over against North Tynedale and Redesdale, that when the thieves from the north were seen descending, hue and cry should be made for assistance to drive them back. Those amongst the dalesmen were most praised and cherished who soonest in youth began to practise themselves in thefts and robberies, for in these they delighted, boasted, and exercised themselves. They were divided into clans, each of which had rank and precedence according to its numerical strength. That of Hall was the greatest and of most reputation; and next to it the Reeds, Potts, Hedleys, Spoors, Daugs, Fletchers. All these were 'lairds,' owners of their own small 'in-field' and Peel-tower, with the right of commonage over the vast unenclosed wilderness around them. A few of these families still exist as lairds on their ancient estates, more still as tenant-farmers on their former properties. They lost their estates through getting into debt by gambling, drinking, and betting on horses and cocks, but the old names, and much of the old pride, haughtiness, and exclusiveness remain. In moss-trooping times, 'If a thief of any great surname or kindred was lawfully executed by order of justice, for stealing beyond the limits of his own province, the rest of his clan would visit his prosecutor with all the retributive vengeance of *deadly feud* as bitterly and severely as if he had killed him unlawfully with a sword.' This frequently led to a sort of civil war in the county; whole townships were burnt; those of whom revenge was sought were murdered; great garrisons were established to check the outrages of the clans, and raids and incursions were made against them and by them, " even as it were between England and Scotland in time of war." Hence persons who were plundered generally chose, when they discovered the thieves who had carried off their goods, to receive a part of

---

* The branches of a valley.   † A sloping hollow between two hills.

them back by way of composition, rather than go against them to the extremity of justice. There is reason to believe that blackmail was paid by many of the Northumbrians even in Queen Elizabeth's reign to these systematic robbers. In 1498 Bishop Fox issued his mandate to the clergy of Tynedale and Redesdale, charging them to excommunicate all those inhabitants of their cures who should, excepting against the Scots, presume to go from home armed 'in a *jack*,* and *salet*,† or *knapescul*,‡ or other defensive armour, or should ride on a horse worth more than six shillings and eightpence, or wear in any church or churchyard, during the time of divine service, any offensive weapon more than a cubit in length.' The same prelate elsewhere describes the chaplains here as publicly and openly living with concubines, irregular, suspended, excommunicated, and interdicted, wholly ignorant of letters, so much so that priests of ten years' standing did not know how to read the ritual. Some of them were nothing more than sham priests, never having been ordained. When such were the morals of the teachers, what produce of virtue was to be expected from the disciples?" §

A beggar in an old play describes himself as "born in Redesdale in Northumberland, and come of a wight-riding surname called the Robsons, good honest men and true, saving a little shifting for their living, God help them!" ‖

The last Act in this reign which calls for any notice is the 34 and 35 Hen. VIII. (1543), entitled "An Acte for thadvauncement of true Religion, and for thabollisshment of the Contrarie," which in some of its sections applies to players, who in the reign of Elizabeth and subsequently were punishable under the Acts against vagrancy. This act imposes a fine of £10 and imprisonment for three months for a first offence upon any person who shall play in interludes, sing or rhyme any matter contrary to the doctrine of the Six Articles, or, as it is commonly called, the Bloody Statute; for a second offence the offender is to forfeit all his goods and be committed to perpetual prison.

"Provided allwayes and be it enacted by thauctorytie aforesaide, that it shalbe lawfull to all and everye persone and persones to set foorthe songes plaies and enterludes, to be used and exercysed

---

* A defensive upper garment quilted with stout leather.
† A light helmet.   ‡ A headpiece, a sort of helmet.
§ Hodgson's Northumberland (1827).   ‖ Scott.

within this Realme and other the Kings Domynions, for the rebuking and reproching of vices, and the setting foorthe of vertue; so allwaies the saide songes plaies or enterludes meddle not with interpretacõns of Scripture, contrarye to the doctryne set foorthe by the Kings Majestie our saide Soveraigne Lord that now is King Henry theight in forme aforesaide."

The wandering ballad-singer, or the strolling player who ventured to take part in a miracle or mystery play must have done so in fear and trembling of this redoubtable enactment, for no one, high or low, was safe from the regal vengeance in this reign. On one occasion, we are told, an actual beggar was thrown into prison, and formal depositions relating to him were sent to the King's minister, because in drinking at a village inn he had said "he wished King Henry's head were boiled in a pot, and he would be the first to drink of the broth."

Villeinage was in this reign fast dying out. In the year 1514 the King manumitted two of his villeins in the following form: "Whereas God created all men free, but afterwards the laws and customs of nations subjected some under the yoke of servitude, we think it *pious* and *meritorious with God* to manumit Henry Knight, a taylor, and John Herle, a husbandman, our natives, as being born within the manor of Stoke Clymmysland, in our county of Cornwal, together with all their issue born, or to be born, and all their goods, lands, and chattels acquired, or to be acquired, so as the said persons, and their issue, shall from henceforth be free, and of free condition." And it appears from the calendar of the Journals of the House of Lords that in the year 1536, and 28 Hen. VIII., a Bill *concerning bondmen* was rejected by the House of Lords on the third reading, which according to this idea (of its being *meritorious with God*) was probably for their general manumission.

The condition of vagabondage in England at the termination of this reign and the commencement of that of Edward VI. may best be judged from the following extract from Harrison's description of England.

"Our third annoiers of the common-wealth are roges, which doo verie great mischeefe in all places where they become. For wheras the rich onelie suffer injurie by the first two, these spare neither rich nor poore; but whether it be great gaine or smalle, all is fish that commeth to net with them, and yet I saie both

they and the rest are trussed up apace. For there is not one
yeare commonlie, wherein three or four hundred of them are not
devoured and eaten up by the gallowes in one place and other.
It appeareth by Cardane (who writeth it upon the report of the
bishop of Lexovia) in the geniture of King Edward the sixt,
how Henrie the eight, executing his laws verie severelie against
such idle persons, I meane great theeves, pettie theeves and
roges, did hang up threescore and twelve thousand of them in his
time. He seemed for a while greatlie to have terrified the rest:
but since his death the number of them is so increased, yea
although we have had no warres, which are a great occasion of
their breed (for it is the custome of the more idle sort, having
once served or but seene the other side of the sea under colour of
service to shake hand with labour, for ever, thinking it a disgrace
for himselfe to returne unto his former trade) that except some
better order be taken, or the lawes alreadie made be better executed,
such as dwell in uplandish townes and little villages shall live but
in small safetie and rest."

The opening of the reign of *Edward VI.* was signalised by a
Draconian statute against vagabondism. It will have been observed
that from the time of Henry VII. the sentimental sympathies of
indiscreet almsgivers were being gradually disregarded and over-
borne by legislation of an increasingly severe character against
vagrants and beggars. But the greatest severities hitherto
enacted were mild in comparison with the severe provisions of the
enactment now under consideration. In fact it is almost impossible
to think that it could ever have been intended as anything more
than an academic fulmination which should act as a deterrent
through the appalling character of its punishments. *Sir John
Cheke,* who was the Greek professor at Cambridge, and was one
of the preceptors of Edward VI., had signalised himself by introducing the study of the Greek language and literature into
England. He entered Parliament as member for Bletchingly in
the year 1547, and it is therefore probable that this enactment is
in a great measure due to the studies which he rendered fashionable,
since the laws of *Lycurgus* would not tolerate mendicants, and
under those of *Draco, Solon,* and other legislators mendicants were
condemned to capital punishment.

The Act to which we allude (1 Edw. VI., c. 3, 1547) commences by reciting: "Forasmuche as Idlenes and Vagabundrye is

the mother and roote of all theftes robberyes and all evill actes and other mischiefs and the multitude of people given therto hath allwaies been here within this Realme verie greate and more in nombre as it maye appere then in other Regions, to the greate impouverishment of the Realme and daunger of the Kings Highnes subgects, the whiche Idlenes and Vagabundrye all the Kings Highnes noble progenitors Kings of this Realme and this highe Courte of Parlament hath often and with greate travaile goon abowte and assayed with godlie Actes and Statutes to represse, yet untill this our tyme it hath not had that successe which hath byn wisshed, but partelie by folishe pitie and mercie of them which shoulde have seen the saide godlie lawes executed, partelie by the perverse nature and longe accustumed idlenes of the parsons given to loytringe, the saide godlie statutes hitherto hath had small effecte, and Idle and Vagabounde persons being unprofitable membres or rather ennemyes of the Cōmen wealthe hath byn suffred to remayne and encrease and yet so doo, who yf theie should be punished by deathe whippinge emprysonement or wth other corporall payne it were not withowt their deserts for thexample of others and to the benefitt of the Cōmen wealth, yet yf thei cowlde be brought to be made proffitable and doo service were much to be wisshed and desired." It then proceeds to repeal all former Acts against vagabonds and beggars, and ordains that every person not impotent, &c., loitering or wandering and not seeking work, or leaving it when engaged, shall be taken up as a vagabond, and every master who has offered such idle person service and labour shall be entitled to bring him before two justices of the peace, who " shall imediatelye cawse the saide loyterer to be marked with an whott Iron in the brest the marke of V. and adjudge the saide parsone living so Idelye to such presentor to be his Slave, to have and to holde the said Slave to him his executors or assignes for the space of twoo yeres then next following." The slave is to be fed on bread and water or small drink and such refuse meats as the master thinks fit. He is to be caused to work by beating, chaining, or otherwise, in whatever work he may be put to, however vile it may be. If such slave runs away his master may pursue him, and punish him with chains and beating; and if he brings him before two justices of the peace they are empowered to cause him to be marked on the forehead or ball of the cheek with a hot iron with the sign of an S. The master can recover £10 and costs from any one knowingly detaining his slave. A slave running away a second time is to suffer pains of death as a felon. Clerks convict, if entitled to benefit of purgation, are only to serve as slaves one year, and if not entitled to purgation for five years. They are liable to the same penalties as other vagabonds, except that they are exempt from burning in the breast. Infant beggars above five and under fourteen may be forcibly taken as apprentices or servants and kept, males till twenty-four, females till twenty. If they run away they become slaves. Masters are empowered to let, sell, or give the services of such children. Fathers, mothers, nurses, or bearers about of such children, who steal such children from their service are to become slaves for life to the master of the child.

All vagabonds who are not taken into any service are to be marked on the breast with a V with a hot iron, and then sent to their birthplace with a pass in the following form :—

"A. B., Justice of Peace in the Countie of S, to the Mayor or cheif officer of the Citie of (Q.) yf it be a citie, or to the hedde Boroughe Bailief or Constable, or hedd officer of the Towne of Q. yf it be a towne, or to the Constable or Tything-man of the Village of C. yf it be a village, greting ; According to a most godlie Statute made in the first yere of the Reigne of our Soveraigne Lord King Edwarde the Sixte &c. We have taken this bearer I. K. vagrauntlie and to the evill example of others withowt Master service or labor wherby to get his living going loytering idellie abowt ; and because the same saiethe he was borne in C. in the Countie of S. wherof youe ar the hedde officer or constable we have sent him to youe to be ordered according to the purporte and effecte of the same statute : and with this writing shall deliver the same loyterer to the Constables or other hed officer of the saide Citie Towne or Village wherin suche loyterer was taken to be saufelie conveyed by them to the next constable, and so from conestables to constables and other hedd officers til he or she be brought to the place to which he or she hath named themselfe to be borne in, and then to be delivered to the hedd officer or Constable of the same Citie Borough or Towne Village hamlett or parishe, there to be nourished and kepte of the same Citie Towne or Village in chaynes either at the Comen workes in amending highe waies or other Comen worke, or from man to man in order til theie which may beare be equallie charged, to be slave to the corporacõn of the Citie or to the inhabitaunts of the Towne or Village that he or she were borne in, after all suche forme condicõn space of yeres orders punishments for runninge awaie and all others as are expressed of a cõmon or private parsone to whome any suche loyterer is adjudged a slave; and the saide Citie Towne or Village shall see the saide Slave being hable to labour sett on worke and not live idelie within the saide precincts, uppon payne that for everie suche defaulte that the said Slave doth live idellye by the defaulte of the Citie Borouge or Towne or Vyllage by the space of three working daies to gether the Citie to forfaicte five poundes, a Boroughe or Towne Incorporate fourtie shillings and other Towne or Vyllage Twentie Shillings, whereof the one halfe to the King our Souveraigne Lorde, the other to him that will sue for the same in anny of the Kings Courtes of Recorde by bill Informacõn, or Action of debte in the which suite no essoyne wager of Lawe or protection shall be allowed."

Cities, &c., are empowered to let or sell such slaves. Vagabonds declaring a false place of birth are to be branded on the face with an S and become slaves there. Foreigners being vagrants are to be treated as English idle persons, except that they are not to be marked on the breast or face. They are to be sent to the next port, and there kept at work until they can be conveyed to their own country at the expense of the inhabitants of the port.

The impotent poor are to be provided with lodging at the cost of the inhabitants of their birthplace, and no others are to be allowed to beg there under a penalty of 10s. for every three days each person begs there, the penalty being recoverable from the head officer of the place. Officers are to examine and remove beggars monthly to their places of birth or residence. All aged poor able to work are to be employed, and a weekly collection of charity is to be made at church on Sunday.

Persons to whom beggars are to be adjudged as slaves are authorised to put a ring of iron about their necks, arms, or legs. Any person helping to take this ring off without the permission of the master forfeits £10.

Two years afterwards *Sir John Cheke* himself attests the failure of this Act in a little work styled the "Hurt of Sedicion howe greveous it is to a commune welth," written at the time of *Kett's* rebellion in 1549. He asks, "What say ye to ye numbre of vagabondes and loitring beggers, whiche after ye overthrow of

your campe and scatering of this seditious numbre, wyl swarme in
every corner of the realme and not only lie loytering under
hedges, but also stande sturdeli in cities, and begge boldly at
every dore, leaving labour which they like not, and folowing
idleness which they should not. For every man is easely and
naturally brought from labour to ease, from the better to the
worse, frome diligence to slouthfulness, and after warres it is com-
munelye sene, that a great number of those whiche wente out
honest, returne home againe like roisters and as though they were
burnt to the warres botome, they have all their lyfe after an
unsavery smacke therof, and smel stil towarde daieslepers, purse
pikers, highwaie robbers, quarelmakers, ye and bloudsheders to.
Do we not se comunely in thende of warres more robbing more
begging more murdering then before, and those to stand in the
high wai to aske their almes whom ye be afraied to say nai unto
honestly, lest they take it awaye frome you violentlye, and have more
cause to suspecte their strength, then pitie their nede. Is it not
then dailye hearde, how men be not onlye pursued, but utterly
spoiled, and fewe may ride safe by the kinge's waie, excepte they
ryde stronge, not so muche for feare of their goodes, whiche menne
esteme lesse, but also for daunger of their lyfe, which everye man
loveth. Worke is undone at home, and loiterers linger in stretes,
lurk in ale houses, range in highewaies, valiaunte beggers play in
tounes, and yet complaine of neede, whose staffe if it be once hoat
in their hande, or sluggishnes bred in their bosome, they wil
never be allured to labour againe, contenting themselves better
with idle beggary, then with honest and profitable labour. And
what more noisom beastes be in a comune wealth? Dranes in
hives sucke oute the honie, a smal matter, but yet to be loked on
bi good husbandes, caterpillers destroye the fruite, an hurtefull
thinge and well shyfted for, by a diligente overseer. Diverse
vermine destroye corne, kyll polleyne, enginnes and snares be
made for them.

"But what is a loyterer? A sucker of honye, a spoyler of
corne, a destroyer of fruite. Naye a waster of money, a spoyler of
vytaile, a sucker of bloud, a breaker of orders, a seker of breakes,
a queller of lyfe, a basiliske of the comune wealthe, whiche by
companie and syght doeth poyson the whole contreye, and staineth
honeste myndes wyth the infection of his venime, and so draweth
the commune wealthe to deathe and destruction.

"Such is the fruites of your laboure and travayle for your pretensed commune wealthe, which justice wolde no man should taste of but yourselves, that ye myghte truelye judge of your owne mischiefe, and fraye other by example frome presumynge the lyke.

"When wee se a great number of flyes in a yere, we naturallye judge lyke to bee a great plage; and having so great a swarminge of loyteringe vagabondes, readie to begge and braule at every mannes doore, which declare a greater infection, can we not looke for a grevouser and perilouser daunger then the plage is?"

On the 6th of August of this year a proclamation was issued for the inhibition of all common players and plays, on the ground that they "do for the moste part plaie suche Interludes as contain matter tendyng to sedicion and contempnyng of sundery good orders and lawes, where upon are growen, and are likely to growe and ensue, muche disquiet, division, tumultes, and uproares in this realme." This inhibition is directed against any kind of interlude, play, or dialogue, in any place public or private, and is to last from the 9th of August until the feast of All Saints next coming.

This was followed by an order from the King to "certain special men in the Shires where tumults and risings have been," directing the proclamation against idle vagabonds to be strictly enforced and stirrers up of tumults to be hanged without delay.

The next enactment on the subject of vagrancy is the 3 & 4 Edw. VI., c. 16 (1549-50), which commences by reciting :—
"Forasmuche as it is notoryouslye seen and knowen, that Vacabonds and Beggars doo dailye encreace within this the King's Highnes Realme in to verye great numbres, chieflye by occation of idlenes, mother and roote of all vyces, wherby doo insue contynuall thefts murthers conspiracies and other sondrye heynous offences, and partelye for that the good and holsome lawes and statutes of this Realme, hath not byn putt in dewe execution, and partelye allso by reason of the multitude of the same (thextremitie of some wherof have byn occation that they have not been putt in use)." It then proceeds to repeal the 1 Edw. VI., c. 3, and revives the 22 Hen. VIII., c. 12, and enacts in addition that labourers refusing to work shall be punished as vagabonds; that the sick and aged poor shall be relieved by the parishes where they were born and not suffered to beg; that the aged poor able to work shall be employed; that the leprous and bedridden poor shall not be forced

to remove, and that they may be allowed to appoint proctors to beg for them; that the Lord Chancellor may grant commissions to leprous people and to persons who have had their houses or barns burnt to gather alms. Children between the ages of five and fourteen may be taken from beggars by any one willing to keep them, and if such children run away they are to be punished by being put in the stocks. Justices may discharge such children from service on misconduct of the master, and foreign beggars are ordered to be removed to their own countries.

With the apparent object of providing more efficient means for the relief of the poor, another statute (5 & 6 Edw. VI., c. 2, 1551-2) was passed in the succeeding year, by which the 22 Hen. VIII., c. 12, and the 3 & 4 Edw. VI., c. 16, are confirmed, and two or more collectors of alms are ordered to be chosen in each city, town, parish, &c., and the alms are to be distributed weekly to the poor and impotent. The mode of collection prescribed is for the collectors, on the Sunday after Whitsun Sunday, when the people are at church, "to gently ask of every man and woman what they of their charity will give weekly towards the relief of the poor," and the same is to be written in a book. If any person being able should obstinately and frowardly refuse to give towards the help of the poor, or wilfully discourage others from doing so, the parson and churchwardens are gently to exhort him, and if he will not be so persuaded, then the bishop is to send for him to induce and persuade him. The collectors are to be chosen by the parishioners, and a penalty of 20s. is imposed on any one who refuses the office.

Immediately after this tinkers and pedlars appear to have attracted the notice of the authorities, and fallen under their ban as troublesome vagrants.

The 5 & 6 Edw. VI., c. 21 (1551-2), recites that "Tynkers, Pedlers and such like vagrant persones are more hurtfull then necessarie;" and enacts that none such shall travel from place to place without license from two justices, under penalty of fourteen days' imprisonment.

On the 28th April, 1551, a further proclamation was issued "for the reformacion of Vagabondes, tellers of newes, sowers of sedicious rumours, players, and printers without license & diuers other disordred persons." In this the King "is moste sory, and earnestly from the botom of his harte doth lament, and so dooe all his counsailors to heare and se many of his subiectes to abuse dayly by their vicious and corrupt conuersations, that most precious Juell the worde of god, and by their licencious behauiors, leude and sedicious talkes, boldely and presumptuously without feare either of goddes plague or the swearde of their Prince, to breake continually the Lawes and statutes of the realme." It then proceeds to say that "the great fault for the continuaunce of the people in euill hath proceded for want of execution of the good Lawes and statutes of the realme, and especially the statutes made against vagaboundes, vnlaufull games, tellers of newes, Inuentors of tales and rumors, vnlauful assembles, riotes, rowtes, huntinges, fishinges, shoting in handgonnes, and Crossebowes, keping of ale houses, eating of flesh on fish daies, regrators, forstallers, breakers of thorder of religion and sundry other like statutes. . . . And for the better aduoiding of al suche inconueniences, his maiestie straightly chargeth and commaundeth all Justices, Mayors, Shirifes, baylifes, Constables, Hedboroughes, Tithing men, and al other Officers and ministers of what estate, degree, or condicion soeuer they be, from hencefurth to loke to their offices, and earnestly, truly, and vprightly, to execute and se executed, al his maiestie's Laws, Statutes, and proclamations . . . And for because that within the citie of London, ther is at this present a great number of idle persons & masterles men, which sek rather by Idlenes & mischief to liue by other mens labours & industries thē to trauail by any paynes takyng, to liue like good and obedient membres of the cōmon welth : His maiesty straightlye chargeth and commaundeth all maner of vagaboundes, and masterles men, vpon the paines, not onelie all ready appoynted by the Lawes and Statutes made for suche maner of menne, but also vpon suche paynes as his maiestie may and wil ordaine to be inflicted vpon them, by his prerogatiue royal, to departe al suche out of the citie of London, and the suburbes of the same, within iiii dayes after the making of this proclamation home to the place where they wer borne, or wher they haue dwelt last thre yeres within the realme, goyng at the least vii miles a day (if they haue so farre to go from London) and passing not aboue ii or iii or iiii at the moste in a company, and not to abide aboue one night in a place, till they come home (except cause of sicknes, the same cause to be allowed by a Justice of the peace, dwelling next to the place where he or they shal fortune to be sicke). And that al vagabondes, and masterles men in al other places, within this realme, shall also within iiii dayes after the making of this proclamation in the next market towne, where they shal fortune to be, departe likewise to the place where they were borne, or last dwelled thre yeres within the realme, without lenger tarieng by the way, or going mo in company together, or fewer miles in a day, then aforesaid: And vpon like paynes as is aforesayd for them which departe from London." The proclamation then prohibits Printers, Booksellers, and Players of Interludes from printing any matter without the permission in writing of the King or his Privy Council upon pain of imprisonment without bail or mainprise. Common players or others are forbidden upon like pains to play any manner of interlude, play, or matter without special license in writing from his Majesty or six of his Privy Council.

In the year 1549 the regulation of the Borders again formed the subject of a convention between the Governments of England and Scotland, and it was provided by Article 7 of the Treaty of Perpetual Peace then concluded—

"That neither of the Princes by any means shall receive, or permit by their subjects to be received, any Murtherers, Thieves, Robbers, Run-a-ways, Rebels, or any other evil Doers whatsoever, which do decline unto any Place from the natural obedience of their Prince; but within Ten days' next, and immediately following after, that one of the Princes hath been required by the Letter of the other Prince, of the which such malefactor is subject, or by his Deputy he shall cause to be delivered, to the bringer of such Letter or Request, the said Murtherers, Thieves, Robbers or Evildoers.

The reign of *Mary* opens with an Act (1 Mariæ, st. 2, c. 13, 1553) for continuing in force the 5 & 6 Edw. VI., c. 2. This was shortly followed by an Act for the punishment of gypsies (1 & 2 Phil. & Mar., c. 4).

On the 18th of August, 1553, the Queen issued a proclamation forbidding the playing of interludes without her special license in writing, "vpon payne to incurre her highnesse indignation and displeasure."

This was followed on the 17th of September, 1554, by a proclamation in the City of London, which ordered "that all vagabonds and maisterlesse men, as well strangers as Englishmen, should departe the citie within five daies: and strictlie charging all in holders, vittelers, taverners and ale-housekeepers, with all that sold vittels, that they (after the said five daies) should not sell anie meat, drinke, or anie kind of vittels or releefe to anie servingman whatsoever, unlesse he brought a testimoniale from his maister to declare whose servant he is, and were in continuall household with his said maister, upon paine to runne in danger of the law if they offend herein." *

This was no doubt rendered necessary by the insurrectionary spirit which was then abroad owing to the unpopularity of the Spanish marriage and the rigorous enforcement of the ecclesiastical laws, as well as to sympathy with the sufferers under Wyat's insurrection.

Disease, deformity, and wounds have always proved a most fruitful stock-in-trade for the beggar, so much so indeed that the afflicted rarely care to be cured. *William Turner*, in his "*New booke of Spirituall physick*," thus expatiates upon this perverse propensity in the year 1555 :—

"When as of late yeares I practised bodely phisick in Englande, in my lorde of Sumersettes house, diuers sick beggers came vnto me, & not knowyng that I was a phisician, asked of me myne almose. To whom I offered to heale their diseases for Goddes sake. But they went by and by awaye from me, and wolde none of that. For they had muche leuer be sick styll with ease and ydlenes, then to be hole & with great payne and labour, to earne honestly theyr lyuing."

The 22 Hen. VIII., c. 12, and the 3 & 4 Edw. VI., c. 16, were confirmed in 1555 by 2 & 3 Phil. & Mar., c. 5, with the following amendments :—

On some day in Christmas collectors of alms are to be appointed yearly in each parish who are to solicit and distribute alms weekly. Collectors refusing to act are subjected to a penalty of 40s.

Persons refusing to give are to be gently exhorted to do so by the parson, vicar, or curate and churchwardens; if this persuasion fails the bishop of the diocese or the ordinary of the place is to send for them, to induce them to extend "their charitee as in this acte is well ment and intended, and so according to discretion to take order for the charitable reformacõn of every suche obstinate person."

* Holinshed.

Gifts by King Henry VIII. for the relief of the poor are to be duly applied.

Where the poor in any parish are too numerous for relief, the justices are empowered upon proper representation to license certain of them to beg outside the parish ; the license to state the exact limits within which the poor person is authorised to resort, and if he transgresses these limits he is to be punished under the statute 22 Hen. VIII., and his license taken from him. Beggars so licensed are ordered to wear badges* to be provided by the mayor or head officer, both on the breast and back of his uppermost garment. All sums gathered in London are to be paid to and distributed by Christ's Hospital. The duration of the Act is limited to the end of the session of the next Parliament, but it was continued by the 4 & 5 Phil. & Mar., c. 9 (1557), because it had been found " good and beneficiall for the Common wealthe of this Realme." At Cambridge, in this year, " the vagabonds, naughtie an jolly persons," are stated to be "farr more in numbre then hath been in tymes past."

* The *almesse* men, instituted by Henry VII. to pray for his "good and prosperous state," wore a gown and hood, on which was embroidered a " scochyn " and a red rose crowned and embroidered thereupon," as appears from an indenture amongst the Harleian MSS. made between the King and John Islipp, Abbot of St. Peter's, Westminster. A similar class of almsmen, called King's Bedesmen or Blue-gowns, were dependent on the Scotch kings, and wore, as distinguishing badges, a cloak of coarse cloth of a light blue colour and a pewter badge.

CHAPTER V.

1558—1603.

Accession of Elizabeth—Legislation against vagabonds—Attempts to settle the rate of wages—General night search for vagabonds, beggars, and gypsies—Action of the City of London—Orders by the Lord Mayor and Aldermen—Returns of vagrants apprehended—Renewed legislation—Licenses to beg—Sir John More on Irish and Welsh vagabondage—The privileges of John Dutton and his heirs—Causes of the legislation against stage players and bearwards—Beggars at Bath and Buxton—Renewed search for vagabonds—Final manumission of bond slaves—Repression of vagrancy in the city—Internal management of houses of correction—Number of rogues and vagabonds—Repressive measures in the City—Treatment of vagrants at the house of a great nobleman—Proclamations against vagrants—Further legislation—Small tenements and beggars—Observance of fish days enjoined as a means of preventing idleness—State of vagabondism in 1596—Further legislation for the relief of the poor and repression of vagrancy—The Border laws—Begging soldiers and mariners.

WE now come to the reign of Elizabeth, a reign distinguished by the wisdom of the Queen's councillors, and by the wisdom of the Queen in accepting such councillors.

The first Act of this reign on the subject of vagrancy is the 5 Eliz., c. 3 (1562-3), which confirms the 22 Hen. VIII., c. 12, and 3 and 4 Edw. VI., c. 16, and practically re-enacts the 2 and 3 Phil. and Mar., c. 5, with the following differences. Collectors of alms are to be appointed on the Sunday after Midsummer day: the penalty on collectors refusing to serve is increased to £10. Recalcitrant almsgivers who refuse to give on the solicitation of the bishop are bound under a penalty of £10 to appear at the next general session of justices, where they may be assessed to the relief of the poor, and on refusal to pay, may be imprisoned until they do pay.

When the poor are too numerous to be relieved by the parish, the justices are empowered to license them to beg outside the parish. The license is to state the exact limits within which the poor person is authorised to resort, and if he transgresses these limits he is to be punished under the statute 22 Hen. VIII. and his license taken from him. Beggars so licensed are ordered to wear badges to be provided by the mayor or head officer both on the breast and back of their uppermost garment.

This was succeeded by another Act (5 Eliz. c., 4, 1562-3) which may be regarded as its corollary, as it aims at compelling every able-bodied person to work. Wages are to be settled annually by the justices in session, aided by such discreet and grave persons as they shall think meet. It further enacts,—

"That none of the said reteyned persons in Husbandrye, or in any the Artes or Sciences above remembred, after the tyme of his Reteyno^r expired, shall departe foorthe of one Cytye Towne or Parishe to another, nor out of the Lathe Rape Wapentake or Hundred, nor out of the Countie or Shire where hee last served, to serve in any other Citie Towne Corporate Lathe Rape Wapentake Hundred Shiere or Countie onles he have a Testimoniall under the Seale of the said Citie or Towne Corporate, or of the Constable or Constables or other Head officer or Officers and of two other honest Housholders of the Citie Towne or parishe where he last served, declaring his laufull departure, and the name of the Shiere and Place where he dwelled last before his departure, according to the Forme hereafter expressed in this acte.

" That no person or persons that shall departe out of Service shalbe reteyned or accepted into any other Service, wthout shewing before his Reteyno^r suche Testimoniall as is above remembred, to the Chief Officer of the Towne Corporate, and in every other Towne and place to the Cunstable Curate Churchewarden or other Head officer of the same where he shalbee reteyned to serve; upon the payne that every suche servante so departing wthout such Certificate or Testimoniall shalbee imprysoned untill he procure a Testimoniall or Certificate, the whiche yf hee cannot doo wthin the space of xxj dayes next after the first daye of his imprysonment, then the sayd person to be whipped and used as a Vagabonde according to the Lawes in suche Cases provided; and that every person reteyning any suche servaunte wthout shewing suche Testimonyall or certificate as ys aforesaid, shall forfaite for every suche Offence fyve poundes: And yf any such person shalbe taken withe any countrefaite or forged Testimoniall, then to be whipped as a Vagabounde.

"That yf any Servant or Apprentice of Husbandrye or of any Arte Science or occupaĉōn aforesaid, unlawfully departe or flye into anye other Shire, that it shalbe laufull to the said Justices of Peace and to the said Maiors Bailiefes and other Head officers of Cities Townes Corporate for the tyme being Justices of Peace there, to make and grante Writtes of Capias, so many and suche as shalbee nedefull, to be directed to the Shriefes of the Counties or to the others Head officer of the Places whither suche Servantes or Apprentices shall so departe or flye, to take theyr Bodies, returneable before them at what tyme shall please them, so that yf they come by suche processe, that they bee put in prisone till they shall finde sufficient suretie well and honestlye to serve their M$^{rs.}$ Maistresses or Dames from they so departed or fledde according to thorder of the Lawe."*

This was shortly followed by another severe enactment against the gypsies (5 Eliz., c. 20).

On the 16th May, 1559, the Queen acting in continuance of the policy displayed in the proclamations of Edward VI. and Mary against stageplayers, by proclamation forbid all manner of interludes to be played either openly or privately, "except the same be notified before hande, and licenced within any citie or towne corporate by the Maior or other chiefe officers of the same, and within any shyre, by such as shalbe Lieuetenaunts for the Queenes Maiestie in the same shyre, or by two of the Justices of peax, inhabyting within that part of the shire where any shalbe played." Offenders are to be arrested and imprisoned for fourteen days or more as cause shall need.

In the year 1569 the northern counties were in a disturbed state owing to the disaffection of the Catholics, who were in expectation of a papal bull for the deposition of the Queen, and as a consequence vagabondage increased not only there but in other parts of the kingdom. Strype says of this—

"Anno 1569.

"As the queen and her council had a jealousy of certain that went about in the north, and in other parts of the nation, as vagabonds, beggars, gamesters, and such like, whereof there were now great store, the lords of the council, in the month of March

* The 2 and 3 Edw. VI., c. 15 (1548-9), imposes penalties on butchers, bakers, &c., conspiring to sell victuals only at certain prices, and on artificers conspiring as to the prices or times of work. The 3 and 4 Edw. VI. enacts that journeymen clothiers, weavers, tailors, and shoemakers are not to be hired for less than a quarter of a year.

last past, had sent to the high sheriff of Yorkshire, to inquire after vagabonds and common rogues, and to punish them, and to make certificate of the same. And now the second time, in the month of June, they sent a larger letter to the said sheriff and the justices of the peace, for the redress of, and taking order about, this sort of people : enjoining this course now to be taken. First, that distributing themselves, with the help of other inferior officers, to cause a strict search, and a good strong watch to begin on Sunday at night, about nine of the clock on the 10th of July, in every town, village, and parish ; and to continue the same all the night, until four of the clock in the afternoon of the next day. And in that search, to apprehend all vagabonds, sturdy beggars, commonly called *rogues* or *Egyptians*, and also all idle, vagrant persons, having no master, nor no certainty how and whereby to live ; and them to be imprisoned. Directions were also given for passports, to send these idle persons home to their own countries. That the same search should be made monthly until the 1st of November, or longer, as they should see cause. And these orders they were to communicate to the officers of every corporate town. They were also to confer, how the statutes provided for avoiding all unlawful games, and especially of bowling, and maintenance of archery, might be speedily and roundly executed. And that if any of themselves were guilty hereof, to forbear for good example' sake ; and that it would be hard for them who were justices to observe their oaths, if they should commit such open hurtful offences themselves, which ought by them in their sessions to be inquired of and punished. They warned, that by no lewd practices of evil disposed, crafty persons, passing by them in the night, by pretences of watchwords, or the like devices, any raising of the people were made, as in some corners of the realm had been attempted, but stayed by the wiser men. That all tales, news, spreading of unlawful books, should be stayed, and sharply punished. And that if any of the justices should be negligent herein, the rest were required to advertise the queen's council thereof. This letter was signed by the lord keeper and many other great counsellors, containing these and other the like matters at large.

" The 21st of June, that is, the day after the date of the former letter, the lords of the council wrote again to the lord lieutenant of the north, signifying that they had sent him the minutes of a letter written from them by the queen's commandment unto divers shires within the realm, concerning the searching for, and punishing vagabonds, rogues, and other idle and disorderly persons. And they required his lordship to cause this order to be notified by his letters unto those shires that were within the compass of his commission, with strait charge to return their certificates unto him of their doings, that he might signify the same unto the council.

"This was a notable search: for it was so ordered, that it was made throughout the whole realm, or at least the most suspicious parts of it, on one and the same day. And I find it had this issue, (which is almost incredible,) that thirteen thousand masterless men throughout the nation, first and last, were taken up upon this search. Which undoubtedly very much brake the intended and attempted insurrections this year."

The City of London especially bestirred itself in the work, as appears by the following order :—

"*Anno* 1569. For the preventing of all idle persons and begging people, whether Men, Women, or Children, or other masterless Vagrants, an effectual Order was made in *April* the said Year, to take them all up, and to dispose of them in some of the four Hospitals of *London*, by the sixteen Beadles belonging to the same. Who had their several Standings and Walks in every Ward. Those that were Vagabonds and sturdy Beggars, they were to carry to *Bridewel*. Those that were aged, impotent, sick, sore, lame or blind, to *St. Bartholomew's* or *St. Thomas's* Hospital. And all Children under the Age of sixteen to *Christ's* Hospital. And this order was made at a Meeting of the Governours of all the Hospitals.

"*Fyrste*. That there do attend at all the Gates of this Cittie everie Morninge from three of the Clocke, until seven in the Forenone, and from seven in the Eveninge, untill eleven at Nyght; and also at the Tyde tymes falling in the Night, as well at *Byllingsgate*, as at *Lyon's Keye*, one of the sayde xvj Beadles thear to watche the coming of all Vagabonnds, Beggers, Children, and Masterles Men and Women: To the intent they may by them be apprehended. *Provided* allwaies, That the saide Beadles so agree and accord together, that they indifferentlie appoynt themsellves for the accomplishment of their Attendance in this behalf, so that one attend as moch, and as often as another.

"*Item*, That the Beadelle (in whose Circuite standeth anie of the Gates of this Cittie) faile not to see the same Gates continually attended all the Daie long, from vij of the Clock in the Forenone until vij at Night: And soche other of them as be not occupied at the Gates, to continue in walking the Circuite whereunto they are appointed.

"*Item*, In walking their circuites before mencioned, that they fail not to go once every Daie to the Collectours Houses, in every Parish within the Circuit; to understand of them or some of their Neighbours, if either Vacabonnde, Beggers, Children, or Masterles Men or Women be in the Streates of their Parrishes; that by them they may be Apprehended.

"*Item*, That one of the said Beadles twyse everie Daie (that is to saie at vij a Cloke in the Morninge, and at one in the Afternone) shall repaire to the Treasurar of the Howse wheare he serveth, to knowe his pleasure.

"*Item*, For *London Bridge*, the Barges of *Gravesende* and other Tide Boates coming up in the Daie tyme, the better to apprehend the Vagabonds, Beggers, Children, and Masterlesse men and Women, and the Bringers of them, *Whereuppon* there is iiij of the same xvj Beadells appoynted to attend every Day; that is to saie, ij of them from vij of the Clocke in the Morninge, untill one at Afternone; and th'other twaine for to be ij of *St. Thomas Hospitall* onlie, for that it is in their owne Circuite; and they to remaine from one of the Clocke until vij at Night; and one of the twaine (when the Tyde happeneth in Tyme of theire Attendance, either in the Forenone or Afternene), shall repaire to *Billingegate*, and to the *Lyon Key*, to the Purpose before declared: *Provided alwayes* that one of the same ij Beadles thear appointed, be one of them last admitted: to th' Intent he may growe the more perfect in his Dewtie, by th' Instruction of his Fellowe." *

About the year 1570 in order to prevent the spread of infection and to hinder "idle persons" from carrying it about with them, the following orders amongst others were issued by the Lord Mayor and aldermen:—

"*Vagrant, Maisterles, and Poore People.*

"1. That all such as be diseased be sent to $S^{t.}$ *Thomas* or $S^{t.}$ *Bartylmewes* Hospital, there to be first cured and made cleane; and afterwards, those which be not of the Cyttye, to be sent awaie according to the Statute in that case provided; and the other to be sett to worke in such Trades as are lest used by the Inhabitants of the Cyttye, for the avoyding all such Vagrant Persons, as well Children Male and Female; Soldiers lame and maymed, as other

* Stow enlarged by Strype.

idle and loytering Persons that swarme in the Streets, and wander upp and downe begging, to the great danger and infecting of the Cyttye, for th' Increase of the Plague, and annoyance to the same.

"2. That all Maisterlesse men who live idelie in the Cyttye, without any lawfull Calling, frequenting Places of common Assemblies, as Interludes, gaming Howses, Cockpitts, Bowling-Allies, and such other Places, maie be banished the Cyttye, according to the Lawes in that case provyded.

"All which Orders abovesaid, the Aldermen and their Deputies are every one in their Place to see performed, both in them selves and others, and in cases of doubt, to yield their Opinions, and gyve Direction."*

In 1570 the State papers furnish returns of beggars apprehended in Fawlesley and Cleyley hundreds in Northamptonshire, and in 1571 numerous returns of vagabonds apprehended and punished in various places in the counties of Essex, Notts, Gloucester, Oxford, Kent, Surrey, Worcester, Northampton, Hereford, Leicester, Stafford, Hunts, Cambridge, and the Isle of Ely. The character of the punishment is set forth in some. In the lathe of Aylesford in Kent "13 men and women were stocked and whipped severely." In Northamptonshire "5 men and 2 women were stocked and whipped," and at Daventry "1 man and 6 women were taken and whipped."

These vigorous measures were succeeded in the year 1572 by a most comprehensive enactment against the evil due probably in a great measure to Cecil, the High Treasurer, as from a memorandum in the calendar of State papers it appears that so early as the year 1566 he had sketched a definition of the term vagabond. This Act, 14 Eliz., c. 5, is styled "An Acte for the Punishement of Vacabondes, and for Relief of the Poore & Impotent."

It repeals the 22 Hen. VIII., c. 12, 3 & 4 Edw. VI., c. 16, and 5 Eliz.,c. 3, and enacts that persons above the age of fourteen "being Roges, Vacabonds, or sturdy Beggers," taken begging shall be committed to gaol until the next session, and that parishes shall pay the expenses of conveying offenders. Rogues and vagabonds on conviction are "to bee grevouslye whipped, and burnte through the gristle of the right Eare with a hot Iron of the compasse of an Inch about," except some honest person will take them into service for

* Stow enlarged by Strype.

a year. A beggar quitting such service is to be whipped and burnt as before ordered.

Beggars offending a second time are to be deemed felons unless some one will take them into service for two years. For a third offence they are to suffer as felons without benefit of clergy. The following classes are punishable under the Act:—

"Proctours or Procuratours goinge in or about any Countrey or Countreys within this Realme, without sufficyent Aucthoritye deryved from or under our Soveraigne Ladye the Queene, and all other ydle persones goinge aboute in any countrey of the said Realme, usyng subtill craftye and unlawfull Games or Playes, and some of them fayninge themselves to have knowledge in Phisnomye Palmestrye or other abused Scyences, whereby they beare the people in Hand they can tell their Destinyes Deathes and Fortunes and suche other lyke fantasticall Imiginacõns; and all and every persone and persones beynge whole and mightye in Body and able to labour, havinge not Land or Maister, nor using any lawfull Marchaundize Crafte or Mysterye whereby hee or shee might get his or her Lyvinge, and can gyve no reckninge howe hee or shee dothe lawfully get his or her Lyvinge; & all Fencers Bearewardes Comon Players in Enterludes & Minstrels, not belonging to any Baron of this Realme or towards any other honorable personage of greater Degree; all Juglers Pedlars Tynkers and Petye Chapmen; whiche said Fencers Bearewardes comon Players in Enterludes Mynstrels Juglers Pedlars Tynkers & Petye Chapmen, shall wander abroade and have not Lycense of two Justices of the Peace at the leaste, whereof one to be of the Quorum, wher and in what Shier they shall happen to wander; and all Comon Labourers being persons able in Bodye using loytering and refusinge to worke for such reasonable wages as ys taxed and comonly gyven in suche partes where such persones do or shall happen to dwell; and all Counterfeytures of Lycenses Passeportes and all users of the same, knowing the same to be counterfeyte; and all Scollers of the Universityes of Oxford or Cambridge y^t goe about begginge, not beinge aucthorysed under the Seale of the said Universities, by the Comyssarye Chauncelour, or Vicechauncelour of the same; and all Shipmen pretendinge Losses by Sea, other then suche as shalbe hereafter provided for; and all persones delivered out of Gaoles that begge for their Fees or do travayle to their Countreys or Freends, not having Lycense from two Justices of the Peace of the same Countye where he or she was delyvered; shalbe taken, adjudged, and deemed Roges Vacaboundes, and Sturdy Beggers."

Any person giving "harboroughe money or lodgynge" to any such is liable to a penalty of 20s.

Shipmen and soldiers licensed* by two justices, cockers or harvest folk in search of work, persons robbed on the highway, servants of honest behaviour turned away by their masters or whose masters had died, are exempted from the Act.

Rogues under fourteen are to be punished with "whippinge or stockinge as heretofore hath been used," and constables neglecting to apprehend vagabonds are liable to a penalty of 6s. 8d.

Justices of peace are ordered to register all aged and impotent poor born or for three years resident in their several districts, and settle them in convenient habitations, and ascertain the weekly charge, and assess the amount on the inhabitants, and yearly appoint collectors to receive and distribute the assessment.

Mayors of cities and constables of hundreds are empowered to receive any poor, not being leprous or bedridden, to their proper districts.

The poor leaving their settlements are to be deemed rogues and vagabonds, and if they refuse such work as they are able, are punishable by whipping and stocking for the first refusal, and as rogues and vagabonds for a second. Persons refusing to contribute to the relief of the poor may be committed to prison until they comply. Beggar's children between the ages of five and fourteen may be taken by any one willing to take them into service, females until the age of eighteen and males until twenty-four. The penalties prescribed by the Statute of Labourers being en-

* The following is the form of a "License to begge," as used in the reigns of Elizabeth and James I.:—"To T. T. C. and J. J. esquires, justices for the conservation of the peace of our Soveraigne Ladie the Queene's Majestie, within the countie of etc. assigned, greeting. Whereas the bearer hereof, M. N. of B in the sayd countie, beeing a very poore man and blinde, by reason whereof hee is not able to labour nor yet to live of himselfe without the charitable relief of others, and being now resident in the said town, is therefore now to be relieved. And being likewise informed that the said towne is at this present charged with more poore and impotent folks than it is well able to relieve; know ye, that wee the saide justices have licenced and allowed the said poore man and his leader to goe abroad to beg, gather, and receive the charitable almes of well disposed people, inhabiting within the Hundred of, &c., in the said countie, requiring you not to molest or trouble the said poore man or his leader for so doing, but desiring you rather to relieve them in their necessitie, as to you shall seeme meete. This our licence to remain in force one whole yeare next ensuing the date hereof."

forceable against any child quitting such service or any one enticing him or her to quit.

"Provyded also that no person or persons havinge chardge of any Viage* in passinge from the Realme of Ireland or from the Isle of Manne into this Realme of England, do from the laste daye of June next comynge, wittingly or wyllingly transporte bringe cary or conveygh or suffer to be transported brought caryed or conveyed in any Shippe Picarde † Vessell Boate or Boates, from and out of the said Realme of Ireland, or from or out of the said Isle of Manne, into the Realme of England and Wales or any parte thereof, any Vacabond Roge or Beggar or any suche as shalbe forced or very lyke to lyve by begging ... on payne ... to forfeyte and lose for every suche Vacabond, Roge Beggar or other person Twentye Shillinges of lawfull Englyshe Money.

"Yf any suche Maniske or Iryshe Roge Vacabounde or Beggar ben alredy or shall at any tyme hereafter be set on Land in any parte of England or of Wales, the same shalbe conveyghed to the next port in or neer whiche they were landed, and from thence be transported, at the cōmon chardge of the Countye where they were set on Land, into those partes from whence they came or were transported.

"Whereas a greate number of pore and dyseased people do resorte to the Cytye of Bath ... and the Towne of Buckston, for some Ease and Reliefe of their Diseases at the Bathes there, And by meanes thereof the Inhabitauntes of the same Cytye of Bathe and Towne of Buckstone are greatly overchardged with the same poore people, to their intollerable chardge ... no dyseased or ympotent poore person living on Almes ... shall resorte or repayre from their Dwellinge places to the said Cytie ... and Towne ... unlesse ... not onely lycensed so to do by two Justices ... but also provided for by the Inhabitauntes of such ... Places from whence they shall be so lycensed to travayle."

If a town has more poor than it can relieve, the justices are empowered to license certain of them to beg beyond its limits.

A proviso appears exempting the privileges of John Dutton and his heirs in the county of Chester from the provisions of the Act.‡ The continuance of the Act is limited to seven years.

* Passage boat.
† A sort of boat of about fifteen tons used on the Severn.
‡ The origin of this curious exemption is as follows. *Randal surnamed Blandeville*, Earl of Chester, was about the year 1210 suddenly besieged by the Welsh, in the castle of Rhuddlan in Flintshire; whereupon he

It will be observed that Manx beggars are for the first time mentioned in this Act. The Irish and Welsh have several times been mentioned before, and according to Sir Thomas More their dishonesty was only equalled by their gross superstition.

"And comenly in ye wild Yrishe and some in Wales to, as men say, whan thei go forth in robbing, thei blisse them & pray God send them good speede y^t they may mete with a good purse and doo harme and take none."*

The principal reason for the ban upon unlicensed players in interludes was to protect the interests of the better class of players, who were nearly all patronised by some of the great lords and attached to their service.

Stow, speaking of actors at this period, says :—

"Comedians and stage-players of former times were very poore and ignorant, in respect of these of this time, but being nowe growne very skilfull and exquisite actors for all matters, they were entertained into the service of divers great Lords, out of which companies, there were xii of the best chosen, and at the request of Sir Francis Walsingham, they were sworne the Queens

sent to his Constable of Cheshire, one *Roger Lacy*, to hasten, with what force he could, to his relief. It happened to be on Midsummer-day, when a great fair was then held at Chester. *Roger* got together a great mob of fiddlers, players, cobblers, &c. and marched immediately to the relief of the earl ; and the Welsh perceiving a great multitude approaching raised the siege and fled. The earl being thus freed came back with his Constable to Chester ; and in memory of this service, by a charter granted to *Roger Lacy* and his heirs, power over all the fiddlers, letchers, whores, and shoemakers in Chester. About the end of the reign of King *John*, or beginning of K. *Hen.* III., Roger Lacy being dead, his son *John* by deed granted to one *Hugh Dutton* his steward, and to his heirs, the rule and authority over all the letchers and whores in all Cheshire, in these words : *Sciant præsentes et futuri, quod ego Johannes Constabularius Cestriae, dedi et concessi, et hac præsenti charta mea confirmavi Hugoni de Dutton et heredibus suis, magistratum omnium leccatorum et meretricum totius Cestriæ, sic ut liberibus illium magistratum teneo de comite, salvo jure meo mihi et hæredibus meis.* Under this grant the heirs of *Dutton* kept a yearly court at Chester on Midsummer-day, being Chester fair, and in a solemn manner rode attended through the city to St. John Baptist's Church, with all the fiddlers of the country playing before the lord of *Dutton*, and then at the court renewed their licenses yearly ; and none were entitled to act as minstrels or fiddlers, either within the city or country, but by an order and licence of that court." The license in 1642 cost 2s. 2d., and in 1666 2s. 6d. ; after this the privilege, probably from the difficulty of enforcing it, must have gradually dwindled in value until it became worthless, as no licensing court appears to have been held subsequent to the year 1756. The last mention of the privilege is in the 17 Geo. II., c. 5 (1743-4), and it therefore continued in force until this statute was repealed by the 3 Geo. IV., c. 40 (June 24, 1822).

* A "Dialogue of Sir Thomas More Knyghte."

servants, & were allowed wages, and liveries, as groomes of the chamber: and untill this yeere 1583, the Queene hadde no players. Amongst these xii players, were two rare men, viz. Thomas Wilson, for a quicke delicate refined extemporall witte, and Richard Tarleton for a wondrous plentifull pleasant extemporall wit, hee was the wonder of his time: hee lyeth buryed in Shoreditch Church."

Minstrels were restrained on account of their being frequently the propagators of seditious ditties, and the reason for including bearwards in the Act is given by Harrison in the following terms :—

"From among which companie our bearewards are not excepted, and just cause: for I have read that they have either voluntarilie, or for want of power to master their savage beasts, beene occasion of the death and devoration of manie children in sundrie countries by which they have passed, whose parents never knew what was become of them. And for that cause there is and have beene manie sharpe lawes made for bearwards in Germanie, whereof you may read in other."

Bear-baiting was under the Tudor sovereigns a very popular amusement, and according to Sir Thomas More was more attractive to many people than church-going.

"At Beverley late, much of the people being at a bear baiting, the Church fell sodenly down at evensong time, and overwhelmed some that were in it. A good fellow that after heard the tale told, 'So,' quod he, 'now may you see what it is to be at evensong when you should be at the bear baiting.'"

And Robert Laneham, in his famous letter from Kenilworth in 1575, thus describes the bear-baitings which took place there:—

"Thursday, the foourteenth of this Iuly, and the syxth day of her Maiestyez cumming, a great sort of bandogs * whear then tyed in the vtter Coourt, and thyrteen bearz in the inner . . .

"Well, syr, the Bearz wear brought foorth intoo the Coourt, the Dogs set too them, too argu the points eeuen face too face: they had learned coounsell allso a both parts: what may they be coounted parciall that are retaind but a to syde?† I ween no. Very féers, both ton and toother, & eager in argument: if the dog in pleadyng woould pluk the bear by the throte, the bear with trauers woould claw him again by the skalp, confess & a list, but a-voyd a

* A variety of the mastiff.   † On one side.

coold not, that waz bound too the bar : and hiz coounsell tolld him that it coold bee too him no pollecy in pleading.

"Thearfore thus, with fending & proouing, with plucking & tugging, skratting,* and byting, by plain tooth & nayll a to side & toother, such exspens of blood & leather † waz thear between them, az a moonths licking (I wéen) wyl not recoouer : and yet remain az far oout az euer they wear.

"It waz a sport very pleazaunt, of théez beastz : to sée the bear with his pink nyez ‡ léering after his enmiez approch, the nimblness & wayt § of the dog too take hiz auauntage, and the fors & experiens of the bear agayn to auoyd the assauts : if he wear bitten in one place, hoow he woold pynch in an oother too get frée : that if he wear taken onez, then what shyft, with byting, with clawyng, with roring, tossing & tumbling, he woold woork too wynde hym self from them : and when he waz lose, to shake hiz earz twyse or thryse wyth the blud & the slauer aboout his fiznamy, ‖ waz a matter of a goodly reléef."

Reasons equally as good as those which prompted the inclusion of Players, Minstrels, and Bearwards in the Act no doubt existed for the inclusion of the rest of the classes specified in the category of vagabonds; in fact we have already seen why in the reign of Edward III. fencers were looked upon as noxious characters. The punishments in this Act, it will be noticed, are increased in severity; but as a counterbalance increased provision is made for the compulsory relief of the impotent poor. The clauses in the Act referring to the number of poor resorting to Bath and Buxton are no doubt due to two causes—the indiscriminate belief among the ignorant poor in remedies of universal virtue, and the certainty that at those places the richer people afflicted with diseases would sympathise with their poorer brethren similarly situated.

During the year 1572 returns continue to be made to the Council of vagabonds apprehended and punished in various counties; and combined with this, in several instances, is a peculiar notification from the justices that they have appointed searchers to detect all persons eating or dressing flesh on fast days. The curious ordinance to which this is a response, and which will be noticed hereafter, was not, as might at first be supposed, an edict in favour of a religious observance of fast days, but a measure intended to benefit fishermen by increasing the consumption of fish.

* Scratching. † A slang term for skin. ‡ Eyes. § Watch. ‖ Face.

The repressive measures against vagrancy were continued during the year 1573, as is apparent from a warrant directed to the sheriff and justices of the peace of the county of Monmouth, which states:—

"Wherein it were not amisse that the order heretofore prescribed to them (the Sheriff and Justices of the Peace) for appointing overseers of good rule in every parish were eftsoon put in execution with no less perseveraunce to thexecution of the lawes against vagabonds, idle persons, loyterers, and such as cannot yeld accompt of their way of livinge within the compasse of the lawe lately provided in that behaulf."

The year 1574 is rendered memorable by a Commission issued by the Queen for the purpose of bringing about the enfranchisement of her bondmen and bondwomen; and though it is possible that isolated instances of this form of servitude may still have continued to linger in a few localities, as this appears to be the last occasion in which villenage is mentioned in a collective form, it is worth while to quote this important document textually. The Commission is directed " To our right trustie and wel beloved Counsellor, *Sir William Cecill* of the Garter Knighte Lord Burghley and High Treasorer of England, and to our trustie and right well-beloved Counsellor *Sir Walter Mildmay* Knight Chauncellor and Undertresorer of our Exchequier, Greetinge.

" Whereas divers and sundrie of our poore faithfull and loyall Subjects, beinge borne *Bonde in Blode* and Regardaunt to divers and sundre our Mannors and Possessions within our Realm of England, have made humble Suyte unto Us to be *Manumysed Enfraunchised* and *made Free*, with theire Children and Sequells, by reason whereof they theire Children, and Sequells may become more apte and fitte members for the service of Us and of our Common Wealthe,

" We therefore,

" Having tender consideration of their said Sute, and well consideringe the same to be acceptable unto Almightie God who in the begininge made all Mankinde free, for the tender Love and Zeale whiche We beare to our saide Subjects, and for the speciall trust and confidence whiche We have in your approved Wisedomes and Fidelities,

" Do name and appoynte you two our Commissioners, and do by these presents, for Us our Heires and Successors, give full Power and Auctoritie to you two our said Commissioners, that you, either by your warrant in writing subscribed with your own Hands and Seales, or otherwise by Commission from Us and in our Name, under the Seale of our Courte of Exchequier, shall and may accordinge to your Discretions nomynate and appoynte any Person or Persons, for Us and in our Name, to enquire of all or any our *Bondmen* and *Bondwomen* with their Children and Sequells, and of all theire Goodes Chattells Landes Tenementes and Hereditaments within the severall Counties of Cornwall Devon Somersett and Gloucester and of what Valewe the same be of, and that suche Person and Persons, so by you named and appoynted to enquyre as aforesaide by force or vertue of any suche Warrante or Commission as aforsaid, shall within convenient tyme make or cause to be made Returne of every suche Warrant and Commission, with true Certificats in Writinge under their Handes and Seales of all their doings concerning the Premisses unto our said Courte of Exchequier.

" And do commytt and give unto you full Power and Aucthoritie by these Presentes, to accepte admitte and Receive to be *Manumysed Enfranchesed* and *made Free,* suche and so many of our *Bondmen* and *Bondwomen* in Blood, with all and every their Children and Sequells, theire Goodes Landes Tenements and Hereditaments as are now apperteynynge or regardaunte to all or any of our Mannors Landes Tenements Possessions or Hereditaments within the said several Counties of Cornwall Devon. Somerset and Glouc. as to you by your Discretions shall seme meete and convenient, compoundinge with them for suche resonable Fines or Sommes of Money to be taken and received to our Use for the Manumyssion and Enfranchesment, and for the Possessions, and enjoying all and singuler theire Landes Tenements Hereditaments Goodes and Chattells whatsoever as you and they can aggree for the same after your Wisdomes and Discretions."

From the list of counties given in this document, it would almost seem as if the bondmen and bondwomen mentioned in it must have been the descendants of South British Celts, who had been enslaved by their conquerors, as it will have been noticed, in the early part of this work, that during the Anglo-Saxon period the Celtic population predominated within the area extending from Cornwall upwards along the estuary of the Severn.

The physical difference between the lowest classes of the two races must originally have been very marked, as *Strabo* says of the British slaves, "The men are taller than the Celti, with hair less yellow; and slighter in their persons. As an instance of their height, we ourselves saw at Rome some youths who were taller by so much as half a foot than the tallest there; but they were distorted in their lower limbs, and in other respects not symmetrical in their conformation." *Giraldus Cambrensis*, writing of Ireland in the twelfth century, says he has "never seen in any other nation so many individuals who were born blind, so many lame, maimed, or having some natural defect." While, on the other hand, we know by the story of *St. Gregory* that the Anglo-Saxon slaves exhibited for sale at Rome in the sixth century were remarkable for their comeliness. The more substantial though coarse fare of the Anglo-Saxons and the gradual amalgamation of the two races no doubt in course of time effected a change in the physical appearance of the conquered tribes.

This Commission may be taken as a record of the extinction of villenage in England owing to natural causes, due partly to the energetic struggles of the labourer to obtain his freedom and partly to the self-interest of the lord, who, finding it impossible any longer to enforce servile labour to his own profit, was no doubt glad to obtain some pecuniary compensation for surrendering rights which must have become of little value to him.

The rigorous repression of vagrancy in the City appears to have been attended with good results, as in the year 1575 Stow tells us that "by the care of *Fleetwood* the Recorder, and the other Magistrates, there were few or no Rogues and Thieves in Goal. For the Lord Keeper *Bacon*, in the month of *August*, sitting in the *Star-Chamber*, and according to the Order calling for the Book of Misbehaviours of Masterless Rogues, Fencers, and such like, there was none to present for *London*. Tho' for *Surrey* there were five or six Strumpets, that had lately been punished at the Assizes at *Croyden*. And *Westminster*, the Dutchy, (that is, the places about *St. Clements* and the *Savoy*) St. Giles, High *Holbourn*, St. *John's Street* and *Islington* (great Harbours of such misdemeaned Persons) were never so well and quiet. For Rogue nor masterless Man dared now once to appear in those Parts. Into such good Order had the Care of the Magistrate at this time brought the City and Suburbs."

In the year 1575-6 some additions were made to the 14 Eliz., c. 5, by the 18 Eliz., c. 3. Under this Act Rogues are to be conveyed by constables from parish to parish until they reach the common gaol, and houses of correction are ordered to be provided for punishing and employing rogues, and unsettled poor. Impotent persons being relieved under 14 Eliz., c. 5, and found begging are to be whipped for the first offence, and punished as rogues and vagabonds for subsequent offences.

The following document* gives an excellent picture of the power vested in the Chief Officer of a House of Correction at this period, and of the internal management of such a house:—

"Orders, Rules, and Directions, concluded, appointed, and agreed uppon by us the Justices of the Peace within the countie of Suffolk, assembled at our Generall Sessions of Peace holden at Bury the 22th daie of Aprill, in the 31st yeare of the Raigne of our Souraigne Lady the Queen's Majestie, for the punishinge and suppressinge of Roags, Vacabonds; idle, loyteringe, and lewde persons; which doe or shall hereafter wander and goe aboute, within the hundreths of Thingo cum Bury, Blackborne, Thedwardstree, Cosford, Babings, Risbridge, Lackford, and the halfe-hundreth of Exninge, in the said countie of Suffolk, contrary to the Lawes in that case made and provided. . . .

"Item, It is ordered and agreed uppon, that the Justices dwellinge in every severall division aforesaid, shall name, appointe, and putt in office, one able and honest man for every of the hundreths and lymitts aforesaid, (yf they shall think good), whoe shal be named or called the Forren officer of the house of correction; and those men so agreed uppon and theire lymitts sett downe and appointed, they shall onely employe the most parte of their travells in goinge or rydinge from towne to towne, and to all faiers, marketts, and other places of meetings and assemblies, from tyme to tyme, within theire severall lymitts to which it is likely that any of the persons aforenamed shall resorte; as also to make diligente search within every place of the limitts appointed unto hym, whether any such person be dwellinge, remayninge, or wandering there; and that all such person or persons which eyther by serch, inquirie, or other intelligence, shal be founde owte, shal be attached, and either by himself or some constable of that place, carried before one of her Majestie's Justices dwellinge in these limitts, to be by hym committed to the gayle or house of correction, as cause shall require.

"Item, We doe order that the said forren officer shall have

* Harleian MSS. British Museum, No. 364.

authoritie within his said lymitts to charge the constable of everie parishe and towne where he shall fynde any of the aforesaid wanderinge or loyteringe persons before recited, to helpe to attach them presently, and to convey them to the next Justice as is aforesaid, whereby he may be committed to the gayoll or house of correction, as the Justice shall thinke good. . . .

"The constables of every towne that shal be charged by any Justice of Peace with the carriage of any of those idle persons to the said house of correction, shall have some allowance, so as the same shall not exceade above one halfpenny the myle, to be accompted from the towne where the same constable shall dwell the next and nerest waie to the said house of correction. . . .

"Item, It is ordered and agreed uppon, that every stronge or sturdie roag, at his or her fyrst enterance into the said house, shall have xij stripes uppon his beare skynne with the said whipp provided for the said house; and every yong roage, or idle loyterer, vj stripes with the said whipp in forme aforesaid. And that every one of them, withowte fayle, at their first comminge into the said house, shall have putt uppon hym, her, or them, some clogge, cheine, collers of iron, ringle, or manacle, such as the keper of the said house shall thinke meete, so as he maie answere for every one, as well for his forth comminge; as also that they shall be quiett, and doe noe hurte for the time they shall contynue in the said house. . . .

"Item, It is ordered, that such whippes as shall be made, ordeyned, or appoynted for the punishment of such idle persons, roags, vacabonds, or sturdie beggers, or such like people, as for theire idlenes, wantones, and lewde demenour, shal be sente thether, shal be made with twoe cordes withowte knotts; and the partie that shall receyve this punishment shall have his or theire clothes turned of theire shoulders to the beare skynne downe to the waste, and then have that correction by the whipp as before sett downe and appointed for them.

"Item, It is ordered, that all unrulie and stubborne persons shal be corrected oft'ner, and used both with harder cloggs, shackles, irons or both, and with thinner diett and harder labour, untyll he or she shall be brought to reasonable obedience and submission to the keper of the said house; and that every person that shall stubbornely refuse to labour and worke, as he or she shal be appointed by the keper of the said house, or shall not be quiett or obedient to his commandement to be ordered accordinge to the rules of the said house, shall, for his or her fyrst refusall, have fower stripes with the said whipp, and shall have a clogge, shackle, or cheine putt uppon him; and for his or her second refusal, shall have vj stripes with the said whipp; and the thurde tyme that he or she shall, after these corrections, refuse, and be still obstinate in obeyeinge the said commaundement of the said keper, then every such person shall, by one of the said Justices of the Peace dwellinge within the hundreths and lymitts, uppon just complainte made unto hym or them thereof, to be committed to the next gayle, there to be punished as a roage accordinge to the statute. . . .

"Item, It is ordered, that every person committed to the said house, shall have for their dietts, theis portions of meate and drinke followinge, and not above, (viz.) At every dynner and supper on the fleshe daies, bread made of rye, viij ounces troye waight, with a pynte of porredge, a quarter of a pound of fleshe, and a pinte of beare, of the rate of iijs. a barrell, every barrell to conteyne xxxvj gallands; and on every fyshe daie at dynner and supper the like quantitie, made eyther of milk or pease or such lyke, and the thurd part of a pound of chese, or one good heringe, or twoe white or redd, accordinge as the keper of the house shall thinke meete.

"Item, It is ordered, that such persons as will applie theire worke, shall have allowance of beare and a little bread between mealtes, as the keper of the house shall fynd that he doth deserve in his said worke. .

"Item, It is ordered, that they which will not worke shall have noe allowance but bread and beare onley, untill they will conforme themselves to worke. . . .

"Item, Yt is ordered, that all such persons as have any notorious infective decease uppon him, shall not be sente to the said house of correction to remayne there, but onely at the discretion of such Justices of the Peace before whome any such person shall be brought, shall and maie by them be sente to the said house, there to be whipped, as they shall appoynte; and thereuppon to be conveied from thence to the place of theire byrth, or last abode three years, according to the statute.

"Item, It is ordered, that all such persons as shall be sent to the said house of correction, and shall have any yonge children that shall wander about with them and not able to worke; that all such children, duringe the abode of such persons within the said house, shall be found with meate, drinke, and lodginge convenient, at the charge of the keper of the said house."

Of the number of rogues and vagabonds wandering about at this period *Harrison*, writing in the year 1577, thus speaks:—

"It is not yet full threescore yeares since this trade began: but how it hath prospered since that time, it is easie to judge; for they are now supposed, of one sex and another, to amount unto above 10,000 persons; as I have heard reported."

The "trade" to which Harrison alludes is that of professional mendicity carried on in a corporate fashion by organised wandering gangs.

In the year 1579 the Council write to the Bishop of Norwich and the justices of Norfolk to commend their exertions in the erecting of a "fourme for the punishment of loyterers, stubborne servantes, and the setting of vagabondes, roagues, and other idle people to work, after the manner of Bridewell."

The repressive measures against vagrancy in the City of London were at this time continued with good effect, as Stow tells us that—

"Recorder *Fleetwood* had set up Privy Searches in *London* for the better finding out of loose and dangerous Persons, who about these times exceedingly pestered the City. In these Privy Searches he employed trusty Officers to go about secretly into the obscurer Parts, to seek for Rogues and Thieves. By which course he at last almost cleared the Town of them. In the year 1581, soon after *Christmas*, were brought into Justice Hall above an hundred Persons taken in one Night's Privy-Search, as we shall hear by and by.

"And as they had these ways to find out and bring to light these idle masterless Beggars and Vagabonds; so they had divers sorts of Punishments for them, namely imprisonment at *Bridewell*, and whipping there; and such as were strong, were sent sometimes to the Milnes* and sometimes to the Lighters to work.

"Upon occasion of a great Parcel of Rogues encompassing the Queen's Coach near *Islington* one Evening in the Year aforesaid, when she was riding abroad to take the Air; (which seemed to put her into some Disturbance) Notice was presently given to the

* Mills.

Maior and Recorder. On that Night and the next Day were taken Seventy Four Rogues, and sent to *Bridewell*. . . .

"Upon *Sunday*, the day after this Twelfth-Day, out of the Dutchy, *Westminster*, *Southwark*, *Lambeth*, and *Newington*, were gathered up a Shoal of Forty Rogues, Men and Women. All sent to *Bridewell*. The same Day Afternoon at *Pauls*, were taken up Twenty cloaked Rogues, that used to keep their Standings there. . . .

"The next Day, Six Fellows were brought out of the *Savoy* Hospital, entertained there as Poor. Who were nothing else but Draymen to Brewers. They were soundly paid,* and sent home to their Masters.

"All *Tuesday*, *Wednesday*, and *Thursday* came in Numbers of Rogues that were rewarded according to their Deserts. The Strong put to Labour and the Weaker dismist into their Countries.

"*Friday* at the Justice Hall were brought in above an Hundred. . . .

"*Saturday* after Dinner, the Recorder went to *Pauls* and other Places, as well within the liberties as elsewhere; and found not one Rogue stirring.

"The Observations the Recorder made to the Lord Treasurer concerning the Transactions of this week, were, That of all these Companies there were not, of *London*, *Westminster*, *Southwark*, *Middlesex* nor *Surrey*, above Twelve; the residue for the most part were of *Wales*, *Salop*, *Chester*, *Somerset*, *Berks*, *Oxford*, *Essex*: And that few or none of them had been about *London* above three or four Months. And that they met not again with any in all their Searches that had received Punishment. So cautious did good Labour and good whipping make them. And further, he observed, that the chief allurers of these evil people were the *Savoy*, and the Brick-kilns near *Islington*.

The laws do not, however, appear to have been put in force efficaciously throughout the country, as *John Northbrooke* in the year 1579 thus complains of the want of vigour in executing them :—

"If these and such like lawes were executed iustlie, trulie, and seuerelie (as they ought to be) without anie respect of persons, fauour or friendship, this doung and filth of idlenesse would easilie be reiected and cast out of this Commonwealth; there would not be so manie loytering idle persons, so manie Ruffians, Blasphe-

---

* Beaten. "I will pay you in cudgels."—*Henry V. Act V. Sc. I.*

mers, & Swinge Buckelers, so manie Drunkards, Tossepottes, Whoremaisters, Dauncers, Fidlers and Minstrels, Diceplaiers, & Maskers, Fencers, Theeues, Enterlude plaiers, Cutpurses, Cousiners, Maisterlesse seruauntes, Juglers, Rogues, sturdie Beggers, counterfait Egyptians, &c., as there are, if these dounghilles and filthe in Common weales were removed, looked vnto, and cleane cast out, by the industrie, paine, and trauell of those, that are set in authoritie, and haue gouernement."

In the year 1587 we get a glimpse in the Derby Household Books of the treatment of vagrants at the house of a great nobleman :—

"Orders touching the gov̄ment of my L. his house sett downe the xiith of Maye, Anno regni reñe Eliz., &c, xxix°. 1587.

"14. It'm, that my Lo. his chiefe officers make a weeklie vewe and take ord^r that noe vagrant p^{s}ons or maisterles men be fostered and kept aboute the house and that noe household srv̄ante of anye degree bee pm̄itted to carie forth of the house or gates any mane^r of victualls bread or drinke."

At the end of 1589 a commission was issued to the lord lieutenants of the several shires authorising them to appoint provost marshals for the apprehension and punishment of soldiers, mariners, and other vagrant and masterless persons and sturdy vagabonds. This was followed in 1591 by a proclamation " that there is a wandering abroad of a multitude of people, the most part pretending that they have served in the wars, though that many have not served at all, or have run away, and therefore ought to be punished instead of relieved."

The severe penalties decreed by the 14 Eliz., c. 5, were modified in the year 1592-3 by the 35 Eliz., c. 7, ss. 6, 7, by which gaoling, boring through the ear, and death in the second degree were abolished, and punishment by whipping under the 22 Hen. VIII., c. 12, s. 12, revived instead. The effective clearances of beggars in the City appear to have caused the authorities to relax the measures taken against them, as *Strype* tells us that "About the year 1593, and before, the City, as well as other Parts of the kingdom, was grievously pestered with Beggars ;. and they many of them poor disbanded soldiers, became poor and maimed by the wars in the *Low Countries* and with *Spain ;* and many more that pretended themselves to be so who committed many Robberies and Outrages. This caused the Queen to set forth a Proclamation in the month of *February*, for the *Suppressing of the Multi-*

tudes of idle Vagabonds, and avoiding mischievous, dangerous Persons from her Majesty's Court. It sets forth—

"It was found in and about the City of *London*, and in the Parts near about her Majestie's Court, that there did haunt and repair a great multitude of wandering Persons. Whereof some were men of *Ireland*, that had these late Years unnaturally served as Rebels against her Majesties Forces beyond the Seas."

The City then again bestirred itself on the subject, as we find on the 17th November, 1594, a letter from the Lord Mayor to the Lords of Council, forwarding for their approval copies of orders to be enforced against vagrants, and on the 30th November another letter from the Lord Mayor to the justices of the peace for the counties of Middlesex and Surrey, appointing, by request of the Lords of the Council, a conference with them upon the measures to be taken for the suppression of vagrancy.

In 1595 we find another letter from the Lord Mayor to the Lords of the Council concerning the number of poor begging within the City, and requesting the assistance of their lordships to prevent the building of small tenements in Southwark and Kentish Street.

The manner in which the Council responded to this appeal may be gathered from the following proceedings in the Star Chamber:—

"In Camera Stellata coram Concilio ibidem, vicesimo die Octobris, Anno Regni Reginæ Elizabethæ quadragesimo, &c.

Præsentibus.

Thoma Egerton. mil.
Dño Custod. Magni.
Sigilli Angliæ.
Dño North.
Dño Buckhurst.
Johanne Fortescue milite Cancellar Scaccarii.

Archiepiscopo Cantuariens.
Popham milite Capitali Justic. de Banco Regis.
Anderson milite Capitali Justic. de Communi Banco.

"This day *Rice Griffin* and *John Scrips* were brought to the Barre, against whome *Edward Coke* Esquire, her Maiestie's Attourney Generall did enforme, That the said *Griffin* had unlawfully erected and built one Tenement in *Hog-lane** in the Countie of *Middlesex*, which hee divided into two severall roumes, wherein were now inhabiting two poore Tenants, that onely lived and were maintained by the reliefe of the parishioners there, and begging abroad in other places: and that the said *John Scrips* had in like sort

* Out of Norton Folgate, now called Worship Street.

divided a Tenement in *Shordich*, into, or about seventeene Tenancies or dwellings, and the same inhabited by divers persons of very poore and base condition, contrary to the intent and meaning of her Highnesse Proclamation, published and set out the seventh day of July, 1580, in the two and twentieth yeere of her Highnesse Reigne, whereby the same, and such maner of buildings and divisions, are altogether forbidden and prohibited, as by her Majesties said proclamation more at large appeareth.

"Moreover, her highnesse said Attourney further informed this Honourable Court, that sithence the sayd Proclamation, sundrie Decrees have been made and taken by this Court, aswell for the prostrating, pulling downe, and defacing of divers new Buildings: as also for reformation of divisions of Tenements: All which notwithstanding, sundry wilfull and disobedient persons, continue in their contemptuous maner of buildings and divisions: by meanes whereof, the City of London, and suburbs thereof, are overcharged, and burdened with sundry sorts of poore, beggerly, and evill disposed persons, to the great hinderance and oppression of the same; So as the Magistrates and Officers in and aboute the Citie, to whom the due execution of the aforesayd Decrees and Orders chiefly appertaineth, cannot performe and doe the same, according to the purport and tenor thereof: And in regard thereof, her Highnesse said Attourney humbly prayed, that the sayd *Griffin* and *Scrips* might receive, and have inflicted on them, some condigne and fit punishment, and that at the humble petition of the Lord Maior and Aldermen of the Citie of London, and other the Justices of Peace of the Countie of *Middlesex* and *Surrey*, the Court would bee pleased to set downe and decree, some last and generall order in this and in all other like cases of new Buildings, and divisions of Tenements. Whereupon the Court gravely considering the great growing evils and inconveniences that continually breed and happen by these new erected buildings and divisions made and divided contrary to her Majesties sayd Proclamation, and well weighing the reasons of the sayd Lord Maior and Aldermen of the sayd Citie and Justices of the Counties aforesayd in that behalfe, greatly tendering the overburdened and distressed estate of the inhabitants that dwell in sundry the parishes where the sayd new Buildings and divided Tenements are, being for the most part but of small ability to beare and sustaine the great charge which is to growe there by meanes of the poore placed in sundry of the new erected and divided Tenements, Have therefore by the whole and general consent of all the honourable presence here sitting, hearing the accusations aforesaid, and the answeres, defences, and allegations of the said *Griffin* and *Scrips*, ordered and decreed, that the sayd *Griffin* and *Scrips* shal be committed to the prison of the Fleete, and pay twentie pounds a piece for a Fine to her Majestie."

It may here not be amiss to notice another cause of vagabondism at this time which is set forth in a very curious document issued by the Privy Council in 1595, entitled—

"A briefe note of the benefits that growe to this Realme *by the observation of Fish-daies : with a reason and cause wherefore the lawe in that behalfe made, is ordained.* Very necessary to be placed in the houses of all men, specially common Victualers."

It then goes on to say :—

"In the first yeere of her Maiesties most gracious raigne, it was ordained that it should not be lawfull for any person within this Realme, to eat any flesh upon any daies then usually observed as fish-daies,* upon paine to forfeit three pounds for euery time he offended, or suffer three months imprisonment without baile or mainprize . . . .

"THE CAVSE AND REASON.

"First for as much as our Countrey is (for the most part) compassed with the Seas, and the greatest force for defence thereof, under God, is the Queenes Maiesties Nauie of ships : for maintenance and increase of the said Nauie, this lawe for abstinence hath beene most carefully ordained, that by the certaine expence of Fish, fishing and fishermen might be the more increased and the better maintained, for that the said trade is the cheefest Nource, not only for the bringing up of youth meete for shipping, but great numbers of ships therein are vsed, furnished with sufficient Marriners, men at all times in a readines for hir Maiesties service in those affaires.

"The second cause, for that many Townes and Villages upon the Sea coasts, are of late yeeres wonderfully decayed, and some wonderfully depopulated, which in times past were replenished, not onely with Fishermen, and great store of shipping, but sundry other Artificers : as Shipwrightes, Smithes, Ropemakers, Netmakers, Sailemakers, Weauers, Dressers, Carriers and Utterers of fish, maintained chiefly by fishing. *That they hereby againe might be renewed, the*

* Friday and Saturday were originally appointed as "fish days," to which Wednesday was added in 1562 by by 5 Eliz., c. 5.

want whereof is, and hath beene cause of great numbers of idle persons, with whom the Realme is greatly damaged : and this happeneth by reason of the uncertainty of the sale of Fish, and the contempt which in eating of fish is concerned."

In 1596 a proclamation was issued against pretended soldiers annoying people by begging. The Queen, it is stated, will appoint a provost marshal with power to execute them upon the gallows without delay. The City authorities followed this up by appointing two marshals for the apprehending "of vagrant and other disordered persons."

In 1598 another similar proclamation was issued.

The state of vagabondism in the country at this period may best be gathered from a letter * written to the Lord Treasurer in the year 1596 by Edward Hext, a justice of the peace for Somersetshire, and which reveals the following among the main causes for the increase of vagrancy—that houses of correction were not kept up, though they had had an excellent repressive effect, that burning in the hand was not permanent, and that the inferior officers of the law did not do their duty.

"Your lordship may behold 183 most wicked and desperate persons to be enlarged : and of these very few came to any good; for none will receive them into service. And, in truth, work they will not; neither can they, without most extreme pains, by reason their sinews are so benumbed and stiff through idleness, as their limbs being put to any hard labour, will grieve them above measure: so as they will rather hazard their lives than work. And this I know to be true : for at such time as our houses of correction were up, (which are put down in most parts of England, the more pity,) I sent divers wandering suspicious persons to the house of correction ; and all in general would beseech me with bitter tears to send them rather to the gaol. And denying it them, some confessed felony unto me, by which they hazarded their lives, to the end they would not be sent to the house of correction, where they should be forced to work. . . . .

"Others, having been burnt in the hand more times than one ; for after a month or two there will be no sign in the world : and they will change both name and habit, and commonly go into other shires, so as no man shall know them. . . . .

"For God is my witness, I do with grief protest in the duty

* Strype.

of a subject, I do not see how it is possible for the poor countryman to bear the burdens duly laid upon him, and the rapines of the infinite numbers of the wicked, wandering, idle people of the land: so as men are driven to watch their sheepfolds, their pastures, their woods, their cornfields : all things growing too, too common.

"Others there be, and, I fear me, emboldened by the wandering people, that stick not to say boldly, *they must not starve, they will not starve.* And this year there assembled sixty in a company, and took a whole cart-load of cheese from one driving it to a fair, and dispersed it among them. . . . .

"And I may justly say, that the infinite numbers of the idle wandering people, and robbers of the land, are the chiefest cause of the dearth: for though they labour not, and yet spend double as much as the labourer doth. For they live idly in the alehouses, day and night eating and drinking excessively.

"And within this three months I took a thief, that was executed this last assizes, that confessed unto me, that he and two more lay in an alehouse three weeks: in which time they eat twenty fat sheep: whereof they stole every night one. Besides, they brake many a poor man's plough, by stealing an ox or two from him: and not being able to buy more, leaseth a great part of his tillage that year.

"Others leese their sheep out of their folds; by which their grounds are not so fruitful as otherwise they would be. And such numbers being grown to this idle and thievish life, there are scant sufficient to do the ordinary tillage of the land. . . . . And when these lewd people are committed to the gaol, the poor country that is robbed by them are forced there to feed them, which they grieve at: and this year there hath been disbursed to the relief of the prisoners in the gaol 73*l.* and yet they allowed but 6*d.* a man weekly. . . . .

"The tinker in his budget, the pedlar in his hamper, the glassman in his basket, and the lewd proctors, which carry the broad seal and green seal in their bags, cover infinite number of felonies: in such sort that the tenth felony cometh not to light; for he hath his receiver at hand, in every alehouse, in every bush. And these last rabble are very nurseries of rogues.

"And of wandering soldiers, there are more abroad than ever were, notwithstanding her Majesty's most gracious proclamation lately set forth for the suppressing of them; which hath not done that good it would, if it had been used as it ought. . . . .

"Your lordship may perceive by this counterfeit pass * that I send you enclosed, that the lewd young men of England are devoted to this wicked course of life: for the man that travelled by colour of it is inheritor to 40*l.* land, after his father; and his name is Limerick. His father a gentleman, and dwelleth at Northlache, in the county of Gloucester. I kept him in prison two months, and examined him often, and yet still confirmed the truth of his passport with most execrable oaths. Whereupon I sent in to Cornwall, where he said his mother dwelt: and by that means discovering him, he confessed all. By which your lordship may see, it is most hard to discover any by examination, all being resolved never to confess any thing, assuring themselves that none will send two or three hundred miles to discover them for a whipping matter, which they regard nothing: for all that were whipped here, upon my apprehension, are all abroad.

"And otherwise will it never be without a more severe course, that liberty of their wicked life is so sweet unto them I may justly say, that the able men that are abroad, seeking the spoil and confusion of the land, are able, if they were reduced to good subjection, to give the greatest enemy her Majesty hath a strong battle, and (as they are now) are so much strength to the enemy. Besides, the generation that daily springeth from them is like to be most wicked. . . . .

* *The False Certificate before mentioned.*

"To all and singular the justices of the peace, mayors, &c., Know, that I Tho. Scroope, knt. lord Scroope of Bolton, lord warden of the middle marshes of England, and captain of her Majesty's city of Carlisle.

"That this bearer, John Manering, lately arrived from Scotland, and came before me, bringing just proof, by his conduct, from the lord warden of Scotland, of the cause of his arrival in England and country: these are therefore to certify of the truth, that the said John, with other of his company, through tempest of foul weather, were driven ashore upon the north parts of Scotland, whereby they were by the northland, called the Scottish Irish, robbed, and spoiled of their bark, and all therein. Wherein the said John lost of his own part the value of threescore pounds and better, and being grievously wounded in the thigh with a dart, and in the arm with an arrow, upon the grappling of the ship: these are therefore, upon consideration of this his loss, his hurt, and great necessity, to request you to permit him to pass unto Wormyl in Cornwall, to his mother and other his friends there; and in her majesty's name require you to relieve him.—Signed with the name and seal of Lord Scroope; and in the names of the Earl of Cumberland, Rich. Louther, and divers other justices in Westmerland, York, Stafford, Worcester, Glocester; and so far as Somerset: when this gentleman and justice, Mr. Hext, found out the cheat, and sent his pass to the lord treasurer, enclosed in his letter to him."

"But the greatest fault is in the inferior ministers of justice, which should use more earnest endeavour to bring them to the seat of judgment and justice."

The evils of indiscriminate charity and the inefficacy of excessively severe punishment had at length become so manifest that a Committee of the House of Commons was appointed to consider the existing laws relating to the poor, and certain amendments proposed upon them. This Committee, apparently acting on the principle that adequate relief must be provided for cases of destitution before mendicity can be suppressed, prepared the 39 Eliz., c. 3 (1597), which for the first time made systematic provision for the relief of the poor by providing for the appointment of overseers of the poor in every parish, who were empowered with the consent of the justices to raise weekly or otherwise by taxation, from every inhabitant and every occupier in the parish, in such competent sum and sums of money as they thought fit, a convenient stock of flax, hemp, wool, thread, iron, and other necessary ware and stuff to set the poor on work; and also competent sums of money for the necessary relief of the lame, impotent, old, blind, and other poor not able to work; and also for the putting out of children to be apprentices.

This Act was immediately followed by the 39 Eliz., c. 4 (1597-8), which repeals all former Acts against rogues, vagabonds, and sturdy beggars, and gives the following definition of rogues and vagabonds:—

"All persons calling themselves Schollers going about begging, all Seafaring men pretending losses of their Shippes or goods on the sea going about the Country begging, all idle persons going about in any Cuntry eyther begging or using any subtile Crafte or unlawfull Games and Playes, or fayning themselves to have knowledge in Phisiognomye Palmestry or other like crafty Scyence, or pretending that they can tell Destenyes Fortunes or such other like fantasticall Imagynacõns; all persons that be or utter themselves to be Proctors Procurors Patent Gatherers or Collectors for Gaoles Prisons or Hospitalls; all Fencers Bearewards comõon Players of Enterludes and Minstrells wandring abroad (other then Players of Enterludes belonging to any Baron of this Realme, or any other honorable Personage of greater Degree, to be auctoryzed to play, under the Hand and Seale of Armes of such Baron or Personage); all Juglers Tynkers Pedlers and Petty Chapmen wandring abroade; all wandring persons and comõn Labourers being persons able in bodye using loytering and refusing to worcke for such reasonable wages as is taxed or comõnly given in such Parts where such persons do or shall happen to dwell or abide, not having lyving otherwyse to maynteyne themselves; all persons delivered out of Gaoles that begg for their Fees, or otherwise do travayle begging; all such persons as shall wander abroade begging pretending losses by Fyre or otherwise; and all such persons not being Fellons wandering and pretending themselves to be Egipcyans, or wandering in the Habite Forme or Attyre of counterfayte Egipcians; shalbe taken adjudged and deemed Rogues Vagabonds and sturdy Beggers. Every such vagabond found begging is to be stripped naked from the middle upwards and openly whipped until his or her body be bloody and then passed to his or her birthplace or last residence, and in case they know neither they are to be sent to the House of Correction for a year, unless some one gives them employment sooner."

Rogues who appear to be dangerous to the inferior sort of people, or who will not reform their roguish kind of life, may be banished the realm or sent to the galleys for life; if they return without license they are to suffer death as felons.

The penalty on constables neglecting to apprehend vagabonds is increased to 10s., and the penalties on masters of vessels for bringing vagabonds from Ireland and the Isle of Man is again fixed at 20s.; those from Scotland are also now included in this prohibition, and the vagabonds themselves so brought are to be whipped before they are sent back.

The regulations for the diseased poor resorting to Bath and Buxton are repeated, and the exemption of the privileges of John Dutton is continued. Shipwrecked mariners provided with proper testimonials, children under seven, and glassmen of good behaviour travelling with a license from three justices, are exempted from the Act.

Though Scottish vagrants are now specifically mentioned for the first time they must have made their appearance in England long previously, as according to Harrison's version of Boece's "History of Scotland," large numbers were expelled from that country as early as the reign of Duffe (A.D. 968), and it was afterwards a favourite remedy with the Scotch for the purpose of disembarrassing themselves of their superfluous rascality. These expatriated vagabonds were not suffered to remain in the Border villages, as is evident from the law against Loiterers in the code of Border laws finally agreed upon by commissioners of both kingdoms specially appointed.

"15. The Wardens shall take good heed in every Marche, that none of the broken borderers (that is, not of any known clan) be suffered to keep in their Companies any idle persons, not employed in any honest service or trade; and likewise that no idle persons be suffered to remain in the Border villages or alehouses, certifying such as shall receipt them on their ground, that they shall be billable for their so doing, as if they had actually receipted the goods so stolen."

As we shall see hereafter, all these rascals in exile from Ireland, Scotland, Wales, and the Isle of Man formed a formidable addition to the ranks of their brethren in England, and furnished them with a large number of words which formed their secret jargon. The proclamation of the year 1596 against pretended soldiers was followed up by a severe enactment against them, the 39 Eliz., c. 17 (1597—8), which recites "that dyvers lewde and lycencyous persons, contemnyng both Lawes Magistrates and Religion have of late dayes wandered up and downe in all parts of the Realme under the name of Soldiers and Marryners, abusing the title of that honourable Profession to countenance their wicked Behavioures, and do contynually assemble themselves weaponed in the High wayes and elsewhere in Troupes, to the greate terror and astonyshment of her Majestyes true Subjects, the ympeachment of her Lawes, and the disturbance of the Peace and Tranquilitye of this Realme," and then commands such persons to settle themselves in service or to repair to their place of settlement upon pain of being reputed felons, and suffering as such without benefit of clergy. Soldiers and sailors wandering without testimonials, and also those bearing forged testimonials, are also to suffer as felons.

Vagabonds falling sick and unable to finish their journey within the time limited by their testimonials are exempted.

Justices are by this Act empowered to license soldiers or mariners to beg on their way home.

The 43 Eliz., c. 3 (1601), styled an "Acte for the necessarie Releife of Souldiers and Mariners," provides that weekly rates shall be raised in every parish for the purpose of relieving disabled soldiers and mariners; it also recites, "that whereas it muste needes fall out that many of suche hurte and maymed Souldiers and Marriners doe arive in Portes and Places far remote from the Counties whence they are by Vertue of this Acte to receive their yeerlie Annuities and Pensions; as also they are prescribed by this Acte to "obtayne the Allowance of their Certificates from the Muster Maister or Receiver Generall of the Muster Rolles, who commonlie is like to abide aboute the Courte or London, so that they shall neede at the firste provision for the bearinge of their Charges to such places." It then enacts, "that it may be lawfull for the Treasurers of the Countie where they shall arrive, in their discrecõn upon their Certificate (though not allowed) to give them any convenient releife for their Journey, to carrie them to the nexte Countie, with a Testimoniall of their Allowance, to passe on towardes suche a place, and in like manner shall it be lawfull for the Treasurer of the nexte Countie to doe the like; and soe from Countie to Countie (in the directe waye) till they come to the place where they are directed to fynde their Maintenance, accordinge to the tenure of this Statute."

It further enacts—

"That everie Souldier or Mariner that shalbe taken beginge in any place within this Realme after the Feaste of Easter nexte, or any that shall counterfeite any Certificate in this Acte expressed, shall for ever lose his Annuitie or Pension, and shalbe taken deemed and adjudged as a common Rogue or Vacabond person, and shall have and sustayne the same, and the like Paynes Imprisonment and Punyshment as is appointed and provided for common rogues and vacabond persons."

The last Act of this reign which it is requisite to notice here is 43 Eliz., c. 2 (1601), which still forms the basis of the English Poor Law, and which provides not only for the relief of the poor, *but for the proper administration of relief*, and for the punishment of those who refuse to work by imprisonment in the house of correction.

CHAPTER VI.

1603—1660.

Accession of James I.—Proclamation against vagabonds and order for their deportation—Legislation against players and vagrants—Acts against conjuration, witchcraft. &c.—Plague-infected persons treated as vagabonds—Stanley's remedy for beggars and robbers—Estimated number of idle vagrants—The whipping of vagrants—Proclamation against overcrowding—Legislation of 1609-10—Deportation of vagrants to Virginia—Action of the City of London—Issue of copper farthings or tokens—Levy of vagrants as soldiers for the war in the Palatinate—Reign of Charles I.—Irish vagabonds—Commission of 1630 for putting in execution the laws for the relief of the poor and the suppression of vagrancy—Beggars in the City—Legislation by the Long Parliament—Acts against players—Prynne's *Histrio-mastix*—Proclamations in the City—Law of 1656.

WITHIN six months of the accession of James I. vagabondism had reached such a pitch that it was found necessary to issue the following proclamation against them:—

"Whereas at a Parliament holden at *Westminster* in the nine and thirtith Yeare of the Raigne of his *Majestie's* late deare Sister deceased, *Queen Elizabeth,* a profitable and necessarie Lawe was made for the repressing of Rogues, Vagabonds, idle and dissolute persons, wherwith this Realm was then much infested, by the due Execution of which Lawe great Good ensued to the whole Common Weale of this Realme; but now of late, by the Remissnes Negligence and Connivency of some Justices of the Peace and other officers in divers parts of the Realm, they have swarmed and abounded everie where more frequentlie than in times past, which will grow to the great and iminent Danger of the whole Realme, yf by the Goodnes of God Almightie, and the due and timely Execution of the said Law the same be not prevented;

"And where, to the end that no Impediment might be to the due and full Execution of the same Law, his Highnes Privie Councell, according to the Power to them in that behalf given by the said Law, have by their order assigned Places and partes beyond the Seas, unto which such incorrigible or dangerous Rogues should according to the same Lawe be banished and conveyed, as by the order in that behalfe made, and under this present Proclamation particulerlie mentioned and set downe, more at large appeareth ;

"His *Majestie* purposing, for the universall Good of the whole Realme, to have the same Lawe dulie and fully executed, doth, by advise of his Privie Councell, require all Justices of Peace, Mayors, Baylifes, Headboroughes, Constables, and other officers whatsoever to whom it apperteineth, to see the said Lawe be in all the Partes and Branches of the same carefully duely and exactly executed, as they and everie of them will answer the contrarie at their uttermost Perills."

This is followed by an Order in Council specifying the following countries as the "Places or Partes to which incorrigible or dangerous rogues shall be banished : The New found Lande, the East and West Indies, Fraunce, Germanie, Spayne, and the Lowe Countries or any of them."

How far this peculiar order was carried out, and how the countries which were made the recipients of these cargoes of English scum treated the matter, does not appear; probably they sent them back again, as was the case with some English gypsies who in the reign of Elizabeth were deported to Norway.

This proclamation was soon after followed by the 1 Jac. I., c. 7 (1603-4), which continues the 39 Eliz., c. 4, but declares that no license by any nobleman shall exempt players from the Act; it also repeals the exemption to glassmen, and declares them to be rogues. It ordains, that in order that incorrigible or dangerous rogues may be identified, they shall be branded in the left shoulder with a hot burning iron of the breadth of an English shilling, with a great Roman R upon the iron, and the branding upon the shoulder to be so thoroughly burned and set upon the skin and flesh that the letter R be seen and remain for a perpetual mark upon such rogue during his or her life, and then be sent to his or her place of settlement. Any rogue again offending is to suffer death as a felon without benefit of clergy. All persons are commanded to apprehend rogues under a penalty of 10s.; the penalty on constables for neglect is 20s. The privileges of John Dutton are exempted from the Act, which is to continue to the end of the next Parliament.

The increased stringency of the regulations affecting plays and players was no doubt greatly owing to the puritanical opposition to them which had long before this shown itself, as *John Northbrooke*, in a Treatise " wherein dicing, dauncing, vaine plaies or Enterludes, with other idle pastimes &c. commonly vsed on the Sabboth day, are reproved," published in 1579, thus inveighs against them, " For I am persuaded that Satan hath not a more speedie way & fitter schoole to worke and teach his desire to bring men and women into his snare of concupiscence and filthie lustes of wicked whoredome, than those places and plaies, and Theatres are: and therefore necessarie that those places and plaiers shoulde bee forbidden and dissolued and put downe by authoritie."

This puritanical feeling was further deferred to by the 3 Jac. I., c. 21 (1605-6), entitled, " An Acte to restraine Abuses of Players. For the preventing and avoyding of the greate abuse of the Holy Name of God in Stageplayes Interludes Maygames Shewes and such like." It enacts that "if at any tyme or tymes after the end of this present session of Parliament, any person or persons doe or shall in any Stageplay Interlude Shewe Maygame or Pageant gestingly or prophanely speake or use the holy name of God or of Christ Jesus, or of the Holy Ghoste or of the Trinitie, which are not to be spoken but with feare and reverence, shall forfeite for everie such offence by hym or them committed Tenne Pounde." Considering that James himself is reported to have made " a great deal too bold with God in his passion, both with cursing and swearing, and a strain higher, verging on blasphemy," this statute seems to embody the conception of Satan reproving sin. Shakspere, it may be stated, mentions the name of God more than a thousand times in the course of his plays.

We may here appropriately take cognisance of the Acts against prophecies and witchcraft, as they form a series of supplementary measures directed against those whom the Vagrant Act of 1530-1 denounces for telling " destinies, diseases, and fortunes." By the 33 Hen. VIII., c. 8 (1541-2), persons using invocations, or other practices of sorcery, to discover treasure, &c., or to destroy or injure any one, or to provoke unlawful love, are declared felons without benefit of clergy. By the 5 Eliz., c. 16 (1562-3), persons using any invocations of spirits whatever, or practising witchcraft whereby death shall ensue, are declared felons, and the penalty enacted for practising witchcraft to the bodily harm of any one is for a first offence one year's imprisonment and pillory; a second offence is declared felony; and the penalty on practising witchcraft to discover or provoke unlawful love is for a first offence one year's imprisonment and pillory, and for a second offence forfeiture of goods and imprisonment for life. This Act was repealed by the 1 Jac. I., c. 12 (1603-4), which then proceeds to enact " for the better restraining the said offences, and more severe punishing the same," that invoking or consulting evil spirits, taking up dead bodies or parts of dead persons for the purposes of witchcraft, or practising witchcraft to the harm of any person, shall be deemed felony, and persons declaring by witchcraft where treasure is hidden, or where things lost or stolen should be found, or provoking any person to unlawful love, or attempting to hurt cattle or persons, are for the first offence to be imprisoned for one year and stand once a quarter in the pillory for six hours, and for a second offence are to suffer death as felons.

By the 33 Hen. VIII., c. 14 (1541-2), persons pretending to make prophecies founded on arms, cognisances, or badges as to the future fate of those who bear them are declared guilty of felony. By 3 & 4 Edw. VI., c. 15 (1549-50), this law is specially directed against those persons who make such prophecies regarding the King for the purpose of raising insurrections. This Act is continued by 7 Edw. VI., c. 11 (1552-3), and by 5 Eliz., c. 15 (1562-3), made especially applicable to the Queen.

The terror generally occasioned by the plague was the cause of another addition to the existing Vagrant Act in the year 1603-4, as by the 1 Jac. I., c. 31, entitled, "An Acte for the charitable Reliefe and orderinge of persons infected with the Plague," it is enacted—

"If any infected person commanded to keepe house, shall contrarie to such Commandment wilfullie and contemptuously goe abroade, and shall converse in companie, havinge any infectious sore upon hym uncured, that then such person and persons shalbe taken deemed and adjudged as a Felon, and to suffer Paines of Death as in case of Felonie; but if such person shall not have any such sore found about hym, then for his saide offence to be punished as a Vagabond in all respects should or ought to be by the Statute made in the nyne and thirtieth yeere of the Reigne of our late Soveraing Ladie Queene Elizabeth for the punishment of

Rogues and Vagabonds, and further to be bounde to his or thiere good behaviour for one whole yeere."

A very curious tract written in this reign, but not published till the year 1646, enables us to form a conception of the state of vagabondism at this period. It is styled, "Stanleyes Remedy, or The Way how to reform wandring Beggers, Theeves, High way Robbers and Pick Pockets," and professes to be "The Recantation and conversion of Mr. *Stanley*, sometimes an Inns of Court gentleman, and afterwards by lewd company became a highway robber in Queen *Elizabeth's* reign, having his life pardoned, hee loaths his wicked course of life, and writes to King *James*, shewing a meanes and remedy, how the poore of his Kingdom may be greatly relieved, by the means of workhouses, in all Cities, Market-townes, and all able parishes in the Kingdome, and how by this meanes wandring begging, idlenesse, and an untimely shamefull end will bee much prevented amongst manie. Idlenesse and prodigality being the grand causes."

"The grand wickednesse of this kingdome, which makes the kingdome not onely poore but also verie wicked, he sheweth to be three sorts, *viz.* :—

" 1. All sorts of roaguish wandring Vagrants.

" 2. All sorts of theeves, high-way robbers, pick-pockets, and such like.

" 3. All such houses as maintaine bawderie, and such like idlenesse, which doth not only wast men's estates, over-throw mens bodies by the French Pox, but also dangers their soules; now to reforme these three grand sins of this Kingdome, he saith will be very easie if his Majestie will ordaine houses of correction or workhouses in everie County, both in Cities and Market-townes;" and so in these words following he writes to the King .... "It is thought by some honourable, grave, and wise Councellours of State, that there are not so few as 80,000 idle Vagrants in this Land, that prey upon the Common-wealth, which losse being estimated and valued, would amount to a very great sum, which reckoned comes to 1,000*l.* a day, which by the yeare amounts to three hundred threescore and five thousand pounds, and there is left no other way to reforme them, but by setting them, or the greatest number of them to worke, in all Market-townes, in houses of Instruction or Correction, and those that will not worke in neither of these houses but are resolved to live a refractorie life, they may be sent either to sea (to rid the land of them) or sold to the English Plantations, to see whether God will turne their hearts and amend their lives, that they may not come to a shamefull end, but rather hope they may return to their Countrey againe with joy. . . . .

" For a good example to all gentlemen in Citie and Countrey, I will embolden my selfe to speake of a godly and charitable Gentleman one Mr. *Harman*,* a Warwick-shire Gentleman, dwelling about Sutton-Colsill, who seeing his Parish to be pestred extreamly with sturdy Beggars, & wandring Rogues, did take order, that they should be all sent to his house, and presently he set them to work, to gather stones forth of his grounds, and gave them some small releefe in meat and drink, and a penny a day, and held them hard to work, (having lustie stout servants to see to them) and when hee had made an end of gathering his owne grounds, hee set them to work in his neighbours grounds, and paid them their wages; which thing, when all the rest of the wandring Beggars and Rogues understood, they durst not one of them come a begging in that parish, for feare they should be made to work : And for the younger sort of the idle poore in his own Parish, this was such a discipline for them, that they did betake themselves to honest labour, and so the old, aged, and true poore of his Parish were verie much the better releeved. . . . .

" The generall rule of all England is to whip † and punish the

---

* This Harman was a descendant of the family of John Voysye, Bishop of Exeter, who died in 1555, at Sutton Coleshill, and is not to be confounded with Harman the author of a " Warning for Common Cursetors."

† It is evident that the beggar had an exciting time of it in the sixteenth and seventeenth centuries. When he appeared in a town he certainly received relief, but it was frequently accompanied by a whipping which must have left so strong an impression upon his mind, as well as upon his body, that he probably did not pay the same locality a visit for some time afterwards.

In the accounts of the constables of Melton-Mowbray, Leicestershire, we find :—

1602. Geven to Robert Moodee for wippin tow pore folks . . . ij^d.
    And gave them when the were wipped . . . . . ij^d.

The infliction of this punishment was sometimes deputed to a boy with what must have been a most tantalising effect :—

1602. Geven to Tomlyn's boy for whippin a man *and a woman* . . ij^d.
    And gave them when the went . . . . ij^d.

1601. P^d· and geven to a poore man and his wiff that was wipped . 0 0 4

Again :—

1625-6. Payd for whippinge 6 vagabonds 00 00 06

After the twopennyworth of whipping and the twopennyworth of alms a pass was given :—

wandring Beggars, and to brand them according to the form of the new statute, and so mark them with such a note of infamie, as they may be assured no man will set them on work, and so many Justices execute one branch of that good Statute (which is the point of Justice) but as for the point of Charitie they leave undone, which is provide houses and convenient places to set the poore to work, which ought to be done in equitie and justice, as well as the other.

"The Poore may be whipped to death, and branded for Rogues, and so become Felons by the Law, and the next time hanged for Vagrancie (by an Act made in the dayes of Queen *Elizabeth* of famous memorie) before any private man will set them to work, or provide houses for labour, and stock and materialls for them. The Publike must joyne their shoulders to the work else it will never be done.

"The right and intent of punishing of Rogues is but the destruction of vices, and saving of men; but here is no care taken to releeve them. The statute commands, that the Vagrants should repair to the places where they were borne, or last dwelled: There are thousands of these people, that their place of birth is utterly unknowne, and they had never any abiding place in their lives, or ever retained in service; but were and are Vagrants by descent.

"To conclude, it is very lamentable that poore Rogues and Beggars should be whipped, or branded according to Law, or otherwise punished, because they are begging, or idle, or do not work, when no place is provided for them to set them to work. I have heard the Rogues and Beggars curse the Magistrates unto their faces, for providing such a Law to whip and brand them, and not provide houses of labour for them; for surely many would go voluntarily to the work-houses to work, if such houses were provided for them: so that the penaltie which the Statute appoints were verie fit to be severely put in execution upon such persons that do

1625-6. Payd: for pass and wax to make passes for wagrants
wch was punished 00 00 03

This pass appears to have saved the back of the recipient at the next place he visited:—

1602. Geven to one that was whipped at buxminster . . . . ij^d.

And from which village he, I presume, brought a pass; but if he did not pass on he took the consequences:—

1601. P^{d.} and geven to bluett that was taken vagrant *after* his
wipping 0 0 2
P^{d.} more for wipping 0 0 2

Notes and Queries, s. 5, v. ix.

releeve a Rogue, or other Vagabonds at their doores, that may go unto a work-house and will not, where he may have reasonable and comfortable maintenance for his labour.

"I make no doubt (most gracious Soveraigne) but it is evident to all men, that Beggerie and Theeverie did never more abound within this your Realme of England, and the cause of this miserie is Idlenesse, and the only meanes to cure the same must be by his contrarie, which is Labour; for tell the begging Souldier, and the wandring and sturdy Beggar, that they are able to work for their living, and bid them go to work, they will presently answer you, they would work if they could get it. But if work-houses were set up in all able great parishes, it will take away all such defensorie and usuall answers, and then it will be tryed whether they will work or not."

In the year 1607, with the object of preventing the overcrowding of pauper residents, a proclamation was issued against new buildings in the City of London in the following terms:—

"The King's Maiestie perceiving the great inconveniences, which dayly do arise by the continuall additions of a multitude of new buildings in the Citie of London and the suburbs and confines thereof, and the filling and pestering of houses with Inmates and several dwellers (and those of the worst sort) almost in every several Roume, whereby both the people increasing to so great numbers, are not well to be governed by the wonted officers and ordinary Jurisdiction of the same, and likewise the prices of Victuals are by that meanes excessively inhanced, and the health of his loving Subjects, not onely those which inhabite in and about the sayd Citie, but also all others repairing thither from all parts, (in respect either of the usuall resiance of his Majesties Court thereabouts, or otherwise for ordinary Justice) indangered (whereof the present Infection in and about this Citie, makes his Majestie the more sensible). . . . .

"And forasmuch as the Dividing of Houses into several Tenements and Habitations, and the letting part of Houses and Chambers to Inmates and Undersitters is no lesse Inconvenient then excessive Building as well in regard of surcharge of people, specially of the worse sort, as for breeding and spreading of Infection, besides other inconveniences proper to this abuse. His Maiestie doeth further charge and straightly commaund, that these Articles following bee also duely observed and obeyed.

"First. That no person within the Citie or Limits aforesaide, doe divide any dwelling House by Lease, sufferance, or otherwise, into any more Tenements or dwellings then are at this present used within the same.

"That no person doe hereafter receive into any House any Inmates or Undersitters, or any more families then one.

"That no man that shall erect a new house upon or within the precincts of an olde foundation, shall divide the same into more Tenements or severall dwellings, then were used in the sayd former Houses."

In the year 1609-10, the non-execution of the law again forms the reason for fresh legislation on the subject of vagrancy, the 7 Jac. I., c. 4, recites that "Heretofore divers good and necessarie Lawes and Statutes have been made and provided for the ereccion of Howses of Correccion for the suppressing and punishing of Rogues Vacabonds and other idle vagrant and disorderly persons, wch Lawes have not wrought soe good effect as was expected, aswell for that the said Howses of Correccion have not been buylte according as was intended, as alsoe for that the said Statutes have not been duly and severely putt in execucion as by the said Statutes were appointed," it directs that all such laws shall be put in due execution and that houses of correction shall be built in every county, "wth convenient Backside thereunto adjoyninge togither wth Milles Turnes Cards and suchlike necessarie Ymplements to sett the said Rogues or such other idle persons on worke," and if before Michaelmas, 1611, such a house is not built or provided in any county, every justice in that county is to forfeit £5. The justices in quarter sessions are to appoint governors of such houses who "shall have Power and Authoritie to sett such Rogues Vagabonds and idle and disorderlie persons as shallbee brought or sent unto the said House to work and labor (being able) and to punishe them by putting Fetters or Gyves upon them, and by moderate whipping of them." Moreover, they "shall in noe sort be chargeable to the Countrie for any allowance either at their bringing in or going forth or during the tyme of their Abode there, but shall have such and so much Allowance as they shall deserve by their owne Labour and Worke."

The justices are further directed to assemble "twice in every yeare at the least and oftener if their be occasion, and commaund to be made a generall privy search in one night wthin their said

Hundreds Townes Villages and Hamletts, for the finding out and apprehending of the said Rogues Vagabonds wandring and idle persons," who are to be brought before the justices to be examined and there to be punished or otherwise to be sent to the house of correction; and " the Constables and Tything men of every Hundred Parish Towne Village and Hamlet shall then appeare " before the justices at their said assemblies, " and there shall give accompt and reckoning uppon Oath in writing, and under the Hand of the Minister of every Parish, what Rogues Vagabonds and wandring and disorderly persons they have apprehended both in the search and alsoe betweene every such Assemblies and Meetings, and howe many have bene by them punished, or otherwise sent unto the Houses of Coreccion." Lewd women having bastards chargeable are to be committed to the house of correction, and there punished and set on work during the term of one whole year. Persons deserting their Families are to be deemed incorrigible Rogues, and "endure the Paines of incorrigible rogues."

In this year (1609), the Lord Mayor received an intimation from the Council informing him that all the ills and plagues affecting the City were caused through the number of poor swarming about the streets, and recommending the Corporation to subscribe with the companies and the several wards, and so to raise a fund to ship out these persons to Virginia ; and he issued his precept to the several companies for the purpose, March 27th, 1609. On April 29th, the Merchant Taylors' Company determined to subscribe £200, and the members of the company advanced £300 more ; the Ironmongers advanced £150. Altogether £18,000 was raised in the City for the purpose of founding this plantation. The scheme, however, failed about 1622.

The burden of a large family appears to have pressed heavily on the labourer at this period, since *Cotgrave*, commenting in 1611 on the proverb, " Children are poor men's riches," says, " In other countries, whose people are industrious, they may perhaps be so ; but in ours, for the most part, store of children make poore men plaine beggers." The relief of such families is recommended in "An Ease for Overseers of the Poore " (1601) in the following terms :—

" When a man is ouercharged with many young children, that though he toile day and night to keepe his family, (as Iacob did for Laban) yet he cannot maintaine his charge with his labour, therefore such an one is to be considered: for if a man in pittie will ease his beast which is oppressed with burthen, he must in nature releeue his neighbour which is oppressed with charge."

The amiable advocates of this policy do not seem to have realised that they were putting a premium on the evil they were seeking to mitigate.

In the year 1613 we find an indenture between Edw. Grent, Robt. More, Martin Smyth, and Fras. Hexham, all of London, patentees of the office of surveyor, for giving in the names of the inmates within three miles of Westminster and London, and for enforcing the laws for maintenance of the poor, and suppressing vagrancy, whereby they agree to divide the said limits into four parts, north, south, east, and west, and each to exercise his office within one of the said divisions; also to hire a house for the business of the office, to keep registers, &c.

In 1614 a letter was sent from the Lord Mayor to the Lord Chamberlain, detailing the steps taken by him since his appointment for reforming what he found out of order in the City.

Firstly. He had freed the streets of a swarm of loose and idle vagrants, providing for the relief of such as were not able to get their living, and keeping them at work in Bridewell, "not punishing any for begging, but setting them on work, which was worse than death to them."

About 1616 we find a letter from the Lords of the Council to the Lord Mayor and Court of Aldermen, stating that, "forasmuch as there were dispersed in and about the cities of London and Westminster, the Borough of Southwark, and other villages and towns adjoining, an infinite multitude of rogues and vagabonds, with other loose and base people, having no certain places of abode and living by no lawful labour or occupation, His Majesty had thought fit, by his Proclamation now published, to command such good laws as were provided in that behalf to be speedily put in execution; and that Provost Marshals should be appointed within the liberties of the City and in the counties of Middlesex, Kent, Surrey, Essex, Herts, and Bucks. It remained for the Court of Aldermen to see the same carefully performed within the City. The Council, therefore, required the City to contribute in some reasonable measure towards the maintenance of Provost Marshals in Middlesex, the charge being but temporary, and not necessary (as they hoped) to be continued for any long time."

"The Council were informed there had been great negligence in constables and such like inferior officers, in not apprehending notorious vagabonds and proceeding with them as the law directed, and they required the Court of Aldermen to reprove the constables sharply and admonish them.

"They deemed it fit that once a week, or as often as convenient, secret and sudden searches should be made in all victualling houses, inns, and other suspected places within the City and liberties."

In 1616 a letter was sent from the Lords of the Council to the Lord Mayor and Court of Aldermen, reciting their former letters for the appointment of Provost Marshals in the City and in the adjacent counties. They had been informed that for the short time such course was tried it did much good, and that it was more necessary than before, seeing that the King was about to make a journey into Scotland with a great part of his Council, and to be absent so long a time. They required the same practice to be adopted till his return.

In 1618 the King writes from Newmarket to Sir Thomas Smyth, who in the subsequent year became governor of the Virginia Company, to the following effect:—

"James R.—Trustie and well beloved wee greet you well, Whereas our Court hath of late been troubled with divers idle young people whoe although they have been twise punished still continewe to followe the same haveinge noe ymploymte. Wee haveinge noe other course to cleere our court from them have thought fitt to send them unto you, desireing you att the next oportunitie to send them away to Virginia and to take such order that they may bee sett to worke there, wherein you shall not onlie doe us good service, but also doe a deed of charitie by ymploying them whoe otherwise will never be reclaimed from the idle life of vagabonds.

"Given att our Court att Newmarket the Thirteenth daie of Januarie, 1618."

Upon receipt of this, Sir Thomas Smyth immediately writes the following letter to the Lord Mayor:—

"Right Hono[ble].—I have this eveninge receaved a lre from his Mat[ie] att Newmarkett requireinge me to send to Virginia divers younge people who wantinge imploym[te] doe live idle and followe the Court, notw[th]standinge they have been punished as by his highnes lres (which I send yo[r] Lp here w[th]to pruse) more att large appeareth. Now for as much as some of theis persouns by his Ma^{ts} royall comand are brought from Newmarkett to London alreadie and others more are comeinge after, and for that the Companie of Virginia hath not anie shipp att present readie to go thither, neither any meanes to imploy them or secure place to detaine them in untill the next oportunitie to transport them (which I hope wilbie verie shortlie), I have therefore thought fitt, for the better accomplishinge his highnes pleasure therein, to intreat y^r Lps favour and assistance, that by yor Lps order theis persons may be detained in Bridewell & there sett to worke untill our next shipp shall depte for Virginia, wherein yor Lp shall doe an acceptable service to his Ma^{ty}, & myselfe be enabled to pforme that which is required of me, soe I comend you to God & rest. Yo^r Lps assured loveinge freind,

"Tho: Smyth."

"This Mundaie eveninge, 18 Januar, 1618."

About 1619-20, the Company for Virginia write to the Lord Mayor, expressing their regret that differences should have arisen between the committees for the City and themselves. Seeing that these differences had no solid foundation, and that the company had now solemnly ratified as much and more than in their former letter was offered, which they understood had been accepted and approved by the Common Council, that on the City's part the money had been collected and the children provided, that the company had supplied a fair ship for transporting them, and the Privy Council had, at the City's desire, granted their warrant for the shipment of such children, the company trusted that the Lord Mayor and Aldermen would proceed to the speedy ending of the differences.

In July, 1619, orders were taken in Council against beggars and vagabonds, who were stated to swarm in every town; they were to be imprisoned for the first offence, branded for the second, and hanged for the third.

The reasons for this increase in vagrancy are thus given by Dekker, in "Greevous Grones for the Poore," published in 1622.

"And thus, though the number of the poore do dailie encrease, all things yet worketh for the worst in their behalfe. For, there hath beene no Collection for them, no not these seven yeares, in many parishes of this Land, especiallie in Countrie townes; but many of those Parishes turneth forth their poore, yea and their lustie Labourers that will not worke, or for any misdemeanor want worke, to begge, filtch, and steale for their maintenance, so that the Countrey is pittifully pestered with them; yea, and the maimed Soldiours, that have ventured their lives, and lost their limbes in our behalfe, are also thus requited: For when they returne home, to live by some labour in their naturall Countrey, though they can worke well in some kinde of labour, everie man sayeth, Wee will not bee troubled with their Service, but make other shifte for our businesse. So are they turned forth to Travaile, in Idlenesse (the highway to Hell) and seeke their meate uppon *Meares* (as the Proverbe goeth) with Begging, Filching, and Stealing for their maintenance, untill the Law bring them unto the fearefull end of hanging."

"The country suffered for centuries from the want of small money. Towards the close of the reign of Henry VII., so much was the scarcity felt that counterfeit coins were put in circulation, and private tokens of lead, which had been previously in use to a limited extent, were more generally adopted. Erasmus, who visited London in 1497 and again in 1499, alludes to these *plumbeos Angliæ*, as he terms them, the money he had observed as being in common circulation. In 1561, during Queen Elizabeth's reign, *silver* coins of the value of three halfpence and of three farthings were issued under her authority; but the want of halfpenny pieces and farthings still compelled the almost general use amongst housekeepers, chandlers, vintners, and other traders, of private tokens of lead, tin, latten, and even of leather. To put a stop to this, various proposals for a copper coinage were made. In 1582 the three-farthing pieces were withdrawn and silver halfpennies substituted; and when King James ascended the throne in 1603, the small coinage seems to have been limited to penny and halfpenny pieces in silver, which were very inconvenient on account of their minute size. In 1613, however, he authorised the making of copper farthings or tokens, for the quaint reason amongst others that they will be a 'relief to the poor as they will thereby receive small alms;' and prohibited by proclamation the use or currency of all private tokens. But he did not oblige his subjects to take these copper farthings or tokens otherwise than 'with their own good liking;' and he expressly says in his Proclamation that he did not make them 'monies or coins.' The object was merely to supersede the private by the royal tokens; but his Majesty's farthings were not looked upon with favour, and the scheme did not meet with acceptance."*

Braithwait, in "Barnabee's Journal," sarcastically alludes to the royal tokens.

> " Thence to *Harrington* be it spoken
> For name sake I gave a *token*
> To a Beggar that did crave it
> And as cheerfully receive it."

Harrington was the cant title for a farthing, and derived its name from Lord Harrington, to whom James granted the first patent for making them; they were originally intended to be of brass.

In the year 1620 English enthusiasm was aroused on behalf of the Elector Palatine, son-in-law of the King, who had accepted the crown of Bohemia, and who was as a consequence assailed by the Catholic powers. James, much against his will, gave him the scantiest assistance compatible with the popular demands.

In 1624 a grant of £300,000 was made by Parliament for the purpose of carrying on the war; and Count Mansfeldt, an experienced soldier, was sent to England to take command of the troops to be raised for this special service.

On the 6th of November, it was reported that—

"The King's ship that was to bring over Count Mansfeldt had been cast away on the 1st of that month, and all in her lost except the Count and two pages, and that the letters to the lieutenants to press men for this expedition were signed with difficulty, and were not yet put in practice. . . . . The press for Count Mansfeldt had begun on the previous night, *amongst vagrants about town.*"

On the 18th December it appears that the soldiers, "a rabble of raw poor rascals," were marching to Dover, but so unwillingly, that they were rather driven than led; some of those pressed having hanged, drowned, or disabled themselves in order to escape the service. It was lamentable to see the heavy countenances, and hear the sad farewells of the pressed men, who were most unwilling to go on account of the bad season, the uncertainty of the employment, and the "ill terms" on which they served, the business in fact appeared to "promise no honour to the nation, and only wretchedness to the poor soldiers."

On the principle that the worm will turn, these waifs and strays

---

* David Murray. The issue of tokens was not prohibited by law until 1817 (57 Geo. III., c. 146).

of society, driven apparently to desperation, in a very few days more assumed the aggressive; for on the 26th December it is reported that "no provisions can come into Dover because the soldiers take all away, and that the town will be ruined by the outrages of the soldiers without an order for the exercise of martial law." On the 27th the official report says that "the misery and fear they cause is indescribable."

The expedition, as might be surmised, ended disastrously, and James died in the month of March following.

In the reign of *Charles I.* little was done in the way of lawmaking owing to the continuous struggle for mastery which went on between the King and the Parliament.

The very first Act of this reign, the 1 Car. I., c. 1 (1625), entitled "An Acte for punishing divers abuses committed on the Lord's day called Sunday," marks a farther concession to the growing puritanical spirit of the age. It recites that—

"Forasmuch as there is nothing more acceptable to God then the true and sincere service and worshipp of him according to his holy will, and that the holy keeping of the Lord's day, is a principall part of the service of God, which in very many places of this Realme hath beene and now is profaned and neglected by a disorderlie sort of people, in exercising and frequenting Bearebaiting, Bullbaiting, Enterludes, Common Playes, and other unlawfull exercises and pastimes uppon the Lord's day; and for that many quarrells bloodshedds and other great inconveniences have growen by the resort and concourse of people going out of their owne Parishes to such disordered and unlawfull exercises and pastimes neglecting Divine service both in their own Parishes and elsewhere." . . .

It then enacts that—

"From and after fortie dayes next after the end of this session of Parliament, there shalbe no meetings assemblies or concourse of people out of their own Parishes on the Lord's day within this Realme of England, or any of the Dominions thereof, for any sport or Pastimes whatsoever; nor any Bearebaiting, Bullbaiting, Enterludes, common Playes or other unlawfull exercises or pastimes used by any person or persons within their owne parishes, and that every person and persons offending in any the premisses, shall forfeit for every offence three shillings foure pence."

In 1628 the 3 Car. I., c. 5, was passed for the purpose of continuing the 14 Eliz., c. 5, so far as related to the levying and employing of gaol-money; the 18 Eliz., c. 3, so far as related to bastards; the 39 Eliz., c. 4, with the proviso regarding the heirs of John Dutton; the 39 Eliz., c. 17, and the 1 Jac. I., c. 7; and this continuing Act was itself again continued indefinitely by the 16 Car. I., c. 4 (1641).

In the autumn of the year 1628 the western counties were annoyed by an influx of Irish pauperism. On the 18th of August the justices of peace for the county of Pembroke write to the Council that "Of late great numbers of Irish poor people have been landed in that county with passes. Being much pestered and burdened by them, the writers have made stay of a bark of ten tons, wherein were carried about 70 of these poor people. They are landed suddenly and some of them secretly in the night, taking after the rate of 3s. for every passenger."

The justices submit "that caution should be given to the Lord Deputy to restrain this confluence into this kingdom."

On the 23rd of October the same justices "reiterate their complaints of the great concourse of Irish people transported into this country. The owners of barks make much gain by transporting them at 3s. a piece for young and old. The reasons they allege for their coming are the last year's death of cattle and dearth of corn; yet they carry cattle into this and other countries, and there is a restraint to send corn from hence into that kingdom. They crave such order that henceforth they be not pestered with these people."

On the 1st of January, 1629, the Mayor and Aldermen of Bristol write to the Council, "The scarcity of corn in Ireland is such that the poor people of that realm are enforced, for avoiding famine, to come over into this kingdom, and are very offensive in all the western parts. They pray permission for merchants of that city to transport corn into Ireland."

On the 18th of March following, the justices for Essex write to the Council that "Their county is much troubled with a multiplicity of Irish men, women, and children, beggars, of whom they cannot learn at what port they were landed, or the cause of their landing. Not being able to dispose of them to their places of last habitation or birth, they crave direction how they may clear the country of so great a grievance."

On the 15th of April the justices of the county of Pembroke again write. "On their previous complaints touching the transportation of poor Irish people into these parts in great multitudes, the Council wrote that they would take order for their restraint. Since which they have continually increased, so that within the last month 300 have been landed thereabouts, for whose passage is paid 5s. a piece. Their ingress cannot be prevented by reason that they land them on rocks and in creeks, and presently return to bring as many more. By ingrossing and transportation corn is grown to a great price and scarcity. Wherefore they pray present order for restraint of licences for transportation."

On the 16th of April the Lords of the Council write to the Lord Mayor, referring to the satisfactory results which had arisen from the steps taken in accordance with their former directions for the suppression of vagabonds and wandering persons in the City. Of late they had very much increased, and they were commanded in the King's name to require him to take speedy and effectual order for their suppression.

On the 20th of April the Lord Mayor and Aldermen reply, detailing the steps taken by them, and stating that they found such persons were mostly foreigners and Irish, very few of whom, when set to work, would undergo the labour with the slender diet in that case allowed. The foreigners, at their own request, had been discharged with correction or relief of money; those who came from the several quarters of the City had been returned to their parishes. They requested the Council to give order to force the Irish vagrants into their own country; and that those who by the strict search which had been made had been driven into Middlesex, Surrey, and Essex, might be so proceeded with that they should not fill the City again.

The evil rose to such a pitch that the judges were consulted as to the mode to be adopted for clearing the kingdom of Irish and other beggars.

Their advice was embodied in a proclamation issued on the 17th of May, expressly commanding that all *Irish Beggars* then in England "wandring or begging shall forthwith depart this Realme and return into their own Countrie and there abide." If at the end of six weeks they are found wandering or begging they are to be apprehended and punished as Rogues and Vagabonds and then to be conveyed from constable to constable to one of the following ports, viz. Bristol, Minehead, Barnstaple, Chester, Liverpool, Milford, and Workington. The proclamation also commands that all officers "use all care and diligence to execute the Lawes against all Rogues and Vagabonds."

On the 11th of June the justices of Pembroke further write that "they have apprehended Edmund Wealsh, master of the Gift, of Dublin, who has transported Irish beggars into those parts, and used unreverent speeches of his Majesty. They have committed him to gaol until they receive further directions. He willingly took the Oath of Allegiance. He has not brought over of Irish beggars above eight."

The evil appears to have been abated, as no further correspondence seems to have taken place on the subject until the 26th of March, 1633, when the justices for the county of Somerset write to the sheriff, certifying their proceedings for relief of the poor and supply of the markets. They report that there are "very few wandering persons amongst them, more than now and then a troop of Irish, that begin again to swarm out of that country, for reformation whereof they desire the lords to take order."

The condition of the peasant in the year 1630 is thus described by John Taylor the Water Poet, in "Superbiæ Flagellum, or, the Whip of Pride:"—

> "The painful Plowmans paines doe neuer cease,
> For he must pay his Rent, or lose his lease,
> And though his Father and himselfe before,
> Haue oft relieu'd poore beggers at their doore;
> Yet now his Fine and Rent so high is rear'd,
> That his own meat, and cloathes are scarcely clear'd,
> Let him toyle night and day, in light and darke,
> Lye with the Lambe downe, rise up with the Larke,
> Dig, delue, plow, sow, rake, harrow, mow, lop, fell,
> Plant, graft, hedge, ditch, thresh, winnow, buy & sell;
> Yet all the money that his paines can win,
> His land-lord hath a purse to put it in.
> What though his Cattell with the Murraine dye,
> Or that the Earth her fruitfulnesse deny?
> Let him beg, steale, grieue, labour and lament,
> The Quarter comes, and he must pay his Rent."

Whipping-posts and stocks appear at the same time to have been plentiful:—

> "In London and within a mile, I weene,
> There are Iayles or Prisons full eighteene
> And sixty Whipping posts, and Stocks and Cages,
> Where sin with shame and sorrow hath due wages."

In this year the King issued a Commission under the great seal, directed to thirty-six of the principal officers of state and nobility, for the purpose of putting in execution the laws for the relief of the poor, and for setting to work idle persons who wander up and down begging, or maintain themselves by filching and stealing. It sets forth :—

"That the defect of the execution of the good and politique Lawes and Constitutions in that behalfe made, proceedeth especially from the neglect of dutie in some of our Justices of the Peace, within the severall Counties, Cities, and townes Corporate of this our Realme of England, and Dominion of Wales, which remissenesse & neglect of duty doth grow and arise from this, That by the most of the said Lawes, there are little or no Penalties or Forfeitures at all inflicted upon the said Justices of Peace, Magistrates, Officers, and Ministers for not performing their duties in that behalfe, or if any be, yet partly by reason of the smalnesse thereof, and partly by reason of their power and authoritie in their severall places, whereby they hold others under them in awe, there are few or no Complaints or Informations made of the neglects and want of due execution of the offices of the said Justices and other Ministers . . . . by reason whereof the said Justices of Peace, Magistrates, Officers, and Ministers, are now of late in most parts of this our Kingdome growne secure in their said negligence . . . . Whereas at this day in some Counties and parts of this Our Kingdome, where some Justices of Peace and other Magistrates doe duely and diligently execute the same, there evidently appeareth great reformation, benefit and safety do redound to the Commonwealth. And likewise when as there was care taken, and diligence used to have the Lawes concerning Charitable uses, wel executed, and all pious gifts to bee imployed according to the good intent of the Donors, these poore people were better relieved then now they are. . . .

"After long and mature deliberation, finding that there is no better wayes or meanes to have the said Lawes and Statutes put in full execution, then by committing the trust and oversight thereof to the speciall care and industrie of certaine persons of principall Place, Dignitie and Order neere unto Our Person; who upon their diligent inquirie how the said Lawes and Statutes are put in execution, may be able upon all occasions to give Us particular information thereof, and by their approved Wisdomes experience and Judgements, give Directions and Instructions from time to time for the better execution of the said Statutes."

It then proceeds to direct the Commissioners to make inquiry, by oath or otherwise, and to inform themselves "how all and every the Lawes and Statutes now in force, which any way concerne the reliefe of impotent or poore people, the binding out of apprentices, the setting to worke of poore children, and such other poore people, as being able or willing to worke, have no stocke or meanes to imploy themselves; the compelling and forcing such lazie & idle persons to worke, as being of bodies able and strong, doe neverthelesse refuse to labour; the maintenance, governement, and well ordering of houses of correction and other places for reliefe of poore indigent and impotent people, the Rating, Collecting, and imployment of all such Summes, as by the Statute of the three and fourtieth of *Elizabeth*, are appointed for the reliefe of Souldiers and Mariners, the punishment or setting on worke of Rogues and Vagabonds: And all Lawes and Statutes now in force for the repressing of Drunkennesse and Idlenesse, the reforming of abuses committed in Innes and Alehouses, the abridging of the number of Alehouses, and the well ordering of such as be licensed, the keeping of Watches and Wards duely, and how other publique services for God, the King, and the Common-wealth, are put in practice and executed."

This is succeeded by orders to the justices to see to the execution of the laws mentioned, to inflict condign punishment on any officers who neglect their duty, and to reward prosecutors and informers. The justices are to report every three months to the High Sheriff, who is in turn to report to the Justices of Assize, who are to report to the Lords Commissioners. Justices failing to send in an account are to be reported to the Commissioners by the High Sheriff, and the Justices of Assize are to inquire and mark what justices are careful and who are negligent.

Attached to these orders are Directions for carrying out the Statutes. Those relating to vagrancy are as follows:—

"That the Lords of Manors and Towns take care that their Tenants, and the parishioners of every Towne may bee releeved by worke, or otherwise at home, and not suffered to straggle and beg up and downe in their parishes.

"That Stewards to Lords and Gentlemen, in keeping their Leetes twice a yeere, doe specially enquire upon those articles that tend to the reformation or punishment of common offences and abuses: As of Bakers and Brewers, for breaking of Assizes: Of Forestallers and Regraters: Against Tradesmen of all sorts, for selling with under weights, or at excessive prises, or things unwholesome, or things made in deceipt: Of people, breakers of houses, common theeves, and their receivers; haunters of Taverns, or Alehouses; those that goe in good clothes, and fare well, and none knowes whereof they live; those that bee night-walkers; builders of Cottages, and takers in of Inmates; offences of Victuallers, Artificers, Workemen, and Labourers.

"That the petty Constables in all Parishes, be chosen of the abler sort of Parishioners, and the office not to bee put upon the poorer sort, if it may be.

"Watches in the night, and Warding by day, and to bee appointed in every Towne and Village, for apprehension of rogues and vagabonds, and for safety and good order.

"And because it is found by dayly experience, that the remissenesse and negligence of petty Constables is a great cause of the swarming of Rogues and Beggers: therefore the High Constables in their severall Divisions are specially to be charged to looke unto the petty-Constables, that they use diligence in their offices, and the High Constables to present to the Justices of Peace, the defaults of the petty-Constables, for not punishing the Rogues, or not presenting those that are Relievers of the Rogues and Beggers, the Law inflicting a penalty upon the Constable for not punishing them, and upon such party as shall relieve them.

"If in any Parish there be found any persons that live out of service, or that live idly and will not worke for reasonable wages, or live to spend all they have at the Alehouse, those persons to bee brought by the High Constables, and petty Constables to the Justices at their meetings, there to bee ordered and punished as shall be found fit.

"That the Correction houses in all Counties may be made adjoyning to the common Prisons, and the Goaler to be made Governour of them, that so he may imploy to worke Prisoners committed for smal Causes, & so they may learne honestly by labour, and not live idly and miserably long in Prison, whereby they are made worse when they come out, then they were when they went in, and where many houses of Correction are in one County, one of them at least to bee neere the Goale.

"That no man harbour Rogues in their Barnes, or Outhouseings. And the wandring persons with women and children to give account to the Constable or Justice of Peace, where they were marryed, and where their children were Christened; for these people live like Salvages, neither marry nor bury nor Christen, which licentious libertie make so many delight to be Rogues and Wanderers."

The other articles in the Directions refer to the apprenticing of poor children, the enforcement of fixed rates of wages* for labourers and servants, the raising of rates for the relief of the poor, and the neglect to repair highways, which are stated to be in great decay in all counties.

Subsequently to these Directions we find in the State Papers reports of the apprehension and punishment of vagrants from the sheriffs of Herts and Kent. One reason no doubt for the toleration of members of the vagrant tribe in rural districts was that many of them were general news-carriers and gossip-mongers. *Cotgrave* says regarding them—

> " If one should refuse to talke with every Begger,
> He should refuse brave company sometimes."

On the 17th of September in this year (1630) a renewed proclamation was issued " for suppressing rogues and vagabonds, and the relief of the poor according to law." It states that, " harvest being ended, the former similar proclamation of the 23rd April last past is to be put in execution against all persons wandering under the names of soldiers, mariners, glassmen, potmen, pedlars, petty chapmen, conyskinmen, or tinkers."

The rogue appears about this period to have devised a legal puzzle for the justices, which they were obliged to submit to the judges for solution, as we find amongst the Resolutions of the Judges of Assize in 1633 the following query, with its answer.

"27 Qu. A rogue is taken at C. and will not confesse the place of his birth: neyther doth it appeare otherwise but that he confesseth the last place of his habitation to be at S. hereupon he is whipped and sent to S. At his comming to S. the place of his birth is there knowne by some to be at W. and thereupon the rogue confesseth it to be so: whether he might without any new vagrancy be sent to W?"

"*Resol.* In this case it is fit to send such a rogue to the place of his birth: for this is but a mistaking and no legall setling."

* The 1 Jac. I., c. 6., s. 2 (1603-4), enacts that Labourers, Weavers, Spinners, and Workmen's wages are to be rated by the Justices.

On January 15, 1633, the Lords of the Council write to the Lord Mayor with respect to their former letters for the execution of his Majesty's Book of Orders concerning charitable uses, and for the punishment of wandering rogues and vagrants, and require him to be more careful and vigilant in the performance of his duty therein.

In March, 1638, the Lords of the Council find it necessary to write to the Lord Mayor and Aldermen with respect to the great number of wandering poor in the city, requiring order to be taken for the relief of the poor according to the laws, that they might have no pretence to wander and beg, and for the punishment of rogues and vagabonds.

In June of the same year the Lords of the Council again write to the Lord Mayor and Aldermen, requiring them to proceed more effectually in the execution of the laws for the suppression of vagrants, and to report their proceedings at the end of every term.

The troublous times which followed were eminently favourable to vagabondage, and until the two great parties in the State had ceased fighting for the supremacy it was useless to expect that any comprehensive measures could be taken to suppress it. In 1647, however, the King had fallen into the hands of the Parliamentary Commissioners, and the civil war was virtually terminated. Towards the end of this year the puritanical sentiment of the Long Parliament caused, on the 22nd October, the passing of an ordinance (c. 97) for the suppressing of Stage plays and interludes. It enacts that Common players shall be committed to the gaol, there to remain until the next general sessions of the peace, or sufficient security entered for their appearance at the sessions, there to be punished as rogues according to law. This was followed, on the 22nd January, 1648, by an order for an ordinance to suppress all Stage Plays, and for taking down all their boxes or seats where they act, and that the Lord Mayor, Sheriffs, and Justices of Peace, and Committees of the Militia, &c., take care to suppress all stage plays for the future.

These ordinances, however, appear to have been entirely inefficacious, and accordingly, on the 11th February, 1648, a more formidable ordinance (c. 106) for suppression of all stage plays and interludes) was passed. It recites that "The Acts of Stage-Playes, Interludes, and common Playes, condemned by ancient heathens, and much less to be tolerated amongst professors of the Christian Religion, is the occasion of many and sundry great ·vices and disorders, tending to the high provocation of God's wrath and displeasure, which lies heavy upon this kingdom, and to the disturbance of the peace thereof; in regard whereof the same hath been prohibited by Ordinance of this present Parliament, and yet is presumed to be practised by divers in contempt thereof." It then enacts, " For the better suppression of the said Stage-Playes, Interludes, and common playes, it is ordered and ordained by the Lords and Commons in this present Parliament assembled, and by the Authority of the same, That all Stage-players, and Players of Interludes, and common Playes, are hereby declared to be, and are, and shall be taken to be Rogues, and punishable, within the statutes of the thirty-ninth year of the Reign of Queen Elizabeth, and the seventh year of King James, and liable unto the pains and penalties therein contained, and proceeded against according to the said Statutes, whether they be wanderers or no, and notwithstanding any license whatsoever from the King or any person or persons to that purpose."

This Act breathes the spirit exhibited by William Prynne in his " Histrio-Mastix " (" The Player's Scourge "),* published in 1633, in which he lays down—

" *That all popular and common Stage-Playes, whether Comicall, Tragicall, Satyricall, Mimicall, or mixt of either (especially as they are now composed and personated), are such sinfull, hurtfull, and pernicious Recreations, as are altogether unseemely, and unlawfull unto Christians.*"

Quoting from *Asterius* he says that " *Playes are the cause of Debt and Usury ; the occasion of Poverty, the beginning of Beggery.*" He afterwards proceeds to maintain that " the effect or product of Stage Playes, is cruelty, fiercnesse, brawles, sedition, *tumults*, murthers and the like ; " and that " the fruits of Stage-playes is this ; that they draw downe God's fearefull judgements both upon their Composers, Actors, Spectators, and those Republikes that tolerate or approve them." He also quotes the following from the sixth Council of Constantinople A.D. 680 :—

Can. 51 : " *This sacred and universall Synode doth utterly prohibit*

* For this book Prynne was imprisoned eight years, fined £3,000, expelled the university of Oxford and Lincoln's Inn, degraded from his profession, stood twice in the pillory, lost both his ears, and had the book burned by the hangman. See his petitions to Parliament.

those who are called Stage-players and their Enterludes ; together with the Spectacles of huntings, and those dances that are made upon the Stage."

Can. 61. " *Those also ought to be subject to sixe yeares excommunication, who carry about beares or such like creatures for sport, to the hurt of simple people ; or tell fortunes or fates, and genealogies, and utter a multitude of such like words out of the toyes of fallacy and imposture : and those also who are stiled charmers, givers of remedies and amulets, and prophets.*"

The public taste for stage plays at this period, judged by the following extracts, appear to have been of a debased character, and must therefore have strengthened the puritanical opposition to them.

" We must have nothing brought now upon Stage
But Puppetry, and pyed ridiculous Anticks.
Men thither come to laugh, and feed fool fat,
Check* at all goodnesse there, as being prophan'd,
When, where ere goodnesse comes, it makes the place
Holy and sacred, though with other feet,
Never so much 'tis scandall'd and polluted.
Let me learn anything, that fits a man
In any stables shown, as well as Stages.

Players
Were never more uncertain in their lives,
They know not what to play, for fearfull fools,
Where to play, for Puritan fools, nor what
To play, for Criticall fools."

In spite, too, of all the official prohibitions, Sir William Davenant opened a kind of theatre in Rutland House, Charterhouse Yard, in May, 1656, and on the 3rd September, 1656, addressed the following letter to Bulstrode Whitelocke, one of the Lords Commissioners of the Great Seal. The opera referred to is the *Siege of Rhodes*, which was given at Rutland House, " the story sung in recitative verse." On this occasion scenes "in perspective" were first publicly used.

" MY LORD,

" When I consider the nicety of the Times, I fear it may draw a Curtain between your Lordship and our opera ; therefore I have presumed to send your Lordship, hot from the Press, what we mean to represent ; making your Lordship my supreme Judge, though I despair to have the Honour of inviting you to be a spec-

* Applied to a hawk when she forsakes her proper game and follows some other of inferior kind that crosses her in her flight.

tator. I do not conceive the perusal of it worthy any part of your Lordship's leisure, unless your antient relation to the Muses make you not unwilling to give a little entertainment to Poetry, though in so mean a dress as this, and coming from, my Lord,

"Your Lordship's most obedient servant,
"WILLIAM DAVENANT."

In the year 1647 the condition of pauperism appears to have necessitated the passing of the following *Ordinance for the Reliefe and Imployment of the Poore; and the Punishment of Vagrants, and other disorderly Persons.*" It recites that " the Necessity, Number and Increase of the Poore is very great within the City of *London* and Liberties thereof, for want of the due execution of such wholsome Lawes and Statutes as have beene formerly made.

" For remedy thereof, and for other the purposes herein after specified; Be it and it is ordained by the Lords and Commons in this present Parliament assembled, That from henceforth there be, and shall be a Corporation within the said City of *London* and Liberties thereof, consisting of a President, Deputy to the President, a Treasurer, and forty Assistants, whereof the Lord Maior of the said City for the time being to be the President, eight of the said Assistants to be of the Aldermen of the said City for the time being; and the other thirty and two to be Free-men of, and Inhabitants in the said City, chosen out of the severall Wards of the said City equally. . . . And be it ordained by the authority aforesaid, for the further reliefe and employing of the said poore within the said City and Liberties thereof, that the said Corporation, or any nine of them, whereof the said President, or any of the said Aldermen or the Deputy to the President, or the said Treasurer to be one, shall have power to Erect one or more Workehouses for receiving, relieving, and setting the poore on work; and one or more houses of Correction for punishing of Rogues, Vagabonds, and Beggers, as they shall think fit. . . .

" And that the said President and Governours, or any nine of them, whereof the said President, or any of the said Aldermen, or the Deputy to the President, or the said Treasurer to be one, shall have power from time to time to make and Constitute Orders and By-Lawes for the better relieving, regulating, and setting the Poore on worke, and the apprehending and punishing of Rogues, Vagabonds, and Beggers within the said City and

Liberties, that have not wherewith honestly to maintaine themselves. . . . And it shall and may be lawfull to and for any County, Corporation, or Boroughes in any County of this Kingdome, or Dominion of *Wales*, to make choise of a fit number of able and sufficient Persons for the like effectuall relieving, and regulating of the Poore in their respective places; and in like manner to draw up and present Orders and By-Laws best suiting to those Counties and places for confirmation as aforesaid, and for the ends and purposes herein above expressed."

A little more than two years later, on the 24th of January, 1650-1, the toleration accorded to vagrants by the parochial authorities in the City seems to have called forth the following proclamation from the Lord Mayor :—

"Forasmuch as of late the constables of this city have neglected to put in execution the severall wholsome laws for punishing of vagrants, and passing them to the places of their last abode, whereby great scandall and dishonour is brought upon the government of this city; These are therefore to will and require you, or your deputy, forthwith to call before you the severall constables within your ward, and strictly to charge them to put in execution the said laws, or to expect the penalty of forty shillings to be levyed upon their estates, for every vagrant that shal be found begging in their several precincts. And to the end the said constables may not pretend ignorance, what to do with the several persons they shal find offending the said laws, these are further to require them, that al aged or impotent persons who are not fit to work, be passed from constable to constable to the parish where they dwel; and that the constable in whose ward they are found begging, shal give a passe under his hand, expressing the place where he or she were taken, and the place whither they are to be passed. And for children under five years of age, who have no dwelling, or cannot give an account of their parents, the parish where they are found are to provide for them; and for those which shall bee found lying under stalls, having no habitation or parents (from five to nine years old), are to be sent to the Wardrobe House,* to be provided for by the corporation for the poore; and all above nine years of age are to be sent to Bridewel. And for men or women who are able to work and goe begging with young

* An ancient building in Vintry Ward known by the name of The Royal, or the Tower Royal, used for a time as the Queen's wardrobe.

children, such persons for the first time to be passed to the place of their abode as aforesaid; and being taken againe, they are to be carryed to Bridewel, to be corrected according to the discretion of the governours. And for those persons that shal be found to hire children, or go begging with children not sucking, those children are to be sent to the several parishes wher they dwel, and the persons so hiring them to Bridewel, to be corrected and passed away, or kept at work there, according to the governour's discretion. And for al other vagrants and beggars under any pretence whatsoever, to be forthwith sent down to Bridewel to be imployed and corrected, according to the statute laws of this commonwealth, except before excepted; and the president and governours of Bridewel are hereby desired to meet twice every week to see to the execution of this Precept. And the steward of the workhouse called the Wardrobe, is authorised to receive into that house such children as are of the age between five and nine, as is before specified and limited; and the said steward is from time to time to acquaint the corporation for the poor, what persons are brought in, to the end they may bee provided for."

Vagrancy, however, continued to increase, and therefore on the 23rd of January, 1655, another proclamation was issued by the Town Clerk of the City to the following effect:—

"Whereas by neglect of executing the good Lawes and Statutes against Rogues, Vagabonds, and Sturdy Beggers, That vermine of this Commonwealth doth now swarme in and about this City and Liberties, disturbing and annoying the inhabitants and Passengers, by hanging upon Coaches, and clamorous begging at the doores of Churches and private Houses, and in the Streets and common Wayes, beguiling the modest, laborious and honest poore (the proper objects of charity) of much reliefe and Almes which otherwise might bee disposed to them by bountifull and well minded people : And by this meanes and their corrupt and prophane communication, doe bring dishonor to God, scandall to Religion, and shame to the Government of this City : And for as much as it is intended and resolved that for Reformation of this living Nusance, the said Lawes and Statutes shall bee henceforth duely and strictly executed within this City and Liberties thereof, and the penaltyes and punishments thereby appointed, imposed and inflicted upon all persons offending against the same : I doe therefore give notice thereof, and in the name of his Highnes the Lord Protector, doe hereby require and command all Constables and other officers and persons whatsoever within this City and Liberties, to bee diligent and watchfull about their duties herein."

The proclamation ends with extracts from 39 Eliz., c. 4, and 1 Jac. I., c. 7, for the information of constables. The means of repression at the disposal of the authorities appears, however, to have been insufficient, for we are told that at "A Common Councell holden . . . the sixth day of March . . . 1656. Upon reading the humble Representation of the President and Governors for the Poore of this City and Liberties thereof, complaining that the number of those Agents (whom their present ability can set forth and maintaine) for clearing the streets of Vagrants cannot effect that work, the Court ordained that the rates for the relief of the poor should be doubled, and payments made to a sufficient number of able warders for apprehending Vagrants and Beggars."

Notwithstanding the good order which generally prevailed under the stern discipline of the Puritan rule, fresh legislation was found necessary, and in the year 1656 a statute (c. 21)* entitled an Act against Vagrants, and wandring, idle, dissolute persons was passed, which recites that, "Whereas the number of wandring, idle, loose, dissolute, and disorderly persons is (of late) much increased, by reason of some Defects in the Laws and Statutes heretofore made and provided for the punishment of Rogues, Vagabonds and Sturdy Beggers (they being seldom taken begging) by means whereof divers Roberies, Burglaries, Thefts, Insurrections and other Misdemeanors have been occasioned ; For the prevention whereof, Be it Enacted by His Highness the Lord Protector and this present Parliament and the Authority thereof, That all and every idle, loose, and dissolute person and persons, which from and after the First day of July one thousand six hundred fifty-seven, shall be found and taken within the commonwealth of England, vagrant and wandring from his or their usual place of living or abode, and shall not have such good and sufficient cause or business for such his or their travelling or wandring, as the Justices or Justice of Peace, Mayors, or other Chief Officers or Officers of the respective Counties or Corporations, before whom such person or persons shall be brought, shall approve of ; That then every such idle, loose and dissolute person and persons, so taken vagrant and wandring as aforesaid, shall be

* This statute is given in its entirety on account of its rarity.

adjudged, and are hereby adjudged and declared to be Rogues, Vagabonds and Sturdy Beggers, within the Statute made in the nine and thirtieth year of the Reign of Queen Elizabeth, c. 4, For the Suppressing of Rogues, Vagabonds and Sturdy Beggers, and shall be proceeded against and punished as Rogues, Vagabonds and Sturdy Beggers within the said Statute, although they shall not be taken begging, any Law, Statute, or Usage to the contrary thereof in any wise notwithstanding. And be it further Enacted by the Authority aforesaid, That if any person or persons commonly called Fidlers or Minstrels, shall at any time after the said First day of July, be taken playing, fidling and making music in any Inn, Ale-house or Tavern, or shall be taken proferring themselves, or desiring, or intreating any person or persons to hear them to play, or make musick in any the places aforesaid, That every such person and persons so taken, shall be adjudged, and are hereby adjudged and declared to be Rogues, Vagabonds and Sturdy Beggers, and shall be proceeded against and punished as Rogues, Vagabonds and Sturdy Beggers within the said Statute, Any Law, Statute or Usage to the contrary thereof in any wise notwithstanding."

CHAPTER VII.

1660—1713.

Accession of Charles II.—Disbandment of the army—The law of settlement—Speech of the King regarding beggars—Results of the new law—Captain Graunt on beggars—Sir Matthew Hale on workhouses—Proclamation against vagrants and beggars and persons carrying combustible matters—Pretended lunatics—Alterations of the law of settlement under James II. and William III.—Highwaymen—The poor receiving relief to wear badges—Bandying about of the poor—Mr. John Cary on the wholesome effect of workhouses—Demoralizing results of passing beggars home—Estimate of the dependent classes—Depravity of beggar children—Legislation under Ann—Consolidation of the laws against vagrants and beggars in 1713.

SOME of the first Acts of the reign of Charles II. had reference to the disbanding of the army, which, owing to its rigid morality and discipline, and its sympathy with puritanical principles, formed a source of danger instead of strength to the restored monarchy. One of these Acts (12 Car. II., c. 16) made it lawful for the disbanded soldiers to exercise trades without having been apprenticed to them, and exempted them from the prohibitory clauses of the 5 Eliz., c. 4, and also from local customs and by-laws to a contrary effect. This enabled them at once to join the industrial ranks, and they availed themselves of it to the fullest extent. Lord Macaulay bears tribute to their good conduct and industry in these apposite terms :—

"Fifty thousand men, accustomed to the profession of arms, were at once thrown on the world: and experience seemed to warrant the belief that this change would produce much misery and crime, that the discharged veterans would be seen begging in every street, or would be driven by hunger to pillage. But no such result followed. In a few months there remained not a trace indicating that the most formidable army in the world had just been absorbed into the mass of the community. The Royalists themselves confessed that, in every department of honest industry, the discarded warriors prospered beyond other men, that none was charged with any theft or robbery, that none was heard to ask an alms, and that if a baker, a mason, or a waggoner attracted notice by his diligence and sobriety, he was in all probability one of Oliver's old soldiers."

We now come to an Act entitled "An Act for the better Reliefe of the Poore of this Kingdom" (14 Car. II., c. 12, 1662), which recites that "the necessity number and continual increase of the Poore not onely within the Cities of London and Westminster with the Liberties of each of them but alsoe through the whole Kingdome of England and Dominion of Wales, is very great and exceeding burthensome being occasioned by reason of some defects in the Law concerning the setling of the Poor and for want of a due Provision of the regulations of releife and imployment in such Parishes or Places where they are legally setled which doth enforce many to turn incorrigible Rogues and others to perish for want togeather with the neglect of the faithfull execution of such Lawes & Statutes as have formerly beene made for the apprehending of Rogues and Vagabonds and for the good of the Poore;" and that "by reason of some defects in the Law poore people are not restrained from going from one Parish to another and therefore doe endeavor to settle themselves in those Parishes where there is the best Stocke the largest Commons or wastes to build Cottages and the most woods for them to burn and destroy and when they have consumed it then to another Parish and att last become Rogues and Vagabonds to the great discouragem^t. of Parishes to provide Stocks where it is lyable to be devoured by Strangers." It then enacts that, "upon complaint made by the Churchwardens or Overseers of the Poore of any Parish to any Justice of Peace, "within Forty dayes after any such Person or Persons coming so to settle as aforesaid in any Tenement under the yearely value of Ten Pounds," for any two justices of the peace "by theire warrant to remove and convey such person or persons to such Parish where he or they were last legally setled either as a native Householder Sojourner Apprentice or Servant for the space of forty dayes at the least unlesse he or they give sufficient security for the discharge of the said Parish to bee allowed by the said Justices." Persons who think themselves aggrieved by such judgment may appeal to the next court of quarter sessions,

AND BEGGARS AND BEGGING.

"whoe are required to doe them justice according to the merits of theire Cause." Next comes a proviso that "it shall be lawfull for any person or persons to go into any County Parish or place to worke in time of Harvest or at any time to worke at any other worke so that he or they carry with him or them a Certificate from the Minister of the Parish and one of the Churchwardens and one of the Overseers for the Poore for the said yeare that hee or they have a dwelling-house or place in which he or they inhabit and hath left wife and children or some of them there." Such work, however, was not to procure such persons a settlement, but they might be removed back again. "And if such person or persons shall refuse to go or shall not remain in such Parish where they ought to be setled as aforesaid but shall return of his own accord to the Parish from whence he was removed," such person so offending may be sent "to the House of Correction there to be punished as a Vagabond, or to a publique Workehouse in this present Act hereafter mentioned there to be imployed in worke or labour."

The president and governors of corporate workhouses, or any person authorised or appointed by them, may apprehend any rogues, vagrants, sturdy beggars, or idle or disorderly persons, and cause them to be set to work in the corporations or workhouses; and the justices of the peace in quarter sessions may signify to the Privy Council the names of such rogues, vagabonds, idle and disorderly persons, and sturdy beggars as they shall think to be transported to the English plantations; and upon the approbation of the Council, any two or more of the justices may, during the next three years, transport them "to any of the English Plantations beyond the Seas, there to be disposed in the usual way of Servants for a terme not exceeding seaven yeares."

It further declares that the laws and statutes for apprehending rogues and vagabonds have not been duly executed for want of officers, because Lords of Manors do not keep court leets every year for making them; and in the case of the death or departure of any officer it empowers two justices to appoint another. It then recites that the 39 Eliz., c. 4, and 1 Jac. I., c. 7, are not duly executed, and it empowers any justice of the peace to whom any rogue, vagabond, or sturdy beggar is brought by a private person, to grant him a warrant to the constable, headborough, or tithingman of such parish where such offender passed through unapprehended, requiring him to pay such person 2s.; and if the constable, headborough, or tithingman refuses or neglects to pay this sum, the justice shall proceed against him to pay such sum as he forfeits under the 1 Jac. I., c. 7, and to allow out of such forfeiture the said 2s., " and such reasonable meanes and allowance for losse of time" as he thinks fit. And if any person shall apprehend any rogue, &c., " att the confines of any County which had passed through any Parish of another County unapprehended," such person may go before some justice of the county through which the rogue passed unapprehended, who is required, upon a certificate of the justice of the county where the offender was apprehended, to grant his order requiring the constable, headborough or tithingman to pay such person two shillings; and if he refuses or neglects to do so, the justice is required to proceed against him and cause him to pay to the person 10s. or " soe much thereof for his expences and losse of time" as the justice shall think fit."

The Act then goes on to state that "Constables Headboroughs, or Tithingmen are or may bee at great charge in releiving conveying with Passes and in carrying Rogues Vagabonds and Sturdy Beggars to Houses of Correction or the Workhouses herein mentioned and as yet have no power by Law to make rates to reimburse themselves." It then authorises them, with the Churchwardens, overseers, and inhabitants of the parish, to make a rate which being confirmed by two justices may be levied by distress.

The Act further authorises the justices, " in any of the Counties of England and Wales in theire Quarter Sessions assembled or the major part of them to transport or cause to be transported such Rogues vagabonds and Sturdy Beggars as shall be duly convicted and adjudged to be incorrigible to any of the English Plantacõns beyond the Seas."

The King, in his speech to both Houses at the prorogation, alluded to this Bill in the following terms: "I hope the laws I have passed this day will produce some reformation with reference to the multitude of beggars and poor people which infest the kingdom. Great severity must be used to those who love idleness and refuse to work, and great care and charity to those who are willing to work. I do very heartily recommend the execution of those good laws to your utmost diligence."

This Act, popularly known as *The Settlement Act*, marks the introduction of a new departure in our Poor Laws, as, except in cases of persons travelling in search of harvest work, it prohibits the poor from wandering, by ordering them to be sent back to their place of settlement. Its main intention undoubtedly is to prevent the rural population from freely resorting to the towns in search of work, and therefore in that sense reintroduces the feudal principle of villenage. Its framers principally had in view the increasing number of poor who resorted to the metropolis, and who thus swelled the ranks of those who mainly propagated the plague, of which every one stood so much in dread; but it was futile in its immediate objects. As *Edmund Waller* the poet remarks regarding it, "The relief of the poor ruins the nation. By the late Act they are hunted like foxes out of parishes, and whither must they go but where there are houses [alluding to London]? We shall shortly have no lands to live upon, the charge of many parishes in the country is so great." The general effect of the Act was, in fact, to drive the poor to London. There was a twofold reason for this: 1st, mendicity was then as now a profitable trade; 2nd, the landlords of small tenements where the poor lodged, and who derived a large profit from their lodgers, would be most unlikely to report them to the overseers or church-wardens within the forty days prescribed by the Act: and the authorities, some from sympathetic tenderness and some to save themselves trouble, would fail as heretofore to put the law in force.

The next Act (15 Car. II., c. 2, 1663) is a corollary of the preceding one, being apparently directed against those who, in the language of that Act, settle in parishes "where there are the most woods for them to burn and destroy." It directs that any person convicted of cutting and spoiling woods, under-woods, poles or young trees, or bark or bast of trees, gates, stiles, posts, pales, rails or hedgewood, broom or furze, shall for a first offence pay a penalty not exceeding 10s., for a second be sent to hard labour in the House of Correction for one month, and for a third be adjudged an incorrigible rogue.

Of the condition of Metropolitan beggars, *Captain John Graunt*, writing in the year 1665, gives us the following picture:—

"My first Observation is, That few are *starved*. This appears, for that of the 229,250 which have died, (of all diseases and casualties during twenty years in London), we find not above fifty-one to have been *starved*, excepting helpless *Infants* at Nurse, which being caused rather by carelessness, ignorance, and infirmity of the Milch-women, is not properly an effect, or sign of want of food in the Country, or of means to get it.

"The Observation which I shall add hereto, is, That the vast number of *Beggars*, swarming up and down this City, do all live, and seem to be most of them healthy, and strong."

In the year 1670 *Sir Matthew Hale*, in a pamphlet entitled, "And England's Weal and prosperity Proposed: Or, Reasons *for the erecting* Publick Work Houses *in every County*, &c.," admirably sums up the condition of the poor at this period, and the reason of the failure of the repressive laws against mendicity. He thus expresses himself:—

"I shall first assert some particulars, which I think are agreed by common consent, and from thence take occasion to proceed to what is more doubtful.

"1. That our poor in *England* have always been in a most sad and wretched condition, some Famished for want of Bread, others starved with Cold and Nakedness, and many whole Families in all the out parts of Cities and great Towns, commonly remain in a languishing, nasty and useless Condition, Uncomfortable to themselves, and unprofitable to the Kingdom, this is confessed and lamented by all Men.

"2. That the *Children* of our *Poor*, bred up in *Beggary* and *Laziness*, do by that means become not only of *unhealthy Bodies*, and more then ordinary subject to many loathsome Diseases, whereof very many die in their tender Age, and if any of them do arrive to years and strength, they are, by their idle habits contracted in their Youth, rendred for ever after indispos'd to Labour, and serve only to stock the *Kingdom* with *Thieves* and *Beggars*.

"3. That if our impotent *Poor* were provided for, and those of both Sexes, and all Ages that can do Work of any kind, employed, it would redound some Hundreds of Thousands of Pounds *per annum* to the Publick advantage. . . .

"*How comes it to pass that in England we do not, nor ever did comfortably Maintain and Employ our Poor?*

"The common Answers to this Question are two:—

"1. *That our Laws to this purpose are as good as any in the World, but we fail in the execution.*

"2. *That formerly in the days of our Pious Ancestors the work was done, but now Charity is deceased, and that is the reason we see the Poor so neglected as they now are.*

"In both which Answers (I humbly conceive) the Effect is mistaken for the Cause: for tho' it cannot be denied, but there hath been, and is a great failure in the Execution of those *statutes* which relate to the *Poor*; yet I say, *the Cause of that failure, hath been occasioned by defect of the Laws themselves*.

"For otherwise, what is the reason that in our late times of the Confusion and Alteration, wherein almost every Party in the Nation, at one time or other, took their turn at the Helm, and all had that Compass (those Laws) to Steer by, and yet none of them could, or ever did, conduct the *Poor* into a Harbour of security to them, and profit to the Kingdom, *i.e. none sufficiently maintained the Impotent and employed the Indigent amongst us*. . . .

"As to the second Answer to the aforesaid Question, wherein *want of Charity* is assigned for another cause why the *Poor* are now so much neglected, I think it is a *scandalous ungrounded accusation* of our *Contemporaries*; for most that I converse with, are not so much troubled to part with their Money, as how to place it, that it may do good, and not hurt to the Kingdom : For, *If they give to the Beggars in the Streets, or at their Doors, they fear they may do hurt by* encouraging that Lazy unprofitable kind of life ; and *if they give more than their Proportions in their respective Parishes, that* (they say) *is but giving to the Rich*, for the *Poor* are not set on Work thereby, nor have the more given them; but only their *Rich* Neighbours pay the less. And for what was given in *Churches* to the *Visited Poor*, and to such as were *impoverished by the Fire;* we have heard of so many and great abuses of that kind of *Charity*, that most men are under sad Discouragements in Relation thereunto. . . .

"Ask any Charitable-minded Man, as he goes along the Streets of *London* viewing the *Poor*, viz., *Boyes, Girles, Men and Women* of all Ages, and many in good Health, etc., why he and others do not take care for the setting those poor creatures to Work ? Will he not readily answer, that he wisheth heartily it could be done, though it cost him some part of his Estate, but he is but one Man, and can do nothing towards it; giving them Money, as hath been said, being but to bring them into a liking and continuance in that way.

"Question 2. *Wherein lyes the defect of our present Laws relating to the Poor ?*

"I answer that there may be many, but I shall here take notice of one only, which I think to be Fundamental, and which until altered, the *Poor* in *England* can never be well provided for, or

Employed; and that when the said Fundamental Error is well amended, it is almost impossible they should lack either Work or Maintenance.

"The said radical Error I esteem to be the leaving it to the Care of every Parish to maintain their own Poor only; upon which follows the shifting off, sending or whipping back the poor Wanderers to the place of their Birth or last Abode; the Practice whereof I have seen many Years in *London*, to signify as much as ever it will, which is just nothing of Good to the Kingdom in general, or the *Poor* thereof, though it be sometimes by accident to some of them a Punishment without effect; I say without effect, because it reforms not the Party, nor disposeth the minds of others to Obedience, which are the true ends of all Punishment.

"As for instance, *a poor idle Person*, that will not Work, or that no Body will employ in the Country, comes up to *London, to set up the Trade of Begging*, such a person probably may *Begg* up and down the Streets seven Years, it may be seven and twenty, before anybody asketh why she doth so, and if at length she hath the ill hap in some Parish, to meet with a more vigilant *Beadle* then one of twenty of them are, all he does is but to lead her the length of five or six Houses into another Parish, and then concludes, as his *Masters* the *Parishioners* do, that he hath done the part of a most diligent officer: But suppose he should yet go farther to the end of his Line, which is the end of the Law; and the perfect Execution of his Office; that is, suppose he should carry this poor wretch to a *Justice* of the Peace, and he should order the *Delinquent* to be *Whipt* and sent from *Parish* to *Parish*, to the place of her *Birth* or last abode, which not one *Justice* of twenty (through Pity or other Cause) will do; even this is a great charge upon the Country, and yet the business of the nation is it self wholly undone: For no sooner doth the *Delinquent* arrive at the place assign'd, but for Shame or Idleness she presently deserts it, and wanders directly back, or some other way, hoping for better Fortune, while the *Parish* to which she is sent, knowing her a Lazy, and perhaps a worse qualified person, is as willing to be rid of her, as she is to be gone from thence.

"If it be here retorted upon me, that by my own confession, much of this mischief happens by the non, or ill Execution of the Laws, I say, Better Execution then you have seen, you must not expect; *and there was never a good Law made that was not well executed; the fault of the Law causing a failure of execution;* it being natural to all men to use the remedy next at hand, and rest satisfied with shifting the Evil from their own Doors ; which in regard they can so easily do, by threatning or thrusting a *poor Body* out of the verge of their own *Parish*, it is unreasonable and vain to hope that ever it will be otherwise."

Partly no doubt to prevent the spread of infection and partly to restrain the disorderly gangs who infested the City for the purpose of plunder during the panic caused by the plague, the Lord Mayor on the 4th of July, 1665, issued the following order to the Aldermen of the wards :—

"That a carefull Watch and Ward be constantly kept at the Gates and Landing Places, to restrain and prevent the ingress of all Vagrants, Beggers, Loose and Dangerous people, from the out parts into this City and Liberties ; and to bring to punishment such as shall be apprehended doing the same, according to Law."

The next public document we have to notice is an order, dated August 19, 1670, from the Court at Whitehall to the Lord Mayor and others, indicating a disturbed condition of the lower orders resulting in incendiarism.

"The said Lord Mayor and Justices of the Peace respectively are required to cause diligent observation to be taken of all Vagrant and Suspicious persons walking at Unseasonable Hours, and to examine and search if they Carry about them any Combustible matters: and in case such persons are not able to give a good accompt of themselves, they are forthwith to be conveyed before the next Justice of the Peace, to be proceeded against and severely punish'd, according to the Law and the quality of the Offences."

So far as London was concerned, the dissolute character of the King and his Court caused a large amount of dissatisfaction in the City, and owing to the non-payment of their salaries many of the inferior attendants about the Court were in a condition of extreme want.

A stringent Act of Parliament (22 and 23 Car. II., c. 7) was also passed at this time to restrain incendiarism.

The City had scarcely been rebuilt after the fire before the beggars again resorted to their favourite haunt, and necessitated the following proclamation by the Lord Mayor on the 7th of November, 1671 :—

"And whereas the Streets and Common Passages, and all Places of Publick Meeting and Resort, are exceedingly pestered and annoyed by Vagrants and Beggars, and that for suppressing and avoiding of that greatest living Nusance, especial resolution is taken to put in execution against them the good Laws in force with all Strictness and Severity : The said Constables, therefore are charged and required to apprehend all Rogues, Vagabonds, and Sturdy Beggars, that shall be found begging, vagrant, wandring, or mis-ordering themselves within their respective parishes and precincts ; and such of them as shall appear to have Dwellings or Abode within the City or Liberties to carry to Bridewel, there to be received and dealt withal according to Law ; " all others are directed to be punished and passed away to their places of settlement.

Simulation of lunacy had from a very early period been a favourite form of imposture, owing to the compassion and sympathy which wandering lunatics excited. In order to endeavour to put down this practice, the governors of Bethlehem Hospital, in June, 1675, inserted the following announcement in No. 1,000 of the *London Gazette* :—

" Whereas several Vagrant Persons do wander about the City of London, and Countries, pretending themselves to be Lunaticks under Cure in the Hospital of *Bethlem* commonly called *Bedlam*, with Brass Plates about their Arms, and Inscriptions thereon. These are to give Notice, That there is no such Liberty given to any patients kept in the said Hospital for their Cure, neither is any such Plate as a distinction or mark put upon any lunatick during their being there, or when discharged thence. And that the same is a false pretence, to colour their Wandring and Begging, and to deceive the People, to the dishonour of the Government of that Hospital."

We now come to the reign of *James II.*, in which we only have to notice one Act, the 1 Jac. II., c. 17, passed in 1685, for continuing amongst other Acts the 13 and 14 Car. II., c. 12. It also makes an addendum to this Act, reciting as a cause " that poore persons at their first comeing to a parish doe commonly conceale themselves," and then enacts that the forty days' continuance in a parish intended to make a settlement is to be accounted from the delivery of notice in writing of the house of his or her abode, and the number of his or her family, to one of the churchwardens or overseers of the poor. A formidable check was thus imposed on poor persons really wandering in search of work ; on the vagrant it could have no effect unless he wanted a gratuitous ride to some place at a distance.

In the next reign the law of settlement received another amendment by the 3 Wil. and Mar., c. 11 (1691), which enacted that the forty days' continuance in a parish or town intended to make a settlement, " shall be accounted from the Publication of a Notice in Writing, which he or she shall deliver of the House his or her Abode" to the Churchwarden or Overseer of the poor, which notice the churchwarden or overseer is required to read or cause to be read publicly on the next Lord's day in the church or chapel of the parish. All the parishioners would therefore be made aware of the arrival of a stranger, and be able if they thought fit, to take steps for expelling him.

In 1692 we are made aware of the disturbed state of the country by an Act " for encouraging the apprehending of highwaymen " (4 Wil. and Mar., c. 8). It declares the highways and roads to be " of late more infested with Thieves and Robbers then formerly, for want of due and sufficient encouragement given and means used for the discovery and apprehension of such offenders, whereby so many Murders and Robberies have been committed, that it is become dangerous in many parts of the Nation for Travellers to passe on their lawfull occasions." It then enacts that a gratuity of £40 shall be given for the apprehension and conviction of every such offender, and in case any person shall be killed in endeavouring to apprehend a robber, his executors or administrators are to be entitled to the reward; and as a further inducement to apprehend, prosecute, or convict such robber, his Horse, Furniture, arms, money, or other goods of the said Robber, taken with him, are given to the person who apprehends him; but this does not take away the right of any person to anything feloniously taken from him by the robber; and it is further enacted, that any robber being at large who shall discover and convict two other robbers is to be entitled to a pardon for his former offences.

In 1696-7 the law of settlement received another amendment by the 8 and 9 Wil. III., c. 30, which recites : " Forasmuch as many poor Persons chargeable to the Parish, Towneshipp, or Place where they live meerly for want of Work, would in any other Place where sufficient imployment is to be had, maintaine themselves and Families without being burthensome to any Parish, Townshipp, or Place ; but not being able to give such Security as will or may be expected and required upon their coming to settle themselves in any other Place, and the Certificates that have been usually given in such Cases having been oftentimes construed into a notice in Handwriting, they are for the most parte confined to live in their owne Parishes, Townshipps, or Places, and not permitted to inhabitt elsewhere, though their Labour is wanted in many other places where the Increase of Manufactures would imploy more Hands." It then enacts that any poor persons, coming to reside in any parish, shall bring with them and deliver to the parish officer a certificate under the hands and seals of the churchwardens and overseers of the parish to which they belong, owning and acknowledging the persons therein mentioned to be legally settled in that parish; and such certificate having been allowed and subscribed by two justices of peace, obliges that parish to receive and provide for the persons mentioned therein, whenever they shall become chargeable, or be forced to ask relief in the parish to which they had come; and then, and not before, such persons may be removed to the parish from whence such certificate was brought, and to the end "that the money raised onely for the Relief of such as are as well impotent as poor, may not be misapplied & consumed by the idle, sturdy and disorderly Beggars," every person receiving relief of any parish, their wives, children, &c., are ordered to wear on the shoulder of the right sleeve of the uppermost garment a badge or mark with a large Roman P, and the first letter of the name of the parish whereof such poor person is an inhabitant, "cutt either in red or blew cloth." Those who neglect or refuse to wear it may have their allowance abridged, suspended, or withdrawn, or they may be committed to the House of Correction, there to be whipped and kept to hard labour for not more than twenty-one days.

In a work on the history of Burton-on-Trent, Mr. Molyneux gives an extract from the vestry book, furnishing an instance of this custom.

"1702, Sept. 6.—Whereas several persons that receive alms out of the poore's levy of this liberty do often omit the wearing the public badge of this town or observe the same; It is therefore ordered that when any such poor person or persons shall, or their, or any of their children bee seen without such badge or to observe the same, that upon the view of either of the overseers or reliable information thereof to them, or either of them, of the neglect of wearing or observing such badge, such poore person or persons shall for a fortnight then after lose his and their allowance out of the poore's levy, and the like penalty shall be continued so often as any such offence shall be comitted and not to be put in pay again till such badge be worne."

Under date June 6, 1703, it is ordered "That Elizabeth Salisbury, Mary Budworth, Hannah Scott, and Ann Hinckley be taken out of constant pay for their stubborn refusal to wear the badge publickly."

The way in which the badged poor were bandied from one parish to another may best be gathered from the following extract from the memoirs of the parish of Myddle (co. Salop).

"Seventh case.—Inter Myddle and Wem, ann. 1700 and 1701.

"Mr. Wase . . . pleaded . . . that Nicholas Hampton had since then procured a settlement in Wem, by receiving money for his maintenance, and wearing the parish badge in Wem for many years. Mr. Fones did not produce the parish book, which in all likelihood would have proved against him, but pleaded that receiving of money could not create a settlement, but paying of money might. That the money was given of charity, and hoped their charity should not bring a burthen on them; and the wearing the badge was only to save the officers harmless from the penalty of the act. Mr. Wase said, that before the Act was made for wearing badges, the parishioners of Wem parish had caused every one of their poor to wear a P. made of tin. And that they caused this Nicholas Hampton to wear one of them, which was then shewed in court; and he said there was then at the giving of that P. no penalty to be inflicted on officers in that case. Mr. Newton said, that what money was given by one or two, or a few persons, might be accounted charity, but what was given out of the parish leawn,* that he did not account charity; for it was what ought by law to be done, and he did not insist so much on the wearing of the badge as the payment of the money out of the poor's leawn.* Mr. Weaver said, this person was born in Wem parish; he came into Myddle parish, and there lived one year, and then returned to Wem parish, and fell lame; if this person turned vagrant, he must be sent to Wem, not to Myddle. Then Mr. Wase desired the judgment of the Bench in this matter; and they all agreed, *nemine contra dicente*, that the order for removing Nich. Hampton into this parish should be reversed."

This ticketing of the poor is, it will be remembered, merely a revival of the provisions in the 2 & 3 Phil. & Mar., c. 5, and the

* Sometimes written *lewn*. A word in use in Shropshire and Cheshire, signifying a tax, or rate, or lay for church or parish dues.

5 Eliz. c. 3, and doubtless enabled the poor in many cases to beg of private persons more effectively on the plea of the insufficiency of the parish allowances.

In the year 1697, through the exertions of Mr. John Cary, a philanthropic merchant, the parishes forming the city of Bristol were constituted into a Union and established a workhouse, where the poor were actively employed in beating hemp, dressing and spinning flax, and in carding and spinning wool and cotton. The wholesome effects of this treatment are thus detailed in a pamphlet on the subject published by Mr. Cary in the year 1700.

"We soon found, that the great cause of begging did proceed from the low Wages for Labour. . . .

"The Success hath answered our Expectation; we are freed from Beggars, our old People are comfortably provided for; our Boys and Girls are educated to Sobriety, and brought up to delight in Labour; our young Children are well lookt after, and not spoiled by the neglect of ill Nurses; and the Face of our City is so changed already, that we have great reason to hope these young Plants will produce a vertuous and laborious Generation, with whom Immorality and Prophaneness may find little Incouragement; nor do our hopes appear to be groundless, for among Three hundred persons now under our Charge within Doors, there is neither Cursing nor Swearing, nor prophane Language to be heard, though many of them were bred up in all manner of Vices, which neither *Bridewell* nor Whippings could fright them from, because, returning to their bad Company for want of Employment, they were rather made worse then bettered by those Corrections; whereas the Change we have wrought on them is by fair means. We have a *Bridewel, Stocks,* and *Whipping-Post* always in their sights, but never had occasion to make use of either."

The example of Bristol was followed in the course of a few years by the adoption of a similar system under Acts of Parliament at Worcester, Exeter, Hull, Norwich, and Plymouth.

In the year 1698-9 the demoralising results of sending beggars home by furnishing them with passes, which entitled them to be passed from parish to parish without further question, necessitated the passing of the 11 Wil. III., c. 18, which recites that "many parts of this Kingdom are extremely oppressed by the usual method of conveying vagabonds or beggers from parish to parish in a dilatory manner, whereby such vagabonds or beggers in hopes of Releife from every Parish through which they are conducted are incouraged to spend their lives in wandring from one part of this Kingdom to another and to delude divers charitable and well-disposed persons very frequently forge or counterfeit passes testimonials or characters whereby the charitable intentions of such persons are often abused." It then provides for the examination by the justices of all bearers of passes in each parish in which they apply for relief or conveyance; if they are punishable they are to be sent to the House of Correction, and if not they are at once to be sent on to their destination. Constables neglecting their duty are liable to a penalty of 20s.

An interesting view of the relative relations of the independent and dependent classes in this reign is furnished in the year 1699 by Charles D'Avenant, from data collected by Gregory King, Lancaster Herald, in the year 1688:—

"The nobility and gentry, with their families and retainers, the persons in offices, merchants, persons in the law, the clergy, freeholders, farmers, persons in sciences and liberal arts, shopkeepers and tradesmen, handicraftsmen, naval officers, with the families and dependents upon all these altogether, make up the number of . . . . 2,675,520 heads.

" The common seamen, common soldiers, labouring people, and out-servants, cottagers, paupers, and their families, with the vagrants, make up the number of . . . . 2,825,000 heads.

5,500,520 heads.

" So that here seems a majority of the people, whose chief dependence and subsistence is from the other part, which majority is much greater, in respect of the number of families, because 500,000 families contribute to the support of 850,000 families. . . . The first class of the people, from land, arts, and industry, maintain themselves, and add every year something to the nation's general stock; and besides this, out of their superfluity, contribute every year so much to the maintenance of others. . . . Of the second class, some partly maintain themselves by labour, (as the heads of the cottage families), but that the rest, as most of the wives and children of these, sick and impotent people, idle beggars and vagrants, are nourished at the cost of others; and are a yearly burthen to the public, consuming annually so much as would be otherwise added to the nation's general stock." *Mr. King* computes the number of vagrants, as gypsies, thieves, beggars, &c., at 30,000, earning an annual income of £10 10s. each.

"The opinion of King William on the state of the poor in his reign may be gathered from his speech to both Houses at the opening of Parliament on the 16th of November, 1699.

"The Increase of the Poor is become a Burthen to the Kingdom, and their loose and idle Life, does in some measure contribute to that depravation of Manners, which is complained of (I fear with too much reason). Whether the ground of this Evil be from defects in the Laws already made, or in the Execution of them, deserves your Consideration. As it is an indispensable Duty that the Poor, who are not able to help themselves, should be maintained; so I cannot but think it extremely desireable that such as are able and willing, should not want Employment; and such as are obstinate and unwilling, should be compelled to labour."*

One of the first enactments of the reign of *Anne* was an Act for continuing for three years the stat. 11 W. III., c. 18. This Act (1 An., stat. 2, c. 13, 1702) "recites that some Justices of the Peace give greater allowances to Constables for conveying Vagrants than may seem necessary, and that the Owners of Horses, Wagons, Carts, or other necessary Carriages for conveying such Vagrants are often extravagant in their rates and demands" and orders "that the Justices in Quarter Sessions shall yearly settle the rates for maintaining and conveying Vagrants."

The precocity and depravity of the children engaged in mendicity at this period appears from a report of the President and Governors for the Poor of London in 1702 to have been very great. It says—

"That people may not be imposed upon by beggars, who pretend to be lame, dumb, &c., which really are not so; this is to give notice, that the president and governors for the poor of London, pitying the case of one Richard Alegil, a boy of eleven years of age, who pretended himself lame of both his legs, so that he used to go shoving himself along on his breeches; they ordered him to be taken into their workhouse, intending to make him a tailor, upon which he confessed that his brother, a boy seven years of

* Chandler.

age, about four years ago, by the advice of other beggars, contracted his legs and turned, them backwards, so that he never used them from that time to this, but followed the trade of begging; that he usually got five shillings a day, sometimes ten shillings; that he hath been all over the West of England, where his brother carried him on a horse, and pretended that he was born so, and cut out of his mother's womb. He hath also given an account that he knows of other beggars that pretend to be dumb and lame, and some that tie their arms in their breeches, and wear a wooden stump in their sleeve. The said president and governors have caused the legs of the said Alegil to be set straight; he has now the use of them, and walks upright. They have ordered him to be put to spinning, and his brother to be kept to hard labour. Several other beggars are by their order taken up and set to work, and when brought into the Workhouse had from ten shillings to five pounds in their pockets."

This condition of things no doubt had a good deal to say to the passing of the Act of 2 & 3 An., c. 6, entitled "An Act for the Increase of Seamen and better Encouragement of Navigation and Security of the Coal Trade," which empowers any two or more Justices of the Peace in their several and respective counties, ridings, or divisions, all Mayors, Aldermen, Bailiffs, and other chief officers of cities and towns corporate, and likewise the churchwardens and overseers of the poor, with the approbation of such justices, mayors, and other chief officers, " to bind and put out any Boy or Boys who is, are, or shall be of the Age of Ten Years or upwards, or who is or are or shall be chargeable, or whose Parents are or shall become chargeable to the respective Parish or Parishes wherein they inhabit, or who shall begg for Alms, to be Apprentice and Apprentices to the Sea service to any of Her Majesty's subjects, being masters or Owners of any Shipp or Vessell used in Sea Service belonging to any Port or Ports within the Kingdom of England, Dominion of Wales, and Towne of Berwick-upon-Tweed, until such boy attains the age of one-and-twenty, and such binding shall be effectual." The Churchwardens are at the same time to pay an apprentice fee of 50s.

The Act also recites that " diverse dissolute and idle Persons, Rogues Vagabonds and Sturdy Beggars notwithstanding the many good and wholsome laws to the contrary, do continue to wander up and down, pilfering and begging through all parts of this

Kingdome to the great Disturbance of the Peace and tranquility of the Realme; for the more effectually suppressing such disorderly Persons, and to the End that they might be made Serviceable and beneficiall to their country," it then enacts "That all lewd and disorderly Men Servants and every such Person and persons both Men and Boys that are deemed and adjudged Rogues Vagabonds and Sturdy Beggars (not being Felons) by the 39 Eliz., c. 4, shall be and are hereby directed to be taken up sent and conducted and conveyed unto Her Majestie's Service at Sea, by such Waies, Methods, and Meanes, and in such Manner and Forme as is directed for Vagrants in the 11 & 12 Wil. III., c. 18, for the more effectuall Punishment of Vagrants and sending them whither by Law they ought to be sent."

By 6 Anne, c. 32 (1706), the 11 & 12 Wil. III., c. 18, is continued for seven years, and courts of quarter session are authorised to raise money by assessment to satisfy constables the expenses of passing vagrants.

We now come to an important statute, the 13 Anne, c. 26* (1713), which consolidates and amends the existing laws regarding vagrancy. It opens by stating "that many parts of the kingdom are oppressed by the usual method of conveying vagabonds or beggars from county to county, by having such persons conveyed as vagrants who ought not so to be. It then gives the following definitions of persons to be deemed rogues and vagabonds, and who, if found wandering and begging, are to be punished as such.

"All persons pretending themselves to be Patent Gatherers or Collectors for Prisons Goals or Hospitals and wandring abroad for that purpose; all Fencers Bearwards Common Players of Interludes Minstrels Juglers all Persons pretending to be Gipsies or wandring in the Habit or Form of Counterfeit Egyptians or pretending to have skill in Physiognomy Palmestry or like crafty Science or pretending to tell Fortunes or like phantastical Imaginations or using any subtile Craft or unlawful Games or Plays all Persons able in Body who run away and leave their Wives or Children to the parish and not having wherewith otherwise to maintain themselves use Loytring and refuse to work for the usual and common Wages and all other idle Persons wandring abroad and begging (except Soldiers, Mariners or Seafaring Men licensed by some Testimo-

* This is Chapter XXIII., 12 Anne, Stat. 2, in the common printed editions, and is cited in Acts of the reign of George II. as 12 Anne.

THE *Hebrews* have extreamly honoured this Science of *Physiognomie*, and the Scripture gives you the Physiognomie of *Jacob, Moses, David, Absalom, Jonathan*, and many others. The Compilers of the *Talmud* have made a Treatise of it, both of *Chiromancie* and *Physiognomie* called מסכת ידים *Massecheth Jadaim*, that is to say, The Treatise of the Hands; where they distinguish *Physiognomie* from *Metoposcopie*, which is indeed but a part of *Physiognomie*, which the *Greeks* understood well, saying, μετωπίσκοπ۰ ἀπὸ τῦ μετώπε ἠ σκοπεῖν, i.e. a Science whereby things to come are known by the aspect of the forehead. These *Greeks* knew also *Umblicometry*, and divers others; but as for *Physiognomie* they placed it according to this Figure:

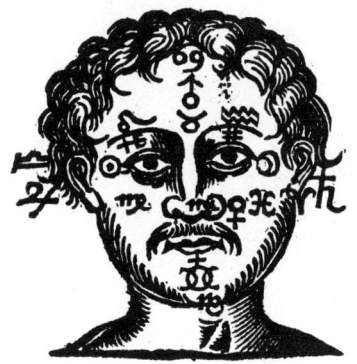

PHYSIOGNOMY

nial or Writing under the Hand and Seal of some Justice of Peace, setting down the Time and Place of his or their Landing and the place to which they are to pass, and limiting the time for such their Passage while they continue in the Direct Way to the Place to which they are to pass and during the Time so limited)."

Any person is at liberty to apprehend any rogue or vagabond found wandering and begging, or misordering him or herself, and is entitled to a reward of 2s. for so doing. Constables or anyone else properly ordered to apprehend a beggar and neglecting to do so are liable to a fine of 10s. Justices before Quarter Sessions, or whenever else needful, are ordered to meet and make order for a general and privy search in one night.

Persons are ordered to be sent to their place of settlement or birth, and if that could not be known, then to the place where they were last found begging or misordering themselves and passed unapprehended.

Any person found wandering and begging after having obtained a legal settlement, is ordered to be stripped naked from the middle and openly whipped, until his or her body be bloody and then to be sent to the House of Correction to be kept to hard labour, according to the nature and merit of his or her offence and then be passed home.

"Any rogue or vagabond apprehended on a privy search and whom the Justices upon examination deem to be dangerous to the People where taken and unlikely to be reformed, may be committed to hard labour at the House of Correction or Gaol until the next Quarter Sessions, and if he is then adjudged dangerous and incorrigible, the Justices may cause him to be publicly whipped Three Market Days successively at some Market Town near, and afterwards keep him to hard labour for such time as they think fit. Any Rogue so committed escaping from prison under such circumstances is to suffer as a felon. Rogues who refuse to be examined on oath or who swear falsely are to be deemed incorrigible rogues.

"Vagrants sent home by pass are ordered to be stripped naked from the middle and openly whipped, or else sent to hard labour for two or three days in each county through which they pass on their way. Exception is made in favour of women great with child, soldiers wanting subsistence having lawful certificates from their officers or Secretary of War, or such Persons as the Justices judge not able to undergo such Punishment, and no

Constable is obliged to receive such persons unless they have been punished.

"Persons sent to their place of settlement and refusing to work, may be punished with hard labour, and if found wandering again the parishes permitting them to escape, may be mulcted in the costs of their apprehension, punishment and conveyance.

"Vagrants without a legal place of settlement may be committed to the custody and power of the person apprehending them, or to any other person or body willing to receive them as apprentices, or servants, for a term of seven years, to be employed in Great Britain, or in any of Her Majesty's Plantations, or in any British Factory beyond the Seas. Such persons are bound under a penalty of £40 to supply the vagrant with proper necessaries and to set him at liberty at the end of 7 years.

"Loose, idle, and disorderly Persons, blind, lame, or pretending to be so, with distorted limbs, or pretending some bodily Infirmity placing themselves to beg in Streets, Highways, or Passages, are on complaint of two or more Inhabitants to be removed, and refusing to be removed, or offending again after removal, are ordered to be stripped naked from the shoulders to the waist and whipped till bloody. Any Constable neglecting this duty is liable to a penalty of 10s.

"Masters of ships bringing Natives of Ireland, the Isle of Man, the Channel Islands, the Foreign Plantations, likely to live by begging are liable to a penalty of £5 for each person, in addition to the cost of their apprehension and conveyance. Any Constable finding such persons wandering or begging, is to cause them to be openly whipped and reconveyed to the place from whence they came.

"Masters are bound to accept the rates settled by the Justices for the Conveyance of vagrants by sea.

"The statutes 39 Eliz., c. 4, 1 Jac. I., c. 7, and so much of 7 Jac. I., c. 4, as relate to privy searches are repealed.

"The privileges of John Dutton are declared exempt."

This Act makes no mention of pedlars, petty chapmen, tinkers, and persons pretending to be soldiers or sailors who were included in the category of rogues and vagabonds in former Acts. Its aim is evidently to repress mendicity by increasing the severity of the penalties against it—a policy which, as we have seen, had proved futile in previous reigns.

CHAPTER VIII.

1713—1760.

Accession of George I.—Inquiry by the House of Commons into the expenditure on the poor in London in 1715—Metropolitan mendicity in 1716—Legislation against idlers under twenty-one and persons deserting their wives or families—End gatherers treated as vagabonds—Mr. Joshua Gee on the employment of the poor—Condition of workhouses—State of mendicity and crime, 1719 to 1734—Enactments against players, and their origin—Special legislation against beggars in the city of Bath—Committee of 1735 on the poor—Legislation of 1739-40, 1743-4, and 1751-2 against vagabonds —Expulsion of vagrants from towns—Mendicity in London in 1753.

AT the commencement of the reign of George I. a committee of the House of Commons was appointed to inspect the Poor's Rates and Scavenger's Rates in the metropolis, it being alleged that they were misspent. By this means some very curious evidence relating to vagabonds and beggars was brought to light, as will be seen by the following extract from the journals of the House :—

" Jovis, 8º dii Martii
Anno 2e Georgii Regis, 1715.

"*Mr. Molesworth* according to Order reported from the Committee appointed to inspect the Poor's Rates, and Scavenger's Rates, within the cities of London and Westminster, and weekly Bills of Mortality. . . . The Committee finding it a work of insuperable difficulty to peruse all the Books and Accounts of the various parishes, report that they have selected the Parish of St. Martin's-in-the-Fields, because it has been represented to them as the most free from Frauds and Abuses, and averred to be under the best regulation of any Parish in *London*. The Committee observe in the course of the report. . . .

" 17. The pensioners, or settled Poor, are given in at between £1,200 and £1,300 *per annum*, for the last three years ; and Multitudes of Names are entered in the Books, which the Committee could find no method of comptrolling ; much less that other vast article of the Casual Poor, amounting to between £1,800 and £1,900 *per annum :* Notwithstanding all which real or pretended Distributions, the Begging Poor about the Streets, in this Parish, are observed to be as numerous as ever. . . .

"That the Increase of Strange Beggars, Cripples, lusty idle Men and Women, Vagabonds, blind People, pretended and real Madfolks and such like, is altogether owing to the Negligence of those that should remedy it, and of the Parish officers who take no due Care to purge their several Parishes of such sort of Vagrants; but connive at them, on purpose that such appearing objects of Charity may give a fair Pretence to these yearly exorbitant Collections of all Kinds; this Kind of Beggars receive little or no settled Parish Alms, but live upon what they can extort by their Cries and Importunities in the Streets, and at Coach-sides; and what they thus get, they are generally obliged to spend at some Tipling-house kept by the Beadles, who have good Salaries allowed them, or their Friends and Relations, who sell unwholesome spirits, which carry off Multitudes of them every year. . . .

"Upon the whole matter, the Committee cannot induce themselves to be of Opinion, that much above One-half of the great sums aforesaid, which are collected by, and paid to, the Churchwardens and Overseers yearly, are really expended on that pious and charitable work of relieving the poor; but that in consequence of the present Methods taken, the Poor are rather increased in this great City of late, than diminished; and those of them which are relieved, are not done so in the manner they ought to be; but that many very miserably perish for want."

This report bears testimony to a state of things which many previous Acts of Parliament have declared to be a cause of vagrancy and mendicity in former times, viz., the neglect or collusive action of the authorities appointed to carry out the Acts.

The tippling-houses kept by the beadles strikingly remind one of the *Scothala* exacted by officers of the forest who kept alehouses in feudal times.

The poet *Gay*, writing at this period, gives us the following picture of metropolitan mendicity in *Trivia* (1716);—

> "If e'er the miser durst his Farthings spare,
> He thinly spreads them through the publick square,
> Where, all beside the Rail, rang'd Beggars lie,
> And from each other catch the doleful Cry;
> With Heav'n, for Two-pence, cheaply wipes his score,
> Lifts up his eyes, and hasts to beggar more.

> Where Lincoln's Inn's wide space is rail'd around,
> Cross not with vent'rous step; there oft is found
>   The lurking Thief, who, while the Day-light shone,
>   Made the walls eccho with his begging Tone :
> That Crutch, which late Compassion mov'd, shall wound
> Thy bleeding Head, and fell thee to the Ground!"

We now come to the 4 Geo. I., c. 11, s. 5, which embodies an extension of the principle contained in the 2 and 3 Anne, c. 6. It recites that—

"Whereas there are many Idle Persons, who are under the Age of One-and-twenty Years, lurking about in divers parts of London and elsewhere, who want Employment, and may be tempted to become Thieves, if not provided for: and whereas they may be inclined to be transported, and to enter into services in some of his Majesty's Colonies and plantations in America: but as they have no power to contract for themselves, and therefore that it is not safe for merchants to transport them or take them into such services; it then enacts that where any person of the age of fifteen years or more, and under the age of twenty-one, shall be willing to be transported, and to enter into any Service in any of his Majesties Colonies or Plantations in America: It shall and may be lawful for any Merchant, or other, to contract with any such person for any such service, not exceeding the term of eight years, on coming before the Lord Mayor or some other justice of the peace of the city or elsewhere before two justices."

The next Act we have to notice is—

"The 5 Geo. I., c. 8 (1717), which commences by reciting 'that divers Persons run or go away from their Places of Abode into other Counties or Places, and sometimes out of the Kingdom, some Men leaving their Wives, a Child, or Children, and some Mothers run or go away, leaving a Child or Children, upon the charge of the Parish or Place where such Child or Children was or were Born, or last legally Settled, although such Persons have some Estates, which should Ease the Parish of their Charge, in whole, or in part.' It then enacts 'that it shall be Lawful for the Churchwardens or Overseers of the Poor of such Parish or Place where such Wife, Child, or Children shall be so left, by warrant of two Justices to 'Seize so much of the Goods and Chattels, and receive so much of the Annual Rents and profits of the Lands and Tenements of such husband, Father, or Mother,' as such Justices shall order, towards the

Discharge of the Parish for the bringing up and Providing for such Wife, Child, or Children."

It thus appears that there were then a class of persons possessed of means, who finding that the law made provision for their wives and families when destitute, determined to avail themselves of this gratuitous privilege.

In the year 1726-7 an Act was passed for the better Regulation of the Woollen Manufacture, and for Preventing Disputes among the Persons concerned therein (13 Geo. I., c. 23).

It enacts a penalty of £5 for each offence upon any clothier or maker of woollen cloths, druggets, or other woollen goods who shall use any ends of yarn, wefts, or other refuse of cloths, druggets, or other woollen goods, or goods mixed with wool, flocks and pinions only excepted. It also recites that "several Abuses have been committed in the Woollen Manufacture by Persons, commonly called End-gatherers, going about the Kingdom collecting, buying and receiving from the Labourers imployed in such Manufacture, ends of Yarn, Wefts, Thrums, short Yarn, and other refuse of Cloth, Drugget, and other Woollen Goods, and Goods mixt with Wooll, Flocks and Pinions only excepted." It then enacts that if from the 1st of June, 1727, " any such person shall be found collecting, buying, receiving or any ways carrying or conveying such matters in any Bag or other Convenience," it shall be lawful for any constable or peace officer " to search and examine such Person, his Bag, or other convenience," and if on search he shall find any such matters he shall carry such person before a Justice of the Peace, and upon due conviction every such offender shall be liable to be punished as a dangerous and incorrigible Rogue, Vagrant, or Person, in the same manner as is directed by the 12 Anne.

The purpose of this enactment was, of course, the protection of the public from frauds by those clothiers who it is evident must have resembled the shoddy manufacturers of our own day. The clothiers themselves had previously received protection by the 7 Geo. I., c. 7 (1720) which in their interests prohibited the wearing or use of printed or dyed calico under a penalty of £5; the sale of it except for exportation was also prohibited under this Act under a penalty of £20.

An interesting work entitled "The Trade and Navigation of Great Britain Considered," was published in the year 1729 by Mr. Joshua Gee, a merchant of London. Under the head of

"Propositions for Better regulating and employing the Poor," he gives us an insight into some of the causes of idleness and mendicity and the condition of mendicity, and makes some very instructive remarks on the remedies which had been found most effective for dealing with the matter.

"Perseverance in the Rules of Industry will change the very inclinations of those idle Vagrant Persons, who now run about the Kingdom, and spend their Time and what Money they can any Way come at upon their Debauches. . . .

"It has been remarked by our Clothiers and other Manufacturers, that when Corn has been cheap they have had great Difficulty to get their Spinning and other Work done; for the Poor could buy Provision enough with two or three Days Wages to serve them a Week, and would spend the rest in Idleness, Drinking, &c. But when Corn has been dear, they have been forced to stick all the Week at it; and the Clothiers have had more Work done with all the Ease that could be desired, and the constant Application to Business has fixed their minds so much to it, that they have not only had Money enough to purchase Food, but also to provide themselves with Cloaths and other Necessaries, whereby to live comfortably. . . .

"Notwithstanding we have so many excellent Laws, great Numbers of sturdy Beggars, loose and vagrant persons, infest the Nation, but no place more than the City of *London* and parts adjacent. If any person is born with any Defect or Deformity, or maimed by Fire or any other Casualty, or by any inveterate Distemper which renders them miserable Objects, their Way is open to *London*, where they have free Liberty of shewing their nauseous sights to terrify People, and force them to give Money to get rid of them; and those Vagrants have for many Years past removed out of several Parts of the three Kingdoms, and taken their Stations in this Metropolis, to the Interruption of Conversation and Business. This must proceed from the very great Neglect of the inferior Officers in and about this City, who ought to put the Laws in Execution; for in those Places where Magistrates take Care to keep Constables and other Officers to their Duty, they have little or no Trouble of this Kind, especially where there are Work-houses.

"The Magistrates of *Bristol* have that City under such excellent Regulation that Foreign Beggars dare not appear; they are not troubled with obnoxious Sights, so common with us; their Work-houses are terrible enough to them; for as soon as any of them are espied in the City, they are taken up and whipt: and wherever Workhouses have been built (if well directed) the Parish Rates have been much lessened; and doubtless when the Master of the Workhouse and others under him come to be experienced in the several Employments the Poor are put to, and perform their Duty with Integrity, there will be little Occasion to waste the Parish Money upon persons that are able to work; and even Children would soon come to spin or do something for a Maintenance. The *Quakers* Work-house in the City of *London* is an Example of this Kind; the poor Orphans among them, as well as the Children of such Poor as are not able to subsist them, are put to their Work-house, where they are taught to read and write certain Hours of the Day, and at other Times are put to spin, or other Employments; and it is found by Experience that the Children who can change their Employments from their Books to their Spinning, &c., are as well satisfied therewith, as if they had so much Time allowed them for play; and the Emulation who shall do most and best seem, to be as much regarded by them, and they have as great a Desire to excel one another, as other Children have at their most pleasing Diversions. And as the Nation has found great advantage by those Workhouses which have been established by Act of Parliament, it is a great Pity that so profitable an Institution was not made general thro' the Nation, that so there might be no Pretence for any Beggar to appear abroad. Their Example is very pernicious; for what they get by begging is consumed commonly in Ale-houses, Gin-shops, &c., and one drunken Beggar is an Inducement to a great many to follow the same Trade.

"There is no place so immediately stands under a Necessity of being relieved from those Vagrants as the City of London, and adjacent Parts, as is before hinted. The Difficulty will be to find out a Method for better putting the laws in Execution. I must confess I think the Error is in depending upon Constables; they are Men of Business, and have Families to support; none of them take the office upon them but with Regret; and if they can find Money, rather buy off than serve in their own Persons; if they are forced to serve, when the Laws against Vagrants should be put in Execution, the Constable is about his own Business; and, if possible, will not be found.

"As to those Creatures that go about the Streets to show their maim'd Limbs, nauseous Sores, stump Hands, or Feet, or any other

Deformity, I am of Opinion, that they are by no Means Objects fit to go abroad; and considering the Frights and pernicious Impressions which such horrid Sights have given to pregnant Women (and sometimes even to the disfiguring of Infants in the Womb), should move all tender Husbands to desire the Redress of this Enormity, and to look upon this as a Charity fit to be provided for in the first Place, by erecting an Hospital on Purpose for receiving and strictly confining such People from all Parts of the Nation, who wander about to extort Money by exposing those dismal Sights."

The pith of Mr. Gee's observations, it will be noticed, is a forcible reiteration of the fact that the increase of mendicity is principally due to the neglect of the constables, and to the inefficacy of mere punishment as a restraint upon the vagrant.

The good effects of well-managed workhouses at this period is clearly set forth in a pamphlet entitled an "Account of several Workhouses for Employing and Maintaining the Poor," published in 1725.

"Wherever Houses have been hired or built, for gathering the Poor into one or more Families, and setting them to Work, under the Inspection of honest Managers, the respective Parishes have found most, if not all, the Advantages following; viz., 200*l*. per annum of the Poor's Rates, under frugal Management, after a House and necessary Accommodations are provided, shall go further in keeping comfortably one or more large Families of Poor, than 300 *or* 400*l*. per annum distributed to the like number of Poor when they live dispers'd.

"Soon after the *Restoration*, in the 13th and 14th years of the Reign of King *Charles II.*, an Act of Parliament past, entituled, *An Act for the better Relief of the Poor of this Kingdom.*

"The Calamities of the Plague, and Burning of the City of London, &c., delay'd the good Effects of this Act, till after the peace of *Ryswick*, when, in the Year 1698, *April* the 4th, in order to put the said Act in Execution, a Corporation was form'd, consisting of the Lord Mayor for the Time being as President, the Aldermen for the Time being, together with fifty-two Citizens, chosen by the Common-Council, to be Assistants, elected a Deputy, President, and Treasurer, as the said Act directs. And for laying a Foundation of so good a Work, a Supply was granted in *December* following, by an Act of the Common-Council."

In *August*, 1699, the Corporation took a house in *Bishopsgate*

Street, and were at great charges in building and fitting the same up for a Work-House, into which they received from the Churchwardens such children as were a charge to the several Parishes, they paying a Weekly allowance towards their Maintenance.

" In *November*, 1700, they began to receive, on the *Keeper's Side*, Vagabonds and sturdy Beggars; and thus they proceeded, by degrees; it being impracticable to execute all Parts of the Act at once. . . .

" The House is divided into two Parts, one call'd the *Steward's Side*, and the other the *Keeper's Side* : In the *Steward's Side* poor Children are taken in from Benefactors, giving 50 or 70*l*. as beforemention'd. . . . .

" In the other Part, called the *Keeper's Side*, Vagabonds, Beggars, Pilferers, lewd, idle, and disorderly Persons, committed by any two of the Governours, have such Relief as is proper for them ; and are imploy'd in beating Hemp for Twine-Spinners, Hemp Dressers, Linnen-Weavers, Shoemakers, and other Trades; as also in picking Oakum, and washing Linnen for the Children in the Steward's Side. . . .

"By the Account of this Work-House, publish'd at *Easter*, 1725, it appears that there have been, since the Year 1701, educated, disdischarg'd, and plac'd forth apprentices

To Officers of Ships, to Trades, and to Services in several good Families. . . . . } 1,782

And in the same time there have been receiv'd and discharg'd of sturdy Vagabonds, Beggars, &c. } 12,265 "

The workhouses then established in the various counties were as follows: in Bedfordshire, 13 ; Berkshire, 1 ; Buckinghamshire 11 ; Cambridgeshire, 5 ; Devonshire, 3 ; Essex, 20 ; Gloucestershire, 2 ; Hertfordshire, 16 ; Kent, 7 ; Lancashire, 1 ; Leicestershire, 5 ; Lincolnshire, 1 ; Middlesex, 14, of which 8 were in the City, 4 in Westminster, and the other 2 at Enfield and Harrow; Norfolk, 1 ; Northamptonshire, 16 ; Oxfordshire, 3 ; Somersetshire, 1 ; Suffolk, 1 ; Warwick, 1 ; Wilts, 1 ; Worcester, 1; York, 2. Total, 126.

The famous *Daniel Defoe*, writing under the pseudonym of *Andrew Moreton*, however, gives us another picture of some of these workhouses.

" These Work-houses, tho' in Appearance Benificial, yet have in some Respects an evil Tendency, for they mix the Good and the Bad; and too often make Reprobates of all alike. We all, alas, are subject to Misfortune! And if an honest Gentleman or Trader should leave a Wife or Children unprovided for, what a shocking Thing it is to think they must be mix'd with Vagrants, Beggars, Thieves, and Night-Walkers! to receive their Insults, to hear their Blasphemous and Obscene Discourse, to be suffocated with their Nastiness, and eat up with their Vermin. And if any Parishioners interpose in their Behalf, they are sure to be shut up and worse treated for the Future."*

Notwithstanding the efforts made to repress mendicity at this period it still continued to flourish, as *Civicus*, writing to the *London Journal* on the 13th February, 1731, speaks of "the multitude of beggers, and the many villainies and robberies committed in this city, the threats of incendiaries, and those threats actually executed; boys of 7 or 8 years old, taken in robbing a shop; and some of 13 or 14, robbing in the streets." He further says, "A few years since *London* was as remarkable for the safety of its inhabitants, as it is now notorious for the danger persons are exposed to who walk the streets after ten at night," and imputes the cause of these evils to the number of poor, whom he divides into two classes—"first, those who are absolutely incapable of working; secondly, those who are able, but not willing. The first sort," he urges, "are real objects of charity, but ought not to be suffer'd to wander the streets, exposing their distorted limbs, and filthy sores, such sights being frequently attended with the worst consequences to women with child."

"The second sort of poor, who are able to work but not willing, are very numerous, and to them, in a great measure, are owing the many villainies daily committed in this *City*."

The audacity and unconcern of beggar boys at this period is illustrated in the *Gentleman's Magazine* for 1734 by the remark of a boy when he was brought to trial for firing the barn of a farmer who had refused him alms.

"'Jack,' said he to one of his companions, upon seeing the *Jury, Judges, Sheriff,* and his *Officers* enter the Court, '*am not I a great man,* Sirrah, *to make such a Bustle as this in the World, and*

---

* "Parochial Tyranny: or the House-keeper's Complaint against the insupportable Exactments and partial Assessments of Select Vestries," by Andrew Moreton Esq. London, 1729.

be thus attended? When will you come to such Preferment, you little inconsiderable Rascal, you?'"

Captain Alexander Smith, in his "Compleat History of the Lives and Robberies of the most Notorious Highwaymen, Foot-Pads, &c.," thus speaks of the condition of crime in the country in 1719 :—

"I acknowledge, Times past were as bad as the present; and four or five thousand Years of Antiquity can furnish us with many Examples of wickedness; for there was many a Man that had his Foible, and could commit a Sin apropos; but yet hath Vice thriv'd more in England since Queen Elizabeth's Days, than ever it did in this Kingdom in all the Reigns before."

This state of things is plainly the cause, for the enactment of the 7 Geo. II., c. 21 (1734), which is entitled, "An Act for the more effectual Punishment of Assaults with Intent to commit Robbery." It recites that "many of His Majesty's Subjects have of late frequently been put in great Fear and Danger of their Lives by wicked and ill-disposed Persons assaulting and attempting to rob them, and that the punishment of such offenders is not adequate to the heinousness of that Crime, nor sufficient to deter wicked Persons from such Attempts." It then enacts "that Persons convicted of assaulting others with offensive Weapons, and a Design to rob, shall be transported for 7 years, and such Convicts breaking Gaol or unlawfully returning from Transportation shall suffer Death."

We now come to two special enactments against Players, the first restraining them from performing at either of the Universities, and the next restraining them from performing in any place in which they have not a legal settlement, and not even there unless they have a license from the Lord Chamberlain.

The first of these, the 10 Geo. II., c. 19 (1736-7), is styled, "An Act for the more effectual preventing the unlawful playing of Interludes within the precincts of the Two Universities." It recites, "that doubts have arisen whether the Letters patent granted by Henry VIII. to the University of Oxford, and by Elizabeth to the University of Cambridge, or other charters, liberties, or laws, sufficiently empowered the Chancellors of either University, or their deputies, to correct, restrain, or suppress common players of Interludes, settled, residing, or inhabiting within the precincts of either of the said Universities, and not wandering abroad." It then declares, "that the Creation of any Playhouse within the Precincts of the said Universities, or Places adjacent, may be attended with great Inconveniences," and enacts "That all Persons whatsoever, who shall for Gain in any Playhouse, Booth, or otherwise, exhibit any Stage Play, Interlude, Shew, Opera, or other Theatrical or Dramatical Performance, or act any Part, or assist therein, within the precincts of either of the said Universities, or within Five Miles of the City of Oxford, or Town of Cambridge, shall be deemed Rogues and Vagabonds, and it shall be lawful for the Chancellor of either of the said Universities or his Deputy respectively, to commit any such Person to any House of Correction within either of the Counties of Cambridge or Oxford respectively, there to be kept to hard Labour for the space of One Month, or to the common Gaol, there to remain without Bail or Mainprise for the like Space of One Month, any Licence of the Chancellor, Masters, and Scholars of either of the said Universities, or anything in this Act or in any other Statute, Law, Custom, Charter, or Privilege to the contrary notwithstanding."

No amount of condonation on the part of the authorities could therefore save the unlucky player from the penalties of the Act.

"The acting of plays was a form of amusement which had long divided opinion in the universities. At Paris we find the austere Gerson interdicting their performance and stigmatising such recreations as 'ludi stultorum;' at Cambridge, however, they were at this time a practice recognised by the authorities and encouraged by statutory enactments—penalties even being sometimes imposed on those who refused to bear their part. The amusement and interest which they excited was in no way diminished by the fact that they were frequently the medium through which one party asserted its own views and satirised those of its opponents."*

"In the second year of King James's reign, a royal letter was issued forbidding 'unprofitable or idle games and plays,' to be carried on 'within five miles compass of and from the university and town,' † 'especially bull-baiting, bear-baiting, common plays, publick shews, interludes, comedies and tragedies *in the English tongue*, games at loggets, nineholes, and all other sports and

* Mullinger. † Of Cambridge.

games whereby throngs, concourse, or multitudes, are drawn together."*

"The design in prohibiting the performance of English plays will be more apparent, if we here note the singular license for which such compositions sometimes afforded scope. The college play was, in fact, far from being an entirely innocent recreation, and was sometimes made the vehicle for satire and gross personalities which were productive of no little ill feeling. Against the townsmen, impervious to such satire when it was clothed in a Latin dress, the English play easily afforded the means not only of ridiculing, but also of making that ridicule felt; and Fuller, in his *History of the University*, has described with more than his usual humour a notable instance of the kind:—

"The young scholars conceiving themselves somewhat wronged by the townsmen (the particulars whereof I know not), betook them for revenge to their wits, as the weapon wherein lay their best advantage. These having gotten a discovery of some town privacies, from Miles Goldsborough (one of their own corporation), composed a merry (but abusive) comedy (which they called *Club-Law*), in English, as calculated for the capacities of such whom they intended spectators thereof. Clare-Hall was the place wherein it was acted, and the mayor with his brethren and their wives were invited to behold it, or rather themselves abused therein. A convenient place was assigned to the townsfolk (riveted in with scholars on all sides) where they might see and be seen. Here they did behold themselves in their own best clothes (which the scholars had borrowed), so lively personated their habits, gestures, language, lieger-jests, and expressions, that it was hard to decide which was the true townsman, whether he that sat by, or he who acted on the stage. Sit still they could not for chafing, go out they could not for crowding, but impatiently patient were fain to attend till dismissed at the end of the comedy. The mayor and his brethren soon after complain of this libellous play to the lords of the Privy Council, and truly aggravate the scholars' offence—as if the mayor's mace could not be played with, but that the sceptre itself is touched therein!" †

"Notwithstanding the stringent enactment against theatrical entertainments at Cambridge, a company of players from the theatres in London performed in 1748, a pantomime called *Harle-*

* Cooper. † Mullinger.

quin's *Frolics or Jack Spaniard caught in a Trap*, in Hussey's Great Theatrical Booth, the upper end of Garlic Row in Sturbridge Fair." *

The second of these statutes is the 10 Geo. II., c. 28, which is entitled "An Act to explain and amend so much of the 13 Anne, cap. 26, as relates to common Players of Interludes." It recites that doubts have arisen concerning so much of the said Act as relates to common Players of Interludes, and then enacts that from and after the 24th of June, 1737, "every Person who shall, for Hire, Gain, or Reward, act, represent, or perform, or cause to be acted, represented, or performed, any Interlude, Tragedy, Comedy, Opera, Play, Farce, or other Entertainment of the Stage, or any Part or Parts therein, in case such person shall not have any legal Settlement in the Place, where the same shall be acted, represented, or performed, without Authority, by virtue of Letters Patent from his Majesty, his Heirs, Successors or Predecessors, or without Licence from the Lord Chamberlain, shall be deemed to be a Rogue and a Vagabond, and shall be liable and subject to all such Penalties and punishments as are inflicted on or appointed for the Punishment of Rogues and Vagabonds, who shall be found wandering, begging, and misordering themselves.

"And if any Person having, or not having a legal Settlement, shall, without such Authority or Licence, act, represent, or perform, or cause to be acted, represented, or performed, for Hire, Gain, or Reward, any Interlude, Tragedy, Comedy, Opera, Play, Farce, or other Entertainment of the stage, or any Part or Parts therein, every such Person shall for every such offence forfeit the Sum of Fifty pounds, and in case this Sum shall be paid, such offender shall not for the same offence suffer any of the Pains or Penalties inflicted by the Act."

No new plays or additions to old ones are to be acted unless a copy is sent to the Lord Chamberlain, and persons acting against his prohibition are to forfeit 50*l.* and their licence. No plays are to be acted in any part of Great Britain except the city of Westminster, or places of His Majesty's residence.

And it is further enacted that "if any Interlude, Tragedy, Comedy, Opera, Play, Farce, or other Entertainment of the Stage, or any act, scene, or part thereof, shall be acted, represented, or performed,

* Wordsworth.

in any house or place where Wine, Ale, or Beer, or other Liquors, shall be sold or retailed, the same shall be deemed to be acted, represented, and performed for Gain, Hire, and Reward."

The legitimate actor and the public-house "spouter" were thus equally brought within the meshes of the law.

The temper and spirit of the times regarding plays and players may be gathered from a debate on the subject in the House of Commons on the 5th of March, 1735.

"Alderman Sir John Barnard (one of the Members for the City of London) moved for bringing in a Bill for restraining the number of houses for playing of Interludes, and for the better regulating Common Players of Interludes. In Support of this Motion he represented the Mischief done to the City of London by the Play-houses, in corrupting the Youth, encouraging Vice and Debauchery, and being prejudicial to Trade and Industry; and how much these Evils would be increased if another Play-House should be built in the very Heart* of the City. Sir John Barnard was seconded by Mr. Sandys (member for Worcester), and supported by Mr. Pulteney (member for Middlesex), Sir Robert Walpole, Sir Joseph Jekyll (Master of the Rolls), Sir Thomas Saunderson, and several other Members; Mr. James Erskine (member for Clackmannanshire) in particular reckoned up the Number of Play-Houses then in London, viz. the Opera House, the French Play-House in the Haymarket, and the Theatres in Covent Garden, Drury Lane, Lincoln's Inn Fields,† and Goodman's Fields;‡ and added, 'That it was no less surprising than shameful, to see so great a Change for the worse in the Temper and Inclinations of the British Nation, who were now so extravagantly addicted to lewd and idle Diversions, that the Number of Play-Houses in London was double to that of Paris; that we now exceeded in Levity even the French themselves, from whom we learned these and many other ridiculous customs, as much unsuitable to the Mein and Manners of an Englishman or a Scot, as they were agreeable to the Air and Levity of a Monsieur. That it was astonishing to all Europe, that Italian Eunuchs and Singers should have set Salaries, equal to those of the Lords of the Treasury and Judges of England. After this it was ordered, *nem. con.*, that a Bill be brought in pursuant to Sir John

---

* There was at this time a project on foot for erecting a play-house in St. Martin's-le-Grand.

† This theatre stood at the back of what is now the Royal College of Surgeons.

‡ Leman Street, Whitechapel.

Barnard's motion, which was done accordingly. But it was afterwards dropped, on account of a clause offered to be inserted in the said Bill, for enlarging the power of the Lord Chamberlain with Regard to the Licensing of Plays.'"

In the year 1738-9, under an "Act for the more easy assessing, collecting, and levying County Rates" (12 Geo. II., c. 29), an addendum is made to the existing Vagrant Acts by authorising the charges for maintaining and conveying vagrants to be paid out of the general county rate.

In the same year we have a further development of the prohibition contained in the 14 Eliz., c. 5, and the 39 Eliz., c. 4, against poor persons who resort to the city of Bath to obtain charity in the form of "An Act for establishing and well governing an Hospital or Infirmary in the City of *Bath*" (12 Geo. II., c. 31).

It recites "that the Medicinal and Mineral Waters of the City of Bath have been found by long experience to give great relief to Persons labouring under, or being afflicted with divers Diseases, Illnesses, or Disorders incident to Human Bodies; but it very often happens that poor persons so afflicted live at a great Distance from the said City, and cannot bear the expense of going thither and attending to use the said waters, by reason whereof great numbers of such poor persons have been prevented from using and trying such waters to their benefit and relief" . . . It then goes on to state that £4,000 having been raised, a hospital or infirmary is to be erected . . . "Every person received into the hospital is to deposit in the hands of the Treasurer a sum of £3 if he comes from any part of England or Wales, and a sum of £5 if he comes from Ireland, in order to cover the expense of conveying him back to his parish, and upon his discharge, after being conveyed by the Beadles, Officers, or other persons employed by the Hospital at least thirty miles, if any person so discharged shall, after being conveyed as aforesaid, be found loitering, wandering, or begging within the said City of Bath, the Constable, &c., shall seize and apprehend him, and the Justice of the Peace or mayor may commit him to the next House of Correction to be kept to Hard Labour for three months."

The Act further recites that "several loose, idle, and disorderly persons daily resort to the said City, and remain wandering and begging about the Streets and other Places of the said City, and the Suburbs thereof, within the Parishes of Walcott and Widcombe under pretence of their being resident at the Bath for the benefit of the said Mineral or Medicinal Waters, to the great Disturbances of His Majesty's Subjects resorting to the said City;" as a remedy it then enacts, "that the Constables, Petty-Constables, Tything-men, and other Peace Officers of the City, and of the Parishes of Walcott and Widcombe, and also the Beadles of the Hospital are to seize, take, and apprehend all such Persons, and to carry them before the Mayor, or some Justice of the Peace, who, upon the oath of one sufficient witness, or upon his own View, or the Confession of the Person found wandering or begging, commit such Person to the House of Correction for any Time not exceeding Twelve Kalendar Months, and to be kept to Hard Labour, and receive Correction as a loose, idle, and disorderly Person."

The vestry minute book of Brislington, near Bristol, in this neighbourhood, records the following order in this year:—

"That no Parish Officer Doe for the future releive any Vagrant or Vagrants, or other travelling person or persons with Passes or otherwise, in order to discourage Strolers and other loose, idle, and Disorderly persons from stroling from their own Parishes."

On the 27th March, 1735, a Committee of the House of Commons was appointed to consider the Laws in Being relating to the Maintenance and Settlement of the Poor, and to consider what further Provisions might be necessary for their better Relief and Employment; this Committee, "having consider'd and examin'd this affair with great Care and Attention," came to several Resolutions:—

"1. That the Laws in being, relating to the Maintenance of the Poor of this Kingdom, are defective; and notwithstanding they impose heavy Burthens on Parishes, yet the Poor, in most of them, are ill taken Care of.

"2. That the Laws relating to the Settlement of the Poor, and concerning Vagrants, are very difficult to be executed, and chargeable in their Execution; vexatious to the Poor, and of little Advantage to the Public, and ineffectual to promote the good Ends for which they were intended.

"3. That it is necessary, for the better Relief and Employment of the Poor, that a public Workhouse or Workhouses, Hospital or Hospitals, House or Houses of Correction, be established in proper Places, and under proper Regulations, in each County.

"4. That in such Workhouse or Workhouses, all poor Persons,

able to labour, be set to work, who shall either be sent thither, or come voluntarily for Employment.

"5. That in such Hospital or Hospitals, Foundlings and other poor Children, not having Parents able to provide for them, be taken Care of; as also poor Persons that are impotent or infirm.

"6. That in such House or Houses of Correction, all idle and disorderly Persons, Vagrants, and such other Criminals as shall be thought proper, be confined to Hard Labour."

These resolutions were agreed to, and as a consequence a new general statute regarding vagrancy was brought forward and passed.

This Act, the 13 Geo. II., c. 24 (1739-40), recites that the number of rogues, vagabonds, beggars, and other idle and disorderly persons daily increases. It makes a distinction between idle and disorderly persons, rogues and vagabonds, and incorrigible rogues. In the first category it places all persons who threaten to run away and leave their wives or children to the parish, all persons who unlawfully return to a parish from whence they have been legally removed, all persons who, not having wherewith to maintain themselves, live idle without employment and refuse to work for the usual and common wages, all persons going about from door to door, or placing themselves in streets, highways, or passages, to beg or gather alms, all of whom may be committed to hard labour for any time not exceeding one month. Any person may apprehend such persons going about begging, and if they resist or escape from the person apprehending them they are to be punished as rogues and vagabonds. A reward of 5s. is to be paid for each person apprehended.

In the second category are placed "all persons going about as patent-gatherers, or gatherers of alms, under false pretences of loss by fire, or other casualty, or going about as collectors for prisons, gaols, or hospitals, all fencers and bearwards, all common players of interludes, and all persons who shall for hire, gain, or reward, act, represent, or perform any interlude, tragedy, comedy, opera, play, farce, or other entertainment of the stage without authority, by virtue of letters patent from his Majesty's predecessors, or from his Majesty, or without license from the Lord Chamberlain ; all minstrels, jugglers, all persons pretending to be gypsies, or wandering in the habit or form of Egyptians, or pretending to have skill in physiognomy, palmestry, or like crafty science, or pretending to tell fortunes, or using any subtil craft to deceive or impose upon any of his Majesty's subjects, or playing or betting at any unlawful games or plays; and all persons who run away and leave their wives or children, whereby they become chargeable to any parish or place ; and all petty chapmen and pedlars wandering abroad, not being duly licensed, or otherwise authorised by law, and all persons wandering abroad, and lodging in barns and other outhouses, not giving a good account of themselves, and all persons wandering abroad and begging, pretending to be soldiers, mariners, seafaring men, or pretending to go to work in harvest, and all other persons wandering abroad and begging." Soldiers wanting subsistence and having lawful certificates from their officers or the Secretary of War, mariners, or seafaring men, licensed by some testimonial under the hand and seal of some justice of the peace, setting down the time and place of their landing or discharge and the place to which they are to pass, and limiting the time of their passage, and persons going abroad to work at any lawful work in the time of harvest *or at any other time*, carrying a certificate in writing from the Minister, one of the Churchwardens or Overseers of the place where they live, declaring they have a dwelling there, are exempted from the Act.

All end gatherers, rogues or vagabonds escaping from custody, prison breakers, rogues, and vagabonds committing any offence under this Act after a first conviction, are punishable as incorrigible rogues.

Any person may apprehend a rogue or vagabond under this Act, and a reward of 10s. is to be paid for each apprehension.

Any officer refusing to use his best endeavours to take such offenders is liable to a penalty of from 10s. to £5. The Justices are to command a general privy search for vagabonds in the night four times a year.

Justices are ordered to pass vagabonds to their last legal place of settlement.

Vagabonds may be kept to hard labour till the next quarter sessions, or such shorter time as the justices think fit, and then sent away by pass. Incorrigible rogues may be sent to hard labour for any term not exceeding six months, and be corrected by whipping in such manner, times, and places as the justices shall think fit. Prison breakers of these classes upon conviction are to be sent to the colonies, and if they return before their time are to suffer death. Incorrigible rogues found begging after being passed home may be sent to the house of correction for three months and publicly whipped, and then sent home again. Masters of ships bringing any rogue, vagabond, or beggar, or any person likely to live by begging, from Ireland, the Isle of Man, the Channel Islands, or the foreign plantations, are liable to a fine of £5 besides the charges of reconveying the vagabonds. They are also obliged to take the rates settled by justices for returning vagrants. Penalties of from 10s. to 40s. are imposed on persons harbouring vagabonds. The privileges of the heirs of John Dutton in the county of Chester are declared exempt from the Act.

The prohibition against minstrels was no doubt primarily intended to protect the privileged members of that class in the same way as the privileged players. At a court of mayoralty held on the 28th November, 1733, we find that the corporation of Norwich passed the following resolution on the subject:—

"That for the future no person or persons be permitted, or do play in the streets upon any musical instrument, to any person or persons within this city or *county* (unless it be the company of musicians belonging to the city), without the licence of the mayor of the said city. This order not to extend to any person or persons that shall be sent for to any private or public house, for the diversion of any person or persons of such private family, or at any such public house : so as such person or persons do not presume to play at any irregular hours."

Like most of its predecessors, the Act appears, however, to have had little effect in mitigating the evils which it was intended to meet, as in the year 1741 we find a presentment to the Court of King's Bench was made by the grand jury of Middlesex "against the unusual swarms of sturdy and clamorous beggars, as well as the many frightful objects exposed in the streets;" in which they state, "that notwithstanding a very strong presentment to the same effect had been made by a former jury in 1728, they had found the evil rather increased than remedied. This they ascribe to negligence in the proper officers, and trust that a proper remedy will be applied, and themselves not troubled with the poor, at the same time that they are every day more and more loaded with taxes to provide for them ; and that his Majesty's subjects may have the passage of the streets, as in former happy times, free and undisturbed, and be able to transact the little business to which the decay of trade has reduced them without molestation."

This was soon after followed by the 17 Geo. II., c. 5 (1743-4), entitled "An Act to amend and make more effectual the Laws relating to Rogues, Vagabonds, and other idle and disorderly Persons." It repeals the 13 Geo. II., c. 24, and repeats the opening statement in that Act.

The categories of persons to be deemed vagabonds are the same as in the previous Act, and the same rewards for apprehension are authorised. The Act is not to extend to soldiers, mariners, or to persons going to harvest-work *only*, provided they carry proper certificates. End gatherers are to be deemed incorrigible rogues. Privy searches for vagabonds are to be made in the night four times a year. Vagabonds committed to the quarter sessions may be punished with a further term of six months' imprisonment and incorrigible rogues with a term of two years and to be whipped at the discretion of the justices. Justices are further empowered to send all above the age of twelve years to be employed in his Majesty's service either by sea or land at any time before their discharge from the house of correction.

Rogues and vagabonds breaking gaol are punishable as in the previous Act.

Masters of ships are bound, under a penalty of £5, to convey one vagrant for every twenty tons burthen, and justices are to limit the rates per mile for passing vagrants.

Wandering lunatics or pretended lunatics are to be kept safely locked up in some secure place, and if necessary to be there chained.

No person is to harbour any rogue or vagabond in any house, barn, or outhouse, under a penalty of 10s. to 40s.

Justices are empowered to place any child of a beggar over the age of seven years as a servant or apprentice with any local person until such child arrives at the age of twenty-one.

The privileges of the heirs of John Dutton are exempted as before, and this is the last occasion on which they are mentioned.

Again the Act was inefficacious, as we shall presently see. At Burton-on-Trent the simple plan of driving vagrants elsewhere was apparently put in force:—

"1749, Dec. 10.—Whereas great numbers of vagrants and sturdy beggars have for some time past frequented this town, and for preventing the same for the future, it is ordered that Robert Hinds be allowed 25s. quarterly, for his care and pains in looking after and driving out of town all vagrants and beggars both by night and day."

This plan was very probably adopted in other localities, as the prevailing sentiment appears to have been for each officer to try to shuffle his responsibilities on to the shoulders of some one else.

During this reign the Vagrant Act received two additions, the first of these, the 25 Geo. II., c. 36 (1751-2), entitled "An Act for the better discovery and bringing to Justice Thieves, Robbers, and other persons maintaining themselves by pilfering and defrauding mankind," authorises justices to examine any rogue and vagabond on oath as to his last legal settlement and means of livelihood, and empowers them to imprison him for six days if he cannot give a satisfactory account of himself. In the meantime an advertisement is to be published describing his person and the things found upon him; if at the end of that time no accusation is laid against him he is to be discharged. This Act is to continue in force for three years, but was made perpetual by 28 Geo. II., c. 19. The next addition was by 26 Geo. II., c. 34, s. 2 (1753), which enacts that the treasurer of the County shall on the production of a proper voucher pay the expenses of conveying vagrants through the county, "it being found that High Constables who are directed to do so often have not enough money in their hands for the purpose."

The condition of mendicity in the metropolis was not in any way improved by all this legislation, as in the year 1753 in "A Proposal for making an Effectual Provision for the Poor," *Henry Fielding* tells us—

"There is not a Parish in the Liberty of *Westminster* which doth not raise Thousands annually for the Poor, and there is not a Street in that Liberty which doth not swarm all Day with Beggars, and all Night with Thieves. Stop your Coach at what Shop you will, however expeditious the Trádesman is to attend you, a Beggar is commonly beforehand with him; and if you should not directly face his Door, the Tradesman must often turn his Head while you are talking to him, or the same Beggar, or some other Thief at hand, will pay a Visit to his Shop!"

CHAPTER IX.

1760—1820.

Accession of George III.—Persons damaging underwood, destroying quicksets or taking bark treated as vagabonds.—Report of the Committee of 1775 on vagrancy.—Condition of workhouses and legislation regarding them.—Persons having a criminal intent, poachers, and unlicensed dealers in lottery tickets deemed vagabonds.—Abuses of the system of passing vagrants.—Permission to soldiers, sailors, &c., to beg.—Mendicity in London in 1796.—Legislation regarding the removal of the poor—Alarming increase of vagrancy in 1814.—Report of a committee of the House of Commons.—Estimate of beggars in the metropolis, and their average receipts.—Encouragement of idleness and vice.—Common lodging houses.—Twopenny post beggars. — Knocker beggars. —Moveable beggars.—Public houses depending for support on beggars.—Impostures practised.—Depravity of beggars.—Irish vagrants in London.—Their idleness and gains as beggars.

By the commencement of the reign of George III., the condition of the labouring classes had materially improved, as is evidenced by the state of the exports, which amounted to nearly double the average of the years 1726-7-8, and by the largely increasing use of many of the necessaries of life.

The first legislation regarding vagrancy in this reign occurs in the year 1766, when we have another addendum to the then existing Vagrant Act in the form of a statute entitled "An Act for the better Preservation of Timber Trees, and of Woods and Underwoods ; and for the further Preservation of Roots, Shrubs, and Plants " (6 Geo. III., c. 48*). It recites that the preservation of timber trees, or trees likely to become timber, is of great consequence to this kingdom, and that many idle and disorderly persons have of late years made a practice of going into woods, underwoods, and wood grounds, and there cut, and carried away, great

---

* This Act is incorrectly referred to in the 45 Geo. III., c. 66, as the 36 Geo. III., c. 36.

WHIPPING STOCKS AT WALTHAM ABBEY (1886)

quantities of young wood of various kinds, for making of poles and walking sticks, and for various other uses; and in beach, and other woods and underwoods under pretence of getting firewood, have cut down, boughed, split off or otherwise damaged or destroyed the growth of the said woods and underwoods to the great injury and damage of the lawful owners, and that the laws in being are not found sufficient to remedy the aforesaid evils." It then enacts that any person who after the 24 June, 1766, shall go into the woods, underwoods, or wood grounds, of any of His Majesty's subjects, not being the lawful owners thereof, and shall there cut, lop, top, or spoil, split down, or damage, or otherwise destroy any kind of wood or underwood, poles, sticks of woods, green stubs, or young trees, or carry away the same, or shall have in his custody any such and shall not give a satisfactory account of how he came by the same, shall on conviction for the first offence forfeit any sum not exceeding 40s. together with the costs, for a second offence any sum not exceeding £5 and costs, and for a third offence shall be deemed an incorrigible rogue and punished as such. This was supplemented in the year 1768 by the 9 Geo. III., c. 41, which recites that great destruction has of late been made of hollies, thorns, and quicksets, growing upon his Majesty's forests and chases to the great prejudice of his Majesty's deer, and also of hollies, thorns, and quicksets growing in the woods, and woodgrounds of his subjects, and then enacts that the 6 Geo. III., c. 48, shall extend to such offences. A final addition was made to this Act in the year 1805 by the 45 Geo. III., cap. 66, which recites that great quantities of bark have of late been taken and carried away out of his Majesty's woods, forests, and chases by persons not having any legal right to take or carry them away. It then enacts that the 6 Geo. III., c. 48, and the 9 Geo. III., c. 41, shall extend to this class of offence, and that any person offending more than three times shall be punished for every subsequent offence as an incorrigible rogue.

According to the *Annals of Winchcombe and Sudeley* in Gloucestershire, six women were in the year 1800 stripped to the waist and flogged till the blood ran down their backs for "hedge pulling" under the Acts of 1766 and 1768; the whipping post is described as being a post in front of the Town Hall fixed in the ground, with iron rings secured in with hinges, leaving just sufficient room for the arms and legs to pass between the iron and the post; the offenders were locked in, and then the whipping commenced.

In the year 1775 a committee of the House of Commons was appointed to review and consider the several laws which concern the relief and settlement of the poor; and the laws relating to vagrants.

This committee reported that the poor were let out in several parishes at from 3s. 6d. to 4s. 3d. per head per week, their earnings being taken by their masters.

They also furnished statistics of the number of vagrants sent to the House of Correction in the years 1772, 1773, and 1774, of which the following is a summary :—

	1772.	1773.	1774.
In Counties in England	2,420	2,766	2,975
,, ,, Wales	14	14	14
In Cities and Towns	503	463	504
	2,937	3,243	3,493

Medium number of persons detained for a year :—

	1772.	1773.	1774.
In Counties in England	117	133	149
,, ,, Wales	—	—	—
In Cities and Towns	7	4	4
	124	137	153

In the north and south divisions of Oxfordshire it is reported that the prisoners have been maintained by their earnings, being employed in the former instance in carding, spinning, knitting, sewing, making skewers and shoemaker's pegs, and in the latter in carding and spinning. At Reading it is stated that their earnings were their only support. At Brecon, Abingdon, Cambridge, Lincoln, and Preston, the prisoners were allowed their earnings for their maintenance, but it is not stated whether the amount was sufficient for the purpose without external charitable supplementation. From Essex, Norfolk, Chester city, and Worcester, it is reported that the prisoners received the profits of their labour *towards* their maintenance.

The following is a summary of the attendant expenses :—

	1772.			1773.			1774.		
	Expenses in apprehending vagrants.	Expenses in passing them.	Expenses relative to those persons within the year.	Expenses in apprehending vagrants.	Expenses in passing them.	Expenses relative to those persons within the year.	Expenses in apprehending vagrants.	Expenses in passing them.	Expenses relative to those persons within the year.
	£ s.	£ s.	£ s.	£ s.	£ s.	£ s.	£ s.	£ s.	£ s.
In Counties in England	1261 14	9687 8	2375 17	1337 9	10514 2	2914 5	1465 3	10311 15	2691 13
In Counties in Wales	6 10	41 13	14 5	5 0	30 16	14 1	5 15	58 2	16 10
In Cities and Towns	93 11	373 4	52 17	88 6	360 4	53 0	91 15	359 3	76 19
	1361 15	10102 5	2442 19	1430 15	10905 2	2981 6	1562 13	10729 0	2785 2

In *Cumberland, Dorset, Essex, Stafford, Wilts,* and the town of *Derby,* the expenses for passing and apprehending are lumped together, but the above return is approximately accurate.

In *Middlesex* the amounts expended for passing vagrants during the above years were £256, £263, and £256 respectively; in *Somerset* £344, £274, and £273. In *Stafford* (the heaviest of all), £617, £694, and £637, the lowest amounts being £43, £71, and £43 in the county of *Dorset*.

From the remarks from *Middlesex* it appears that the returns included the city of *Westminster,* and that there was then an annual allowance to a person for passing vagrants, " which had reduced the expense about three-fourths, it having been about £1,000 per annum. The contractor cleared some of the Bridewells four times, and others twice a week, and amounted to about 1,200 in the year."

From *Somerset* it is stated that the Way Vagrants are generally passed from *Cornwall* and *Devon* to *London, Bath, Bristol,* &c.

Merioneth in the year 1774 returns its expenses relative to vagrants at 25s., which sum it is stated was incurred for one old Irish vagrant, who cost that amount in nursing.

From *Bury St. Edmunds* it is stated that those who could not spin were maintained by charitable contributions and victuals from the workhouse.

The report from *Newcastle upon Tyne* appears to raise a suggestive question as to the amount of supervision then exercised over houses of correction, as it states that during the years 1772 and 1773 the keeper was insane, and no books or accounts were to be found. In 1774 it states that fourteen men, nine women, thirteen boys, and one girl were sent to the house. This is the only instance in which a detailed return of persons is given, and if it in any way represents the proportions between children and adults in other places, it shows the great care which was necessary in their separation and supervision.

The resolution of the committee upon the information furnished to them is " that the said Abstracts may be a Foundation for this House to make effectual Provision for the better Employment, Relief, and Maintenance of the Poor; the Apprehending and Passing of Vagrants; and for regulating Houses of Correction within that part of *Great Britain* called *England*."

By this time the workhouses appear to have degenerated in their management to a lamentable extent, as Mr. John Scott, the benevolent Quaker poet who took great interest in the condition of the poor, writing in the year 1773 " On the present state of the parochial and vagrant poor " thus speaks of them :—

"A thorough acquaintance with the interior economy of these wretched receptacles of misery, or rather 'parish prisons,' called workhouses, is not easily to be acquired : in these, as in other arbitrary governments, complaint is mutiny and treason, to every appearance of which a double portion of punishment is invariably annexed : particular incidents shocking to humanity may have sometimes transpired ; but the whole mystery of iniquity perhaps never has been, nor ever will be developed. One thing is too publicly known to admit of denial, that those workhouses are scenes of filthiness and confusion; that old and young, sick and healthy, are promiscuously crowded into ill-contrived apartments, not of sufficient capacity to contain with convenience half the number of miserable beings condemned to such deplorable inhabitation."

The recital to the next Act, 22 Geo. III., c. 83 (1782),* entitled " An act for the better Relief and Employment of the Poor," gives us a clue to the cause of this shocking state of things, as it states "that notwithstanding the many Laws now in being for the Relief and Employment of the Poor, and the great Sums of Money raised for those Purposes, their Sufferings and Distresses are nevertheless very

---

* This Act is commonly known as *Gilbert's Act*, from the name of its framer, who was member for Lichfield from 1768 to 1796, and greatly interested himself in measures for improving the condition of the poor.

grievous; and by the Incapacity, Negligence, or Misconduct of overseers, the Money raised for the Relief of the Poor is frequently misapplied, and sometimes expended in defraying the Charges of Litigations about Settlements indiscreetly and inadvisedly carried on." By section 31 it then enacts that "all idle or disorderly persons, who are able but unwilling to work or maintain themselves and their Families, shall be prosecuted by the Guardians of the Poor of the several Parishes, Townships and Places, wherein they reside, and punished in such Manner as idle and disorderly Persons are directed to be by the 17 Geo. II., c. 5. Any Guardian who shall neglect to make complaint against such person to some neighbouring Justice within Ten days after it shall come to his Knowledge shall forfeit a sum not exceeding £5 nor less than 20s. a moiety of which is to go to the Informer."

We now come to a series of enactments bringing persons having a criminal intent within the purview of the existing Vagrant Act; the first of these, the 23 Geo. III., c. 88, (1782-3), recites that " divers ill-disposed Persons are frequently apprehended, having upon them Implements for Housebreaking, or offensive Weapons, or are found in or upon Houses, Warehouses, Coachhouses, Stables or outhouses, areas of Houses, enclosed yards or gardens belonging to Houses, with intent to commit Felonies; and although their evil Purposes are thereby manifested, the power of His Majesty's Justices of the Peace to demand of them Sureties for their good Behaviour, hath not been of sufficient Effect to prevent them from carrying their evil Purposes into Execution." It then enacts that persons found with implements for housebreaking, or offensive weapons, with felonious intent, or found in any dwelling-house, warehouse, coachhouse, stable or outhouse, or in any enclosed yard or garden or area with an intent to steal are to be deemed rogues and vagabonds under the 17 Geo. II., c. 5.

The next is the 39 and 40 Geo. III., c. 50 (20 June, 1800), which recites that "idle and disorderly Persons frequently associate themselves to support and assist each other in the Destruction of Game in the Night, and are, if interrupted, guilty of great Violence by shooting, maiming, and beating, to the great Terror of His Majesty's Subjects, and to the Encouragement of Idleness and Immorality; and such Practices are found by Experience to lead to the commission of Crimes and Felonies." It then enacts that persons to the number of two or more found in any forest, chase, park, wood, plantation, paddock, field, meadow, or other open or enclosed ground, in the night, having any gun or engine with intent to kill or take game, or persons aiding them with offensive weapons may be apprehended, and on conviction before a justice shall be deemed rogues and vagabonds.

This was followed by the 39 and 40 Geo. III., c. 87 (28 July, 1800), which is styled " an act for the more effectual prevention of depredations on the river *Thames*, and in its vicinity." It recites under s. 12 that " divers ill-disposed and suspected Persons, and reputed Thieves, frequent the said River, and the Quays and Warehouses adjoining thereunto, and the Avenues to the same Quays and Warehouses, and the Streets and Houses leading thereto with Intent to Commit Felony." It then enacts that all such persons are to be deemed rogues and vagabonds.

The last of this series is the 42 Geo. III., c. 76, s. 18 (June 22, 1802), which recites that " divers ill-disposed and suspected Persons and reputed Thieves frequent the Avenues to Places of public Resort, and the Streets and Highways, with Intent to commit Felony on the Persons and Property of His Majesty's Subjects there being: and although their evil Purposes are sufficiently manifest, the Power of His Majesty's Justices of the Peace to demand of them Sureties for their good Behaviour, hath not been of sufficient Effect to prevent them from carrying their evil Purposes into Execution." It then enacts that every such person shall be deemed a rogue and vagabond.

This Act was only temporary, to last for five years. It was re-enacted in 1811 by the 51 Geo. III., c. 119, which in its turn was repealed by the 54 Geo. III., c. 37, s. 18 (Dec. 17, 1813), which, however, re-enacted its provisions.

Another class of persons who were brought within the purview of the Vagrant Act in this reign were unlicensed dealers in lottery tickets.

The 27 Geo. III., c. 1 (1787), styled " An Act to render more effectual the Laws now in being for suppressing unlawful Lotteries," recites that " the good and wholesome Laws from Time to Time made and provided for the Suppression of unlawful Lotteries, and against adventuring in Lotteries established by Acts of Parliament, in Great Britain or Ireland, by unlawful Sales of Chances of Tickets, and by Insuring for or against the Drawing of such Tickets, have not been found effectual for the purposes intended thereby."

It then enacts that all persons who deal in any lottery tickets, or sell chances without taking out a license from the Commissioners for managing the duties upon stamped vellum, parchment, and paper, are to be deemed rogues and vagabonds, within 17 Geo. II., c. 5, and punished as such.

The motives which prompted this enactment were partially moral and partially fiscal, as in the year 1778 an Act was passed by which every person keeping a lottery-office was obliged to take out a yearly license costing £50. This reduced the number of such offices from 400 to 51, and as a natural consequence numerous evasions of the law were from time to time perpetrated.

In 1802, minor lotteries held in public houses and similar places were dealt with by the 42 Geo. III., c. 119, styled "An Act to suppress certain Games and Lotteries not authorized by Law." It recites that "evil disposed persons do frequently resort to public houses and other places to set up certain mischievous games or lotteries, called little goes, and to induce Servants, Children, and unwary persons, to play at the said games, and thereby most fraudulently obtain great Sums of money from Servants, Children, and unwary persons, to the great impoverishment and utter ruin of many families." It then proceeds to enact that all games or lotteries called "little goes" shall be deemed public nuisances and against law. Persons keeping any office or place for any game or lottery not authorised by law shall forfeit £500, to be recovered by information, and are to be deemed rogues and vagabonds within the meaning of 17 Geo. II., c. 5. Persons so offending, against whom no such information shall have been made, are to be punished as rogues and vagabonds. Persons assisting offenders and persons employing others, though not discovered in the premises, are also to be deemed rogues and vagabonds.

Reverting to general enactments against vagrancy, we come to the 27 Geo. III., c. 11 (1787), which recites that doubts have arisen whether the 6 Geo. I., c. 19, gives a discretionary power to justices to commit vagrants and other criminals either to the Common Gaol or House of Correction, and authorises them to commit to the Common Gaol as well as the House of Correction.

This must have had a most pernicious effect in the case of young offenders, as the gaols at this period were perfect sinks of iniquity. We now come to a further evidence of the misconduct of the inferior officers appointed to carry out the Vagrant Acts.

The 32 Geo. III., c. 45 (1792), recites that "great abuses are committed in conveying from one place to another by passes persons who are not rogues or vagabonds, or in conveying such persons who are rogues and vagabonds without complying with the directions of 17 Geo. II., c. 5." It then enacts that all rogues and vagabonds ordered to be conveyed by pass are first to be publicly whipped, or confined in the House of Correction: that no reward is to be paid for apprehending rogues or vagabonds until they have been punished: that no female vagabond is to be whipped: that as the present mode of conveying vagrants in the custody of constables is frequently insufficient, from the misconduct and negligence of constables, justices may order vagrants to be conveyed by masters of Houses of Correction, or their servants: that justices at Sessions are to regulate the rates for passing vagrants: that the permission formerly accorded to soldiers and mariners is highly improper, and that those of them who beg shall be deemed rogues and vagabonds. It also enacts that any person who spends his money in alehouses, or places of bad repute, or in any other improper manner, and does not apply a proper proportion of the money he earns to the support of his wife and family, by which they become chargeable to the parish, is to be considered an idle and disorderly person. The wholesome provision regarding permitting soldiers and sailors to beg was, however, soon abrogated by the 43 Geo. III., c. 61 (24 June, 1803), styled "An Act for the Relief of Soldiers, Sailors, and Marines, and of the Wives of Soldiers, in the Cases therein mentioned." It recites that " Soldiers and Marines, and Sailors, or Persons discharged from such, having Occasion to return to their respective Homes or Places of Legal Settlement in *England*, which are frequently at a considerable Distance, are under the necessity of soliciting alms for their Relief, and that such solicitation is forbidden by the 32 Geo. III., c. 45," and then enacts that Every Soldier, Marine, or Sailor on carrying his Discharge out of any Regiment, Ship, or Vessel, within three Days to the nearest Chief Magistrate, shall receive a Certificate of his Place of Settlement, fixing the time he is to reach it at the rate of 100 miles in 10 days and so in proportion, on producing of which, being in his Time and Route, he shall not for asking Relief, be deemed a Vagabond. Wives of non-Commissioned Officers or Soldiers on making Proof of not being permitted to embark with their Husbands, shall receive from the nearest Chief Magistrate a like Certificate of their Place of Settlement, which will entitle them to ask Relief while in their Time and Route. In case of duly proved accident or sickness, by which the holder of the certificate is prevented from proceeding on his or her journey, the Magistrate of the Place where the person shall be, shall grant a new Certificate." This economical measure, though it relieved the treasury of a charge which it ought to have borne, is by no means creditable to the Government of the day, and is in striking contrast to the spirit of the 43 Eliz., c. 3, which authorises the treasurers of counties to help disabled soldiers and mariners on their way, and forbids the latter to beg under severe penalties.

The effect of enforcing the whipping of vagrants before passing them was to increase the crowd of beggars in London.

A writer in the "Gentleman's Magazine," in December, 1796, says: "In my late walks about London and its environs, I have observed with concern the multiplied swarms of beggars of every description. That concern is increased by the menacing approach of this winter. Impressed with the idea that more of these miserable objects are beggars by choice than by necessity, I leave them with the wish that our laws, or the magistrates, whose business it is to put these laws in execution, would at least endeavour to lessen their number, or by some badge or other means of distinction enable kind-hearted Christians to discern their proper objects."

In a work by Mr. P. Colquhoun, a magistrate, styled "A Treatise on the Police of the Metropolis," and published in the year 1797, the following estimate is given of the number of vagrants in London at this period :—

Strangers out of work, who have wandered up to London in search of employment, and without recommendation, generally in consequence of some misdemeanor committed in the Country ; at all times above	1,000
Strolling Minstrels, Ballad-Singers, Show-men, Trumpeters, and Gypsies	1,500
Grubbers, Gin-drinking Women, and destitute Boys and Girls wandering and prowling about the streets and bye-places after Chips, Nails, Old Metals, broken Glass, Paper, Twine, &c., &c., who are constantly on the watch to pilfer when an opportunity offers	2,000
Common Beggars and Vagrants, asking alms, supposing one to every two streets	3,000
Total	7,500

In another work, styled the "State of Indigence, and the Situation of the Casual Poor," Mr. Colquhoun remarks—

"The expense of the class of persons denominated *Casual Poor*, who have no settlement in any parish in the Metropolis amounts to a large sum annually. In the united parishes of St. Giles in the Fields and St. George, Bloomsbury, this expense amounted to £2,000 in the year 1796. It arose from the support of about 1,200 poor natives of Ireland, who but for this aid must have become vagrants. The shocking abuse of the vagrant passes previous to the year 1792, produced the Act of the 32 Geo. III., c. 45, which requires that Vagrants should be first publicly whipt, or confined seven days in the House of Correction (females to be imprisoned only, and in no case whipped) before they are passed, as directed by the Act of the 17 Geo. II., c. 5. Hence it is that so many who are either on the brink of vagrancy or have actually received alms, are permitted to remain a burden on the parishes, the Magistrates being loth to incur the charge of inhumanity, by strictly following the letter of the Act, in whipping or imprisoning poor miserable wretches, whose indigence has rendered relief necessary."

"In all the 146 parishes within and without the walls, including the Bills of Mortality, &c., it is not improbable that the casual charity given in this way may amount to £10,000 a year."

The country was as badly infested with beggars as London itself. "Common beggars are greatly multiplied from the same cause of general neglect. The Traveller now passes near no populous village, without being assailed by this new species of parish Mendicants. These are encouraged under that general relief, which officers indiscreetly give to paupers, whose children are suffered to grow up around them without any other employ than begging of the passengers, breaking fences for fuel, or other idle habits, which invariably attach to them through life." *

It is also stated "that it is a common practice for children, put out to nurse in the country by London parents, to be compelled to bring home firing for their nurses by such means, and even to take up, in their richer neighbours' names, articles of grocery, &c., at the shop where they dealt."

This is followed in the year 1807 by another doleful cry from London: "Surely something will be done to cleanse the streets from that Augean filth, the beggars; a most indelible disgrace to

* Dudley.

these enlightened times, a dreadful imposition on the public, in which the cause of real charity is not served, and which only tends to the increase of the nuisance—I mean, as to the charity bestowed on these very improper though unfortunate objects." *

Legislation now again claims our attention, this time of a humanitarian character.

The 35 Geo. III., c. 101 (22 June, 1795) recites the powers of removal given by the 13 and 14 Car. II., c. 12, and the 8 and 9 Will. III., and "that many industrious Poor Persons chargeable to the Place where they live, merely from Want of Work there, would in any other Place, where sufficient Employment is to be had, maintain themselves and Families without being burthensome to any Parish, and such Poor Persons are for the most part compelled to live in their own Parishes, and are not permitted to inhabit elsewhere, under Pretence that they are likely to become chargeable to the Parish into which they go for the Purpose of getting Employment." It then enacts that thenceforth "no poor person shall be removed until he has become actually chargeable to the parish he then inhabits."

It also recites that Poor Persons are often removed or passed to the Place of their Settlement during the Time of their Sickness, to the great Danger of their Lives; and then enacts as a remedy "that if any poor person shall be brought before a Justice for the Purpose of being removed by virtue of any Order of Removal, or of being passed by virtue of any Vagrant Pass, and it shall appear to the Justice that the Poor Person is unable to Travel, by reason of Sickness or other Infirmity, or that it would be dangerous for him or her so to do, the Justice is required and authorised to suspend the execution until he is satisfied that it may be safely executed. The charges incurred by such Suspension to be paid by the Officers of the Parish to which the poor Person is ordered to be removed." The Act is not to alter the powers of justices to pass or punish vagrants by 17 Geo. II., c. 5.

It further enacts, "Every Person who has been convicted of any Felony, or who appears on the oath of a credible witness to be a Person of evil Fame, or a reputed Thief, not being able to give a satisfactory account of himself or his way of living shall be liable to be removed to the Parish of his last legal settlement by order of the Justices.

* "Gentleman's Magazine."

The 49 Geo. III., c. 124 (20 June, 1809), makes a technical alteration in the 35 Geo. III., c. 101, and then enacts "that in order to avoid any Pretence for forcibly separating Husband and Wife, or other Persons nearly connected with or related to each other, and who are living together as one Family at the Time of any Order of Removal made, or Vagrant Pass granted during the dangerous Sickness or other Infirmity of any one or More of such Family, on whose account the Execution of the Order of Removal or Vagrant Pass is suspended;" such order shall be suspended for the same Period with respect to every other Person named therein, as already described.

The next acts regarding the poor are conceived in the same spirit, as the 50 Geo. III., c. 52 (9 June, 1810), repeals the 8 and 9 Wil. III., c. 11, which requires poor persons receiving alms to wear badges, and the 52 Geo. III., c. 31 (1812), repeals the 39 Eliz., c. 17, against lewd and wandering persons pretending themselves to be soldiers or mariners, and which directed that they should suffer as felons.

At the end of the year 1814 a further alarming increase of vagrancy took place, owing to the disembodying of many militia regiments, the reduction of the army in general, and the dismantling of a large portion of the navy.

The practice of begging in London had arrived at such a pitch that on the 8th of June, 1815, the Rt. Hon. George Rose called the attention of the House of Commons to the state of mendicity in and about the metropolis. He said that a recent institution of great utility had been the means of many inquiries into the subject. Mr. Martin, a gentleman connected with it, had calculated, from pretty good sources, that there were more than 15,000 beggars in and about the metropolis. Of these, some had settlements; they amounted to 6,690, of whom 4,150 were children, and 2,540 adults. There were 2,604 who had settlements in the country of England, of whom 1,137 were adults and 1,467 children. Those without settlement were estimated at 5,310, of whom 3,273 were children. There were Scotch and Irish; the Scotch amounted to 504; 177 had no settlement whatever, and were foreigners. On the whole, there were 9,288 children, and 6,000 adults, living by begging, making 15,288. Some of these could occasionally earn as much as forty shillings a week; but, not belonging to benefit societies, when they were ill their wives and children went a-begging. The support of all these people, taking them at 3s. a day, and he knew many received much more, would come to £328,000 a year for the adults. The inconvenience in the streets was the least part of the evil. The great mischief was, that the children were brought up in all sorts of idleness and vice. The beggars would seldom send a child to the new schools; which, in many cases, had been of incalculable benefit: there were even instances of the children educated therein having reformed their parents. The most importunate beggars were seamen who were wounded, and who were, therefore, entitled to their pension of £18 a year. He then moved for "a committee to inquire into the state of mendicity in the metropolis and its neighbourhood," which was agreed accordingly.

The report of the committee was presented to the House on the 11th of July, from which the following particulars are extracted.

The number of mendicants in the metropolis was estimated at 30,000, and most of these persons gained more than many industrious individuals of the lower classes of the community. One man actually acknowledged that his profits were about thirty shillings a day. This might be a singular case; but it was proved by the strongest evidence, that the average receipts of mendicants in London were from three to six shillings a day. This money was spent in the most exceptionable manner, in dram shops, at feasts, and even in the purchase of luxuries of all sorts, eatable as well as drinkable. Many parishes farmed their poor; about one hundred parishes in the City did so. Six or seven shillings a week each were allowed to those by whom they were taken, and who sent them out to beg during the day for the purpose of saving their provision.

Mr. Stevenson, who was overseer of St. Giles's parish the preceding year, said: "Most of these beggars have no lodging. There are houses where there are forty or fifty of them, like a gaol. The porter stands at the door and takes the money; for threepence, they have clean straw, or something like it; for those who pay fourpence there is something more decent; for sixpence they have a bed. They are all locked in for the night lest they should take property. In the morning there is a general muster below. The servants go and examine all the places, to see that all is safe; and then they are let out into the street, (just as you would open the door of a gaol,) forty or fifty of them together, and at night they come again : they have no settled habitations, but those places to which they resort, but there are numbers of those houses in St. Giles's."

The evidence of the Rev. W. Gurney, rector of St. Clement Danes, a gentleman of well-known humanity and consideration for the poor, is very interesting, "I am rector of St. Clement Danes, and minister of the Free Chapel in West Street, St. Giles's. In the Free Chapel there is accommodation for 600 poor. In the course of my ministry there I have had occasion to visit persons in very great distress, and have seen a great deal of suffering. I have ascertained that there are four different sorts of beggars, or persons not having habitations, or rather four different ways of begging. Some are by letters: these are called *twopenny-post beggars*. Some are what we call *knocker-beggars*, who go from house to house, knocking at every door. They contrive to get a knowledge of persons from others residing in the same street; and, if they can get information of any one residing in a street, they go to that house, and, if they succeed, or even if they do not get anything, they say, 'I have been to Mr. Gurney's or some other person's, and I want to make up a sum of money to pay rent;' whereas perhaps they pay no rent. A third sort of beggars are *stationary* the whole day; they come to their stand at a certain hour, and they stay so many hours, and then are led perhaps to another stand. These persons get a great deal of money, and live very well, especially if they are pretty well maimed, or if they are blind, or if they have children. There is a fourth sort, women and children, who are *moveable beggars*; they move about with the people, not particularly by the street, but with the people: for instance, at the time of the play they are always very near the theatres; and, if they see a gentleman and lady walking together in deep conversation, they will pester them, and run before them till they get a penny or twopence to get rid of them. Those people at other times of the day, if it is a Sunday for instance, will be found near chapels where there are large congregations; they know as well where the large congregations are as possible; not that they ever go within side the doors, they keep without-side, and there they speak of the benevolence and charity of the people coming out, and pray for them. If they get anything it is well, if not, perhaps they will afterwards utter imprecations against them, which I have frequently heard."

Mr. Gurney might have added that these beggars are of all persuasions. There was one who regularly stood at the door of the Catholic Chapel of Lincoln's Inn Fields, petitioning "for the love of the Holy Virgin," and other Catholic saints; in half-an-hour afterwards he was at the door of a dissenting meeting house bawling "for the love of Christ." The evening placed him at West Street, or at some other chapel belonging to the Established Church.

"There are five large gin-shops, or wine vaults as they are called, close to the Seven Dials, which are constantly frequented. There is one where they go in at one door and out at another, to prevent the inconvenience of returning the same way, where there are so many. A friend of mine, who lived opposite, had the curiosity to count how many went in the course of one Sunday morning, before he went to church, and it was 320."

The following information was given by Joseph Butterworth, Esq., M.P., one of the committee of the Strangers' Friend Society. "In the course of my observations I have noticed the condition of many beggars, and in the general way they have been found to be impostors; and I am persuaded they are the most profligate and idle description of character. I am convinced that very few, if any, honest, industrious, and sober people ever have recourse to begging. In the neighbourhood where I live there is a great resort for beggars; and I have made some inquiries into their condition. There are two public-houses in Church Lane, St. Giles's, whose chief support depends upon beggars; one called the *Beggar's Opera*, which is the Rose and Crown public-house, and the other the Robin Hood. The number of beggars that frequent those houses, at various times, is computed to be about 300. I have been credibly informed they are divided into companies, and each company is subdivided into what are called *walks*, and each company has its particular walk; if this walk be considered beneficial, the whole company take it by turns, each person keeping it from half an hour to three or four hours; their receipts at a moderate calculation cannot be less than three to five shillings a day each person, frequently more. They cannot be supposed to spend less at night than half-a-crown, and they generally pay sixpence for their bed. It is their custom to sally out early in the morning, and those who have any money left of the preceding day's earnings treat the rest with spirits before they begin the operations of the day. I have been informed, that they have a kind of committee to organise the walks to be frequented by each person, and they generally appropriate the best walks to the senior beggars in rotation. There is an Irishman who pretends to be a sailor, and frequently cuts his legs to excite compassion; he begs shoes and then sells them; he is a most audacious fellow, and has several times been imprisoned. Another man, half naked, and who generally appears in that condition, has, I am credibly informed, a considerable sum of money in the funds; he is a young man with a long beard; he frequently has flowers in his hand, and limps, he will not act with the gang, but preserves his own independence, and is one of the greatest boxers in St. Giles's. I understand that, after the business of the day is over, they frequent those houses and partake of the best food they can obtain; they spend their evenings in a very riotous manner; the food that is given them by benevolent persons they do not eat, but either throw it away or give it to the dogs. Women have been frequently known to assume an appearance of pregnancy, in order to obtain child-bed linen, which, in many cases, they have done eight or ten times over. I know a sober hackney-coachman, upon whose veracity I can depend, who has frequently conveyed beggars to their lodgings; and formerly, when he plied in St. Giles's, has been called to the houses I before mentioned, to take them from thence, being so intoxicated they could not walk home. A fact lately came under my observation of a person in Charles Street, Drury Lane, who, with his wife, obtained their living by begging; she lately lay-in; a benevolent neighbour, perceiving she had no bed or bedstead, furnished her with them, but he soon found they were not used. The bedstead was cut up and made into a rabbit-hutch; and the reason assigned by the beggar was this: that benevolent persons would occasionally visit them, and finding that they had neither bed nor bedstead, would be more disposed to give them money; and he wished to appear as mean as possible.

"The visitors of the Strangers' Friend Society, on the eastern part of the town, report that they never knew any worthy characters found in the streets begging. I have known several instances of persons obtaining considerable sums, daily, by begging. About two months ago some children in Russell Square attracted my attention; I inquired particularly into their history; and I found the mother supported by a daughter, a girl about twelve years of age, who also appeared very dirty and offensive. The girl informed me she had been six years engaged in begging for her mother; that on some days she gets three or four shillings, besides coppers; that on Christmas Day last she earned four shillings and sixpence, that she usually gets about eighteen pence a day. I inquired of the mother whether the child had any instruction; she said she had not, and she gave as the reason that she had no suitable clothes to go to school in. The mother was furnished with money to procure suitable clothing, and the child was sent to the Sunday school in Drury Lane, which she attended two or three Sundays; but, like many other similar cases, she then absented herself.

"A boy, aged fifteen years, was placed by his mother by the wall near Whitechapel workhouse. On application to the mother, entreating her to let him be taken into the workhouse, she would not consent unless they would allow her 36s. or 38s. a week, as, she stated, that upon an average was but a part of his gains. The Society well knew a negro beggar, who, about two years since, used to stand by Messrs. Elliott and Robinson's tea warehouse, near Finsbury Square, who has retired to the West Indies, with a fortune, it was supposed, of about £1,500 obtained by this way of life."

Mr. S. Roberts, watch-house-keeper, Bloomsbury, said: "My opinion is, that a great number of the beggars who go about are not in distress, that they are impostors: I have knowledge of one man in particular, that goes about and pretends to be in fits in the street: he chews soap, and has been taken several times in imposing upon people; he was taken in Lincoln's-inn-Fields about a fortnight ago, and committed for a month: his name is John Collins; he is known by the beadles by the name of the soap-eater. There is another, a woman, a good deal in Lincoln's-inn-Fields, of the name of Anne Phillips; she has been passed to St. Sepulchre's a number of times, but it is impossible to keep her away from that neighbourhood. There is a little black man who has frequently been brought into the watch-house for begging. I have seen him have a bag with silver, and another bag with copper; and at other times he has come to fetch me to take up people who have robbed him of a great deal of money, as he stated: and I have been told at the public house he would spend fifty shillings a week for his board, he would spit his own goose or his own ducks, and live very well."

Mr. Cooper, connected with the Spitalfields Benevolent Society, stated "that in January, February, and March, 1814, the Spitalfields Society was called upon for very particular exertions. A committee, consisting of about sixteen persons, visited, in the course of those three months, I suppose at least 800 different families. From the observations I made upon the state of poor families, I have no idea at all that, in any individual case, persons that were worthy objects, however, distressed they were, have had recourse to street begging."

Mr. John Daughtry, in the same connection, was asked what his general opinion was as to the character of street-beggars, derived from any information he had acquired.—"That they are idle and worthless; the visitors of the Spitalfields Benevolent Society, with which I am connected, having been led to adopt as a maxim, 'That street-beggars are, with very few exceptions, so utterly worthless and incorrigible, as to be undeserving the attention of such a Society.' I would beg to state as a general observation, that, when persons are by any means driven to the practice of street begging, their characters become so depraved, that they are seldom of any use to society or their families afterwards; they generally become openly depraved and immoral to a very great degree. But the instances in which worthy, honest, industrious, persons have recourse to begging, are extremely rare; they will in general rather starve than beg. A person of veracity, who some time ago visited 1,500 poor families in the neighbourhood of Spitalfields, affirms that out of 300 cases of abject poverty and destitution, and at least 100 of literal starvation, not a dozen had been found to have had recourse to begging: many of the most wretched of the above cases had been not long before able to support themselves in some comfort, but want of employ had completely ruined them; they were at that moment pressed by landlord, baker, and tax-gatherer; had pawned and sold everything that could be turned into money; were absolutely without a morsel of food for themselves or family; but still had not had recourse to begging. As a general fact, the decent poor will struggle to the uttermost, and even perish, rather than turn beggars.

"After some of the preceding observations, it need scarcely be stated, that the class of persons under consideration is believed to consist almost exclusively of the idle and profligate, the greater part depraved and abandoned beyond description, only less vicious and injurious to society than professed thieves and housebreakers. In most cases, idleness and hypocrisy are so wrought into their natures, that they are absolutely incurable. Living by hourly deception, *they have less character than even thieves*, and are more hopeless as to moral reformation: they are known to be *too idle even to beg when they have a shilling left to spend*, or can find a public-house or chandler's shop that will trust them."

Mr. William Hale, of Spitalfields, said: "I have known instances of my own work people who have left good looms of work to go out begging. Some time back, in Old Broad Street, leading to the Royal Exchange, where there are a number of merchants who walk about four o'clock towards the Exchange, coming towards Spitalfields I met a woman, as I was crossing the street in a hurry; she had an infant in her arms, and asked charity; I looked her in the face, and she was very much confused; she and her husband worked for me at the time; he had a good loom's work, and she silk-winding, which I was at the time very much in want of.

"There was a woman who used to go to a chapel in the City Road, as she said: one of our overseers was coming out in the evening after service, when he heard a voice, 'Pray, remember a poor blind child; have pity on a poor blind child.' Knowing the voice, he turned round, and recognized her to be one of our paupers, who had borrowed or hired this blind child for the purpose of exciting pity; for it is a very common thing for them to hire or borrow children to go out begging; and if you meet with a woman who appears to have twins, in ninety-nine cases out of a hundred they are not her own, or not both her own. *I have known a woman sit for ten years with twins; they never exceeded the same age.* Some, who are well practised in the art of begging, will collect three, four, or five children, from different parents of the lower class of people, and will give those parents sixpence or even more per day for those children to go begging with; they go in those kind of gangs, and make a very great noise, setting the children sometimes crying in order to extort charity from the people. Many children also are sent out by their parents as soon as it is possible for them to extort relief, and distributed about.

One perhaps takes a broom; and if they do not bring home more or less, according to their size, they are beaten for it. A family is the greatest resource of such persons.

"Some mendicants employ a certain portion of their time in finding out the committee-days of the respective parishes, when they meet and relieve their out-door poor; and it is very well known they go to one vestry on a Monday, a second on Tuesday, and a third on Wednesday, and so on. They will tell such tales of distress, which appear so interesting to gentlemen not deeply versed in their duplicity, that they are sure to gain upon their feelings, and they get 1s. or 1s. 6d. or 2s. 6d. from each."

Mr. G. H. Malme, of St. John's, Westminster, said: "Going along the High Street, Borough, I saw a number of persons, whom, by their appearance, I knew to be itinerant beggars, travelling by passes. Observing a man and his family divide, close to the church, and the woman take a pass out of her pocket, I guessed the business they were upon; and, on paying a little attention to their further proceedings, found this family were making use of two passes; the woman went into the shop where one of the overseers resided, taking with her all the children; and the man went afterwards with some of them; by which means they got double allowance."

Mr. Hale was asked, "What is your opinion of the best means to prevent mendicity?" "To take every possible means of informing the public of what description these individuals are, and their sheer depravity; that they are not fit objects of their benevolence; *that in no instance should an individual give anything to a person that applied to him in the streets.* But the advantages arising from begging are such a temptation to the idle poor, not willing to work, that they would sooner be imprisoned three months in the year, than be deterred from the practice of begging the other nine."

The following evidence was given with regard to the earnings of beggars:—

Mr. Philip Holdsworth the senior City Marshal stated: "One officer, the week before last, in taking up a sailor whose dog carries his hat was seriously hurt by the populace. We proved on the average that that man with his dog got thirty shillings a day; that was proved by his own assertion when in Bridewell."

Mr. John Cooper, calico printer, 8, Queen St., Cheapside, said: "A female on being remonstrated with for pursuing such a course, stated that it was a bad street that would not produce a penny, and that she could travel sixty of those in a day; that that therefore was a better livelihood than any other she could follow."

Samuel Roberts, watch-house keeper of St. Giles's, stated: "He had heard some of them say it was a poor day they could not go through forty streets; and it was a poor street that would not turn out twopence."

John Furzman, round-house keeper in St. Giles's, said "He had many times heard them say, that it is a very bad day if they do not get eight shillings, and more than that."

The following estimate of the number of metropolitan beggars and their earnings was presented to the commitee by Mr. Matthew Martin.

I. Parochial Individuals.

a. of Home Parishes; inclusive of about 4,152 children, about	6,693
b. of Distant Parishes; inclusive of about 1,467 children, about	2,604
Total Parochial Children, about 5,619	
Total Parochial Individuals, about	9,297

II. Non-Parochial Individuals.

a. Irish; inclusive of about 3,273 children, about	5,310
b. Scotch; inclusive of about 309 children, about	504
c. Foreign, inclusive of 87 children, about	177
Total Non-Parochial Children about . . . 3,669	
Total Non-Parochial Individuals, about	5,991
Total Children about 9,288	
Total Individuals about	15,288

And the gross amount of the sums annually extorted from the public by their importunities cannot be computed at a lower estimate than what is *absolutely necessary* for the *maintenance* of such a body of people, although in beggary.

For 6,000 grown persons, at 6d. a day each, lodgings and clothes, inclusive	£54,750 0 0
„ 9,288 Children, at 3d. a day each, clothes inclusive	42,376 10 0
About 15,288 Individuals, at a gross annual expense of about	£97,126 10 0

It appears by the evidence of the person who contracts for carrying vagrants in and through the county of Middlesex that he has passed as many as 12,000 or 13,000 in a year;* but no estimate can be formed from that, as many of them are passed several times in the course of a year.

In 1817 a select committee was appointed to inquire into the working of the Poor Laws; from the evidence taken before this committee we gather some instructive evidence regarding Irish vagrants in the metropolis.

John Smith, one of the beadles of St. Giles's parish, stated that he conceived it would be a great relief if the Irish could be sent to their own country. They go into a cheap lodging-house that lets out lodgings at twopence, threepence, and fourpence a night, where they are accommodated if they have money, the people taking good care not to do it if they have not. Then the next day if they have no more money, " Go down to the workhouse, and you will get relieved." It is possible the beadle is sent to inquire into the circumstances: if he goes to the landlord, the landlord will coincide with the man if he says he has been in the parish a fortnight or a month, though he has not been there a night. When they have run a week's rent, and are not able to pay their lodgings, they are sent down to the Board; if eighteenpence or two shillings is given the landlord is ready to take it: the poor people are not the better for it, except by being allowed to stay a week longer. The wife will come on the Board day; she will get her money regularly at the Board, and the husband will come afterwards and get relieved too. They wander into the parish, and gain no settlement there, but stay as long as they can get a shilling; some of them will hardly move about to look after work. Among the casual poor there are some who practise these deceptions, who get double and treble what other respectable people do; if they go to inquire, they may find a bed of straw, and their clothes all rags—all appearance of distress. Saturday night comes, and the husband brings home a guinea, and the wife will perhaps get five or six shillings a week more, but it is all gone on the Sunday in making merry; and then by Monday morning they have nothing left, and they live upon a potatoe and a herring, or anything during the week, and the children are deserted.

He had no doubt that if there was a power of removing these people, on their becoming chargeable, it would get rid of a great weight on the parish; but he has found that a woman has been

---

* At an average cost per head of 6½d. to 7d.

drawing relief from their parish who has been living at Bow, and her husband has been receiving money for working at a soap manufactory at Bow, at a guinea a week. Many cases of that kind have occurred. He is of opinion that a large portion of those people could gain a livelihood if they were disposed. They might live very comfortably, and the parish would not be burthened in the manner it is.

To meet this state of things a clause was inserted in the 59 Geo. III., c. 12 (March 31, 1819), which recites "that poor persons, born in *Scotland* and *Ireland*, and in the isles of *Man, Jersey,* and *Guernsey*, frequently become chargeable to parishes in *England*, and no provision is made for the removal of any such poor person, unless he shall have committed some act of vagrancy, and shall be adjudged a rogue and vagabond, and that no person so adjudged can be lawfully removed without having been first publicly whipped or imprisoned in the House of Correction;" it then authorises justices to pass such persons in the form prescribed by 17 Geo. II., c. 5, without their having been first whipped and imprisoned. Regarding rogues and vagabonds born in *Scotland, Ireland,* or the isles of *Man, Jersey,* and *Guernsey,* it also authorises the justices to exercise their discretion, according to the circumstances of the case, as to whipping or imprisoning them prior to their removal.

CHAPTER X.

1820—1837.

Accession of George IV.—Report of the Select Committee of 1821 on Vagrancy—Review of previous legislation—Abuses tolerated and frauds practised—Cozenage and fraud connected with the system of conveyance by pass—Number of vagrants passed from 1807 to 1820—Vagrant Act of 1822—The existing Vagrant Act and the additions made to it—Irish and Scotch vagrants in England, and the cost of their removal—The Poor Law Amendment Act of 1834—Abuses connected with the removal of vagrants.

THE lower orders were in a disturbed condition on the accession of George IV., both from political causes and from the stagnation of trade. The Spafields Riots, occasioned by a meeting of distressed manufacturers and mechanics, had occurred in 1816, and a bread riot had taken place at Bridport in the same year. The windows of the Prince Regent's carriage were broken by missiles on his return from opening Parliament in 1817, and in consequence of the alleged disaffection of large bodies of the people repressive measures were passed through Parliament, giving the executive amongst other things the right of imprisonment without trial. This was immediately followed by the "Blanketeer" riot at Manchester and another in Derbyshire. In 1819 came the "Peterloo" Riot, and in 1820 the Cato Street Conspiracy. All of these disturbances being naturally favourable to the spread of vagrancy and vagabondism.

In 1821 another Select Committee was appointed to consider the existing laws relating to vagrants. The report of this Committee is instructive as to the abuses then prevailing. It says:—

"An attempt was made in the reign of George II. to simplify the then existing laws upon this subject, which produced the General Act of 17 George II., c. 5. But this Act has since been found to be extremely loose in its definitions and enactments, and

VAGRANTS AND VAGRANCY. 229

in several of its provisions of very doubtful intendment; and the difficulties thence arising have been abundantly increased by the addition of eighteen statutes* since passed, all bearing more or less upon the same subject.

" The inadequacy of these Acts to attain their object, numerous as they are, is clear from the increasing number of vagrants, and the enormous expense annually incurred by different counties in their apprehension, maintenance, and conveyance by pass.

" The abuses tolerated and the frauds practised under these laws have been unquestionably proved by the evidence which has been taken before your Committee, and are in fact but too general and notorious.

" The county reward of 10s., at present payable, has in some instances converted the apprehension of vagrants into a regular trade, so disgraceful in all its branches as even to prevent the more respectable constables from interfering with vagrants, from a dread of sharing the obloquy attached to their apprehension: It is in evidence that it has led to a system of collusion between the apprehender and the vagrant, and that the latter has voluntarily entered, or been invited, into the district of the former, and even been bribed to commit an act of vagrancy with the view of procuring the reward of 10s., which in some cases has actually been divided between the parties.

" The threat of commitment has lost its terror. The vagrant himself, so far from shrinking, throws himself in the way of it, is apparently solicitous for it, and in fact steps forward as a volunteer for prison.

" The system of conveyance by pass has been found to be one of inefficiency, cozenage, and fraud; it is in complete consonance with the wandering habits of vagrants, and is made a matter of trade. Their returns to the same place are frequent, and some of them within periods which evidently show that they could not have reached their parishes. From the accommodation afforded by the law as it stands, or at least by the administration of it as now enforced, a vagrant is enabled to migrate at the expense of the public, by putting himself in the way of apprehension, and he thus obtains a pleasurable jaunt to any part of the kingdom he

* The list of statutes handed in by the chairman enumerates sixteen only, the real number being twenty-two. The statutes omitted from the list are 28 Geo. II., c. 19; 6 Geo. III., c. 48; 9 Geo. III., c. 41; 22 Geo. III., c. 83; 35 Geo. III., c. 101; 42 Geo. III., c. 119.

may choose. If during his progress he wishes to change company or vary his route, no impediment prevents him, it being understood equally by the offender and the officer who has him in charge, that he is under no control. He has his summer and his winter haunts, to which he repairs at stated periods; and he has been known to remark, 'Why should I work for 1s. or 1s. 6d. a day, while I can be thus amused with seeing and laughing at the labours of others?' It would be irrational to expect the active services of a man who, supposing him to have a wife and four children, *would be in some counties conveyed free of expense*, and in a state of perfect indolence, with an allowance of £1 18s. 6d. per week from the county stock. Under such a course of proceeding the country is plundered, the law is violated, and its object unattained; for in a majority of cases it is fairly to be presumed that the vagrant seldom reaches the parishes to which he *really belongs*, and if he does he is rarely, if ever, detained there by the parish officers.

"The short periods of confinement for which most vagrants are committed, operate rather as a bounty upon delinquency than an actual chastisement. And what the law intended as a punishment has in many instances been contemplated not merely with indifference, but with satisfaction. The further punishment authorised by the law upon a repetition of the offence is generally prevented by the non-attendance of either prosecutor or witnesses at the Quarter Sessions. The constables have observed that it would be folly to get a man committed for six months when he is so likely within that time to give them the means of earning another 10s., and very few, if any, instances are to be found (in London) of rogues and vagabonds having been prosecuted at the sessions, until the establishment of that useful institution, 'The Mendicity Society.'"

In his evidence before this Committee, Mr. *Thomas Davis* says that he has happened to be present when many of these vagrants have been searched, and has known instances where they have had £20 or £30 about them at a time. He means the Irish particularly, and no others. With respect to the £20 or £30 which he has seen about them, it has been in silver or notes; in different ways it is all locked up in their boxes and in their little concerns; some of them have a great deal of money. The Scotch vagrants are as bad as the Irish vagrants; they are very shy about their money; they will not tell him much about it. Those persons who have money go home for good; they do not return. They ride home free of expense with all their little matters. He handed in the following statement:—

Number of vagrants passed from the year

1807 to 1808 amounted only to				540
1808 ,, 1809 ,, ,,				592
1809 ,, 1810 ,, ,,				721
1810 ,, 1811 ,, ,,				922
1811 ,, 1812 ,, ,,				1,014
1812 ,, 1813 ,, ,,				1,532
1813 ,, 1814 ,, ,,				1,973
1814 ,, 1815 ,, ,,				2,346
1815 ,, 1816 ,, ,,				2,894
1816 ,, 1817 ,, ,,				3,429
1817 ,, 1818 ,, ,,				5,401
1818 ,, 1819 ,, ,,				5,852
1819 ,, 1820 ,, ,,				6,689
Total passed in the above years				33,905

Mr. *Thomas Davis* was a contractor for the removal of vagrants to the borders of Middlesex, and had been so for fourteen years. He received at first £250 a year, which was afterwards advanced to £350; in addition, he received 6d. a day for the maintenance of each vagrant for a period not exceeding three days. He kept four receiving-houses, one at Egham, one at Colnbrook, one at Ridge, and one at Cheshunt, for which he paid six guineas a year each. His establishment consisted of seven horses, four men and a boy, three carts and two covered vans.

G. B. Mainwaring, Esq., acting magistrate of the county of Middlesex, said:—

The amount paid as ten-shilling rewards by the County of Middlesex in the year 1820 was £986, which gives a number of vagrants apprehended of 1,972
Take these 1,972, without considering those not apprehended, as exciting a daily contribution of at least 6d. per day, or £9 per annum, each on an average (exclusive of what they may have received from parish officers as casual relief) may be estimated at £17,748
Rewards for apprehension 986
Expenses of passing, subsistence, &c., paid 1,429
As each vagrant was confined one week in the House of Correction previously to being passed, 1,972, say, at 2s. 6d. per week . 246

Estimated present annual expense in Middlesex, exclusive of wages of parochial officers £20,409

Mr. *Cartwright*, a member of the committee, delivered in the following statement. A return of the number of vagrants passed through the county of Northampton for the quarter ending at Christmas, 1820 :—

Total number of passes	446
Ditto of individuals passed	686
Ditto of single men	276
Cost to the county	£352 1s. 8d.

Of these passes 149 were to Ireland, containing 241 individuals, of whom 93 were single men.

In the returns for the years 1772, 1773, 1774, the expenses incurred in passing vagrants through this county in those years are stated to be £377 10s. 2d., £414 5s. 6d., and £389 11s. 10d. respectively. In a little less than half a century the expense had therefore increased nearly fourfold.

The chairman delivered in a return of all vagrants passed from Liverpool to Ireland from the year 1814 to the year 1820, both inclusive :—

From Jan., 1814, to June, 1814	1,044
,, June, 1814, to June, 1815	4,294
,, June, 1815, to June, 1816	5,257
,, June, 1816, to May, 1817	6,654
,, May, 1817, to June, 1818	6,484
,, June, 1818, to June, 1819	6,637
,, June, 1819, to June, 1820	6,146
,, June, 1820, to Jan., 1821	2,897
Total	39,413

(Signed) R. CHAMBERS,
Pass-master, Liverpool.

The chairman read the following extract from a letter from Mr. Barrow, secretary to the committee for the suppression of vagrancy at Kendal, dated April 22nd, 1821 :—

"I think about the time we began the office, the vagrants in England had been reckoned at 60,000 (and the increase in the number relieved by the overseers between 1816 and 1817 was alarming—from 3,234 to 5,050), and that they were supposed on an average to collect *in money*, exclusive of clothes, £50 a year each, which, from the scenes of drunkenness in the streets and in the neighbourhood of the lodging-houses, does not appear to me to be a high estimate: these sums multiplied give £3,000,000 !!

"As to the number, I think it under-rated, for no one can suppose one-twelfth of the vagrants in England would pass and re-pass this place in the course of a year. Of this 60,000 I suppose one-third might be Irish and Scotch, who have no claim for parochial maintenance; but even supposing the whole 60,000 to belong to England, and that by the general refusal of relief, except at vagrant offices, they could be driven to their settlements, and allowing 3s. 4d. a head weekly for parochial maintenance, or one-sixth of their gains, the amount would be £500,000, leaving a balance of £2,500,000!! even supposing they were kept in a state of idleness; but if employed in almost any kind of labour, the value of that labour ought to be equal to their maintenance, which would leave a balance of £3,000,000.

"The situation of children brought up in vagrancy and mendicity struck me as being truly deplorable. Perhaps out of 60,000 about 15,000 or 16,000 may be reckoned as under fifteen years of age: from the wandering and dissolute lives of their parents they can have no means of instruction; bred up in lying, deceit, and every kind of art and trick to excite or extort charity; exposed to all the horrors of the common lodging-houses; their parents without the means or inclination to put them out to learn any honest trade, and if they had, who would receive the children fresh from the habits of vagrancy into their employ? And with little inclination to labour themselves, what chance is left for these unfortunate children (about 1,500 of whom may be thrown on the public annually) but to continue the vagabond life they have been brought up to, and increasing by marriage, or most likely without it, the number of vagabonds, or to seek their fortunes in large towns, or in the metropolis (where so many temptations abound). and swell the list of juvenile offenders so loudly complained of? . . .

"The unfortunate blind, objects of the greatest compassion, and who ought to have every attention paid to them at their own settlements, and who, I believe, by the care and attention of their neighbours and parish officers, would never be suffered to want anything that could add to their real comfort, are too often dragged about in all weathers (indeed, I believe the worse the weather the better the success), for the sake of gratifying the gin-drinking propensities of their wives and trulls. What used to be got by beggars of this description would scarcely be credited: I have frequently seen them get from 6d. to 8d. or 1s. in the street, in the course of five minutes; and have every reason to believe that no blind beggar ever got less in this town than a guinea a day, and on market days considerably more; and I was informed by a respectable lady, that a few days before we began the office she saw a woman who attended a blind beggar take *three guineas* worth of copper, at one time, to a shop in the town to get changed for more portable cash. I made inquiries through the town and Kirkland, and found that there was not a person almost who ever refused relief to the blind, and that the poorer classes frequently borrowed halfpence to give to them, and that people receiving parochial relief always gave their mite. I have reason to believe that the women who go about with the blind beggars are seldom their wives, and often treat them improperly; and know, that in the early part of 1818, a woman who attended one of them was seen beastly drunk three different times in one day.

"The blind beggars, those wanting a leg or arm, who have generally pensions of 1s. a day, the maimed, and those (and there is no inconsiderable number of them) who by tight bandaging the left arm, wrist, and hand, twisting the wrist and fingers, and making artificial sores from the elbow to the fingers, make themselves appear objects of compassion, extorted great sums of money, especially from the poor, who call them *great objects*, which was generally spent in dissipation.

"In mentioning those impostors, who by twisting the fingers and wrist of the *left* hand and bending the arm at the elbow joint, so as to *appear* to be crippled, I must call your particular attention to the subject; you cannot fail to have observed beggars of this description, and I can almost venture to assert that you never saw one of them exposing the *right* hand thus. I have for very many years noticed this species of imposition, and can imitate it tolerably well; and by exposing this trick and explaining it to the lower orders, found it very useful in getting their support to the plan adopted here. Except an officer, and this is the only exception, I never saw a person wounded to produce this particular appearance in the *right* arm; and out of the hundreds I have inquired of, I cannot find one who ever saw a beggar expose a *right* hand and arm in this way."

The report of the Committee was immediately followed by a temporary Act (3 Geo. IV., c. 40, 24th June, 1822). It recites "that it is expedient to amend the laws in force relating to Vagrants, and that it would tend to simplify them if the several provisions relating to such offenders were consolidated into one Act." It then repeals all former provisions relating to Rogues, but excepts the laws for the removal of persons born in *Scotland, Ireland,* or the

Isles of *Man*, *Jersey*, and *Guernsey*, who have not committed acts of vagrancy.

The following classes of persons who are not included in the present Vagrant Act are deemed idle and disorderly persons under this Act. All persons who threaten to run away and leave their wives or children chargeable, all common prostitutes or night-walkers wandering and not giving a satisfactory account of themselves. The following classes are treated as rogues and vagabonds. All persons going about as gatherers of alms, under pretence of loss by fire or other casualty, or as collectors under any false pretence, all bear-wards, all common stage players, and all persons who shall for hire, gain, or reward, act, represent, or perform any interlude or entertainment of the stage, such persons not being authorised by law; all persons pretending to be gypsies, all persons playing or betting at any unlawful game, or wandering abroad and lodging in alehouses.

Idle and disorderly persons may be committed to the House of Correction for any time not exceeding one calendar month.

Any person may apprehend offenders, and the penalty on any officers neglecting or refusing to execute their duty, or on any person obstructing them in the execution of their duty is a sum not exceeding £5 nor less than 20s., or in default hard labour for any time not exceeding three calendar months. Any person charged by a justice to use his best endeavours to apprehend an offender and refusing or neglecting to do so, is liable to a penalty of 20s. The justice may order an overseer of the parish to pay a reward of 5s. to any officer or other person apprehending an offender. Vagrants are to be searched, and their trunks and bundles inspected. Rogues and vagabonds and incorrigible rogues may be committed to the House of Correction until the next General or Quarter Sessions, or for any time not exceeding three months with hard labour; if committed to the sessions the justices there may order a rogue and vagabond to be detained for any time not exceeding six months, and an incorrigible rogue for any time not exceeding one year or less than six calendar months, and (except in the case of females) "to be corrected by whipping at such times and places within their jurisdictions as according to the nature of such person's offence they in their discretion shall think fit." Lodging-houses may be searched, and suspected persons brought before a justice. justices are not to grant certificates enabling persons to ask relief on route except to soldiers and sailors, under 43 Geo. III., c. 61. Persons asking alms under certificates, except soldiers and sailors, are to be deemed vagrants.

The Act is not to repeal the 10 Geo. II., c. 28, or any Act relating to players.

This Act was abrogated by the present Vagrant Act, the 5 Geo. IV., c. 83 (June 21st, 1824), which "recites that the 3 Geo. IV., c. 40, will expire on the 1st September, 1824," and that it is expedient to make further provision for the suppression of vagrancy and the punishment of idle and disorderly persons, rogues, vagabonds, and incorrigible rogues in *England*. It then repeals all previous Acts and enacts the following classification:—

Idle and Disorderly Persons.—Those able to maintain themselves and wilfully refusing or neglecting to do so, by which they become chargeable to any parish; those who return to a parish and become chargeable to it after being legally removed; pedlars and petty chapmen trading without license; common prostitutes behaving publicly in a riotous or indecent manner; those who beg or encourage any child to do so. *Punishment*, imprisonment with hard labour for any time not exceeding a month.

Rogues and Vagabonds.—Those who repeat any of the above offences; those who pretend or profess to tell fortunes, or use any subtle craft, means, or device, by palmistry or otherwise, to deceive and impose on any one; those who publicly expose any obscene print, picture, or other indecent exhibition; those who publicly expose their persons obscenely; those who endeavour by the exposure of wounds or deformities to gather alms; those who endeavour to collect charitable contributions under any false or fraudulent pretence; those who run away and leave their wives or children chargeable to any parish; those who publicly play or bet at any game or pretended game of chance; those who have in their possession implements for house-breaking or offensive weapons for the purpose of committing a felony; those who are found in any dwelling-house, warehouse, coach-house, stable, outhouse, inclosed yard, garden, or area, for an unlawful purpose; suspected persons or reputed thieves frequenting any public place with intent to commit felony; idle and disorderly persons who resist apprehension. *Punishment*, imprisonment with hard labour for any time not exceeding three months.

Incorrigible Rogues.—Those who break out of prison before the expiration of their term; those who have already been convicted

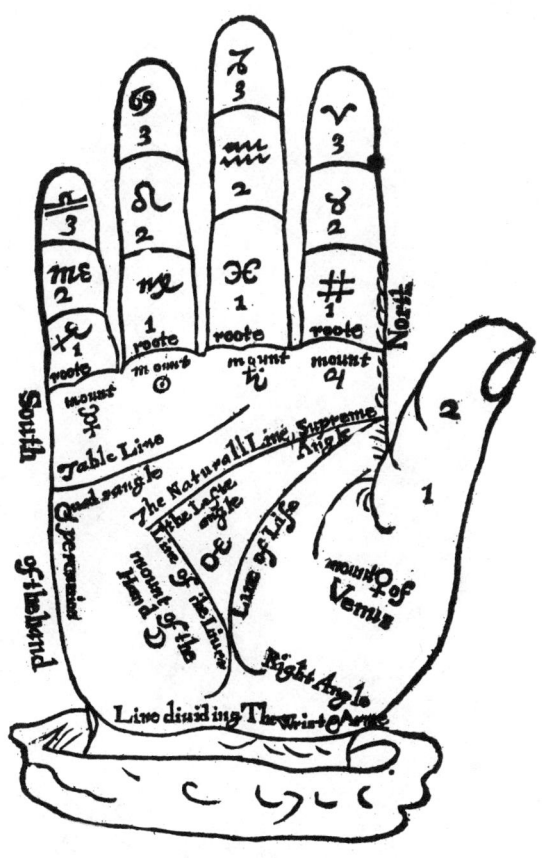

The Explanation of the fore-going Figure.

HEre visibly appears (in the foregoing Figure) the general division of the Hand, according to Art, as also the appellation of the parts thereof, from the roots of the fingers, to the Line dividing the Wrist and the Arm

PALMISTRY, OR CHIROMANCY

as rogues and vagabonds; and rogues and vagabonds who resist apprehension. *Punishment*, imprisonment with hard labour for any time not exceeding twelve months, with (in the case of males only) whipping at the discretion of the Justices in Quarter Sessions.

Any person may apprehend offenders, and constables who neglect their duty are liable to a fine not exceeding £5, or imprisonment for three months. Vagrants and their trunks, bundles, &c., may be searched, and money and effects found on them applied towards the expense of apprehending and maintaining them. Lodging-houses suspected to conceal vagrants may be searched, and suspected persons brought before a justice. Visiting justices of gaols may grant certificates to persons discharged to receive alms in their route to their place of settlement, any such persons loitering upon their route or deviating from it are to be deemed rogues and vagabonds and punished accordingly. Magistrates are empowered to grant certificates under the 43 Geo. III., c. 61, to soldiers, sailors, marines, and their wives, to ask alms in their route to any place.

Nothing in the Act is to alter any law in force for the removal of poor persons born in *Scotland, Ireland,* or the Isles of *Man, Jersey,* or *Guernsey,* and the Act is not to apply to *Scotland* or *Ireland.*

The former prohibition against bearwards is omitted in this Act, probably because it had proved futile for the purpose intended, as a writer in " Notes and Queries," speaking of this period, says :—

" I was never a witness of a bear-bait, but I well remember a poor brute who was kept alive for this sole purpose, at F——, in Lancashire. He was confined, as a general rule, in a small back-yard, where, sightless, dirty, stinking, and perhaps half-starved, his sole and constant exercise appeared to be moving his head and forequarters from side to side. When taken to other villages to be baited, his advent there was announced by a wretched fiddler, who walked before him and the bear-ward. Upon one occasion the story goes that he and a second champion of the like kind arrived at W. on the wakes day, before the evening church-service was completed. This, however, was rapidly brought to a close by the beadle calling to the preacher from the church door: ' Mestur, th' bear's come ; and what's more, there's two of 'em.' This freedom of speech in a holy place is less to be wondered at when it is known that the good rector and a party from the rectory usually witnessed the bear-bait from the churchyard adjoining the village green."

The 1 and 2 Vict., c. 38 (July 27, 1838), extends the Vagrant Act to those who expose obscene prints in shop windows.

The 31 and 32 Vict., c. 52 (1867-8), provides that those who game in public with any coin, card, token, or other means of wagering or gaming, are to be deemed rogues and vagabonds. This was repealed by 36 and 37 Vict., c. 38 (1873), so far as regards punishment, which allows magistrates at their discretion to impose a fine not exceeding 40s. for a first offence, and of £5 for a second in lieu of imprisonment.

A further extension was made by the 34 and 35 Vict., c. 112 (1871), which, with regard to every suspected person or reputed thief frequenting any highway or place adjacent, enlarged the construction of these words so as to include any place adjacent to a street or highway; and with regard to proof of his intent to commit a felony, it enacted that it should not be necessary to show that the person suspected was guilty of any particular act tending to show his purpose or intent, and he might be convicted if from the circumstances of the case and from his known character as proved to the court that his intent was to commit felony.

Other additions to the Act have also been made for the purpose of punishing idle or fraudulent persons in receipt of poor law relief.

By 5 and 6 Vict., c. 57, s. 5 (1842), any person relieved in a workhouse neglecting or refusing to perform a task of work suited to his age, strength, and capacity, or wilfully destroying or injuring his own clothes or damaging the property of the guardians, is to be deemed an idle and disorderly person.

By 7 and 8 Vict., c. 101 (1844), women able to maintain their bastard children, and neglecting to do so, are to be deemed idle and disorderly persons; and persons received into a houseless poor asylum giving a false name, or making a false statement, or giving different names on different occasions, are to be deemed rogues and vagabonds.

By 11 and 12 Vict., c. 110 (1848), persons applying for poor law relief and not making a correct disclosure of their means are to be deemed idle and disorderly persons.

By 12 and 13 Vict., c. 103 (1849), persons chargeable to the common fund of a union are to be regarded as persons chargeable to a parish, in regard to proceedings under the Vagrant Act.

By 28 and 29 Vict., c. 79, s. 7 (1865), paupers removed under an order of removal who return and become chargeable to the union within twelve months, are to be deemed idle and disorderly persons.

By the Poor Law Amendment Act, 1866 (29 and 30 Vict., c. 113, s. 15), persons relieved out of the workhouse who refuse or neglect to perform a prescribed and duly authorised task of work suited to their capacity, or wilfully destroy or damage tools, materials, or other property belonging to the guardians, are to be deemed idle and disorderly persons.

By 39 and 40 Vict., c. 61, s. 44 (1876), the word "pauper," in the Poor Law Amendment Act of 1834 is to include any person who obtains relief by wilfully giving a false name or making a false statement, and such person may be proceeded against as an idle and disorderly person.*

During the reign of George IV., Irish and Scottish vagrants continued to swarm in the kingdom, and a Select Committee of the House of Commons was, in the year 1828, appointed to consider the matter.

The report of this Committee states that—

"The number of Irish and Scotch paupers conveyed by the county of Buckingham was, in the last year, 4,904, and in the five years, 14,698. By the county of Lincoln, in the last year, 2,336, and in the five years 4,562. The total cost of the five years has been to Buckingham £1,532 11s., while it has only amounted in the county of Lincoln to £418 6s. 11d.

"In the counties situated on the western coast of England the burthen falls still heavier, partly owing to their being the general thoroughfare as regards the Irish, and being also charged with the entire expense of the transit of those persons by sea to the sister island.

"The numbers passed through the county of Lancaster amounted, in the last five years, to 22,045, of which 20,414 were Irish, and 1,631 Scotch. . . .

"It appears to your Committee that the expense of these removals is rendered much larger than necessary by the number of individuals to whose care the paupers are consigned, and of the counties who have to sustain this burthen, which, on reference to the returns transmitted by the different counties, will be found to extend, in the course of the last five years, to the amount of £56,120 4s. 2d.

* Proceedings under this Act are also authorised by 34 and 35 Vict., c. 108, and 45 and 46 Vict., c. 36.

" It might in fact be shown, that upon a calculation of the rates allowed for conveyance alone, by the different counties through which he would have to be passed, the removal of a single adult pauper from the metropolis to Liverpool amounts to £4 11s. 3d., a sum which, from the present facilities of communication is manifestly far beyond what the circumstances of the pauper can require. The present charge for an inside place in the mail being only £4 4s."

According to a return ordered by the House of Commons to be printed on the 14th of March, 1833, the number of Irish poor shipped under passes from the Port of *Liverpool* to *Ireland*, and the charge for passing them in each year, from 1824 to 1831 inclusive, was as follows:—

	No.	£ s. d.
1824	2,481	802 11 10
1825	3,028	1,078 14 9
1826	6,428	2,695 12 6
1827	6,055	2,196 11 0
1828	4,349	1,644 19 3
1829	5,086	2,224 12 3
1830	5,679	1,809 7 3
1831	5,863	1,800 11 8
	38,969	14,253 0 6

According to another return the number of Irish poor passed by sea from *Bristol*, from the 25th March, 1823, to the 25th March, 1832, was as under:

Names of Places and Date.		Male and Female of 10 years of age and upwards.	Male and Female under 10 years of age.	Male and Female under 2 years of age.	Total.	Charge for passing them in each year.
Commencing 25th March. There has been no distinct account kept of the number and charges of those brought from places not within the City of Bristol; but it is believed that nearly the whole of the numbers here enumerated were principally brought from London.						£ s. d.
	1823	806	111	82	999	702 13 3
	1824	610	170	83	863	471 15 8
	1825	650	189	95	934	506 14 2
	1826	834	221	106	1,161	563 17 9
	1827	1,161	338	144	1,643	621 8 2
	1828	693	247	93	1,033	326 12 0
	1829	891	278	131	1,300	412 0 0
	1830	1,524	388	193	2,105	687 4 0
	1831	2,628	643	277	3,548	1,179 16 0
		9,797	2,585	1,204	13,586	£5,472 1 0

In the year 1834 a sweeping change was made in the Poor Laws by the Poor Law Amendment Act (4 and 5 Wm. IV., c. 76). This change had long been necessary owing to the abuses current under the existing laws for the relief of the poor, which tended to foster idleness and improvidence on the part of the poor, and jobbery and peculation on the part of those placed in authority over them.

Vagrancy was generally in a flourishing condition, the Poor Law Inquiry Commissioners being of opinion that it had "actually been converted into a trade, and that not an unprofitable one." The commitments to gaol having been more than doubled in six years, being in 1825 7,092, and in 1832 15,624. The principal increase was in London, where the committals rose from 2,270 in 1829, to 6,650 in 1832. On the other hand, at Norwich the numbers had diminished, owing to the magistrates giving the vagrants asking for relief a small sum instead of committing them.

The abuses connected with the removal of vagrants still flourished in full force, as the following reports of the year 1834 amply testify:—

From the Overseer for Speenhamland, Newbury.

"There are frequent disputes between the carrier and the vagrants. The poor miserable horse which conveys them can scarcely get up the hills; when the driver requires them to walk to ease him, they refuse to do so. Hence disputes; they would ill-use and beat the driver did he not carry fire-arms."

From the Pass Master for the City of London.

"The paupers frequently come to me with boxes containing clothes, &c., but if they are large I refuse to carry them, and make them sell the boxes and put the things in a bag. While this interchange has been making, I have repeatedly seen lace caps and pellerines, and, in fact, whole wardrobes, better than that of my wife, in possession of women passed in this way. This, however, applies to the bonâ-fide cases: the old hands never have any luggage with them; they take care to keep it out of sight.

From the Pass Master for the Parish of St. Giles's.

"The greater part of the persons who are passed are, I believe, very poor; but there are many who not only have good suits of clothes on, but large bundles, band-boxes, and even trunks and chests, containing property. They always keep these out of sight until they have been sworn before the magistrates, because if they did not it would be at once seen that they had the means of getting on very well without passes.

"These people, especially the Scotch, stand up for their rights very much; they often refuse to get out of the carts to walk up hill, and insist upon carrying all sorts of luggage. A few weeks ago my partner and I, who were on our way to Barnet, had great difficulty in rescuing an old man who passes paupers from one of the neighbouring parishes from the hands of a party of them, who were 'pegging into him' because he required them to walk up Highgate hill owing to his cart being so heavily laden with women, children, and luggage. The lower class of the Scotch are, I think, the most dirty but the best educated. Their chief subsistence is salt fish, which they get at 1d. per pound, butter-milk at 1d. a quart, and potatoes."

From the Pass Master for the Parish of St. Luke's, Middlesex.

"Some of the vagrants behave very ill. They will come with luggage amounting perhaps to half a hundredweight, and they complain sadly, and often riotously, if I make any difficulty as to removing the whole. I have no power to search their luggage, but if I had, I have no doubt that I should find good clothes, and other useful property there; indeed, not long since a man whom I was passing as a pauper laughed at me for not dressing better than I did, and told me that he had in a bag which he carried with him a much better suit of clothes than any I had. Women, too, will often make great difficulties, because they think I do not take sufficient care of their bonnet-boxes, large pasteboard boxes, in which they have fine bonnets with plenty of ribbands, and all of which they expect to be conveyed in the cart with them, and *with the utmost care.*"

CHAPTER XI.

1837—1848.

Accession of Victoria—Circulars of the Poor Law Commissioners—Report of 1839 relative to vagrancy by the Constabulary Commissioners—Number of vagrants, begging-letter writers and bearers of begging letters—Habits of vagrants—The three sorts of cant—Style of living amongst tramps—Vagrancy and juvenile delinquency—Naked beggars—Ring droppers—Pretended rag sellers—Quack doctors—Umbrella menders—Turnpike sailors—Act to provide asylums for the homeless poor—Report of the committee of 1846 on the non-establishment of these asylums—Increase of vagrancy owing to the inducements held out to agricultural labourers to migrate to large and populous towns—Irish vagrants—Increase of vagrancy brought about by night refuges—Profitable character of these asylums—Revelations of "A. B."—General conduct of vagrants—Their lawless character—The Irish famine and consequent influx of poor Irish into England.

THE accession of Queen Victoria marks the commencement of an era of social legislation and of systematic efforts to improve the condition of the poorer classes hitherto unparalleled. Amended regulations were in 1837 framed for regulating emigration under the Poor Law Amendment Act, and providing for the migration of agricultural labourers to the manufacturing districts, so as to diminish the distress in rural districts. In the same year the Poor Law Commissioners issued a circular directing relief to be given to the vagrant poor without attention to settlement; they likewise advised that every vagrant should as far as possible be required to perform some work in return for the relief he obtained. In 1838 they issued another circular to Boards of Guardians in the metropolis, recommending that the wandering poor should be relieved in workhouses. In 1839 they issued a warning to the officers, that in case of any neglect on their part to receive destitute persons on application at the workhouses, the officers of the workhouse would be dismissed.

The neglect and dereliction of duty on the part of local constables had made it long evident that for the purpose of effectively checking crime, a paid and efficient police force was necessary throughout the country. Accordingly Commissioners were appointed to inquire as to the best means of establishing an efficient Constabulary Force in the Counties of England and Wales.

The report made by these Commissioners in the year 1839 is most instructive on the subject of Vagrancy and Mendicity in the country. It opens with a

TABLE SHOWING THE CHARACTERS OF PERSONS OF THE THREE FOLLOWING CLASSES.

1. Persons who have no visible means of subsistence, and who are believed to live wholly by violation of the law.
2. Persons following some ostensible and legal occupation, but who are known to have committed an offence, and are believed to augment their gains by habitual or occasional violation of the law.
3. Persons not known to have committed any offences, but known as associates of the above classes, and otherwise deemed suspicious characters.

	Metropolitan Police District.			City of Bristol.			City of Bath.			Town of Kingston-on-Hull.			Town of Newcastle-on-Tyne.		
	1st Class.	2nd Class.	3rd Class.	1st Class.	2nd Class.	3rd Class.	1st Class.	2nd Class.	3rd Class.	1st Class.	2nd Class.	3rd Class.	1st Class.	2nd Class.	3rd Class.
Vagrants	1089	186	20	263	..	..	2	45	42	27	7	261	192	92	..
Begging-letter Writers	12	17	21	8	..	3	1	..	..	..	..	..	4	2	..
Bearers of Begging Letters	22	40	24	11	..	..	9	22	18	2	1	..	..	..	..

TABLE SHOWING THE NUMBER OF HOUSES FOR THE PURPOSE OF DELINQUENCY OR VICE KEPT IN THE YEAR 1837 IN THE FOLLOWING PLACES:—

	Metropolitan Police District.	Borough of Liverpool.	City of Bristol.	City of Bath.	Town of Kingston-on-Hull.	Town of Newcastle-on-Tyne.
Mendicants' Lodging Houses	221	176	69	14	11	78
Average daily number of Lodgers at each house	11	6	7	9	3	3

The report next states that "The most prominent body of delinquents in the rural districts, are vagrants, and these vagrants appear to consist of two classes; first, the habitual depredators, house-breakers, horse-stealers, and common thieves; secondly, of vagrants, properly so called, who seek alms as mendicants. In the borough of Chesterfield "There are many vagrants. The number cannot be stated. Their habits are to prowl about the borough and immediate adjacent villages, under pretext of begging or seeking work, but whose real objects are to look at the premises where they call to see what booty can be gained by plunder at night."

The evidence regarding the habits of vagrants in other towns, such as Lincoln, Ludlow, Chesterfield, Devizes, and Maidstone, is of a similar character.

Extracts are then given from the confessions of four depredators of the migratory class, and one mendicant.

A thief aged 21 in Salford Gaol says:—

"For the last four years, up to 1839, I have 'travelled' for a maintenance. I carried a covered hawker's basket, with an oil-case on the top, with cutlery, trinkets, braces, Birmingham fancy goods, buttons, pearl, bone, and wood; it was the excuse for travelling. There are cant words for everything you use or do. I have seen some old cant in print, but it is nothing to the cant now used. There are three sorts of cant, the gypsies, the beggars (such as pretended sailors and others), and the thieves'. The cants are distinct in many words, but alike in others. A stranger to the cant words could not understand the gypsies or others, save a few words here and there. The gypsies have a cant word for every word they speak. The vagrant cant is a lower style than the thieves'; they use it to tell one another what they get at different houses; they are not always thieves, they will not push themselves forward to steal, and one-half of them if they saw another stealing would tell of him, and yet, if they could do it themselves, they would. The Manchester and Liverpool thieves are reckoned the most expert; they are thought to be of Irish parents, and to have most cunning. In fact, I'll be bound to say, that three parts of those who are travelling now throughout the kingdom have Irish blood in them, either from father, mother, or grandmother.

"I stayed till about February, when I started by Stockport, Macclesfield, and begged my way up to London; about seven days on the road. I went to Covent Garden market; I lived for six weeks by stealing fruit and selling it."

Next come the confessions of a young thief:—

"At every lodging house on the road H—— met plenty of trampers, and he did not see one face he had not seen at St. Giles's. They also recognised him and compared notes. Some were hawkers, some were going half naked, some were ballad singers, some were going about with false letters, others as broken-down tradesmen, some as old soldiers, and some as shipwrecked sailors; and every night they told each other of *good houses.* They all lived well, never eat any broken victuals, but had meat breakfasts, good dinners, hot suppers, and frequently ended by going to bed very drunk. Not one spent less than 3s. a day, many a great deal more. They sometimes make 5s., and average 3s. 6d. per day; some often get a sovereign where humane people reside." (All this is confirmed by P——.)

A boy of fourteen, a prisoner in Knutsford Gaol, then states:—

"Sometimes I have been sent begging to different houses; the people have been watched upstairs to make the beds; I have then gently opened the door, pulled the key out of the lock, and pressed it against a piece of tempered clay which I had in my hand. We could then cut a key and go in when we liked."

The report then goes on to say:—

"The next classes of depredators who perambulate the country are the vagrants, properly so called. Upwards of eighteen thousand commitments per annum of persons for the offence of vagrancy mark the extent of the body from which they are taken."

It will be seen that vagrancy, or the habit of wandering abroad under colour either of distress or of some ostensible though illegal occupation, having claims on the sympathies of the uninformed, constitutes one great source of delinquency, and especially of juvenile delinquency. The returns show that the vagrant classes pervade every part of the country, rendering property insecure, propagating pernicious habits, and afflicting the minds of the sensitive with false pictures of suffering, and levying upon them an offensive impost for the relief of that destitution, for which a heavy tax is legally levied in the shape of poor's rates.

The following confession, taken by Mr. Miles from B——, an experienced travelling vagrant, furnishes a more particular account of their habits than is contained, or could be expected, in a return to official queries.

"Beggars tramp about from town to town: there is a low lodging house for travellers in every village: they tell the people that they are travelling to find work, but pray to God they may never get it. They all go about 'to walk' in the mornings, and return at night to their lodging houses, where they live well, and spend the day's produce in drinking. They are merry fellows, money or no money, and laugh at the people for 'flats.' They tell each other what houses are 'good,' and arrange their districts so as not to interfere with each other. Every tramper is accompanied by his fancy girl or his wife. A black fellow, who is well-known about Deptford, and goes about the streets singing and dancing, takes his country journeys with two women, and makes plenty of money to pay all their expenses.

"The women who travel about with the trampers seldom go out begging; they sometimes disguise themselves as Gypsies, and go fortune-telling. It is very profitable; they watch for the master and mistress to leave the house, and then try to get hold of the servants. They beg money, food, clothes, or anything; and if a silver spoon is in their way they will not 'tumble over it;' they will steal it.

"The price of their bed is threepence; always two in a bed; sometimes ten or fifteen in a room. 'Yokels' (countrymen) were seldom or never seen in the lodging houses; but he has seen many during the last two months. Does not know why. They manage very badly, cannot get enough to find themselves in food. The regular trampers give them scraps to eat if they have been unlucky in the day. . . . They all have their appropriate cant names. B—— describes these classes as follows :—

"1st. Men who go about the country almost naked begging clothes or food. They get about 3s. a day. They have good clothes at their lodging house, and travel in them from town to town, if there are not many houses in the way. Before they enter the town, they take them off, as well as their shoes and stockings, put on their Guernsey jackets, send the bundle and the woman forward to the lodging house, and commence begging at the first house they come to. Knows a man who was recently clad from head to foot in new clothes at a shop in Billericay, by the son of the rector in a neighbouring village, all of which clothes, including hat, shoes, and stockings, he sold about half an hour afterwards, by auction, in the tap-room of a low public-house, to his companions, and they all got drunk together with the proceeds. These fellows always sell a gift of clothes.

"2nd. Men who are ring-droppers. Travelling tinkers make sham gold rings out of old brass buttons. H—— D—— is a noted fellow at this work; his wife and mother go with him and drop the rings.* They live in St. Giles's, and travel for a month or two. They sometimes make 20s. or 25s. a day.

"3rd. Fellows who go round to different houses, stating their master's stock of rags has been burnt, or that a sudden supply is wanted, and that they are sent forward to collect them. The rags are called for, and one fellow marches off with the bundle, leaving one or more talking with the housewife, who is gravely cavilling about the price, and as gravely informed that the master is coming round, and they leave some private mark on the doorpost which they say is the sign to indicate to him the quantity and quality taken and the amount to pay; so they walk off and 'never tip her anything.' The rags are carried to the keeper of a rag-shop, who gives quires of paper in exchange, which they carry round to small villages, and sell to small shopkeepers, or at farmhouses. All rag-shops 'stand fence for anything,'† and buy any stolen property. . . .

"4th. A set of fellows who go about in decent apparel, leaving small printed handbills at cottages and farmhouses, wherein are set forth the wonderful cures of all sorts of ailments effected by medicine which they sell. The following day these bills are called for, and the credulous people buy small phials of this nostrum, at various prices from 10s. to 6d., according to the tact of the beggar, and the folly of the party. The mixture is only a decoction of any herb or rubbish that may be at hand. He (B——) was told by one of this class that he had just sold a bottle of 'stuff' to a poor woman who lived in a cottage on Warley Common, Essex, and who had been long ailing. She gave 10s. for it, and it was only salt and water, some tea, and coloured green with nettle-tops. These fellows obtain more money than any other class of impostors, sometimes as much as £2 a week, and they seldom go to London.

"5th. Men who travel about the country in shabby-genteel attire, stating that they have been well off formerly, but are reduced by recent misfortune. Some are burnt-out farmers or shopkeepers; some first-class workmen out of work, owing to the bankruptcy of their employers, some captains who have just lost

---

* For an explanation of this practice, see pp. 595, 630.
† Receive stolen goods of any kind.

their ships upon the coast. This story is always used after a heavy gale of wind. Some carry begging letters which are written for them, price 1s. This is very profitable, if well managed. The 'Lady Bountifuls' are great supporters of these fellows.

"6th. Fortune-tellers. Many women, when tramping with the men dress themselves like Gypsies, and contrive to get a tolerable daily booty, at least 3s. or 4s. a day.

"7th. Trampers who have nothing to sell, but manage to live merely by begging.

"8th. Thieves—'prigs'—generally go in couples; walk into a country shop, where there is an old woman and a candle; buy something, drop a sixpence; get the old lady to bring the candle round to look for it, while the other fellow is filling his pockets with whatever he can lay his hands on.

"9th. Match sellers.   "10th. Ballad singers.

"11th. Fellows who boil up fat and a little soap over night, run it out in a cloth, and next morning cut it up like cakes of Windsor soap. It's all bad, but they drive a good trade.

"12th. Fellows who go from house to house stating that they live in some neighbouring town, and ask for 'umbrellas to mend.' An active fellow in this line will make a clean sweep of all the umbrellas in a village before dinner. These umbrellas are produced in the London market on wet days and dusky evenings."

The Commissioners then go on to say—

"Instances have been stated to us where travelling mechanics have been seduced from their occupations into the career of mendicancy from the temptation which it offers. Labourers have gone to the vagrants' lodging houses to purchase, for their own use, the meat and refuse food which they could obtain there at a cheap rate. The contrast of the advantages enjoyed by the dishonest, under comparative impunity, against the industrious, is depicted by a witness who relates an instance which came to his knowledge, where an agricultural labourer sitting by the roadside eating dry bread with a little cheese, was observed by a vagrant, who asked him if he had no meat to eat with his bread; being answered in the negative, the beggar pitied him, and offered to him some of the meat which he had obtained by begging at the doors of the surrounding houses of the gentry, from which doors the labourer said that he or his children, who were known to be industrious, would have been spurned if they attempted to beg.

"At Llanfyllin there are three lodging houses for tramps,

the most notorious is kept by a woman known by the name of 'Old Peggy.' One man told Mr. D——, a druggist in the town, that for twopence 'Old Peggy' would give him scraps enough to keep his dog for a week or more. The druggist stated that 'Old Peggy' has often come to him saying, 'God bless you, doctor, sell me a hap'orth o' tar.' When first applied to, he asked, 'What do you want with tar?' The reply was, 'Why, to make *a land sailor*. I want a hap'orth just to daub a chap's canvas trousers with, and that's how I makes a land sailor, doctor.'

"In Fifeshire a preventive police has been established, with almost the sole object of looking after vagrants. It appears to have worked well, and to have been productive of great advantages.

"Having investigated the general causes of depredation of vagrancy and mendicancy, as developed by examinations of the previous lives of criminals or vagrants in the gaols, we find that in scarcely any cases is it ascribable to the pressure of unavoidable want or destitution, and that in the great mass of cases it arises from the temptation of obtaining property with a less degree of labour than by regular industry."

In the year 1842, with a view to impose some check on the vagrants who obtained food and shelter at the workhouse without compensation of any kind, and who frequently extorted clothes from the parochial authorities by destroying those they wore, the Guardians of any Parish or Union are, by the 5 & 6 Vict., c. 57, "empowered, subject always to the Poor Law Commissioners, to prescribe a Task of Work to be done by any Person relieved in any Workhouse, in return for the Food and Lodging afforded; but not to detain any Person against his Will for the Performance of such Task of Work for any Time exceeding Four Hours from the Hour of Breakfast in the Morning succeeding his Admission; and if he refuses or neglects to perform a Task of Work suited to his Age, Strength, and Capacity, or wilfully destroys or injures his own Clothes, or damages any of the property of the Guardians, he is to be deemed an idle and disorderly person within the meaning of the Act 5 Geo. IV., c. 83, s. 3."

This was followed in the year 1844 by the 7 & 8 Vict., c. 101, which enacts that every woman neglecting to maintain her bastard child shall be punishable as an idle and disorderly person; and that every woman convicted a second time of such an offence, or deserting her bastard child, shall be punishable as a rogue and vagabond under 5 Geo. IV., c. 83. It also provides that asylums may be formed for the temporary relief of poor persons found destitute and without lodging in London, Liverpool, Manchester, Bristol, Leeds, and Birmingham; and that if they desire it, poor persons admitted to any such asylum shall be relieved with food and lodging for the night; and no such person shall be detained longer than the ordinary hour of breakfast and four hours afterwards, unless he has become punishable for misbehaviour, when he may be confined for twenty-four hours. If any person received into such an asylum gives a false name, or makes a false statement, or gives different names on different occasions, he is to be deemed a rogue and vagabond.

In 1846 a Select Committee was appointed to inquire into the manner in which the Poor Law Commissioners had exercised the powers for the establishment of District Asylums for the Houseless Poor of the Metropolis confided to them by this statute; and also to inquire into the effects of any Asylums supported by voluntary subscriptions which might have been formed for the same purpose.

Mr. Richard Hall, assistant Poor Law Commissioner, stated before this committee that he thought " the tendency of the circular which it had been found necessary to issue to the masters of workhouses in 1837, 1838, and 1839, to relieve destitute applicants, had been to increase vagrancy and mendicancy." He was also of opinion "that a great increase of tramps and vagrants took place from transient circumstances, such as the beginning of the hay season in Middlesex, Essex, and Hertfordshire, or of the hop season in Kent and Sussex, or some local fair or horse-race."

Mr. Thomas Thorne, Secretary to the Workhouse in Marylebone, attributed the increase of vagrancy to the acts and orders of the Poor Law Commissioners, by inducing hundreds and thousands of persons to migrate from their places of settlement to large and populous towns.

The migration was carried out by the direction and encouragement of the Poor Law Commissioners, and he thought it was carried out under the influence of threats and delusive promises that were made to the migrants, which failed to be realised.

For example, the first communication that was made with reference to migration was to be found in the report of 1835, where a circular letter was addressed to the manufacturers in

Lancashire and other districts, where the Poor Law Commissioners were informed there was the greatest demand for labour, with a view to labour being supplied from agricultural districts; and the Commissioners proceeded to state that the first trial of the measure was made in the parish of Bledlow, in Buckingham, where it had been reported to them that numerous families were existing in extreme distress, and where land would be thrown out of cultivation in consequence of the increasing burthen to the rates. It was admitted by Mr. Muggeridge, the agent for migration, that many of these parties returned from the manufacturing districts again, and had become wanderers in the country.

Mr. Muggeridge stated, "Extravagant and unfounded promises, and where these failed, threats had been, he was informed, in some cases held out to induce persons to migrate; and instances had, as must have been expected, already occurred, in which families brought down under such circumstances had been returned to their parishes at an expense far greater than the amount saved by their temporary absence from their settlements." That was confirmed also by the statement of Mr. Baker, another migration agent in Yorkshire, who said, "The objections which have been urged against the system are three: 1st. By the poor, from misstatements which have been made by idle returners, or persons incapacitated from working by bodily infirmities, and who have been therefore obliged to return, having been sent by their parishes on the fallacious reasoning of 'out of sight out of mind.'"

Mr. *Thorne* attributed the increase of vagrancy partly to the unsettling of the résidence of these parties at the time. Upwards of ten thousand persons had been removed in the short space of two years.

But he principally attributed the increase of vagrancy to the issue of the circular of the Poor Law Commissioners in 1839, which took away all discretion from officers as to the relief of persons, whether deserving, or persons who were known to be professed vagrants.

Mr. (*afterwards Sir Richard*) *Mayne*, Commissioner of Police, stated that the number of destitute poor persons found in the streets by the Metropolitan Police, from the 1st January to the 31st December, 1845, was 1,111—574 males and 537 females. Of these 34 males and 20 females were taken to hospitals, and 540 males and 517 females to Workhouses.

Mr. *Thomas Brushfield*, chairman of the Whitechapel Union,

stated that the number of casual poor who applied for relief in that union had increased from 3,982 in 1842 to 6,073 in 1845; and evidence was given of a great increase in other unions.

William Jones, a constable in plain clothes specially detailed to apprehend beggars, stated that the greater part of them were Irish, and this was corroborated by the secretary of the Mendicity Society.

Strong evidence was given that the night asylums attracted vagrants to the metropolis and were otherwise demoralising.

Lieutenant T. L. Knevitt, secretary and assistant manager to the Mendicity Society, said, " During the time the night refuges were open they had considerably more applicants; they multiplied immediately; and the moment the refuges were closed they decreased." The way in which he accounted for it was that a great number of persons came to London in November, when the refuges were generally opened, hoping to get lodgings in those refuges at night, and to go about begging during the day. It was not an unfrequent answer, when they were asked, " How is it you have come to London again; you were here last year?" " Oh, I thought the ' Houseless' was open."

He put in the following statistical return of the number of applicants for two weeks before the ' Houseless' was opened, and for two weeks afterwards:—

Years.	Cases two weeks previous to the Houseless Institution opening.	Cases two weeks after the Houseless Institution opening.	Cases two weeks previous to the Houseless Institution closing.	Cases two weeks after the Houseless Institution closing.
1840 and 1841	1,031	1,457	846	461
1841 and 1842	1,717	1,847	1,541	1,534
1842 and 1843	1,422	2,970	2,031	1,057
1843 and 1844	731	1,218	1,014	499
1844 and 1845 closing	529	699	965	372
1845; did not open in 1845	...	...	...	...
1846	2,203	2,875	...	...

When the private asylums were open, the number of applicants to the Mendicity Society undoubtedly increased. These establishments were decidedly not useful in lessening vagrancy; they rapidly increased it, and did harm instead of good. He knew that many of the applicants were young prostitutes that followed the railroad and other labourers round the country; they travelled round the country in summer, and came into London in November. If they came before the refuge was open they went to Peckham; then they went to St. Olave's; and then to Greenwich and other unions. That was ascertained by questioning them.

The public report of the Mendicity Society for 1829 states:—

"The surplus of those who have applied for work arose partly from the severity of the season, partly from the absence of those ordinary resources of employment from which the vagrant poor derive subsistence at other periods of the year, and partly from the tendency of that humane and valuable institution, the Society for the Houseless Poor, to attract persons to the metropolis by the offer of nightly lodging. The office has been thronged by such applicants. The managers cannot advert to the operations of a Society so closely interwoven with those of this institution without expressing, with every friend of humanity, their testimony to its beneficial influence; at the same time, convinced by their experience of some years of its tendency to increase the number of street mendicants, they feel it their duty to impress upon its directors the expediency of using the utmost circumspection and vigilance in regard to the persons whom they may admit as objects of their benevolent attention."

In the report of 1844 the managers say:—

"It would not be difficult, perhaps, to assign some of the causes which have apparently prevented this town from partaking in the benefits which reviving trade seemed calculated to confer on every part of the country; and the managers are of opinion that the great facility now afforded to the idle and profligate to obtain food and shelter has greatly diminished their anxiety to seek for employment, and that very many have been drawn up to London, who would never have ventured to come there without the security now offered to them against the evils to which improvidence would formerly have exposed them. The experience of those managers who have taken their rota of duty in the office where beggars with tickets are referred for examination, has been, that a very large proportion of the applicants are persons who lodge in the unions or refuges for the houseless, where they get their supper, bed, and breakfast, wander about the streets all day, apply with a mendicity ticket at the society's office for a dinner, and in the evening seek their lodging again in one of the unions or refuges, to repeat the same proceeding for days and weeks together. A life more suited to the habits of the young and profligate of both sexes can hardly be conceived."

The report of 1845 states :—

"Early in the month of December there was a very large influx of mendicants of both sexes from the country, most of them young, who having begged their way to London, sleeping at the union houses by the way, have taken up their abode in or about London, sleeping at the different refuges which have been opened for the destitute, or at the union houses in or near the metropolis, and applying in great numbers daily for food and other assistance at the office of this society. Many of these applicants appeared to be of very questionable character, and are known to have remained two or three months in London, making no exertion whatever to obtain work. Those managers on whom the duty has devolved of examining the persons applying with tickets for relief, have been led, by what they have witnessed, to the conclusion that a large floating population has been created by the facilities now given to vagrancy, who are driven from their homes by the discipline of the workhouse, and encouraged to lead a vagrant life by the certainty that they shall find a nightly refuge in the vagrant wards of the different union-houses whilst on the tramp, and an asylum in the refuges of London when they arrive there."

Mr. James Jopp, City of London Union, said :—

"It appeared to him that while the refuges were open the number of applications were decreased, partially so; but immediately they closed he had found the numbers increased more than they were before the refuges were opened. In 1842, before the asylum was opened in Playhouse-yard, the number admitted was 966 in one week. In the week after the asylum was opened there were only 701 cases, showing a decrease of 265 in the week. Again, the week before the refuge closed in March, 1843, the number admitted in their union was 339; the week after it closed it was 615."

William Jones, constable 157 D, said that the superintendent had ordered him to look to the night asylums at the time the vagrants came out, when the inhabitants complained of the nuisance they caused. He found that the persons who generally attended at the night refuges were the worst of vagrants, the lowest of beggars, who were begging about all day, principally young persons of both sexes.

Mr. *John Sard*, secretary to the committee for affording Shelter to the Houseless, said they had three asylums, one in Playhouse-yard, Whitecross Street, accommodating 550; one in Glasshouse Street, East Smithfield, accommodating 340; and one in Ogle Street, Marylebone, accommodating 300. The average number they had in the three asylums was 1,000. They were only open during the inclement part of the year.

As to the profitable character of these asylums to their managers the following suggestive evidence was elicited:—

Mr. George Guyerette, manager of the West End Nightly Refuge for the Houseless Poor, 60, Market Street, Edgware Road, admitted that he was both collector and manager, and that in the former capacity he received £79 18s. and in the latter £75 out of a total of £893 15s. He also lived in the house attached to the premises rent free, and procured the provisions for the house. The refuge was only open from the 27th December to the 1st April. During the rest of the year he did nothing in particular, but acted as a general dealer, dealing in jewellery and plate. The treasurer and auditor was his brother-in-law, and the committee, consisting of four members, appointed themselves.

Mr. Henry Smith, chairman of the St. Olave's Union, gave a curious reason for the attraction of poor persons from the country to that union. He said that their situation being so near the Borough hospitals brought an additional burden upon them in the shape of a better description of poor. Persons came up from the country with a view to gain admission to the hospitals, who, if they did not gain their point, immediately applied to the relieving officers, who admitted them into the workhouse; and when they came out of the hospital, if they were too weak and too poor to find their way home, they were received till they were able to go home. That was a very common occurrence.

As to the general conduct of the vagrants who came to them, he said they were very troublesome during all the night; they came in in gangs; and if a wayfarer to whom this protection was afforded happened to be introduced in the ward after dark, immediately they knew that he was not one of them they set upon him, and stole his neckcloth or his shoes, and behaved to him in such a way that frequently the poor fellow cried to be allowed to come out.

It was impossible to identify the wrongdoer, or to separate

WILLIAM READ, ALIAS "A. B."
A Vagrant, examined before a Committee of the House of Commons in the Year 1846.

those cases in such a way that the really destitute should not be subject to that kind of treatment.

Some very remarkable evidence was given before the committee by an anonymous vagrant, who was examined as "A. B."*

"He stated that he was then an inmate of the Marylebone Workhouse, and went into service as a page at the age of seventeen or eighteen, and remained three years. He then ran away to 'see the country,' went round Kent, and returned to London at the end of three months, and took a situation as potboy and waiter, in which he continued for about two years in two places, until at last he got such a character for becoming intoxicated that he could not get a place. He was taken dangerously ill, and was taken to the infirmary at Marylebone. After his discharge he tried to get something to do, but having lost his character he found it very hard, and was therefore obliged to take to a rambling life, and get food where he could. He had been in all the refuges for the destitute in London, and believed that the vagrants liked the gaols better than the workhouses.

"The class of persons who usually got admission to the union workhouses and the houses of refuge consisted of all sorts: there were a few countrymen among them, and some were sailors, and some were very bad characters. Not ten out of every hundred of them would be really deserving persons. If a deserving poor man was admitted, if he had anything about him, such a thing as a handkerchief or knife, they would have it in the course of the night. They hustled about him, they would strike him, being so many of them. He had had his food taken away at places he had been at.

"He applied at Newington about the beginning of this year, on a Sunday evening. He was given half a pound of bread, and a rug to cover him. He was then put into a very filthy place; and the moment he got inside the door the bread was snatched out of his hand, and the rug too. He expostulated a little concerning it, and they heaved a pail of water over him, and two or three began attacking him because he did not belong to the gang.

"There was a gang called Spevin's gang; there were not so many then as there used to be; some had been transported for

* This man has been identified as a crossing-sweeper named *William Read*, who is still alive (February, 1887).

different things, particularly since the place that they used to cohabit in—Smithfield—had been broken up. They were in the habit of committing petty robberies, and of arranging and concocting them in the vagrant ward.

"Vagrants did not stand in the least fear of the police, at least the most part of them. Persons who made application at night for admission into the vagrant ward of the workhouses were mostly begging in the daytime.

"He considered that houses of refuge tended to increase vagrancy to a frightful extent, considering there were many vagrants who, well knowing they could get a lodging anywhere at night, would spend their money in drinking and all sorts of debauchery.

"Most vagrants lived very well; they had houses where they got food in the daytime.

"The best dress for a beggar to wear in the streets of London was a smock-frock; it excited more compassion; though they might perhaps have been in London two or three years.

"The best and most successful garb for a man to assume was that of a country labourer. Such a man might get five or six shillings a day. If they spent the whole of that money in drink and dissipation, they could easily gain admission into the workhouse at night. He had known many of them come in quite intoxicated.

"When he was in the country begging he pretended to be a servant out of place. In going about and getting so very little food at the different unions he got to feel very bad. You have a comfortable bed in prison, and he preferred going there at times to get a little rest.

"They are very riotous in the Kensington Union sometimes; they rob one another very much. A gang went down there once for the express purpose of robbing a bread store in Hammersmith. At the Greenwich Union a clothes place there was broken into, not a great while previously.

"A great many persons who live by vagrancy leave the country from doing something wrong; they are afraid to go back again; they come up to London, and they find there are so many places of refuge that they can get a better living and an easier one in London.

"The principal number are English, a considerable number Irish, and a great many Scotch.

"The facility of getting a night's lodging is a great inducement for strangers to come up to London. Vagrancy had been on the increase during the past four years."

In the autumn of 1846 great destitution prevailed in Ireland, owing to the almost universal and entire failure of the potato crop. The consequence of this was an immense influx of Irish pauperism into England.

Mr. Edward Rushton, stipendiary magistrate of Liverpool, gave the following evidence on the subject in the year 1847, before the Select Committee on Settlement and Poor Removal:—

"The history of the influx of the Irish into Liverpool may be given in a few words. In the month of November, 1846, I was sitting in the police-court every day, and I was much struck with the increase of Irish vagrants, and on inquiry I found that the arrivals were very numerous. The practical operation may be perhaps elucidated by one case. The overseer brought up a woman for begging, for being very importunate in the street. I said, ' It is a clear case, a very bad case; send her to gaol.' The overseer then said, ' She has six children; if you send her to gaol I must take the children, and it will be a great loss to me.' I said, ' If this is to be the process, there is an end of the Vagrant Act in Liverpool.' He would have had to hire a nurse for the young children, if sent into the workhouse without their mother, and the mother had been sent to gaol. I did not send her to gaol, and they were all sent into the workhouse; and that case illustrates practically the working which has attended the influx, and its effect upon our parochial funds. The influx of Irish into Liverpool became day by day so much increased that on the 13th of January, 1847, I ordered the officers to be stationed when the boats arrived from Ireland, to count the number of poor people who came; and from the 13th of January to the 19th of April inclusive, there had arrived in Liverpool 131,402 poor persons, many of them shockingly debilitated, all of them in a most distressful condition, and some of them diseased. The emigration from the port during this period amounts to 43,146, nearly all Irish; nineteen-twentieths, certainly; so there remain in Liverpool and the adjacent country a balance of about 90,000.

"A great many of them have remained in Liverpool, though the town is already overcrowded; we have an unhappy notoriety about our habitations for the poor, cellars and places of that description, where of course there is great mortality, and they have been crammed into those places in a way that is perfectly frightful to think of.

"A good many of the 90,000 have passed into other parts of England, but not anything like half. A gentleman called upon me, sent by Lord St. Vincent, the other day, to inquire what we were doing, as the Irish paupers were coming into Staffordshire so fast, and they have gone to Manchester in great numbers, and into Yorkshire.

"It would be physically impossible to administer the Vagrant Act; the gaol in Liverpool is, under ordinary circumstances, quite inadequate; it ought never to have within it more than 460 people, and there are more than 700 in it, and hardly one from vagrancy, except in peculiar cases which I can state, that is to say, when a man came to solicit charitable aid with money tied up in his trousers, the relieving officer found him out, then I have committed him under the Vagrant Act, but otherwise the Vagrant Act is a dead letter in the whole place; we are choked out.

"There has also been a great increase in the numbers of Irish coming into Liverpool under peculiar circumstances. An American ship called the *Rochester*,* having on board 250 Irish people going to the United States, was wrecked last week on the Arklow Bank on the coast of Wexford. These poor people were taken to the town of Wexford. The captain of the *Rochester*, who is, I understand, part owner of the ship, and who would be looked to for a return of the passage-money, was on the spot, yet notwithstanding this, the Mayor of Wexford put all these destitute persons on board a steamer, and sent them consigned to the Mayor of Liverpool, as he said, to obtain justice and charity in Liverpool.

"I am persuaded that the local authorities and landowners have sent over the Irish destitute poor to a large extent."

* This vessel was wrecked on the north end of the Blackwater Bank, April 13, 1847.

CHAPTER XII.

1848—1854.

Reports of the Poor Law Inspectors in 1848 on the existing condition of vagrancy—Character and conduct of vagrants—Immense increase of vagrancy and its causes—Description of the Irish poor in England—Effect of sending Irish vagrants home—Intercommunication amongst vagrants—Gaol a favourite resort of the vagrant—Concealment of property by tramps—Social demoralisation produced by vagrancy—Poor Law accommodation for vagrants—Report of the committee of 1854 on the removal of the Irish and Scotch poor from England—Decrease of vagrancy in Ireland and its causes—Irish paupers sent home from Liverpool—Results of the influx of Irish poor into Liverpool.

In the year 1848 a series of valuable Reports and Communications on Vagrancy was made to the Poor Law Board by the Inspectors and several Boards of Guardians and individuals.

The general character of the vagrants is thus depicted:—

"For the most part these vagrants are the refuse of society; spending the day in idleness, begging, plunder, and prostitution, and repairing at night to the workhouse on their route, or where they expect the best treatment, instead of to the low lodging houses to which they used to resort; they thus traverse the country in every direction, to the great prejudice of the industrious poor; this system of relief affording great encouragement to sturdy beggars and vagabonds, who prefer a life of idleness and vice to honest industry. There can be little doubt, that as the certainty of obtaining a night's lodging and food gratuitously has become more generally known amongst this class, coupled with the entire absence of any effectual inquiry into their habits or course of life, their resort to workhouses has greatly increased, and will no doubt continue to do so." *

"In describing the class of persons commonly called Vagrants, but in the Poor Law vocabulary designated 'Tramp;' I give pre-

* Report of Mr. Grenville Pigott.

cedence to the sturdy English mendicant. He, though not a constant occupant of the tramp ward in the workhouse, is frequently there, either having relied on that shelter when he has spent his last penny in dissipation, or having the calculating selfishness to save the cost of his lodging, that he might have the more to spend in debauchery. The man of this class is easily recognised by his patched but warm and ample coat, with a number of pockets, and many appliances for his personal comfort suggested by his long experience. He never visits a workhouse where labour is exacted (unless it may be on Saturday night, work not being done on Sunday), but leaves early without work or breakfast; dry bread, or even gruel not being to his taste when he can resort to the wallet, left well stored with broken victuals in the custody of some friend in the village.

"The class next, and more important from increasing numbers, is that of the young English vagabond, generally the native of a large town, probably an 'idle apprentice,' who, from crime or abandoned conduct, has made himself an outcast. Having no ties to bind him, he finds it most agreeable to travel about the country, being sure of a meal and a roof to shelter him at night. The men of this class are principally of from 17 to 25 years of age. They often travel in parties of two or three, having frequently a young woman or two, as abandoned as themselves, in company; begging, or extorting money during the day; but making no provision for the night or the morrow.

"This is a very numerous, and, I fear, rapidly increasing class, and to them principally belong the defiers of authority, who break windows, and abuse the officers, refuse to work, and incite others to rebel. For these the gaol has no terrors; but it is a desirable retreat from the winter cold, or as affording a sanitary asylum, where the best medical skill and the most proper diet for the cure of disease engendered by filth and immorality may be obtained.

"These, as a class, are of the lowest moral character, not possessing the honour generally attributed to thieves, and not only robbing and cheating each other, but shamelessly claiming applause for it. Their habits are noisy, disturbing the fellow-lodgers at night, by singing and shouting in chorus, and corrupting or disgusting all within hearing by the tales of crime, and boasts of debauchery in which they emulate each other." *

* Report of Mr. W. D. Boase.

Captain Carrol, chief of police at Bath, says :—

"The generality of tramps go from Union to Union, calling at Bath on their way, and watching the ladies in their walks; soliciting alms, which are afforded to get rid of the importunity. These characters generally come and go with the fashionable visitors, whose inconsiderate charity affords great encouragement to them."

Mr. Boase adds the following observations :—

"Approaching these in character are the young countrymen who have absconded, perhaps for some petty poaching offence, and to whom the facility for leading an idle vagabond life has proved too great a temptation. The tale of the profligate and the applause of the young aspirant has frequently been overheard in tramp words.

"There are a few calling themselves agricultural labourers, who are really such; and who are to be readily distinguished. There are a few mechanics also, chiefly tailors, shoemakers, and masons, who are occasionally destitute; but as much from improvidence and improper reliance upon workhouse relief as from any misfortune or necessity.

"Of the female English tramps little can be said, but that they are in great part prostitutes of the lowest class. . . .

"At Aylesbury the master of the workhouse told me that he had frequently heard them using the most obscene language, and singing songs of the same character, and that he overhears them relating their stories of depredation and theft, emulating each other as the most abandoned, to earn the applause of the audience. It would be endless to multiply the statements to this effect which have been made by officers at nearly all the workhouses I have visited, and I will only add, that the English are considered as much worse in character than the Irish. The statement of the relieving officer at Neath, Mr. Bentley, will illustrate the general opinion. He says, 'The Irish behave best, and the greatest blackguards come from the large towns in England. If I refuse relief, the Irish will lie at the door for hours, and the English will break the windows.' "

The *Clerk of the Stockport Union* is of opinion that—

"The majority of the trampers and vagrants are professional mendicants, wandering about the country, without any ordinary and daily trade in life to get their living by. This is openly avowed by most of them, who boldly say they have been in every workhouse in the kingdom, and will never work so long as they can get a bed, a pound of bread, and a pint of gruel a day; and they visit the different workhouses at periodical intervals of from two to six months."

The *Clerk of the Chesterfield Union* observes that—

"Amongst the officers of different Unions the calculation is that three-fourths of those who partake of the relief given (night and morning), the moment they leave the wards begin to beg, and so continue through the country they traverse to the next union, during which journey the moneys, food, &c., they obtain is deposited in the care of the most confidential of each party, who repairs to the lodging house for its safe keeping until the morning.

"These remarks apply altogether to the English vagrants, and generally young men and women without families; in fact, it is rare to find an aged English man or woman amongst the applicants, plainly showing that the class of persons most likely to require assistance are rarely found the recipients of this relief."

The *Clerk of the Shardlow Union*, in Derbyshire, says—

"It is found that at least nine-tenths of them are wandering about without any settled purpose, and upon being discharged from the workhouse in the morning it frequently takes them some time to decide whether they shall travel towards the north or the south. The evil is not only confined to workhouses, which are now resorted to regularly as common lodging houses, but in a rural district like ours it is seriously felt by the inhabitants: nearly all these trampers beg during the day, and frequently extort alms from the residents at odd houses (particularly if the latter are females) by threats of violence."

At *Lutterworth* the relieving officer states "that many of these vagrants and trampers have applied for assistance in a state of intoxication, and have been very abusive to him."

The *Master of the Cosford Union*, in Suffolk, says—

"Above four years ago, I admitted into the house a bold beggar, almost in a state of nudity. On the following morning I endeavoured to elicit from him his mode of life. Among other things he observed, that he found it to his advantage to travel in that state, with a view to excite the compassion of the public. He further added, that the greatest sum he ever realised in one day by begging was ten shillings; but when begging through a large town, he thought it a poor day's work if he did not beg five shillings.

"A few weeks since, I admitted into the house two of the most impudent vagrants I have ever met with. On questioning them respecting their religion, one of them observed that he was no religion; the other, that he was a horse's religion. I inquired what he meant by a horse's religion; his reply was, that he worked from Monday morning till Saturday night like a horse, and on Sunday he rambled about the fields. I merely mention this to show the impudent bearing of this class."

The *Chairman of the Ruthin Union* observes—

"Too often has it been found that many of the vagrants are portions of regular gangs of housebreakers, who rob the dwellings of cottagers when the family are at work in the fields."

Mr. Boase thus sums up the evidence on the subject:—

"The belief resulting from all my inquiries and experience on this subject is, that at the least 90 out of every hundred occupants of the tramp wards have no claim upon the honest poor man's fund."

The following testimony is furnished of the immense increase of vagrancy at this period:—

Number of vagrants admitted into workhouses—

During the six months ending 30th Sept., 1846   18,533
,,   ,,   ,,   ,,   1847   44,937

Increase of in 1847 26,404

WATFORD UNION.

Number of vagrants relieved:—

1841	1842	1843	1844	1845	1846	1847	1848 (first six months)
422	810	558	627	918	953	2,486	3,487

A return of the tramps relieved in the township of Warrington between March 25, 1847, and March 25, 1848:—

English.	Irish.	Scotch.	Natives of other places.	Total.
4,701	12,038	427	156	17,322.

Mr. Hawley furnishes the following observations as to the social character of the individuals who were then augmenting the ranks of vagabondism:—

"Of the increase of vagrancy since the autumn of 1846, and the alarming height at which it has arrived at the present time, the returns which have lately been transmitted by the clerks of the Unions to the Poor Law Board will afford sufficient evidence without producing any further statistical proofs of the fact. At the period above alluded to, the evil which had always existed in a mitigated degree was aggravated by the failure of the potato crop in Ireland, and the distress consequent upon that great national calamity, and thousands of the labouring natives of that portion of the empire, allured by the prospect of employment and that charitable aid which the sympathy and benevolent feelings of the people of this country always prompt them to extend to the needy and helpless, flocked to its shores, pouring a torrent of immigration over it which it has since been found difficult, and even impossible under existing enactments, to repress. Notwithstanding the enormous grants from the public funds destined for their support in *their own* country, the hand of charity was freely, and perhaps with too little consideration of the consequences, extended to them in *this*, and that which was intended only as a temporary alleviation of their sufferings has been converted into an incentive to a permanent system of mendicancy, with its usual accompaniments of idleness, vice, and disease.

"These observations are intended to apply to the Irish immigrants, but the partial distress in the manufacturing districts, and the want of funds to carry on the works on railroads now in the course of construction, have lately introduced another class of English mendicants into the northern counties, who, allured by the success which attended the irruption of the Irish, have established a similar system of professional vagrancy, but are found far more difficult to deal with, being for the most part persons of previously worthless character, for whom a prison has no terrors, and who set all law and authority at defiance."

Mr. Aneurin Owen supplies the following supplementary information:—

"The irruption of vagrants of every description into the towns and country places has reached to a great and annoying extent.

"That class of them composed of Irish, generally squalid, miserable, and frequently fever-stricken, met with the most compassionate treatment; and although the burden was heavily felt, complaints respecting it were not loudly expressed. Their destitution was generously relieved, trusting the New Irish Poor Law would in future prevent such an immigration of miserable objects.

"Concomitantly with them, another class, that of importunate sturdy tramps, has been perambulating the country, composed generally of young, idle, and insolent able-bodied men, unamenable to discipline, threatening and committing lawless acts of violence in the workhouses where they obtain nightly shelter, frequently refusing to perform any task of work unless, which can seldom be the case, a force be at hand to overpower their resistance. They stroll in bodies through the country places, committing depredations, and terrifying the inmates of lone farmhouses and cottages into giving them money. Since the establishment of a more effective police in the large towns, an additional number of them appears to have been driven into the country, at least it is supposed so."

The reasons for the increase of vagrancy, apart from the irruption of Irish pauperism, appear to have been twofold: first, the general facilities for wandering afforded to vagrants by providing them with food and shelter at the workhouse; and second, the special attractions furnished by the Night Asylums. *Mr. Stockdale*, superintendent of Police at Cardiff, supplies the following evidence on the second of these points:—

"For the first three or four years of my being here vagrancy was unknown; at least the style of it which exists now. The present system commenced, (I should think) between eight and nine years ago, in a trifling degree; perhaps one or two of a night. There had first been a refuge in Swansea, established by private subscription. In the winter following, one was opened here by similar means. .... The majority went from this towards Swansea, having come from Newport. .... The majority of these were those who made vagrancy a profession, which profession was entirely induced here by the opening of night asylums in Swansea, Newport, and here. The majority of applicants were single men, generally from 18 to 30; the greater part of whom came from England, mostly from Somerset and Wilts. One or two whom I knew in London (and particularly one who used to sweep a crossing in the Strand), told me that they had heard of the accommodation, and had come down to see the country. The crossing-sweeper told me that he had heard from tramps that he would be sure of breakfast and supper and a night's lodging. At first, when we began to search them, we generally found small sums of money, but after a week or two they used to know and manage differently."

The *Guardians of Burton-upon-Trent* state that "they have been greatly disappointed in the practical results of the system established in the year 1839, for relieving vagrants by tickets at the Union Workhouse. Instead of operating as a check on vagrancy and mendicity, it holds forth a direct encouragement to the idle and dissolute to wander from place to place throughout the kingdom. The ready means of obtaining lodging and food at each Union Workhouse hath given that facility for wandering, that advantage hath been taken of this system of relief by reputed thieves, attendants at races, fairs, and other public meetings, on their way to these places of resort."

Mr. Boase makes the following supplementary remarks :—

"The increase of vagrant applications appears to have commenced by a few applying to the workhouse in 1841; since which time it has grown each year in a rapidly progressive ratio. The increase for the two first quarters of the present year over the corresponding ones of the year 1846 is general. The number in the year 1847 is not used for comparison, being considered as greatly affected by the Irish famine. But in many cases the increase has, for the last few months, exceeded the corresponding months of even that year."

The Guardians of the Metropolitan Parish of *St. Martin* state in a memorial to the Poor Law Board that—

"Previously to the year 1839, the parish of St. Martin-in-the-Fields experienced but little inconvenience from applications for relief from what are called casual poor. Such applications were of rare occurrence until the year above mentioned; when persons having no known place of abode applied before this date, their demands were generally met by the affording some relief in food, and occasionally a night's lodging. The numbers of these vagrants applying for relief began gradually to increase during the year 1839, when 767 such persons received admission into the workhouse of St. Martin-in-the-Fields.

"In 1840 the number of such admissions was nearly doubled, as in that year it amounted to 1,376. The mischief rapidly extended, until, in 1846, as many as 6,308 casuals or vagrants were admitted, and in the last year, 1847, no less than 11,574 admissions of tramps, including wives and children, took place. . . .

"The vagrancy seems to have become a habit and system with vast numbers of idle mendicants and others, who, while they can procure a night's lodging and a meal, will continue to prowl about the metropolis during the day begging or stealing, and remaining content with this lazy and vicious existence."

The *Clerk of the Thirsk Union* reports:—

"Last year the increase (of vagrants) was principally occasioned by the Irish, this year they are of a different class, mostly English from the southern counties, young, idle, and lawless. This increase may in part be accounted for from the number of men dismissed from public works; but there can be no doubt that when in full work, the characters relieved in the workhouse have spent their money in dissipation, calculating on the assistance of workhouse accommodation in getting home again, or in rambling about the country ostensibly seeking work. It, however, shows the lamentable condition of this class, that many of them commit offences for the purpose of being sent to prison. During the last quarter, fifteen have been committed to the House of Correction for breaking windows or destroying their clothes. The vagrant ward window-frames have been pulled entirely out and destroyed, as well as the form for sitting on in the room. The yelling, shouting, and disorder in the ward has occasionally been such as to prevent the inmates from getting any rest, and the officers of the workhouse have been wholly unable to quell the disorder."

Mr. Boase furnishes the following description of the Irish poor who came over at this time:—

"The Irish, who form by far the majority of the applicants for casual relief, remain now to be described. These can scarcely be classified in any other way than as those who come to England to labour and those who come to beg. To the former class, as a class, I cannot go so far as to attribute settled habits of industry or pride of self-dependence. I fear they yield too readily to their disposition to idleness;—the difficulty of providing supper, breakfast, and lodging for themselves being removed by the workhouse. This class are physically superior to the mass of Irish vagrants, wear better clothing (generally the grey frieze), and are, at least, less disgustingly filthy and infested with vermin. It appears that for very many years considerable numbers of these have annually come to England in the spring, to work at hay-harvest, remaining for corn-harvest and hop-picking, and then have carried home their earnings in the autumn, seldom resorting to begging. Formerly this course was general, until within the last four or five years, and especially since the failure of the potato crop; when greater numbers were brought to England, more than there was work for; consequently the tramp-ward became the refuge of the surplus, and the inducement to many to remain in England. A great many harvest-men land at Newport and the Welsh ports; but by far the greater proportion of the Irish I saw in Wales were women with small children, old men apparently feeble, pregnant women, and girls and boys about ten years old. Great numbers of Irish are landed on the Welsh coast; but the amount cannot be ascertained or even guessed at. They are brought over by coal vessels as a return cargo (*living ballast*), at very low fares (2s. 6d. is the highest sum I heard of), huddled together like pigs, and communicating disease and vermin on their passage. Thrust on shore clandestinely, perhaps in the night (for there is great odium attached to the traffic), landed in the mud in some obscure part of the river,* exhausted, faint, and feverish from privation of food and air, is it to be wondered at that these become the medium of extending fever and contagion into the heart of the kingdom, into the asylums of the poor, where it finds its most susceptible victims and its greatest stronghold in the overcrowded rooms?

"Those landing in Wales are nearly all helpless and burdensome to the community. The incredible number of widows with three or four small children, who came over to 'get a bit for the children;' others professing to be married women whose husbands are supposed to be in London; young girls and boys looking for parents, brothers, and uncles, who may or may not be found; and again, a very numerous class of old women who have tried the basket of tapes in vain for a livelihood, and who now undisguisedly say, when asked where they are going, 'I don't know; just going up and down everywhere, your honour.' There are a great many, perhaps nearly half of the Irish now in England, who have abided with us all last winter, filling the refuges and absorbing the greater part of the charities distributed at that season. I have

---

* Much of this experience appears to be a repetition of a similar state of things in August, 1628, and April, 1629. See p. 148.

no hesitation in expressing as my opinion that many called English vagrants are of Irish origin.

"Of the young female Irish tramps many are undoubtedly prostitutes, having been corrupted by vile associations which not even the national character for chastity could shield them against.

"My suspicions were much more excited by the appearance of the Irish landing in Wales, that they had been got rid of as burdens, or probable burdens, upon society at home. And some evidence exists to support the supposition. Speaking of the influx in 1847, Superintendent Stockdale, of the Newport police, says, in his examination, 'A great many told me that Mr. *** of ***, near Cork, had paid 2s. 6d. for their passage; I think in hundreds of instances I was told this.'

"A remarkable fact is, that all the Irish whom I met on my route between Wales and London, said they came from Cork county. This is also confirmed by the officers who relieve them at Chepstow, Newport, and Cardiff. Mr. John, the relieving officer at the latter place, told me, in his examination, 'That not one out of every 100 of the Irish came from any other county than Cork. There are a few Tipperary men, but these do not trouble us; they are more industrious in their habits than Cork people.' And further,—'Not one-half of the Irish are able-bodied; I believe that they are sent here because they are likely to become chargeable at home.'"

Superintendent Stockdale further says—

"The Cork vessels used to land the Irish poor at Cardiff; at first 13 or 14 in a vessel, then increasing to upwards of 200 in one vessel. I made various reports to the Marquis of Bute, our late Lord Lieutenant, at the time; a great many told me that Mr.—— of ——, near Cork, had paid 2s. 6d. for their passage. I think in hundreds of instances I was told this. They came direct to me or to the relieving officer; having been told in Ireland that they might depend upon being relieved immediately. They were many of them apparently starving, and many in advanced stage of disease. One was found dead in the bottom of the hold, and an inquest was held on the body; many died shortly after landing.

"*Harriet Huxtable*, the manager of the tramp-house at Newport, says, 'There is hardly a family that have come over and applied to me but we have found a member or two of it ill. They are chiefly troubled with dysentery now, not fever; some in a shocking filthy state; they don't live long with it, there is a sort of dropsy attends with it.

" 'They are very remarkable: they will eat salt by basins' full, and drink a great quantity of water after. I have frequently known them (children and grown-up people), those who have been stopping with us, and who could not have been hungry, eat cabbage-leaves and other refuse from the ash-heaps. I prevent them now. I really believe they would eat almost anything.'

"*Mr. Joseph Lewis*, master of Chepstow Workhouse, says, 'There are more women than men with the Irish. I think the men go on before their wives and families without calling here (perhaps to escape work, which we make them do). Some of the Irish families appear to be making for no place, and we see them often in their rounds.'

"The *Master of Stafford Union Workhouse* remarks, 'The Irish are extremely filthy in their habits, generally swarming with vermin. The Irish women are even more filthy than the men. The younger Irish women appear to be generally prostitutes.' Similar statements to this have been repeated, without exception, at all the workhouses visited."

The *Oxford Mendicity Society* state that—

"Questions have been made regularly to the Irish paupers who are now flocking into Oxford to ascertain who has furnished the means for making their passage. There is a general unwillingness to answer the question at all, but it has been admitted in some cases that some persons in authority, who seem from the description to have been Poor Law Officers, have given money."

Mr. Broadhurst, relieving officer of the Congleton Union, thus characterises both the English and Irish vagrants at this period:—

"During the quarter ending 25th December, 1847, 1,594 tramps were admitted to the Congleton Union, of which 80 per cent. were Irish. Many of the Irish state they are in search of work; yet one of them told Pickford, the manager, that the greater part would curse any man who offered them employment. (The man made the same statement to me.) An Irishman, a few weeks back, told Pickford that he had lived by begging for the last fifteen years, and never done a day's work. The English vagrants are cotton-workers, wool-combers, hatters, &c., though at times habitual mendicants are amongst those who are admitted. Pickford states he has been told by some of the tramps, that if food was given in every case the applicants would be sixfold. No labour is imposed; each morning they are taken out of the town by the beadles.

The effect of sending the Irish vagrants home seems to have stimulated the flow of vagrancy instead of stopping it, as *Mr. Boase* observes :—

"With regard to the riddance of tramps hanging about a town, nothing appears to be effectual. Even those removed under the law for Irish removals will return again after a few days, as has been experienced at Cardiff and at Liverpool ; and, in my opinion (founded on what I have gleaned from tramps), this remedy re-acts upon itself, doubtless inducing many to venture the journey from Ireland, confiding that at the worst, should England turn out not to be the Dorado represented to them, they will be forwarded home again gratuitously, and inducing many Irish tramps to resort to the towns where this practice is adopted, from the most distant parts of the kingdom, with the avowed purpose of obtaining gratuitous passage home."

If any testimony were needed by those who have studied the question of the utter worthlessness of the whole fraternity of tramps, it would be afforded by the intimate fellowship they maintain, a fellowship and interchange of information carried on for every evil purpose and for no good purpose. The following is a typical revelation of the freemasonry which exists amongst them:—

"It is remarkable, however, with what telegraphic despatch the whole corps of tramps become acquainted with any altered circumstances bearing upon their relations with particular unions. In the North Witchford Union, for example, it happened that two months ago the stock of junk for oakum-picking was exhausted, and the guardians, not then appreciating sufficiently the necessity of enforcing the provisions of 5 and 6 Vict., c. 57, s. 5, delayed to authorise the master of the Doddington Workhouse to procure a fresh supply. In the very next week the number of vagrants, which had for some time previously averaged about 20 per week, increased to 45, in the second week to 57, in the third week to 75, and then, oakum-picking having been resumed, the number as steadily decreased till it reached the usual average." *

Hardened in vice and frequently graduated in crime, gaol has no terrors for the vagrant; *Sir John Walsham* thus writes upon the subject :—

* Report of Sir John Walsham

"It is now, I apprehend, becoming a system with the vagrants to pass away the cold months by fortnightly halts in different gaols. I have no doubt that the men who have just been sent to Ipswich from Stow Union will, as soon as their fourteen days have expired, make their way to Blything or Wangford Union houses, and commit the same depredation there, in order to be sent to Beccles Gaol; from thence they will proceed to Yarmouth, and so on.

"In the summer months vagrancy is a pleasanter occupation, and then they find the workhouses such convenient lodging-houses or hotels, that they behave better; nevertheless, work is their special aversion, and in most of my workhouses now they are set to work, whilst in Ipswich and other gaols work has been abandoned. They are often found, at all times of the year, destroying whatever they can in all union houses where work is required. I feel almost convinced that this estimable fraternity have bound themselves by a vow always to resist, even to being committed to prison, the prescribed task of work."

This is also the opinion of *Mr. Hawley*, who observes :—

"Refusals to work, and destruction of clothing for the purpose of getting a better outfit, have been common practices amongst the vagrants; and in several instances the workhouse windows have been wantonly broken, and articles of furniture destroyed. Magisterial interference has been generally called in to suppress and punish these outrages, but it has been found that they have frequently been committed for the purpose of incurring a punishment which the lenient discipline, liberal dietary, and general comforts of the county gaol render a desirable object with these persons."

Before the Government took over the management of gaols, and established uniformity of treatment in them, vagrants naturally exhibited a preference for those gaols in which the treatment was of a superior character, as the following statement made by Mr. Evans, M.P. for Derbyshire, in the House of Commons in 1876, conclusively shows.

"In his own county (Derbyshire) they had done their best to make the gaols efficient; but as opinions differed it was inevitable that gaols should be managed in different ways throughout the country. He might claim to be pretty well acquainted with the wishes, tastes, and fancies of the prisoners in our gaols, and he could assure the House that the discrimination they showed in their appreciation of different prisons was almost beyond belief. About five or six years ago an old offender, who was intimately acquainted with all the prisons in the country, was brought before him for fowl-stealing. He had stolen the fowls in the night, had cooked one for supper at a furnace, and had then lain down to sleep with the other fowls near him. About five in the morning a policeman, who had heard of the robbery, shook him by the collar and said, ' I take you into custody on the charge of stealing these fowls.' He was found just on the borders of the two counties, and the prisoner's first question was, ' What county am I in ? ' The policeman replied, ' Derbyshire,' whereupon the man exclaimed, ' Thank God for that ! ' As one of the magistrates of Derbyshire he confessed he felt humiliated. They had been racking their brains to make their prisons as unpleasant as possible, yet here was a man who thanked God that he was going to Derby instead of Leicester Gaol."

The mode in which tramps conceal their property when applying for relief is thus described by *Mr. Boase* :—

"Searching is not general ; at Brentford and some other places it is entirely abandoned. In some few places it is kept in practice chiefly for the purpose of preventing danger from lucifer matches, pipes, tobacco, and knives. It is still occasionally resorted to where there is a suspicion of concealed property ; but the general practice of it has been defeated by the tramps, who expect and prepare for it, and hide their money, or appoint a banker to lodge out of the Workhouse ; or deposit it at small hucksters' shops and marine-store shops. Some time ago the master at Eton Workhouse found a considerable sum, which several tramps had hidden under a stone before applying.

" The *Master of Stafford Union Workhouse* says : ' The Irish have a practice of leaving their money at some small huckster's shop. They hide it also ; they have almost pulled down a hedge near the workhouse by hiding money in it. I have no doubt that all the Irish we get have (but with few exceptions) money somewhere. Sometimes one of a party will be ' captain,' and stay at a lodging house with the money ; sometimes the mother and children will come alone. The men almost invariably have lucifer matches, a pipe and tobacco, and a knife ; seldom are any tools found, sometimes a few cottons and tapes ; but they now appear to give up these ostensible pretences of living.'

" The *Master of Kensington* has found poaching snares and picklocks, and the night before I was at Cookham, dice and thimble-rig * apparatus were found upon tramps going to Reading Fair."

---

* A cheating game performed on a small table with a pea and 3 thimbles. The

The following statement of *Mr. Wilkinson*, relieving officer of the Congleton Union, shows the mode in which keepers of tramps' lodging houses actually profit by the establishment of casual wards :—

"This at first may appear strange, that the lodging-house keeper is benefited by others going to the Union workhouse for the night; but when you know that those who apply for a ticket for the night first give up their money, clothes, trinkets, &c., besides a quantity of food they have begged during the day, to those who stay at the lodging house, and he is commissioned to sell for them the food so charitably disposed. Thus the lodging-house keeper often gets more than one-half the provisions for himself and family, and I have frequently heard Irishmen who have lodged in this township say they often get good bargains of this sort; it is high time that some means should be taken to prevent these people imposing on the public, as you see last year there was a percentage of more than 57 direct from Ireland, and this year not 4 per cent., although the vagrants are 50 per cent. increased."

The social demoralisation produced by vagrancy is thus strikingly set forth by the *Master of the Cosford Union* :—

"From all that I have witnessed in the general behaviour of vagrants, I take for granted that a vast amount of demoralisation is carried into every part of the country by the streams of vagrants and mendicants constantly floating therein.

"A large number also of this class is to be found in the gaols of the rural districts, the other portion being chiefly agricultural labourers, who, whilst they may be considered pupils in the school of crime, learning from these vagrants to carry back to their villages the amount of knowledge theoretically acquired in felonious practices, and which, I am sorry to add, is speedily brought to bear in reality after their liberation.

"My experience leads me to believe vagrancy to be the first step towards the committal of felony. I have known numerous cases where the career in crime commenced in vagrancy; and I am further of an opinion, that the suppression of vagrancy would go far in suppressing a great amount of imposition and depredation."

The accommodation provided for vagrants in the various work-

pea is openly passed from one thimble to another, and then bystanders are tempted to bet that they can indicate the particular thimble under which the pea is. They are sometimes allowed to win at first, in order to inspire them with confidence, but are speedily cheated by the performer, who on each occasion removes the pea under one of his finger nails.

houses at this period seems to have been of an inferior and demoralising character.

Mr. *Grenville Pigott* says—

"In some workhouses there are still no distinct vagrant wards, and in none can those appropriated to that purpose be deemed sufficient for the accommodation of the numbers who occasionally demand admission, amounting sometimes to 20, 30, or even 40 a night."

Sir *John Walsham* remarks—

"I have now accomplished the establishment of vagrant wards in most of the workhouses of my district. Some of these wards are, I am sorry to say, very bad."

Mr. *Boase* observes—

"The buildings appropriated to tramps are generally brick buildings, of one story; in the range, and attached to the back part of the yard. In general they have brick floors and guard-room beds, with loose straw and rugs for the males and iron bedsteads with straw ties for the females. They are generally badly ventilated and unprovided with any means of producing warmth. All holes for ventilation in reach of the occupants are sure to be stuffed with rags or straw; so that the effluvium of these places is at best most disgustingly offensive, and has more than once produced illness to myself when visiting them in the morning, just after their being opened.

"In some workhouses but small provision, or none, has been made for the reception of tramps, and a sudden influx has filled the stables and outhouses; the general impression among the Poor Law officers being, that they are bound to provide for all who apply, and considerable sums have been paid for lodging tramps at public-houses and in barns at such crises."

Upon receiving this evidence the Poor Law Board issued a Minute, in which it was stated that "a sound and vigilant discrimination in respect of the objects of relief, and the refusal of it to all who were not ascertained to be destitute, were the only effectual remedies against the continued increase of vagrancy and mendicity." The exercise of this discrimination by the officers of the Poor Law which immediately followed appears at the time to have had a favourable effect in reducing the ranks of vagrancy.

In order to remove doubts as to the power of the Poor Law officials to search vagrants, it was enacted by the 11 & 12 Vict., c. 110, passed in this year, that "any destitute wanderer or wayfarer applying for admission to the workhouse may be searched, and if found in possession of money or other property, the money is forfeited to the guardians: and if he has not disclosed the possession, he is liable to punishment as an idle and disorderly person." In the year following (1849) it was enacted by the 12 & 13 Vict., c. 103, s. 3, that where a poor person is chargeable to the common fund of a union it shall have the same effect as chargeability to a parish in respect of proceedings under 5 Geo. IV., c. 83.

In the year 1854 a Select Committee of the House of Commons was appointed to inquire into the operation of the Act 8 & 9 Vict., c. 117, relating to removal from England of chargeable poor persons born in Scotland, Ireland, the Isles of Man, Scilly, Jersey, or Guernsey, and also into the operation of the Act 8 & 9 Vict., c. 83, relating to the removal from Scotland of chargeable poor persons born in England, Ireland, or the Isle of Man.

At the outset of the inquiry it was evidently the desire of the Irish witnesses to prove that mendicity in Ireland and the immigration of Irish pauperism into England and Scotland had so far decreased that it was not worth while to maintain the existing regulations for returning Irish paupers to their places of settlement.

Mr. Alfred Power, Chief Commissioner of the Poor Law in Ireland, stated, "It was notorious that a very large number of poor Irish used annually to proceed to England and Scotland in search of work in time of harvest, but the number was diminished now very much.

"The actual price paid for a deck passage for an Irish pauper coming from Dublin to Liverpool in the year 1847 was 1s., and the price back again, under orders of removal, was 2s. 6d. Public mendicancy had much diminished in Dublin since he came to reside there about ten years ago, and he believed that it had much diminished in other parts of Ireland. He thought there was a strong and growing feeling throughout the country to discourage mendicancy."

Mr. R. L. Jameson, guardian of the Cork Union, stated, "Mendicancy had been very much discouraged of late in the south of Ireland. He considered that mendicancy was dying out very much; they did not see one beggar in the streets of Cork now, he thought, for twenty that were seen a few years ago."

The Earl of Donoughmore, guardian of the Clogheen Union,

said, "He did not think it probable that any large number of persons would leave Ireland to go to England for the purpose of begging there, they having to pay their passage money of 10s. or 12s. to England; and even supposing they could get to England for little or nothing, he did not think that they would go, because it struck him that a beggar had a much better chance in Ireland than he had in England. It was the habit of the people (it might perhaps partly be the consequence of the religion of the people), even of the very poorest in Ireland to give to beggars. He had observed beggars going through his own estate; he had seen them go from door to door of the cottages of the farmers, and had scarcely ever seen them go away empty. He thought it was very much to be deplored, for he thought it encouraged that kind of wandering life which beggars lead; but if he was asked in which country a beggar had the best chance of picking up relief, if he was a beggar himself, he would certainly much rather live in Ireland than in England.

" He thought the system of roving mendicancy was becoming gradually diminished, but not to the extent he should wish. It had diminished in Clonmel, and been very much discouraged in Limerick, Waterford, and all great cities and towns."

This evidence is generally corroborated by the reports of the Irish Poor Law inspectors in the year 1856, as will be seen on referring to the concluding chapter on the History of Vagrancy in Ireland.*

From the following evidence adduced before the Committee it appears, however, pretty certain that this reduction of mendicity in Ireland was brought about by its transference to England and Scotland.

Sir John M'Neil, chairman of the Board of Supervision for the Relief of the Poor in Scotland, stated, " He had returns of the number of vagrants and beggars challenged by the police in the counties of Haddington and Edinburgh, exclusive of the city of Edinburgh, during the eight years ending 30th June, 1853. In these two counties, which are on the east coast of Scotland, in the first four of those eight years, that is, in 1846, 1847, 1848, and 1849, there were challenged for vagrancy and begging by the police—Scotch, 4,395; English, 1,317; making together of Scotch and English 5,712; of Irish in those four years, 4,810. He understood that it was stated that vagrants had nearly dis-

* Pp. 422—426.

appeared from Ireland. He thought he could account for some of them. In the four years, 1850, 1851, 1852, and 1853, in those two counties the number of vagrants were: Scotch, 7,251; English, 839; English and Scotch together, 8,090; Irish, 11,248. It would be observed that in the first four years, which were the four years of great distress, but were also the four years of lavish relief in Ireland, the whole number of Irish vagrants in those two counties was 4,810 In the last four years, after the cessation of that relief in Ireland, when the vagrants began to disappear from Ireland, the number in those two counties was 11,248—more than double what it was in the first four years. He thought that would therefore probably show what had become of the vagrants who had disappeared from Ireland, or a considerable number of them. The number of persons apprehended by the police of the City of Edinburgh, and tried for begging in the four years, 1850 to 1853, both inclusive (the records did not furnish the means of giving the returns for the first four years for the City of Edinburgh, they only furnished returns for the last four years), were 2,015 Scotch, 220 English, 1,427 Irish. Therefore, adding the City of Edinburgh to the two counties for those four years, the numbers would stand thus: Scotch, 9,266; English, 1,059; Scotch and English together, 10,325; Irish, 12,675. The number of Irish exceeded, therefore, by 2,300 the aggregate number of English and Scotch together. Those were two counties, it would be observed, not on the west coast of Scotland, but on the east coast of Scotland.

"In respect of the western counties, he was desirous to have obtained similar information with regard to the county of Lanark, but unfortunately the county of Lanark had no county police.

"He thought that the increase of Irish vagrancy in Scotland at the very time when Irish vagrancy began to decrease in Ireland, and its continued increase during the past four years, while it had been diminishing in Ireland, afforded at least a very strong presumption that they had in Scotland a considerable number of the vagrants who had disappeared from Ireland."

Mr. William Smythe, formerly secretary to the Board of Supervision of the Poor in Scotland, said, "The chief inducement operating upon the poorer Irish to come to Scotland was, he thought, that they heard from their friends who had come over that there was some employment likely to be got for them. He thought that they came in search of employment, that there were very few cases, excepting those who might come to their relations, of parties who did not come seeking employment. They were very likely uneasy at home, and they thought that any change which they might have would be for the better; they fancied that Edinburgh and Glasgow were wealthy places, and that there were many odd jobs there by which they could pick up a livelihood. After having come, he would wish to observe that the vagrancy laws in Scotland were by no means stringent, and that if they found that they could not obtain a livelihood by industrious labour there was very little check upon their going about the country begging.

"One of the complaints which were made with respect to the Irish who came over—and a complaint that certainly had some grounds for existence—was that the men found employment; but that while the men were employed, the women and children went out begging. He had heard that complaint often made in all parts of the country.

"They were very anxious to pick up money from any quarter whatever, during the period that they were resident in a district.

"He did not think that they entertained the same repugnance to mendicancy—they did not fancy that it was so degrading a profession as the native Scotch did."

The Rev. Augustus Campbell, rector and chairman of the Select Vestry of Liverpool, presented the following return:—

NUMBER OF PAUPERS PASSED TO IRELAND, SCOTLAND, ISLE OF MAN, AND GUERNSEY, FROM 26TH DECEMBER, 1845, TO 25TH DECEMBER, 1853, WITH THE EXPENSE.

	Total passed.	Ireland.	Scotland.	Isle of Man.	Guernsey.	TOTAL COST.
						£ s. d.
26 Dec. 1845 to 25 Dec. 1846	5,649	5,313	330	6	—	1,197 1 6
,, 1846 ,, 1847	15,472	15,008	443	21	—	4,175 11 3
,, 1847 ,, 1848	8,239	7,607	612	20	—	2,459 8 6
,, 1848 ,, 1849	10,071	9,509	543	19	—	2,568 3 10
,, 1849 ,, 1850	8,102	7,627	463	12	—	1,487 15 6
,, 1850 ,, 1851	8,232	7,808	406	13	5	1,968 19 10
,, 1851 ,, 1852	6,004	5,506	483	9	6	1,460 2 6
,, 1852 ,, 1853	4,820	4,503	302	13	2	1,124 13 6
	66,589	62,881	3,582	113	13	16,441 16 5

He also read the following letter from the late *Mr. Rushton* to the Home Secretary, dated April 21, 1849 :—

"You already know the results of this accumulation of misery in the crowded town of Liverpool, of the cost of relief at once rendered necessary to prevent the thousands of hungry and naked Irish perishing in our streets, and also of the cost of the pestilence which generally follows in the train of famine and misery, such as we then had to encounter. I do not enter into the details of this misery, further than to say that though the pecuniary cost to the town of Liverpool was enormous, the loss of valuable lives was yet much more to be deplored; hundreds of patients perished, notwithstanding all efforts made to save them, and ten Roman Catholic* and one Protestant clergyman, many parochial officers, and many medical men who devoted themselves to alleviating the sufferings of the wretched, died in the discharge of those high duties.

"I believe I have in my former letters to you, stated my conviction that the presence of this miserable population would materially affect the health and character of our own labouring classes; my worst anticipations have been realised. I am unfortunately enabled, by the results of my daily experience, to show you how much the health of the people has suffered, and I am enabled by exact details to show you how greatly the Irish misery has increased crime in Liverpool. In the year 1846 18,171 prisoners were brought before the police-court; in 1847 the number increased to 19,719; and in 1848 a further increase took place, and the numbers were 22,036. In the year 1845 the number of committed for trial, and summarily convicted for felony, amounted to 3,889; in 1846 the number increased to 4,740, in 1847 to 6,510, and in 1848 to 7,714. I do not possess the means of accurately distinguishing the countries to which the criminals belong before the year 1848; previous to that time I had, however, directed my attention to the subject, and I saw from day to day that the poor Irish population, forced upon us in a state of wretchedness which cannot be described, would within twelve hours after they landed be found among one of three classes, viz. paupers, vagrants, or thieves. Few became claimants for parochial relief, for in that case they soon discovered they might be at once sent back to Ireland. Many of these forlorn creatures became beggars, many of them thieves."

* Mr. Campbell stated his belief that this was an error, and that the number of Roman Catholic clergymen who died was *six*, and not one Protestant.

Mr. Campbell then stated that "his belief was that a great proportion of the mendicants in Liverpool were Irish; and in times of great pressure they had found it absolutely necessary, on the part of the Select Vestry, to put placards upon the walls entreating the inhabitants not to give money to unknown beggars in the street, but to send them when they applied for relief in the street, either to the parish officers or to the District Provident Society.

"It was a matter of notoriety that the Irish poor generally very willingly applied for out-door relief; in ten years £74,078 was expended in out-door relief to the Irish; the workhouse relief to them was £44,505, the industrial school £5,424."

Mr. John Evans, assistant overseer of Liverpool, stated that, "The class of Irish who came merely for the purpose of begging did not come now in any number as compared with former years."

Mr. James Salter, relieving officer of the Newport Union, Monmouthshire, said that, "The class of Irish who applied to him for removal orders were men who had been up to London, or in different parts of the country to work during the harvest; they generally got some little money and went back in the winter. He had had many of them searched, and had scarcely ever found anything upon these individuals; but he had subsequently found that they had employed a man that they had confidence in, and this man had been their cashier; he had had the whole of the money; he himself had preceded them by a vessel, having purchased his own passage to Ireland, and left these parties to apply to him (the relieving officer) for orders of removal to send them home, or for assistance: they asked more for assistance to send them home than anything else."

CHAPTER XIII.

1854—1882.

Arguments in favour of establishing industrial schools for vagrant children—Legislation of 1857—Subsequent amendments of the Industrial Schools' Act—Evasion of the maintenance of vagrants by Metropolitan Boards of Guardians—Attempted remedy by the Houseless Poor Act of 1864—Accommodation provided for vagrants—Reports on vagrancy by the Poor Law Inspectors in 1866—Character of tramps and their conduct in the vagrant wards—Estimated proportion of vagrants who devote themselves to idleness, crime, &c.—Average ages of vagrants—Arson by tramps—Systematic communication amongst them—Increase of vagrancy—Legislation of 1871—Vagrant Italian children in England—Committee of 1879 on settlement—Decrease of Irish vagrancy in England and its causes—Further increase of vagrancy and its causes—The Casual Poor Act, 1882.

In the course of the year 1854 Mr. Dunlop, M.P. for Greenock, brought in and carried a Bill for rendering Reformatory and Industrial Schools more available for the benefit of juvenile delinquents and vagrant children in Scotland.

In 1857 the subject was taken up on similar lines as regards England by Sir Stafford Northcote, afterwards Earl of Iddesleigh, who moved for leave to bring in a Bill to make better provision for the care and education of vagrant, destitute, and disorderly children and for the extension of industrial schools. He said that, "The large class of children to whom the Bill referred was one peculiarly demanding their care and attention, not simply from motives of humanity, but from reasons of State policy connected with our criminal legislation. The difficulty of dealing with our criminals would be materially diminished if we could cut off the supply of those criminals at its source; and, as the worst of them were those who had been trained to crimes from their earliest years, the best interests of society would be consulted by taking them in hand before they became hardened.

"The reports of our prison inspectors appeared to show that about 7,000 were annually added to the criminal class of this country;

that might be, and he hoped was, an over-estimate; but the number, whatever it was, represented a much larger body of children who ran about the streets, getting constantly into trouble, and continually coming into the hands of the police, and on whom our present schools failed to make any impression. In Bristol, last year, there were apprehended of this class 525 children under sixteen years of age, of whom only 126 were committed for trial or summarily convicted, the remainder being left to wander about uncared for. In Liverpool, Manchester, Birmingham, and other populous towns, a similar state of things unhappily prevailed. This class not only constituted a dangerous element in our society, but, from their neglected condition, had a strong claim on our pity. How, he asked, did our existing institutions meet the wants of this class! The national schools did not meet the demand, for they were too high to meet the children in question. The children with whom his Bill proposed to deal would not choose to mix in their rags with the children of a superior class who now attended the national schools, neither was the discipline of those schools such as was necessary for the proper government of children of the lowest class, who required not a high scale of education, but the training of strict discipline and control. . . . . In support of this Bill he would call the attention of the House to the successful working of the Scotch Act, the operation of which had been attended by a marked decrease in the committals of juvenile offenders. In Aberdeen, before the establishment of the free schools, the average annual number of juvenile vagrants taken into custody by the police was 342, while the average annual number in five years after their establishment was only six. In Edinburgh and Glasgow similar results had been produced."

This Bill fell through in consequence of the dissolution of Parliament, but on the assembling of the new Parliament in the same year was reintroduced by Mr. Adderley, afterwards Lord Norton, who stated that, "It was calculated that the number of children, in this kingdom alone, who might be dealt with under a measure of this nature, was about 50,000. At present no means of education whatever were provided for these unfortunate children. The late Mr. Tufnell said that they were the class of children for whose education it was most important that the State should make provision, and that their redemption from idle and dissolute habits would do more to promote the true interests of the country than any number of gaols and gibbets. In fact, these children formed the basis of an hereditary class of criminals, the insuperable difficulty of disposing of whom the House had to-night been discussing for some hours." *

The Bill subsequently became law as the Industrial Schools Act, 1857 (20 and 21 Vict., c. 48), entitled an Act to make better Provision for the Care and Education of Vagrant, Destitute, and Disorderly Children. It enacts that any child who, in the opinion of the justices, is above the age of seven and under fourteen taken into custody on a charge of vagrancy may be sent to a Certified Industrial School for any period not exceeding one week while inquiries are made for the parent, guardian, or nearest adult relative of the child. At the end of this period the justice may order the child to be discharged altogether, or may deliver him up to his parent or guardian on his giving an assurance in writing that he will be responsible for the good behaviour of the child for any period not exceeding twelve months. In default of this assurance the child may be sent for such period as the justices may think necessary for his education and training to a Certified Industrial School. If a child again commits an act of vagrancy after an assurance given by the parent or guardian and through his neglect within the period for which he has become responsible, the justices may inflict a fine upon him not exceeding 40s. Children may be discharged on good security being found. Parents may be ordered to pay a sum not exceeding 3s. a week until the child attains fifteen. Children absconding may be sent back to school, and any person who induces them to abscond or knowingly conceals or harbours them is liable to a penalty not exceeding £2. The Committee of Council on Education may certify Industrial Schools.

In 1860 a proposal was sent from the Privy Council Office to the Home Office to transfer the schools to the latter department on the ground that they were schools having a penal character, and this was carried into effect by the 23 and 24 Vict., c. 108. In the year 1861 Sir George Lewis, as Home Secretary, introduced a new Bill, stating as a reason that some technical objections rendered the existing Act difficult to be carried into execution, and that the present Bill, attempted to put the enactments of the Act into a more working form. This Bill subsequently became law as the Industrial Schools Act, 1861 (24 and 25 Vict., c. 113), and

* Alluding to the discussion on the Transportation and Penal Servitude Bill introduced earlier in the evening by Sir George Grey.

entitled an Act for amending and consolidating the Law relating to Industrial Schools. It enacts the following description of children liable to be sent to school.

Any child apparently under the age of fourteen begging or receiving alms or being in any street or public place for that purpose.

Any child of the same age found wandering and not having any home or settled place of abode, or any visible means of subsistence, or who frequents the company of reputed thieves.

Any child apparently under the age of twelve who has committed an offence punishable by imprisonment, but who ought in the opinion of the justices to be sent to an Industrial School.

Any child under fourteen whose parent represents that he is unable to control him and that he desires him to be sent to an Industrial School and will pay for his maintenance.

Any person may bring a child coming within these descriptions before a Justice, who may send him to the workhouse for a week pending inquiries, and then commit him to an Industrial School until he attains the age of fifteen. The Justices may order the parent to pay any sum not exceeding 5s. a week towards his maintenance. Any child absconding from school may be sent back or committed to a Reformatory School, and any person who directly or indirectly withdraws a child from school, or who induces or aids him to abscond, or knowingly conceals or harbours him, is liable to a penalty not exceeding £5. This Act repeals the 20 and 21 Vict., c. 48, and 23 and 24 Vict., c. 108. The Act is to remain in force until January 1, 1864.

The 25 and 26 Vict., c. 10 (1862), continues this Act until January 1, 1867.

In the year 1866 it was resolved to consolidate and amend the Acts, and this was effected by the 29 and 30 Vict., c. 118 (10th August, 1866), known as the Industrial Schools Act, 1866, and entitled an Act to consolidate and amend the Acts relating to the Industrial Schools in *Great Britain*. It enacts that any person may bring before two Justices or a Magistrate any child apparently under the age of fourteen that comes within any of the following descriptions:—

" That is found begging or receiving alms (whether actually or under the pretext of offering anything for sale), or that is found in any street or public place for a similar purpose.

" That is found wandering and not having any home or settled place of abode or proper guardianship or visible means of subsistence.

"That is found destitute, either being an orphan or having a surviving parent who is undergoing penal servitude or imprisonment.

"That frequents the company of reputed thieves.

"Any child apparently under twelve charged with an offence punishable by imprisonment may also be sent to an Industrial School. Refractory children under the age of fourteen in the charge of their parents or in workhouses or pauper schools may also be sent to Industrial Schools. A child may be sent to the workhouse pending inquiries. A child apparently above ten who refuses to conform to the rules of the school may be sent to hard labour for any term not less than fourteen days nor more than three months and at the expiration of the time he may be sent to a reformatory. A child escaping from the school may be sent back, or if apparently above ten may instead be sentenced by the Justices to hard labour for any time not less than fourteen days nor more than three months, and at the expiration of this time he may be sent to a Reformatory. Any person who knowingly assists a child to escape or induces him to do so, or harbours or conceals him or prevents him from returning to school, is on conviction liable to a penalty not exceeding £20, or imprisonment not exceeding two months with or without hard labour. Parents, step-parents, or other persons legally liable to maintain a child may be ordered to contribute a sum not exceeding 5s. a week towards his maintenance. The detention is to cease on the child attaining sixteen. This Act repeals the 24 and 25 Vict., c. 113, 24 and 25 Vict., c. 132 (Scotland), and 25 and 26 Vict., c. 10."

The following additions have since been made to this Act. The 35 and 36 Vict., c. 21 (1872), enacts that "Section 12 of the Industrial Schools Act, 1866, shall extend to authorise the prison authority in England themselves to undertake anything towards which they are authorised by that section to contribute."

The 34 and 35 Vict., c. 112, s. 14 (1871), provides that, "Where any woman is convicted of a crime, and a previous conviction of crime is proved against her, any children of such woman under the age of fourteen years who may be under her care and control at the time of her conviction for the last of such crimes, and who have no visible means of subsistence, or are without proper guardianship, shall be deemed to be children to whom in Great Britain the provisions of the Industrial Schools Act, 1866, and in Ireland the provisions of the Industrial Schools (Ireland) Act, 1868, apply."

Under the Elementary Education Act, 1870 (33 and 34 Vict., c. 75, s. 27), "A School Board shall have the same powers of contributing money in the case of an Industrial School as is given to a Prison Authority by Section 12 of 'The Industrial Schools Act, 1866.' A School Board may also establish an Industrial School, and may appoint officers to bring children before two justices or a magistrate in order to their being sent to an Industrial School."

Under the Elementary Education Act, 1876 (39 and 40 Vict., c. 76), "If either the parent of any child above the age of five years prohibited from being taken into full time employment, habitually and without reasonable excuse neglects to provide efficient elementary instruction for his child; or,

"Any child is found habitually wandering or not under proper control, or in the company of rogues, vagabonds, disorderly persons, or reputed criminals, it shall be the duty of the Local Authority, after due warning to the parent of the child, to complain to a court of summary jurisdiction, and the court may order the child to attend some certified efficient school willing to receive him.

"Where an attendance Order is not complied with, without any reasonable excuse within the meaning of this Act, a court of summary jurisdiction, on complaint made by the Local Authority, may,

"In the first case of non-compliance, if the parent of the child does not appear, or appears and fails to satisfy the court that he has used all reasonable efforts to enforce compliance with the order, impose a penalty not exceeding with the costs five shillings; but if the parent satisfies the court that he has used all reasonable efforts, the court may, without inflicting a penalty, order the child to be sent to a Certified Day Industrial School, or if it appears to the court that there is no such school suitable for the child, then to a Certified Industrial School; and

"In the second or any subsequent case of non-compliance with the order, the court may order the child to be sent to a Certified Day Industrial School, or if it appears to the court that there is no such school suitable for the child, then to a Certified Industrial School."

By Section 16 of the "Elementary Education Act, 1876," authority is given to the Secretary of State to Certify a Day Industrial School if he is satisfied that, "owing to the circumstances of any class of population in any school district, a school in which industrial training, elementary education, and one or more meals a day, but not lodging, are provided for the children, is necessary or expedient for the proper training and control of the children of such class."

The same legal power of detention is given to the managers of Day Industrial Schools, during the hours authorised by the Rules of the School and approved by the Secretary of State, as the Managers of other Certified Industrial Schools have.

Magistrates did not in the first instance make use of the Industrial Schools to the extent that had been contemplated by the framers of the Act. In the year 1861 only 358 children were committed in England and 650 in Scotland; in 1865 the numbers amounted to 475 and 300 respectively. After the passing of the Act of 1866 the numbers, however, rose rapidly. In 1867 the number committed in England was 1,378 and in Scotland 605. After the passing of the Elementary Education Act they increased in 1871 to 1,957 and 926 respectively, and in 1884 they amounted to 3,059 for England and 936 for Scotland, of whom 3,114 were boys and 881 girls. Concurrently with the establishment of these schools the number of juvenile offenders under sixteen years of age committed to prison for crime decreased from 13,981 in 1856 to 8,977 in 1871.

The influence of the Day Industrial Schools is also said to be good, and that the children rapidly improve in decency and good order.

In the meantime the adult Vagrant was regarded as a nuisance by most Metropolitan Boards of Guardians, and the policy generally adopted was to endeavour to evade the responsibility of entertaining him. In one case a board was hung outside a workhouse with "Take Notice—the Casual Wards are Full," when there was not a casual ward in the place. In another parish, cold water was poured on the vagrants when they assembled outside the workhouse for the purpose of obtaining admission. An inquiry undertaken by direction of the President of the Poor Law Board in 1863 showed that in the whole metropolis there was accommodation for 997 destitute vagrants and wayfarers, and that that accommodation was very unevenly distributed. It was also estimated that there were 1,400 persons homeless and destitute every night. Meantime the number of voluntary night refuges for this class had increased from 3 to 12 in number, accommodating at least 1,000 persons.

In the year 1864 the Right Hon. C. P. Villiers, then President of the Poor Law Board, introduced a Bill for remedying this state of things, observing that the 7 and 8 Vict., c. 101, had never been enforced, because the machinery was found to be cumbrous and costly. Fears were expressed that the proposed Bill would increase vagrancy, and Mr. Briscoe, M.P., stated that "some time ago he had met a party of people going about begging. They told him they were bricklayers from Windsor, and their reason for coming to London was that they understood they should get at any workhouse food and a night's lodging, so that they could 'chance it' for the day." The Bill, however, became law under the title of the Metropolitan Houseless Poor Act, 1864 (27 & 28 Vict., c. 116). It recites that it is expedient that provision should be made for distributing the charge of the relief of certain poor persons in the Metropolis during the ensuing winter otherwise than is now lawful. It then enacts that Guardians of Parishes or Unions in the Metropolis may keep account of relief to destitute wayfarers, wanderers or foundlings during the hours from 8 p.m. to 8 a.m., and obtain reimbursement from the Metropolitan Board of Works. This relief is to include food and articles of necessity and the cost of lodging or shelter, but not money given to them. Where no adequate accommodation exists the Guardians are required to provide wards or other places of reception for destitute wayfarers and foundlings having regard to the number of such persons likely to require relief; in default they are not to be entitled to the benefit of this Act.

In 1865 this Act was made perpetual by 28 Vict., c. 34. This Act also gave power to the police to conduct destitute wayfarers to the wards which were ordered to be open for their admission from 6 p.m. to 8 a.m. from October to March inclusive, and from 8 p.m. to 8 a.m. from April to September inclusive.

The result of the passing of these Acts was that accommodation was provided for 1,539 males, 974 females, and 32 children, or a total of 2,545, which the returns furnished to the Poor Law Board showed was ample, and as a consequence the misery and distress previously observable about the London streets largely decreased.

The number of admissions rapidly rose. In *Marylebone*, for the half-year to Lady Day, 1865, they amounted to 4,749; at Michaelmas, 1865, to 10,676; at Lady Day, 1866, to 19,322; and at Michaelmas, 1866, they fell to 10,012. The increase at the commencement was attributed to the closing of the Night Refuges, and the decrease in 1866 to the fact that the police began to be employed as Assistant Relieving Officers on the 21st February, 1866, and that the vagrants disliked having to go before them in order to obtain admission to the wards. A temporary check occurred in December, 1864, owing to the baths for the use of vagrants being then completed, and their being compelled to use them. For two months preceding the erection of the baths the number of casuals admitted was 2,429, while for four months afterwards, or double the time, the number only amounted to 2,320. In 1865 about 50 per cent. of the casuals at Marylebone stated that they had not been in London three days; 3,122 were English, 984 Irish, 103 Scotch, and 45 Welsh. Nearly all the male applicants were able-bodied, between the ages of 18 and 35, and a very large number of women were refused admission for being in a state of intoxication. In the *Whitechapel Union* the numbers relieved gradually rose from 5,411 in 1864 to 20,343 in 1869. Upon observation being made on the 25th October, 1869, it was found that of 71 vagrants relieved, 55 (or 77 per cent.) were personally known to the superintendent as habitual wanderers or professional vagrants.

The principal influx in the metropolis it was found occurred on the eve of public executions, important horse-races such as the Derby, and other public spectacles of a popular character. The first of these attractions, however, ceased to exist in 1868, as the last public execution took place on the 26th of May in that year.

In the year 1866 a fresh series of valuable Reports on Vagrancy was made to the Poor Law Board by the Poor Law Inspectors. The character of the tramps is thus described :—

"Among the tramping community are many wretched beings who could not, if they would, take any effective step to escape from their condition. Outcasts from society by their crimes or vices, or unpleasant ways, or unbearable temper, they would seek in vain for employment. Who would willingly employ a filthy jailbird or a ragged deserter? What respectable labourer would willingly work with such a vagabond? Some tramps have been from birth in the lowest grade, and have never been able to surmount the obstacles arising from early vicious association, or inferior bodily or mental organization. They exhibit an excessive misery and squalor which inspire disgust rather than compassion."*

"Tramps are for the most part, if not criminals, at least on the verge of crime. The greater portion of them have never done a week's work consecutively in their lives, and, if they can help it, never intend to do one. From many who have been taken ill on their journey, and had, for a time, to remain in the Wrexham Workhouse, it has been ascertained that they have, since shortly after the passing of the new Poor Law, passed their time circling from union to union, and either begged or stole to eke out an existence." †

"As a general rule, the 'casual ward' of a workhouse so far from being the temporary refuge of deserving poor, is a place of rendezvous for thieves and prostitutes and other vagabonds of the lowest class, gangs of whom "work" allotted districts, and make their circuits with as much regularity as the Judges." ‡

The *Master of Atcham Workhouse*, in Shropshire, says—

"The class of persons received there as vagrants are, generally speaking, men who hardly ever do any sort of work, but who go about the country from workhouse to workhouse, to beg, intimidate, or steal, as opportunity offers. As an illustration, he mentions the case of two strong men, well known both to the police and himself. These men had between two and three pounds of food each when searched on their admission. The Master remarked to them that theirs seemed to be a profitable occupation; their reply was, 'We are the men to make it so, for if we cannot get it by fair means we will have it by foul; if we cannot beg we steal.'"

The opinion, founded upon experience, of the *Master of Newport* (Salop) *Workhouse* of tramps who come there for casual relief is that they are the most worthless and reckless class that he has any knowledge of, and that they are composed of thieves of every sort, deserters from the army, bad characters discharged

---

* Report of Mr. John T. Graves.
† Statement of Mr. Kemp, previously master of the Wrexham Workhouse.
‡ Report of Mr. Andrew Doyle.

from the army as such, runaway apprentices and idle vagabonds of every kind who will not work, and prefer the vagabond life of a vagrant to any other.

The *Master of Wem Workhouse* instances the case of a young woman who was put into the vagrant ward. A short time after came a young man; he inquired if a young woman had been put up; the porter said " Yes ; " he said, " Where is she ? " the porter replied, " Up-stairs ; " he said, " I am going to sleep with her ; " the porter said, " I am sure you are not ; " he said, " I shall," and was impertinent, and the Master was fetched, who spoke to him and told him he could not allow anything of the kind. The young man was very abusive, and said he would have his 3d., as he gave the young woman 3d. before she came in, to sleep with her The Master sent for the policeman, but he left before the policeman came. The Master further adds, " Almost all tramps are filthy, dirty, and covered with vermin. They get so dirty that they cannot wear their clothing any longer, so go into the tramp wards, and in the course of the night tear up their clothing; this has occurred many times there. One evening (and this had happened several times) there came a vagrant; he was shown into the vagrant wards ; he said, ' Is this the place where I am going to sleep ? ' the porter said ' Yes ;' he said, ' Then go to hell, and sleep there yourself,' and so left."

The *Master of Walsall* says he has many times listened at the tramp ward doors to overhear their conversation. At odd times he has heard as follows: " How did you get in, Bill ? " " Oh, I told the b——y gaffer that I walked from Stone to-day ; he said he didn't believe me, but he let me in." He heard another say, himself and So-and-so stole a loaf out of a baker's shop at Abergavenny, and how they knocked the " Bobby " * down and got away. He heard another say that he would tell them a " stunning " † workhouse for a good supper and breakfast. " Much Wenlock (Madeley), lads, that's the place." Another said, " I'll tell you a house always good for twopence. Do you know that big white house on the right-hand side as you go into Lichfield ? " " Yes." " Well, then, I have had it there many a time, and I know it's always good for it." Another said Dudley Workhouse was the worst place for skilley ‡ that he ever was at, &c., &c.

The *Master of Wrexham* considers that for low cunning, outward immoral conduct, obscene language, and, in many cases, bare-

---

* Policeman. † First rate. ‡ Gruel.

faced lying and stealing, vagrants in general are not to be surpassed by the most depraved outcasts of the metropolis.

The *Relieving Officer of Birkenhead* says—" Vagrants are young and old unmarried persons of both sexes who gain their living by any means but honest industry." He classifies them as follows:—

"Thieves on the look out, low prostitutes, beggars of both sexes and all ages, hawkers of petty articles, such as watches, caps, laces, bead ornaments, steel pens, writing paper (or anything which will serve to approach a house, to find what can be obtained by fair or foul means); and begging-letter writers, smashers,* ballad singers, travelling tinkers, china menders, umbrella repairers,† either of which description of business can be much more profitably carried on if the person be aged, lame, or can gracefully assume to be so, or be successful in just keeping alive a delicate child, because greater sympathy will be thereby excited."

Their general conduct in the vagrant wards at night is thus depicted:—

The *Master of Great Boughton,* in Cheshire, says he frequently hears them about 9 o'clock at night singing obscene songs, cursing and swearing, or relating some begging adventure.

The *Master of Madeley* observes that—

"The police of that town are of opinion that the greater part of the vagrants who come before them are men who never want work, and make a trade of tramping the country, begging, and stealing. They frequently see them in different public-houses before they come to have their tickets signed. . . . Many of them spend a great part of the night in singing and dancing, and telling each other their adventures and the whereabouts of other acquaintances. They all go by slang names, and are known to each other by them."

The experience of the *Master of Shiffnal* is, that "Tramps sometimes obtain orders from the relieving officer between 6 and 7 o'clock, get them countersigned by the police constable, and then stop at public-houses in the town till between 11 and 12, when they come to the workhouse and disturb the inmates by violently shouting and kicking at the outer doors. The early part of the night in the ward is spent in giving each other an account of the previous day's route, frauds, and success, inquir-

---

* Persons who pass counterfeit coin.
† Styled in " Tramps' cant " *Mushroom fakers.*

ing after companions, and repeating obscene and disgusting tales and songs. That some have received a liberal education or are possessed of great natural gifts is evident from some good drawings sketched with pencil upon the walls of the ward, or verses nicely written, but on the most obscene subjects. Parties who have been in the tramp ward are frequently taken into custody by the police within an hour after their discharge on charges of vagrancy."

The *Master of Wem* states that—

" A great many of the tramps that come there swear most fearfully ; only tell them of something that they may have done wrong, and then you get your eyes and limbs cursed fearfully. He has stood at the door after locking up tramps, and has many times heard them telling where they have called at that day, and saying, ' You must take care when you go, there' (describing the house) ' is a large dog ;' also, at another place, ' You will get plenty to eat and to bring away ; but don't go to such a place, you will get nothing ;' so that, generally, the places are marked out, which is good and which is bad ; also, saying they are going to such places, to the races, and stating what arrangements they have made with others to meet at certain places. A woman and three children came there about three weeks previously ; she was so drunk that she could scarcely walk, and swore most dreadfully."

The following estimates are given of the proportion of vagrants who devote themselves exclusively to idleness, begging, or crime.

The *Chief Constable of Chester* is " decidedly of opinion that, estimated roughly, 75 per cent. of vagrants *never* work, but spend their time in tramping from union to union. In fact, he had at that moment the names, or rather the nicknames, of between 30 and 40 men and women known as the ' Long Gang,'* and who ' worked' Cheshire and North Wales in pairs, visiting Liverpool when they got possession of anything that they could not safely dispose of elsewhere. Most of these were thieves, robbing clothes-lines, stables, &c."

The *Master of Great Boughton* is of opinion " that at least 18 out of every 20 vagrants are either thieves, or have fully given themselves up to a life of idleness and vagrancy. They have some every week who admit they have been in gaol."

---

* A criminal confederacy, in which the members of the gang assume the characters of thriving tradesmen, at different addresses, and frequently in different towns. They act as referees for one another for the purpose of obtaining credit, and dispose of all goods consigned to them the moment they obtain them.

The opinion of the *Master of Burton-on-Trent* of the character of the vagrants is, "that about two-thirds of them are regular beggars, very coarse in their manner and language, many apparently uneducated, very badly clothed, and appear to have done no work for a long time."

The *Master of Ellesmere* is clearly of opinion "that a very great majority of the males are thorough idle scamps, and the females generally appear to be disreputable characters, both sexes giving the most absurd names and routes. For instance, on the 13th of May, 1865, three young fellows gave the names of George Fordham, Jemmy Grimshaw, and Luke Snowdon, three of the most noted jockeys of the day, and whom they afterwards acknowledged as having seen riding at Chester Races during the week."

The *Master of Leek* states as his opinion that "about two-thirds of the number of males are idle youths and young men who pretend to be in search of employment, but who really do not want to obtain work. He finds that many of them have been regularly admitted inmates of workhouses, and disliking the discipline and employment they meet with there, they leave, and take to tramping about the country, living by begging in the daytime, and trusting to getting shelter for the night in the tramp wards of workhouses."

The *Master of Stafford* states—

"Two-thirds of them are a lazy, indolent, and vicious set of persons, hardened in every kind of vice and infamy, insomuch that when work is offered to them they refuse the offer and curse you for your pains. Their chief characteristic seems to be to lounge about the streets by day begging, and then spend what they can get in tobacco and beer, and finally resort to the different unions at night."

The *Superintendent of the Ludlow Police* says "that 90 per cent. of the vagrants who apply to him for tickets of admission to the Union House consist of that class of tramps who go wandering from town to town under the pretence of looking for work, but praying at the same time '*that they may never find any.*'"

The following evidence is furnished as to the ages of tramping vagrants:—

The *Master of Newport* (Salop) says—

"The average age of the vagrants admitted into this house is about 30 years, and there are about as many youths under 20 as there are men about 40. Very few old men indeed, and still fewer old women."

The *Relieving Officer of Birkenhead* states—

"The great majority are young men and women from 16 to 27 years of age, *unmarried*, but travelling together as man and wife. It does not require long acquaintance to form this connexion, and it is as soon broken up, their only home being a prison, a vagrant shed, or a night lodging-house; in this way they travel from town to town the kingdom over, staging it from workhouse to workhouse, calculating as certainly on the provisions which the law has made for them, as if they had the means at their own disposal."

The *Constable at Congleton*, who acts as relieving officer, says that —"Seventy per cent. who apply to him for relief are able-bodied, from 16 to 35 or 40 years of age, and are of a class he may call confirmed vagrants. On searching them he generally finds about $1\frac{1}{2}$d. in money, a good supply of bread, cheese, and other eatables, tobacco, one or two knives, constructed so as they could easily be used for housebreaking, a memorandum book, which contains a list of the principal towns, unions, &c., which they travel through, and the names of friends, low lodging-house keepers, whose houses they frequent."

The following examples of the reckless resort to the crime of arson on the part of tramps are given:—

The *Master of Ellesmere* mentions the case of two young vagrants, who slept there on the 27th of August, 1865, and set fire to a haystack, close to the town, on the next day, for which they were each sentenced to five years' penal servitude at the Shropshire Winter Assizes. One of them, Thomas Smith, aged 19, proved to be the same person whom the Master got committed to gaol for a month's hard labour, only on the 2nd of May previous, for tearing up his clothes.

The *Master of Newport* (Salop) says—

"One night, the beginning of last winter, several tramps were admitted into that house. He knew most of them as regular vagrants, two of them especially. The next morning but one a police officer came there to inquire after two men who had set fire to, and burnt down entirely, a large stackyard about four miles from there, and from his description he at once knew them to be these two tramps. They were taken at Market Drayton, where they were in custody for tearing up their clothes. When charged with the arson they coolly confessed it, and gave as a reason that the farmer refused to give them alms when they went to his house to beg."

The *Master of Shiffnal* gives the following instances of this vicious manifestation of spiteful malignity :—

"*February*, 1863.—William Woodward and Thomas Kent, after leaving the tramp ward, set fire to a stack of hay in a field adjoining the workhouse garden, and went direct to the police station and stated what they had done.

"*August*, 1864.—Two tramps set fire to the rickyard of Mr. Edwin Edwards, Brockton Grange, Sheriffhales, in this union, and were taken into custody in Market Drayton tramp ward the day after.

"*August*, 1865.—Two tramps, after leaving this tramp ward, set fire to a large barley rick, the property of Mr. Boulton, of Lea Farm, Albrighton, in this Union."

The *Master of Wrexham* supplies the following examples :—

"About three months ago, two, who had passed the night at this union, were committed for setting fire to a stack of hay, and another for the same offence last week. One who has often visited here was lately committed for an attempt at highway robbery, and another is now lying in Ruthin gaol under a sentence of transportation for theft."

The system of inter-communication amongst tramps alluded to in the reports of 1848 is thus further illustrated by the *Chief Constable of Chester* :—

"The perfect system of communication among tramps is surprising. I have tested it, and find that about two days are sufficient to promulgate a new regulation, &c., among the fraternity. My first test was causing every male to be searched, and burning pipes and tobacco found upon them. Every professional tramp carries a favourite pipe, and, as a rule, has half an ounce of tobacco per day. After two or three nights not one of the applicants had either pipe or tobacco, having hidden these luxuries before entering the police-office. The second test was searching for money, and with a like result."

If confirmation were wanted of the truth of the representations as to the character and habits of the vagrant class, it is furnished by themselves in the notices which they usually leave behind them upon the walls and doors of the vagrant wards. Here are some of the notices copied from the vagrant wards of different workhouses :—

"*Private Notice.*—Saucy Harry and his moll * will be at Chester

* Girl.

to eat their Christmas dinner, when they hope Saucer and the rest of the fraternity will meet them at the union.—14th November, 1865."

"*Notice to Long Cockney, or Cambridge, or any of the fraternity.*—Harry the Mark was here from Carmarthen, and if anybody of the Yorkshire tramps wishes to find him, he is to be found in South Wales for the next three months.—17th August, 1865."

"Yankey Ben, with Hungerford Tom and Stockport Ginger.—The oakum was tried to be burned here on 28th October by Messrs. John Whittington, Joseph Walker, Thos. Pickering, Jas. Hawthornwaite."

"Wild Scoty, the celebrated king of the cadgers, is in Newgate, in London, going to be hanged by the neck till he is dead; this is a great fact.—*Written by his mate.*"

"Never be ashamed of cadging. I was worth five hundred pounds once, and now I am glad to cadge for a penny or a piece of bread.—*Lanky Tom.*"

"If ragtailed Soph stays here (Shiffnal), come on to Stafford."

"Shaver here, bound for Salop to see the Rev. Henry Burton, a most benevolent minister of the Church of England, and may the devil fetch him soon."

The late Mr. Burton, who is very correctly described, was also a magistrate well known amongst that class by his frequent conviction of them.

"George Day and William Jackson, 7th November, 1865, bound for Portmadoc."

From a report in a local newspaper in the following week, it appears that "George Day" and "William Jackson," upon arriving at their destination, were captured and sent to gaol for robbery.

"Poor hould Salford prig* Frank, was here on the 20th June, 1865, bound for the hill of good country, Wales, so no more at present from your poor Frank. Amen."

"Browney will not have none of Prince Charles this winter, he is bound for Westmoreland and Cumberland, all padding cans† in that country, no dirty rugs and boards."

"Bow Street and two other ragamuffins slept here on the night of the 12th April, and was quite shocked at the clownish impudence of the old pauper at the lodge. The thundering old thief denied us a drink of water. So help me Bob."

* A thief. † Tramps' lodging houses.

"Bishop's Castle Union Workhouse is a good one to be down in, but a damned bad lot of paupers about it."

"The Dutchman was here on the 21st September, ragged and lousey, padding the hoof* and getting the mange quite fast.— *The Dutchman.*"

"I should dearly like to marry if I could find
Any gay old donner † suited to my mind.
Jack Sheppard, from York."

"This is a rum place for a fellow to come to for a night's lodging; you will never catch me here again.—*Old Bob Bridley Oh!*"

The internal arrangements of the Vagrant wards at this period, as in 1848, were still favourable to the spread of demoralising influences, as by herding all classes together at night, the most depraved tramps were enabled to tutor others in the worst forms of vice and crime. The insanitary condition of the wards must also have had a debasing effect.

Dr. *Edward Smith* furnishes the following description of the wards in country districts. "The Vagrant wards vary in character greatly. They are for the most part placed in detached low buildings, which, if of one story only, are low and open to the roof. In others they are placed in the roof of a building. Hence they are usually cold in winter and hot in summer, and when placed upon the ground floor are seldom quite dry. The ventilation is almost universally defective. There is rarely more than one window except in large workhouses, and that is usually placed in a position ill adapted for ventilation. It is very commonly small, and if made to open and the bed is placed near to it, the vagrants close it. The cubic space allowed is usually sufficient, but at certain periods of the year the number of vagrants so greatly increase that the room becomes crowded, and not one-half of the proper cubic space is allowed. Thus it very frequently occurs that the maximum number admitted is three or four times greater than the average number."

The principle of making the cost of maintaining vagrants a common charge upon the metropolis, introduced by the Houseless Poor Act of 1864, was reaffirmed by the Metropolitan Poor Act of 1867 (30 Vict., c. 6), which empowered the Poor Law Board to unite Unions and Parishes into districts for the relief of any class of poor, and enacted that the expenses of providing any

* Tramping. † Woman (Italian *donna*).

asylum for the reception and relief of casual paupers should be repayable from the Metropolitan Common Poor Fund.

In the year 1871, in consequence of the increase of vagrancy, the Earl of Kimberley introduced a Bill into the House of Lords for the purpose of increasing the stringency of the provisions of the Houseless Poor Act of 1864. In the course of his introductory remarks Lord Kimberley said—

"There was some misconception in the public mind as to the existing number of vagrants. The number actually relieved in the workhouses of England and Wales was not so large as was popularly imagined. Taking the night of the 1st of July, when it was usual to take a Census, the number relieved in 1866 was 1,086 in the metropolis, and 4,075 in the rest of England and Wales. In 1867, the numbers were 1,573 and 5,248 respectively; in 1868, 2,085 and 7,946; in 1869, 1,802 and 7,020; and in 1870, 1,627 and 5,430. They did not, however, show the whole number of vagrants in England and Wales. As far as could be ascertained by the police, the whole number on the night of the 1st of April, 1867, was 32,528; and in 1868, 36,179.* No later Returns had been published; but it was believed that such Returns would show a diminution corresponding with that exhibited by the Poor Law returns. . . . .

"One of the defects of the present law was, that the Poor Law Board had no power of securing uniformity of treatment as regarded food, lodging, and the labour test. Nothing could be worse than what now happened; that the treatment was comparatively inviting in one Union and deterrent in another."

This Bill passed into law as "The Pauper Inmates Discharge and Regulation Act, 1871" (34 and 35 Vict., c. 108).

It recites that doubts are entertained as to the length of time for which paupers may be lawfully required to remain in workhouses after giving notice of their intention to discharge themselves: and then enacts that paupers who have not discharged themselves within one month before giving notice may be detained twenty-four hours; those who have discharged themselves once within that period, forty-eight hours; and those who have discharged themselves more than twice in the preceding two months, seventy-two hours. A "casual pauper," who is defined to be a

* The number of tramps' lodging houses in England and Wales in 1867-8 was 5,648, and wards for casuals are attached to nearly every workhouse (more than 600 in number).

destitute wayfarer or wanderer applying for relief, may not discharge himself before eleven A.M. on the day following his admission nor before he has performed the work prescribed for him, and a casual pauper who has been admitted on more than two occasions during one month shall not be entitled to discharge himself before nine A.M. on the third day after his admission, and may be at any time removed to the workhouse for the remainder of his detention.

For the purposes of the Act every casual ward in the metropolis is to be deemed to be a ward of the same Union. Casual paupers absconding, or escaping, refusing to be removed to any workhouse or asylum, refusing or neglecting the work prescribed for them, or wilfully giving a false name, or making a false statement for the purpose of obtaining relief, are to be deemed idle and disorderly persons, under 5 Geo. IV., c. 83, and any pauper who repeats these offences, or wilfully destroys or injures his own clothes, or damages the property of the guardians, is to be deemed a rogue and vagabond under the same Act.

In the year 1877, in consequence of a great number of Italian children being reported to be employed for mendicant purposes throughout the country, the Charity Organisation Society appointed a Committee to inquire into the matter. This Committee reported that the ordinary circumstances under which the system was carried on was as follows:—Persons known as padroni, acting generally two together and working alternate six months in Italy and England, obtained the children from their parents in the Neapolitan districts, which are the least advanced of the Italian kingdom. They entered into a verbal contract with the parents to pay a fixed sum for the services of the children at the end of two years, and undertook to clothe and feed them during that period, and to teach them a "virtu," that is, to sing and play a musical instrument, "so that they might become as rich as the padroni themselves." They were not brought by railroad, but were made to walk the whole way through France, singing, playing, and dancing in the towns and villages through which they passed, and within the previous three years there had been at least four authenticated instances of children having died of sheer exhaustion after their arrival in England. They were then placed in depôts in London, whence they were distributed throughout the country in suitable groups, under experienced members of the fraternity. They were sent into the streets by day to play, or to pretend to play, a musical instrument, singing and dancing in time to it, and at night they performed in like manner in public-houses. They also exhibited guinea-pigs or white mice, and sometimes, in order to excite compassion, a child of a few months old was carried about on the top of an organ placed on a barrow. On their return to their temporary abode the children had to deliver up the whole of their earnings to the padroni, of whom they stood in great awe, being threatened and otherwise ill-treated if they did not bring back enough to satisfy them. In recent years the importation of Italian girls had much increased. They slept in the same room as their padroni, and, sad to say, were used, under various pretences, for the most immoral purposes.

A deputation was appointed to wait on the Home Secretary on the subject, and Sir Charles Trevelyan, in introducing it, said—

"We are come to lay before you a case of slave trade and slavery in the midst of our English Christian civilisation. That this should have been possible is owing to two causes; first, the extremely youthful, almost infantile, age of the unhappy children; and secondly, their total ignorance of our language, and the general ignorance of their own language in England. These poor children are thus completely cut off from verbal intercourse with our people, so that, even if they were of sufficient age, and had the courage to claim our protection, they have no means of doing so for want of speech. This system has all the characteristics of a slave trade and slavery. In the first place the children are bought from their parents, on a two or three years' lease, by a class of professional persons who go by the most unsuitable name of 'padroni.' They are also often transferred from one of these professional persons to another for pecuniary considerations. Occasionally they are stolen by one padrone from another; for the attractiveness of many of these children makes their services extremely lucrative; and there are degrees of respectability even among the padroni. The poor children can often stand it no longer, and run away, which is their only resource; and when they run away they are advertised for as if they were cattle. In fact, the practice is the same as formerly prevailed among our Liverpool and Bristol West Indian proprietors when the negro footmen and valets brought home by them to England thought they might take advantage of what was supposed to be a free country. Although the poor children earn from day to day considerable sums of money, yet they do not get a sixpence of it;

neither are they allowed any wages, but only obtain their necessary keep. They are also coerced by harsh treatment and punishment. If they do not bring in as much money as the padroni expect, they rebuke them, stint them of their food, and too often severely whip them. They therefore live in constant fear of them." The Home Secretary (Sir R. A. Cross), in reply, promised that everything that could be done should be done to put an end to such a scandal, and as a result, through the efforts of the police, the traffic was suppressed — the Italian Government having previously done all in its power to put a stop to this abominable speculation.

In the year 1879 a Select Committee of the House of Commons was appointed to inquire into the operation of the existing laws in the United Kingdom relating to the settlement and irremovability of paupers, with special reference to the case of removals to Ireland.

The evidence given before this Committee showed that the immigration of Irish paupers into England had largely diminished. *Mr. H. J. Hagger*, vestry clerk of Liverpool, furnished the following statistics of the number of paupers removed from Liverpool from 1869 to 1878, inclusive:—

	England.	Ireland.	Scotland.
1869	15	204	20
1870	15	120	9
1871	19	67	13
1872	15	82	—
1873	5	53	—
1874	26	95	2
1875	27	118	4
1876	18	112	3
1877	34	102	4
1878	29	88	6
	203	1,041	61

He also stated that a Parliamentary Return made in pursuance of an Order of the House of Commons in 1854, signed by the Mayor of Liverpool, showed that during the year 1849, 80,000 persons came over from Ireland to Liverpool as deck passengers, who presented all the appearance of paupers; the return being headed, "Deck Passengers, apparently Paupers;" and there being a separate return for other deck passengers. In the following year, 1850, 77,700 of the same class came over; in 1851, 68,100 came over; in 1852, 78,400 came over; and in 1853, 71,300 came over; and then they seemed to have begun to fall off very rapidly, for the three months of 1854 given in the returns showed that the number was 4,500.

Every year the pressure upon Liverpool and other ports caused by people coming from other countries and from Ireland was becoming one of less importance.

Mr. Andrew Doyle, inspector of the Local Government Board, said, when he was first appointed upon the Commission, Liverpool was labouring under what was certainly a very great grievance in 1848, viz. an enormous influx of the very lowest and most miserable class of Irish poor. He believed that the feeling of Liverpool had been ever since and was now influenced very much by the recollection of the difficulty of that time. He did not think that the Liverpool people made sufficient allowance for the change that had taken place in the condition of the Irish poor from that time. In 1845 and 1846, just before the famine year, there was a population in Ireland of between 8,000,000 and 9,000,000. The exact number, according to the census of 1841, of the population of Ireland was 8,175,000; in 1851 there was a diminution to 6,552,000; and in 1871 it had fallen to 5,400,000, showing a reduction, from the period when Liverpool was under this apprehension of 2,700,000 people, and that of exactly the class of people who were likely to become chargeable; for, looking at the Census Return, it would be found that the holders of small holdings, of from one to five acres, numbered in 1841, 310,346, and in 1875, the number was 69,098. That was the class of people who would be likely to come in large numbers.

He had known Ireland tolerably well forty years before, and had revisited it, for the first time, two years previously, and he could scarcely imagine that he was passing over the same country, the whole character of the population and the aspect of the country had so completely changed; and from inquiries amongst the labouring classes as to the rate of wages and as to the condition of the people, he did not think there was any ground for apprehending an incursion of Irish pauperism into either England or Scotland.

In the month of July a large immigration of Irish labour annually took place for the hay harvest, and then came the corn harvest, followed by the potato-getting. Their families would then come over, and they would get what they could in potato-getting and other employments of that sort, and put their money all together and send it over to Ireland. They would then go to Liverpool, and would get sent over by a free passage at 10s. per head. That was exceedingly agreeable to them and to the boat companies that had the carriage of them; but it was an unfair thing for the Liverpool authorities to point to that and say that that was an evidence of pauperism. It was the evidence of something totally different from pauperism; it was the evidence of craft and imposition upon the one side, and of great simplicity upon the other.

Mr. Zachary Myles, guardian of the Limerick Union, said he remembered when wages were from 6d. to 1s. a day, and now they got 2s. and 3s.; what is commonly called a "handy man" would get 3s., and a common labourer would get 2s. wages. There was not, to his knowledge, any emigration of vagrant paupers from the Limerick Union to England. The vagrancy laws were applied in the unions in the county and through the kingdom. Travelling from one union to another for the purpose of obtaining relief was illegal, and punishable under the Vagrancy Act.

Mr. Peter Beattie, inspector of the Barony Parish in Glasgow, said, at that time they were relieving a great number of Irish who had no settlement and who were removable, but who were not removed. The total number of persons of that class treated in the poor-house and receiving indoor relief for the previous year was 439, entailing an expenditure of an amount of money equal to £909. Those were all Irish, with no settlement in Scotland, and persons eligible for removal, so far as settlement was concerned. On the outdoor roll they had 73 Irish and 120 dependants, the amount of money paid being £153. Their Irish-born poor were one-third of their total poor. For the month of May, 1879, they had in Glasgow, in the barony parish, 4,391 poor families, comprising 7,307 individuals, and one-third of those were Irish-born people.

In the year 1882 a discussion on vagrancy took place in the House of Commons.

Sir Baldwyn Leighton, in introducing the subject, said, that notwithstanding the regulations of the Local Government Board dealing with the relief which was to be given to vagrants, during the last 20 years there had been a great, he might say an alarming and continuous, increase in their numbers. What made it more serious was the terrorism which they began to exercise over orderly and respectable persons; some roads being so infected by them as to be inconvenient, if not unsafe, to travel upon. In 1869 and 1870 the numbers decreased, owing to the great amendment that then took place in Poor Law administration; but while in 1873 the numbers were 1,900, in 1880 they were 7,000. That showed great fluctuation; but at the same time a very serious increase. The present vagrant army sleeping in workhouses was between 6,000 and 7,000; about three times as many more were known to the police as vagrants—say, 20,000—half of whom were more or less wayfarers, and half of whom were undistinguishable from the workhouse tramp, making the vagrant body about 16,000 or 17,000, at least. Now, the fluctuations of the number of the workhouse tramps were very remarkable. Without giving each year, and taking the rise and fall since 1861, there were, according to the Return, of those sleeping on January 1st in workhouse wards—1861, 1,179; 1867, 3,566; 1868, 6,053; 1870, 4,147;. 1873, 1,987; 1880, 7,041. Then, as regards separate Unions, he had obtained Returns from about 20, showing the increase since 1876 for the half-year. These were ten typical ones:—

	1876.	1881.
Atcham, Shropshire	450	1,880
Tenbury, Worcester	350	1,118
Langport, Somerset	160	410
Hatfield, Herts	550	2,133
South Molton, Devon	110	312
Burton-on-Trent, Stafford	592	6,986
Stafford, Stafford	1,838	3,041
Tamworth, Stafford	740	2,430
Uttoxeter, Stafford	929	1,327
Seisdon, Stafford	118	369

Showing an increase amounting to 300 per cent. in the five years. By Returns obtained over a month or two in one Union, he found that one-fifth of the vagrants were short-service soldiers, and o' these one-quarter, or thereabouts, were actually Reserve men. So that out of every 1,000 tramps about 200 were discharged soldiers, and 50 of them actually Reserve men—that was, if the proportion of other Unions tallied with his own. Now, what were the causes of that increase? It was not easy exactly to define them, but two or three were apparent. Depression of trade was no doubt one; stricter or laxer administration might be another and a local cause. The short-service Army system might have something to do with it, in de-industrializing young men, and afterwards giving them just enough to be idle upon, and, possibly, the want of industrial training in their school children might have something to answer for. But the danger of the matter seemed to be that it was growing; and those who took to that life did not return to regular and industrial habits. It seemed to him difficult to imagine a more certain way of inculcating idle habits and vagabond life than taking a young man of 18 or 20, keeping him for six years, when he might be learning some trade, in a somewhat idle profession, and then turning him loose, with just sufficient to live a roving life, living in tramp wards and on what could be begged; and if that was so, the short-service system might have to answer not only for destroying the efficiency and solidarity of their regiments, but also de-industrializing the young men who were enlisted, and forming a pauper Reserve, or proletariat reservoir.

Mr. Salt said he had observed this very remarkable feature in respect to vagrancy throughout the country—that if they kept their attention fixed on some particular district—for instance, on some great centre of the iron industry—they would find that a year or so after the adverse circumstances of trade commenced vagrancies spread gradually from that particular point throughout the Kingdom. What happened was this. Men who were thrown out of employment from the bad times held to their homes as long as they could, hoping for a return of better trade; but at last they left their homes, and started on a journey, sometimes in search of work. They went a certain distance; some of them got work, others did not.

Sir Henry Fletcher said he could prove that since the introduction of the short-service system vagrancy had increased. He had, in his own Union, in the county of Sussex, taken pains to ascertain the number of tramps who had been short-service men, and he was sure that Sir B. Leighton under estimated rather than exaggerated the number. What happened was this: a man enlisted as a soldier at the age of 18 or 19; he served for a period which up to now had been seven years, and at the end of that time he received his discharge and returned to his village, his town, or his parish. He went to his old master, and asked to come back to his former employment; but the master replied—" I have filled up the place, and I have nothing for you to do." The man, during his soldier life with the Colours, had contracted a restless mode of life, and finding he could not get employment in his own parish, he started off and wandered over the country, living a restless, unprofitable existence.

Mr. J. G. Talbot said, in his capacity as chairman of the Vagrancy Committee in the county of Kent, it had been his duty to watch the alarming increase of this great evil. It was not only an evil, in so far as it was a disgrace to the community that a large number of persons should be wandering about without visible means of support; but it was also an evil because vagrants were usually persons who preyed in some way upon society.

This discussion was shortly after followed by a measure giving increased powers of detention as regards the casual poor: the 45 & 46 Vic., c. 36, known as "The Casual Poor Act, 1882." It amends the 34 & 35 Vic., c. 108, by enacting that a Casual pauper shall not be entitled to discharge himself before 9 A.M. of the second day following his admission, nor before he has performed the work prescribed for him; and where he has been admitted more than once during the month he shall not discharge himself before 9 A.M. on the fourth day after his admission, and he may at any time be removed to the workhouse for the remainder of his period of detention. In computing the number of days of detention, Sunday is to be excluded. Any person who for the purpose of obtaining poor relief for himself or any other person wilfully gives a false name or makes a false statement to the guardians or their officers is to be deemed an idle and disorderly person under 5 Geo. IV., c. 83.

CHAPTER XIV.

1882—1886.

Modern begging.—Its various divisions—Average earnings of beggars—The effect of free night refuges and soup kitchens—The rules of trades unions regarding travelling members—Average improvement of the working classes during the last fifty years—Various systems for the repression of vagrancy adopted in Berks, Cumberland, Dorset, Gloucester, Hants, Kent, Wilts, &c.—The cause of failure of the Poor Law system—Contempt of the vagrant for the inmate of the workhouse—Increased nomadic habits of the agricultural labourer—The teachings of history regarding the vagrant—Suggested remedy for vagrancy.

MODERN begging is quite as much an organised profession as it was more than three hundred years ago; it has of course adapted itself to the spirit of the times, but it is wonderful how little adaptation has been called for. The credulity of the charitable is the stock-in-trade of the beggar, and it never fails him. Like the "confidence trick" of the London sharper, the very staleness and antiquity of the beggar's dodges appear to give them a sanctity in the eyes of many, a sanctity derived from the belief that others might be deceived by counterfeits, but that the person appealed to cannot: he or she has found the genuine honest, long-suffering and unappreciated object of charity, and having found this priceless treasure is bound to reward it.

Others again adopt the fallacious reasoning that it is better to reward 999 impostors rather than miss the chance of relieving one genuine case of distress, thus altogether ignoring the fact that the deserving poor *never* beg, and prefer to die rather than incur such a degradation.

The principal varieties of begging are now termed *lurks* (from the Welsh *llerc*, a fit of loitering): the fire lurk (pretended losses by fire), the shipwrecked or disabled sailors' lurk, the accident lurk, the sick lurk (pretended illness; some tie up their arms in a very clever way, others feign fits, others remain in bed simulating illness while they send out their companions to beg for them), the foreigners' lurk, the frozen-out gardeners' lurk, the servants' lurk (pretended loss of place as a domestic servant), the family man lurk (parading a number of children in a state of feigned destitution), the lucifer, air balloon, picture, or bread-and-butter lurk (dropping in the mud or otherwise damaging by an apparent accident boxes of lucifer matches, air balloons, cheap pictures in frames, or slices of bread-and-butter), the deaf and dumb lurk, the colliers' lurk (pretended loss of employment through an explosion), the weavers', the calenderers', and cotton spinners' lurks ("Come all the way from Manchester, and got no work to do.") To these may be added the "shallow cove" or "shivering Jemmy," who goes about half naked, the "cab touter," who begs at cab doors as they are leaving theatres, and the "high-flier," who simulates the broken-down gentleman, officer, or tradesman.

It is difficult to draw the line between the habitual vagrant, the petty hawker, and the street swindler, as the pursuits of the vagrant are of the most protean character. One day he is the "lurker," another day he is the "crocus" or "sham doctor," selling potions flavoured with salt, or some form of nastiness, or " vegetable pills," obtained ready made from the rabbit warren and rolled in flour, or he is the card sharper of the public-house or the race-course, or he is the hop-picker just returned from the country with "genuine ketchup," made from " Cattle Market mushrooms " (*i.e.* decayed pigs' livers), or he is the sham smuggler, who sells brandy or tobacco, the samples of which are genuine, but the bulk of which consists principally of coloured gin or hay.

"The men and women who, disguised as gypsies or country folk, come to the kitchen entrance of one's house and offer for sale what they are pleased to term fresh fruit, vegetables, or poultry, are too often arrant frauds. The duck purchased at many shillings below the price charged by the local poulterer is discovered, when too late, to be a vile specimen of a bird and perfectly worthless; the eggs palmed off as 'new laid' turn out to be venerable enough to have come out of the ark; and so on with everything else. A vendor of apples and potatoes tried this little game on last week, but the purchaser of his goods was a match for him, and the itinerant merchant was given into custody and charged with fraud. The samples exhibited to his customers he pretended were representative of the bulk of the fruit and vege-

Parish of Hampstead, Middlesex.
March 7th 1873.

The sympathy and assistance of a few Benevolent friends are earnestly entreated on behalf of the Widow and family of the late Mr. James Atkinson, for many years a District Visitor and Scripture Reader in this parish, and who in the Summer of last Year during the prevalence of Small Pox in this locality in his humane endeavours to impress on the minds of the dying and afflicted the necessity of Prayer to the Lord and Saviour, he fell a Victim to the Malady.

The deceased Mr. Atkinson in 1871 became security for a Relative to a considerable amount hence arises the necessity of this appeal in order to realize by voluntary contributions the sum of £70. to establish Mrs. Atkinson & family in a small way of business to be disposed of for that amount. We earnestly recommend her case to the Charitable notice of the Gentry and Clergy.

F. W. Tremlett. D C L £2
Vicar of St. Peter's

Revd. H. Sharpe £2 —
P. Turner 2.0.0

Revd. W. Sargent 1.0.0

Revd Charlton Lane.
£3.0.0

Mrs B. Wodd Smith £2

Mr Janius J. Smith 2.2.0
P.h Bearer

A. H. Wodd 2.0.0

Miss E. 1.0.0

Capt Thos Freeman 21/-

J. F. Anderson MD 1—1—0
pd

Wm H. Tagart 1 Guinea
P.h Bearer

Sundry small Donations previously received on beh of the Widow & family.
£19.11.6

tables, but whereas the former was fresh and good, the latter were in a state of decay and dissolution." *

There is hardly a source of human suffering or a passing calamity of any magnitude which these rascals do not endeavour to turn to their advantage.

Mr. Gomm, the chief officer of the Mendicity Society, is of opinion that the present average earnings of a professional beggar are from 5s. to 20s. a day, and that those who write begging letters average still more.

Vagrants in many instances still continue to communicate with one another by scribbling on the walls of their dormitories, as described in the report of 1866, and they "are still for the most part, if not criminals, at least on the verge of crime." Reports from country districts testify that arson continues to be their favourite method of venting their spite, and that a large number of discharged soldiers annually swell the ranks of vagrancy. Night refuges, which admit applicants at all hours of the night, continue to exist, as in the year 1846, and lend their aid in promoting vagrancy. Their managers turn a deaf ear to the warning that the casual wards of the workhouse are available for all such cases, and that no amount of cross-questioning will enable them to arrive at the real character of the applicants, as the most undeserving, from skill acquired by long practice, are always able to make themselves out to be the most deserving.

Another promoter of professional vagrancy is the indiscriminate free soup kitchen, the tickets for which are distributed broadcast, being frequently given to the deputy landlords of common lodging-houses.

"These tickets have, like those of the bread, grocery, coal, and blanket charities, a market value in spirits at the public-houses, and are used as authoritative licences to beg for the penny which has to accompany them to the counter. One person was watched while he begged for and received nine pennies in the neighbourhood of one of these soup houses, under the pretence of purchasing a penny basin. The most thriftless tramps and vagrants are collected at the distribution, and even the class above them learns how much easier it is to live at the expense of others than by their own labour."

A further development of this system is thus commented upon by the *Globe* newspaper in February, 1886:—

* " Modern Society," February, 1886.

"Who would have the heart to refuse a copper to some little tatterdemalion begging for the price of a halfpenny dinner? It would be taken for granted in any locality where this admirable form of charity has come into existence, that the money would be spent for the desired purpose. Coventry tells a different tale, however. It has been ascertained there that, since the establishment of half-penny dinners, juvenile mendicancy has greatly increased. As the hour for the cheap feast draws near, crowds of children turn out in the adjacent streets, and importune every person who passes for "only a halfpenny." At first, few resisted the pathetic appeal, but latterly the nuisance became so great that inquiry was set on foot, with the result of proving that very few of the half-pennies found their way to the dinner room. Many went to supply luxuries to idle and worthless parents, while the sweetstuff shops came in for a share. In short, the halfpenny dinner was merely made the excuse for extracting alms from the public in such a way as would not come under police cognisance."

The same demoralising system prevails to a large extent in London, where children during the summer months present cards in the streets, which apparently authorise them to beg for assistance for a school treat.

The honest travelling mechanic or labourer in search of work is no longer in need of assistance from the outside public. *Mr. George Howell, M.P.*, in his work on "The Conflicts of Capital and Labour," gives the following particulars of the travelling relief afforded by trades unions to their members:—

"In addition to the extremely useful and legitimate provision for supporting their members when out of work, there is in most societies an allowance to members going from home in search of employment: this is called travelling relief. At one time tramping was systematic and general, and it became a great nuisance, for many men merely used the society as a means for enabling them to tramp all over the country, living upon the funds of the union, supplemented, as it usually was, by collections made by the workmen in several towns through which they passed. This practice has greatly diminished of late years; if properly used the system of tramp relief is a good and useful one, but in the past it was little better than a kind of professional mendicity, excepting that the mendicants begged from those least able to afford assistance, and urged their claims for contributions with a kind of authority as though it was a right to which they were justly entitled. The method of relieving those on tramp is pretty much the same in all societies, although the amounts slightly differ, and the distances to be travelled before the relief can be obtained is greater or less according to the trade, and the several 'stations,' that is lodges, on the route taken by the "journeyman" member. Bed and breakfast are generally provided, but it is not a universal rule, in addition to which they get a shilling or eighteen-pence towards their maintenance until they reach the next relieving station. These vary in distance; they may be sixteen or they may be twenty-five miles apart, but on the average the amount paid is about one penny per mile. In some societies it is usual to pay the railway fares, third class, to some distant place in search of employment: this mode of relief has been in operation for some time in the Amalgamated Carpenters' and Joiners' Society, and it is stated that it has had the effect of greatly diminishing the system of tramping from place to place. The custom of tramping from one town to another is a very old one, it existed under the old guilds and was general all through Germany until very recent times, and is still practised there to a much greater extent than it is in England. The origin of the term journeyman may be traced to this ancient custom, one of the objects of which in olden times was to acquire experience in the craft or mystery in which the traveller was engaged by seeing the different methods of work in various parts of the country."

The *Agricultural Labourers' Union* pays the fare of its members when they move from one place to another to better their condition.

In the *Amalgamated Society of Engineers* the unemployed members receive what is termed donation benefit from the Society. This ranges in amount from 10s. per week down to 6s. per week, according to the length of time a member remains unemployed. Should any member in receipt of this benefit wish to travel in search of work he is provided with a travelling card. On the presentation of this card to any of the Branch Secretaries in any part of the world in which the Society has a branch, he will be paid the amount of donation benefit that may be due to him. A branch secretary waited upon by a traveller is bound to direct him to the places where he is most likely to obtain work.

In the *Amalgamated Society of Tailors* free members out of work are entitled to a travelling card on giving the secretary six hours' notice of their requirements. A member whilst on travel is entitled to 1s. 4d. in any Branch belonging to the Amalgamation, but a member who has only been in the society three months and under six is only entitled to 4d. Members refusing employment in a shop where such employment is acceptable to the branch are suspended from travelling benefit for seven days.

In the *Operative Stone Masons' Society* members when travelling in search of employment are provided with a bed at any lodge they call at, and they are paid money relief in proportion to the distance they have travelled from the last lodge at which they have been relieved. In each lodge a list of builders' yards, or the buildings in course of erection, in the town is provided as a guide for the unemployed to seek employment. In many large towns the traveller can remain some two, three, or four days, so as to give him a good opportunity of seeking employment. On Sundays the members do not travel, as the Society allows them extra pay for not doing so. The travelling relief averages about 9s. per week.

In the *Iron Founders' Society* each two years' member receives 1s. 4d. per day for thirteen weeks, and for the next thirteen weeks 1s. 2d., and if he still continues out of work he receives 10d. a day for six months. A one year's member receives 8d. per day. Each member on travel, in addition to these allowances, is also allowed a bed at each club-house and one for Sunday once in three months, and where the next branch is more than twenty-five miles distant he is allowed one day's donation in advance for every additional twenty-five miles. Members under twelve months are only entitled to beds. If the distressed artisan or mechanic is not a trades unionist he readily obtains relief from members of his own calling at the workshops of the town through which he is passing, and as a rule he does not scruple to apply for it.

The conditions of society are now entirely changed. The legitimate vagrant of the Middle Ages, or even of fifty years ago, no longer continues to exist under the old conditions; he has improved his status and looks down with contempt, if not with disgust, on the base parasite who now usurps the place he formerly occupied. At a meeting of the Statistical Society in January, 1886, *Mr. Giffen* said the estimate of 50 to 100 per cent. as the average improvement of the working classes in fifty years was not only not excessive, but under the mark. On a broad survey of the facts, the composition of the people of the United Kingdom was entirely changed from what it was fifty years ago. Whereas fifty years ago one-third of the working masses were Irish peasants, earning a doubtful 4s. a week on the average, and the agricultural population of Great Britain constituted another third of the total, this class likewise earning much smaller incomes than the third class, consisting of the non-agricultural workers of Great Britain; now the Irish labourers were less than one-eighth of the total, the British agricultural labourers were also one-eighth only, and the remaining three-fourths were artisans and other non-agricultural workers. In Ireland, the improvement in the wages or earnings of small farmers and labourers was at least 100 per cent., the doubtful average, 4s., of fifty years ago having been converted into a much less doubtful 8s., or its equivalent, at the present time. In Scotland and Wales the average improvement in agricultural labour had equally been about 100 per cent., from 9s. in the former case to 18s., and from 7s. 6d. in the latter case to 15s. In England the changes were not so extreme, but from 8s. to 13s. and from 10s. to 16s. were not uncommon figures, fully justifying the conclusion as to there having been an improvement of 60 per cent. The worst-paid labour in Great Britain of a non-agricultural kind had equally undergone improvement. In the Metropolis and the leading manufacturing towns, the rise ranged from 15s. to 25s., or about 70 per cent.; but in the other parts of the country, as in Glasgow, there were cases of an advance of 100 per cent. There had also been a great increase in the number of income-tax assessments, implying an improvement of the artisan and other classes just above the income-tax limit. There had been a simultaneous improvement in France, Germany, and other countries. While the total income of the country fifty years ago was about five hundred millions only, of which two-fifths were derived from agriculture, the present income, on the authority of Mr. Dudley Baxter and Mr. Leone Levi, might be placed at about 1,270,000,000, of which only one-sixth was from agriculture. At the same time the agricultural labourer was better off, because, whilst his numbers had diminished, the net income from agriculture and his share of that income had increased. Further, the working masses of Great Britain had more than doubled their number in the interval, simultaneously with a vast diminution in Ireland, whose aggregate income remained much the same, though with a diminished number to share it.

Professor Leone Levi said not only did the working classes earn more, but they worked less, the Factory Acts having reduced by 20 per cent. the amount of time given to labour. There was no doubt whatever that they were consuming more. They got with the same amount of money a great deal more food and clothing. Taking them as a whole, his impression was that the labouring classes were much more elevated in character—socially, intellectually, and politically—than ever they were before.

Vagrancy and crime bear an important relation to each other. Mr. Snowden remarks in his "Police Officers' and Constables' Guide," "that it is his firm opinion that if poaching and vagrancy were put down, and more especially in the rural districts, crime would be of very rare occurrence."

Various County systems for the repression of vagrancy have from time to time been tried; the best known of these are the Dorset system and the Berks system.

The DORSET SYSTEM was established in January, 1870, by Captain Amyatt, the able chief constable of Dorsetshire. It consists in the relief of the vagrant by means of tickets, which up to the year 1881 were exchangeable at distances of about five miles apart for one pound of bread; since 1881 the allowance has been reduced to half a pound. The tickets are not exchangeable in towns unless signed by the police, and no more than half a pound can be obtained by one person in exchange for any number of tickets. The system is worked by the police, under the direction of the magistrates and guardians, and is combined with a uniform enforcement of the Vagrant Act. The following have been the results of the system so far as regards the admissions to casual wards in the county.

Year.	Number of admissions to casual wards.	Year.	Number of admissions to casual wards.
1869	11,248	1878	9,208
1870*	8,107	1879	11,287
1871†	5,850	1880	13,231
1872	2,840	1881‡	13,054
1873	2,600	1882§	10,053
1874	2,847	1883	5,483
1875	2,490	1884	7,251
1876	3,971	1885	8,927
1877	6,931		

* Introduction of the system.
† Pauper Inmates Discharge and Regulation Act, 1871, passed.
‡ Reduction of the allowance of bread from 1 lb. to ½ lb. ordered.
§ Casual Poor Act, 1882, passed.

The following are the results so far as regards crime :—

Year.	Number of persons charged.			Number of criminals to each thousand of population.
	Summarily.	Upon indictment.	Total.	
1869	2,668	139	2,807	17·58
1872	1,997	98	2,075	12·67
1873	2,126	125	2,251	13·75
1882	2,292	80	2,372	15·20
1885	2,330	79	2,407	15·43

It will be observed that the subsequent decrease in numbers in the list of admissions to casual wards is coincident with the introduction of increased methods of repression—in 1872 owing to the coming into force of the Pauper Inmates Discharge and Regulation Act, 1871; in 1882 owing to the reduction in the allowance of bread from one pound to half a pound; and in 1883 owing to the Casual Poor Act, 1882, coming into operation. It should be remembered that as under this last-mentioned Act vagrants can be detained two nights, the present number of admissions represents twice that number under the previous system, that is, that the numbers for 1885 to be fairly compared with those of 1882 should be reckoned as 17,854 against 10,053, instead of 8,927 against 10,053.

In the year 1880, 7 tons 15 cwt. 46 lbs. of bread was given away.

The BERKSHIRE SYSTEM was instituted by Colonel Blandy, the able chief constable of Berkshire, in August, 1871. It consists in way-tickets, containing a description of the vagrant or tramp, and showing the place he came from and his final destination, which are issued to all who enter a workhouse in the county. Relief stations are formed at the police constables' houses between the workhouses. On the production of the way-ticket the vagrant receives eight ounces of bread, provided he is on his specified route. The ticket is signed by the constable or person administering the relief, and entry of the matter is made in a book. Punishment of not less than fourteen days' hard labour is inflicted on conviction for vagrancy. The system has been in abeyance in Berks since the passing of the Casual Poor Act, 1882, owing to the withdrawal of one of the leading unions. Vagrancy, it is stated, has much increased in consequence.

The system was adopted in 1884 throughout North Wales under the following conditions. On entering the North Wales Counties District the wayfarer received a ticket which recorded his description, the place he came from, and his final destination. The union he should next go to was endorsed on his ticket, and so on throughout the district. The police were in all cases where practicable employed as assistant relieving officers, and afforded to vagrants at each relief station, along the route one pound of bread for each adult and eight ounces for each child. At workhouses, in cases where the wayfarer's account of himself and his conduct was satisfactory, and his ticket was in order, he was discharged as soon as he had performed a task of work not exceeding in value the cost of his maintenance. In all other cases full advantage was taken of the powers conferred by the Casual Poor Act of 1882, under which vagrants may be detained two or four days. The police apprehended all persons found begging or otherwise infringing the Vagrant Act. Not less than ten days' hard labour was the recognised punishment for offences against the Vagrant Act, except in the case of threats having been used, when the offender was sent for trial under 24 and 25 Vict., c. 96, s. 45. Union officers gave all possible information as to where employment could be obtained, and employers of labour were invited to communicate their wants to them. The following is the reported number of vagrants relieved under this system :—

County.	1883.	1884.	Decrease.
Anglesey	310	236	74
Carnarvon	4,328	3,367	961
Denbigh	4,710	3,333	1,377
Flint	4,521	3,719	802
Merioneth	3,222	2,822	400
	17,091	13,477	3,614

In the first six months of 1885 the numbers of vagrants relieved as compared with the corresponding period of 1884 showed an increase of 721, viz. 9,040 in 1885 as compared with 8,319 in 1884, and a further increase was subsequently noticeable. The plan was abandoned at Lady Day, 1886, owing to want of funds to pay for the bread rations, and to the want of combined action and active interest on the part of boards of guardians.

The following other systems have also been adopted at different times with a view to repress mendicity.

THE CUMBERLAND AND WESTMORELAND SYSTEM, established 1867, consists in a rigid enforcement of the Vagrant Act, with assistance and protection to poor people travelling in search of work. The police act as assistant relieving officers, and whenever persons of the latter description apply for relief, the police supply an order which secures relief at the workhouse, if it is situated sufficiently near to be available; but if not, the necessary relief is supplied by the police, and the expenses incurred in this way are paid by the board of guardians of the district. The Chief Constable remarks that "the class of people who make begging a trade are not the honest workpeople who travel from county to county in search of work. They are people who will not work when work is offered to them, they travel through the country, they make begging a trade, and whenever an opportunity occurs they steal whatever they can lay their hands upon."

THE GLOUCESTER SYSTEM, established in August, 1866, consisted at first of the way-ticket system, combined in June, 1869, with an enforcement of the Vagrant Act, every vagrant found begging being sent to gaol for ten days.

The Berkshire system was introduced in July, 1882.

The following tables, compiled from information furnished by Admiral Christian, the chief constable, show the effects of this system under his effective management.

NUMBER OF PERSONS WHO SLEPT IN CASUAL WARDS AND COMMON LODGING HOUSES IN GLOUCESTERSHIRE ON THE FIRST TUESDAY IN APRIL IN EACH YEAR.

	Total No.	Number who slept in Casual Wards.						Remarks as to the truth of their statements.	
		Males.	Females.	Under 16 years of age.	16 years of age and above.	Number of Strangers.	Num. of known residents.	Supposed to be true.	Entirely living by tramping.
1st Tuesday in April, 1878	139	128	11	9	130	—	—	—	—
,, ,, 1879	137	123	14	8	129	—	—	—	—
,, ,, 1880	161	133	28	22	139	—	—	—	—
,, ,, 1881	126	116	10	1	125	—	—	—	—
,, ,, 1882	171	—	—	—	—	—	—	—	—
,, ,, 1883	83	65	18	9	74	77	6	50	33
,, ,, 1884	63	48	15	8	55	61	2	40	23
,, ,, 1885	92	76	16	11	81	92	—	62	30
,, ,, 1886	111	87	24	20	91	106	5	58	53

	Total No.	Number who slept in Lodging Houses.						Remarks as to the truth of their statements.	
		Males.	Females.	Under 16 years of age.	16 years of age and above.	Number of Strangers.	Num. of known residents.	Supposed to be true.	Entirely living by tramping.
1st Tuesday in April, 1878	598	426	172	76	522	—	—	—	—
,, ,, 1879	551	383	168	74	477	—	—	—	—
,, ,, 1880	505	377	128	46	459	—	—	—	—
,, ,, 1881	593	424	169	96	497	—	—	—	—
,, ,, 1882	553	391	162	75	478	417	136	424	129
,, ,, 1883	463	332	131	53	410	279	184	348	115
,, ,, 1884	561	399	162	62	499	397	164	469	92
,, ,, 1885	570	400	170	83	487	409	161	504	66
,, ,, 1886	597	421	176	91	506	444	153	484	113

ANALYSIS OF TRADES OF THE PERSONS WHO SLEPT IN CASUAL WARDS.

Trades.*	1883	1884	1885	1886
Bricklayers	1	—	1	1
Carpenters	—	—	—	2
Charwomen	5	2	4	4
Children	8	7	10	20
Field hands (females).	2	1	—	—
Fitters	—	—	2	—
Labourers	44	36	39	56
Laundresses	5	1	4	2
Married women	—	3	1	2
Masons	1	1	2	—
Painters	1	—	4	2
Plasterers	1	1	—	2
Printers	1	—	2	—
Seamen	6	2	1	1
Tailors	—	—	2	4
Tailoresses	—	—	1	2
Tramps (avowed)	1	2	3	—

* The other callings represented during this period were :—
One member once—Blacksmith, boatman, buttonmaker, cabinetmaker, cane chair seater, carver, chandler, coachmaker, coach trimmer, collar maker, dressmaker, fireman, flax dresser, hatter, hawker, lacemaker, needlewoman, pianomaker, printer, rag sorter, rivetter, ropemaker, seaman, servant, shoemaker, shoe finisher, stoker, stone sawyer, striker, tinman, upholstress, wire drawer.
One member twice—Brickmaker, clerk, currier, gardener, groom, moulder.

AND BEGGARS AND BEGGING.

ANALYSIS OF THE TRADES OF PERSONS WHO SLEPT IN COMMON LODGING HOUSES.

Trades.*	1882.	1883.	1884.	1885.	1886.
Blacksmiths	10	3	3	—	6
Bricklayers	—	1	1	5	2
Cabinet Makers	4	1	1	3	6
Carpenters	3	5	1	6	3
Children	64	45	53	56	80
China menders	1	4	2	3	—
Charwomen	10	10	11	15	9
Colliers	3	—	3	1	4
Drovers	12	8	9	11	11
Field hands (females)	2	—	2	3	4
Fitters	1	1	4	6	6
Gardeners	6	5	7	3	7
Grooms	2	4	3	1	3
Labourers	141	146	162	159	150
Laundresses	7	3	—	3	5
Married women	61	38	46	53	49
Masons	—	—	3	2	2
Musicians	14	13	28	27	17
Nailmakers	7	1	3	4	3
Needleworkers	1	13	10	2	3
Painters	6	6	5	15	5
Pedlars and Hawkers	74	75	86	94	97
Pensioners	1	4	2	—	1
Plasterers	1	—	3	1	1
Plumbers	—	—	2	3	1
Rag and bone gatherers	5	5	9	6	7
Saddlers	3	1	2	1	1
Sawyers	1	3	2	—	2
Shoemakers	8	6	9	7	9
Street singers	—	4	4	1	14
Seamen	5	2	4	—	—
Tailors	8	4	11	3	6
Tailoresses	1	—	--	3	2
Tinkers	—	1	—	5	1
Tinmen and Tinworkers	2	2	1	3	2
Tramps (avowed)	5	5	4	—	2
Umbrella menders	—	4	4	1	4
Wireworkers	3	—	—	2	5

* The other callings represented during this period were :—

One member once—Actor, artist, baker, bellhanger, bootcloser, boot-lace cutter, brickmaker, cane worker, carriage trimmer, carver, chimney sweep, clogger, coach wheeler, confectioner, cook, cork cutter, dealer, decorator, dye-wash maker, dyer, engine driver, engraver, errand boy, farrier, fern maker, galvanist, glover, harness maker, hoop roller, hurdle maker, iron turner, jeweller, lathrender, locksmith, mechanic, mill-stone dresser, navvy, nurse, nut forger, packman, paper maker, parish relief, pattern maker, photographer, potter, sail maker, slaughterman, tanner, upholstress, waggon builder, warehouseman, waterman, well sinker, whip maker, wood gatherer, wood turner.

Returns of Persons arrested for Begging.

	Arrested.	Discharged.	Convicted.	Average amount of money found on them.	Remarks.
				d.	
1881	341	95	246	$4\frac{1}{4}$	91 tramps had food in their possession when arrested £9 9s. 1½d. was found on one beggar, which would have raised the average sum to 10¼d.
1882	303	68	235	$3\frac{1}{2}$	47 tramps had food in their possession when arrested.
1883	203	50	153	$5\frac{1}{2}$	
1884	278	78	200	$5\frac{3}{4}$	
1885	292	102	190	$4\frac{3}{4}$	

	1881.	1882.	1883.	1884.	1885.
Tramps committed for offences other than begging	248	244	259	259	240
Average amount of money found on them	$5\frac{3}{4}$d.	$6\frac{1}{2}$d.	1s. 0¼d.	$6\frac{1}{4}$d.	$10\frac{1}{2}$d.

Effects of the Adoption of the Berkshire System.

Number of Vagrants relieved by the police before the Berks system commenced. Years.				Number of Vagrants relieved by the police after the Berks system commenced. Years.				Proportion per cent. who brought way tickets with them in the first quarter of the year			
1878	1879	1880	1881	1882	1883	1884	1885	1883	1884	1885	1886
25,653	29,918	43,267	43,772	38,027	19,101	18,317	22,189	70	60	54	54

One member twice—Basketmaker, brass finisher, brushmaker, boatman, clock cleaner, coachmaker, herbalist, ironworker, living on means, maltster, miller, miner, printer, rivetter, striker.
One member three times—Shoeblack, thatcher.
One member four times—Engineer.
One member once and two members once—Boxmakers, dressmakers, hatters, machinists, pipemakers, porters, quack doctors, servants, wheelwrights.
One member once and two members twice.—Coopers.
One member once and three members once—Clerks, factory hands, washerwomen, weavers.
One member twice and two members once—Billposters, boilermakers, compositors, knitters, skinners, stablemen.
One member twice and three members once—Puddlers.
One member three times and two membere once—French polishers, glaziers, saw sharpeners.
Two members once—Acrobats, actresses, butchers, iron-holder makers, lace cutters, prostitutes, rag sorters, travellers with a performing bear.
Two members twice—Smiths, stokers, watchmakers.
Three members once—Chairbottomers, cutlers, needlemakers, watercress sellers.
Four members once—Costermongers, flowermakers, grinders.

AND BEGGARS AND BEGGING.

NUMBER OF VAGRANTS SUPPLIED WITH BREAD AT THE DIFFERENT POLICE STATIONS IN THE COUNTY.

Year ending 31st March, 1884.		Year ending 31st March, 1885.		Year ending 31st March, 1886.	
Number supplied with bread.	Cost.	Number supplied with bread.	Cost.	Number supplied with bread.	Cost.
10,438	£ s. d. 64 16 2	12,664	£ s. d. 74 15 2	13,782	£ s. d. 79 0 5

An analysis of the callings of those who slept in *Casual Wards*, gives the following proportionate constituent elements:—

Labourers, 50 per cent.; children, 13; charwomen, $4\frac{1}{2}$; laundresses, $3\frac{1}{2}$; seamen, $2\frac{1}{2}$; painters, 2; married women,* tailors, and avowed tramps together, 5; masons and plasterers together, 2; making a total of $82\frac{1}{2}$ per cent. The next $7\frac{1}{2}$ per cent. is made up of 11 callings, and the remaining 10 per cent. of 32 callings.

A similar analysis of those who slept in *Lodging Houses* yields the following results:—

Labourers, $27\frac{1}{2}$ per cent.; pedlars and hawkers, $15\frac{1}{2}$; children, $10\frac{1}{2}$; married women, 9;* musicians, $3\frac{1}{2}$; charwomen, 2; drovers, 2; shoemakers, painters, rag and bone gatherers, and tailors together, 5; gardeners and needleworkers together, 2; blacksmiths and street singers together, $1\frac{1}{2}$; carpenters, fitters, laundresses, and nailmakers together, $2\frac{1}{2}$; cabinet makers and avowed tramps together, 1 per cent.; making a total of 82 per cent. The next $3\frac{1}{2}$ per cent. is made up of 13 callings, the next $2\frac{1}{2}$ of 16 callings, and the last 12 per cent. of about 100 callings. The *ratio per cent.* of the sexes was, in *Casual Wards :* male 79, female 21; in *Lodging Houses*, male 71, female 29; the aggregate ratio being male 72 and female 28 per cent. It is curious to note, as the issue of an investigation, in the year 1867, into the relative proportion of the sexes then attending a notorious metropolitan place of entertainment, which was supposed to be a place of assignation for men of the middle class, that the result obtained was very similar: 24 per cent. of women to 76 per cent. of men—the women being all of the prostitute class.

That the personal descriptions given above are often the

---

* In the majority of instances, it need hardly be said that the records of these marriages are not to be found in the archives of the Registrar-General.

offspring of the exuberant inventive powers of the tramp is abundantly clear, as in spite of the fact that numbers of discharged soldiers are known to be amongst them, not one, it will be observed, announces himself as such. Nevertheless, accepting these descriptions as accurate, it will be seen that the largest proportion of the vagrant class consist, *according to their own showing*, of those employed in the lowest or least skilled ranks of labour, and who, if bound to labour compulsorily, could as a consequence be easily provided with suitable employment. It will also be noticed from the average returns of money and food found on country tramps arrested, that, *apart from the provision made for the by the local Poor Law and Police Authorities*, they had not even the excuse of immediate and temporary want for begging. As to the sums of money discovered, it should be observed that the begging gains of a tramp are as a rule smaller in open country districts than they are in towns; moreover, the first idea of a tramp directly he gets money, is to spend it in sensual enjoyment by indulging in a drink, or even in a feast, for as a rule he despises the food he collects, and will only eat what he most relishes cooked in the way he likes best.

THE HANTS SYSTEM, established October, 1870, consisted in an agreement between the chairman and vice-chairman of boards of guardians and a committee of magistrates appointed by the Court of Quarter Sessions. Every vagrant was received, lodged, and fed in the casual wards of each union, and on stating that he was journeying in search of work, was provided with a way-ticket indicating his route to the next workhouse, and with a sufficient lunch for his support during the day. The task of work in the workhouse was remitted in his case, but enforced in all other cases. Acts of vagrancy were punished by fourteen days' imprisonment. This system was given up after a short trial in consequence of objections raised by the then Poor Law Board.

THE KENT SYSTEM, established March, 1871, is the same as the Dorset system. It is thus reported on by the *Standard* in February, 1886.

"Streams of vagrants are passing daily from town to town in Kent, having, it is stated, come from London. They are apparently in search of work, but a large proportion of them are undoubtedly tramps. Many of the men are discharged soldiers. Those who apply for work cannot obtain any, as there is not sufficient employment either in town or country for the resident labouring classes. The vagrants find shelter at night in the casual wards of the workhouses, and on their discharge they move on to another town, obtaining assistance on their way either through begging or by means of tickets issued by subscribers to the Mendicity Society.

THE WILTS SYSTEM, established in 1881, is the same as the Berks system.

THE MALVERN SYSTEM, established 1862. The head officers of police appoint an assistant relieving officer. The public assume that the really necessitous will be supplied with food and shelter. The funds are raised by public subscription, and the Vagrancy Act is strictly enforced.

In towns various methods of repression have from time to time been tried, the best known of them in the present day are those of the Mendicity Society and the Charity Organisation Society. The London Mendicity Society, established in 1818, issues tickets to subscribers to be given to street beggars instead of money, and referring them to the Society's office, where their cases are investigated and disposed of. The Charity Organisation Society, established in 1869, adopts the same method in principle except that it does not limit its operations to subscribers, and the scope of its work in dealing with the poor generally is of the widest extent. About 60 other societies, founded more or less on the model of this latter society, are scattered through the principal towns in the provinces.

None of the methods hitherto adopted have, however, had any permanent effect in reducing vagrancy.

The Whitechapel Guardians appear to have arrived at the pith of the cause of failure in a report made by a Committee specially appointed to consider the matter in 1880. They expressed an opinion—

"That the discipline and arrangements of existing casual wards are unassociated with any influence calculated to improve the habits of the vagrant poor; that they are not sufficiently elastic to meet the necessities of exceptional cases of distress; and that the labour test imposed upon vagrant paupers is not calculated to induce a spirit of independence, a habit of work, nor to impart physical power to enter upon industrial employment.

"That habitual vagrancy cannot be repressed by severe discipline and treatment, unassociated with means for dispauperisation."

Mr. W. C. Glen, the well-known writer on the Poor Laws, makes the following observations in the preface to his treatise on the Casual Poor Act, 1882.

"In former times the sturdy vagrant was dealt with by the parish constable and the justices of the peace under the provisions of the criminal law; but now vagrancy has become an institution and part of the poor law system, which the poor law authorities have hitherto failed to grapple with, at any rate to grapple with successfully. Every applicant professing to be destitute and to have no home, is at once and without undergoing any ordeal other than being searched for money or valuables, admitted into the casual ward, placed in a bath, housed for the night, fed, and after performing a prescribed task of work discharged, as destitute and forlorn as when admitted, without a character and without a word of kindness to cheer him on his way. If when he was in the casual ward he became sick the doctor prescribed for him, and if necessary he was taken into the body of the workhouse and treated as an ordinary sick pauper; but, failing to be on the doctor's list, there was no visitor to his dreary cell (miscalled ward) to offer counsel or advice, for the Workhouse Chaplain's footstep is never heard crossing its threshold in the ordinary course of his duties. No wonder that under such a system vagrancy increases, or, if it does not increase, that it is driven into active crime, for however desirous the 'professional vagrant' may be to change his course of life, he cannot do so any more than the leopard can change his spots. Compulsory detention is no doubt a step in the right direction; but the distinction between 'casual poor' and ordinary pauperism should be abolished, and all should be treated alike in the Workhouse—all being there by one common right—the right of destitution; and if destitution does not exist, neither wanderer nor inhabitant should be received into the workhouse as an inmate."

One curious result of the present system appears to be that the vagrant looks upon the inmate of the workhouse as something beneath him in the social scale. Mrs. Douglas, the mistress of the Marylebone Workhouse, on visiting the Houseless Poor Wards on one occasion, expressed to an old woman whom she saw there, an opinion that she would be much better off in the workhouse, to which the old lady replied that "thank God she hadn't come down to *that* yet."

At present the danger of a further accretion to the ranks of vagrancy seems to come from the agricultural districts. *Mr. Thomas Hardy*, writing on the Dorsetshire labourer, says—

"Ten or a dozen families, with their goods, may be seen halting simultaneously at an out-of-the-way inn, and it is not possible to walk a mile on any of the high-roads on Lady Day without meeting several. This annual migration from farm to farm is much in excess of what it was formerly. For example, on a particular farm where, a generation ago, not more than one cottage on an average changed occupants yearly, and where the majority remained all their lifetime, the whole number of tenants were changed at Lady Day just past, and this though nearly all of them had been new arrivals on the previous Lady Day. Dorset labourers now look upon an annual removal as the most natural thing in the world, and it becomes with the younger families a pleasant excitement. . . . .

"They come and go yearly, like birds of passage, nobody thinks whence or whither. This dissociation is favoured by the customary system of letting the cottages with the land, so that, far from having a guarantee of a holding to keep him fixed, the labourer has not even the stability of a landlord's tenant; he is only a tenant of a tenant, the latter possibly a new comer, who takes strictly commercial views of his man and cannot afford to waste a penny on sentimental considerations.

"The changes which are so increasingly discernible in village life by no means originate entirely with the agricultural unrest. A depopulation is going on which in some quarters is truly alarming. Villages used to contain, in addition to the agricultural inhabitants, an interesting and better-informed class, ranking distinctly above those—the blacksmith, the carpenter, the shoemaker, the small higgler, the shopkeeper (whose stock-in-trade consisted of a couple of loaves, a pound of candles, a bottle of brandy-balls and lumps of delight, three or four scrubbing-brushes, and a frying-pan), together with nondescript workers other than farm-labourers, who had remained in the houses where they were born for no especial reason beyond an instinct of association with the spot. Many of these families had been life-holders, who built at their own expense the cottages they occupied, and as the lives dropped, and the property fell in, they would have been glad to remain as weekly or monthly tenants of the owner. But the policy of all but some few philanthropic landowners is to disapprove of these petty tenants who are not in the estate's employ, and to pull down each cottage as it falls in, leaving standing a sufficient number for the use of the farmer's men and no more. The occupants who formed the back-bone of the village life have to seek refuge in the boroughs. This process, which is designated by statisticians as 'the tendency of the rural population towards the large towns,' is really the tendency of water to flow uphill when forced. . . . .

"The system is much to be deplored, for every one of these banished people imbibes a sworn enmity to the existing order of things, and not a few of them, far from becoming merely honest Radicals, degenerate into Anarchists, waiters on chance, to whom danger to the State, the town—nay, the street they live in, is a welcomed opportunity."

Mr. Richard Jefferies, writing on the subject of the Wiltshire labourer, expresses himself in very similar terms.

"Ceaseless effort to obtain wages causes a drifting about of the agricultural population. The hamlets and villages, though they seem so thinly inhabited, are really full, and every extra man and youth, finding themselves unable to get the weekly stipend at home, travel away. Some go but a little distance, some across the width of the country, a few emigrate, though not so many as would be expected. Some float up and down continually, coming home to their native parish for a few weeks, and then leaving it again. A restlessness permeates the ranks; few but those with families will hire for the year. They would rather do anything than that. Family men must do so because they require cottages, and four out of six cottages belong to the landowners and are part and parcel of the farms. Farmers are more given to changing their men than was once the case, and no longer retain the hereditary faces about them. The result is that the fixed population may be said to decline every year. The total population is probably the same, but half of it is nomad. It is nomad for two reasons —because it has no home, and because it must find wages."

If we look back through the long vista of legislation on vagrancy what do we find? The vagrant has been threatened with every species of punishment known to the law, and he has at different times been stocked, scourged, branded, imprisoned, and hanged, but he still survives with his old tricks as merrily as ever, and if music really has charms to soothe a savage breast, the *Rogue's March*, which appears to have been specially composed to honour his progresses through the land, ought to have tamed him long ago. He was in the first instance largely the offspring of harsh and repressive laws, now he is the noxious parasite fostered by indiscriminate and baneful charity.

All history plainly teaches us that so long as the vagrant is tolerated and acknowledged so long will he continue to flourish in spite of any temporary checks he may experience. That familiarity breeds contempt is especially true of the tramp, for no sooner has he become practically acquainted with any new law or regulation intended to repress him than he rises superior to it, he in fact resembles a shying horse who, directly he becomes familiarised with the object which at first startled him, goes on without heeding it in the future. The Houseless Poor Act of 1864, the appointment of the police as assistant relieving officers, the Pauper Inmates Discharge and Regulation Act of 1871, and many minor checks all intended to curb him, had only a temporary effect, and their latest successor, the Act of 1882, is so far as effect is concerned apparently following in the track of all its predecessors, as it will be noticed that the admissions to casual wards are again rapidly on the increase.

Vagrants frequent the casual wards as a matter of economy, when they are flush of funds or whenever they wish for a debauch with their paramours they frequent the lodging house. As the vagrants therefore oscillate between the tramp ward and the tramps' lodging houses, no real distinction can be made between the occupants of either. A good proportion, too, revolve between the casual ward and the gaol.

Under our Poor Law system we still recognise the right of an unlimited number of people to travel over the country and to receive lodging and supper and breakfast at the public expense.*

---

* While at the House of Correction at Hohnstein, in Saxony, in the year 1875, the Governor told the author that one of the inmates had informed him that he greatly admired the English workhouse system, and thought it worthy of imitation elsewhere. This man, it appeared, had been incarcerated at Hohnstein, and when released was, as usual, ordered to report himself to the police in the different districts through which he had to pass. He, however, failed to report himself and was lost sight of by the police for some time, but was at last found, recaptured and brought back to undergo a further sentence. "But," said the Governor, "how do you know anything of the English workhouse system?" and he replied that he had been to England. "How did you get there?" he was asked, and he answered that after leaving Hohnstein he went

The idea is that they are in "search of work," but no sort of verification is attempted to be made regarding their statements.

Our regulations with regard to vagrants seem to be framed with a sublime disregard for an age of cheap newspapers, halfpenny postage, and railways, and recognise a state of things compatible only with the condition of the country in the seventeenth and eighteenth centuries, when districts were isolated from one another, and when our high roads were our only means of intercommunication.

No one ought to have a right to travel through the country at the public expense; but if a man is destitute and can get work in another locality it is obviously to the public interest that he should be helped to his destination and thus be made a contributor to our taxation instead of remaining a drag upon the public purse.

But it is plain that this system will be grossly misused—as it is at present—if care is not taken to ascertain—

1st. That work is to be had in the locality to which the intending wayfarer states his wish to go.

2nd. That the intending wayfarer is destitute, and is a proper person for the work both as regards character and capacity.

If we refuse permission to travel at the public expense to all but those legitimately in search of work, it is evident that a tremendous residuum of idle vagabondism and criminality will be prevented from circulating, and will have to be dealt with in some shape or form; but we have established industrial schools for vagabond children—why not, then, houses of industry for vagabond adults? Compulsory labour ensured for lengthened periods without any other wage than sustenance, clothing, and lodging ought to be remunerative; if it is not it reflects discredit on the administration which fails to make it so. Mere punishment has no beneficial effect upon the vagrant, while the cost of it is a heavy tax upon the community, but a thorough industrial training, however simple in kind, would be of advantage both to the

to Hamburg, where he met a friend who asked him if he would like to go to England. He said he had no means of paying his passage. "Oh," replied his friend, "you won't want that. I am going on board a steamer as a cattle drover, and I can get you a similar place. In England you will not have to pay for your living; you will find splendid public lodging houses there where they will give you a bed and breakfast and make no charge at all. Come over and enjoy yourself!" Acting on the advice of his friend, he came over. He saw London and some of the principal country towns, and then, having become tired of his trip, he was duly passed back by the consul to his own country.

public and to the vagrant. It would in the long run be an immense saving to the country in rates; would tend to reduce crime, and would, to a large extent, reserve the flow of private charity for the deserving poor, whose condition might then be much ameliorated. The subject is one well worthy the attention of the practical philanthropist, who, if he wishes to do real good to the poor must be prepared to act on the principle that the highest and truest function of charity is to raise people above the necessity of receiving it.

CHAPTER XV.
SCOTLAND.
968—1885.

The condition of bondmen—Vagrancy in the reigns of Duffe, Kenneth III., and David II.—Legislation under Robert II. against caterans and vagrants—Laws of James I. against sorners and beggars—Laws of James II. against masterful beggars with horses and hounds and feigned fools—Further Acts of James III., IV., and V.—Laws of James VI.—The punishment of vagabonds shooting at game—Legislation against vagabondism in the Borders and Highlands—Further laws against vagabonds and beggars and gypsies—Students with weapons to have them confiscated—Masters of Coalheughs empowered to apprehend and employ vagabonds—Innkeepers not to receive masterless men, rebels at the horn, &c.—Charles I.—Complaints of the non-enforcement of the Acts against beggars—Correction houses, &c., to be established—Enforcement of the laws under the Commonwealth—Charles II.—Re-enactment of measures against vagabonds—James VII.—Magistrates of Edinburgh to purge the streets of beggars—William III.—Re-enactment of measures against vagrants—Attempts to regulate the rate of wages—Legislation of 1845, 1862, and 1865—Account of vagrancy from 1815 to 1878—Existing condition of vagrancy in 1885.

IN order to understand some of the leading causes of vagrancy in Scotland in early times we must first take a view of the condition of the lowest orders of people; and of the rights of compulsory hospitality, which did not differ very materially from the state of things in England in Anglo-Saxon times.

" The different ranks of the bondmen or unfree class have been preserved in the code of laws termed ' quoniam attachamenta.' They are there termed native men (nativi), and we are told that there are several kinds of nativity or Bondage (nativitatis sive bondagii) . . . . In the Chartulary of Scone, King William the Lion grants a mandate directing that if the abbot of Scone or his sergands shall find in the lands or in the power of others any of the Cumlawes and Cumherbes pertaining to his lands, he may reclaim them; and in the Chartulary of Dunfermline, the foundation charter by King David the First grants that all his serfs and all his Cumerlache from the time of King Edgar shall be restored to the Church wherever they may be found, and the scribe interprets the word Cumerlache by 'fugitivi' on the margin; and in a mandate by the same king to the same effect the title is 'of the fugitivi' which are called Cumerlache. In the last syllable of the name 'Cumherbes' or 'Cumarherbe' we can recognise the Irish word 'Orba' applied to that part of the tribe territory which had become the private property of the chiefs; and this name was no doubt applied to that class of serfs whose bondage was derived from their possessing servile land. They were the 'ascripti glebæ' of feudal times. The term 'Cumlawe' or 'Cumarlawe' is simply a translation of the Latin term 'manutenencia,' which characterised the third kind of bondage above described, and whose tie to their master being a personal one, led to their frequently escaping from hard usage and being reclaimed as fugitives. Thus among the laws of King William the Lion we find one declaring that anyone who detains a native fugitive man (nativi fugitivi) after he has been demanded by his true lord or his bailie, shall restore the said native man with all his chattels, and shall render to his lord the double of the loss he has sustained."

Conveth was the Irish Coinmhedha or Coigny, derived, according to O'Donovan, from "Coinmhe," which signifies feast or refection. It was the "Dovraeth" of the Welsh laws, and was founded upon the original right which the leaders in the tribe had to be supported by their followers. It came to signify a night's meal or refection given by the occupiers of the land to their superior when passing through his territory, which was exigible four times in the year; and when the tribe territory came to be recognised as crown land, it became a fixed food contribution charged upon each ploughgate of land. Thus in the charter by King Malcolm the Fourth, confirming the foundation of the abbey of Scone, he grants to the canons from each ploughgate of the whole land of the church of Scone in each year, at the feast of All Saints, for their "Coneveth" one cow and two pigs, and four "Camni" of meal, and ten threaves of oats, and ten hens and two hundred eggs, and ten bundles of candles, and four pounds of soap, and twenty half meales of cheese.

In the reign of Alexander the Third this word seems to have assumed the form of Waytinga, and appears in the Chamberlain Rolls of his reign as a burden upon the Thanages. Thus the Chamberlain renders an account of the Waytingas of Forfar and Glammis, of the Waytinga of one night of Fettercairn, of the Waytingas of four nights in the year of Kinross, and " of the rent of cows of two years," that is to say of the Waytingas of two nights in the year of Forfar, forty-eight cows, and of the Waytinga of (one) and a half nights of the Thanage of Glammis, twenty-seven cows.

Another name for this exaction was " Cudoidhche," or a night's portion, corrupted into Cuddiche or Cuddicke. It appears under this name mainly in the Highlands and Islands, and was continued as a burden on the lands to a late period.*

According to Harrison's version of Boece's " History of Scotland," the first historical indications regarding vagrancy are to be met with in the reign of King Duffe, A.D. 968, when " he called the Thanes of the Isles afore him commaunding straytly as they would avoyde his displeasure to purge theyr countreys of such malefactours, wherby the husbandmen and other commons might live in quiet without vexation of such barrettours † and idle persons as sought to live only upon other men's goodes. The Thanes upon this charge given them by the King tooke no small number of the offenders, partely by publike authoritie, and partely by lying in awayte for them where they supposed theyr haunt was to resort, the which being put to execution according to that they had merited, caused ye residue of that kind of people eyther to get them over into Ireland, eyther els to learne some manuall occupation wherewith to get theyr living, yea though they were never so great gentlemen borne."

In the reign of King Kenneth III. (A.D. 976), " If any idle person were espied abroad in the streetes, straightwayes the sergeants would have him to warde. The nobles remayned in the Kings house or in other lodgings to them assigned, procuring by their freendes and ministers to have suche offenders as used to robbe and spoyle the husband man, apprehended and brought to the King unto Bertha,‡ theyre to receyve judgment and punition according to theyr demerites: for so they perceyved they must needes worke, if they minded the safegard of their own lives. Hereof it followed also, that within short space there were brought unto Bertha, to the number neare hande of v.₡.§ of suche idle loyterers as used to live by spoyle and pillage, many of them being discended of famous houses, all whiche companie being condemned for theyr offences to die, were hanged upon gybets aboute

---

* Skene
† Old French *barrateur*, a deceiver. A common mover of suits and quarrels in disturbance of the peace.
‡ Perth. § 500.

the towne, and commaundement gyven by the King, that theyr bodies shoulde not be taken downe, but there to hange still, to give ensample to other, what the ende was of all suche as by wrongfull meanes sought to live idelly, by other men's labours."

In 1331 David II., "that vertue might be cherished within the realme, commaunded that no vagabunde nor ydle person should be received into any towne or place, except they had some craft or science wherewith to get their lyving. By this means he purged the realm of Scotlande of many idle and slouthfull roges and vagabundes."

By the 12th statute of Robert II., made in 1385, those persons are deemed rebels "quha* travellis as Katheranis,† eatand the cuntrie, and consumand the gudes of the inhabitants, takand their gudes be force and violence."

By an Ordo Justiciare of this year sorning‡ is to be made a point of dittay § at the justice ayre.||

During the limited personal reign of *James I.* that monarch made strong efforts to improve the administration of justice and to protect the lower orders against the rapacity and oppression of the great. Three enactments were specially directed against the vagabond catherans or sorners who had long greatly abounded. The first, 1424, c. 7, forbids that "ony cumpanyis pas in the cuntre lyand apone ¶ ony the Kingis lieges or thig ** or soiorne‡ horses oupon Kirkmen †† or husbandes ‡‡ of the lande " and orders the sheriff to arrest and challenge them as breakers of the King's peace, and if they are convicted they are to find sureties to assithe §§ the King and the complainer. The second, c. 21 (repeated by c. 26 of the year 1457), creates an important distinction between those who are able to earn their own livelihood and those who are obliged to resort to the charity of others for their subsist-

* *Quha,* who.
† *Gael.* Ir. *Ceatharnach,* a soldier. Bands of robbers, especially such as came down from the Highlands to the low country, and carried off cattle, corn, or whatever pleased them, from those who were not able to make resistance. —JAMIESON.
‡ *Sorne, soiorne,* to obtrude one's self on another for bed and board. Ir. *Searbhan,* a tribute, oats.
§ *Dittay* (dictay) indictment, line of accusation.
|| Itinerant court of justice. Eng. *eyre.*
¶ Lying upon.
** *Thig,* to ask, to beg. *Thiggar,* a beggar. Swed. *tigga,* to beg, to ask alms.
†† *Kirkman,* one who has an ecclesiastical function or an office in the Church.
‡‡ *Husbands,* husbandmen.
§§ *Assithe,* to compensate, to satisfy.

ence. It directs that "na thiggar be thollyt* to thyg nother †
in burgh nor to land betuix xiiij & lxx yeres of age bot thai
be sene be the counsall of the town or the commons of the cuntre,
that thai may not wyn thar leffing ‡ otherwayis; and they that sa
beis fundyn,§ sall haue a certane takyn "|| on them, while all
others, "haifande na takynis" are to be charged by open proclamation to labour and "pass to craftis for wynning of thar
leving, and that under payn of birninge on the cheyk and banyssing
of the cuntre." By a subsequent statute of the same monarch,
1425, c. 20, it is ordained that "ilk¶ scheref of the realme,
within his balgery,** inquire diligently, gif ony ydil men, that
has not to live of thare awin to leif apon be resett †† within the
lande: eftir the quhilk‡‡ Inquisicion, the scheref sal ger §§ arrest
sic ydil men, ande ger kep thaim in festynance |||| quhil ¶¶ it be
knawin, quhare on*** thai leif. . . . . the scherif sall assigne xl dais
to sic ydil men to get thaim masteris, or to festyn thaim to leful†††
craftis. Ande thai xl. dais beande gane, gif thai be fundyn mars ‡‡‡
ydil, the scheref sal arrest thaim agayn, ande sende thaim to the
Kingis preson, to byde ande be punyst at the Kingis will."

These rigorous enactments do not seem to have been carried
into execution, for in 1427 there appears an Act (c. 4) which
directs former laws against beggars to be enforced, and inquisition
to be made and a fine imposed on those magistrates who had
neglected them: it was likewise enacted, c. 8, "that na§§§ lippir |||||
folk, nothir man nor woman, fra thyn furth enter, na §§§ cum in to
na burgh of the realme, but thrise in the wolk,¶¶¶ that is to say
ilk Monunday, ilk Weddynisday, & ilk Friday, fra ten houres, to
twa efter none;**** ande quhar fares ande mercates †††† fallis on
thai dais, at thai leif thare enterri in the borowis,‡‡‡‡ and gang on
the morne to get thare leving. Item, that na lippour folk sit to

---

* *Thole, thoill,* to suffer. A.S. *teolan,* to toil, to labour; *teolian,* to take care of, to mollify. † Neither.
‡ Living. § Found. || *Takyn,* token, mark, sign.
¶ *Ilk,* each, every. A.S. *œlc, etc.*
** *Balgery, baillerie,* bailiwick, jurisdiction of a bailiff.
†† *Resett,* to receive, to harbour, to entertain.
‡‡ *Quhilk,* which. §§ *Ger, gar,* to cause, to make. Icel. *göra.*
|||| *Festynance,* confinement, durance. A.S. *faestenes.* ¶¶ *Quhil,* until.
*** *Quhare on,* whereon. ††† Lawful.
‡‡‡ *Mars,* more. A.S. *mare.* Gael. *mor.* §§§ *Na,* no, nor.
||||| *Lippir* or *lippour folk,* leprous people. ¶¶¶ *Wolk,* week. A.S. *weoce.*
**** *Efter none,* afternoon. †††† *Mercates,* markets. Lat. *mercatus.*
‡‡‡‡ *Borowis,* boroughs.

thig, nothir in Kirk nor in Kirk-yarde, na in nane uthir place within the borowis, bot at thare awin hospitale, and at the porte* of the toune & uthir places outewith † the borowis."

Mr. *Tytler* says "these statutory regulations are, with a few changes, to be found amongst the Statutes of Richard II. and the fourth and fifth Henrys; and prove that the King, during his long detention in England, had made himself intimately acquainted with the legislative policy of that kingdom."

During the minority of *James II.* numbers of the nobility, like many of their brethren in England in the reign of the earlier Plantagenet kings, indulged in plunder and robbery. The administration of the kingdom was venal and corrupt; famine and pestilence added to the disorders of the State, and as a result numbers of the poor perished from hunger and disease.

In the year 1449 the following stringent law against vagabonds was passed (c. 9): "It is ordainit, for the away putting of sornares, overlyars,‡ and masterful beggars,§ with horses, hundes, or uthir gudes, that al officiares, bath schereffes, baronis, alderman, balyeis, als wele within burgh, as utwith, tak ane inquisicione at ilk court that thai hald of the forsaid thinges : ande gif ony sic be fundyn, that thar horses, hundes, and uthir gudes be eschet to the King, and their personis put in the Kinges warde quhil the King haf said his wil to thaim. Ande alsua that the said schereffe balyeis, and officiares inqueres at ilk courte, gif thar be ony that makis thaim fulis ‖ that ar nocht bardes,¶ or sic lik utheris rynnares aboute.** Ande gif ony sic be fundyn, that thai be put in the Kinges warde,†† or in his yrnis,‡‡ for thar trespasses, als lang as thai haf ony gudes of thar awin to leve apon, and fra thai haf nocht to lefe apon that thar eris §§ be nalyt to the trone ‖‖ or to ane

---

* *Porte*, gate. A.S. *port*. † *Outewith*, outside.

‡ *Overlyars*, beggars that "overlie" other people's crofts or tenements, *i.e.* occupy or sleep in them against the will of the owner.

§ *Masterful beggars*, such as take by force, or by putting householders in fear. ‖ Feigned fools.

¶ *Bardes*, a poet or bard ; a name contemptuously applied in the old laws to those strolling rhymers who were wont to oppress the lieges. Ir. *bardas*, a satire, a song.

** *Rynnares about*, runners about, *i.e.* vagabonds.

†† *Waird*, a prison. As. *weardian*.

‡‡ *Yrnis* = irons, *i.e.* fetters. §§ *Ears*.

‖‖ *Trone*, the pillar or post on which the town scales were hung. Icel. *tjalds trönur*, a platform on which to pitch a tent, allied to *trana*, a framework.

uthir tre,* and cuttit of; and bannyst the cuntre. And gif thareftir thai be fundyn again, that thai be hangit."

The mounted vagabonds here legislated against appear to realise the conception of the proverb which declares that " set a beggar on horseback and he will ride to the devil." A very similar state of things was legislated against in Ireland in 1634.

The disturbed political state of the country, together with the low moral condition of the people, not only prevented the due execution of the laws, but otherwise tended greatly to augment the number of the disorderly gangs which these statutes were intended to suppress. The Legislature, however, seem to have hoped, by the increasing severity of their enactments, to supply the want of moral restraint on the part of the people; and accordingly we find, in a few years, that sorners are ordered to be summarily put to death as thieves and reivers, by 1455, c. 8, which ordains that "quhar ever sornoures be overtane in tyme to cum, that thai be deliveryt to the Kingis schereffes, and that thai furthewith as the Kingis Justice do law apone thame as apone a theif or reffar" †; and by a statute of the same year (c. 13), the King on going to any head burgh is to inquire whether there be any sorners or oppressors of the poor, and to punish them. By 1457, c. 26, the King's Justices at the justice aires are directed to "tak Inquisicione of sornares, bardes, maisterfull beggars, or fenzeit fulys: ‡ and other bannysh thame the cuntre, or sende thame to the Kingis presone."

During the minority of *James III.* the venality of the ruling faction conduced to the revival of oppression and crime. Royal pardons were sold for the most outrageous crimes, resembling the condition of things legislated against in England in 1328, and the country was frequently distracted with the havoc and plunder arising out of private feuds. To add to the public distress, the coinage was debased at a time of serious dearth. In the midst of all this social confusion the laws against masterful beggars and sorners were re-enacted in the year 1478, by the Statute 1478, c. 10, which has for its professed object the " staincheing § of

* Any other post.

† *Reffar, rever, ryfir*, a robber, a pirate, corresponding to the English *ruffler*. A.S. *reafere*.

‡ The *fenzeit fulys*, or feigned fools, were common in the northern parts of England up to the middle of the eighteenth century. *Shakespeare* calls them *Bedlam beggars*, and they were generally known in England as *Abraham-men*.

§ *Staunch*, to stop, to assuage. Old Fr. *estancher*.

masterfull beggars and sornares, that daily oppressis and heryis * the Kingis pur lieges."

Legislation and social improvement in Scotland appear to have followed English precedents at long intervals of time. The oath of peace which Hubert, Archbishop of Canterbury, sent throughout England in 1195 seems to have been imitated in Scotland in the year 1487, when "the lords spiritual and temporal, with the barons and freeholders, gave their promise that in all time coming they should cease to maintain, or stand at the bar with traitors, men-slayers, thieves, or robbers, always excepting that they must not be prevented from taking part in 'sober wise' with their kin and friends, in the defence of their honest actions. They engaged also to assist the King and his officers to bring all such offenders to justice, that they might 'underly' the law." The exception introduced in this pledge must, however, have enabled all who gave it to "keep the word of promise to the ear and break it to the hope."

During the minority of *James IV.* open spoliation was again resorted to by the party in power. When, however, the King attained full authority, his energy and activity in the administration of justice, and in the suppression of crime, were productive of good effect. He adopted a system not uncommon in those times of engaging the most powerful of the resident nobles and gentry in a covenant or "band," which under severe penalties obliged them to maintain order throughout the country. The rigorous treatment which the King meted out to all who disturbed the peace of the country had also a wholesome effect. In the year 1503, by c. 14, it was ordained "that the statute of King James the First, maid upoun stark † beggars be observit and kepit. And that the schereffis, provestis, ballies within burrowis, baith of rialte‡ and regalite,§ spirituale and temporale, see that this Act be execute and keipit: and that thai thoill nane to beg within thame, except crukit folk,‖ blind folk, impotent folk, and waik folk, ¶

---

* *Herry, hery, harry,* to rob, to spoil, to pillage. Icel. *herja.*
† *Stark,* able-bodied. A.S. *stearc,* stiff.
‡ *Rialte,* territory immediately under the jurisdiction of the King, as distinguished from that to which the privileges of a regality were annexed.—*Jamieson.*
§ *Regality,* a territorial jurisdiction granted by the King with the lands given *in liberam regalitatem*; and conferring on the persons receiving it, although commoners, the title of *Lords of Regality.   Jamieson.*
‖ *Crukit-folk,* cripples.
¶ *Waik folk,* weak folk, infirm people.

under the pane of payment of ane mark,* for ilk uther beggar, that beis fundin."

In none of these enactments, subsequent to the statute 1424, c. 21, is there any mention made of the regular poor, who, by that Act, were permitted to beg—a privilege at a future period exchanged for the right to parochial support. No Act relative to this subject appears till the statute 1503, c. 14, just cited, which points out more distinctly the class who were to enjoy the privilege of begging, including those only who, by reason of physical disability, and of mental or bodily weakness, were incapable of maintaining themselves.

The premature death of James IV. on the field of Flodden again let loose disorder in the kingdom, and bands of robbers openly traversed the country. Lord Dacre, the warden of the English marches, in order to distract the Scottish Government, kept four hundred Scottish outlaws in his pay, who caused daily burning and destruction. Some of the venal nobility, seduced by the bribes of the English Government, also indulged in numerous acts of oppression under which the people groaned without means of redress. The house of Douglas exercised despotic power, and the excesses of its representatives rendered the life and property of all opposed to them insecure; the Highlands too were in a state of the utmost disorder.

Immediately upon the accession of *James V.* to power in the year 1528, the King proceeded to establish law and order throughout the kingdom. The most notorious Border chieftains, who had long subsisted by rapine and violation of the laws, were hanged, amongst them being the famous freebooter *Johnnie Armstrong.* In the year 1535 a very important restriction was imposed on the privileged beggars by c. 29 of that year, which enacts "that na beggaris be tholit to beg in ane parochine † that ar born in ane uther; and that the hedismen ‡ of ilk parochine mak taikynnis § and geve to the beggaris thereof, and that thai be sustenit within the boundis of that parochine; and that nane uther be servit with almous ‖ within that parochine, but thai that bearis that takin alanerlie." ¶

* *A mark*, 6s. 8d.
† *Parochine*, parish. Lat. *parochia*.
‡ *Hed'sman*, headsman, the principal man in the district.
§ *Taikynnis*, takings, collections. ‖ *Almous*, alms. A.S. *ælmesse*.
¶ *Alanerlie*, sole, only.

Statute 21 of the year 1540 recites that a multitude of vile, unhonest, and miserable creatures are said to frequent the meal market at Edinburgh daily to get sustentation, and orders the market to be removed in consequence.

During the minority of *Queen Mary* the kingdom was again in a distracted condition. The English invasions in the years 1544-45—47-48 caused widespread devastation in the train of the army. The instructions of Henry VIII. in 1544 being "to sack Leith and burn and subvert it, and all the rest, putting man, woman and child to the sword."

The Act of 1535, c. 29, was repealed in 1551 by Statute 16, and again in 1555 by Statute 38 of that year. This latter Act was passed under the regency of *Mary of Guise*, when many wise and judicious laws were introduced for the administration of equal justice throughout the country.

Notwithstanding, however, the provisions for the suppression "of sorners and masterful beggars," their number seems greatly to have increased during the disorders of the subsequent unfortunate reign of Queen Mary.

By the year 1567 murder, robbery, and offences of all kinds prevailed to an intolerable degree on the Borders, and men who had been publicly outlawed, walked abroad, mocking at the powers of justice. The great centre of crime was Hawick. The Earl of Mar at length pounced on the principal offenders and executed them, thus reducing the disturbed districts to peace and quietness. In this year a Statute (c. 17) was passed ordaining that vagabonds having no goods and shooting with culverin, crossbow, or handbow, at "Da,* Ra,† Hart, Hynde, ‡ Hair, § Cuning, ‖ Dow,¶ Herron," or fowl of the river, are to be imprisoned for forty days for the first offence, and to have their right hand cut off for the second.

In the year 1570 the kingdom was in a wretched condition owing to its being torn by the two contending factions of the captive Queen Mary and the infant King supported by English intrigue.

In 1573-4 the justice ayres were the organs of rapacity by encouraging informers to discover offences which laid the unhappy

* Doe. A.S. *da*.   † Roe. A.S. *ra*.
‡ Hind.   § Hare. A.S. *hara*.   ‖ Rabbit. Lat. *cuniculus*.
¶ Dove. A.S. *duua*.

defendants under heavy fines. A little later, however, the vigour and success of the Government of the Regent Morton brought about security to property and person. Under his regency, in the year 1574 an enactment was introduced against vagabonds, strong and idle beggars, which orders those between the ages of fourteen and seventy to be apprehended and tried, and on conviction to be scourged and burned through the gristle of the right ear with a hot iron, unless some responsible person will take them into his service for a whole year. Any vagabond quitting such service is to be burnt as aforesaid for the first offence, and if he offends again, after seventy days he is to suffer pains of death as a thief. Egyptians or gypsies are for the first time included among the classes of persons who are to be deemed vagabonds. Persons who give money, harbouring, or lodging to vagrants are to pay a fine not exceeding five pounds. Any person impeding the execution of the Act is to suffer the same penalty as the vagabond would have incurred. The inhabitants of every parish are to be taxed for the relief of the aged and impotent poor. All impotent beggars, except leprous and bedridden people, are to be passed to their place of birth or common resort during the last seven years; those who refuse or neglect to go are to be punished by scourging, imprisonment, and burning through the ear. Collectors of alms refusing or neglecting their office are to be liable to a penalty of twenty pounds. Any person may take a beggar's bairn between the ages of five and fourteen into his service, and keep a male to the age of twenty-four and a female to the age of eighteen. No Irish or Highland bards or beggars are to be brought into the Lowlands, under a penalty of twenty pounds upon the bringers.

Shortly after King James VI. assumed the reins of government, an attempt was made to form a more regular system for the remedy of the evil which had so long grievously oppressed the people of Scotland. This was done by the Act, 1579, c. 12, which appears to be modelled on the English Statute 14 Eliz., c. 5 (1572), and which is the foundation of the present system of Scotch poor laws. It is, to this day, the only authority (with the exception of a proclamation of the Privy Council) for enforcing a compulsory provision for the support of the ordinary poor; the later statutes, which direct assessments to be levied, being for entirely different purposes, having now fallen into total desuetude.

This Statute entitled an Act "For pwnishment of the strang and ydle beggaris, and releif of the pure and impotent," proceeds on the narrative, that the "sindrie lovable actis of Parliament maid be our Soverane Lordis maist noble progenitors, for the stancheing of the maisterfull and ydle beggaris, away-putting of soirnaris, and provisioun for the puyr," "in tyme bigane hes not bene put to dew executioun, throw the Iniquitie and troublis of the tyme bipast, and be ressone that thair wes not heirtofoir ane ordor of pwnishment sa specialie devisit as neid requirit; bot the saidis beggaris, besydis the utheris inconvenientis quilke they daylie produce in the commounwelth, procuris the wraith and displesure of God, for the wiked and ungodlie forme of leving, usit amangis thame, without mariage or baptizing of a greit nowmer * of thair bairnis."† It then goes on, "Thairfoir, now, for avoiding of thir inconvenientis and eschewing of the confusioun of sindrie lawis and actis concerning thair pwnishment, standing in effects, and that sum certane executioun and gude ordor may follow thairanent, To the greit plesure of Almichty God, and commoun weill of the realme, It is thocht expedient, statute and ordanit, alsweill for the utter suppressing of the saidis strang and Idle beggaris, sa contageous Innemyes to the commoun weill, As for the chearitable releving of aiget ‡ and impotent puyr people, that the ordor and forme following be observit." The "ordor" of pwnishment appointed for these "sa countageous innemyes to the commoun weill," was, that in being convicted for the first time, "they be adjudget to be scurget,§ and brunt throw the ear with ane hett yrne," ‖ "except sum honest and responsall man will of his charitie, be contentit then presentlie To act himself befoir the judge To tak and keip the offendor in his service for ane haill zeir;" ¶ "and gif the offendor depart and leif the service within the zeir, aganis his will that ressavis him in service, he shall then be scurgit and brunt throw the ear, as is befoirsaid; quilk pwnishment being anys ressavit,** he sall not suffer the lyk agane for the space of lx dayis thairefter; Bot gif, at the end of the saidis lx dayis, he be found to be fallin agane in his ydill and vagabund trade of lyf, then, being apprehendit of new, he salbe adjudget, and suffer the panes of deid †† as a theif." The Act then sets

---

* *Nowmer*, number. Lat. *numerus*. † *Bairnis*, children. A.S. *bearn*.
‡ *Aiget*, aged. § *Scurget*, scourged. ‖ *Hett yrne*, hot iron.
¶ *Haill zeir*, whole year. ** *Ressavit*, received. †† *Deid*, death.

forth who are to be considered "as strang and idle beggaris and vagabunds, and worthie of the pwnishment befoir specifijt;" and these are generally all persons between fourteen and seventy years of age, going about the country idle, and not following any lawful mode of winning their bread.

This Act, which first establishes a regular "ordor of pwnishment" for sorners, masterful beggars, and vagabonds, gives the following list of those who shall be held to be such, viz., "All ydle personis ganging about in ony cuntrie of this realme, using subtill, crafty, and unlauchfull playis, as Juglarie, fast-and-lowiss,* and sic utheris. The Idle people calling thame selffis Ægyptianis,† or ony utheris that feinzies ‡ thame selffis to have knawlege of prophecie, charmeing, or utheris abusit sciences, quhairby they persuaid the people that they can tell thair weardis,§ deathis, and fortunes, and sic uther fantasticall Imaginationes, and all personis being haill and stark ‖ in body, and able to wirk, allegeing thame to have bene heryit or brunt in sum far part of the realme, Or allegeing thame to be banist for slauchter, and utheris wicked deidis; and utheris nouthir having land nor maister, nor useing ony lauchfull merchandice, craft, or occupatioun, quhairby they may wyn their leavingis, And can gif na rekning how they lauchfullie get thair leving; and all menstrallis,¶ sangstares, and tailtellaris,** not avouit †† in speciall service be sum of the Lordis of Parliament or greit barronis,‡‡ or be the heid burrowis and cieties, for thair commoun menstralis; All commoun lauboraris,§§ being personis able in body, leving ydillie, and fleing laubor; All counterfaittaris of licenses to beg, or useing the same, knawing thame to be counterfaittit; all vagabund scolares of the Universities of Sanct Androis,‖‖ Glasgow, and Abirdene, not licencit be the rector and deane of faculties of the Universitie to ask almous." It is declared that these, "and all schipmen and marinaris, allegeing thame selffis to be schipbrokin, without they have sufficient testimoniallis, salbe takin,

* *Fast-and-lowiss*, fast and loose, a cheating game practised by vagrants and gypsies, known in England as *pricking the garter*. A garter is made up into a number of intricate folds, and the victim tries to prick the centre for a wager.
† *Ægyptianis*, gypsies.   ‡ *Feinzie*, to feign.
§ *Weird, werd, weerd*, fate, destiny.   A.S. *wyrd*, the fates; fate, fortune.
‖ *Stark*, strong.   ** *Tailtellaris*, taletellers, resembling
¶ *Menstrallis*, minstrels.   the Irish *skelaghes*.
†† *Avouit*, avowed.   ‡‡ *Barronis*, barons.
§§ *Lauboraris*, labourers.   ‖‖ *Sanct Androis*, Saint Andrews.

adjudged, estemit, and pwnist, as strang beggarris, and vagabundis." The same statute farther declares, that any person who "disturbis or lettis * the executioun of the Act," shall suffer the same pains as the vagabond whose correction he has impeded would have incurred.

Besides the penalties to be inflicted on the vagabonds themselves, the Act declares, that every person who "gives money, harbry or ludeging, settis † houses, or shawis ony uthir rcleif" to them, shall be liable to a fine not exceeding 5 pounds Scots ‡ to the poor of the parish.

The Act further provides, that if the "aiged and impotent persones, not being so diseased, lame, or impotent, but they may wirk in sum maner of werk," shall, nevertheless, refuse to perform the work appointed to them by the overseer, they shall be punished as vagabonds. It also allows any of the lieges to take beggars' children between the ages of five and fourteen years into their service, and gives a right to their labour till the age of twenty-four in males and eighteen in females. It makes provision for allowing to persons shipwrecked, licenses to proceed to their own homes, and permits testimonials to be given to such of the poor as may be judged proper, authorising them to ask alms in their own parishes. It declares that vagabonds, while imprisoned, shall be maintained by the parishes in which they were apprehended—"allowing to each person ane pund of aitbreid § and watter to drink."

There are also included among vagabonds (by this and subsequent enactments) those poor persons who, though entitled to parochial relief, either refuse to perform such work as they are able for when required by the parish, or persist in begging without a license, or beyond the bounds of the parish to which their license extends, or refuse to pass to the parish of their own settlement.

The law against bards was, we are told, put into force on the

* *Let*, to hinder, to impede. A.S. *lettan*. † *Set*, to let, to lease.
‡ Up to 1355 the Scottish money was equal in value to the English; after this, owing to the impoverishment of the kingdom, it sunk in value. In 1390 Scotch coin passed for only half its nominal value in England; and in 1393 it was ordered that its currency as money in the latter should cease. After this it became gradually more debased, until in 1600 it was only a *twelfth* part of the value of English money, and remained at that point until the union of the two kingdoms.
§ *Aitbreid*, oatcake.

12th of August, 1579, by the Earl of Morton under the following circumstances.—

"Aug. 12. Twa poets of Edinburgh, remarking some of his (the Earl of Morton's) sinistrous dealing, did publish the same to the people by a famous libel written against him; and Morton, hearing of this, causit the men to be brought to Stirling, where they were convict for slandering ane of the King's councillors, and were there baith hangit."

By the 59th Statute of 1587, s. 7, vagabonds and "unanswerable" men in the Borders, Highlands, and Isles are to find security to underlie* the law, and failing to do so are to be denounced rebels and fugitives. Action is to lie at the instance of the parties injured against the magistrates where they are reset. This Act was repeated in 1593, "unanswerable" men being there termed masterless men.

In the year 1591 crime was again rife, as the King, speaking on the 1st of June in that year, says, "I must advertise you what it is that makes great crimes to be so rife in this country, namely, that all men set themselves more for friend than for justice and obedience to the laws."

The next Statute relating to the poor, 1592, c. 69, grants power to certain persons to be appointed by the sheriff in each parish, to hold courts, and summon an assize for the trial and punishment of vagrants, strong and idle beggars and vagabonds.

In 1593, owing to the factions and family feuds amongst the nobility, the kingdom was in a miserable state. The law was powerless against such influential offenders. Nevertheless, the Acts of 1579 and 1581 against vagabonds and beggars are ordered to be enforced by the ordinary judges or justices, who are empowered to punish them by death or otherwise at their discretion. The magistrates of Aberdeen found it necessary to take order this year with "a great number of idle persons, not having land nor masters, neither yet using ony lawful merchandise, craft, nor occupation, fleeing as appears frae their awn dwelling, by reason of some unlawful causes and odious crimes whereof they are culpable, whilk are very contagious enemies to the common weal of the borough." The town was ordered to be cleared of them, and the future harbonage by the inhabitants was forbidden.

* *Underlie*, to be subjected to, to undergo.

In 1594, by the 33rd Statute, students "vagand" or wandering night or day armed with swords, pistolets, and other weapons are to have them confiscated. This somewhat resembles an early ordinance published at *Heidelberg*, which expressly forbids the students to go about the city with arms at evening, and after the tolling of the bell which calls the night watch to their duty.

C. 37 of the same year commences by reciting that "nochtwithstanding the sindrie actis maid be his hienes and his maist noble progenitors for punischement of the authoris of thift reif* oppressioun and sorning and masteris and sustenaris of thevis. Yit sic has bene and presentlie is the barbarous cruelties and dalie heirschippis † of the vickit thevis and lymmaris of the clannis and surnames following inhabiting the hielandis and Iles, Thay ar to say Clangregor, Clanfarlane, Clanlauren, Clandowill, Clandonnochie, Clanchattan, Clanchewill, Clancharron, Clanronald in Lochaber, Clanronald in Knoydert Moidart and Glengarry, Clanleyid of the Lewis, Clanleod of Harris, Clandonald South and North, Clangillane, Clanayioun, Clankinnoun, Claneal, Clankenzie, Clanandries, Clanmorgun, Clangun, Cheilphale and also many broken men of the surnames of Stewart in Atholl Lorne and Balquhidder Campbells, Grahams in Menteith, Buchans, McCauls, Galbraiths, McNabs, McNabricks, Menzies, Phersons, Spadings, McIntoshes in Atholl, McThomas in Glensche, Farquharsons in Brae of Mar, McPhersons, Grants, Rosses, Frasers, Monroes, Neilsons and others inhabiting the sheriffdomes of Argyll, Bute, Dunbarton, Stirling, Perth, Forfar, Aberdeen, Banff, Elgin, Forres, Nairn, Inverness and Cromartie, stewartries of Strathearn and Menteith, and likewise a great number of wicked thieves oppressors and peacebreakers and resetters of theft of the surnames of Armstrong, Elliott, Nickson, Crossar, Graham, Irving, Bell, Carlisle, Batson, Littles, Thomsons, Glendonnings, Carruthers, Johnstones, Jardines, Moffats, Latimers and others inhabiting the borders 'foiranent' ‡ England, In the sheriffdoms of Roxburgh, Selkirk, Peebles, Dumfries, and stewartry of Annerdale, In the murder 'heirschip' and daily oppression of his Highnesses peaceable and good subjects in the whole countries adjacent to the Highlands and Borders to the displeasure of God, contempt and dishonour of

---

* *Reif*, robbery, rapine. A.S. *reaf*.
† *Herschip*, *heirschipp*, the act of plundering, devastation.
‡ *Foiranent*, directly opposite to. A.S. *foran*, before, and *ongean*, opposite to.

his Highnesses person and authority and to the wasting and desolation of a good part of the plentiful ground if speedy remedy be not provided. And understanding that this mischief and shameful disorder increases and is nourished by the oversight, 'hounding out,* resett,' maintenance and not punishment of the thieves limmers and vagabonds partly by the landlords masters and baillies of the lands and bounds where they dwell and resort and partly through the counsel directions resett and partaking of the chieftains principals of the branches and householders of the said surnames and clans which bear quarrel and seek revenge for the least hurting or slaughter of any one of their unhappy races although it were by order of justice or in rescue and following of true men's gear stolen or reft. So that the said Chieftains Principals of the branches and householders worthily may be esteemed the very authors fosterers and maintainers of the wicked deeds of the vagabonds of their clans and surnames." It then enacts that a roll and catalogue should be made with all possible diligence of all persons of the surnames aforesaid suspected of slaughter, theft, reif, resett of theft or thieves or sorning. That all landlords" . . . . "and baillies are to find surety to make their men, tenants, and servants answerable to justice. Such householders of the clans as compere,† to find caution,‡ such as do not to be denounced rebels and fugitives. Chieftains, principals of the branches, and householders who do not compere, or compering do not find sureties, are to be denounced rebels and their goods to be disponed to their landlords for their better relief."

By the next Statute (1597, c. 39) the period during which strong beggars and their children may be employed in common works is extended to their whole lifetime.

The next Act (1600, c. 28) complains, that the Statute 1579 has received "litill or na effect or executioun," and declares "that the strang and idill beggaris, being for the maist pairt theiffis, bairdis, and counterfitt lymmeris,§ levand maist Insolentlie and ungodlie without mariage, or baptisme of a great number of thair bairns, ar sufferit to vaig ‖ and wander throuchout

---

* *Hound out*, to set on, to encourage to do injury to others.
† *Compere*, to appear in the presence of. Fr. *comparoir*. Lat. *comparere*.
‡ *Caution*, security. Lat. *cautio*.
§ *Lymmer, limmar*, a scoundrel, a worthless fellow, used in the laws as equivalent to *thief riever*. Dan. *lommier, looby, lubber, lout*.
‖ *Vaig*, to wander, to roam. Icel. *vaga*, to waddle.

the haill cuntrey, and the pure and impotent persones ar neglegit, and na cair had, nor provisioun maid, for thair intertenement and sustentation;" and attributing to the neglect of the persons to whom the execution of the Acts of Parliament had been committed, what was truly the consequence of the state of the country and the moral condition of the people. It then orders the session of the Kirk (equivalent to the English vestry) to put the said Acts of Parliament into execution.

The 10th Statute of 1606 authorises masters of coal-heughs* and saltpans to apprehend and put to labour all vagabonds and sturdy beggars.

In his Institute of the Law of Scotland, *Mr. John Erskine*, so late as the year 1773, lays down that "colliers, coal-bearers, salters, and other workmen necessary for the carrying on of collieries and salt works are by the law itself, without any paction, bound, merely by their entering upon work in a colliery or salt manufactory, to the perpetual service thereof; and if the owner sell or alien the ground upon which the works stand, the right of the service of these colliers, salters, &c., passes over to the purchaser, as *fundo annexum* without any express grant."

In the year 1743 there appears to have been a disposition among the bondsmen of the coal-mines in Fife and Lothian to assert their freedom. Fifteen men who worked in the Gilmerton coal-works having absented themselves in October and gone to work at other collieries, their master, Sir John Baird, of Newbyth, advertised them, so that no other master might break the Act of Parliament by entertaining them, and also that the deserters might be secured. In the same year, the Marquis of Lothian had to complain of three boys who ran away from his colliery at Newbattle, and took refuge amongst the people of another estate. The restraints upon the personal freedom of salters and colliers— remains of the villainage of the Middle Ages—were not put an end to till 1775, when a Statute (15 Geo. III., c. 28) extinguished them. In the year 1820, an old man explained how he came into a particular part of the country, by saying that the father of his interrogator took a liking to him, and that his then master took a fancy to a very nice pony belonging to the father; so they agreed on the subject, and *he was niffered*† *away for the pony*. The

---

* *Coal-heugh*, from *heugh*, a crag, precipice. Icel. *haugr*, a mound. *Coal-heugh*, a coal-shaft.   † *Niffer*, to exchange.

man had in short been a slave, and was exchanged for a pony.*

In the year 1606, George, Earl of Dunbar, his Majesty's Commissioner for ordering the Borders, took such a course with the broken men and sorners (there), that, in two justiciary courts halden by him, he condemned and caused hang above a hundred and forty of the nimblest and most powerful thieves in all the Borders, and fully reduced the other inhabitants there to the obedience of his Majesty's laws.†

This happy state of things did not, however, last long. In the year 1609 a representation went up to the King from the well-disposed inhabitants of the Borders, which says, "The thieves are like the beasts of the field. Lord Dunbar being now gone with his justice-courts, they are returned to their old evil courses, and there is nothing which they will not attempt. Wild incests, adulteries, convocations of lieges, shooting, and wearing of hagbuts, pistolets, and lances, daily bloodsheds, oppression and disobedience in civil matters, neither are nor has been punished . . . . there is no more account made of going to the horn than to the ale-house. If diligent search were made . . . . there would be found ane grit number of idle people, without any calling, industry, or lawful means to live by, except it be upon the blood of the poorest and most obedient sort."

In 1609, by the 20th Statute, vagabonds, sorners, and common thieves, commonly called Egyptians, are ordered to quit the kingdom by the 1st of August; those who return or who remain after that date are to be executed as common, notorious, and condemned thieves.

As to gypsies or Egyptians, so infallible was deemed the presumption that they must necessarily be by habit and repute thieves, that by this Act they are declared liable to be put to death, merely on its being proved that they are Egyptians, without any evidence of their having committed a specific crime.

In the year 1612 some of the principal Border gentlemen had a meeting at Jedburgh, with a view to make a final and decisive effort for stopping that system of blood and robbery by which the land had been so long harassed, even to the causing of several valuable lands to be left altogether desolate. They entered into a sort of bond, declaring their abhorrence of all the ordinary

* R. Chambers. † Sir James Balfour.

violences, and agreeing thenceforth to shew no countenance to any lawless persons, but to stand firm with the government in putting them down.*

An Act of Privy Council against beggars, March 5, 1616, describes Edinburgh as infested with them—"strang and idle vagabonds"—"having their resets in some parts of the Cowgate, the Canongate, Potterrow, West Port, Pleasance (and) Leith Wynd, where they ordinarily convene every night, and pass their time in all kind of riot and filthy lechery, to the offence and displeasure of God." By day, they are said to present themselves in great companies on the principal streets. Numbers of them "lie all day on the causey of the Canongate, and with shameful exclamations and crying, not only extort almous, but by their other misbehaviour fashes† and wearies as weel his majesty's nobility and councillors, as others his majesty's subjects repairing to this burgh; sae that hardly ony man of whatsomever quality can walk upon the streets, nor yet stand and confer upon the streets, nor under stairs, but they are impeshit ‡ by numbers of beggars." The Council therefore ordered the magistrates of Edinburgh and Canongate to get these wretched people expelled from their respective bounds, and suffer them no longer to seek alms on the streets. In like manner, they commanded that "the Laird of Innerleith and his bailies cause their streets and vennels § to be kept free of beggars;" as also, that "Mr. Patrick Bannatyne and Mr. Umphra Bleenseillis remove the haill beggars out of their houses at the foot of Leith Wynd, and suffer nane to have residence, beild, or reset there." All this under threat of pecunial fines.

Dec. In anticipation of the King's visit, it now became necessary to repeat the above orders, "because it is like enough that when his majesty comes to this country next summer, they will follow his court, to the great discredit and disgrace of the country."

In those days, the wretched and the insane went freely about the highways and thoroughfares, a constant source of annoyance, disgust, and even terror.‖

---

* R. Chambers.
† *Fash*, to trouble, to molest. Fr. *fâcher*.
‡ *Impesh*, to hinder, to prevent. Fr. *empêcher*.
§ *Vennel*, an alley, a lane. Fr. *venelle*.
‖ R. Chambers.

In the year 1617 an enactment was passed, c. 8, "anent the Justices for Keeping of the King's Majesty's peace and their constables." S. 7 orders justices of peace to put in execution the Acts against wilful beggars and vagabonds, solitary and idle men and women without calling or trade lurking in alehouses, tied to no certain services, and reputed and held as vagabonds, and against persons who are commonly called "Egyptians." S. 11 enjoins upon Hostlers* not to receive masterless men, rebels at the horn,† vagabonds or other persons guilty of known crimes, under a penalty of forty shillings for the first fault, four pounds for the second, and ten merks for the third together with the loss of liberty of brewing. Justices of the peace are to pursue and fine such delinquents. SS. 5 and 6 of the part "anent constables," order constables to arrest all vagabonds, sturdy beggars and Egyptians, and all idle persons whom they know to have no means to live upon and will not take themselves to any labour, trade, or occupation, and carry them before a Commissioner of Peace for judgment and punishment.

Notwithstanding the additional assistance of the justices of the peace, who by this Act are instructed to put the Acts of Parliament into due and full execution against vagabonds, and to punish and fine their receptors and setters of houses to them, the very next Statute, 1617, c. 10, sets out with narrating that "the number of the saidie beggaris hathe daylie incresced more and more," and that the evil arose from not educating the children of poor parents in habits of industry, with a view to effect which, it models into a more complete form the system of temporary slavery introduced by the preceding Acts.

At the commencement of the reign of Charles I., in 1625, a missive from the King is enrolled stating " that he understands that the laws against beggars are not properly enforced, and that as he is coming to Scotland shortly to be crowned he commands the former Acts to be put in execution."

---

* *Hostler,* an inn-keeper. Old Fr. *hostelier.*

† *To put to the horn,* to denounce as a rebel ; to outlaw a person for not appearing in the court to which he is summoned. The phrase originated from the manner in which a person was denounced an outlaw. A king's messenger, legally empowered for the purpose, after other formalities, gave three blasts with a horn, by which the person was understood to be proclaimed rebel to the king for contempt of his authority, and his movables escheated to the king's use. *At the horn,* put out of the protection of the law, proclaimed an outlaw.

In 1630 complaint is made that the Acts against beggars are not enforced, and it is ordered that penalties for non-execution of the Acts are to be enforced by the Secret Council. On the 7th September, 1639, a petition by the General Assembly anent idle beggars is presented and remitted to a committee. On the 13th September this committee are ordered to give in their overtures. On the 1st October it is noted that the Act, "that all vagabond knaves without passes be apprehended," is delayed.

In 1641, by Statute 100, the Commissioners for manufactories are to appoint correction houses for the restraint of idle and masterless beggars; masterless men are to be compelled to work at manufactories at such reasonable rates as the Commissioners shall appoint. In the same year the Commissioners of the Kirk petition that order may be taken with sturdy beggars, Egyptians, and vagabonds, and a solid course be laid down for removing the horrible villanies committed by such persons.

By c. 290 of the year 1646 the Acts and Articles for the erection and encouragement of manufactories are ratified as being the best ways and means of restraining idle and sturdy beggars and masterless vagabonds, who are a burden to the country.

In 1647, by c. 341, the procurators of state are directed to consider all the Acts of Parliament relating to idle and sturdy beggars and gypsies, and to report to the next session what is further necessary to be done to make these Acts effectual.

The next Act calling for notice is c. 161 of 1649, styled an Act of Charles II. It orders all able-bodied beggars to be compelled to work, and begging to be punished as directed in former Acts. Persons supplying or receiving beggars are to pay five pounds towards the maintenance of the poor. Sturdy beggars are to be sent home to their own parishes.

The succeeding Acts are stated to be "Acts and Ordinances of the Government." The 9th Statute of 1655 orders the commissioners of the peace to put in execution the laws against the classes described in 1617, c. 7, s. 7. By the 13th Statute of this year, innkeepers or "hoastlers" receiving masterless men or vagabonds or persons guilty of known crimes are to be fined forty shillings for the first offence, four pounds for the second, and ten merks for the third, together with the loss of their license. Constables are to arrest all vagabonds, sturdy beggars, and Egyptians. Each parish is ordered to maintain its own poor, so that none go begging to the scandal of the Christian religion. Masterless idle vagabonds and robbers are to be apprehended and transported to the West Indies and elsewhere. Such vagabonds are to be maintained by the parishes where they have been apprehended until they are transported. Lists of idle masterless vagabonds and robbers are to be given in from time to time to the Governors of Inverlochy and Inverness, and to the Commander-in-Chief on the south side of the Forth.

The next Act, passed in 1656, is a counterpart of the English Act of the same year. It enacts that "all idle loose and dissolute persons found wandering after the first of July are declared to be Rogues, Vagabonds, and Sturdy Beggars, and punishable as such under 39 Eliz., c. 4. Fidlers or Minstrels playing in any Inn, Alehouse or Tavern are to be punished as Rogues and Vagabonds."

The first Act after the accession of Charles II. (1661, c. 275) has for its object the employment of vagabonds. Persons are to be appointed in each parish to instruct poor children, vagabonds, and other idlers to fine and mix wool, spin worsted, and knit stockings. By c. 338 the commissioners of the peace are again ordered as in 1655 to put the laws in execution against the classes described in 1617, c. 7, s. 7. "Hostlers" are forbidden to receive masterless men, rebels " at the horn," vagabonds, or other persons guilty of known crimes under the penalties set forth in 1655, c. 13, and constables are again instructed to arrest all vagabonds, sturdy beggars, and Egyptians.

By the next Act, 1663, c. 52, which recites and ratifies c. 74 of the sixth Parliament, c. 268 of the fifteenth Parliament, and c. 10 of the twenty-second Parliament, all of the reign of James VI., power is given to persons or societies having manufactories to seize all vagabonds and idle persons, and employ them as they shall see fit, "the same being done with the advice of the respective Magistrats of the place wher they shall be seized upon." And to induce the societies and manufacturers to employ these persons, it is enacted that they shall have right to their service for seven years without paying them any wages, giving them meat and clothes only; and besides this, that they shall receive from the parish for the persons so employed by them two shillings Scots* per day for each person during the first year after his

* Equivalent to 2d. English.

apprehension, and one shilling per day for the next three years, when the allowance to be paid by the parish is to cease.

In the months of January and February, 1664, there were many robberies throughout the country, and even in the streets and closes of Edinburgh, occasioned by the poverty of the land and heavy burdens pressing on the people; "the haill money of the kingdom being spent by the frequent resort of our Scotsmen at the court of England." *

The next Act, 1672, c. 42, for establishing correction houses for idle beggars and vagabonds, like all which preceded it, complains of the inefficiency of former enactments, and ordains the magistrates of certain burghs to build sufficient correction houses within a certain period for receiving and entertaining of the beggars, vagabonds, and idle persons within the burghs, and such as shall be sent to them.

If the contributions of the parish kirk are not sufficient to maintain the poor, the ministers, elders, &c., are to provide them with a badge or ticket to beg in their own parish only. Coalmasters, salt-masters, and others who have manufactories are authorised to seize vagabonds and beggars and put them to work, and are to have the same power of correcting them as masters of correction houses.

In April, 1683, "at the funeral of the Duke of Lauderdale at Haddington, while the usual dole of money was distributing among the beggars, one, named Bell, stabbed another. He was apprehended, and several stolen things found on him; and, he being made to touch the corpse, the wound bled afresh. The town of Haddington, who it seems have a sheriff's power, judged him presently, and hanged him over the bridge next day."

In the reign of James VII., by c. 22 of the year 1686, the magistrates of Edinburgh are ordered to lay down effectual ways for freeing and purging the streets, wynds,† and closes of the numerous beggars which repair in and about them, under pain of 1,000 pounds Scots yearly.

Three Statutes relative to the poor, 1695, c. 74, 1696, c. 29, and 1698, c. 40, merely contain directions for carrying the former Acts (which are thereby ratified) into more rigorous execution, grant power for that purpose to the Privy Council, and ratify

* Nicoll.   † *Wynd*, a narrow lane.

their proclamations. By c. 64 of 1695, idle, loose, and vagabond persons are to be compelled to serve as soldiers.

These proclamations were issued in consequence of the distress occasioned by a succession of bad harvests for several years, thence called "the seven ill years." The first proclamation (Aug. 11, 1692) makes provision for the transmission of beggars to their own parishes, and imposes fines on persons giving alms to beggars beyond their parish. The second proclamation (Aug. 29, 1693) renews the directions as to beggars repairing to their own parishes under pain of being imprisoned as vagabonds, and fed on bread and water for a month. By the third proclamation (July 31, 1694) power is given to the sheriffs, justices of the peace, and magistrates of burghs, to impose fines on all persons not obeying and carrying into execution the several Acts and proclamations relative to the poor.

By c. 23 of 1696, sheriffs are again ordered to cause vagabonds to be seized for service in the army.

Mr. Robert Chambers remarks nothing, in the former state of the country, is more remarkable in contrast with the present, than the miserable poverty of the national exchequer. The most trivial furnishings for the troops and garrisons remained long unpaid, and became matter of consideration for the Lords of the Privy Council. A town where a regiment had lain, was usually left in a state of desolation from unpaid debt, and to make known its misery in the same quarter with but small chance of redress

In the year 1700 overtures for providing the poor and repressing beggars are remitted to the committee for security to bring in an Act. This is followed by a petition from Roxburgh that the laws already made be put in execution for maintaining the poor in ilk shire and restraining idle and vagrant persons. The last Act passed in 1701 ratifies the Acts for maintaining the poor and repressing beggars. It orders heretors* to provide and lay down rules for the maintenance of the poor, and to appoint such rules and methods as they shall find most effectual for keeping vagrant beggars out of the parish.

Andrew Fletcher of Saltoun, in his "Second Discourse concerning the Affairs of Scotland," thus speaks of the poor at this period.

"There are at this day (1698) in Scotland (besides a great

* *Heritour*, a proprietor or landholder in a parish.

number of families very meanly provided for by the Church-boxes, with others, who by living upon bad Food, fall into various diseases) 200000 People begging from door to door. These are not only no way advantageous, but a very grievous burden to so poor a Country. And, tho the number of them be perhaps double to what is formerly,* by reason of this present great distress, yet in all times there have bin about 100000 of those Vagabonds, who have lived without any regard or subjection either to the Laws of the Land, or even those of God and Nature; fathers incestuously accompanying with their own Daughters, the Son with the Mother, and the Brother with the Sister. No Magistrate could ever discover, or be informed which way one in a hundred of these wretches died, or that ever they were baptized.† Many murders have bin discovered among them; and they are not only a most unspeakable oppression to poor Tenants (who, if they give not Bread, or some kind of Provision, to perhaps forty such Villains in one day, are sure to be insulted by them), but they rob many poor People who live in Houses distant from any Neighbourhood. In years of Plenty, many thousands of them meet together in the Mountains, where they feast and riot for many days; and at country Weddings, Markets, Burials, and other the like public occasions, they are to be seen both Men and Women, perpetually drunk, cursing, blaspheming, and fighting together. . . . And for example and terror three or four hundred of the most notorious of those villains which we call Jockys,‡ might be presented by the Government to the State of Venice, to serve in their Gallies against the common enemy of Christendom. . . . And the Highlands are such a vast and unsearchable retreat for them, that if strict and severe order be not taken to prevent it, upon such an occasion these Vagabonds will only rob as much food as they can out of the Low-country, and retire to live upon it in those Mountains, or run into England till they think the storm of our resolutions is over. . . . This part of the Country being an inexhaustible source of Beggers, has always broke all our measures relating to them."

On the 20th of March, 1728, Alexander, ninth Earl of Eglin-

* As an opponent to the Union, Fletcher was bound to make the best of former times.
† This resembles the description of wandering persons in England in the Directions of Charles I. "who live like salvages." See p. 154.
‡ *Jockie,* a name formerly given in Scotland to a strolling minstrel.

toun, was buried in the family tomb in the west country, with the parade proper to his rank, according to the ideas of the age. One feature of the ceremonial was considered so peculiar that the *Caledonian Mercury* makes a paragraph of it alone. "There were between nine hundred and a thousand beggars assembled, many of whom came over from Ireland, who had £50 of that nobleman's charity distributed amongst them." *

Until the close of the eighteenth century, according to *Professor Eadie*, " the agriculture of Scotland was at a very low ebb. The feudal system of land tenure, which was introduced into Scotland about the eleventh or twelfth century and continued in existence five or six hundred years, was a formidable barrier to improvement in agriculture. The tenants held their lands on the condition that they should be ready to follow their landlord to the field whenever he required their services; and as peace was never of long duration in those days of foreign war and intestine feud, the tillers of the soil were liable at any moment to be summoned to the field. In these circumstances, even though they had possessed the desire to improve their small patches of ground, which few of them did, they had little or no encouragement or opportunity to do so. The crops too, were often destroyed by the English invaders, or rendered comparatively worthless by inclement weather.

"The agricultural classes in Scotland until the present century were always so closely on the brink of poverty, that any failure of crops at once reduced them to a state of starvation. Throughout the whole course of the history of Scotland periodical famines decimated the people."

Mr. Robert Chambers observes " there was a great amount of hospitality in those old times, the poverty had less effect on the entertainments of the higher classes than might have been expected. What helped the gentlefolks in this respect was the custom of receiving considerable payments from their tenants in *kind*."

In the year 1793 the *Gentleman's Magazine* gives the following account of poverty in Scotland:—

" Inverness, to a very distressing degree, abounds in common beggars. We had remarked the same circumstance in almost all the towns we had passed through in coming hither from the Tweed, and had imputed it, probably, to its true causes, the defi-

* Sir John Lauder.

ciency of agricultural employments and the want of manufacturers, to furnish subsistence to the lower ranks of people, joined with the total absence of all provisionary laws, compelling, as in England, every Parish to take care of and support its poor. To these causes might be added those impolitic severities, and that thriftless thirst of wealth, by which, whilst many a wretch has been driven to the uncertain miseries of emigration, others, clinging perhaps to an ungrateful soil, or despairing to better their condition by flying from it, have remained to certain misery, and a lingering death at home."

A little later we get a graphic picture of the condition of matters in the "History of Peeblesshire," by William Chambers.

"Acts of kindness to poor people are very frequent in the town-books. For example, June 28, 1803, the council having heard 'that Widow Henderson at Whinnyknowe has got two houses totally brunt, agree to give her spars for roofing the houses from the town's plantation.'

"There was need for these small benevolences. At this and a later time, the parochial succour to the poor was on that niggardly footing which at length provoked the establishment of the new poor-law system. Besides the native poverty, too modest to make itself known, mendicancy of every kind was still common—aggravated, indeed, by the mishaps of the war. Old soldiers with wooden legs, and blinded of an eye, from the campaign in Egypt; sailors with one arm, and long queues hanging down their backs, who were always singing ballads about Lord Nelson and his marvellous battles; houseless nondescripts carrying wallets for an 'awmous' of meal; blue gowns, who presented themselves with professional confidence; and real or affectedly lame aged women, who were carried about on hand-barrows from door to door, were all a pest to the community, and continued their perambulations in defiance of a functionary, designated the 'beggar-catcher,' who was specially appointed for their suppression. Fasten's E'en and Beltane Fairs, at which there was still a considerable concourse, usually attracted fresh groups of mendicants, who arrived from Edinburgh along with the shows, and the gingerbread and wheel-of-fortune men. . . . . Besides these mendicants and peripatetic minstrels, natural idiots, or 'daft folk,' as they were called, haunted the town and county, some harmless and amusing, and others vicious and troublesome."

Vagrancy in Scotland does not appear to have been affected to any material extent by the regulation of the rate of wages—probably owing to the fact that the labouring population was nearly always in excess of the requirements of the soil.

The first Statutes appear to be directed only against artificers and idlers.

Under *James I.* the aldermen and town councils are to fix the wages of craftsmen (1426, c. 3, 4). Under *James IV.* craftsmen, such as masons, wrights, and others, making rules for payment of wages on holidays are to be indicted as common oppressors (1493, c. 14). Idle able-bodied men are to be compelled to serve for wages as sailors in ships or boats (busses) suitable for the taking of great fish, or to be banished from the burgh (1493, c. 20). Craftsmen taking exorbitant prices are to be punished by taking one unlaw* for the first time, one unlaw and the forfeiture of the stuff that is exorbitantly sold for the second time, and the third time by depriving and suspending them from their craft (1496, c. 5). Under *Mary,* "My Lord Governor and three Estates of Parliament regarding the exorbitant prices that every craftsman within Burgh raises upon our Sovereign Lady's Lieges in all such things as pertains to their craft so that the prices are doubled and trebled by many of them to the great hurt of the said lieges," ordains that all Provosts and Bailies shall ordain reasonable prices (1551, c. 18). Under *James VI.* actions for servants' wages are to prescribe † in three years, after which the debt can only be proved by writ or oath of the debtor (1579, c. 21).

It is not until the year 1617 that any need seems to have been felt for fixing the rate of wages by authority. In that year it was enacted that "Justices of the Peace shall appoint at their quarter sessions, to be kept in August and February, the ordinary hire and wages of labourers, workmen, and servants; and those who shall refuse to serve upon the prices set down by them, shall be imprisoned and farther punished at their discretion, and the said Justices shall have power to decern and compel the masters to make payment of the fees appointed by their ordinance (1617, c. 8, s. 14). A price is to be set on craftsmen's work and upon the 'Ordinaris of Pennye brydellis,' together with the price of shearers' fees, and the contraveners are to be punished (s. 18)."

* A fine or amerciament.
† Applied to property when lost by the lapse of time.

The effect of this attempt to regulate wages was speedily made evident by a subsequent Statute (1621, c. 21) which recites that "Our Sovereign Lord and Estates of Parliament understanding the great straits and necessities whereunto the poor Labourers of the Ground are driven and constrained especially by the fraud and malice of Servants who either refuse to be hired without great and extraordinary wages promised them or otherwise hire themselves only from Martinmas to Whitsunday after the which term of Whitsunday they cast them loose of purpose and intention to make their gain and advantage by the extraordinary works which befall in that season betwixt Whitsunday and Martinmas such as casting and winning of petty turves faill dovettis* building of fold dykes † shearing in the harvest for doing whereof they know the said husbandmen who have necessarily ado therewith will be forced to hire them at daily and oulklie ‡ wages and such high rate as they please to the great harm of the laborers of the ground and all his majesty's subjects. For remedy it then ordains that it shall not be lawful for any hired servant to leave his master at the term of Whitsunday except he is able to verify to the Justice or Constable that he is hired to another Master from Whitsunday to Martinmas and if he is not then it shall be lawful for his present master to keep and detain him from Whitsunday to Martinmas on payment to him of such wages as he paid to him before and if the servant break loose from his master it shall be lawful for his master to take and apprehend him and present him to the Constable or Justice upon the ground where he shall be found who shall have power to compel the servant to return to his former master (if it be found that he be masterless and not otherwise) and it shall be lawful for all his Majestys lieges to take apprehend and employ in their works whatsoever loose and masterless men and women whom they shall find within their own bounds and the Justices and Constable shall have power to force and compel all loose men and women to serve for competent hire and wages."

Under Charles I., in 1630, an estimate is made of the wages of herring fishers. The wages of sixteen men in every ship is set down at £74 for four months. In 1639 the Commissioners of the Assembly are ordered to inquire into the instructions given to

* Thin flat turves and clods covered with grass.
† Walls built of sods or turves.   ‡ Weekly.

justices to deal with wages. In 1641 the Commissioners for Manufactories are ordered to set masterless beggars to work at such reasonable rates as they shall appoint, c. 100. In the same year the maximum wages of colliers are fixed at twenty merks a year. In 1655 the Commissioners for the Peace are ordered to appoint the ordinary hire and wages of labourers, workmen, and servants, in terms identical with the Act 1617, c. 8, s. 14.

Under Charles II., it is declared not to be lawful "for any Coalmasters to give any greater fee than the sum of twenty merks in fee or bounteth, under any colour or pretext, and because the said coalhewers, and salters and other Workmen in Coalheughs, do lie from their work at Pasch,* Yule,† Whitsunday, and certain other times in the year which times they employ in drinking and debauchery. It is therefore ordained that the said Coalhewers, salters, and other workmen in the Coalheughs, work all the six days in the week except the time of Christmas, under the pain of twenty shilling scots to be paid to their master, for every day failure and other punishment of their bodies" (1661, c. 333).

In 1663 beggars and vagabonds are ordered to work in manufactories for food and clothing only (c. 52).

Modern legislation on the subject of adult vagrancy in Scotland is contained within the brief compass of three Acts of Parliament. The first of these, the 8 & 9 Vic., c. 83, s. 70 (1845), provides that destitute persons are to be relieved, although having no settlement in the parish to which they apply.

This Act draws no distinction between the different classes of applications for relief, but lays down the same rule for dealing with all applicants, whether they are residents in the parish or of the vagrant class. A great source of annoyance to inspectors, is the class of beggars, tramps, and packmen, who, arriving at night in a town, try to get a bed and supper at the expense of the parish, and are off next morning. As to these, the Board of Supervision has observed that inspectors may do much to repress improper applications for relief by applying the statutory rules to families.

The too common practice of giving to every vagrant applicant a ticket to a private lodging-house is highly objectionable, even when the applicant is entitled to relief, and is nearly as objectionable as that of giving a sum of money to each.

* Easter. A.S. *pasche*, Heb. *pesach*, the passover.
† Christmas. A.S. *geól*, Icel. *jól*.

On the same subject the Board further observes :—" It is well known that imposition is frequently and in various ways practised by applicants. Sometimes illness is feigned ; at other times destitution is pretended, although the applicants are possessed of money which they conceal; women or children are frequently sent forward to make application, and represent themselves as single or deserted, as the case may be, while the husband or father is at hand and keeps out of sight merely for the purpose of strengthening the application. Every such or any other instance of detected imposition should be reported to the police, with a view to prosecution. If such arrangements as these are firmly and judiciously carried through, the Board have no doubt that the number of applications by vagrants will be very soon reduced to their proper limits, *i.e.* to those in which the applicants either have a legal right to relief or a *prima facie* case for inquiry. It is feared that many inspectors give relief to vagrants much too easily." *

The second, the Lindsay Act, 25 & 26 Vic., c. 101, s. 331 (1862), empowers "any Constable to apprehend and bring before the Magistrate all Persons found begging, or exposing Wounds or Deformities, or exposing Children of tender age to the inclemency of the weather, or placing themselves or otherwise acting so as to induce or for the purpose of inducing the giving of Alms, and all persons conducting themselves as vagrants, having no fixed place of residence and no lawful means of gaining their livelihood within the Burgh, and all persons who, after having been convicted of vagrancy, or of Housebreaking or Theft, are found in possession of any Picklock, Key, Crow, Jack, Bit, or other Implement usually employed in Housebreaking, or who, although not previously so convicted, are found in possession of any such Implement, or of any lethal weapon, or in any building or part of a building or other enclosed space for any unlawful purpose, or who, after having been convicted of Housebreaking or Theft, are found in any public or private street, or other place, with Intent to commit any Penal or Police Offence, or in possession of any article without being able to give a satisfactory account of their possession thereof; and such persons upon conviction, shall be liable to be imprisoned for any period not exceeding Thirty Days, and for a second or any subsequent offence to imprisonment for a period not

* Guthrie Smith.

exceeding sixty days : and any money or article found upon their persons may be forfeited."

The third, the 28 & 29 Vic., c. 56, deals with vagrants, and is styled an Act to provide for the better prevention of trespass in Scotland (1865).

"Persons who lodge in any premises or encamp or light a fire on or near any private road or enclosed land, without the consent of the owner or occupier, are for a first offence liable to a penalty not exceeding twenty shillings or fourteen days' imprisonment, and for a subsequent offence to a penalty not exceeding forty shillings or twenty-one days' imprisonment."

The punishment usually inflicted on vagabonds in Scotland is a short term of imprisonment, and sometimes laying them under surety for their good behaviour.

Sheriff Watson, of Aberdeen, gives the following description of Scottish mendicity between 1815 and 1878 :—

"Between 1815 and 1840 there had been several seasons of great agricultural, commercial, and manufacturing distress; and from want of employment and want of food, great numbers must have resorted to vagrancy for support. But in those days the vagrants had it all their own way, as there was no one to stop them; and it was useless on the part of the authorities to find fault with them. The preservation of the peace of the country was intrusted to a few sheriffs' officers, distributed here and there among the large villages. Such offences as simple assaults and breaches of the peace were then thought not worth the attention of a criminal officer; and unless the assaults were of a very serious nature they were altogether unheeded. And the men who, at fairs and feeing-markets, while contending for the goodwill of some country beauty, exchanged a few blows more in fun than with bad feeling, were left to settle their differences in their own way without the interference of the sheriff's officer.

"In 1839 the Commissioners of Supply of the County of Aberdeen took the great increase of vagrancy under their consideration, and resolved to establish a rural police force as the most effectual means for its prevention. To that end they appointed a police committee, which reported that not less than one thousand persons were continually wandering about the country preying upon the inhabitants: that in some districts gangs of five, ten, or fifteen masterful beggars established themselves for days and even weeks in a place, and levied contributions on all around; and who, if not supplied with what they wanted, helped themselves, and were withal so formidable that the tenants were afraid to meddle with them, and rather submitted to their exactions than incur their vengeance by complaining to the magistrate. And being thus forced to contribute to the sturdy vagrant, many of them were unable to assist their poor and deserving neighbours. To remedy this alarming state of things a rural police was accordingly established in April, 1840; but, unfortunately, the causes of vagrancy were not taken into consideration, and the effect of the police on the vagrancy of the county was most disappointing, as during the first four years after its establishment there was scarcely any diminution in the number of vagrants. The first report by the chief constable for the year ending April, 1841, stated that the number of vagrants was 2,459: 914 men, 1190 women, 328 children travelling with adults and 27 travelling alone. But about the end of 1841 a preventive check came into operation which had a sensible effect in diminishing the vagrancy of the county. The average yearly number of vagrants reported during the five years ending 1850 were 470 men, 479 women, 238 children with adults, and 6 travelling alone. Vagrancy continued to decrease from year to year, though with two or three interruptions, and it may now be said to have altogether disappeared; the average yearly number reported during the five years ending 1875 having been 141: 67 men, 47 women, 16 children travelling with adults, and 11 travelling alone. But though pure vagrants had disappeared, large numbers of tinkers, men, women, and children, continued to infest the county till about 1867, when they greatly diminished, and in 1870 they ceased to exist, having been converted into certificated pedlars, and so freed from the control of the police.

"We have no information about the vagrancy of the other counties prior to 1860. In 1858 an Inspector of Constabulary was appointed, and from his reports to the Secretary of State, which are published yearly by order of the House of Commons, we shall show the vagrancy of the country subsequent to 1859. During the year ending 15th March, 1861, the number of vagrants reported was 53,534; during the following year it was 57,350; and in his fifth report the Inspector says that vagrancy is still on the increase,—the number of vagrants reported during the year ending 15th March, 1863, having been 62,278, including men, women, and children of all ages. There was a slight decrease during the year ending March, 1864, the number of vagrants reported having been 59,254; of these there were 12,265 children, though some of the counties made no separate return of children. But as some cases are reported more than once in the same county, it is impossible to ascertain the exact number of persons set down as vagrants, but the actual number may be estimated at about one-third, or 20,000 persons. A serious feature in the system of vagrancy is the great proportion of children who are brought up from their very infancy as tramps and vagabonds, with little or no education. He adds that legislation is loudly called for to check the vagrancy in Scotland, and particularly the continuance of juvenile vagabondism.

"Vagrancy continued to decrease, and the number of vagrants reported during the year ending 15th March, 1867, was 49,374: but it made a great rise during the following year, 1868, when the number of vagrants reported was 62,076, of whom 13,762 were children, being 22 per cent. of the whole number, fast treading (the Inspector says) in the footsteps of their parents, without education of any kind except in begging and pilfering.

"He goes on to say that the Trespass Act* is found to be very easily evaded, as vagrants find so many people ready to allow them to lodge on their premises. The amount that is given to these people by farmers, cottagers, their wives and servants, in the country, in money, food, and other perquisites, and lodgings (from a mistaken feeling of charity), would keep more than double the number of the unfortunate paupers in their parish poorhouses. So long as this custom prevails the police are powerless, and vagrancy increases as a profitable occupation and trade.

"There was a considerable increase of vagrants during the following year ending March, 1869, the number reported having been 33,096 men, 20,756 women, and 13,584 children.

"The Inspector says: 'The evil of vagrancy is loudly complained of from one end of Scotland to the other.' The term vagrant has not been legally defined. There is no Vagrancy Act as in England, but the term vagrant is generally applied to tinkers, gypsies, muggers, unlicensed hawkers, and all persons who live by begging, or have no apparent profession, calling, or

* 28 and 29 Vict., c. 56.

means of supporting themselves. The fluctuations and changes in the annual number of vagrants reported cannot be satisfactorily accounted for. There was a slight decrease last year in the number of children reported under fourteen years of age; but the number, 13,584, is still very great, and taking them at one-third of the number of cases reported, which is as near the truth as can be estimated, there are 458 juvenile vagabonds, with little or no education, brought up as professional mendicants and tramps.

"The number of females is also very large—20,756, or 6,918, taking them at one-third of the number of cases. Vagrancy must be a profitable trade to those who pursue it, and its apparent vicissitudes and hardships are in reality made up; for it is well known that these people live far better than not only the paupers supported by the enforced charity of the poor laws, but also better than many of our honest and industrial classes.

"Vagrancy reached its maximum during the year ending 15th March, 1870, when the number reported was 74,755. There was a decrease of 3,416 the following year, the number reported having been 71,339: 40,286 men, 26,638 women, and 14,360 children. This decrease is accounted for partly by the unusually long and severe winter, which prevented vagrants from travelling about the country so much as they otherwise would have done, and partly from the fact that, during the period from 1st January to 15th March, 1871, many of these persons, who had hitherto been reported as vagrants, had become certificated pedlars under the Pedlars' Act, 1870, and were, with their wives and children, legally authorised to wander all over the country, many of them merely on the pretence of obtaining a livelihood, with a stock-in-trade of no intrinsic value.

"There was a great reduction in the number of vagrants reported during the year ending 15th March, 1872, the number having been 25,979 men, 18,275 women, and 8,002 children. This decrease was owing to the Pedlars' Acts of 1870 and 1871. By the former, a pedlar's certificate cost sixpence; by the latter, it was raised to five shillings, which, the inspector says, would diminish the number of licensed pedlars, and about as much increase the number of vagrants to be reported by the police. This turned out to be the case, though not for a year or two, as the number of vagrants reported during 1873 was 40,678, and the number reported during 1874 was 40,827; but during 1875 the number reported was 42,223. After this there was a great increase, the number reported during 1876 having been 43,893; and during 1877 the number was 47,520, of whom 12,197 were women and 6,063 children; and during 1878 the numbers were 54,236, of whom 12,380 were women and 6,543 children. This great increase was in men out of employment. It thus appears that the rural police are altogether incompetent to deal with the vagrancy of the country, and that, exclusive of English and Irish vagrants, and tinkers, muggers, and unlicensed hawkers, who are now converted into certificated pedlars, there are at least 10,000 bonâ fide Scotch vagrants, who are in a manner forced out of the large towns to prey, during a great part of the year, upon the country farmers, crofters, and cottagers, who have their own poor to maintain, and who are ill able to bear this grievous burden, to which they are unjustly exposed. As there has been an increase of vagrancy, so there has been an increase of crime. The average yearly number of commitments for definite periods to all the prisons in Scotland during the five years ending June, 1861, was 10,482; the yearly average during the four years ending June, 1876, was 13,910; and the number committed during 1877 was 14,999.

"The great increase has been of commitments for short periods. The number committed for terms not exceeding sixty days during the first periods was 9,301; during the second it was 12,003; and during the third it was 13,774; while the commitments for a year and upwards were 265 during the first period, 326 during the second, and 317 during the third. So that while there has been a great increase of petty offences, there has been a diminution of serious crime; and it is satisfactory to observe that there has been no increase of commitments of juvenile offenders under sixteen.

"There has been a very great increase of commitments for indefinite terms for non-payment of fine, the number committed during the first period having been 4,753, during the second 21,081, and during the third 28,512. These punishments, however, seem to have been of little avail, as recommitments are rapidly increasing, the number recommitted twenty times and upwards during the first period having been 634; during the second it was 1791; and during the third 2,332."

In the annual report of the Inspector of Constabulary for

Scotland, made up to March 15, 1885, the numbers of vagrants returned by the police are—

	59,214 males
	21,513 females
	10,840 children
Total	91,567

In March, 1875, the total was 40,817. It will therefore be observed that the numbers have more than doubled during the last ten years. The Inspector states in his report that "this estimate was not very reliable, as the same vagrant may be counted over and over again by constables in the same day, but the number of tramps and vagrants has undoubtedly increased to an alarming degree, and something will have to be done with regard to them."

The cause for this increase is doubtless (1) the bad state of trade; (2) the encouragement given to vagrants and beggars by the public giving them money, food, and old clothes. The Inspector classes them as follows:—

1st. The professional tramp, vagrant, or beggar.

2nd. The destitute and really needy.

3rd. Those going from one place to another seeking work, and destitute of means to supply their daily wants.

4th. The blind or maimed, who are fit subjects for the poorhouse, but prefer their liberty, and obtain a living by begging.

5th. A class who hawk small wares, and no doubt beg under the cloak of selling bootlaces and matches.

There are doubtless prostitutes amongst them. As a rule they are very filthy, and will do anything for money. There are also idle apprentices, worthless characters who find it difficult to obtain honest employment.

Old soldiers also tramp the country, and always know where retired officers live, and where they can generally be sure of getting money.

Tinkers in Scotland are a peculiar class, they are generally tinsmiths, and some deal in horses.

There used to be a regular colony of gypsies at Yetholm in Roxburghshire, where their Queen, Esther Faa Blyth, died in July, 1883. There are not many left now. Large camps of English gypsies have been seen in Midlothian, the men dealing in horses, and the women telling fortunes.

There are a few English vagrants in Scotland, and a great number of Irish, or of Irish extraction. When they can they steal, especially game, fish, or clothes from drying-greens, and doormats.

Cases are known where vagrants commit offences in order to get locked up and obtain a night's lodging, or when ill or diseased, in order to get into a prison hospital to be treated without cost.

Parochial relief no doubt encourages vagrancy to a certain extent, while at the same time this relief is very necessary for the really destitute and needy. . Short periods of imprisonment do not appear to act as deterrents, judging from the frequency with which these short terms are inflicted again and again on the same persons.

Many Scotch vagrants have their winter quarters in towns in the south of Scotland. They generally start off on their rounds in April, and return south again about the end of September or in October. They generally separate to beg, meeting again in the evening, or at some previously arranged place. They avoid towns that have the Lindsay Act of 1862 in force.

In 1854, by 17 and 18 Vict., c. 74, the Industrial School system was introduced into Scotland, and since this time various Acts have been passed for improving and developing the administration of the laws regarding them. Great success appears to have attended the working of the Acts.

CHAPTER XVI.

IRELAND.

438—1701.

The Brehon laws.—Regulations of the *Senchus Mor* and *Corus Bescna* in favour of almsgiving and against fugitives.—Regulations of the *Book of Aicill* relating to compulsory hospitality and proclaimed persons.—*Crith Gabhlach* respecting the rights of chiefs to compulsory hospitality.—Social condition of Ireland at the English Conquest.—Description of the class of persons with whom the "kings" surrounded themselves.—The " crumb-fox."—Laws of Edward II. against maintaining idle men and cearns.—Laws of Henry VI. against coigny and livery.—Act to compel the sons of labourers to work as their fathers did.—Laws of Henry VI. and Edward IV. allowing liege men to kill or take notorious thieves.—Extortionate practices of the soldiery.—Henry VII.—" Poynings' Law" and the law to render English Statutes operative in Ireland.—Henry VIII.—Acts to regulate servants' wages and to suppress vagabonds.—Law of Elizabeth against idlers.—Laws of Charles I. against rogues, vagabonds, and cosherers.—Condition of the country in the reign of William III.

IN Ireland, "the English law, introduced by King Henry II. in the twelfth century, for many years scarcely prevailed beyond the narrow limits of the English Pale, comprising the present counties of Louth, Meath, Westmeath, Kildare, Dublin, and Wicklow. Stat. 13 Hen. VIII., c. 3 (1522), recites that at that time the English laws were obeyed and executed in four shires only. But Meath then included Westmeath, and Dublin included Wicklow. Throughout the rest of Ireland the Brehons* still administered their ancient laws amongst the native Irish, who were practically excluded from the privileges of the English law. The Anglo-Irish, too, adopted the Irish laws to such an extent that efforts were made to prevent their doing so by enactments first passed at the Parliament of Kilkenny in the fortieth year of King Edward III. (1367), and subsequently renewed by Stat. Hen. VII., c. 8, in 1495. So late as the twenty-fourth and twenty-fifth years of the reign of King Henry VIII. (1534), George Cromer,

---

* *Breitheamh*, a judge.

Archbishop of Armagh and Primate of Ireland, obtained a formal pardon for having used the Brehon laws. In the reign of Queen Mary (1554) the Earl of Kildare obtained an eric of three hundred and forty cows for the death of his foster brother, Robert Nugent, under the Brehon law.

"The authority of the Brehon laws continued until the power of the Irish chieftains was finally broken in the reign of Queen Elizabeth, and all the Irish were received into the King's immediate protection by the proclamation of James I. This proclamation, followed as it was by the complete division of Ireland into counties, and the administration of the English laws throughout the entire country, terminated at once the necessity for and the authority of the ancient Irish laws.

"The wars of Cromwell, the policy pursued by King Charles II. at the Restoration, and the results of the Revolution of 1688, prevented any revival of the Irish laws; and before the end of the seventeenth century the whole race of judges (Brehons) and professors (ollamhs) of the Irish laws appears to have become extinct." *

The *Senchus Mor* or *Great Law*, supposed to have been compiled at the instigation of *St. Patrick* between the years 438 and 441, contains the following provisions bearing on almsgiving and vagrancy:—

"Alms. There are three things which are paid, *viz.*, tythes, and first-fruits, and alms, which prevent the period of a plague, and the suspension of amity between a king and the country, and which also prevent the occurrence of a general war. . . ."

The explanation of preventing the period of a plague is, " that they prevent that a plague or carrying off of the people such as follows famine should take its course."

This superstitious inculcation seems to furnish the keynote to the almost reverential treatment which the beggar even now experiences in Ireland, while at the same time it also appears to denote the underlying pagan origin of the Brehon laws.

This declaration is repeated in the *Corus Bescna* or *Customary Law* in very similar terms.

"There are three periods at which the world is worthless; the time of a plague; the time of a general war; the dissolution of express contracts.

"There are three things which remedy them: tithes, and first-

* "Ancient Laws of Ireland."

fruits, and alms; they prevent the occurrence of a plague; they confirm peace between the king and the people; they prevent the prevalence of a war; they confirm all in their good contracts and in their bad contracts; they prevent the worthlessness of the world."

The next law reminds one of the clause in *Magna Charta*, saving to the villein his wainage.

"No labourer, no fuidhir,* no imbecile vagrant, no shepherd, no cowherd, no cart-boy is destrained in a decision about debts due of himself or others, or for the regulations of a territory, but his foot is fettered or a chain put about his neck."

The imbecile vagrant is defined to be an honest person who is moving from place to place; the term imbecile being probably used in the primitive sense of weak, feeble.

The next law deals with the removal of the vagrant.

It is in it (*the rule of one day's stay*) were included *distresses for* .... the difficult removing of a vagrant.

"*Gloss.* For the difficult removing of a vagrant, *i.e.* for the difficult journey (tenn uide) which removes the person who has no habitation but the road. A notice of one day is to be served on him, or *he is* to be in his company for the space of one day, or to *accompany him to* the mearing of the territory holding him by the collar."

We now come to the regulations in the *Corus Bescna* relating to "banquets" or entertainments, which are divided into three classes: (1) godly banquets; (2) human banquets; and (3) demon feasts.

"The godly banquets are feasts or refections connected with the performance of religious sacraments or rites, or the works of charity enjoined by Christian doctrine. The former class includes—(1) the Sunday meal given by a married pair to their church, which might be given weekly 'without ale,' or monthly 'with ale;' (2) the celebration by a feast of the high Festivals, such as Easter or Christmas; (3) the feast given as the price of baptism; (4) the feast on the consecration of a church. The latter class comprises—(1) tithes and first-fruits, &c.; (2) feeding a pilgrim; (3) charity to the poor. For the payment of tithes, first-fruits, and alms by their people, the chiefs gave pledges to the church, which the parties primarily subject to the payment were required

* Hereditary bondsman.

to redeem, in case of their failure to perform the service. The usual confusion between what is morally right and legally exigible appears in this section, to understand which it is necessary to realise how very small must have been the territory and following of a large proportion of those who are designated as 'chiefs.'

"Under the term 'human feasts' are included the customary entertainments given by the tenant to the chief, the origin of all the abuses subsequently known under the general term of cess,* and the duty of providing provisions for the assembled body of the tribe on particular occasions, *e.g.* 'when the forces of a territory were assembled for the purpose of demanding law and proof, and answering to illegality.'

"The third species of banquets are not a subject of law in any sense; they are defined as demon feasts, *i.e.* banquets given to the sons of death and bad men, *i.e.* to lewd persons and satirists, and jesters, buffoons, and mountebanks, and outlaws and heathens and harlots, and bad people in general. 'Such a feast,' it is added, 'is forfeited to the demon.' There is not in the text any enactment or rule prohibiting these entertainments, which are merely placed under a moral censure. Here possibly may be recognised some early prohibition against the celebration of heathen usages. The portion of the text commencing with '*i.e.* to lewd persons,' &c., is probably a late interpolation after Christianity was generally established, and the celebration of heathen rites had ceased to be usual. It may be remarked, that the introduction of the term 'heathen' into this portion of the text shows that at a date long subsequent to the introduction of Christianity there were existing in the island some who still adhered to the old worship, and as such were classed by the church among 'bad people in general.'"

The penalty on persons who entertain fugitives is the subject of the next regulation.

Five " seds " † is the fine upon a person who entertains a fugitive who is known. As to every crime which he (*the person entertained*) shall commit notwithstanding "bán-apadh," ‡ proclamation, while with the tribeman, the third of the fine shall be upon

---

* *Cios*, rent, tribute, revenue, tax.   † *Sed*, a cow.

‡ *Bán-apadh*, literally "white notice," is explained to be "feeding and sheltering the proclaimed person before he has committed the crime; feeding and sheltering him after he had committed the crime was called *derg-apadh*, literally "red notice."

him (*the tribeman*). If he is with him in violation *of law* his full crime shall be upon him (*the tribeman*). If he (*the proclaimed person*) be entertained by a man of another tribe while under "bán-apadh" proclamation, half of the fine for his crime shall be upon him *who entertains;* but full crime *is committed if he be entertained* in violation *of law.*

In the *Book of Aicill,* which may be considered as the Code of Ancient Irish Criminal Law, the following regulations relating to compulsory hospitality are ordained :

"Every person under obligation of hospitality (brewy) * must have roads to his house.

"That is, some of these following are exempt *from compulsory hospitality* for their nobility,. some for their nonage, some for the shame of it, some for their madness, *and* some for their old age.

"Kings and the septenary grades,† and the 'airchinnechs' ‡ of the 'cill'-churches, whether they have or have not taken protection,§ are exempt from the liability of *supplying* food, and from liability on account of kinsmen.

"The chieftain grades, if they have not taken upon themselves protection, are exempt from the liability of *supplying* food, and from liability on account of kinsmen. If they have taken upon themselves protection, they are not exempt from the liability of *supplying* food, but they are from liability on account of kinsmen. And that is a privilege of the septenary grades, because the other chieftain grades are not exempt.

"The inferior grades, if they have not taken protection upon them, are exempt from the liability of *supplying* food, but are not exempt from liability on account of kinsmen. If they have taken protection upon them, they are not exempt from liability on account of kinsmen, and they are entitled to nothing but a 'screpall' ‖ in right of their worthiness, if they be worthy, and if they be not worthy, they are not entitled to anything.

---

* *Bruighe,* an independent farmer keeping an open house.

† Any grade or degree entitling a person to seven "*cumhals*" (three cows) of "eric" fine and to seven "*cumhals*" of penance.

‡ *Airdcindeach,* a superior, prior of a convent, provincial of a religious order.

§ *Taken protection.* This in English would mean "to have become vassals or placed themselves *in manu* of some one." It indicates some act by which the status was lowered.

‖ A *screpall* was equal to three *pinghims,* and a *pinghim* of silver weighed 8 grains of wheat.

"The farmers, if they have undertaken to support obligatory hospitality, but have not taken protection upon them, are exempt from the liability of *supplying* food and liability on account of kinsmen. If they have taken protection upon them they are not exempt from the liability of *supplying* food, nor from liability on account of kinsmen; and they have no honor-price save only the honor-price of the middle 'bo-aire'* chief, or of the best 'bo-aire'-chief; *and this* when they make good use, in hospitality of their wealth beyond the protection; and if they do not, they are entitled only to a 'screpall' in right of their worthiness if they be worthy, but if they be not worthy they are not entitled to anything."

The following penalties are enacted in the *Book of Aicill* against those who feed proclaimed persons or their sons or daughters.

"Six cows with an ounce *of silver is the penalty* upon a person who shall diet a proclaimed man beyond the territory, *i.e.* this is a 'cumhal' † of white proclamation, for supporting and advising a fugitive who does not come under the oath of 'cain'-law, ‡ and his partner's share of the ounce; but it is without violating the 'cain'-law of Patrick it is given, *i.e.* there is a condition that this *fine* is imposed upon the feeder when nothing that is forbidden in this rule of Patrick is committed; and moreover, if he (*the fugitive*) committed trespass, 'eric'-fine § for the trespass is *due* from him in addition.

"A cow with an ounce *is the fine* upon the person who feeds a son or daughter of another after being proclaimed, *i.e.* this is the fourth of a 'cumhal' for supporting and advising the women and sons of the foreigners who do not come under the oath of 'cain'-law, until they themselves (*i.e. the parents*) visit them; but if they visit them, he (*the person who feeds them*) is exempt.

"A cow and fifteen 'screpalls' *is the fine* upon the person who feeds a houseless person. This is the same as the foregoing, except that the share of the pledge of a king of a province is brought forward here; two 'screpalls' for the cow, and one 'screpall' for the 'samhaisc' ‖ heifer."

The responsibility for sheltering a violator of the King's laws appears to have been of a very far-reaching character.

* The lowest rank of chief derived from the possession of cows—equivalent to the rank of "ceorl" amongst the Anglo-Saxons.
† Equal to three cows. ‡ A statute law, a rule.
§ Honour fine. ‖ A heifer in her third year.

"*As* to a man who violates the King's laws, his crimes are adjudged on the seven houses in which he gets beds."

The probable meaning of which is that the giving a bed to a culprit renders the parties giving it liable, until he has been entertained thus in seven houses.

A vagabond is defined to be one who does not observe "the corus-fine"* law, and a proclaimed person one who is proclaimed by his nearest kinsman.

The following were the rights of the chiefs as regards compulsory hospitality according to the *Crith Gabhlach*.

"The 'aire ard' chief had twenty tenants, ten 'giallna'† tenants and ten 'saer'‡ tenants. His full company in his territory was seven men, his half company five. Twenty couples were his right on a feasting (*coshering*) from Calends to Shrovetide. The 'aire tuisi'§ chief had twenty-seven tenants, fifteen 'giallna' tenants and twelve 'saer' tenants. His full company in his territory was eight, his half company ∥ six. Twenty-seven couples were his right on a feasting from the Calends to Shrovetide."

A careful study of these ancient regulations will enable us better to understand the complex causes of vagabondage in Ireland in later times.

The social condition of Ireland at the time of the English Conquest is thus set forth by *Giraldus Cambrensis* :—

"The Irish are a rude people, subsisting on the produce of their cattle only, and living themselves like beasts—a people that has not yet departed from the primitive habits of pastoral life. In the common course of things, mankind progresses from the forest to the field, from the field to the town, and to the social condition of citizens; but this nation, holding agricultural labour in contempt, and little coveting the wealth of towns, as well as being exceedingly averse to civil institutions—lead the same life their fathers did in the woods and open pastures, neither willing to abandon their old habits or learn anything new. They, therefore, only make patches of tillage; their pastures are short of herbage; cultivation is very rare, and there is scarcely any land

---

* Tribe law. † Service tenants. ‡ Free tenants. § Leader in battles.
∥ Half company. On this Professor O'Curry remarks, "Every gentleman according to his rank was entitled to entertainment for himself and his prescribed company for one night in any house in the territory. Were he to stay any longer he could keep but half his company, and one, two, &c., in addition according to rule."

sown. This want of tilled fields arises from the neglect of those who should cultivate them; for there are large tracts which are naturally fertile and productive. The whole habits of the people are contrary to agricultural pursuits, so that the rich glebe is barren for want of husbandmen, the fields demanding labour which is not forthcoming. Moreover, I have never seen in any other nation so many individuals who were born blind, so many lame, maimed, or having some natural defect. The persons of those who are well-formed are indeed remarkably fine, nowhere better; but as those who are favoured with the gifts of nature grow up exceedingly handsome, those from whom she withholds them are frightfully ugly. No wonder if among an adulterous and incestuous people, in which both births and marriages are illegitimate, a nation out of the pale of the laws, nature herself should be foully corrupted by perverse habits.

"The impression produced by the *Crith Gabhlach* * as to the condition of the Irish people at the date of its composition is very unfavourable. Their houses must have been small and ill-furnished; the length of the house of an "og-aire" † is set down as seventeen feet—about the size of the cottage of the poorer class of farmers of the present day—and the house of the head king is stated to measure only thirty-seven feet in length; from this we must conclude that the habits and mode of life of the upper and lower classes were very similar; the houses would seem to have consisted each of one room only; the description of a house, as having so many "beds," not rooms, in it, shows that they all slept in one chamber; the houses were wood, or wattle-work of a very unsubstantial character; the back house so often alluded to was probably a detached kitchen; the furniture described is of the simplest nature, and in insignificant quantity; although some golden and silver articles are mentioned, there is scarcely an allusion to rich dresses, jewels, personal ornaments, or works of art; the ordinary diet seems to have been of the coarsest description; and it is remarkable there is no allusion to wine throughout."

"At the south end of the King's house were posted the body guards of the King, four in number; these were not men of his

* The opinion of the editors of the *Crith Gabhlach* is, that its internal evidence leads to the conclusion that the date of the work must be brought down to some date after the English invasion, or at the earliest to the first quarter of the fourteenth century.

† A young "aire" who has lately acquired the rank of a "bo-aire."

house, or of his tribe, but broken, landless men, whom he had freed from dungeon or gallows, or from servitude of the lowest grade, men without tribe or home, who existed only as the hirelings of their masters; the man whose life the king had spared in battle, was not considered as sufficiently in his power, 'for he may lay hands upon him and kill him out of devotion *to his own chief or people*,' such a man could not be trusted, for he had a tribe and home to which he might return."

The description of the class of persons with whom the kings surrounded themselves, proves that they were selected precisely because they were not members of the tribe, and, therefore, bound to the lord by simply personal interests.

The freeman who had " lost his patrimony, his lands, and his stock, and did not possess anything throughout the territory visibly or invisibly. By the loss of all his property the freeman lost also his status.

A " cow grazier of a green," a term used metaphorically to express the case of the freeman who has lost his status, not from poverty, but by reason of disgraceful cowardice.

A " Baitse " tenant, a man who is not freed by profession or residence.

A man matched with a bad wife, by whom he is rendered deranged and unsteady; such a person is defined as an " oinmit." *

A " midhlach " person, an effeminate, unwarlike man, a coward or an imbecile.

A clown, mountebank, or buffoon, not a jester simply, but what we should call an itinerant tumbler, dishonoured because he "went out of his shape before hosts and crowds."†

A " rias-caire " man, " a robber whom his race and family shun, a violator of ' cain '-law, and of law, who goes from marsh to marsh, and from mountain to mountain," or as it is also explained,

---

* A fool, an idiot.

† The regulations of the *Ancient Customary of Brittany* throw some further light on the reasons which caused this vocation to be looked upon as discreditable.

" Art. 151. Amongst those who are regarded as infamous in the eye of the law, and incapable of acting as witnesses, are lewd women, hangmen of thieves, vagrants, horse-knackers, hawkers of pastry, and among others *retailers of wind*, that is to say performers on the violin and bagpipe, mountebanks and players, who lead a life full of infamy and scandal. *Because in point of fact there is no profession more infamous and more remote from the natural duty of all men than that of devoting one's life to the amusement of others.*"

expressive of the latter fate of such an one, "a rath-builder who is enslaved to a chief and a church."

And lastly, the person described as "'a crumb-fox,' who gets the crumbs of all food natural and unnatural, whatever he crunches or eats is his;" by which may be meant a starving roguish outcast ready to appropriate and consume the fragments of other's victuals.

"The old tribal organisation continued to be the supposed form of their social system. We read of the King calling his people together for various purposes, and of the people themselves declaring the "Fenechus" law, but the universal system of commendation extending from the low 'mbidboth' man to the king of companies (every one of whom received cows from a superior, and paid his food-rent), and the masses of non-free tenants who swelled the retainers of the '*flaith*,'* prove that the new system of personal relation was being rapidly substituted for the bond of tribal union; the tribe lands had been monopolised by the noble class; whether by grant or force, fairly or unfairly, is unimportant. As a natural consequence, landless men and 'fuidhirs' abounded; the general instability is proved by the custom of hostages, and the presence of the foreign retainers who surround the King; and the rules, as to the maintenance of the wife of the mercenary soldier, show that the hired gallowglass,† the curse of Ireland, was not unknown."‡

The earliest English legislation of which we have any record begins in the reign of Edward II. in the year 1310, when Sir John Wogan, who had been re-appointed Lord Justice for the third time, summoned a Parliament which met at Kilkenny.

The first Statute passed by this Parliament (3 Edw. II., c. 1) is entitled "An Act to restrain great Lords from taking of Prises§ lodging, or sojourning against the will of the owner." It recites, "That merchants and the common people of this land are much impoverished and oppressed by the prises of great lords of this land, which take what they will throughout the countrey without paying anything, or agreeing with the owner of the same; and that they will sojourn and lodge at their pleasure with the good people of

---

* Lord.
† A heavy armed foot soldier. Erse, *Gallo-glach*, a servant; a heavy armed soldier.
‡ Introduction to *Crith Gabhlach*.
§ Purvevances.

the countrey against their wills, to destroy and impoverish them." It then enacts, " That no such prises be henceforth made without ready payment and agreement, and that none shall harbour nor sojourn at the house of any other by such malice against the consent of him, which is owner of the house, to destroy his goods; and if any shall do the same, such prises and such manner of destructions shall be holden for open robbery, and the King shall have the suit thereof, if others will not nor dare sue."

The next (3 Edw. II., c. 2) is entitled "An Act against the keeping of idle Men and Kearns in time of Peace." It enacts, " That none shall keep idle people nor kearn* in time of peace to live upon the poor of the countrey, but that those, which will have them, shall keep them at their own charges, so that their free tenants, nor farmers, nor other tenants be not charged with them. And if any idle man or kearn take anything of any person against his will in the form aforesaid, the wardens of the peace, and the sheriff of the county, where such an act shall be done, shall do with him as an open robber, as often as they shall have notice thereof, by indictment, or by the suit of the King or the party."

Sir John Davis in his " Discoverie of the State of Ireland," tells us that it was *Maurice Fitz-Thomas of Desmond*, chief commander of the army against the Scots, who in this reign " began that wicked extortion of *Coigne*,† and *Livery*,‡ and pay, that is : He and his army tooke Horse-meate and Mans-Meate and money, at their pleasure, without any Ticket or other satisfaction." He further says—

" The English Lords to strengthen their parties, did ally themselves with the Irish, and drewe them in to dwell among them ; gave their Children to be fostered by them ; and having no other meanes to pay or reward them, suffred them to take Coigne and Livery uppon the English Freeholders ; which Oppression was so intollerable, as that the better sort were enforced to quit their freeholds and fly into England ; and never returned, though many Lawes were made in both Realmes, to remaunde them backe againe : and the rest which remained, became degenerat and meer Irish, as is before declared. And the English Lords finding the

---

* A foot soldier of the lowest rank. Erse, *cearn*, a man.
† *Coinnimh*, entertainment.
‡ An allowance to keep horses at livery.

Irish exactions to be more profitable than the English rents and services; and loving the Irish tyranny, which was tyed to no rules of *Law* or *Honor*, better than a just and lawfull Seigniory, did reject and cast off the English Law and Government, received the Irish Lawes and Customes, took Irish Surnames, as *Mac William, Mac Pheris, Mac Yoris*, refused to come to the Parliaments which were summoned by the King of England's Authority, and scorned to obey those English Knights which were sent to commaund and governe this Kingdome; Namely Sir *Richard Capel*, Sir *John Morris*, Sir *John Darcie*, and Sir *Raphe Ufford*."

In the year 1440 another Act (18 Hen. VI., c. 3) was passed by which those who brought or led hoblors,* kearns, or hooded men,† English rebels, or Irish enemies, or any other people, or horses, to ly on horseback or on foot upon the King's subjects, without their good wills and consents, but upon their own costs, and without hurt doing to the commons of the country, were to be adjudged as traitors.

The attractions of a vagabond and plundering life seem to have operated as an inducement to many labourers to give up honest labour, as the 25 Hen. VI., cap. 7 (1447), recites, "That the commons are much grieved with this, that the sons of husbandmen and labourers, which in old time were wont to be labourers and travaylers upon the ground as to hold ploughs, to ere‡ the ground, and travayl with all other instruments belonging to husbandry to manure the ground, and do all other works lawful and honest, according to their state: and now they will be kearnes, evil-doers, wasters, idle men, and destructioners of the King our sovereign lord's liege-people, to the great decay of the said commons, and impoverishment of their state." It then enacts that "the said persons from henceforward shall be labourers and travailers upon the ground, as they were in old time, and in all other works and labours lawful and honest, according to their state. If it fortune, that any such son of husbandman or of labourer in time to come do the contrary of this, and thereof be lawfully convicted, he shall have the imprisonment of one year, and over that he shall make a fine to the King, or to the lord of the franchise.

* Light horsemen mounted on hobbies or ponies.
† Outlaws with hooded mantles in the Irish fashion, which enabled them to elude recognition.
‡ To till, to plough. A.S. *erian*.

The evidence of the state of the country and the woeful condition of the common people afforded by the two following Acts remind one forcibly of the condition of England in the reign of King Stephen.

Richard, Duke of York, who was the lieutenant of the kingdom, was at the same time Earl of Ulster and Lord of Connaught and Meath. He is stated to have "kept the borders and marches of the Pale with much adoo, and to have held many Parliaments wherein sundry Lawes were made for erecting of Castles in Louth, Meth, and Kildare, to stop the incursions of the Irishrie."

"At a certain Great Council holden at *Dublin* before *Richard* Duke of *York*, the King's lieutenant of *Ireland, anno dom.* 1450.

"An Act that no Marchour,* nor other Man, shall keep more Horsemen or Footmen, than they shall answer for, and maintain upon their own Charges and their Tenants; and for presenting the names of their Men; and that none shall take Coynee, Cuddies,† or Night-suppers, nor shall take no Pledges of them; the offenders shall be Felons, &c.

"At the request of the commons, that where the marchours of the county of Dyvelyn,‡ and other marchours of sundry countries, and other men within the land of Ireland, do keep horsemen and footmen, as well Irish as English, more than they can maintain upon their own costs, or upon their own tenants, and from day to other do coynee them upon the poor husbands and tenants of the said land of Ireland, and oppress and destroy them; and namely in time of harvest upon their cornes and meadows with their horses both day and night, and do pay nothing therefore, but many times do rob, spoyl, and kill the said tenants and husbands as well by night as by day; and the captains of the same marchours, their wives and their pages, certain times of the year do gather and bring with them the King's Irish enemies, both men and women, and English rebels, with their horsemen and footmen, as well in time of war as of peace, to night suppers called cuddies, upon the said tenants and husbands; and they, that are the chief captains of the said marchours, do lead and lodge them upon one husband one hundred men, horsemen and footmen, some night, and upon one other tenant or husband so many one other

---

* President of the Marches.
† *Cuid*, a part, share, supper. *Cuideadh*, help, aid.
‡ Dublin (Erse, *Duibh-linn*, the black pool; *pr.* Div-lin or Duv-lin).

night, and so every captain and their wives, pages, and their sons, as well as themselves, and every of them, do lead and bring with them so many of the said Irish enemies and English rebels, with their horsemen and footmen, upon the said husbands and tenants, and so they espy the secrecie of the said land: and after that every of the said marchours and their wives, pages and sons, have overgone the said husbands and tenants of the said marches in the form aforesaid; then they go to the captains aforesaid, and there the thieves of the said marcheours do knit and confeder together. And that the said marcheours thieves do steal in the English countrey they do put out to them in the march, and in time of war the men of the said marcheours, as well horsemen as footmen, do guide the said Irish enemies and their thieves into the English countrey; and what tenant or husband will not be at their truce, they do burn, they do rob, spoil, and kill, and for the more part the said land is wasted and destroyed. And if such rule be holden not punished, it is like to be the utter destruction and undoing of the said land. Wherefore the premisses considered, it is ordained and agreed by the authority of the said council, that no marcheour nor other man of the said counties shall keep more men, horsemen or footmen, but that they shall answer for them, and shall maintain them upon their own costs, or their own tenants. And what men they do keep, horsemen or footmen, the marcheours of the county of Dyvelyn, and in like case, all marcheours and other men of every county within Ireland, to the sheriffs or justices of peace of the counties, and they to present them to the mayor and bailiffs of the said cities within the said counties, soveraigns or provosts of the best borough-towns within the said counties. And that the said marcheours, nor no other man, shall any more use such coynees, suppers, cuddies, nor shall take no pledges for them, nor none of their thieves or men shall guide none of the King's Irish enemies in the form aforesaid. And what marcheours or other men do contrary to the ordinances aforesaid, that they shall be judged as felons." (28 Hen. VI., c. 1.)

The 28 Hen. VI., c. 3, passed on the same occasion, recites, "The thieves and evil-doers increase in great store, and from day to other do increase in malice more than they have done heretofore, and do destroy the commons with their thefts, stealings, and manslaughters, and also do cause the land to fall into decay and poverty, and waste every day more and more." It then enacts that notorious thieves, or thieves found robbing by night or day may be killed by any liege man, who shall receive a reward to be levied on every plough or cottage."

A still more ferocious Act, commonly known as the "Head Act" (5 Edw. IV., c. 2), was passed in the year 1465. This Statute declared it lawful to take, kill, and decapitate thieves, robbing the liege people by day or night, or going or coming, having no faithful Englishman of good name or fame in their company, in English apparel. The head was to be carried to the portreve of the town of Trim, who was bound to set it on a stake or spear upon the castle, and to give his writing, under the common seal, attesting the delivery. By this document the bringer of the head was authorised to distrain and levy by his own hands, in the barony where the thief had been taken, twopence from every plough land, and from every man having a house or goods to the value of forty shillings one penny; and one halfpenny from every other cottier having house and smoke.

The Earl of Desmond, the deputy governor, through whose instrumentality this Act was passed, was attainted by the Parliament at Drogheda for alliance and fostering with the Irish and for taking coigne and livery, and beheaded 14th February, 1467-8.

In the reign of Henry VII. the independence of the Anglo-Irish Parliament was abolished by the 10 Hen. VII., c. 4 (1495), entitled, "An Act that no Parliament be holden in the land until the Acts be certified into England," and known as "Poynings' Law," owing to its being passed through the initiative of Sir Edward Poynings, who was then Lord Deputy. This was followed by the 10 Hen. VII., c 22 (1495), entitled, "An Act confirming all the Statutes made in England," the preamble to which runs thus:—

"Item, prayen the commons, that forasmuch as there been many and diverse good and profitable statutes late made within the realm of England by great labour, studie, and policie, as well in the time of our sovereign lord the King, as in the time of his full noble and royal progenitors, whereby the said realm is ordered and brought to great wealth and prosperity, and by all likelyhood so would this land, if the said estatutes were used and executed in the same." It then ordains "That all estatutes, late made within the said realm of England, concerning or belonging to the common and publique weal of the same, from henceforth be deemed good and effectuall in the law, and one that be acceptyd, used, and executed within this land of Ireland in all points at all times requisite." *

It does not appear that the laws thus rendered operative were ever put in force on a comprehensive scale; otherwise, within the English pale they could only have rendered confusion worse confounded, and to have attempted to bring the native Irish within their scope would have been as impracticable a proceeding as would have been the sudden introduction of English Statute Law into India in the last century.

In the year 1536 in his despatch announcing the destruction of O'Brien's bridge across the Shannon (which opened a highway from Thomond into the English territories), the Lord Deputy (Lord Gray) complains bitterly of the insubordination of his English soldiers, who frequently mutinied in the field to obtain money or plunder. "I am in more dread of my life amongst them that be soldiers," he wrote, "than I am of them that be the king's Irish enemies."

Sir John Davis thus speaks of the extortionate practices of the soldiery and their effects.

"But the most wicked and mischeevous Custome of all others, was that of *Coigne* and *Livery*, often before mentioned; which consisted in taking of *Mansmeat, Horsemeat,* and *Money* of all the inhabitants of the Country, at the will and pleasure of the soldier, who as the phrase of Scripture is, *Did eat up the people as it were Bread*: for that he had no other entertainment. This Extortion was originally Irish, for they used to lay *Bonaght* † upon their people, and never gave their Soldier any other pay. But when the English had Learned it they used it with more insolency, and made it more intolerable; for this oppression was not temporary, or limited either to place or time; but because there was every where a continuall warre, either Offensive, or Defensive, and every Lord of a Countrey, and every Marcher made warre and peace at his pleasure; it became Universal and Perpetuall; and was indeede the most heavy oppression, that ever was used in any

---

* In 1331, the 5 Edw. III., cc. 11—14, together with the statutes previously enacted in the same reign, was sent into Ireland in form of letters patent "to be publicly proclaimed, and so much as to the people of those parts belongeth to be firmly kept and observed."

† *Buanacht*, subsidy, quartering of soldiers; living on free quarters. *Buanadh* a soldier, an unwelcome guest.

Christian or Heathen Kingdom. And therefore *Vox Oppressorum*, this crying sinne, did drawe downe as great or greater plagues upon Ireland, then the oppression of the *Israelites* did draw upon the Land of *Egypt*. For the plagues of *Egypt*, though they were grievous, were but of a short continuance. But the plagues of *Ireland* lasted 400 yeares together. This Extortion of Coigne and Livery did produce two notorious effects. First, it made the Land wast; Next, it made the people idle. For when the Husbandman had laboured all the yeare, the soldier in one night did consume the fruits of all his labour, *Longique perit labor irritus anni.* Had he reason then to manure the Land for the next yeare? Or rather might he not complaine as the Shepherd in *Virgil*—

> 'Impius hæc tam culta novalia miles habebit?
> Barbarus has segetes? En quo discordia Cives
> Perduxit miseros? En queis consevimus agros?'

And hereupon of necessity came depopulation, banishment, and extirpation of the better sort of subjects; and such as remained became idle, and lookers on, expecting the event of those miseries and evill times: So as this extreme Extortion and Oppression, hath beene the true cause of the Idlenesse of this Irish Nation; and that rather the vulgar sort have chosen to be Beggers in forraign Countries, then to manure their own fruitful Land at home.

"Lastly, this oppression did of force and necessity make the Irish a craftie people: for such as are oppressed and live in slavery, are ever put to their shifts; *Ingenium mala sæpe movent;* and therefore, in the old Comedies of *Plautus* and *Terence,* the Bond slave doth always act the cunning and Craftie part. Besides, all the Common people have a whyning tune or Accent in their speech, as if they did still smart or suffer some oppression. And this Idlenesse, together with feare of imminent mischiefes, which did continually hang over their heads, have bin the cause, that the Irish were ever the most inquisitive people after newes, of any nation in the world. As *St. Paule* himselfe made observation upon the people of *Athens;* that they were an idle people, and did nothing but learne and tell Newes.* And because these

---

* This is a common idiosyncrasy with uneducated people. *Mayhew* says that "among English costers not one female in twenty can read, and not one in forty can write. But they are fond of listening to any one who reads the newspaper or any exciting story."

Newes-Carriers did by their false intelligence, many times raise troubles and rebellions in this Realme, the Statute of *Kilkenny*, doth punish newes-tellers (by the name of *Skelaghes*) * with Fine and ransome.

"This Extortion of *Coigne* and *Livery*, was taken for the maintenaunce of their men of warre; but their Irish exactions extorted by their Chieftaines and *Tanists*,† by colour of their barbarous Seigniory, were almost as grievous a burthen as the other; namely, *Cosherings*,‡ which were visitations and progresses made by the Lord and his followers, among his Tenants: wherein he did eate them (as the English Proverbe is) *Out of House and Home*. Sessings of the *Kerne*, of his family called *Kernety*, of his Horses and Hors-boyes; of his Dogges and Dog-boyes, and the like: And lastly, *Cuttings*, *Tallages*,§ or *Spendings*, high or low, at his pleasure; all which, made the Lorde an absolute Tyrant, and the Tennant a very slave and villain; and in one respect more miserable then Bond slaves. *For commonly the Bond slave is fed by his Lord, but heere the Lord was fedde by his Bond slave.*"

In the year 1542 we meet with the first Act for the regulation of servants' wages (33 Hen. VIII., c. 9). This Act recites, "That as prices of victualls, cloth, and other necessaries for labourers, servants at husbandry, and artificers yearely change, as well sometime by reason of dearth and scarcenesse of corne and victuall as otherwise, so that hard it is to limit in certain what wages servants at husbandry should take by the yeare, and other artificers and labourers by the day; by reason whereof they now aske and take unreasonable wages within the land of Ireland." It then enacts, "For reformation whereof, that the Justice of Peace in every County, yearly in their sessions to bee holden within one moneth next after the feast of Easter, and one moneth next after the feast of Saint Michael the Archangel, shall make proclamations by their discretion, haveing respect to such prices as victualls, cloth, and other necessaries then shall be at, how much every mason, carpenter, sclauter, and every other artificer and labourer, shall take by the day, as well in harvest season, as any other time of the yeare, with meate and drinke, and how much without meate and drinke, betwixt both the said sessions; and also at the sessions

---

* *Scealaidhe*, a story-teller, tale-bearer.
† *Tanaiste*, the second person in rank, the presumptive or apparent heir to a prince. ‡ *Coisir*, a feast, entertainment.
§ *Talladh*, a cutting or lopping off.

to be holden next after the feast of Easter, how much every servant at husbandry shall take by the yeare following, with meate and drinke; and that every of them shall obey such proclamations from time to time, as a thing made and established by Act of Parliament for a law in that behalfe, upon paine of forfeyture, every one of the said carpenters, sclauters, artificers, labourers, and servants, that shall take any thing contrarie to the said proclamation or proclamations, the thing so taken, and imprisonment of their bodies by the discretion of the said justice." This Statute was revived and made perpetual by 11 Eliz., c. 5, Sess. I. (1569).

In this year an Act against vagabonds was also passed by 33 Hen. VIII., c. 15, Sess. I. This Act is a reproduction of the English Statute, 22 Hen. VIII., c. 12, and it further provides that "Gaolers shall have a seal engraved with the name of the gaol, and give licence to beg for six weeks to persons delivered, not able to pay fees, nor get work, nor born in that hundred. Afterwards they shall be compelled to go within a limitted time to the hundred where born, or dwelt last three years."

At the commencement of the reign of Elizabeth, the practice of many English lords in encouraging the native Irish to harass their rivals in authority appears to have produced its inevitable results in an increase of vagabondage. This was attempted to be put down by 11 Eliz., c. 4, Sess. I. (A.D. 1569), styled, "An Act that five Persons of the best and eldest of every Nation amongst the Irisherie, shall bring in all the idle Persons of their Surname, to be justified by Law."

"Whereas we, your Majesties most humble and obedient subjects, have been these many years past grieved with a generation of vile and base conditioned people, bred and maintained by (coynie and liveries) the aunciont enemies to the prosperitie of this your Majesties realm, of which sort the lords and captains of this land hath to raise and stirre up some to be maintained as outlaws to annoy each others rules, and so serving the iniquitie of the time, hath not onely in attending those practices, imbased their owne particular estates, but also brought the whole publike wealth of their supposed rules to ruine and utter decay; for remedie whereof, your said subjects most lowly and humbly beseech it may bee enacted, ordeyned and established, that from henceforth, five persons of the best and eldest of everie stirpe* or nation of

* A race, a family.

the Irishrie, and in the countries that bee not as yet shire grounds, and till they bee shire ground, shall be bound to bring in to be justified by law, all idle persons of their surname, which shall bee hereafter charged with any offence, or else satisfie of their owne proper goods, the hurtes by them committed to the parties grieved, and also yield to the Queen's Majestie, her heires and successours; such fines as by the lord deputy, governour or governours, and the councell of this realm for the time being, shall be assessed for their offences."

In July, 1633, Viscount Wentworth, whose obnoxious memory is better preserved by his subsequent title of Earl of Strafford, commenced his duties as Lord Deputy of Ireland. He came to Ireland with feelings of thorough contempt for all classes in that country, and his supercilious bearing gave great offence to the Council and the nobility. In July, 1634, he assembled a Parliament, the subserviency of which he endeavoured to secure by having a number of persons in the pay of the Crown, chiefly military officers, returned as members.

One of the first measures of this Parliament was an Act against vagabondage (the 10 & 11 Car. I., c. 4) for the better suppressing of rogues, vagabonds, and other idle and disorderly persons, which directs houses of correction for setting idle people to work to be built in every county. The following are to be deemed rogues and vagabonds:—

"All persons calling themselves schollars, going about begging, all idle persons going about in any country, either begging or using any subtile craft, or unlawfull games or playes, or faigning themselves to have knowledge in phisiognomie, palmestry, or other like crafty science, or pretending that they can tell destinyes, fortunes, or such other like phantastical imaginations, all persons that be or utter themselves to be proctors, procurers, patent-gatherers or collectors for gaols, prisons, or hospitalls, all fencers, bear-wards, common players of enter-ludes, and minstrels, wandering abroad, all juglers, wandering persons, and common-labourers, being persons able in body, using loytering, and refusing to work for such reasonable wages as is taxed and commonly given in such parts, where such persons doe or shall happen to abide or dwell, not having living otherwise to maintaine themselves, all persons delivered out of gaols that beg for their fees, or otherwise travaile begging, all such as shall wander abroad, pretending losse by fire or otherwise, all such as wandering pretend themselves to be Egyptians, or wander in the habite, forme, or attire of counterfeit Egyptians. These are all to be punished under Stat. 33 Hen. VIII., c. 15, or by sending to the House of Correction." Persons able to labour running away and leaving their families upon the parish, or threatening so to do upon proof by two witnesses, are to be sent to the House of Correction unless they find surety.

The next Act we have to notice (the 10 & 11 Car. I., c. 6) reads like a grim piece of political satire.

It recites that "divers statutes of force within this kingdome are now by reason of the blessed change of times grown out of use, and many of them not fit to be continued, as not sorting with the condition of the present times, and the happy government under which the subjects of this kingdome doe live." It then repeals, among others, 28 Hen. VI., c. 1, and 5 Edw. IV., c. 2.

This Parliament also legislated against another form of the practice of coshering by the 10 & 11 Car. I., c. 16, entitled an Act for the suppressing of Cosherers and Idle Wanderers. This Statute recites that "there are many young gentlemen of this kingdome that have little or nothing to live on of their owne, and will not apply themselves to labour, or other honest industrious courses to support themselves, but doe live idely and inordinately, coshering upon the country, and sessing themselves, their followers, their horses and their gray-hounds upon the poore inhabitants, sometimes exacting money from them, to spare them and their tenants, and to goe elsewhere to their eaught* and edraugh,* *viz.* supper and breakfast, and sometimes craving helps from them; all which the poore people dare not deny them, sometimes for shame, but most commonly for fear of mischief to be done or procured them so refusing, and therefore doe bare it although unwillingly, and many times when they are scarce able so to doe, and yet dare not complaine for feare of the inconveniencies aforesaid, and to that end doe make cuts, levies, and plotments upon themselves to pay them, and give such entertainment and helps to the utter impoverishing and disablinge of the poore inhabitants to pay their duties to the

* *Eaught* is a corrupt form of the old Irish word *óigedacht*, hospitality or maintenance, also written *aoidheacht*, from *oegi*, a guest. The derivation of *edraugh* is probably the Gaelic *edrath* (a shortened form of *eadar-thrath*), mealtime in the morning, a word now obsolete in Ireland.

King's Majestie, and their rents unto their landlords; and by that lawlesse kind of life of these idle gentlemen and others, being commonly active young men, and such as seek to have many followers and dependants upon them, many other inconveniences are likely to arise, for they are apt upon the least occasion of disturbance or insurrection, to rifle and make bootie of his Majesties loyall subjects, and to be heads and leaders of outlawes and rebels, and in the meantime do and must sometimes support their excessive and expencefull drinking and gaming, by secret stealths, or growing into debts, oftentimes filch and stand upon their keeping, and are not amesnable to law." It then enacts that such persons may be apprehended and bound to good behaviour and committed to gaol till they find bonds with very good sureties returnable at the next sessions.

These cosherers bear a strong family likeness to the *Scotch sorners*, and are probably identical with the gentlemanly idlers who, in the year 1596, are thus described by Spenser in his "View of the State of Ireland":—

"All the Irish almost boast themselves to be gentlemen, no lesse then the Welsh; for if he can derive himselfe from the head of any sept, (as most of them can, they are so expert by their Bardes,) then he holdeth himselfe a gentleman, and thereupon scorneth to worke, or use any hard labour, which he saith, is the life of a peasant or churle; but thenceforth becommeth either an horse-boy or a stocah * to some kerne, inuring himselfe to his weapon, and to the gentlemanly trade of stealing, (as they count it). So that if a gentleman, or any wealthy man yeoman of them, have any children, the eldest of them perhaps shall be kept in some order, but all the rest shall shift for themselves, and fall to this occupation. And moreover it is a common use amongst some of their gentlemens sonnes, that so soon as they are able to use their weapons, they straight gather to themselves three or foure straglers, or kearne, with whom wandring a while up and downe idely the countrey, taking onely meate, he at last falleth unto some bad occasion that shall be offered, which being once made known, he is thenceforth counted a man of worth, in whome there is courage; whereupon there draw to him many other like loose young men, which, stirring him up with incouragement, provoke him shortly to flat rebellion; and this happens not onely some-

* *Stocach*, an idle fellow who lives on the industry of others.

times in the sonnes of their gentle men, but also of their noblemen, specially of them who have base sonnes. For they are not onely not ashamed to acknowledge them, but also boaste of them, and use them to such secret services, as they themselves will not be seene in, as to plague their enemyes, to spoyle their neighbours, to oppresse and crush some of their owne too stubburne freeholders, which are not tractable to their wills."

A little later Sir William Petty bears testimony to the unhappy condition of the country. " About 504,000 of the Irish perished, and were wasted by the sword, plague, famine, hardship, and banishment between the 23d of October 1641, and the same day 1652."

The temptations to intemperance, with all their pauperising consequences, seem to have been very great, as a " Declaration of the Lord Deputy and Council" in the year 1655 states, "That the Multitude of Ale-houses in this Nation (being the shops and nests of wickedness) are no whit restrained in number, nor reformed in their abuses, but (according to the old usual Irish manner) almost every house in every Village and Town is an Alehouse." It then orders the authorities to take special care to lessen the number.

The Vagrant Acts of 1542 and 1634 appear to have made instruments for oppression and extortion in many cases, as the Declaration further states, that under colour of warrants granted by Justices of the Peace " many poor innocent persons of the Irish nation that do follow their labour are taken away and sent to the English plantations; and many are forced to give money for their deliverance, contrary to law and the power and directions given for apprehending such persons." Persons so offending are then ordered to be proceeded against.

The wild state of the country is evidenced by two Proclamations of the Lord Deputy and Council in the years 1654 and 1656 " for the better destroying of wolves, which of late years have much increased in many parts of this Nation," and offering the following rewards to all persons who shall take, kill, or destroy any wolf. For every bitch wolf six pounds, for every dog wolf five pounds, for every cub which preyeth for himself forty shillings, and for every sucking cub ten shillings.

In the early years of the reign of William III., the country was again desolated during the struggle for supremacy with the adherents of James II.

The 7 Will. III., c. 21 (1695), recites that "by the late rebellion a great part of the kingdom hath been left waste and desolate, and the frequent robberies, murders, and other notorious felonies committed by robbers, rapparees* and tories † upon their keeping, hath greatly discouraged the replanting of this kingdom." It then enacts that the inhabitants of every barony or county are to make full satisfaction for such matters. Any person presented by the grand jury as a tory, rapparee, or robber out on his keeping, and not surrendering within a time limited by proclamation by the lord deputy is to be convicted of high treason, and any person concealing or aiding him is to be guilty of felony without clergy. The justices at assizes or sessions with the assent of the grand jury may tax the inhabitants for a reward to those who take, convict, or kill such offenders.

Defects in this Act are supplied by 9 Will. III., c. 9 (1697); by 9 Anne, c. 11 (1710); it is extended to cattle maimers, and the 6 Geo. I., c. 12 (1714), continues and amends the Acts for suppressing tories, robbers, and rapparees.

The prohibitions on Irish commerce were also another fruitful source of misery at this period. Sir William Petty, writing in 1691, pertinently asks, "Why should they (the Irish) breed more cattle, since 'tis penal to import them into England . . . and how should merchants have stock, since trade is prohibited and fettered by the statutes of England?"

* *Rapparee.* Erse, *rapaire*, a robber, a thief, a name formerly given to certain armed plunderers in Ireland.

† *Tory.* Erse, *tóruidhe*, a pursuer, hence a plunderer, a robber.

CHAPTER XVII.

IRELAND.

1701—1885.

Reign of Anne—Provision for erecting a workhouse in Dublin—Treatment of vagabonds—Act for suppressing tories, robbers, and rapparees—George I.—Act to punish idle and disorderly servants and to authorise vagrant children to be apprenticed to Protestant housekeepers, &c.—Evil results of the lax punishment of offenders—Acts against idle and disorderly persons in the city of Dublin—Condition of mendicity in 1729—George II.—Acts to regulate wages and to authorise the transportation of vagabonds or their compulsory service in the fleet—Act to restrain vagrants labouring under bodily disorders—George III.—Vagrants to be kept apart from children—Condition of vagrancy in 1752—Further Acts to regulate the rate of wages—The helpless poor receiving relief to wear badges—News cryers, shoe cleaners, basket carriers from market, &c., without licence deemed vagabonds—Estimate of the number of beggars in Dublin in 1784—Punishment of persons harbouring rogues—Act to authorise the detention of suspicious strangers as vagabonds—Act against unlawful oaths—Social condition of the poor in 1797—Reports of the Committees of 1803 and 1828 as to existing provision for the support of the aged and infirm poor and punishment of vagrants—The "Bang Beggar"—State of Dublin in 1818—Act of 1836 against persons deserting their wives or children—Meeting in 1842 on the increase of vagrancy—Act of 1847 for the repression of vagrancy—Report of the Poor Law Inspectors on the condition of vagrancy in 1856—Number of vagrants relieved in 1870 and 1885.

In the year 1703 we meet with a Statute which contains the first germs of a legal provision for the relief of the poor (2 Anne, c. 19); it is styled "An Act for erecting a workhouse in the City of Dublin for imploying and maintaining the Poor thereof," and recites that "the necessities, number and continuall increase of the poor within the city of Dublin, and liberties thereto adjoyning, are very great and exceeding burthensome for want of workhouses to sett them at worke, and a sufficient authority to compell thereto." It then establishes a corporation consisting of the principal Court and City and County officials, who are to elect out of themselves "a treasurer and seven assistants without any reward or sallary," who are to have power to make by-laws "for relieving, regulating and setting at worke all vagabonds and beggars which shall come within the city and liberties," and to provide necessaries and materials for the setting to work the poor of the city and liberties, or any that shall be found begging therein; and to apprehend all idle or poor people begging or seeking relief or who receive parish alms to dwell in such hospital or workhouses and to do such work and labour there as the court shall think them able and fit for, and also to detain and keep in the service of the corporation until the age of sixteen any poor children found or taken up above the age of five, who shall be left to be maintained by any parish, or who are unable to support themselves; and after they have attained the age of sixteen the court is to have power to bind or put out such children apprentices to any honest persons, being Protestants, within the realm: (that is to say) every male child, until he attains the age of twenty-four; and every female child until she attains the age of twenty-one, or for any lesser time.

"The court or assembly is to have power to inflict reasonable punishment or correction from time to time on any vagabond or poor person within the workhouse who shall not conform to the rules, orders, and ordinances, and is to have the care of the maintenance of the poor of the city, of what age or kind soever they be, infants under the age of five years only excepted: and is to have full power to examine, search and see what poor persons are come into, inhabiting, or residing within the city or liberties; and to apprehend any idle vagrants and beggars, and to cause them to be kept and set to work in the workhouses for any time not exceeding seven years."

A proviso in the Act, however, shows that private charity had already been attempting to cope with the evil, as it specially exempts from the provisions of the Act any almshouses, hospital, or any other charitable gift or use already settled or erected.

The treatment of the unfortunate wretches who were confined under this Act is graphically described by *Mr. W. D. Wodsworth* in his "History of the Ancient Foundling Hospital of Dublin":—

"*Vagabonds.*—Before quitting and here losing sight of the poor 'Vagabonds and Beggars,' who were at first consigned to the care of the Governors, it may be as well to recall what was thought fitting and meet for them in the early part of the last century, especially as their treatment forms part of this famous Statute of Anne.

"*Their Accommodation.*—The accommodation fitted up for their reception consisted of 'the vaults and other convenient places' under the hall of the workhouse.

"These vaults, or cellars, are specified as having been 240 feet long by 17 wide, with an 'airy' sunk at the outside of the building for the purpose of affording light and to carry off the rainwater, and they were to have a double row of beds 'two tire' high to admit of sleeping 100 men and 60 women, and also to be used for their working and day accommodation.

"Any one fond of calculation can form a good idea of what the sanitary aspect of these low-pitched, dark, damp, and dreary lodgings must have been.

"Any vagabond that thought fit to have the 'Fallen Sickness' was to be turned out, and 'disabled poor people' were not to be admitted under any pretext whatsoever.

"*Transportation.*—The law required Vagrants and sturdy Beggars 'to be employed and to work' voluntarily; but there was no work or employment to be had, and then, Poor Beggars, they were to be flogged, imprisoned, receive 'severe usage' and be treated with 'proportionate rigour,' and finally were to be transported beyond the seas 'without trial or traverse.'

"*Burial.*—Until the year 1731, their bodies, when they died, were buried without coffins; but after that time it was ordered that they should have coffins allowed them.

"*Dyet.*—Their diet was perhaps the most merciful thing in their treatment. It consisted of fair quantities of gruel, bread, milk, porridge, and 'Burgoo' with some milk, and one pound of meal a day extra to those who could do a hard day's work and earn 8d. This Burgoo consisted of some oatmeal stirred up in cold water, seasoned with salt, and enlivened with pepper. Poor vagrants! It was not a very pleasant thing to be 'on tramp' in those days."

The next Act we have to notice, the 6 Anne, c. 11 (1707), for the more effectual suppressing tories, robbers, and rapparees, and for preventing persons becoming tories or resorting to them, affords evidence that "the young gentlemen that have little or nothing to live on" were by no means suppressed by the 10 and 11 Car. I., c. 16.

It enacts that "all loose, idle vagrants, and such as pretend to be Irish gentlemen, and will not work nor betake themselves to any honest trade or livelihood, but wander about demanding victuals, and coshering from house to house amongst their fosterers, followers, and others, and also loose persons of infamous lives and characters, shall on presentment at assizes and sessions be sent to gaol till sent on board the fleet, or to the plantations in America, unless they give sufficient security to be of good behaviour." It also recites that "many persons have made a trade of obtaining robbery money from the country, pretending to have been robbed, whereas they never were robbed, or were not robbed of near the value and sum they alledge; and enacts that all persons pretending to be robbed shall not only give notice to a neighbouring justice, but also within five days to the high constable of the barony, who is to publish it in all market towns. The act is to continue for seven years."

We now come to the reign of George I., the opening of which was signalised by a formidable Jacobite uprising in Scotland. This rebellion did not, however, meet with any sympathy in Ireland; the country, in fact, remained so completely undisturbed that a considerable body of troops was withdrawn for service in Scotland, and the Irish Parliament, to testify its loyalty, set a price on the head of the Pretender. The first Act of this reign which calls for observation is the 2 Geo. I., c. 17 (1715), entitled "An Act to impower Justices of the Peace to determine Disputes about Servants, Artificers, Day-Labourers, Wages, and other small Demands, and to oblige Masters to pay the same, and to punish idle and disorderly Servants," recites that "several persons do refuse or neglect to pay the wages due to servants, artificers and day labourers; and there being no remedy, whereby they can in a summary way, without much charge or delay, recover what is due for their service." It then enacts that justices may summon the master, not being a peer, and determine and enforce the demand by warrant. It also recites that several servants are drunkards, idle, or otherwise disorderly in their services, or waste and purloin their masters' goods, or lend the same without their masters' or mistresses' consent or knowledge, or depart their masters' or mistresses' service within the time, for which they had obliged themselves to serve. It then enacts that on proof of the offence they may be put in the parish stocks for six hours, or be sent to the house of correction for ten days and then ordered to return to service if desired by the master; on refusal they may be again committed and corporally punished during the time they ought to serve. Masters are forced to give certificates of discharge from service, and no servant can be hired without one under a penalty. Servants counterfeiting discharges are to be imprisoned for three months and whipped.

The Act further recites that "there are in almost every part of this kingdom great numbers of helpless children, who are forced to beg their bread, and who will in all likelihood, if some proper care be not taken of their education, become not only unprofitable but dangerous to their country: and that it is hoped that many of them may be entertained in comfortable services, and others may be bound out to and bred up in useful callings, if well disposed persons could have any fair prospect of receiving hereafter by the labours of such poor children any return, suitable to the trouble and charges they must necessarily undergo in bringing them through that state of childhood." It then enacts that the minister and churchwardens of any parish may bind out any child begging, or any poor child in the parish with the consent of the parent, to a Protestant housekeeper or tradesman as a menial servant till the age of twenty-one or as an apprentice to a tradesman till twenty-four.

This proselytising measure must have been most unpalatable to the poor, who were mainly Roman Catholics.

The lax punishment of offenders and the evil consequences resulting from it forms the subject of two enactments at this period.

The 6 Geo. I., c. 12 (1719), recites that the punishments inflicted by the laws now in force against the offences of robbery and felony, have not proved effectual, and that many offenders to whom royal mercy has been extended on condition of transporting themselves to the West Indies have often neglected to perform the same, and by that means several gaols of the kingdom are at the time filled with such offenders. It then enacts stringent measures for the transportation of such offenders.

The 8 Geo. I., c. 9 (1721), recites that "some felons and vagabonds who have been ordered to be transported, have already, and others may hereafter, come on shoar, and return to the kingdom, or may break gaol or escape before transportation." It then enacts that any such person being convicted shall suffer death as in cases of felony without benefit of clergy.

The next four enactments treat of idle and disorderly persons frequenting the city of Dublin and the methods by which they are to be repressed.

The 10 Geo. I., c. 3, s. 17 (1721), recites that "great numbers of idle and vagrant persons daily resort from the country to the city of Dublin and suburbs, who, by reason of the correspondence they generally keep with the beadles of the several parishes, and the neglect of such beadles in the performance of their duty, are permitted to beg in and throughout the city." It then enacts that the Lord Mayor, two aldermen, and one of the sheriffs may make rules, orders, and regulations for clearing the city and suburbs of sturdy, idle, and vagrant beggars and inflict pecuniary penalties not exceeding ten shillings for the breach of any bye-law by any beadle.

Under the 1 Geo. II., c. 27, s. 30 (1727), the Court of Assistants of the workhouse or any five of them are empowered to depute "so many persons as they shall judge necessary to seize, and apprehend, and bring before them any sturdy beggar or other idle vagabond, begging, strowling, or frequenting any of the streets or houses in the city or suburbs of Dublin;" and any five or more of the Assistants may commit such person to hard labour in the workhouse until the next general court of assembly, when any fifteen of them may confine him for any term not longer than four years with hard labour or other employment.

The 3 Geo. II., c. 17, s. 4 (1729), recites that several sturdy beggars and vagabonds have escaped punishment before a warrant could be obtained from five members of the Court of Assistants for their commitment to the workhouse. It then enacts that one Assistant shall have the power to commit to the workhouse, and that any beadle, bell-hour,* or constable neglecting or refusing to seize any beggar or vagabond is to forfeit the full sum of 20s. The provisions of this Act are repeated by 19 Geo. II., c. 21, s. 11

* A public officer whose business it was to parade streets and ring a bell, and then to bellow or shout any public news, an auction, a sale, a take of perishable fish, reward for the apprehension of some offender, &c. Called in 11 and 12 Geo. III., c. 11, a "*bellower.*"

(1745). By 9 Geo. II., c. 25, s. 15, similar regulations are established for the City of Cork.

The 5 Geo. II., c. 14, s. 12 (1731), recites that from the great number of vagabonds and beggars from time to time committed to the workhouse it often happens that very great disorders are committed there. It then enacts that any five members of the Court of Assistants may commit persons guilty of such disorders to the gaol or house of correction commonly called Bride-well.

With a natural *penchant* for disorder in any guise, the vagabond classes appear at this period to have affected a devotion for Jacobitism, as on the 8th of June, 1728, the Lord Mayor of Dublin issued a proclamation, which states that "great numbers of idle, vagabond Persons have of late years assembled themselves on the 10th Day of June,* in a riotous manner in the streets and other places of this city, particularly in St. Stephen's Green, wearing white roses and other marks of distinction, which has occasioned great disorders and disturbances in the same." The constables are then ordered to apprehend all such persons.

Inconsiderate charity then, as now, appears to have done its utmost to nullify the laws for the suppression of mendicancy. In January, 1729, a Mr. James Southwell left by will "3 pence a-piece to 60 common beggars the day after his funeral." The deceased evidently knew by experience that such a number could easily be collected.

As a species of counterblast the Grand Jury, in July, 1730, presented several persons then in Newgate as vagabonds in order to their being transported, and in the month of October following fifty-two men and twenty-nine women were duly transported to the plantations in America.

In September, 1729, the Rapparees gave proof of their audacity by attacking and robbing Major-General Naper and his retinue near Dungiven. Rewards of £20 each were offered for the capture and conviction of the robbers, with the result that Owen O'Donnelly, a proclaimed tory and the commander of the gang, was shot by one O'Cahan on the 4th of October, 1729, and his head was cut off and fixed on the gaol of Derry.

The following graphic picture of the condition of mendicity in Ireland at this period occurs in an "Essay on the Trade and Improvement of Ireland," by Arthur Dobbs, published in 1729.

* This was the birthday of the Pretender.

"Another evil very necessary to be remedied is the idleness of our poor. The hurt this kingdom suffers from the number of idle and sturdy vagrants is greater than is commonly imagined. It is not easy to give a detail of the several arts and stratagems they use to induce the opulent and industrious to be charitable to them. They are an oppression to the truly industrious poor, who endeavour to maintain their families and support the public; from whom they extort something out of compassion, and frequently, where they find women alone, by force. They appear in various forms, mostly affected or brought upon them by particular management, as blind, lame, dumb, distorted, with running sores, pretended fits, and other disorders. They frequently pretend loss by fire, or to have numerous families lying sick. They exercise the greatest barbarities upon children, either their own or those they pick up, by blinding them or breaking and disjointing their limbs when they are young to make them objects of compassion and charity. Not to mention their debauching the girls when grown up, who go about big-bellied, pretending their husbands are dead or sick, and they have them to maintain. Nor the robberies and thefts they commit, and the lewdness, debauchery, and drunkenness that is to be found among them at their merry-meeting. And to sum up all, imagine the most complicated scene of wickedness in low life and it will be found among them. . . .

"To make this article somewhat clearer I will show how the above increase of beggars happens in the summer season. It is very well known that great numbers of the native *Irish* in the mountainous parts of the kingdom that have houses and small farms, by which they might very well maintain themselves when they have sown their corn, planted their potatoes, and cut their turf for firing, do either hire out their cows or send them to the mountains, then shut up their doors and go a begging the whole summer until harvest, with their wives and children, in the most tattered and moving condition they can appear in, and disperse themselves over all the richest parts of the kingdom. This practice has been so much encouraged of late by the success these strollers have met with, that in several places many who pay at least 4*l*. *per ann*. rent, hire three or four servants, and give to each of them 3*l*. for their chance of the summer's begging. These have their fixed stations, from time to time, where to beg and where to rendezvous to divide their booty. . . .

"Since this trade of begging has become so general, and proves so easy and beneficial to them, it has been known that servants have quit their service and have gone a strolling with them, and day-labourers have quit their labour and refused to be employed, giving it for a reason that they get more by begging than they get by working. And the children of many small farmers, though they are settled in farms where they may live comfortably, have frequently so little conscience as to allow their parents, when grown old, to go about as vagrants."

The horrid devices of maiming the children appear to be the same as those described in the "Vision of Peers Ploughman."

In 1729 we meet with another Act for regulating the rates of wages (3 Geo. II., c. 14) entitled, "An Act to prevent unlawful Combinations of Workmen, Artificers, and Labourers employed in the several Trades and Manufactures of this Kingdom, and for the better Payment of their wages, &c." It recites that "great numbers of workmen, artificers, and others concerned in the several trades and manufactures of this kingdom have without any charter or other licence or authority lately formed themselves into unlawful clubs and societies, and have presumed contrary to the law to enter into combinations, and to make by-laws and orders, by which they pretend to regulate the trade and the prices of goods, and to advance their wages unreasonably, and many other things to the like purpose: and that it is necessary that more effectual provision should be made against such unlawful combinations." It then enacts that contracts and by-laws by unlawful clubs of artificers, &c., regulating the trade, settling prices, advancing wages, or lessening the hours of work, shall be null and void; and that offenders prosecuted within three months after the offence before two justices shall be liable to be committed to the house of correction for any time not exceeding three months with hard labour, or to the common gaol for three months without bail or mainprize.

The next remedy tried for vagrancy seems to have been transportation, or service on board the Royal Navy.

The 9 Geo. II., c. 6, s. 2 (1735), recites that "the power given by 6 Anne, c. 11, to grand juries, to make presentments of loose and vagrant persons at general quarter sessions has been found to be inconvenient." It also recites that "there are great numbers of loose idle vagrants, and of loose persons of infamous lives and characters in the city and county of Dublin, to the disturbance of the peace and annoyance of the localities." It then enacts that on presentment by the grand jury, or on a warrant from a judge of the court or justice of the peace, such persons may be committed to the county gaol, there to remain without bail or mainprize until they shall be sent on board His Majesty's fleet, or to some of the plantations in America, for any term not exceeding seven years, unless they give sufficient security to be of good behaviour. Such persons breaking gaol or returning from transportation before the expiration of their term are to be liable to the same punishment as vagabonds ordered to be transported at the assizes. Grand juries are not to make such presentments at general quarter-sessions except for Dublin and the county.

The bodily disorders of vagrants legislated against in the following Act remind one forcibly of the description of the Irish people given by *Giraldus Cambrensis.*

The 23 Geo. II., c. 11, s. 10 (1749), recites that "several strolling beggars and vagrants labouring under various disorders, which render them not only offensive to the sight, but also dangerous to the health, daily resort from different parts of the kingdom to Dublin, and beg alms in the public streets to the great annoyance of the inhabitants, and especially women with child, by exposing their infirmities in order to move compassion ; that the workhouse is not capable of containing the great numbers of such persons who resort to the city; and that a hospital for incurables has been erected, where such miserable objects are attended by physicians." It then enacts that any member of the Court of Assistants may commit such persons to the workhouse for thirty-one days, and if any three physicians or surgeons shall within that space certify that such persons labour under any incurable or dangerous disorder or infirmity, such persons if curable may be confined in any house appointed for the purpose until they are cured, and such as are incurable for the space of five years.

Owing to the dearness of provisions at this period the poor suffered greatly, but professional beggars, trading on the compassionate sympathies of the public, naturally fared well. In September, 1756, a marriage is recorded between Judith Redmond, an old beggar-woman, aged sixty, and John Doran, a boy seventeen years of age. Before the ceremony was performed he ripped out of her under-petticoat thirty guineas, and they afterwards set out for the country to regale themselves.

The Bishop of Cloyne, writing in the year 1752, thus speaks of the able-bodied vagrants:—

"It is a shameful thing and peculiar to this nation, to see lusty vagabonds strolling about the country, and begging without any pretence to beg. Ask them why they do not labour to earn their own livelihood, they will tell you, they want employment; offer to employ them, and they shall refuse your offer; or, if you get them to work one day, you may be sure not to see them the next. I have known them decline even the lightest labour, that of haymaking, having at the same time neither clothes for their backs nor food for their bellies."

A humane provision for preserving children from contamination by associating with adult vagabonds forms the subject of the next Statute.

The 11 and 12 Geo. III., c. 11, s. 13 (1771-2), which recites that "the reception of vagabonds and strolling beggars into the same house, or the same walls with children, will be manifestly injurious by setting a bad example." It then enacts that no such offender is to be sent to the same house or kept within the same walls with children, but that every such offender shall be sent to Bridewell or such other place as the governors shall think fit to appoint. The governors or Court of Assistants are empowered to inflict reasonable punishment on any vagabond, beggar, or poor person who does not conform to the rules and regulations of the house. Any sturdy strolling beggar or other idle vagabond may be apprehended and committed to Bridewell by a governor or justice of the peace until the next general Court of Assembly, at which any eleven governors may confine him for any term not exceeding three years. Any beadle, bellower,* or constable neglecting or refusing to seize any such offender is to forfeit the full sum of 20s.

In the year 1763, by 3 Geo. III., c. 34, ss. 23, 24, a further attempt was made to regulate the price of labour in two of the principal Irish industries. This Act is entitled an Act for the better Regulation of the Linen and Hempen Manufactures, and prescribes that "if any person shall summon any manufacturer, artificer, journeyman, apprentice or labourer to appear at any

* Called in 3 George II., c. 17, a "*bell hour*" which see.

meeting in order to consult upon, or to enter into any rule, agreement, or combination to ascertain or fix the price of labour or workmanship, or shall administer any oath or declaration tending to fix the price of wages of labour or workmanship or shall deliver any ticket, certificate, or token (except such certificate or token delivered by order of the corporation of which such manufacturer artificer or labourer is a member) to any manufacturer, artificer, or labourer of his being licensed to work at his trade or who menaces or hinders such manufacturer artificer or labourer to work at his trade at such prices as he shall agree for with his employer shall be liable to be committed to gaol for six months and to be three times publickly whipped at some publick place."

By the 11 and 12 Geo. III., c. 18, s. 40 (1771-2), the same provisions are extended to the city of Cork.

The six following Acts constitute the remaining legislation of the Irish Parliament with regard to wages.

By the 11 and 12 Geo. III., c. 33 (1771-2), "Journeyman tailors and shipwrights in and about Dublin leaving service without cause, or combining as to wages or work are to pay a fine of £10 or may be imprisoned for three months. The hours of work appointed for tailors are from 6 A.M. to 8 P.M. with 1 hour for dinner and ½ an hour for breakfast at wages not under 1s. 4d. nor above 1s. 8d. per day except at a season of scarcity when the wages shall be appointed by the justices. The work hours of shipwrights are to be from 6 to 6 save for dinner and breakfast and wages not under 2s. nor above 2s. 6d. a day."

The 19 and 20 Geo. III., c. 19 (1779-80), entitled "an Act to prevent combinations, and for the further encouragement of trade" declares that "in order to secure every man the full enjoyment of that property he has in his own labour, to find employment for the industrious, and bread for the poor, and to extend throughout this ancient kingdom all the benefits of free trade, all and every sort of combinations in trade as well among master manufacturers as among journeymen are publick nuisances, and ought to be suppressed, and that it is the duty of all civil officers to prosecute to conviction all such persons."

By 19 and 20 Geo. III., c. 27 (1779-80), journeymen ordered to be whipped in the city of Cork are only to be whipped after conviction by a jury.

By the 19 and 20 Geo. III., c 36, combinations to fix the price

of labour, &c., among butchers, coopers, salters, journeymen,
apprentices, labourers, or others concerned in the *provision trade*
in the city, liberties, and county of Dublin are to be punished by
imprisonment for any time not exceeding two months. The wages
to be paid are to be ascertained yearly every Midsummer at
quarter sessions. No more than the amount thus allowed is to be
taken on pain of forfeiting any sum taken over and above. If
wages are withheld double the amount may be recovered from
the party withholding them. This Act was amended by the 21
and 22 Geo. III., c. 22 (1781-2), which was continued to 1786
by the 23 and 24 Geo. III., c. 54, but then expired.

The general effect of the attempts to regulate wages would naturally be to drive workmen and servants into vagrancy, either from
detestation of the conditions under which they were compelled to
work or from a desire to carry their labour to a better market.
This does not, however, appear to have been the case to any extent
in Ireland, as none of the Acts make any mention of a dearth of
labour, which probably arises from the fact that the population
has always been in excess of the needs of the native labour
market, partly no doubt owing to the unwise and unjust restrictions imposed upon trade.

The condition of Irish mendicity seems to have become inten-
sified by the year 1771. In order to meet it the authorities
appear to have deemed it best to conciliate the almsgiver by
legitimatising begging on the part of the impotent poor while
punishing able-bodied vagrancy.

The 11 and 12 Geo. III., c. 30 (1771-2), recites that "strolling
beggars are very numerous in the kingdom, and that it has become
equally necessary to give countenance and assistance to those poor
who shall be found disabled by old age or infirmities to earn their
living, as to restrain and punish those who may be able to support
themselves by labour or industry, and yet may choose to live in
idleness by begging; and it is just to call upon the humane and
affluent to contribute to the support of real objects of charity."
It then creates a corporation for the relief of the poor in every
county, and requires such corporations to grant to the helpless poor
who have resided for one year within their respective counties,
badges or marks of such materials and of such a stamp or impression
as they shall think fit, and also a licence to beg in such barony or
limits of the corporation for such time as they shall think fit, speci-

fying the names and characters of the persons so licensed, and the causes, as nearly as may be collected, of their poverty, and whether reduced to that state by sickness or misfortune. The corporations are required to build workhouses, to be divided into four parts, one for poor helpless men, another for poor helpless women, a third for vagabonds or sturdy beggars, and a fourth for idle, strolling, and disorderly women. Every male beggar above the age of fifteen found begging without a license, or who does not wear his badge exposed to public view, is to be committed to stocks for any time not exceeding three hours for a first offence, and not exceeding six hours for any subsequent offence, and every old persevering offender may be indicted and tried, and on conviction imprisoned for any time not exceeding two months, and for a new offence may be sentenced to be publickly whipped in any market town, and again imprisoned for any time not exceeding four months, and the same for every subsequent offence. Females found begging without licence and badge are to be confined in any place appointed for the purpose for any time not exceeding three hours for a first offence, six for a second, and for subsequent offences to be proceeded against as in the case of men. Fatherless or deserted poor children under the age of eight found strolling and begging may be sent to charter school.

Strolling vagrants capable of labour, who have no place of abode, and every person above the age of fifteen who begs publickly without a licence or badge, or after the term of the licence is out, are to be committed to the workhouse, where for ill-behaviour they may be corporally punished; they are also to be kept in restraint upon a first commitment for any time not exceeding two months; second, four months; third, one year; fourth, two years; and afterwards four years.*

The system of wearing badges prescribed by this Act appears to have already existed in many parts of Ireland. In England it was practised so far back as the reign of *Queen Mary*. The Byelaws of Galway in the year 1628 enact "that sturdie beggars and

* This Act and the 13 & 14 Geo. III., c. 46, have been amended as to details of administration by the 21 & 22 Geo. III., c. 45 (1781-2); 23 & 24 George III., c. 58 (1783-4); 27 Geo. III., c. 57 (1787); 37 Geo. III., c. 34 (1797); 38 Geo. III., c. 34 (1798); 38 Geo. III., c. 35; 39 Geo. III., c. 38 (1799); 40 Geo. III., c. 33 (1800); 40 Geo. III., c. 40; 41 Geo. III., c. 50 (1801); 46 Geo. III., c. 95 (1806); 50 Geo. III., c. 192 (1810); 1 Geo. IV., c. 49 (1820); and 1 & 2 Vict., c. 56, s. 3 (1838).

poor scholars be banished; and that such poor and needie men, borne in the towne, as shall be allowed to begge, shall have leden tokens fastened to their caps, to distinguish them from others."

"The paupers' badges of old brass or bronze are to be met with sometimes in collections. In the Museum of the Royal Irish Academy there is a circular badge three inches in diameter, inscribed, 'No. Parish of Tidnavet, 1742.' Tidnavet is in Co. Monaghan.

In 1750 the proper officers were ordered after February 23 to take up all beggars in the streets of Dublin that had no badges, and to take all children of beggars, and put them into the Protestant charter schools.

The 13 & 14 Geo. III., c. 46 (1772-3), commences by reciting the expediency of removing empediments to the execution of 11 & 12 Geo. III., c. 30, by different jurisdictions. It then enacts that beggars in Dublin may be sent to the House of Industry. It subsequently recites that a number of young and able-bodied persons follow the several occupations of news crying, cleaning shoes, and carrying baskets from the markets, and are in the intervals of such employment exposed to idleness and vice, and that such persons might be more usefully engaged in labour, and such employments might be executed by persons partly disabled, who must otherwise be taken into the House of Industry. It then enacts that any person following any of the said occupations without a license from the poor corporation, granted without fee, shall be deemed an idle person and liable to commitment as a vagabond. It further recites that a number of persons in order to evade the penalties against vagrant beggars, and at the same time to excite compassion and avoid betaking themselves to useful labour, have recourse to hawking about small wares, whereby they cannot earn a subsistence. It then enacts that such person who has not a license shall be deemed an idle person, and liable to commitment as a vagabond.

It also enacts that beggars apprehended and clothed at the expense of the poor corporation may be detained until by their labour they have reimbursed the expense of their clothes.

It also enacts that the 33 Hen. VIII., c. 15, 10 Car. I., c. 4, repealed by 11 & 12 Geo. III., c. 30, shall be in full force in Wexford, Armagh, Wicklow, and King's County, where that Act is not carried into execution.

The Foundling Hospital, established by the 2 Anne, c. 19, for the purpose of receiving the children of the poor, partly for the purpose of saving their lives, and partly for the purpose of bringing them up in the Protestant faith, had by this time begun to yield unmistakable evidence of failure in its intended objects; the mortality was appalling, and the proselytism in many cases problematical. Nevertheless the numbers of children admitted continued to augment annually.

The 15 & 16 Geo. III. (1775-6), c. 25, recites that the number of poor children of the age of six years and under received into the Foundling Hospital has increased so far that the expense of supporting them has exceeded every provision that could be made. It then amends 11 & 12 Geo. III., c. 11, by enacting that no child appearing above one year old shall be received there. This Act was further amended by the 54 Geo. III., c. 128 (1814), which empowered the governor to suspend the admission of infants for six months in the year. Between the years 1797—1818, 43,254 infants were admitted. Out of 25,352 children admitted between 1784 and 1796, 17,253 died; the rate of mortality being consequently at the rate of 68 per cent.

Popular sympathy in Ireland appears always to have been on the side of the beggar as against the constituted authorities. On the 26th April, 1774, the Dublin Corporation for relieving the poor—

"Resolve—That their thanks be returned to the Churchwardens and other gentlemen of the Parochial Committee of the parish of St. Werburgh's for their spirited conduct in publickly supporting their Beadle in apprehending and endeavouring to carry to the House of Industry, the noted beggar, commonly known by the name of Hackball. And whereas the said Hackball was rescued from the hands of the said Beadle by a riotous mob,

"Ordered—That the sum of five guineas be given to any Beadle, or any other legal officer, who shall apprehend the said Hackball in the act of begging, and lodge him in the House of Industry.

"Ordered—That the sum of five pounds be paid to any person who shall discover and prosecute to conviction any person concerned in the rescue of the said Hackball, or any other beggar who shall hereafter be taken by the officers of this Corporation."

In February, 1784, the following gloomy picture of the condition of poverty and mendicity in Dublin appears in *Saunders's News Letter*.

"It is estimated that no less than 50,000 souls are now in real want in this metropolis, 18,000 of which number are beggars. The relief they receive at the House of Industry, and at the different parish churches, can only serve to prolong a miserable existence, if some means of employment are not devised to keep them from recurring to the scanty pittance of charity. Had the able number of those mendicants been employed to clean the dirtiest streets in Europe, we would not be held up in the eyes of strangers as a filthy people wading through mire in the day, and groping by half glimmering lamps at night; but this city seems devoted to the perpetual curse of nastiness."

The 30 Geo. III., c. 32 (1790), is "an Act for rendering the Transportation of Felons and Vagabonds more easy," and enacts that the Lord Lieutenant or other chief governor may cause felons and vagabonds under sentence of transportation to be transported to any part beyond the seas in such manner as he shall think proper. The 31 Geo. III., c. 44 (1791), is an Act for reviving and continuing several Temporary Statutes, and revives the 6 Anne, c. 11.

The next Act, in spite of its professing to be merely a measure for the repression of vagabondage in various forms, appears to bear a political complexion, as the description of a person "not giving a satisfactory account of himself" would apply to any rebel sympathiser.

The 35 Geo. III., c. 36 (1795), is entitled "An Act for more effectually preserving the Peace within the City of Dublin, and the District of the Metropolis, and establishing a Parochial Watch in the said City."

It enacts that every person on whose premises a rogue or vagabond shall be found knowingly and wilfully harboured or concealed shall upon conviction for the first offence forfeit the sum of fifty pounds, and for every subsequent offence the sum of one hundred pounds, or in default be committed to prison for any time not exceeding six months; that any superintendent magistrate, or constable may enter ale-houses and apprehend journeymen, apprentices, servants, or labourers drinking or gaming at unseasonable hours, and take them before any justice to be dealt with as vagabonds; that all night-walkers, all suspicious persons in the day-time, loitering about, without any visible means of maintaining themselves, all persons not giving a satisfactory account of themselves, all persons notoriously suspected of being thieves, and all persons gambling or tippling in the public streets, by-places, or fields, if they shall not give sufficient surety for their good behaviour, shall be adjudged to be rogues and vagabonds; friendless and deserted boys under the age of fourteen may be sent to the Marine Hospital to be placed in the sea service or be put to some useful occupation, and common beggars are to be sent to the House of Industry.

In April, 1795, the recall of Earl Fitzwilliam, who had surrounded himself with liberal-minded men, and had promised the Catholics complete emancipation, caused widespread dissatisfaction, and brought about a new organisation of the revolutionary party who were now bent upon republicanism, of which France had recently set them an example. Baronial, county, and provincial committees were established with oaths of secrecy and mutual fidelity. The English Government was thoroughly informed of everything, and immediately enacted new laws to meet the emergency.

The three following enactments, though they class the offences at which they are aimed under the head of vagabondage, are entirely political both in their origin and application.

The 36 Geo. III., c. 20 (1796), is entitled, " An Act more effectually to suppress Insurrections, and prevent the Disturbance of Public Peace."

It enacts that magistrates may arrest any stranger and examine him on oath respecting his place of abode and manner of livelihood; if he does not account satisfactorily, he may be committed to prison until he find a surety for good behaviour; that magistrates or peace officers may arrest any person found out of his place of abode from one hour after sunset to sunrise, and bring him before two justices of the peace, and unless he can prove that he was out of his house upon his lawful occasions he is to be deemed an idle and disorderly person and transmitted to the appointed officer at some port as a recruit for his Majesty's navy; that justices may authorise the demand for admission and if refused the forcible entry into houses in proclaimed districts from one hour after sunset until sunrise if the inhabitants are suspected to be absent, and if any of them are absent they are to be deemed idle and disorderly persons unless they can prove that they were absent on their lawful or proper occasions; that persons who cannot upon examination prove themselves to exercise some lawful employment or to have some substance sufficient for their support are to be deemed idle and disorderly persons; that any persons tumultuously assembling in the day-time are to be deemed idle and disorderly persons; that all persons found assembled in any proclaimed district, in any house in which malt or spirituous liquors are sold, not being inmates or travellers, between nine at night and six in the morning, are to be deemed idle and disorderly persons; that men or boys hawking or dispersing any seditious hand-bill, paper, or pamphlet, or paper required by law to be stamped and not duly stamped, shall be deemed idle and disorderly persons, and that women guilty of like offences shall be committed to prison for three months unless they sooner discover the persons from whom they received the papers or who employed them.

The 37 Geo. III., c. 38, s. 5, is entitled, "An Act to explain the 36 Geo. III., c. 20," and enacts that any person who takes or administers an unlawful oath binding to any association or brotherhood, and who may have been ordered to serve on board his Majesty's fleet, may be ordered to serve in the land forces.

The 38 Geo. III., c. 21, 1798, recites the 36 Geo. III., c. 20, and 37 Geo. III., c. 38, and enacts that justices and persons authorised by them may search for pikes, pike-heads, daggers, or dirks in any suspected house or place, and persons found in possession of them may be sent to serve in the army, or navy, in the same manner as disorderly persons.

The social condition of the country at this period is thus depicted by Mr. Ruggles in his "History of the Poor" (1797).

"Ireland presents, in your accurate and particular account of its internal police, no very flattering prospect of the situation of the poor, either with respect to their modes of life, their moral habits, or their industry. In the first instance, they are, in general, what the English peasantry were five hundred years ago; the cottage, which affords neither window or chimney, where cows, calves, pigs, children, men, and women, all lie on straw together, on the same floor; their raggedness, which approaches to nakedness, and the general disuse of shoes and stockings, give one no refined ideas either of their cleanliness or their comforts: and a country where pilfering is carried to that excess, that turnips are stolen by the poor in cart-loads, and acres of wheat carried away in a night, is not a country of well-regulated police or good moral principles: neither will the dance in the evening, or the last polish which they receive from the dancing-master, who is essential to their system of education, compound for that excess of laziness, and that weakness in their exertions, when *encouraged* to work, which has occasioned you to doubt of the heartiness of their food,—potatoes, oatmeal, and milk; although the athletic forms of the men, and the swarms of children in their miserable cottages, bespeak vigour and health.

We have now arrived at the last enactment of the Irish Parliament relating to mendicity which calls for special notice.

The 38 Geo. III., c. 34, s. 3 (1798), which recites that "persons committed as common beggars to the House of Industry are immediately and frequently by undue means discharged therefrom and return to beg in the streets," it then enacts that no person so committed shall be discharged without the consent of three governors.

The next Act (48 Geo. III., c. 140), passed in 1808, emanates from the legislature of the United Kingdom. It orders (s. 53) that—

"All night-walkers, all persons notoriously suspected of being thieves, and all persons gaming or tippling in the publick streets, bye places, or fields in Dublin, are to be deemed rogues and vagabonds, and if any such person so apprehended shall be a friendless and deserted child under the age of fourteen, the justices may bind such child an apprentice for seven years, or if a boy tender him to the Governors of the Marine Hospital to be placed in the sea service, and if any of the persons so apprehended shall be a Common Beggar he or she shall be sent to the House of Industry."

Warburton, in his "History of Dublin," draws the following deplorable picture of the conditions of the city in the year 1818:—

"It is probable, then, that the great distress of the poor of the metropolis for the last two years, may be the principal cause that has crowded our courts and prisons with culprits. The prejudices of the common people of Dublin against the House of Industry, or, as they call it, 'Channel-row,' were some years ago insuperable, and it was necessary to use compulsion to fill its apartments. The well-known black cart was constantly seen in the streets, surrounded by the officers of the Institution, dragging the reluctant vagrant along, and compelling him to accept of shelter and protection. The pressure of calamity was so great for the last years that the cart was no longer seen. The poor people themselves came voluntarily to beg admission till 3,100 persons were crowded into the house, and its extensive accommodation could contain no more. Still they pressed for admission; and the governors were reduced to the afflicting, and to them extraordinary necessity of rejecting those who begged to be let in; and in this way 450 persons were in a few months thrown back into the streets, where many of them were known to have perished. Provisions were a common object of theft, and to protect them was the constant employment of the police."

Alluding to the natural position of Dublin he says—

"From all these circumstances then of free air, dry soil, mild climate, pure water, and wholesome and abundant provisions, Dublin should be a very healthy residence, and the usual distempers arising from the contrary causes be absent. But though nature has done much for its salubrity, art has done more to counteract it. Nineteen church-yards attached to as many parish churches, and nine slaughter-houses behind or within their respective shambles, in the heart of the city, expand the noxious effluvias of animal putrefaction in every direction, and so taint the air as to render it highly offensive to all the neighbourhood, and frequently to compel the inhabitants to seek another residence. Where these are wanting, offals of every kind are suffered to accumulate in the front and rear of every narrow lane till they become impassable and intolerable, and engender and perpetuate the germs of contagion among a population which is here more crowded than elsewhere, and sometimes averages at twenty-eight to a house. To this is to be added, the extreme distress of some of these poor people, arising from frequent suspension of industry and want of employment. The privations they suffer of every comfort, the bad quality and scanty quantity of the food they are able to procure, their exposure to wet and cold, with scanty and insufficient covering both night and day; habits of intoxication, which are promoted by 900 houses licensed to vend spirits, and 300 more, perhaps, unlicensed, together with those moral effects which arise from anxiety and depression of mind and irregular passions, all these latter circumstances predispose them to receive diseases which the preceding causes had engendered. Hence it is, that sickness is prevalent in Dublin, and twelve hospitals and five dispensaries cannot afford adequate accommodation and relief."

In 1803 a Select Committee of the House of Commons was appointed to consider the legislative provision already existing for the support of the aged and infirm poor in Ireland, and for the punishment of vagrants, and as part of the result of their labours they reported—

" That the several Acts passed in the Parliament of *Ireland*, and particularly that of the 11th and 12th of His present Majesty, directing the Establishment of a House of Industry in every County, County of a City, and County of a Town, have not been complied with, nor any Presentment made by the several Grand Juries to assist in the support of such Establishments for the Relief of aged and Infirm Poor, and the Punishment of Vagrants and Sturdy Beggars, except in the Counties of *Cork, Waterford, Limerick,* and *Clare,* and in the Cities of Cork, Waterford, and Limerick.

No further notice, however, appears to have been taken of the matter until the year 1828, when the House of Commons ordered a return to be made of the corporations in the counties, and in the counties of cities and towns in Ireland, instituted for the relief of the poor, and for punishing vagabonds and sturdy beggars in pursuance of the Act 11 & 12 Geo. III., c. 30, passed in 1771-2. The response made to this return is characteristically Irish.

Out of 35 counties and counties of cities, &c.—

Clare had established a hospital and a house of industry; *Cork County and City*, a house of industry; *Kilkenny County and City* and *Limerick County and City*, a county infirmary and fever hospital each; and *Waterford City* a hospital or house of industry.

Out of 47 cities and towns—

Clonmel had established a lunatic asylum and infirmary, and *Wexford* a lunatic asylum.

The rest had done nothing.

Corporations for the Relief of the Poor had been established in 3 counties, viz. *Cork County and City, Kilkenny County and City,* and *Waterford City,* and in 2 towns, *Clonmel* and *Wexford.*

It should be remembered that one of the main purposes of the Act was to require Corporations to make provision for helpless men, women, vagabonds, or sturdy beggars, and idle, strolling, and disorderly women.

This requirement appears to have been carried out in one place only, and in a characteristically humorous fashion of its own, as the return from *Dundalk* states that "all sturdy Beggars strolling are turned out upon their entering; and a constable is kept by the Corporation for that purpose, and is called a *Bang Beggar*."

In the year 1836 Sir George Nicholls thus describes the general condition of mendicancy in Ireland :—

"One of the circumstances that first arrests attention on visiting Ireland, is the prevalence of mendicancy. It is not perhaps the actual amount of misery existing amongst the mendicant class, great as that may be, which is most to be deprecated; but the falsehood and fraud which form a part of their profession, and spread by their example. To assume the semblance of misery is the business of the mendicant, and his success depends upon the skill with which he exercises deception. A mass of filth, nakedness, and squalor is thus kept moving about the country, entering every house, addressing itself to every eye, and soliciting from every hand.

"The suppression of mendicancy is necessary for the protection of the peasantry themselves. No Irish cottier, however poor, closes his door whilst partaking of his humble meal. The mendicant has free access, and is never refused a share. There is a superstitious dread of bringing down the beggar's curse, and thus mendicancy is sustained in the midst of poverty, perpetuating itself among its victims."

The next legislation on the subject is the 1 & 2 Vict., c. 56 (31 July, 1838), entitled "An Act for the more effectual Relief of the Destitute Poor in *Ireland*." S. 59 enacts that persons deserting their wives or children so that they become destitute and are relieved in the workhouse shall on conviction be committed to hard labour for any term not exceeding three months.

This Act, while providing effectively for the compulsory erection of workhouses in every union in the country and the reception of the poor in them, makes no other provisions regarding vagrancy, which in consequence became a rampant evil. There was therefore a general feeling throughout the country that means ought to be taken for its suppression. The citizens of Dublin held a meeting on the 12th of March, 1842, at which it was agreed that the following resolutions should be submitted to the Lord Lieutenant :—

" 1st. That mendicancy has long been recognised by the Irish Parliament as a great public evil which it was expedient to suppress, various Acts having from time to time been passed for the purpose, terminating in the great Act of 1772 (11 and 12 Geo. III., c. 30), which established corporations for the poor in every county and city of Ireland, and gave ample powers to its members and to magistrates for coercing sturdy mendicants, and accommodating the willing poor in houses of industry.

"2ndly. That under said Act the House of Industry in Dublin was for many years more or less efficiently conducted *with both views*, until a popular outbreak destroyed the "black cart" employed for conveyance of the sturdy mendicants, apprehended in the streets by the 'servants' of the Governor, whose actual presence being deemed necessary to legalize the acts of the officers, led to the cessation of the practice and to the conversion of the House of Industry (under the sanction of Government) to a receptacle for willing paupers only, and for incurable lunatics.

" 3rdly. That mendicancy having in consequence thereof greatly increased in Dublin, led to the establishment of the Mendicity Institution in 1818, which, besides giving relief to thousands annually of *voluntary* applicants, coerced likewise the sturdy mendicants by enforcing against them the existing laws, so far as '24' cells in the House of Industry (their legal prison), in place of 110 cells, to which, under the Act of 1772, they were entitled, could enable them to enforce those laws.

" 4thly. That under the 45th section of the Poor Law Act, all the laws regulating the House of Industry and Foundling Hospital in Dublin were, on the opening of its two workhouses, forthwith repealed, and with that repeal expired all the effective powers of the magistracy to coerce sturdy beggars, who have consequently taken advantage of the immunity thereby afforded them, and now crowd the streets of Dublin in unprecedented numbers, and will continue to do so until the old powers of the magistracy shall be restored with such modifications as existing circumstances may demand, and until a Vagrancy Act shall be passed for Ireland, where, for various reasons (religious as well as political), such an Act is more necessary than in England, and without which the Poor Law Act itself can never be popular, while our streets are exposed to the disgusting and demoralising exhibitions of mendicancy."

Forty Boards of Guardians also expressed opinions favourable to such a measure, and the Poor Law Commissioners reported that—

"In some of the Unions, after the stock of habitual mendicants had for the most part been taken into the Workhouses, the Ratepayers of particular Electoral Divisions finding that the removal of what may be called their own established poor did not protect them from mendicancy, but was followed by inroads of beggars from the surrounding districts, or even from those more distant, have deemed it better that their own poor should be permitted to levy contributions from house to house as heretofore, rather than that the Ratepayers should incur the charge of maintaining them in the Workhouses, and at the same time be compelled to make contributions to casual vagrants or mendicant strangers by whom their doors were beset.

"The prevalence of such a feeling has been exemplified in occurrences in the Kilmallock Union, where *the Ratepayers of a certain Electoral Division came in a body to the Workhouse, and demanded to have their poor delivered up to them, which was accordingly done, and they were carried back with great demonstrations of rejoicing, to be supported by almsgiving in the accustomed mode.* The Ratepayers in this case no doubt expected that, when they had their own beggars about them, they would be protected from the inroads of beggars from other districts, to which they were liable, so long as their own habitual stock were maintained in the Workhouse."

As a consequence of these representations the 10 and 11 Vict., c. 84 (22 July, 1847), was passed, which recites that it is expedient to make further provision for the punishment of Beggars and Vagrants and persons offending against the laws in force for the Relief of the destitute Poor in *Ireland*. It then repeals the provision in 1 & 2 Vict., c. 56, for the punishment of persons deserting their wives or children, and enacts that persons deserting or wilfully neglecting to maintain their wives or children so that they have to be relieved in any union, shall be liable on conviction to hard labour in the House of Correction for any time not exceeding three months; that Persons wandering abroad or begging in public places or causing children so to do, or going from one union to another for the purpose of obtaining relief, shall be sent to hard labour for any time not exceeding one month. Any person may apprehend offenders against this Act without a warrant."

In the autumn of 1845 the potato-rot again set in, and scientific investigation showed that the evil was beyond the reach of human skill. A dreadful famine was the result, and the workhouses were filled to overflowing. The English Government did its utmost to allay the evil by despatching cargoes of corn and Indian meal to the distressed districts, and English charity contributed large sums for the purpose of aiding the good work. Unfortunately, in 1846, the disease again made its appearance, much earlier than in the preceding year, and the misery and distress became so extreme that multitudes perished. To add to the horrors of the time, crime and outrage again broke forth, and steeped the unhappy country with augmented calamity. Several millions of money were expended by the Government in relief and in public works, organised for the purpose of providing employment for the poor, and private charity further endeavoured to mitigate the distress. Many thousands of the Irish emigrated to America, and many came over to England, where they became mendicants, or joined the ranks of the London street-sellers, taking up those callings requiring the least amount of speculative judgment.

The population was, in fact, largely in excess of the requirements of the country, and the least failure of any of its ordinary resources brought about misery and starvation to the lower orders. The only effective cure for such a state of things was necessarily a reduction of the population.

In 1856 the Ninth Annual Report of the Poor Law Commissioners in Ireland supplies the following evidence regarding the condition of vagrancy and mendicity at that time:—

Report for the Counties of Leitrim, Mayo, Roscommon, Sligo, and Donegal.

"During the last three years there has been a gradual, but steady, diminution of mendicancy in this district, and at the present time it is confined, almost entirely, to professional beggars and vagrants. In the year 1853, whilst the effects of the previous years of famine continued to be felt, the mendicants in this district may be considered as having belonged to four classes.

"1st. The professional beggars, comprising persons maimed in limb, or suffering from blindness or other bodily defect, who made a trade of exposing their deformities in the thoroughfares adjoining towns where fairs or markets were held, and mendicants who frequented towns, clamouring for alms at shop-doors or coach offices.

"2nd. Vagrants who rambled through rural districts, sometimes extorting charity from the timid by the importunity with which it was claimed.

"3rd. Persons rendered destitute by the famine, who had been ejected from their cabins and were wandering through the country with their families, preferring a life of mendicancy to the restraints of the workhouse.

"4th. Women and children abandoned by the head of the family whilst he sought employment in England or Scotland: this class being chiefly met with during spring and summer.

"Of these four classes the third was the first to disappear; and families of beggars, without homes, are now very rarely met with in this district.

"The fourth class continued longer; and, until within the last two years, women and children were to be met roaming through the country and maintaining themselves by begging, whilst the head of the family was employed at harvest-work in England or Scotland. These persons were usually possessed of a cottage, and a small quantity of land planted with potatoes before the head of the family went to England or Scotland, and to which they returned when he came back."

Report for the Counties of Clare, Limerick, and Tipperary.

"During the early part of the four preceding years the dole of the beggar (potatoes) was scarce, and the small holders of land had barely recovered from the effects of famine; they were, moreover, then compelled to pay high rates, which operated in checking alms-giving, and mendicants were necessitated to seek workhouse relief. Since that period the condition of the farmer and the peasant has favourably progressed, and mendicancy, with its attendant evils, again exists to a large extent.

"The great majority of mendicants are a helpless class—widow-women burthened with children of tender years, the cripple, blind, and impotent. On fair and market days, this class may be seen, on the outskirts of towns, exposing their wretchedness to commiseration, and extorting by their prayers and importunities pittances of potatoes, turf, and such other commodities as may be passing to the market; the exception is to give money, the rule is to give small quantities of the commodities described; and at night ready access to the cabin is afforded, where the beggar is permitted to cook his meals and shelter himself. This voluntary and pernicious system is generally preferred to the compulsory one of requiring the destitute to be supported by poor rates in workhouses.

"Irrespective of the system being a direct infraction of the Vagrant Act, the provisions of which are seldom enforced, it is fraught with many evils to the community at large. It perpetuates mendicancy, prostitution, and thieving; for it is notorious that the offspring of persons who subsist by begging, are incapable of exertion, become demoralised, and rarely, if ever, seek any other occupation."

Report for the Counties of Antrim, Armagh, Cavan, Down, Londonderry, Monaghan, and Tyrone.

"During the last few years mendicants have diminished in number in this part of Ireland, and are still decreasing.

"This change is, however, not to be altogether attributed to the improved condition of the labouring classes, or to the rise in the rate of wages, as the persons who resort to begging for their support are a class not much affected by the state of the labour market. They are either professional and habitual mendicants, who have no inclination for work, and whose previous habits of life unfit them for it, or they are poor persons unable to earn a maintenance in consequence of age, infirmity, or some mental or bodily defect; but labourers and mechanics, when in distress from want of employment, have generally sought relief from the Poor Law Guardians, and have, when destitute, obtained admission to the Union Workhouses.

Report for the Counties of Dublin, Kildare, King's, Longford, Louth, Meath, and Westmeath.

"Mendicancy has been progressively and *rapidly* declining in this district during the last three years, and at the present time it no longer can be considered to exist as a substantive or general evil.

"A few 'shoulers'* still clinging to the obsolete notion as expressed in the old song, that

> 'Of all the trades agoing,
> A-begging is the best;
> For when a man is weary,
> He can sit him down and rest,'

continue to ply about in some places; and who, for old acquaintance' sake, and from old habits, still pick up a few halfpence, especially in and about towns; but virtually the occupation of a vagrant beggar is gone, as a trade—as a great and wide-spread evil it has ceased to exist; it is no longer productive. A beggar's child is now rarely as a beggar bred. No millionaire of a beggar (if such there are now) would give £100 for a beggar's right to beg on Palmerstown Hill, near Chapelizod, as was reported several years ago. Real want, caused by infirmity or age, can now find a shelter in a workhouse, and ratepayers have not, and will not continue, to give alms to beggars and pay rates for poor-houses; and it is now generally felt and known, that every one who can work, and is willing to work, can live by the hire of their labour."

Report for the Counties of Galway, Roscommon, King's, Westmeath, and Tipperary.

"In the rural districts, professional mendicancy had almost ceased to prevail during the famine period, but as the condition of the farming classes has gradually improved, and food has become more abundant and cheaper, symptoms of a revival of the system have been observable, and both individuals and families, formerly habituated to this mode of life, are now not uncommonly found to leave the workhouse during the periods of the year most favourable for the purpose, and seek a living by begging through the country from house to house, and, as frequently happens, from Union to Union."

Report for the Counties of Cork, Kerry, and Limerick.

"Numerous mendicants are not now, as formerly, seen going from house to house in search of eleemosynary assistance, in the shape of food and shelter; nor are travellers by public or private conveyances so frequently importuned for alms by beggars of every age and sex, at every town or stoppage on the road.

* Wandering beggars are called "Shoulers" in the south of Ireland. Ir. *siubhlach*, a traveller. *Siubhal*, going, moving, march, walking.

"Except in large towns committals for vagrancy have become of comparatively rare occurrence; and a greatly improved tone, in point of self-reliance and a spirit of independence, is observable in the conduct of the industrial classes generally.

"This important decline in mendicancy, and the favourable progress in the condition of the peasantry and industrial classes, within the last three years, must certainly be attributed, in a great measure, to there having been, during the whole of that period, a constantly growing demand for labour of all kinds at an improved rate of wages."

Report for the Counties of Cavan, Donegal, Fermanagh, Londonderry, and Tyrone.

"Mendicancy is generally on the increase throughout this district, especially so in the county of Donegal, and there are more strolling beggars now than there have been for some time past. The abundant supply of potatoes and other provisions in the hands of the small farmers is the principal cause of this state of things."

Report for the Counties of Dublin, Carlow, Tipperary, Kildare, Kilkenny, Queen's, Wexford, and Wicklow.

"The number of professional mendicants has everywhere very considerably decreased, and but few of this class are now to be met with in the district. They may be said to be confined to some parties belonging to the aged and infirm class, who, during the period of fine weather in summer, take their discharge from the workhouses, to return again, in a short time, when the weather becomes broken."

In the year 1868 the Industrial School system was extended to Ireland by the 31 and 32 Vict., c. 25.

In 1870, the comparative condition of vagrancy in Ireland and in England is thus alluded to in the 23rd Annual Report of the Irish Poor Law Commissioners :—

"In the last Annual Report we mentioned the subject of the relief of tramps and vagrants and the large proportion of that class alleged in the volume entitled 'Judicial Statistics, Ireland,' to exist in Ireland in comparison with the same in England and Wales, and also the theory advanced that this excess was due in some measure to the limited extent of out-door relief in Ireland.

For the reasons which we have already stated, and which it is unnecessary here to repeat, we continue to think that the number of tramps and vagrants in the two countries, if it has been accurately ascertained and compared, has no connexion with the more limited practice of out-door relief in this country.

"As to the number of tramps and vagrants or casuals relieved in the two countries, we have had the weekly number in Ireland carefully noted since the 6th March, 1869, and we find that the average weekly number received into the Irish workhouses in the course of twelve months has been 968, and the maximum number so relieved in one day only 211. In England and Wales the number relieved in workhouses on the 1st January, 1869, was 5,346, besides 1,674 who received on the same day out-door relief."

According to the Report for 1886 the largest number of "night lodgers" or "casuals" relieved in any one week between the 7th of March, 1885, and the 6th of March, 1886, was 3,802, comprising 2,637 males, 606 females, and 559 children under 15, and the smallest 2,944. The maximum number in workhouses at the close of any week was 529, comprising 377 males, 79 females, and 73 children under 15, and the minimum 364, the estimated population for 1885 being 4,924,342. The average per week being 3,358, and per day 480, or an increase of 342 per cent. per week on the number relieved in 1869, the estimated population in 1869 being 5,536,217. This increase is attributable to the unsettled state of the country.

In reviewing the condition of the lowest class of the Irish poor from whom the vagrant and mendicant are recruited, it is impossible to avoid remarking that it differs essentially from the parallel social strata in England, Wales, and Scotland. Wales and Scotland formerly combined with Ireland to supply, though in a lesser degree, a large contingent of the idle or dependent poor in England. They have long ceased to do so, and the number of Welshmen and Scotchmen in London workhouses is comparatively infinitesimal. The reverse is, however, the case with the Irish, or people of Irish descent. In nearly all the London workhouses they form a large contingent of the inmates,* and throughout the

* In the *Marylebone Workhouse* in August, 1886, out of 1,540 inmates, 265, or 17½ per cent., were born in Ireland, and about a similar number were of Irish descent in the first generation. Accepting this as a fair average of the metropolis at large, which there is good reason to believe it is, it would appear that one-third of the pauperism of London consists of Irish-born people and

metropolis, while the Welsh, the Scotch, and the Germans are conspicuous as traders or merchants, the aboriginal Irish follow the most servile occupations, and seem to aspire to little higher. The names on our shop-fronts testify to the energy and enterprise of the Germans and Italians, who frequently arrive in this country almost penniless, while Irish names are only rarely to be met with, and even as street-traders the Irish only pursue the inferior callings.

Religion is certainly not the cause, because the number of English Roman Catholics in London workhouses is by no means large.

The same social phenomenon is observable in Ireland itself. Taking, for instance, an important trade—that of woollen-draper—we find in the Dublin Directory of 1766, which is the earliest accessible, that out of 57 names, not more than 11, or one-fifth, are of Irish origin.

The habits, too, of the lowest class of Irish are unfortunately such that they are looked upon as undesirable tenants in model dwellings.

Such being the case—though some further social improvement may still be looked for—the teachings of history unfortunately forbid any hope that until the primitive portion of the race is completely amalgamated with a more vigorous stock its individual members can ever attain that flourishing independence which has characterised the other races in Great Britain.

---

their immediate descendants. There were in this workhouse at the same period only 9 natives of Scotland and 2 of Wales, together with 76 English Roman Catholics. In the Whitechapel Workhouse, out of 203 inmates at this period, there were 3 English Roman Catholics, 2 natives of Scotland, and none of Wales.

CHAPTER XVIII.

WALES.

A.D. 943—1284.

The Laws and Institutes of Wales—The Venedotian, Dimetian, and Gwentian Codes and the Anomalous laws relating to Gwestva dues, harbouring of guests, and description and treatment of bondmen—The fine for an offence against a homeless beggar—Welsh hospitality in the twelfth century.

THE laws and institutes of Wales, such as they have been handed down to us, are comprised in several distinct codes, that of Gwynedd, or Venedotia, comprising the greater part of what is now called North Wales; that of Dyved, Dimetia, or West Wales, the country comprised in the see of Menevia; that of Gwent or Gwentia, the district inhabited by the Silures, comprising the diocese of Llandaff; and the Cyvreithiau Amryval or Anomalous Laws, comprehending legal dicta and decisions, pleadings, and elucidatory matter.

These laws are originally ascribed to Howel Dda, or Howel the Good, " a conspicuous king in South Wales, in the government of which he succeeded his father Cadell. He inherited from his mother Elen possessions in Powys, and his influence appears to have been powerful throughout North Wales. Perceiving the laws and customs of the country to be violated with impunity and falling into desuetude, he caused them to be examined, that so what was wholesome and beneficial might be retained, what was ambiguous might be expounded, and what was superfluous or prejudicial might be abrogated."

"Having summoned the Archbishop of Menevia, other bishops and the chief of the clergy, the nobles of Wales, and six persons (four laymen and two clerks) from each comot, to meet at a place called Y Ty Gwyn ar Dav, or the White House on the river Tav, near the site of Whitland Abbey, in Caermarthenshire, he repaired thither in person ; and having spent all the Lent in prayer and fasting, he selected from the whole assembly twelve of the most experienced persons, and added to their number a clerk or doctor of laws named Blegwryd. To these thirteen was confided the task of examining, retaining, expounding, and abrogating. When completed, that nothing might be wanting to strengthen the observance of these laws, sentence of excommunication was denounced against all transgressors." The date usually assigned to this Congress is the year 943.

The Venedotian Code is said to be the compilation of Iorwerth, son of Madog, son of Raawd, from alterations of the laws of Howel Dda by Bleddyn, Prince of North Wales, about 1080.

The Dimetian Code is founded upon alterations made by Rhys, son of Grufudd, Prince of that district, about 1180.

The Gwentian Code is asserted to be the compilation of Cyvnerth and his father Morgenau, both of whom are enumerated among the judges summoned by Howel to attend his Congress.

The Custody and Entertainment of Guests.

Dimetian Code.

There are three fours. . . . one of them is, legally harbouring a guest, that is, keeping him from dusk until the morning, and if his bedfellow puts his hand over him three times in the course of the night, and he swears to the fact with the people of the house, in that rhaith.* The third fours are, the four persons for whom there is no protection, either in court or in church, against the king. . . . The third is, a person to whom the king is a supper guest, who ought to supply him with food that night, and who does not supply him ; the fourth is, the King's bondman.†

Cyvreithiau Amryval (Sundry or Anomalous Laws).

These are the various cases wherein guardians‡ are required.

---

* *Rhaith, verdict.* There were various kinds of rhaiths, composed of from five to three hundred compurgators. † Bk. II. c. 8, s. 13.

‡ *Ceidwad (cadw-ad), a guardian*—a term taken in an extensive sense. In suits for land guardians and evidences were produced, the distinction between them being slight. A guardian swears to the thing in dispute, to his certain knowledge, being the property of the person he names ; an evidence, that a certain person was dispossessed by another. A guardian charges no one with wrongdoing ; an evidence speaks to the outrage. The guardian proves the matter of action ; the evidence the cause of action.

For custody of birth and rearing; for custody before loss; for custody of guests.*

Here are the nines of law, which are . . . . 8, the nine nights of the guest house (gwesty).†

Here is further notice of legal (defences). . . . The second is, an arwaesav; ‡ that is, where a person shall give his arwaesav to exonerate his guest from wrong; that is, as to night theft, and absence, and ferocious or horrid deeds; although an arwaesav can likewise be called for theft in hand. §

There are three thieves subject to dirwy, ‖ that is three cases where a dirwy for theft occurs : . . . or a man who fails to confine his lawful guest during the night; or where there is evidence of theft against him.¶

In three ways there is a dirwy for theft: by the confession of the party spontaneously; by the failure of a rhaith; by the failure of guardians, in exonerating lawful guests, for night theft.**

In three various modes one kind of kindred is competent to a full denial: one is, to keep the ownership of property for a person; the second is, to prove his being, on the night he was reputed to do the deed, in such and such a house, and thus lawfully exonerate his guest; the third is, an arddelw,†† that is, a way to prove an alibi.‡‡

Three things which accord in law, although it may be deemed extraordinary that they do so: guardians, after prosecution, and that means, to exonerate a guest against theft in absence. §§

Three cases where guardians are appropriate: for living or dead property; for privilege, or lack of privilege, in another; and for lawful guests.¶¶

Three arddelws which accord with denial: an arddelw of an established rhaith; an arddelw of custody of guests unimpeached; and an arddelw of innocency, according to justice and country.

---

* Bk. IX. c. 35, s. 1. † Bk. X. c. 8.

‡ *Arwaesav* (ar-gwaesav), *support*. The person, or authority, a defendant avouches to be the guarantee of the right to property with which he is charged to be unlawfully possessed. § Bk. XIV. c. 2, s. 3.

‖ *Dirwy*. There were two kinds of fine imposed upon offenders. The dirwy was twelve kine, or three pounds; the other, or *camlwrw*, three kine, or nine score pence. *Dirwy* signifies sometimes, but rarely, various amounts of fine.

¶ Bk. XIV. c. 12, s. 7. ** Bk. XIV. c. 12, s. 11.

†† *Arddelw* (ar-delw), a vouchee of various natures in defence. Such kind of defence was abolished by 26 Hen. VIII. c. 6.

‡‡ Bk. XIV. c. 15, s. 6. §§ Bk. XIV. c. 15, s. 22.

¶¶ Bk. XIV. c. 16, s. 9.

Three arddelws which comprise confession: an arddelw of arwaesav, and failing the party; an arddelw of innocence, and undergoing a rhaith, and it failing, that is equivalent to a confession; and an arddelw of custody of guests, and it failing, the claim is confessed.*

There are three arddelws: an arddelw which shall take the thing out of the hand of a defendant, and set him free from the claimant; an arddelw of innocence, and to which pertains a rhaith or the custody of guests; and an arddelw of a surety.†

XXX. Here is further of theft absent, for which an arddelw is not had, and against which guardians are to be had, that is, theft absent which shall be imputed to a person.

1. "Verily," says he then, "on such and such a night, thou art charging the theft upon me, there are for me enow of lawful guardians to clear me of illegality out of such and such a house; to wit, the owner of the house." He is to clear him, swearing with the men of the house to putting a hand three times in the night (over him), and thus clearing him from the time of securing the byres until the morning: securing the byres implies, from the time of tying the cattle until the morning.

2. Guests can only be cleared for night theft.

3. These guardians may be charged as disreputable, like others; for the disreputable cannot clear.

4. If he fail to clear the guest; three pounds to the lord, and his property to the complainant.‡

The Protection of a Beggar.
Gwentian Code.

In three ways a silver rod is paid to the King, and a golden vessel with a golden cover to it: for violating a woman; for breaking the protection of the road towards a beggar without a home; and for saraad§ to the King. ||

The Bondman.
Dimetian Code.

In what place soever a fugitive bondman shall be overtaken, twenty-four pence, as a rescue fee, is to be paid on his account;

---
* Bk. XIV. c. 21, s. 3.   † Bk. XIV. c. 21, s. 14.   ‡ Bk. XIV. c. 30.
§ *Saraad*. The fine for contempt in its legal sense.
|| Bk. II. c. 39, s. 46.

and fourpence for every comot he shall have passed over: if he go to another kingdom, twenty-four pence shall be paid in hand to any one that shall release him; and out of that the captor is to retain a third; and the owner of the land is to have the two parts.*

Three persons who are to receive saraad, and who are not to receive galanas: † . . . the third is a bondman, there is no galanas for him; only payment of his worth to his master, like the worth of a beast.‡

Cyvreithiau Amryval.

An adventitious bondman, is one who shall be in the house of an uchelwr, at spade and fork; and such a one is a domestic bondsman, who shall remain with the uchelwr § unbought, uninvited: and the worth of such a one is twice as much as that of a bondman who shall be bought. ||

A serving bondman is one who shall be in the house of an uchelwr who goes not to spade, nor quern: such is a domestic bondman, one who shall remain by invitation, without buying, with an uchelwr: his worth is the same as the worth of a bought bondman.¶

Howel the Good permitted every uchelwr to hold his own land according to its privilege, and to rule his bondmen according to conditional bondage in South Wales, and perpetual bondage in Gwynedd. The King's villeins are to be regulated according to the privilege and law of the taeog-trev** in which they may dwell, and that according to bond service and bond rent.††

Conditional bondmen and alltuds‡‡ can be sold by their lord, and given, by law.§§

---

* Bk. II. c. 17, s. 49.
† *Galanas, homicide.* The sum assessed upon the criminal and his relatives as the retribution for murder.
‡ Bk. III. c. 3, s. 8.
§ *Uchelwr* (uchel-wr), *a high man.* Variously styled "gwr rhydd," a free man; "gwr da," a good man; and "breyr," a mote man, in different parts of Wales.
|| Bk. V. c. 2, s. 111. ¶ Bk. VI. c. 1, s. 72.
** *Taeog-trev, villein trev.* A trev was a division of land containing four gavaels or 256 erws, equal to about 228½ acres.
†† Bk. X. c. 13, s. 1.
‡‡ *Alltud* (all-tud), *of another land.* A person, either from foreign parts or from another part of the island, in villenage under the King or a freeholder.
§§ Bk. XI. c. 2, s. 2.

PENALTY FOR ENTERTAINING A FUGITIVE.

Cyvreithiau Amryval.

If a man feed a person who is banished by the sentence of the law, or who is food-forbidden by the injunction of the lord, some say he is liable to a dirwy; the law, however, says, that he who shall feed him is only liable to a camlwrw.* †

ENTERTAINMENT PRIVILEGES OF THE KING AND THE CHIEFTAINS.

Venedotian Code.

Of the Land Maer (land bailiff).

He is entitled to "gwestva" from the men of the maer-trev (the demesne). ‡

Privileges of Arvon. That there shall be no payment for horses of guests or for men on their progress.

Whoever shall reside in Arvon a year and a day, if he be a man of substance, he acquires the same privilege as a man of the country. §

Gwentian Code.

The King is to have thirty-six persons on horseback in his retinue: the twenty-four officers, and the twelve gwestais; ‖ likewise his household, his gwrdas,¶ his youths, his minstrels, and his suitors.**

Cyvreithiau Amryval.

Three cows which the King is to have: a cow which the canghellor †† shall take by distress for the King's gwestva. ‡‡ §§ . . .

Three dues a lord is to have from his man without doing injustice to him: one is, the geld of his territory due to him and his household, which happens in various modes: the first is, his

---

* *Camlwrw* (cam-llwrw). *Mulct for wrong.* A fine of three kine, or nine score pence, sometimes doubled and tripled.   † Bk. XI. c. 1, s. 12.
‡ Bk. I. c. 34, s. 11.   § Bk. II. c. 2, ss. 12, 14.
‖ *Gwestai,* a visitor or guest.
¶ *Gwrda* (gwr-da), *a good man.* A freeholder.   ** Bk. I. c. 4.
†† *Canghellor* (cancellarius). An officer in every canghellor-ship who held pleas to determine disputes among the King's villeins and secured his waste.
‡‡ *Gwestva* (gwest-ma), *entertainment place.* A term used for the provision, or money payment in lieu of it, due to the lord from the uchelwyr or freeholders.   §§ Bk. XIV. c. 3, s. 31.

gwestva from the privileged maenols;* and his supper, or payment for it, that is, one pound, if not had between the calends of winter and Martinmas.†

Giraldus Cambrensis gives the following account of the hospitality and liberality of the highest classes in Wales in the 12th century:—

"No one of this nation ever begs, for the houses of all are common to all; and they consider liberality and hospitality amongst the first virtues. So much does hospitality here rejoice in communication, that it is neither offered nor requested by travellers, who, on entering any house, only deliver up their arms. When water is offered to them, if they suffer their feet to be washed, they are received as guests; for the offer of water to wash the feet is with this nation an hospitable invitation. But if they refuse the proffered service, they only wish for morning refreshment, not lodging. The young men move about in troops and families under the direction of a chosen leader. Attached only to arms and ease, and ever ready to stand forth in defence of their country, they have free admittance into every house as if it were their own.

"Those who arrive in the morning are entertained till evening with the conversation of young women, and the music of the harp; for each house has its young and harps allotted to this purpose. Two circumstances here deserve notice: that as no nation labours more under the vice of jealousy than the Irish, so none is more free from it than the Welsh; and in each family the art of playing on the harp is preferable to any other learning. In the evening, when no more guests are expected, the meal is prepared according to the number and dignity of the persons assembled, and according to the wealth of the family who entertains. The kitchen does not supply many dishes, nor high-seasoned incitements to eating. The house is not furnished with tables, cloths, or napkins. They study nature more than splendour, for which reason, the guests being seated in threes, instead of couples as elsewhere, they place the dishes before them all at once upon rushes and fresh grass, in large platters or trenchers. They also make use of a thin and broad cake of bread, baked every day,

---

* *Maenol, stony.* A territorial division, consisting of four trevs or 1,024 erws. It seems analogous to a manor.

† Bk. XIV. c. 10, s. 6.

such as in old writings was called *lagana*;* and they sometimes add chopped meat, with broth. Such a repast was formerly used by the noble youth, from whom this nation boasts its descent, and whose manners it still partly imitates, according to the words of the poet :

'Heu ! mensas consumimus, inquit Iulus."

"While the family is engaged in waiting on the guests, the host and hostess stand up, paying unremitting attention to everything, and take no food till all the company are satisfied ; that in case of any deficiency, it may fall upon them. A bed made of rushes, and covered with a coarse kind of cloth manufactured in the country, called *brychan*, is then placed along the side of the room, and they all in common lie down to sleep; nor is their dress at night different from that by day, for at all seasons they defend themselves from the cold only by a thin cloak and tunic. The fire continues to burn by night as well as by day, at their feet, and they receive much comfort from the natural heat of the persons lying near them; but when the under side begins to be tired with the hardness of the bed, or the upper one to suffer from cold, they immediately leap up, and go to the fire, which soon relieves them from both inconveniences ; and then returning to their couch, they expose alternately their sides to the cold, and to the hardness of the bed."

In the *Dream of Rhonabwy*, in the *Mabinogion*,† a rather different picture is, however, given of the hospitality of the lower ranks of society. "And Rhonabwy and Kynwrig Vrychgoch, a man of Mawddwy,‡ and Cadwgan Vras, a man of Moelvre in Kynlleith § came together to the house of Heilyn Goch the son of Cadwgan the son of Iddon. And when they were near to the house they saw an old hall, very black and having an upright gable, whence issued a great smoke ; and on entering they found the floor full of puddles and mounds, and it was difficult to stand thereon, so slippery was it with the mire of cattle. And where the puddles were a man might go up to his ankles in water and dirt. And there were boughs of holly spread over the floor, whereof the cattle had browzed the sprigs. When they came to the hall of

* Bara llech and Bara llechen, or griddle bread, from being so baked.
† Translated by Lady Charlotte Guest.
‡ *Mawddwy* was one of the western districts of ancient *Powys*; it now forms part of one of the hundreds of Merionethshire.
§ *Kynlleith* is a division of the hundred of Chirk in Denbighshire.

the house they beheld cells full of dust, and very gloomy, and on one side an old hag making a fire. And whenever she felt cold she cast a lapful of chaff upon the fire, and raised such a smoke that it was scarcely to be borne, as it rose up the nostrils. And on the other side was a yellow calf-skin on the floor—a main privilege was it to any one who should get upon that hide.

"And when they had sat down they asked the hag where were the people of the house. And the hag spoke not, but muttered. Thereupon behold the people of the house entered, a ruddy, clownish, curly-headed man, with a burthen of faggots on his back, and a pale, slender woman, also carrying a bundle under her arm. And they barely welcomed the men, and kindled a fire with the boughs. And the woman cooked something, and gave them to eat barley bread, and cheese, and milk and water.

"And there arose a storm of wind and rain, so that it was hardly possible to go forth with safety. And being weary with their journey they laid themselves down and sought to sleep. And when they looked at the couch it seemed to be made but of a little coarse straw, full of dust and vermin, with the stems of boughs sticking up there-through, for the cattle had eaten all the straw that was placed at the head and the foot. And upon it was stretched an old russet-coloured rug, threadbare and ragged, and a coarse sheet, full of slits, was upon the rug, and an ill-stuffed pillow, and a worn-out cover upon the sheet. And after much suffering from the vermin and from the discomfort of their couch, a heavy sleep fell on Rhonabwy's companions. But Rhonabwy, not being able either to sleep or to rest, thought he should suffer less if he went to lie upon the yellow calf-skin that was stretched out on the floor. And there he slept."

Detailed information as to the social customs of the Welsh prior to the conquest of Wales is almost altogether wanting, and can only be supplied to a limited extent by a study of the Laws and of the Mabinogion.

It appears to have been a practice with the Welsh to group the leading principles of every branch of knowledge according to the number of cardinal points they contained, such, for instance, in law, as the threes of the law, the fours of the law, the three fours, &c.

The cherished sin of the vagabond section of the community appears to have been the pursuit of cattle-lifting, and the restraints sought to be imposed on the entertainment of guests seem to have been mainly directed at placing obstacles in the way of this philobovian avocation, by requiring the host to declare that he had extended the hand over his guest three times during the night, and found him in his "lair," which would be the most correct description of his night couch. Hard swearing—which was doubtless frequently forthcoming—would apparently exonerate the guest in most instances.

Unless the signification of "the nine rights of the guest house" is, that this was the extreme limit of the permissible entertainment of strange guests, there does not seem to have been any other legal limit to their entertainment as such.

It is difficult to understand what the penalty for breaking the protection of the road towards a homeless beggar could have meant. If the penalty of a silver rod, and a golden vessel with a golden cover, was not a mythological or bardic ideal of what such a penalty ought to be, the alternative of non-payment—whatever that may have been—must in most cases have been enforced. The penalty for disgracing the King of Aberfraw on account of his wife was of the same character, viz. "a gold cup with a gold cover to it, as broad as his face, and as thick as the nail of a ploughman who has been a ploughman for nine years; a golden rod as tall as himself, and as thick as his little finger, and a hundred kine for each cantrev in his possession." *

Now the person who was hardy enough to commit such an offence, and wealthy enough to pay such a penalty, would scarcely be the kind of person to submit to its enforcement. In fact, it looks very much as if the idea had been borrowed from the *Mabinogion*, as in the tale of *Branwen the Daughter of Llyr*, Bendigeid Vran sends to tell Matholwch "that as an atonement for the insult, he shall have a staff of silver as large and as tall as himself, and a plate of gold of the breadth of his face."

Both laws, as they at present stand, appear to be riddles; they could hardly have promoted morality, as they could easily be made engines for extortion in the hands of a needy and unscrupulous prince.

The laws regarding bondmen appear to reflect the condition of things prevailing in England at the same period, when the status of the bondman had so far improved that the savage penalty of

* *Venedotian Code*, Bk. III. c. 1, s. 24.

death was no longer exacted for absconding, and milder treatment prevailed in every other respect. The *allîtuds* alluded to on page 433 were evidently English bondmen in captivity.

The privileges of compulsory hospitality appear to have been very similar to those prevailing in Scotland and Ireland, and no doubt encouraged truculent vagabondism on the part of those who could in any way claim to be retainers or dependents of a chieftain of consequence.

The *Westour*, who was legislated against by various English sovereigns, was originally the *Gwestwr*, or officer appointed to collect the King's *Gwestva* dues, or *Cymhorth*,* or purveyance, and who went about eating and drinking at the expense of the public, and afterwards procuring food and supplies for his master. After the annexation of Wales the *gwestwrs* seem to have multiplied, and to have carried on business on their own account, until they became an intolerable pest.

The *Commorthas*, legislated against by 26 Hen. VIII., c. 6, appear to have been of two kinds : illegal feudal commutations claimed by lords of manors—which they endeavoured to enforce—and fees which, by ancient custom, were paid to bards on their periodical circuits or *cylch clera*, and which were subsequently claimed by the priesthood. The bards were originally instructors of the people, but at last degenerated into wandering minstrels and mendicants of the lowest type. After the conquest of Wales *Cymhorth* was, up to the time of Henry VIII., no doubt frequently made the excuse for bringing together assemblies which, while professing to be for the purpose of assisting some person or persons in any work or need, were often made the medium for collecting the partisans of an insurrectionary movement, and were therefore discountenanced by the Government. On such occasions *cwrw cymhorth* or *bidale* was distributed.

* *Cymhorth* (cyn-mhorth) is derived from *Cyn*, a prefix in composition, giving force to words which denote a mutual act, quality, or effect ; and *porth*, aid, sustenance, provision. In the present day cymhorth means a gathering of people to assist a neighbour in any work such as mowing, harvesting, coal-carrying, &c.

CHAPTER XIX.

THE ISLE OF MAN AND THE CHANNEL ISLANDS.

THE ISLE OF MAN, 1422—1885.—Reign of Henry V.—No one to leave the island without a licence—All Scots to avoid the land—No man to bring in beggars or vagabonds—Reign of Elizabeth—No alien to pass without a licence—Loitering Irishwomen to be banished—Reign of James I.—Statute to regulate the rate of wages—Reign of Charles II.—Vagrant servants and their punishment—Poor not to beg out of their parishes—Apprentices to serve for five years—Further attempts to regulate wages—Reign of Victoria—Masters of vessels bringing over paupers to be punished—Condition of mendicity in 1879 and 1885.
JERSEY, 1669—1885.—Letters patent of Charles II. providing for the setting to work of poor and idle people—Code of 1771—Provision for the maintenance of the poor—Infirm people to be licensed to beg—Pauper children not to be taken out of the island—Inhabitants not to receive strangers more than one night—Tavern-keepers not to tolerate vagabonds—Condition of mendicity in 1885.
GUERNSEY, 1534—1885.—1534, penalty for harbouring strangers—1537, poor strangers to be banished—1542, young men and young women to take service—1566, orphans, &c., to be apprenticed—1566, strange servants not to be received—1583, banished criminals to quit the island—1588-9, vagabonds to quit the island—1597, infirm poor to be relieved—1611, begging without a licence forbidden—1684-5, ordinances relating to the poor and mendicants—Condition of mendicity in 1885.

THE ISLE OF MAN.

THIS island, judgèd by the character of its language, appears to have been originally peopled by a tribe of Gaelic or Erse origin.

The Druids sought refuge here after the conquest of Anglesey by the Romans under Suetonius Paulinus in the year 61. It is said to have been subsequently governed by a series of Welsh kings, who in the tenth century were superseded by Norse chiefs, from whom the peculiar constitution of the island is derived. In 1270 the Scots obtained possession of the island, lost it to the English, again retook it in 1313, and again lost it in 1344.

In 1406 Henry IV. bestowed the island on Sir John Stanley, whose son, John Stanley II., adopted measures for establishing the law and the executive government on a fixed footing, and for inducing the inhabitants to cultivate and transform the country, which had fallen out of tillage during the Scottish domination. Up to this period the laws remained unwritten, being dispensed by the lord and the deemsters and local parliament by a law termed "breast law,"* a relic no doubt of Celtic rule. The island is and always has been governed by its own laws, enacted by the three estates, viz. the Queen in Council (formerly the Lord of the Island), the Governor in Council, and the House of Keys, which consists of 24 members. These two last estates are termed when assembled a Tynwald Court, and the concurrence of the three is absolutely necessary to establish the validity of any law, which is even then without force until proclaimed from Tynwald Hill.

The first law we have to notice appears to have been passed with the twofold object of preventing the depopulation of the island and also of restraining bondmen from quitting their lords.

"The Court of all the Tennants and Commons of Man, holden at Kirk Michaell, upon the Aill of Reneurling,† before our Doughtfull Lord Sir John Stanley, by the Grace of God, King of Mann and Th'Isles, the Tuesday next after the Feast of St. Bartholomew, in the year of our Lord God 1422 . . . . Alsoe it is ordained and proclaimed in the same Court, that noe Man of what Condition soever he be, goe out of the Land, without special Lycense of the Lord or his Lieutenant, with Vessell, upon Paine of Forfeiting the Vessell and all the Goods therein."

The next law reminds one of the law of King Alfred as to the men that chapmen were allowed to take with them. The order for the expulsion of the Scotch, and for the future exclusion of beggars and vagabonds, affords a presumption that the Scotch expedient of banishing vagabonds so often resorted to, had resulted in the establishment of a number of them in the island.

"Our most Gratious and excellent Lord, Sir John Stanley, King of Man and the Isles. In the Vigill of your Lady Sct. Mary, Anno Domini 1422, att his Castle of Rushen, asked his Deemsters and the xxiiij the Laws of Mann in these Points under written. To the which the said Deemsters, with the xxiiij gave for Law, that these be Points of your Prerogatives.

* "Breast" law is supposed to mean the traditional and unwritten law, of which the knowledge was in the breast of the judge.

† *Aill* in Manx means a place, a stead. The *Aill of Reneurling* is now called *Cronk Urley* (the Hill of the Eagle). It was formerly occasionally used, as the Hill of Tynwald is now, for assemblies of the Legislature.

"Therefore be it ordained that every Chapman and Shipman have Lycense as oft as his Profitt serveth, for England, Ireland and Wales, soe that he warne the Lieutennant, and have Lycense, to goe, and knowe if he have any Business and Cause to the Coast they goe unto, or backe again. Alsoe that they take noe Tennants nor Servants out of the Land without Lycense of the Lieutennant, for noe Offence to them made, upon Paine of Forfeiture of his Vessell, and to pay the Farme of them that he carryeth away, and his Body to Prisson: And also that he find Sureties to come againe if he have no Lycense.

"Also that all Scotts avoid the Land with the next Vessell that goeth into Scotland, upon Paine of Forfeiture of their Goods, and their Bodys to Prison. . . . .

"Alsoe that no Man bring Beggars or Vagabonds into the Countrey, upon Pain of Forfeiture of his Boate."

We have next an order made by the Commissioners of the Lord principally directed against Irish female vagabonds, many of whom had probably been made homeless by the extortionate practices of the English soldiery in Ireland. Sir Richard Sherburne, mentioned in the order, was the lieutenant-governor of the island at the time, as though the lords of the house of Stanley made frequent visits to it, the governorship was usually vested in their lieutenants.

"The Book of Orders made by the Comissioners, Anno Domini 1561, at the Castle Rushen, in the Isle of Mann, the 16th Day of July, in the year afforesaid, by Sir Richd. Sherburne, Knight, Gilbert Parr, Hugh Diconson, William Stopforth, and Alexander Rigby, Comissioners to Edward, Earle of Derby, Lord Stanley, Lord of Mann and the Isles, and of the most noble Order of the Garter, Knight.

"Itm. That no Alien, coming into any Haven in Mann, with Merchandize, or otherwise, shall after warning to him given, pass any further into the Island, without Lycence of the Councell, but to the next Parish Church, upon Paine of Forfeiture of his Goods, and Body to Prison: and that Irish Women, loytering and not working, be commanded forth of the said Isle, with as much convenient speed as may be; and no Boat hereafter to be suffered to bring any of the said loytering Persons into the said Isle; but that he, upon paine of Forfeiture of his Boate and Goods, after warning him given, take the said Persons to him againe."

Writing of this order in the year 1879, the Attorney-General says: "It might be doubtful how far this order of itself could be considered as a law. It does not professedly appear to be a declaration of the common law, and it is not a Statute. I look upon it, however, as setting forth what the common law was as to foreign vagrants generally, and it but shows the mode in which the law as declared in 1422 was applied, namely, that persons who conveyed vagrants to the island were obliged to remove them again, and if they did not do so their boats were liable to forfeiture."

The first attempt to regulate the rate of wages by Statute appears to have been made in the year 1609.

"Castle Rushen, The Tenth Day of October, 1609.

"Att an assembly of the Lieutenant and other the Officers, with the 24 called the Keyes, of the Land, for the consulting and determining of Matters concerning the State of the Land, there was these Statutes ensuing made and enacted.

"First as concerning the Wages General of Servants. It is agreed upon by the Generall Councell of the Land, with the Consent of the said 24, that every Man Servant, being a Plowman, shall have by the yeare for his wages xiijs. iiijd. and not above, every Driver xs. and every Horseman viijs. and not above; provided that every of these shall be reputed sufficient by the Deemsters and the Jury for Servants;* and although that a Plowman or Driver be by the said Jury made and allowed for want of better, yet notwithstanding, as before spetified, he must be allowed and held sufficient by the Deemster; and for every woman according as she shall be thought to deserve by the Deemster and Jury.

"Itm. That every head Taylor working by the Day shall have for his wages, with Meat and Drink, iiijd. and not above; and every apprentice Taylor, with Meat and Drink, ijd. and not above; and every Taylor working for Servants shall have with Meat and Drink, ijd. and not above; and his apprentice jd. and not above; and if any refuse to work after the Rate above spetifyed, or refuse to come, being sent for by the Farmer, (except he be in other Men's Work,) shall, upon Complaint sufficiente proved, be put to be a Servant.

"Itm. Every Woolen Weaver shall have for every yard of

* The jury probably consisted of ordinary jurymen summoned by the coroner.

Woolen Cloth for Blankett sufficiently wrought an Ob.; for every four great Hundred Breadth of Keare,* Ob. Qs.; for every yard of Medlie † 1*d*. Qs., being five Hundred, which is for every great Hundred Qs.

"Itm. That every Linen Webster shall have for every yard of Clouth sufficiently wrought according to the old Custome after, as the yard shall be in Smallness or Greatness.

"Itm. Every Walker or Fuller of Cloath shall have for every yard of Blanket Cloath sufficiently pulled an Ob. of the great Hundred; for every yard of Keare Cloath three Farthings; every Yard of Medlie j*d*. Ob.; and every yard of white Cloath j*d*.

"Itm. Every Mazon, Carpenter, Shipwright, Hooper, Slater, Thatcher, thatching after the English Fashion, and Joiner, shall have the Day, with Meat and Drink, iiij*d*. and not above, being sufficient Workmen.

"Itm. Every Blacksmith shall have for laying of every Coulter j*d*.; for making of every Coulter ij*d*.; for making of every new Sock ij*d*.; ‡ for making and laying of every Wing an Ob.

"If any farmer or other having Occasion to use any of the said Servants or Handicrafts Men shall give any greater Wages than before is mentioned, otherwise than upon the good Desert of his Servant, in way of Bountie, and not by set Hyre or Wages, then every such Person so offending contrary to the true Meaning of this Statute, shall for every Time forfeit soe much to the Lord of Land as the whole wages or Day's work cometh unto."

During the civil wars the lordship of the island changed hands. James, Earl of Derby, being taken prisoner at the battle of Worcester, was tried and beheaded October 16, 1651, and the lordship was conferred on Lord Fairfax. His commissioners took possession of the island in 1652, but on the accession of Charles II. it again reverted to the Derby family. These changes, however, no doubt produced a certain amount of social disorder which is always favourable to vagabondage, and accordingly in the year 1664 fresh legislation regarding refractory servants and vagabonds appears to have been found necessary.

At a Court of Tinwald,

"Holden at St. John's Chappell within the Parish of Kirk

---

* A dark grey colour in wool.   † Of a mixed stuff or colour.
‡ A ploughshare.

German, in the Isle of Mann, the xxiiijth Day of June, in the Year 1664, before the Right Reverend Father in God Isaac Lord Bishop of Sodor and Mann, and Governor of the said Isle; Henry Nowell, Esquire, Deputy Governor of the same under his Lordship; and before the Officers, Deemsters, and the 24 Keyes, the Representative Body of the said Isle: these ensuing Orders, Acts and Statutes, were ordained, enacted and proclaimed, as wholesome Lawes to be observed in this Island in future.

"Itm. It is hereby ordered and enacted in Observance of former antient Statutes and Orders within this Isle, That whosoever shall transport any Person or Persons, inhabitting within this Isle, and in particular Men and Women Servants, or young Persons, without spetiall Lycence first had and obtained from the Governor of this Isle, shall for every Time soe offending be proceeded against and forfeit as by the ancient Law and Statutes of this Isle is already declared and provided; and such Servant or Servants, or young Persons, presumeing to transport themselves out of the Isle without such Leave or Lycence, shall be proceeded against either in Person or Goods, or both, at the Discretion of the Governor and Officers of this Isle.

"Itm. Fourthly, it is also ordered, That Servants who are wilfull and refractorie to do their Service to their lawfull Master, that Claime by Hireing, or are made by a Jury of Servants, or by Yarding,* shall be punished by Imprisonment as the Governor and Deemsters shall appoint, and soe to continue until the said Servant do yield Obedience, and perform his Service, who for his Allowance is to have but one Cake a Day and a Proportion of water as afforesaid; which allowance is to be deducted out of his Wages by the Master who is to send the said Relief daily unto him, either from himself, or some Friend entrusted in that Behalf; and likewise the Master to have allowance out of the Servants' wages afforesaid, during the Time of his Imprisonment, for want of his or her Labour, or for to give another in his or her Place for the said Time of Imprisonment, at the Discretion of the Deemster.

"Itm. Tenthly, That Juryes for Servants be impannelled all Times in the Yeare as often as there will be just Cause for the

* This term is derived from the "yard" or staff of office, which the coroners of the "sheadings" or districts formerly carried with them, as the symbol of their authority. The "yarding" was the summoning of servants by the coroner on behalf of the Deemsters and others entitled to a priority of choice of servants.

same; and that the Vagrant Servants by the said Jurors found be first made liable and put to Service, otherwise to suffer Punishment until they submit, having for Allowance in that Time as is ordered for refractory Servants: and that the Days of St. Catharine's in Winter for Men Servants, and St. Collumbe's in Summer for Maid Servants, be noe Hindrance thereunto for the future; provided nevertheless, that this Liberty be not granted to any but such as are driven thereunto through manifest necessity; for that many relying on this Liberty forbear to keep any Servants in the Winter and Summer Season till towards Harvest Time, when Servants are scarcely to be had, and then to the Prejudice of poor People, as Cotlers, Intackholders, Prentices, and the like, who are engaged by Trades, and giving Shearing for Crofts and Nooks of Ground for the Relief of a poor Family, they are mollested by such negligent Farmers, by endeavouring to compel them to their Service by Juries of Servants, provided therefore that no Man Servant be made to any by Jurys of Servants, or otherwise but in the Time of Winter, nor a Maid Servant but within a reasonable Time of Summer, except in respect of Death, or other just and lawful Cause or Reason, (and that made known to the Governor and Deemsters) a further Liberty be granted for the same.

"Forasmuch as notwithstanding the severall Orders heretofore made to restrain the Poor of this Isle for ranging and begging from Parish to Parish, they doe nevertheless not observe the same, whereby the said former laudable Orders are neglected, and the Charity of the respective Parishioners not extended and afforded to the Relief of their own Poor, as is most expedient to be distributed, it is therefore ordered and ordained at this Court of Tinwald, That the Poor of the Isle shall not range or begg out of their own Parish into any other Parish; wherein if they do offend contrary to this Order, then the Constable, Coroners, or Lockman * of such other Parish, is for the first Time to warne and require such Beggars back to their own Parish, which if they neglect and refuse, then they are to be compelled and whipped to their said Parish; and if they continue refractory, and be disobedient, then are they to be brought by any of the said officers into the next Gaole, there to continue until they declare themselves conformable to this Order; And it is also ordered, That none be relieved as the

* *Guilley-gliash*, an officer answering to a constable in England, whose business it is to serve summonses, &c.

Poor of any Parish but such as are blind, lame, mayme, or decrepitt in respect of Age, or other Infirmity; and that all young and Sound Persons shall either labour for their Livelihood, or be made to serve by a Jury of Servants, or otherwise to be committed untill they submitt thereunto; and this Order to be observed from the last Day of this Month, upon the Pain and Penalty contained herein; and if the said Constable, Coroners or Lockman of any Parish, do neglect their Duty, contrary to what is before expressed, they and every of them so offending and neglecting is, upon Complaint and Proof made, to be fined and punished at the Discretion of the Governor and Officers of this Isle for the Time being.

"These Lawes made and subscribed by my officers of my Isle of Man, I doe allow and approve off, and give my assent, that from henceforth they doe become Lawes. Given under my Hand at Knowsley this 16th of June 1665. CHA. DERBY."

The Attorney-General, writing in 1879, says, "This enactment is still the law; but I never heard of its enforcement in modern times." The next enactment reminds one in some measure of the 14 Car. II., c. 12, which recites that " poor people do endeavour to settle themselves in those parishes where there is the best stock, the largest commons or wastes to build cottages, and the most woods for them to burn and destroy."

"INSULA MONÆ. *Anno* 1665.

"Notwithstanding the several Statutes, Orders, Acts, and Ordinances already contrived, and made at sundry Times for Laws to be observed and kept within this Isle, Experience (nevertheless) finds it requisite by the Observation of severall Occurrences in the Progression and Transaction of divers Matters, beside what the Necessity of the Times doth require, that further or other Orders and Lawes be enacted, some to be repealed, and other to be enlarged or explained, as the present Government, with the Approbation of the Right Honourable the Lord of the Isle, shall think fit and requisite to be put in Execution."

"Itm. Whereas it is observed that a great Cause of Differences and Complaints in this Isle touching Servants is, the frequent binding of Youth to Trades for two or three Years, and then, before they well understand the same, setts up for themselves and marry, and so live meanly and poorly, and turning Cottlers* or

* Cottagers or villeins.

Inclosurers on some Highway Side, are commonly given to pilfering and stealing and intertainers of Vagabonds, and of Men's Children and Servants, at unseasonable Times, in dishonest Manner; and also, for want of Judgment, spoils, if not pilfer, some Part of the Country's Work and Goods put unto them; and becoming thus to be Tradesmen, assumes an Exemption from being Servants, and in that Manner cause a great Scarcity both of Servants and of honest and able Tradesmen in the Isle: It is therefore ordered, ordained, and enacted, That no person or persons within this Isle shall for the future, after Proclamation hereof, take or entertaine any Apprentice to learn any Science or Trade, without such Apprentice, with sufficient Surety, do first enter into a Penalty by Bond to the Lord's Use in the Sum of tenn Pounds at the least to serve for the Time, Term and Space of five Years; and further, when the said Terme of Years is run up and expired, such Apprentices are (nevertheless) hereby inhibited, forbidden, and barred to receive and entertaine any other Apprentice or Apprentices with, unto or under him for the space and Terme of one Year afterwards; and that to be nevertheless upon the Approbation of three of the same Faculty at least for the Sufficiency to take and teach an Apprentice for the Terme of Years afforesaid; neither is such Apprentice serving such Number of Years allowed or permitted to marry for One Year's Time and Space without the special Lycence of the reverend Ordinary, or his Substitutes or Spiritual Officers so impowered for the Time being, first had, procured, and obtained for the same; and upon a true Certificate under the Hand of the Minister of the Parish, and two sufficient Neighbours where such Tradesman doth live and reside, of his Condition, Honesty and Abillity, according to their Knowledge and Common Feme and Report, and all this upon Pain of severe Punishment upon the person of the Offender or Offenders, and a pecuniary Mulct besides for a Fine to the Lord of the Isle.

"Approved June 16, 1665."

Notwithstanding the apparent failure of the previous attempt to regulate the rate of wages another effort was made to accomplish the object in the year 1667.

At the Court of Tynwald,

Holden at St. John's Chappell, within the Isle of Mann, the 21st day of September, 1667.

3. Itm. Whereas notwithstanding the Statute of the year 1609 for Limittation of Servants Wages, to wit, a Plowman to have by the year xiijs. iiijd., a Driver xs., and a Horseman viijs., and to a Woman Servant as she should be reputed to deserve, &c.; at which Time the Farmer was of better Abillity than of late Times, since the enhancing of the Wages, to pay the same by the Rares afforesaid for their Corn and other Comodities; that nevertheless the Servants will not of late yeares hire for double the Wages so mentioned, unless they may receive what wages they please, not considering that the Farmer is far more unable now than formerly to pay the same, in respect of the scarcity of Money, and the cheap Rates both of Corn and Cattle; and yet are the Servants in a better Condition to subsist, by the cheapness of Cloath, both Woolen and Linnen, and all the Comodities they stand in need of: and whereas it may be conceived, that the Wages mentioned in the said Statute was only intended for such Servants as were made by Jurys and Yarding, albeit the foresaid Statute is plain to the Contrary, being for the Wages Generall of Servants, &c.; be it therefore hereby ordered, enacted, and declared, That there be a Restraint of such Exorbitancy in the Servants, That (considering both the Cheapness of all Comodities at present, and that probably the same may rise higher hereafter, and so continue for some Time) there be this Moderation made on both Parts, viz. That every sufficient Plowman shall have for his Wages fifteen Shillings and not above; every Driver ten shillings; every Horseman, or Horse Lad, eight Shillings; every Household Fisherman xiijs. and not above; and every Maid Servant of Abillity to undertake and perform her Master or Mistress's Service, the wages of nine Shillings by the Year, and not above; and that the allowance of Wages to other Maid Servants of meaner Capacity and Abillity, and to Shepherds and the like, be estimated by the Deemster, and in some Things both by the Deemsters and the Standing Jurys for Servants in each Yeare, if such last sort of Servants will not be otherwise reasonably satisfied by their Master or Mistress; and no other certain Wages to be given above the Rates and in Manner as aforesaid, unless it be by way of Bounty, at the Discretion of the Master or Mistress, as they shall understand the Servant worthy of, or himself deserve, according as is mentioned in the foresaid Statute: And if any Servant be refractory, and refuse to serve at the Wages and Rates aforementioned, such Servants

(upon complaint to the Governor, or his Deputy) are to be imprisoned, and so to continue with the Dyett of disobedient Servants untill they submit to the Statute thus made, and give security for their honest and careful Labour as Occasion shall require; and besides, to pay such Fees for their Contempt as by the Governor or his Deputy shall be thought fitt.

"And it is provided, That the said Wages is Conditional in case the Servants be not able to perform the work, otherwise to be lessened at the Deemster's Discretion.

"4. Itm. Whereas divers, under the Pretence of old and decrepit Persons, do make entrance of Choice Children for their Freedom from Service, when as such Challenge and Claime by many of those Entrys is contrary to the true Intent and Meaning of the Statute made in that Behalf, by Means whereof a Scarcity of Servants are occasioned, and an obstruction both to the Farmers, Deemsters, and other Officers, who should have the Benefit of yarded Servants, &c.; Be it therefore hereby ordered, enacted, and declared, That no Person shall have the Benefit of Entrance of a Choice Child for the future, but such as shall have the Approbation for the same under the Hands of the Jury of Servants in their own Parish for the just Necessity thereof."

As compared with England, the wages of a mason, carpenter, &c., are the same as those ordered by Statute in the year 1495, to be paid in that country from Easter to Michaelmas (from Michaelmas to Easter they were 3*d*. a day only). The wages of a ploughman as fixed by the justices of Rutlandshire in 1610 were 29*s*., very nearly double those now under consideration. This would of itself in a great measure account for the dissatisfaction on the part of servants, and their consequent endeavours to escape from service where the statutory regulations were enforced; as the dazzling prospect of largely augmented wages generally appears to outweigh in the popular mind considerations regarding consequent increase in the cost of living.

In 1765 the lordship of the island was purchased from the then possessor, the Duke of Atholl, by the British Government, and in the year 1829 all his manorial rights were also acquired. No further legislation on the subject of vagabondage took place until the year 1846, when a bye-law was made with a view to prevent alien vagrants from landing in the island.

Bye-laws for the Regulation and Government of Towns made under Authority of Act of Tynwald, 6 *Wm. IV.*

"XL. In case Information is given to any Justice of the Peace, or High Bailiff, that any Pauper or Vagrant has, within three Months preceding, been brought over to the *Island,* and still remains there, the Justice or High Bailiff is to cause the Pauper or Vagrant, and the Master of the Vessel (if known), by which he or she was brought over, to be apprehended and brought before him; and unless good Cause be shewn to the contrary, the Master is to be imprisoned, until he enters into a Bond, with two sufficient Sureties, to find and provide at his own Expense suitable Maintenance and Lodging for the Pauper or Vagrant, while he or she remains on the *Island;* and, within fourteen days, to cause the Pauper or Vagrant to be conveyed back to the Port or Place wherefrom he or she was brought, or until the Master is discharged from Gaol; and in case any Master refuses to enter into a Bond, or that any Delay arises in discovering or apprehending the Master of such Vessel, the Justice or High Bailiff may direct the Pauper or Vagrant to be found and provided with decent Maintenance and Lodging, and to be forwarded to the Place from which he or she was last brought, and the Expenses incurred thereby are to be levied under Execution, out of the Goods and Chattels of the Owner of the Vessel."

This bye-law was repealed in 1870, being considered in excess of the power given for making bye-laws, and none has since been made.

The recent condition of mendicity in the island may be gathered from a most interesting report of a *Commission on Medical Aid and Poor Relief* in the island, presented to the Tynwald Court by order of the Lieutenant-Governor in the year 1879. From this report it appears that "the funds available for charitable relief throughout the island are raised by voluntary subscription, and seem to be fully adequate for the purpose, too much so it would appear in one instance at least, as there is a local saying that "if the devil himself came to Kirk Michael they would not starve him." Nevertheless begging seems to be extensively and profitably practised. One enterprising individual, who keeps a small shop in the parish of Santon, not satisfied with an allowance of 9s. a month from the parish, and 2s. a day and his meat when he goes out to work, sometimes goes begging. Another woman, partly imbecile, who is boarded out with a man and his wife out of parish funds, acts partially as their domestic servant, and regularly goes out begging, bringing home the amount thus obtained to the people with whom she boards.

In the town of Douglas, the most effective system of organisation at present in existence would seem to be that of the beggars and tramps who, in organised gangs, go round the town every Monday morning begging contributions from the shopkeepers and other respectable inhabitants, which they appear to be afraid to refuse.

One witness says: "On Monday mornings you will see strings of beggars going from door to door, 30 to 50 of them at a time. They find it a more profitable business than working for a living." Another says: "He is aware that there is a system of going round to the shopkeepers every Monday morning, and that it has been the habit of shopkeepers to give them money to get rid of them. These people, in fact, levy a kind of black mail on the trade of Douglas. Most of these beggars are inhabitants of the town, and he knows that many of them do not deserve any relief at all."

After their regular Monday's raid in Douglas, those who have not expended their last sixpence in drink, appear to take the train in the direction either of Castletown or Peel in search of other "happy hunting grounds," but Castletown no longer presenting a profitable field of action, they usually stop short at some of the villages *en route*, in search of more victims—as at Santon, where a landowner states, "We have no beggars belonging to the parish, but very often tramping vagrants come from Douglas and elsewhere to beg. In no case, however, are these beggars parishioners, they are always tramps. Some of them travel by train."

Or they proceed a little further—as to Arbory, where, says the vicar, "We have tramping vagrants coming from all parts. Some come from so far off as Douglas, and there are a few from Castletown. These are generally drunkards, and the very worst of characters. They must make a great deal of money, as they seem well able to pay their railway fares. They come out by train, and go back by train."

At Peel the same system of house-to-house begging prevails as at Douglas. Saturday is here the favourite raiding day. The secretary of the Peel Artificers Society, is of opinion that the example of putting a stop to street begging would do good, for they find little ones growing up as beggars following in the footsteps of their parents. The present system is a great evil, and he perceives that under it begging is becoming professional and hereditary. If what they say themselves is to be believed, some of the beggars make a very good thing out of it, earning as much as from 10s. to 20s. a week. A great proportion of the money finds its way into the public-houses. Another witness from Peel says, "As a rule, these begging tramps get money in the morning, and get drunk in the evening; he has himself seen them lying drunk in the middle of the road, and has removed them to the side of the hedge, so that they might not be run over. There is no place of shelter in Peel for these tramps. Some of them are given shelter in some of the farmhouses. There used to be a general custom of giving shelter to tramps, but it is passing away. *The police do not interfere with beggars.* He has seen the beggars selling the meal which has been given to them in charity at the farmhouses, and most likely they drank the money.

Mr. Kermode, a shopkeeper of Peel, says he knows the system of begging that is practised there. He has often asked beggars what they considered was a fair day's relief to receive, and how much they would earn in a day. They have frequently told him that it would be a poor day if they did not earn half-a-crown, besides as much meat as would last them two or three days. Most of them would make no secret of what they got in this way, but used to tell it in a boasting way. They generally sell the meal they receive. Tramps invariably carry a bag or basket, in which to carry meal and scraps which they get at the various houses they call at. *They think nothing of making 14s. or 15s. a week and their "grub," as they describe it.* He is visited at his shop regularly once a week by these tramps, to the number of some fifteen or eighteen. It costs him from fifteen to eighteen pence a week to satisfy their demands. He gives a penny a week to those he considers the most deserving. *Some of them "tried on" coming fortnightly, and demanding the double allowance. He refused to agree to that.* They said *they could not go round on Peel and Castletown in one day; and, as they only came once in two weeks, they thought they were entitled to the double allowance.* He did not fall in with their proposal; but would rather give it to them than subject himself to the abuse they very frequently give you if you refuse to give them relief. Most of them are strangers to Peel. The incumbent of St. Paul's Church, Ramsey, says that before a well-organised system of relief was established in that town, there was a most elaborate system of begging in vogue there. A black stream of beggars might be seen going round one after the other.

A lady witness says it is reported that a man named Blind Tom made as much as 7s. a day by begging, and that there is no doubt that the poor are very much petted and spoiled in Douglas. At one time the Manx poor would not beg from door to door at all; but now they do it regularly. She thinks that they have been taught to beg by the Irish. There are still a good many Manx who will not beg. A great many Irish beggars come to Douglas, and they never return to their own country, because *they find such a lot of charity going on in Douglas.* They get so much there in charity that they never think of going back. One woman who applied for relief, and was told that if she did half a day's work a shilling would be given to her, replied, "*What! work for a shilling! It is not worth while going there to work for that.*"

In the year 1880 the Central Poor Relief Board for Douglas decided "that with a view to the total suppression of mendicity and vagrancy, begging from door to door in town and country, relief at the hands of the public shall be discouraged, and ordinary applicants for relief be sent to the officer to be appointed to act as the general poor inspector of the town.

The Chief Constable of the island, writing in April, 1886, says: "I do not think there is any of that abject poverty which one hears of in England, though there is considerable improvidence amongst a portion of the population of the towns, chiefly those of Irish nationality, who earn large wages as porters, &c., during the season, but never think of the winter. The Manx are, I think, very provident. During the summer season we have of course our full share of itinerant musicians, disabled sailors, &c., and in the winter a few professional beggars, who are encouraged by the well-meant but unwise generosity of the more wealthy, but these mendicants are not really poor."

JERSEY.

In the year 1669, Charles the Second by letters patent, allowed an impôt on brandies and wines, in which it is stipulated that

300 livres tournois, part of the revenue derived from the impôt, should be yearly employed in the erecting and building of a convenient house, and for and towards the raising and maintaining of a stock of money to be used for the setting to work and orderly governing of poor and idle people, the relief of decayed tradesmen, and the correction and restraint of vagabonds and beggars in the Island. The revenue arising from the impôt was not applied, from its insufficiency in amount, to all the purposes originally intended. No portion of it was specially appropriated for the poor, nor any portion devoted for the correction and restraint of vagabonds, till the erection of the present house of correction in the year 1838.

The subsequent enactments relating to Mendicants and Vagabonds are to be found in a Code of Laws for the Island of Jersey approved by His Majesty in Council, March 28, 1771, from which the following extracts are taken :—

Regulations.

For Mendicants.

"The Constable, Principals,* and officers in each Parish, are to provide respectively for the maintenance of their Poor, in letting out, or setting to work those who are able-bodied; and in furnishing the infirm, with the necessaries of life from week to week; and for this purpose, such of the inhabitants of their respective parishes, as are in a position to contribute to make a rate in the same way as other necessary rates are imposed, for charges and disbursements in connection with public matters, are authorised to act conjointly with the Assembly of Principals and Officers.

"The Minister, Constable, and Churchwardens of each Parish may grant a licence under their hand to infirm poor people to beg from house to house in their own Parish only.

"The Poor will not be permitted to beg outside their parishes on any pretext whatever, nor in their own parish without the above-named licence, under the penalty of being put in the stocks by the Constable for the first offence and brought before the Court for the second to receive such punishment as they may be found to deserve.

* The term Principal is applied to the ratepayers in a parish contributing above a certain amount. The amount varies in each parish, but is fixed by law.

"Persons who through mistaken charity, give alms to persons who are forbidden to beg, are liable to pay sixty sous for each offence, of which one-third is to go to the informer and the other two-thirds to the poor of the Parish, which is to be levied by the Constable on the principal chattels of the offenders, and if they resist, by seizure and sale of their goods in the same way that rates are levied for the maintenance of the poor and other public taxes.

"Strangers and other persons who are not residents, or their agents, are not allowed to hire or take out of the island, any children who are chargeable to the parishes, or permitted to beg; and when strangers or non-residents or their Agents have hired any other children, they must produce them to the Constable or to one of the Centeniers * of their parish, before taking them on shipboard, so that it may be ascertained if they are chargeable, under a penalty of fifty pounds for each child.

"The able-bodied poor who are let out or hired by the Constables, by the advice and with the consent of the Principals of their Parish, shall only be so if they are thirteen years of age or younger, until they attain the age of twenty; and those who are more than thirteen, shall only be let out for seven years at the utmost, and less when it is possible.

"The above-mentioned penalties shall be appropriated half to the King, and half to the poor of the parish where the offence was committed."

Strangers.

"In accordance with a certain order of the King and the Council, dated the twelfth day of June, 1635, registered in the Rolls of the Royal Court the twenty-fourth day of September following : and a certain letter from the Lords of his Majesty's Council dated the twentieth day of February, 1660, registered the twenty-seventh of April, 1665—

"It is decreed that no inhabitant of this island, whether a Tavern Keeper or otherwise, shall receive a stranger into his house, nor allow any one to remain in it more than one night, without giving notice to the Constable of the Parish, under a penalty of ten pounds, a third to the King, a third to the poor, and a third to the informer.

"The Constable of the Parish of S. Helier, shall be liable to

---

* The Centeniers are assessors and rate gatherers.

make a report to the Governor within twenty-four hours of notice being given to him of the arrival of strangers, or as soon as it is possible for him to do so : and the Constables of other parishes within a week at the latest, or as soon as possible, if such strangers are suspicious persons.

"Strangers shall not be allowed to remain in the island nor to marry the women of the country without the permission of the Governor, as is directed by the said order of His Majesty and his Council of the twelfth of June, 1635; and if they offend they shall be compelled to quit the country."

Tavern-keepers.

"Tavern-keepers shall reserve at least two good beds for the accommodation of strangers and those of the residents who may require them; and are in general required not to tolerate in their taverns any drunkards, blasphemers, vagabonds, idlers and persons of bad repute, nor to allow riots or assaults, but are bound to inform the police officers thereof with all speed.

"They shall not harbour the young men of any family, or male or female servants without the knowledge of their fathers, mothers, masters or mistresses; nor permit the frequenting of poor persons to drink beyond their visible means, under a penalty of ten pounds, and suspension or revocation according to circumstances.

The Lieutenant-Governor, writing in August, 1885, says, "There are so few beggars in the island, that it is not necessary to enforce the law contained in the code of 1771, and I have not, since I have been here, now two years, heard of any proceedings being taken before the Police Magistrate for simple begging, or for begging combined with any other offence, such as drunkenness or threatening. Each parish provides for its own poor."

GUERNSEY.

The royal Court of this island has always claimed and exercised the right of passing ordinances for regulating the manner in which the Common Law is to be carried out, and the written records of the Court, commencing early in the 16th century, contain many regulations respecting paupers and mendicants not differing materially in spirit from contemporary legislation in England.

As early as 1534 an enactment appears to the following effect :—
"It is ordered by the Court that no one shall harbour any stranger to reside in the island, under a penalty of sixty sols, unless it be as his man-servant or maid-servant."* But this may possibly refer only to aliens, and not to English subjects.

In 1537, "It is ordered by the Court that all poor strangers who cannot live in the island without begging, having arrived within a year and a day, shall quit the country under pain of being scourged and whipped, and the Constables, each in his parish, are enjoined to bring them and deliver them to the Sheriff, to be turned out of the island; and that all paupers who are beggars, natives of the island, shall beg and ask alms each in his own parish." †

In the same year precautions also appear to have been taken against needy strangers settling in the island.

"It is ordered that the Sheriff shall have the supervision of all vessels that come into the island as well from Jersey, as from Normandy and other places, that is to say, that he shall go into the said vessels and shall see and set down in writing those who come into the island, by name and surname; and shall take their rudder until their departure, in order to see that each passenger returns from whence he came, and does not go away without his leave." ‡

---

* "Il est regardez par Justice que nulluy ne logera nul estrangier pour demeurer en l'isle sur peyne de LX. souls,[1] se che n'est pour son serviteur ou sa servante."

† "Il est regardez par Justice que touts pouvres gens estrangers qui ne peuvent vivre en ceste isle sans mandier, y venus depuis an et jour, vuyderont hors du pays sur peynne de estre fustigués et foytés, et en ayra les Connestables, chacun en sa paroesse, charge de les amener et les delivrer au Prevost pour les mettre hors de l'isle; et que tous pouvres mandians, natifs de ceste isle, quaiteront et demanderont l'aumosne chacun à sa paroesse."

‡ "Il est regardez que le Prevost du Roy ayra la surveue de tous bateaulx qui viennent en ceste isle, tant de Jersy que de Normandie et autres lieux,

---

[1] With respect to the value of the money in which fines for infraction of ordinances are assessed in Guernsey, it is still legally the ancient "livre tournois," or currency of Tours, which differed from the "livre Parisis" in value, inasmuch as it was, or was supposed to be, of greater weight or purer metal. The Normans, proverbially keen in all matters of business, made all their contracts in it, and so it became the legal tender in the island, and is still retained as a measure of value, although, like the pound sterling, it had disappeared as a coin many years ago. Fourteen livres tournois are in the present day equivalent to the pound sterling; 1 sol 3 deniers tournois are equal to 1 penny; 60 soulx is about 4s. 3½d. sterling.

The following ordinance was passed at Michaelmas, 1542, and had probably reference only to strangers :—

"It is ordered by the Court that all young men and young women who live by themselves, shall take service by All Saints' day next coming, under pain of quitting the island, and of a fine of sixty sols on those who harbour them every time they do so."*

In 1566 a system of parish apprentices was instituted by the following ordinance :—

"That from henceforth if there are found in the town, and in any of the parishes of the island, any poor orphans or children of poor persons who have not the means of supporting them, or of sending them to England, to learn suitable trades by which in time to come they may live and assist their parents, the constables of the said parishes and town shall have the responsibility and charge of finding them masters in their parishes, and if they cannot find any, shall send them to England at the cost of the said parishes." †

The Governor, to whom the defence of the island was entrusted, had always a discretionary power to expel aliens or to prevent their settling there in too great numbers, and the following order may possibly have been made in consequence of the number of French driven to the islands by the persecution against Protestantism in their country. This ordinance was enacted in January, 1566-7 :—

"It is ordered that none for the future, of whatever nation they may be, shall be received to remain and dwell in this island as servants, who do not bring a proof of the country from which they come and of their good behaviour; and that they shall be examined by those who shall be appointed by the Governor and

c'est asavoer, que il yra dedans les dits bateaulx et voera et mettra par escript ceulx qui viendront en ceste isle, par nom et par surnom, et prendra leur gouvernail jusques à leur departement, pour voer chacun passager retourner dont yl soet venus ni s'enyront point sans son congy."

* "Est regardez par Justice que tout jeune homme ou jeune femme qui demeurent à leur part se mettront en louage dedans le jour de la Toussaint prochain venant, sur la paine de vuyder hors de l'isle et de LX. souls d'amende à ceux qui les logeront toutes foes et quantes."

† "Que dorenavant s'yll trouve en la ville et en toutes les paroesses de l'isle aulcuns paupvres orphelyns ou enffants de paupvres gents qui n'ont pas les moyens de leur nourrir, ne de les envoyer en Angleterre aprendre bon mestiers par lesquels en temps advenir ils en puyssent vyvre et ayder à leur parens, les Connestables des dites paroesses et ville auront la charge et soing de leur chercher mestres en leurs paroesses, et ce ils n'en peuvent trouver, les envoyer en Angleterre ès coustages des dites paroesses."

the Court, and that none of them shall be received into the service of any inhabitant of the island, before they have produced their leave and licence from the said appointed authority, under a penalty of a fine of ten livres from those who have the ability to pay it, and those who have not the ability to pay the said fine shall be punished corporally at the discretion of the Court. And similarly no masters of vessels, from whatever port they may come, shall put on shore any passengers after having been warned, without having first consulted with the said appointed authorities, under a penalty of a fine of one hundred sols for the use of the harbour. The said appointed authorities are the Bailiff or his Lieutenant and two Jurats."*

According to the "Approval of the laws, customs, and usages of the island of Guernsey differing from the customary law of Normandy from time immemorial observed in the said island, compiled at Richmond the 9th day of October, 1580, and at Greenwich the 30th July, 1581, and completed the 22nd of May, in the year of grace 1582, and ratified at the Privy Council the 27th day of October, 1583," Book 12, Chapter 34, "We have no asylum to which criminals can retire; but with regard to those who are banished and ordered by the Court to be sent out of the island, the Sheriff is accustomed to ask the exile to what country he wishes to go, and to order him under pain of capital punishment to leave in the first passage-boat for the port to which he intends to proceed." †

---

* "Il est ordonnez que nulls pour l'advenir, de quelconque nation que ils soient, ne sera rechu pour rester et demourer en ceste isle pour servir, qui n'aporte rellation du pays d'où il est, et de son bon comport, et qu'yls seront examynés par ceulx qui seront apoyntés par Monsieur notre Cappitaine et la Justice, et que nuls d'yceulx ne seront recheus à servyr, de nuls des habytans de l'isle, que premier ils ne monstrent leur congy et lycence des dits apoyntés, sur la peine de dix livres d'amende à ceulx qui airont la puyssance de la poyer ; et ceulx qui n'airont la puyssance de poyer ladite amende, ils seront pugnys corporellement à la discretion de Justice. Et semblablement null mestre des bateaux, de quelque lyeu que ils soient, ne metteront nuls passagiers à terre après avoir estey garnys, que premièrement ils n'ayent parlé aulx dits apoyntés, sur la peine de cent souls d'amende à l'usage de la chaussée. Et sont apoyntés au dit faict Monsieur le Bailyff ou son Lieutenant et deulx Jurés."

† "Approbation des lois, coutumes et usages de l'ile de Guernesey, différentes du coutumier de Normandie d'ancienneté observé en la ditte Ile. Fait à Richmond le 9 jour d'octobre, l'an 1580, et à Greenwich le 30 Juillet, 1581, et achevé le 22 Mai, l'an de grace 1582, et ratifié au conseil privé, le 27e jour d'octobre, 1583, et du règne de Sa Majesté Notre Souveraine Dame Elizabeth, par la grâce de Dieu, Reine d'Angleterre, France, et Irlande, &c., Défenseur de la Foi, le 25 me." Livre Douzième. Chapitre Trente Quatrième. "Nous

In January, 1588-9, the following regulations were made:—
"Item, that all vagabonds and idle persons who will not work, and those who are known not to gain their living honestly, who have a bad name and reputation, or who are guilty of lewdness or adultery, if they are strangers, natives of places beyond this island, shall quit the island within forty days after having been publicly ordered so to do, and not return afterwards, upon pain of being whipped in the public places of the town, and their ears nailed to the pillory: and after the said term of forty days, that no person shall harbour one or any of such who shall be ordered to depart, under the penalty of a fine of twenty livres tournois, half to Her Majesty, and half to the informer." *

"Item, that no strangers shall let lodgings, or keep a tavern, or keep open shop for retailing any merchandise in time to come, except those who have a special licence formerly granted by the Governor during the troubles in France, and without prejudice to

n'avons aucun lieu de franchise pour les criminels à se retirer ; mais quant aux bannis et mis sous le plein Mars[1] par ordre de Justice, le prévôt a accoutumé de demander au banni en quel pays il veut passer, et lui commander sur peine capitale de partir dans le premier passage vers le lieu où il prétend passer."

* "Item, que tous vagabonds et fayneants qui ne veulent travailler, et ceux qui sont nottez de ne gaigner loyallement leur vie, qui ont mauvais bruit et renommée, ou qui ont commis paillardize ou adultère, s'ils sont estrangers, natifs hors de ceste isle vuideront hors de ceste isle dans quarante jours aprez avoir esté publié. Sans aprez y retourner, sur peine d'estre fouettez par les quarrefours de la ville, et leurs aureilles attachées au pillory: et aprez le dit terme de quarante jours, qu'aucune personne ne logera aucun ni aucuns de ceux qui seront commandez de vuider, sur la peine de vingt livres tournoys d'amende, moytié à Sa Majesté, et moytié au trouveur."

---

[1] The literal meaning of "*sous le plein Mars*," more usually "*le plein de Mars*," is "below the mark which the sea reaches at the spring tides in March," which are generally the highest in the year, and is still in common use as an equivalent to "below high-water mark." The term seems to have been used as equivalent to "out of the island."

The sentence of banishment, even in the commencement of the present century, was by no means an unusual punishment, and for natives of the island a very severe one, as banishment for seven years or a longer term was followed by confiscation of all the property, real and personal, of the delinquent to the Crown. It was a convenient method of getting rid of strangers; but as for the most part, they reached the neighbouring seaports in England without a penny in their pockets, they were soon obliged to have recourse to begging ; and complaints were made by the towns where they landed, that Guernsey sent all her rogues and vagabonds to them. Banishment has ceased to be inflicted on natives, in consequence of their being liable to be sent back to their place of settlement; but strangers who have not acquired a settlement in the island are still liable to be sentenced to banishment after an imprisonment, or other punishment, if they are notorious evil livers whom it is desirable to be rid of.

the chapmen or other merchants, who coming into the island shall expose their merchandise for sale for the trip."*

"Item, that no foreign strangers shall be permitted to marry in this island, to dwell amongst us." †

"Item, that no strangers shall in future be permitted to live in this island, unless they shall first have produced proof of their good behaviour, and delivered sufficient sureties from inhabitants that neither they nor their children nor family shall thereafter be a charge to the church or the parish where they dwell, but that if they come to want, their sureties shall be compelled to maintain them and to provide for all their necessities." ‡

"Item, that no young children, nor others of more mature age, shall go begging in the island, but that their nearest relations shall be compelled to receive them and to keep them or place them in service, or send them out of the country to learn a calling by which to earn their living; or if they have no relations, or that they are poor and without the means of supporting them, the constables shall take charge of them, and shall do their duty towards them at the common and public cost, each in his parish; and that the poor aged persons who have no means of livelihood or work, shall be relieved, each in his parish, by the alms of the church, without going out to beg, if they have not the special license of the Court for it." §

* "Item, que nuls estrangers ne garderont logis, ne tiendront taverne, ne garderont boutique ouverte pour retailler aucunes marchandizes en temps advenir, excepté ceux lesquels ont eu de ce specialle licence par cy devant de Monsieur le Gouverneur durant les troubles de la France ; et sans préjudice des colporteurs ou autres marchands, lesquels venants en ceste isle exposeroynt leurs marchandizes en vente pour le voyage."

† "Item, que nuls estrangers forains ne seront permis de se marier en ceste isle, pour habiter entre nous."

‡ "Item, qu'aucuns estrangers à l'advenir ne seront permis demeurer en ceste isle, sinon que premièrement ils ayent apparu d'attestation de leur bon comport, et baillé pledges suffisants des habitants qu'eux ne leurs enfants ne famille ne seront puis aprèz en aucune charge à l'eglize ne à la paroysse où demeureront ; ains que s'ill leur advenoyt necessité, leurs pledges seroynt contraints de les nourir et leur subvenir de toutes leur necessitez."

§ "Item, que nuls jeunes enfants, ne aultres de plus competent age, n'yront mandiant par l'isle, ains que leur prochains parens seront contraints les recueillir et garder ou mettre en service, ou envoyer hors le pays apprendre mettier à gagner leur vie ; ou s'ils n'ont parens, ou qu'ils soyent pauvres et sans moyens de leur subvenir, les connestables auront de ce le soin, et en feront leur devoyr aux frais communs et publicks, chacun en sa paroysse ; et que les pauvres anciennes personnes qui n'ont moyen de vivre ne travailler, seront subvenues, chacun en sa paroysse, des ausmosnes de l'eglise, sans aller mandiant s'ils n'ont de ce specialle licence de Justice."

The foregoing regulations appear somewhat severe towards strangers and aliens, but with such a dense population as then existed in the island and such limited means of subsistence, there was no doubt some necessity for them. With respect to aliens, their residence in any large number might have been dangerous in case of a sudden outbreak of war between England and France.

In 1597 the first clear indication of a poor rate appears, the necessitous up to this time having been apparently relieved by private charity, collections made at the church doors, legacies, and rent charges on land. It is contained in the following article:—

"Item, that the persons who languish in their homes and have not the means of soliciting charity from those in their parish who might be inclined to assist them, shall be supported at the common cost of the public, every one in his parish, and for this purpose contributions shall be made and levied by the said Constables and Douzaine, of which they shall also keep a good account."*

In 1611 all these ordinances were revised and consolidated into one, by the 1st Art. of which no person whatever above the age of fourteen was allowed to beg without a licence, and if found so doing was to be put by the Constables into the stocks for the first offence, whipped with rods in private by order of Justice for the second, and flogged publicly by the hangman, by the same order, for the third, all at the expense of the parish in which they were taken. By the 2nd Art. children under fourteen found begging without the knowledge of their parents were to be taken to the nearest parish school and then whipped; but if their parents or guardians had allowed them to go begging then these were to be brought before the Royal Court and punished as if they had themselves been found begging. By the 3rd Art. the Constables and Douzeniers of each parish are bound to make a rate twice a year for the relief of the poor.

* "Item, que les personnes qui languissent en leurs maisons et n'ont moyen de demander la charité de ceulx qui en leur paroysse les vouldroyent assister, seront entretenus aux communs frais du publicq, ung chacun en sa paroysse, et pour ce faire sera faicte et levée une contribution par les dits connestables et Douzeine,¹ du quoy aussy ils garderont ung bon lyvre."

¹ The "Douzaine" is a parochial body of twelve men, elected by the ratepayers, and presided over by the senior of the two constables, who are similarly elected. They have the superintendence of the roads, the assessment of taxes, and the assessment of the value of land for the purpose of division among co-heirs, and they also assign to the eldest son the portion (called "le préciput") to which he has a right beyond the portion allotted to his brothers and sisters.

The civil wars in the reign of Charles I. appear to have had a very disastrous effect on the prosperity of the island, and the restoration found it very much impoverished. In 1684-5 the provisions of the ordinances relating to the poor and mendicants were re-enacted with the following preamble:—

"Upon complaint made by the Crown officers of the great abuses and disorders committed in this island by many persons who, under the pretence of poverty, give themselves up to evil practices and lead a scandalous life, preferring to remain idle and to be vagabonds than to apply themselves to any employment, through the habit which they have acquired of begging, diverting by this means the charity due to the poor and necessitous, to the intolerable vexation of the public, the scandal of good people, and the dishonour of the inhabitants. To remedy which, &c."*

It will be seen by these extracts that the treatment of paupers and beggars did not differ much, if at all, from what was customary at the same period in England. Mendicity has always been discouraged, and may be said scarcely to exist in the present day. It would probably disappear entirely were it not for the mistaken kindness of some and the laziness of others who will not take the trouble of inquiring into the circumstances and characters of those whom they relieve. Pauperism has certainly increased very considerably since the beginning of the present century, and that in a great measure from the influx of strangers. The Guernsey men, as a rule, are thrifty, and in many instances will bear with great privations rather than apply for Parish relief, but it is not so with strangers. They soon get demoralised by the temptation afforded by the cheapness of spirits, and, neglecting their children, these grow up in habits of idleness, and often end in becoming paupers and chargeable. In the town and parish of St. Peter Port, the population of which by the last census was about 17,000, there is an institution combining a Hospital for sick and infirm persons with a poor-house, and in this, in which, except in cases of accident or sickness, none but parishioners are admitted, out of 233

---

* "Sur la plainte faite par les Officiers du Roy des grands abus et desordres quy se commettent en cette Isle par plusieurs personnes quy, souls pretexte de pauvreté, s'adonnent à mal faire et mennent une vie scandalleuse, aymant mieux se tenir oyseux et être vagabonds que de se mettre à quelque travail, par l'abitude qu'ils ont prinse de gueuser, derobant par ce moyen la charité deüe aux pauvres et necessiteux, à l'intolerable vexation du public, scandalle des gens de bien, et deshonneur des habitants. Pour à quoi remedier, &c."

inmates, 135 bear names which do not originally belong to the island. Of 194 parishioners receiving out-door relief, 118 bear also appellations which prove that either they or their ancestors came from without. Besides these, who may be looked upon as permanent paupers, there are others to about the number of 190 who are receiving casual and temporary relief, and of these 152 appear to be strangers to the island, judging at least from their names. Probably before the beginning of the present century, there were not many strangers of low degree residing in the island, but during the long wars on the Continent there were frequently four, five, or more regiments stationed there. The men were sometimes discharged there, and remained as residents in the island, or if discharged at any neighbouring ports in England returned thither, especially if they had chanced to marry natives of Guernsey. Many farm-labourers have at different times gone over from Dorsetshire, Devonshire, and Hampshire, and quarrymen from Cornwall. The decline of some manufactures too in the southern counties has driven several of the factory hands over to the island, and about thirty years ago many of the men brought up for theft and even burglaries came from Crewkerne and its neighbourhood. A good many low Irish too find their way to the island. It is perhaps fortunate that the islands are not as near Ireland as the Isle of Man, or they would probably be inundated with Irish beggars. A little time ago, a lady who gave some trifling relief to an old Irishwoman was thanked in the most effusive manner, the recipient ending her speech by saying " that she would write to her friends in Ireland to come over, as the gentry were so very kind to the poor." The foregoing facts show the nature of the pauperism that exists in the island ; the greater part of it is distinctly traceable to intemperance, the cheapness of spirits there being an irresistible temptation to men, and women too, who have always been accustomed to look upon them as a luxury.*

* With the exception of the translation of the ordinances, the whole of the account of *Guernsey* is due to the kindness of Sir Edgar MacCulloch, Bailiff of the island.

CHAPTER XX.

THE SECRET JARGON OF THE VAGRANT AND MENDICANT.

First accounts of the cant language in England—Harman's vocabulary, 1567—Constituent elements of the vocabulary—Derivation of the words beggar and rogue—Derivation of cant words from the Welsh, Gaelic, Erse, Manx, Lowland Scotch, Latin, Provincial English, Gypsy, and from foreign languages—Metaphorical terms—Modern cant.

THE first account we have of the Cant language in England is that published by *Harman*, in his *Caveat for Cursetors*, in the year 1567. Speaking of its origin he says—

"As far as I can learne or understand by the examination of a number of them their languag—which they terme peddelars Frenche or Canting—began but within these xxx yeeres, or lytle above; and that the first inventer therof was hanged, all save the head; for that is the fynall end of them all, or els to dye of some filthy and horyble diseases: but much harme is don in the meane space by their continuance, as some x., xii., and xvi. yeares before they be consumed, and the number of them doth dayly renew."

Harrison, in his description of England (1577), says, "Moreover in counterfeiting the Egyptian roges they have devised a language among themselves, which they name Canting but others pedler's French a speach compact thirtie yeares since of English, and a great number of od words of their owne devising, without all order or reason: and yet such is it as none but themselves are able to understand. The first deviser thereof was hanged by the necke a just reward no doubt for his deserts, and a common end to all that profession." And Samuel Rowlands, writing in the year 1610, thus speaks of the foundation of this jargon: "First of all they thinke it fit to devise a certaine kinde of language, to the end their cousenings, knaveries villanies might not be so easily perceived and knowne, in places where they come: and this their language they spunne out of three other tongues, viz. Latine, English, and Dutch: these three especially, notwithstanding some few words they borowed of the

Spanish and French. They also gave names to such persons of their Company according to the kind of life that he undertooke: as for example a common begger or rogue they termed a Clapperdudgeon."

All these statements regarding the origin of the language are little better than guesses at the truth. It is probable that after the arrival of the gypsies in England, about the year 1505, the example of their language, which was perfect in itself, stimulated English vagabonds to polish and improve their Cant so as to make it a current medium of speech; but no single individual has ever yet invented a spoken language, and cant words must have existed long before the time of Henry VIII.

The earliest specimen of Cant as yet discovered in a concrete form is to be met with in the following extracts from the *Hye way to the Spyttel House*,* written by *Robert Copland* about the year 1535, in the form of a dialogue between himself and the porter of St. Bartholomew's Hospital:—

Copland. Syr, yet there is another company
Of the same sect, that live more subtylly
And be in maner as mayster wardayns
To whom these rogers[1] obey as capytayns
And be named clewners,[2] as I here say
* * * * *
Come none of these pedlers this way also,
With pak on bak, with their bousy[3] speche
Jagged and ragged with broken hose and breche?

Porter. Inow, ynow; with bousy coue maimed nace *[4]
Teare the patryng coue *[5] in the darkman cace[6]
Docked the dell[7] for a coper meke[8]
His watch *[9] shall feng[10] a prounces[11] nobchete *[12]
Cyarum[13] by salmon *[14] and thou shalt pek my jere *[15]
In thy gan *[16] for my watch it is nace gere[17]
For the bene bouse *[18] my watch hath a coyn
And thus they babble, tyll theyr thryft is thyn
I wote not what with their pedlyng frenche.*[19]

* This was in 1609 plagiarised with some errors by *Dekker* in his "*Lanthorne and Candle-light*" as the original poetry of a canter making rhymes in his own language. *Dekker* does not, however, attempt to decipher the cant.
[1] Rogue. Erse, *ruagaire*, an outlaw.
[2] Gael. *cluainear*, Erse, *cluainire*, a cunning fellow, a hypocrite.
[3] Crapulous.   [4] Drunken.   [5] Priest.   [6] Night.
[7] Deflowered the girl.   [8] For a copper halfpenny.
[9] He (*his watch*—he; *my watch*—me).
[10] Steal. A.S. *feng*, a grasp, hug. Icel. *fengr*, a haul, take, gain, booty.
[11] Prince. Erse, *prionnsa*.   [12] A hat or cap.
[13] Lowland Scotch, *Keerie-oam*, the equivalent of the English game of I spy I.
[14] Oath, Gipsy, *sauloholomus*.   [15] Gael. *inneir*, excrement.
[16] A mouth. Cornish, *ganow*.   [17] Certainly. A.S. *gere*.   [18] A good drink.
[19] Cant language.   The words marked * appear in Harman's work.

The following list of cant words is given by Harman at the end of his work:—

Nab, a head.
Nabchet, a hat or cap.
Glasyers, eyes.
A smelling chete, a nose.
Gan, a mouth.
A commission, a shierte
Drawers, hosen.
Stampers, shooes.
A mofling chete, a napkyn.
A belly chete, an apern.
Dudes, clothes.
A lag of dudes, a bucke of clothes.
A slate or slates, a shéete or shetes.
Lybbege, a bed.
Bunge, a purse.
Lowre, monye.
Mynt, golde.
A bord, a shylling.
Halfe a borde, sixpence.
Flagg, a groate.
A wyn, a penny.
A make, a halfe peny.
Bowse, drynke.
Bene, good.
Benshyp, very good.
Bufe, a dog.
The lightmans, the daye.
The darkemans, the nyght.
Rome vyle, London.
Dewse a vyle, the countrey.
Rome mort, the Quene.
A gentry cofe, a noble or gentleman.
A gentry morte, a noble or gentle woman.
The quyer cuffyn, the Justicer of peace.
The harman beck, the counstable.
The harmans, the stockes.
Quyerkyn, a pryson house.
Quier crampringes, boltes or fetters.
Tryninge, hanginge.
Chattes, the gallowes.
A pratling chete, a tounge.
Crashing chetes, teeth.
Hearing chetes, eares.
Fambles, handes.
A fambling chete, a rynge on thy hand
Quier, nought.
A gage, a quarte pot.
A skew, a cuppe.
Pannam,* bread.

Cassan, cheese.
Yaram,† mylke.
Lap, butter milke or whey.
Pek, meate.
Poppelars, porrage.
Ruff pek, baken.
A grunting chete or a patricos kynchen, a pyg.
A cakling chete, a cocke or capon.
A margery prater, a hen.
A roger or tyb of the buttery, a goose.
A quakinge chete or a red shanke, a drake or duck.
Grannam, corne.
A lowhinge chete, a cowe.
A bleting chete, a calfe or sheepe.
The hygh pad, the hygh waye.
The ruffmans, the wodes or bushes.
A smelling chete, a garden or orchard.
Crassing chetes, apels, peares, or anye other frute.
To fylche, to beate, to stryke, to robbe.
To nyp a bounge, to cut a pursse.
To skower the cramp rings, to weare boltes or fetters.
To heve a bough, to robbe or rifle a boeweth.
To cly the gerke, to be whypped.
To cutte benle, to speake gently.
To cutte bene whydds, to speake or geve good wordes.
To cutte quyre whyddes, to geve evell wordes or evell languáge.
To cutte, to saye.
Quaromes, a body.
Prat, a buttocke.
Stampes, legges.
A caster, a cloke.
A togeman, a cote.
A prauncer, a horse.
Autem, a church.
Salomon, a alter or masse.
Patrico, a priest.
Nosegent, a nunne.
A gybe, a writing.
A larke, a seale.
A ken, a house.
A staulinge ken, a house that wyll receave stolen ware.
A bousing ken, a ale house.
A lypken, a house to lye in.

* The 1573 edition reads *yannam*.

† The 1573 edition reads *param*.

AND BEGGARS AND BEGGING. 469

A lybbege, a bedde.
Glymmar, fyre.
Rome bouse, wyne.
Lage, water.
A skypper, a barne.
Strommell, strawe.
A gentry cofes ken, a noble or gentleman's house.
A gygger, a doore.
To towre, to see.
To bowse, to drynke.
To maunde, to aske or requyre.
To stall, to make or ordaine.

To cante, to speake.
To myll a ken, to robbe a house.
To prygge, to ride.
To dup the gyger, to open the door.
To couch a hogshead, to lye down and sléepe.
To nygle, to have to do with a woman carnally.
Stow you, holde your peace.
Bynge a waste, go you hence.
To the ruffian, to the devell.
The ruffian cly the, the devyll take thee.

The following cant words are also used in the work, though not included in the vocabulary :—

Abraham men, those that feign themselves to have been mad.
Autem mortes, married women, "they be as chaste as a cow."
Baudye baskets, women who go with baskets and cap cases on their arms.
Beck, a constable.
Bena bowse, good drink.
Beray, dung, dirty.
Booget, a travelling tinker's basket.
Bottel of strawe, a truss.
Bucks, baskets.
Chete, a thing.
Clapper dudgeon, another name for a palliard.
Cly, to take, or have.
Cofe, an individual.
Cranke, the falling evil.
Cuffin, a man.
Dell, a young wench.
Dock, to deflower.
Doxes, unchaste girls.
Factors, tax-gatherers.
Frater, a pretended collector of alms for some benevolent object.
Freshe water mariners, sham sailors.
Gerry, excrement.

Gyllot, a prostitute.
Jarkeman, one who makes writings and set seals for licences and passports.
Kynchin co, a young boy brought up to vagabondage.
Kynching morte, a little girl brought up to vagabondage.
Lycke, to beat.
Lyp, to lie down.
Morte, a woman.
Nase, drunken.
Pallyard, a beggar with manufactured sores.
Pelte, clothes.
Prigger of prauncers, a horse stealer.
Prygges, a name applied to drunken tinkers.
Quire bird, one who has lately come out of prison.
Rome, good.
Togemans, a cloak.
Watch : my watch, me ; our watch, us.
Whyddes, words.
Whip Jacke, a sham sailor.
Wylde roge, a born beggar.

The constituent elements of this vocabulary, and the cant words shown in the extract from the "Spyttel House," are in accordance with the historical testimony of the Statutes.

The Act 5 Edw. III., c. 14, affords evidence of the advent of the Welsh *Gwestwr*, or unbidden guest, into England prior to the year 1331; and we should accordingly expect to find that he had contributed his quota towards the formation of a secret vocabulary of rascaldom—an expectation which would be well founded, as a number of the words are Welsh.* The same anticipation would be verified with regard to Irish, Scotch, and Manx vagabonds who are legislated against at a later period; though as their languages are so much alike it is almost impossible to discriminate between their respective contributions, except in the case of the Lowland Scotch, which is also represented. The suppression of the monasteries sent a number of dissolute monks and monastic dependents wandering over the country, and they no doubt supplied the Latin roots found in the jargon. The gypsies contributed a few words; a small number of French words have probably come from the Channel Islands; and the remainder appear to be made up of provincial English, a few foreign words, and a good many ordinary words used in a metaphorical sense.

It seems curious that two of the words which represent the class as a whole, namely, the words *beggar* and *rogue*, should hitherto have eluded the skill of the etymologist in determining their origin.

As to the word *beggar*, in the Norman-French of our law courts we find the word *beogaunt*, begging, but the word is not French. *Webster* and other authorities appear to think that it must have sprung either from the Anglo-Saxon word *biddan*, to ask, to pray; or from *bœlg*, a bag, referring to the bag which mendicants carried for the purpose of conveying victuals or food. Another derivation, but an improbable one for many reasons, is from the *Béguards* or *Béguins* and the *Béguines*. The first two of these names appear to have been borne in the thirteenth century both by certain heretics who pretended to be immaculate, and also by converts to the fraternity of the third order of St. Francis. The *Béguines* were an order of nuns who are said to have derived their name from *Sainte Beggha* or *Begghe*, a Duchess of Brabant who adopted a religious life in 680, and died about 692.

The two most probable sources of the word appear to be the Welsh or the Swedish or Danish or German through the Lowland Scotch.

The Welsh *begegyr*, a drone, which is also used metaphorically

---

* In *Peers Ploughman*, circa 1362, *Griffin the Welshman* is described as sitting on the alehouse bench in company amongst others with Sisse the Sempstress; Wat the Warrener and his wife drunk; Tom the Tinker; Dawe the ditcher, with a dozen strumpets kept by pig-drivers and pickpockets and knavish tooth-drawers.

for an idle vagabond, as in the following extract, would aptly represent the occupation of the beggar :—

> "Mab Gwgan, mae begegyr
> Gyda chwi, o gedwch wyr."
>
> "Son of Gwgan, there is a drone with you : O Good men fly from him."
> *D. ab Gwilym, am y Bwa Bach* (circa 1369).

It should be noticed that until within the last hundred years the word is almost invariably spelt *begger*, which accords very closely with *begegyr*. On the other hand, we have in Swedish *begär*, desire, appetite ; in Danish *begjær*, to desire, to demand ; and in German *begier*, desire, longing ; all of which bear an analogy to the vocation of the beggar. One or other of these words may have found its way into our language through the Lowland Scotch, though there is no direct evidence of the fact. The origin of the word is evidently due to one or other of these sources, and I am inclined to award the palm to the Welsh, on account not only of the early introduction of Welsh slang into England, but also of the fact that *begegyr* is a descriptive noun, which the others are not.

Still it is not at all impossible that the noun and the verb may have sprung from different sources, the noun from the Welsh and the verb from the Danish.

As to the word *rogue*, which appears in our Statutes for the first time in the 14 Eliz., c. 5 (1572), *Lambard* in his *Eirenarcha*, published in the year 1602, says : " The woord Rogue is but a late Guest in our Law : for the elder Statutes call such a one, a valiant, strong or sturdy Begger and Vagabond, and it seemeth to be fetched from the Latin *Rogator*, an asker, or Beggar, and in which sense Martial the Poet long since used it saying :

> *Inter raucos ultimus Rogatores*
> *Oret caninas panis improbi buccas.*
>
> And ranged last among the roaring Rogues
> In vaine a morsell may he begge of bread
> So bad, as hungry Dogs disdaine to byte."

This derivation appears to be the one generally adopted by Horne Tooke, Dr. Johnson, Webster, and other commentators, almost the only other offered being the Icelandic *hrokr*, a rook ; a croaking. Now the word is a slang word, and therefore of low parentage. In the year 1567 the rogue is described as " carrying health and hypocrisy about him," as being a "picker and stealer," and as being ready "to bid a man forthwith to deliver all that he had, or else that he would with his staff beat out his brains." The signification of the descriptive title which he and his comrades would adopt would therefore have to accord with the characteristics of his vocation, for it must be remembered that "they gave names to such persons of their company according to the kind of life that he undertook."

Now in the Manx language we find the word *rueg*, the meaning of which, according to *Dr. Kelly*, the eminent Manx lexicographer, is "An enemy, a plunderer, an invader, a band of invaders. When Christianity was first established in the Isle of Man, the infidels that retired to the mountains and lived by plunder were called the *rueg;* and when a body of them appeared, the sentinel gave the alarm by calling *yn rueg, yn rueg.*"

This word is intimately allied with the *Gaelic, ruaig,* a pursuit; *ruaigair,* a pursuer, chaser, hunter; the *Erse, ruaig,* a chase, incursion, descent; *ruagaire,* an outlaw, a pursuer. It is the Lowland Scotch *rugger,* as in the following extract from a "Description of the Western Isles of Scotland in the year 1549," by Donald Monro. Speaking of Ronay, he says, "the same havein is guyed for fostering of theives, *ruggairs,* and reivairs." Though not of cognate origin, the Welsh *herw,* a going about for pillage; *herwr,* a depredator; *herwriaeth,* vagrancy; and *herwrian,* to lead a roving life, convey pretty much the same meaning. In former times the *porthiant herwr,* or subsistence of the fugitive, was a contribution levied by the lords marchers in certain districts towards the support of vagrants, with a view to preserve the country from their depredations.

The extracts from the "Spyttel House" show that "roger" * (the *g* evidently pronounced *hard*), another form of the word, was also early in use among the vagabond classes, which establishes a still closer relationship with the Erse *ruagaire.*

The meaning of the word would therefore be understood by the rascals of all these nationalities; and it consequently seems natural and feasible to conclude that the word is of Manx or Erse origin.

As regards the vocabulary, the Welsh or Cornish appear to have supplied the following:—

* See also the extract on p. 81.

Baudye, obscene ; *baw*, dirt, mire, excrement.
Bufe, a dog ; *bwch*, a buck, the male of several animals.
Bowng, a purse ; *bwng*, an orifice.
Clapper dudgeon,* a beggar with manufactured sores ; *dygan*, a chaunt, a hymn, a song. The clapper dudgeon evidently used the leper's alms basket with a *clapper* and chaunted his afflictions to the passers-by.
Fylche, to steal ; *yspeilio*, to rob † (Lowland Scotch, *pilk*, to pilfer, to take away).
Gan, a mouth ; Cornish, *ganow*, a mouth ; Welsh, *gen*, an opening, a jaw.
Gygger, a door ; *Gwyddor*, a gate.
To couch a hogshead, to lie down and sleep ; *hepiad, hephun*, a slumber or doze.
Lycke, to beat ; *lluchio*, to throw, to cast or fling about, or *llachio*, to throw or lay about, to cudgel.
Morte, a woman ; *modryb*, a matron ; *morwyn*, a virgin, a maid.
Mot huys is a brothel in Dutch, but *mot* is not a word of Dutch origin.
Quier, nought, bad, or evil ; *chwired*, craft, deceit, or cunning.
Skypper, a barn ; *ysgubor*, a barn.
Tryning, hanging ; *tranc*, cessation, end, decease, death.
Whyddes, words ; *Chwedle*, a saying or sentence ; *Chwedla*, to talk, to gossip.

The *Gaelic, Erse,* and *Manx* languages appear to be responsible for the following :—

Abraham man, a feigned madman. Gael. and Erse, *bramanach*, a noisy fellow.
Clewner, a master vagabond. G. *cluainear*, a cunning fellow, a hypocrite. E. *cluainire, cluainaire*, a seducer, a flatterer. M. *cleaynagh*, a tempter ; *cleaynaght*, knavery.
Cly, to take or have. Erse, *cloib*, a snatch.
Commission, a shirt. G. and E. *caimis*, a shirt.
Dock, to deflower. G. *torraich*. E. *toirrchigh*.
Iere, excrement. G. *inneir*, manure, dung, ordure.
Lybbege, a bed. G. and E. *leabadh*, Manx, *lhiabbee*, a bed.
Lyp, to lie down. G. and E. *luidhe*, a lying down.
Nosegent, a nun. G. *nuas*, from on high, and *gean*, a woman.
Pelte, clothes. G. and E. *peall*, a covering.
Towre, to see. E. *tòirigh*, G. *tòirich*, to search after, pursue.
Wyn, a penny. E. *pinghin*, M. *ping*, a penny.
Yaram, milk. G. *uaran*, fresh water.

The *Lowland Scotch* appears to have been the source of the following terms :—

Bottel of straw, a bundle of straw, from the Fr. *botteler*, to make into bundles. In Scotland the word is used both as a noun and a verb, in England as a noun only, the Scotch being evidently the older and more perfect usage.
Bucks, baskets. This appears to be an instance of compound metonymy. *Bouk* or *buck* originally signified a lye in which foul linen was steeped in order to its being cleansed or whitened. In course of time the bulk of linen so washed came to be called a *buck*, and the basket in which it was carried a *buck basket*, and finally in the present instance the name appears to have been re-transferred from the linen to the basket itself. *Hansom* for *Hansom cab* is an instance of simple metonymy of a similar character.

---

* Also called a " Pallyard."
† The change of *p* or *sp* to *f* is not uncommon. The Gr. *sphonggos* becomes the Eng. *fungus ;* Lat. *pileus*, Eng. *felt ;* W. *pysg*, A.S. *fisc*.

Bynge a waste, go you hence ; *Bynge, beenge*, to cringe, in the way of making much obeisance. This is evidently a transmutation of the preliminary to an act into the act itself, namely, the bow made on going away into the act of going away. *A waste* or *avast* (It. and Ger. *basta*, enough) seems to be added for the purpose of intensifying the meaning. A similar transmutation occurs in the meaning of the word *restive*, which originally meant at rest, or in a condition of stubbornness, but now in the case of horses signifies the frequent sequence of stubbornness, namely, restlessness or unruliness.

Chattes, the gallows ; *chats*, a cant name for the gallows (Aberdeen).

Cranke, the falling evil ; *crank*, infirm, weak, in bad condition.

Cyarum ; Keerie-oam, a game common in Perth. One of the boys, selected by lot, takes his station by a wall with his face turned to it and covered with his hands. The rest of the party run off to conceal themselves in the closes in the neighbourhood, and the last who disappears calls out *Keerie-oam*. The boy, who has his face to the wall then leaves his station, and searches for those who have hid themselves; and the first whom he lays hold of takes his place in the next game, which is carried on as the preceding one.—*Jamieson*.

Doxy, a prostitute ; *doxie*, lazy, restive, slow.

Dudes, clothes ; *duds*, rags, clothing. Regarding this word, *Jamieson* remarks : " It seems probable that a considerable number of what are called cant E. words or slang, and which are generally viewed as formed by the mere scum of society, have been borrowed by them from the lower classes residing in the different provinces by whom they have been transmitted from time immemorial. *Duds* seems to be of this description."

" He took out his knife, loot a' his *duddies* fa',
And he was the brawest gentleman that was amang them a'."
The Jolly Beggar, attributed to *James V.*

Fambles, hands ; *femmel*, to select the best, including the idea of the refuse being thrown out. Swedish *famn*, arms, embrace ; *famla*, to grope, to fumble. Danish, *famle*, to grope, to fumble, to finger, to handle.

Myll, to rob ; *mill*, to steal (Renfr.).

Rome, good ; *rum*, excellent in its kind. Swed. and Dan. *rum*, vast, large, wide.

Slate, a sheet ; *slait*, slitted, cut.

Strommell, straw ; *strammel*, straw. Dan. *strimmel*, slip, strip, ribbon, shred.

The Latin appears to have been the progenitor of the following :—

Bene, good ; *Bene*, excellent, well.
Gerry, excrement ; *gerræ*, trifles, stuff, nonsense.
Grannam, corn ; *granum*, grain, seed.
Nase, drunken ; *nausea*, sickness.
Patrico, a priest ; *patrice*, paternally.
Peck, meat ; *pecus*, cattle.
Quaromes, a body ; *corium*, a skin, hide.
Pannam, bread ; *panis*, bread (ac. *panem*).

Provincial English appears to have supplied the following :—

Beray, dung, dirty ; *bewray*, to defile with ordure.
Booget, a travelling tinker's basket ; *budget*, a basket.
Chete, an affix used in the formation of names such as *crashing chetes*, teeth ; *cackling chete*, a cock or capon, &c., which appears to be equivalent to the Gypsy affix " *engro*," *e.g. kaun-engro*, an ear fellow or hare, *ruk-engro*, a tree fellow or squirrel ; *pov-engro*, an earth thing or potato. The derivation seems

to be the A.S. *cið*, a germ, sprig, sprout, now employed in the common phrase, " the whole *kit* of them." The change of the initial *c* to *ch* is very common. (*Skeat*.)

Dup, to open ; *dup* (do open), to open :—

"Then vp he rose, and dond his close,
And dupt the chamber doore."—*Hamlet* (1604).

Feng, to steal, to snatch. A.S. *feng*, a grasp, a hug. Icel. *fengr*, haul, take, gain, booty.

Gage, a quart pot ; *gage*, a bowl or tub for cream.

Glymmar, fire. A.S. *gleam*, a trembling light, from *glawan*, to shine.

Kynchen co ⎫ A.S. *cyn*, offspring. O. Sax. *kind*. Modern English, *kid*,
Kynchen morte ⎭ a child.

Nygle, to have to do with a woman carnally ; *niggle*, to play with, to trifle.

The following words are probably of gypsy origin :—

Gyb, a writing ; *jib*, tongue. (Hin. *Jiv*.)
Lowre, money ; *luvvo*, money.
Maund, to ask or require ; *mang*, to beg. (Hin. *Māgna*.)
Salomon, an altar or mass, an oath ; *Sauloholomus*, an oath.

The following words may be of foreign extraction :—

Couch, to lie down. French, *coucher*, to lay, to lay down.
Nab, a head. Danish, *næb*, beak, bill.
Vyle, a town. French, *ville*, a town.

The undermentioned words evidently owe their origin to one or other of the sources indicated, but on account of the near resemblance of many of the root words it is almost impossible to identify the relationship with greater precision.

Beck, a constable. Welsh, *bwg*, Erse, *bocán*, Manx, *boag*, a bugbear.

Bowse, to drink. Erse and Gaelic, *baois*, water ; Dutch, *buysen*, to drink, great drafts, or quaff ; *buyse*, a gutter or channel ; Arabic, *būza*, beer.

Cant, to talk. Latin, *canto*, Welsh, *canu*, to sing.

Cassan, cheese. Latin, *caseum*, Welsh, *caws*, Manx, *caashey*, Gipsy, *kaes*, cheese.

Casters, a cloak. Latin, *casula*, Welsh, *casul*, a cloak, a chasuble.

Cove, Cuffin, an individual. Welsh, *cyfaill*, a friend, an associate, a companion ; Gaelic, *comhlan*, an assistant, a colleague ; Lowland Scotch, *coffe, cofe, coife*, a merchant, a hawker. This latter term is evidently allied to the German *kauf*, a purchase, a bargain ; *kaufmann*, a merchant, a tradesman. In Swedish *kofsa* means a wench.

Dell, a young wench. Welsh, *del*, pert, smart ; Lowland Scotch, *dilp*, a trollop, a slattern, from the Swedish *toelp*, a clown, an awkward fellow ; Provincial English, *dell*, a young wench. *Docking the dell*, dangling at a wench's tail.

"As interest or usurie plaieth the devil
So hil-back* and fil bellie biteth as evil :
Put dicing among them, and *docking the dell*,
And smell of a begger where ever ye dwell."

Good Husbandlie Lessons, by *Thomas Tusser*, 1577.

* Extravagance in apparel.

Dummerer, a pretended dumb man. Welsh, *dymunwr*, one who entreats or solicits ; Lowland Scotch, *domeror*, a madman (Teviotdale).

Gyllot, a prostitute. Lowland Scotch, *giglottis*, playful, wanton wenches; Provincial English, *giglot*, a romping wench.

" Yong *Talbot* was not borne
To be the pillage of a *Giglot* Wench."
Shakespeare, Hen. VI., Pt. I., 623.

Ken, a house. Persian, *khân*, for *khāna*, a house; Arabic, *kanāt*, the walls of a tent or canvas enclosure with which a sort of courtyard is formed in a camp ; a screen. Gypsy, *ken*, a nest ; Hebrew, *kin*.

Lag, water. Welsh, *llwch*; Erse, *logh*; Gaelic, *loch*, a lake.

Lap, milk. Welsh, *llaeth*; Erse, *lacd*, milk.

Make, a halfpenny. Provincial English, *mag*, or *make*; Lowland Scotch, *mag* or *maik*, a cant term for a halfpenny in the West of Scotland, especially among boys.

Pallyard, a beggar with manufactured sores. Gaelic, *paeled*, a plaister or salve ; French, *paillard*, a wanton, a rake, from *paille*, straw, the underlying idea, according to *Scheler*, being one who sleeps or wallows in the straw, an indication of idleness and beggary as well as of lewdness and debauchery.

Poppelars, porridge. Lowland Scotch, *poble*, to bubble or boil up like porridge ; Welsh, *pobi*, to bake, to roast, to toast; Cornish, *pobas*, to bake ; Latin, *pappo*, to eat pap.

Prygger, a thief. Provincial English or Lowland Scotch, *prig*, a thief (from the A.S. *priccian*, to prick).

Skew, a cup. Latin, *scutula*, a little dish or platter; Manx, *sgillad*, a small kettle ; Gip. *scourdilla*, a platter.

Togmans, a coat. Latin, *toga*, a covering, a garment; Lowland Scotch, *tokie*, an old woman's head-dress ; French, *toque*, a cap ; *toquet*, a head-dress.

In the extract from *Copland* the *patrico*, or priest, is termed *pattering cove*. If this is the original form of the expression the meaning would be the " muttering man," derived from the practice of the priests in reciting the *Pater Noster*, which up to the time of the Reformation they repeated in a low voice as far as " and lead us not into temptation," when the choir took it up.

In the same extract the Cant language too is termed *peddling French*, or petty French. This by no means implies that there was supposed to be any relationship between the languages, as amongst the lower orders the word French used to be a generic term for anything foreign or outlandish. A similar strain of meaning underlies the word *walnut*. Now the walnut-tree is a native of Persia, and is of course not a tree that grows against a wall, but the *Wealh* or Welsh, or foreign nut-tree. In Welsh the converse rendering occurs, as in that language the tree is styled *cneuen ffrengig*, or French nut-tree. Of 215 names of vagabonds in Harman's book, who are stated to travel in Essex, Middlesex, Sussex, Surrey, and Kent, 27 at least are undoubtedly of Welsh origin, and 7 of Irish or Scotch.

The following terms are evidently founded on metaphor :—

Belly chete, an apron ; *bleting chete* (bleating thing), a calf or sheep ; *cakling chete* (cackling thing), a hen ; *crashing chetes,* teeth ; *darkemans,* the night, and *lightmans,* the day ; *dewse a vyle* (deuce a town), the country ; *gentry cofe* and *gentry morte* (gentleman and gentlewoman) ; *glasyers,* eyes ; *hearing chetes,* ears ; *lowing chete,* a cow ; *mofling chete* (muffling thing), a napkin ; *mynt,* money ; *grunting chete* or *patricos kinchen* (priest's child), a pig ; *pratling chete,* a tongue ; *a prauncer,* a horse ; *quacking chete* (quacking thing) or red shank, a duck ; *quyer cramprings,* fetters ; *quier cuffin* (a queer or bad man), a magistrate ; *quire bird,* one lately come out of prison ; *quyer kyn* (queer or bad house), a prison ; *red shanke,* a drake or duck ; *Rome bowse* (good drink), wine ; *Rome mort* (good woman), the queen ; *Rome vyle* (good town), London ; *ruff peck* (rough meat), bacon ; *ruffian,* the devil ; *smelling chete* (smelling thing), the nose ; *stampes,* legs ; *stampers,* shoes ; *stow,* to hold ; *to cly the jerke* (to receive the jerk), to be whipped.

A similar strain of allegorical meaning is observable in the cant of other nations. For instance, in German cant *schwartz* (black) means night; *breitfuss* (broad foot), a duck ; *plattfuss* (flat foot), a goose ; and in French, *brune* (dark) means night, *cuit* (cooked) signifies condemned.

Margery prater, a hen, and *Roger* or *Tib of the Buttery,* a goose, seem to be pet names of the same type as *Tom tit, Jenny wren, Robin redbreast, Poll parrot, Dicky bird, Billy goat, Nanny goat, Jack ass,* and many others. *Madge Howlet,* for owl, occurs in the works of Ben Jonson and Taylor the water-poet.

"I'll sit in a barn with madge-howlet, and catch mice first."—*Every Man in his Humour.*

The personal pronouns seem to be formed by adding the word "watch" to the possessive pronouns. My watch, "me;" his watch, "he;" our watch, "us," as in the following examples :—

" I saye by the Salomon I will lage of it with a gage of bene bouse then cut to my nose watch."
" I swear by the masse I will washe it of with a quart of good drynke, then saye to me what thou wylt."
" That is beneshyp to our watche."
" That is very good for us."

The same system prevails in North Country cant in the present day : " my nabs," myself ; " his nabs," himself.

The purposely corrupt jargon of the scum of society must always present analytical difficulties to the etymological inquirer ; it will, however, be perceived that in the foregoing list a great many words are identified beyond the possibility of doubt, and the remainder are traced as nearly as human possibilities will admit.

Several cant words occur in the works of *Skelton,* whose poetry began to appear in 1483, so that they must have been in current use at the time he wrote.

For instance, he stigmatises the Duke of Albany as a "proude *palyarde.*" In "the boke of Phyllyp Sparowe" he uses the expression " to fyll *bougets* and males" (to fill baskets and trunks). In Elynour Rumming we find "her face all *bowsy*" (*i.e.* bloated by drinking), and—

"It was a *stall* to take
The deuyll in a brake,"

stall being used in the sense of a lure or decoy.

And he styles *Garnyche* a "*bawdy* babyone" (baboon).

The words bawd and bawderie are, however, to be found in *Chaucer.*

"This false theef, this Sompnour, quod the frere
Had alway *baudes* redy to his hond."

"In punishing of fornication
Of witchecraft, and eke of *bauderie.*"

Since the date of Harman's book great alterations have taken place in the Cant language; many words have dropped out of use, many more have been introduced.* For instance, Hebrew words have found their way into it through Jew "fences," or receivers of stolen goods; Italian words through the organ-grinders; Oriental terms through Hindoo vagabonds. In addition to this there are also varieties of cant known as *Back Slang, Centre Slang,* and *Rhyming Slang.* Back slang consists in pronouncing words as they are spelt backwards, *e.g.* nam = a man, namow = a woman.

In *Centre Slang* the central vowel of a word is taken as its initial letter, and letters or syllables are added to give the word a finish, as *lock* becomes *ockler; pitch, itcher,* and so on. *Er,* it need hardly be said, is a favourite cockney termination.

Rhyming Slang consists in finding a rhyme for the word intended, *e g. apples and pears,* stairs; *Cain and Abel,* a table.

Of modern cant, the origin of the following leading words deserve a passing notice:—

Billy, a silk pocket-handkerchief. Gaelic, *bille,* a rag.
Bone, to appropriate, to steal. Gaelic, *buain;* Erse, *buainim,* to cut, to reap, to loose.
Bull, a crown piece. Welsh, *bwl,* rotundity.
Buzz, to pick pockets. Welsh, *bysio,* to finger or touch with the fingers.
Cadger, a beggar. Banff. *cadger,* a hawker of fish; Manx, *cadjer,* a hawker.
Cly, a pocket. Erse, *claib,* a mouth.
Croaker, a beggar. Welsh, *crwydrwr,* a vagrant, a wanderer.
Doss, a bed. Banffshire, *dossick,* a small truss or bundle; Manx, *doss,* a bunch; *dossagh,* bushy, or perhaps Welsh, *diddos,* a shelter.

* In the seventeenth and eighteenth centuries many Dutch words were introduced. See extracts on pp. 627—31.

Fake, to cheat. Welsh, *ffug*, guile, deceit, fraud.
Gad, a going about. Welsh, *gad*, quitting or leaving.
Gammy, bad. Erse and Gaelic, *cam*, deceit; Manx, *cam*, crooked, bent; Welsh, *cam*, wrong, false, crooked.
Jagger, a gentleman. Erse and Gaelic, *sagart*, a priest.
Kip-house, a common lodging-house. Lowland Scotch, *kip*, a cant term for a brothel (Clydes). Welsh, *cwb*, a hut, a kennel.
Lurk, a going about with some species of imposture. Welsh, *llerch*, a fit of loitering.
Moll, a girl. Erse and Gaelic, *maol*, a servant; Manx, *meyl*, a female servant.
Scranning, begging. Erse and Gaelic, *scram*, a snatch, a grasp.
Shallow coves, fellows who go about half naked. Welsh, *salw*, frail, poor, ill, sick.
Smasher, a person who passes counterfeit coin. L. Scotch, *smacher*, trash.
Snid, sixpence. Erse and Gaelic, *sneidh*, little, small.
Twig, to understand. Gaelic, *tuig;* Erse, *tuigim*, to understand, perceive, discern.

The characteristics of the *crocus* or vagabond quack doctor appear to find a sardonically appropriate origin in the Erse *cruach-bhas*, a bloody death.

Modern cant also owes the undermentioned words to the gypsy tongue:—

Blowen, a flaunting hussy.
Bosh, a fiddle.

Cuttor, a sovereign.
Drum, a road, a street, a house.
Hook ·and snivey, an imposture by means of pretended illness and other dodges.
Muns, the mouth.
Pal, a companion, a friend.
Parny, rain or water.
Sturabin, a prison.

Bloen, a sister in debauchery.
Bosh, a fiddle, a contraction of Báshom-angri.
Cuttor, a piece, a guinea piece.
Drom, a road. Wallachian, *drom*.
Hukni, ringing the changes; the fraudulent changing of one thing for another.
Mui, face, mouth. (Hin. *munh*).
Pal, a brother. (Hin. *Pala*, a son).
Pani, water. (Hin. *Pani*).
Staripen, a prison.

The word *jingo* may also possibly have been introduced by the gypsies. It is the Basque word *Jinkoa*,* God, literally "He who is on high," and is used in that sense by the gypsies in the north of Spain and south of France. Another mode, however, by which the word might have travelled to England would be through the "many thousands of soldiers" who, *Matthew of Westminster* tells us, "were sent to the assistance of King Edward I. from Guienne and the Basque provinces and other foreign countries," for the purpose of completing the conquest of Wales in 1284.

Misplaced ingenuity is the leading characteristic of the vagabond, and nowhere is it more conspicuous than in the jargon of his calling.

* A contraction of *Jaungicoa*.

CHAPTER XXI.

THE MENDICANT OR BEGGING FRIARS.

Vagrant monks in the year 390—Institution of mendicant friars in 1209—John Wickliffe's opinion of them.

THE Abbé Fleury, in his "Ecclesiastical History," tells us that in the year 390, "Among the vagrant Monks, who at that time infested the East, may be reckoned the Massalian heretics, who made profession of renouncing the world, though really they were not all monks. . . . Those who bore the name of Christians, began about the reign of Constantius, but their origin is uncertain. They came from Mesopotamia, and some of them were at Antioch when St. Epiphanius wrote his treatise *Against Heresies*," i.e. A.D. 376. He ascribes their error to the extreme simplicity of some among them, who had taken in too literal a sense the precept of our LORD, of forsaking all to follow him, and selling their goods and distributing to the poor. They indeed abandoned everything; but they afterwards led an idle and vagabond life, asked alms, and lived together men and women promiscuously, sleeping in the open street during the summer nights. They never fasted, but would eat as early as eight or nine in the morning, and even before daybreak as they felt hungry. They rejected all manual labour as wicked, abusing these words of our Saviour, *Labour not for the meat which perisheth, but for that meat which endureth unto everlasting life.*" *

The modern institution of an order of mendicant friars seems to have originated with St. Francis of Assisium in the year 1209, who obtained the verbal approbation of Pope Innocent IV. Their leading characteristics were contempt of the world, renouncing of their own will, and mortification of their senses. They were to

* St. John vi. 27.

remain entirely destitute of all fixed revenues and possessions; though in process of time their number became a heavy tax on the people. The older orders of monks had at this time lapsed into luxury and indolence, and as these monks exhibited in their outward appearance and life more self-denial, learning, and religious zeal, they were soon regarded with the greatest esteem and veneration. Innocent III., to increase their respectability and usefulness, released them from the jurisdiction of the bishops, and rendered them responsible to the See of Rome only, and their privileges were confirmed by a bull of Pope Honorius III. in 1223. Admitted as confessors into the confidence of all classes, they gradually absorbed much of the power of the regular clergy. Their influence spread rapidly, but unfortunately their success made them arrogant and presumptuous. They declared that they had a divine impulse and that their indulgences were of superior efficacy and virtue, and that they had familiar intercourse with the saints, the Virgin Mary, and the Supreme Being. A spirit of hatred on the part of the clergy broke out against them, and at a General Council at Lyons, in 1272, Gregory X. reduced their many orders to four, namely, the Dominicans, Franciscans, Carmelites, and Augustinians. Their influence did not decrease for some time, but the determined hostility of the clergy coupled with the exposures of the Reformation at last completely undermined their prestige, and in the sixteenth century the newly instituted Society of Jesus practically usurped their functions.

John Wickliffe, in his "Treatise against the Orders of Friars," circa 1380, thus speaks of them:—

"Also *Friers* saien and manintainen, that begging is lawful, the which is damned by God both in the old testament & in the new. For in the fifth booke of holy writ God saies to his people *Algats a needy man an begger shal not bee amongst you.** Also the holy ghost tawght Salomon to pray these two thinges of God : *God make vanitie and leasinge wordes farre fro me, and give not to me begging or beggingnesse ; but give only thinges that beene needfull for my livelode : perauenture lest I be fulfilled, be drawen to renaye and saie who is Lord? As who say, I knowe no Lord : and lest I be compelled, or made of force by needines, to steale, and to forswere the name of my God.*†

"Also *Friars* beggen withouten need for there own rich Sect,

* Deut. xv. 7, 8.   † Proverbs xxx. 8, 9.

& not for there poore bedradden men that maie not goe and have no man to sende for their livelode: but rather drawen rich mens almes fro such poore men. And therefore charitie is outlawed among them, and so is God: & leasings, & covetise and Fiends beene enhabited among them, for they deceaven men in there almes to make costlie houses, not to harbour poore men but Lords, and mightie men. . . . .

"Also Friars maken our Lond lawles; for they leaden Clarks and namely rulen Prelats and Lords and Ladies and Commons also; and they beene not ruled by Godes lawe, ne lawes of the Church, ne lawes of the King. For they glosen Gods lawes as them likes, and been exempt fro Byshops and other ordinaries & leaden the Byshops of *Rome*, as them likes. And men saien they beene not liege men to the King, ne subject to his lawes. For thowgh they stealen mens children, it is said there goes no lawe uppon them, and that seemes wel; for they robben the Kings liege men by false begginge of sixtie thowsande marke by yeare as men dowbten reasonablie, & yet they be not punished therefore."

Mr. *Matthew*, in his introduction to the hitherto unprinted works of Wickliffe, thus comments on this condition of things:—

"Nothing can have been more trying to a parson who was doing his best to keep alive the flame of spiritual religion in his flock, than the visit of one of these vagrant friars, preaching a catch-penny sermon, shriving men of sins which they were ashamed to confess to their own pastor, and generally encouraging the belief that a few easy benefactions to the convent would take the place of penitence and good life. I would not for a moment suggest that friars were always or even mostly of such a type, but very many such were to be seen in the villages. Jealousy once aroused was likely to be increased by the reports of Wyclif's poor priests, between whom and the friars there was a constant rivalry which often came to open quarrelling. If we take into account besides the permanent antagonism between regulars and seculars at the University, from the influence of which Wyclif can scarcely have escaped, we shall find both public and personal causes enough to set him against the friars long before they led the attack on his sacramental doctrines."

CHAPTER XXII.

THE GYPSIES IN ENGLAND.

Various names by which they are known—Their origin—Arrival in England—Act of 1530-31 against them—Letter from Lord Cromwell to the President of the Marches in 1537—Letter to the Earl of Essex—Act of 1554.—Arrest of Gypsies in the reign of Elizabeth—Act of 156?-3 against them—Execution of Gypsies under this Act—Letter of Mr. Hext regarding them in 1596—Robbery of Gypsies by Tom Waters, a highwayman—Subsequent history, according to Borrow—Description of the English Gypsies in the years 1858-9 by a City Missionary—Their Homes—Ignorance—Gambling propensities—Drunkenness—Absence of marriage—Residence during the winter months—Condition of their children—Employments—Fortune-telling.

THE *Gypsies* are styled in the Lowlands of Scotland *Tinkler*, in the Highlands *Ceàrd* (tinker), in Wales *Sipsiwn* or Egyptians, in Ireland *Giofog*, which also means a female servant, and in the Isle of Man *Faaishleyder* (a fortune-teller, a juggler). In France they are styled *Bohémiens*, because they were believed to be Hussites expelled from their country; in Spain they are called *Gitanos* and *Zincali*, the meaning of which is believed to be *the black men of Zend or Ind;* in Italy *Zingari;* in Germany *Zigeuner*, or wanderers; in Holland *Heyden*, or heathens; in Denmark *Kjeltring*, or scoundrels; amongst the Moors and Arabs *Charami*, or robbers; in Hungary *Pharaoh nepek*, or Pharaoh's people, and *Cygani*; in Transylvania, Wallachia, and Moldavia, *Cyganis;* in Russia *Zigani;* in Turkey and Syria *Chingana;* and in Persia *Kauli* (an inhabitant of Cabul), *Luri* (Hindí *lohari*, a smith), *Karashmár* and *Karachi* (swarthy).

It is now placed beyond doubt that the Gypsies are of Indian origin and come from Hindostan, where such tribes as the *Bazeegurs*,* *Panchpeerees*,† *Cheere-Mars, Sumperas, Bundur Nachwya,*

---

* Jugglers or tricksters.
† Five Races or Families.

Qulundur, and *Dukyt* are still to be found, having the same characteristic and speaking a similar language. The English Gypsies call themselves *Romany Chals* and *Romany Chies*, that is, sons and daughters of Rome, a word derived from the Sanskrit Rama, a husband. The gypsies were established in Cyprus and the Grecian Archipelago in the beginning of the fourteenth century; they are found in Bohemia as slaves about 1370, and probably appeared there between 1245 and 1250. These were pioneers of the great body which appeared in Europe at the beginning of the fifteenth century, and the cause of whose migration is attributed to the cruelties practised upon the natives upon the conquest of India in 1400 by *Timur Lenc*, incorrectly styled *Tamerlane*. They have also been looked upon as springing from the degraded caste called pariahs, who from this cause may have gone into voluntary exile. This supposition is founded on the actual habits of the gypsies, which are contrary to the sanitary laws of the Indian religion, and, amongst others, on their custom of eating the flesh of animals dying of disease. Colonel David Richardson believes them to be nearly identical with the *Panchpeerees*, one of the Indian tribes included under the generic title of *Nuts*. Speaking, however, of their musical and sleight-of-hand characteristics, he says—

"The *Conjurors* or *Jugglers* who arrived in Europe about the thirteenth century, and who introduced the viol of three strings, appear to have been a race almost exactly similar to what the *Bazeegurs* are at this day.

"The word *juggler* may be of Indian extraction, although there exist, according to Johnson, both French and Latin originals against it, as well as the word *jug* in our own tongue. *Cups, jugs, mugs*, might all have been used at first by conjurors in various ways, whence to *juggle*, as a verb, stands on nearly the same ground with *handle*, and many more. In the Hinduwee dialects *jugg* is applied to a particular act of worship, which the *Bruhmuns* alone can perform, and by virtue of which they pretend to acquire sometimes preternatural powers. In this way they hope for the success of their *muntur* or incantations, and in imitation of them the Gypsies may have preserved the name, on their arrival in the European territories, with many other mysterious customs and lofty pretensions."

In the Middle Ages the gypsies were generally looked upon as Egyptians, of which their English name is a corruption. They themselves pretended that they had to accomplish a pilgrimage in expiation of certain crimes. It is probable that they acted thus in order to take advantage of the superstitious credulity of the age and procure for themselves toleration, which they not only effected by this means, but in many places also obtained safe-conducts.

The gypsies are generally supposed to have arrived in England about the year 1505.

The following account of their arrival appears in " The Art of Jugling or Legerdemaine," published in 1614 :—

" Heretofore we have runne over the two pestiferous carbuncles in the commonwealth, the Egiptians and common Canters : the poore Canters we have canvased meetly well, it now remaines to proceed where I left.

" These kind of people about an hundred yeares a goe, about the twentieth yeare of King Henry the eight,* began to gather an head, at the first heere about the Southerne parts, and this (as I am informed) and as I can gather was their beginning.

" Certaine Egiptians, banished their Contry (belike not for their good conditions) arived heere in England, who being excellent in quaint trickes and devises, not knowne heere at that time among us, were esteemed and had in great admiration, for what with strangenes of their atire and garments, together with their sleightes and legerdemaines, they were spoke of farre and neere, insomuch that many of our English loyterers joyned with them, and in time learned their craft and cosening. The speach which they used was the right Egiptian language, with whom our Englishmen conversing, at last learned their language. These people continuing about the country in this fashion, practising their cosoning art of fast and loose† and legerdemaine, purchased to themselves great credit among the country people, and got much by Palmistry and telling of fortunes; insomuch they pittifully cosened the poore Country Girles, both of money, silver spoones, and the best of their apparrel, or any good thing they could make, onely to heare their fortunes."

The statement that the English rogues learned the gypsy language is a mistake arising from the ignorance which prevailed as to the origin and nature of the gypsy tongue—an ignorance which was not dispelled for more than two centuries after their

* Evidently an error for Henry VII.
† For an explanation of this form of cheating, see note on p. 346.

arrival. Very few gypsy words were acquired by native vagabonds, as will be seen by a reference to the Cant vocabulary published by *Harman*.

By the year 1530-1 the gypsies had made themselves so generally obnoxious that the 22 Hen. VIII., c. 10, entitled " An acte concernyning Egypsyans " was passed to repress them. This Act recites—

"For as mouch as afore this tyme dyverse and many outlandysshe People callynge themselfes Egyptians usyng no crafte nor faicte of marchaundyse have comen into this Realme, and gone from Shire to Shire and Place to Place in greate company and used greate subtyll and crafty meanes to deceyve the people, beryng them in hande, that they by Palmestre coulde telle menne and womens fortunes, and so many tymes by crafte and subtyltie have deceyved the people of theyr money, and also hath comytted many and haynous felonyes and robberies to the greate hurte and deceyte of the people that they have comyn amonge : Be it therfore, by the Kynge our Sovereign Lorde the Lordes Spirituall and Temporall and by the Comons in thys presente parliament assembled, and by the auctorytie of the same, ordeyned establysshed and enacted that from hensforth no suche persones be suffred to come within this the Kynges Realme, And yf they do (than) they and every of them so doynge shall forfayte to the Kynge our Sovereign Lorde all theyr goodes and catalls and then to be comaunded to avoyde the Realme wythin xv. dayes next after the comaundement upon payne of imprisonament. . . . .

"Provyded alwaye that the Egyptians nowe beynge in thys Realme have monycyon to departe within xvj dayes after proclamacyon of thys estatute amonge them shalbe made, upon payne of imprisonament and forfeyture of theyr goodes and catells, and yf they then so departe that then they shall not forfayte theyr goodes nor any parte therof."

Though the Act styles them an outlandish people, it specifically deprives them of the benefit of the Statute 8 Hen. VI., c. 29, *de medietate linguæ*, and orders them to be tried by an English jury. Any goods they have taken are to be restored to the parties robbed, and of other goods seized in their possession one moiety is awarded to the seizor and the other to the King.

This Act, however, appears to have been inefficacious for the purpose intended, judged by the following letter from Cromwell to the Lord President of the Marches of Wales, dated December 5, 1537 :—

"After my right hertie commendacions, whereas the kinges majestie aboute a twelfmoneth past gave a pardonne to a company of lewde personnes within this realme calling themselves Gipcyans, for a most shamfull and detestable murder commytted amonges them, with a speciall proviso inserted by their owne consentes, that onles they shuld all avoyde this his graces realme by a certeyn daye long sythens expired, yt shuld be lawfull to all his graces offycers to hang them in all places of his realme where they myght be apprehended, without any further examynacion or tryal after fforme of the lawe, as in their lettres patentes of the said pardon is expressed. His grace, hering tell that they doo yet lynger here within his realme, not avoyding the same according to his commaundement and their owne promes, and that albeit his poore subjects be dayly spoyled, robbed, and deceyved by them, yet his highnes officers and ministres lytle regarding their dieuties towardes his majestye, do permyt them to lynger and loyter in all partys, and to exercise all their falshodes, felonyes, and treasons unpunished, hathe commaunded me to signifye unto youe that his most dreade commaundement is that ye shall laye diligent espiall throughowte all the partes there aboutes youe and the shires next adjoyning, whether any of the sayd personnes calling themselfes Egipcyans, or that hathe heretofore called themselfes Egipcyans, shall fortune to enter or travayle in the same. And in cace youe shall here or knowe of any suche, be they men or women, that ye shall compell them to repair to the next port of the see to the place where they shalbe taken, and eyther wythout delaye uppon the first wynde that may conveye them into any parte of beyond the sees, to take shipping and to passe to owtward partyes, or if they shall in any wise breke that commaundment, without any tract to see them executed according to the kinges hieghnes sayd lettres patents remaynyng of recorde in his chauncery, which with these shalbe your discharge in that behaulf: not fayling taccomplishe the tenour hereof with all effect and diligence, without sparing uppon any commyssion, licence, or placarde that they may shewe or aledge for themselfes to the contrary, as ye tender his graces pleasure, which also ys that youe shall gyve notyce to all the justices of peax in that countye where youe resyde, and the shires adjoynant, that they may accomplishe the tenour hereof accordingly. Thus ffare ye hertely wel. From the Neate, the vth day of December, the xxix^th yere of his majesties most noble regne

"Your lovyng ffreende,

"Thomas Crumwell.

"To my verye good lorde, my lorde of Chestre, president of the counsaile of the Marches of Wales."

Another letter of the same period shows that a good many Gypsies were deported to Norway.

"*To Thomas earl of Essex, lord prevey seal.*

"Right honorable and my singuler good lorde, my dutie remembred, this is to advertise your honorable lordshipp that one maister Paynell, baylyff of Bostone, is com bi your lordshippes commaundment, as he seithe, for to convey up certeyne persones namynge them sellffes Egiptians that shulde be here in prison at Bostone. So it is, right honorable lorde, that the Mondaie in the Rogacion weeke laste paste, there cam to Bostone foure Egiptians whiche did com the daie before from the towne of Lenn, whiche forseide persones the undermarshall of the kynges marshallsee caried from hence to London to your lordshipp from other of ther company that wer here then in prisone before Cristynmas laste paste, and the reste of their company wer shipped by the kynges commaundement (as your lordshipp knoweth) from Bostone and landed in Norwey. And now at these persones commynge laste to Bostone, the constables of the same town immediatly not onely sett them in the stockes as vagaboundes, but also serched them to their shertes, but nothinge cowde be found uppon them, not so muche as wolde paie for their mete and drynke, nor none other bagge or baggage, but one horse not worthe iiij^s; and then I did examen them why thei cam hither, and did not get them owte of the kynges realme, as other of their company was, and thei shewed me that of late thei were demytted owte of the marshallsee where thei wer in prisone, and commaunded bi your lordshipp (as thei seide) to departe owte of the realme as shortely as thei myght gett shippinge. And thei thinkinge to have had shippinge here at Bostone as their company

A Stockes to staye sure and safely detayne,
Lasy lewd Leuterers that lawes do offend:
Impudent persons, thus punished with payne,
Hardly for all this, do mean to amende.

STOCKING AND WHIPPING (1567)

had, did com hither, and here beynge no shippinge for them, the forseide constables of Bostone did avoide them owte of the town as vagaboundes towards the nexte portes, which be Hull and Newcastell. And this I certefie your lordship of truethe, as knowes our Lorde, who ever preserve your honorable lordshipp. Written at Bostone the Thursdaie in Whitson weeke.

"By yower oratour with my pore servys

"Nicolas Robertson."

Notwithstanding this partial deportation of the gypsies others speedily took their places, which in the reign of Mary occasioned the passing of another Statute against them, the 1 & 2 Phil. and Mar., c. 4 (1554), which recites the Act of Hen. VIII., and then states that "dyvers of the sayd Companie and suche other lyke persons not fearing the penaltie of the said Statute, have enterprised to come over againe into this Realme using their olde accustomed develishe and noughty practises and devises, with suche abhominable lyving as is not in any Christian Realme to be permitted named or knowen." It then enacts a penalty of £40 on any one willingly bringing them in; Egyptians so brought remaining one month and those already in the kingdom who do not depart in forty days are declared felons without benefit of sanctuary or clergy. Exception is made in favour of such as shall leave that "noughtye idle and ungodly lyef and company, and be placed in the service of some honest and able Inhabitante."

In "The Art of Jugling," the effects of the Act are thus described—

"These Acts and Statutes now put forth, and come to their hearing, they devide their bands and companies, into divers parts of the realme: for you must immagine and know that they had about two hundred roagues and Vagabonds in a regiment: and although they went not altogether, yet they would not be above two or three miles one from the other, and now they dare no more bee known by the name of Egiptians, nor take any other name upon them then poore people. But what a number were executed presently upon this statute you would wonder: yet notwithstanding all would not prevaile: but stil they wandred, as before up and downe, and meeting once in a yeare, at a place appointed: sometimes at the Devils arse in peak in Darbishire, & otherwhiles at Ketbrooke by Blackheath, or elsewhere, as they agreed stil at their meeting."

At the commencement of the reign of *Elizabeth* instructions appear to have been issued for active measures against Gypsies and other vagabonds, as we find the Queen on the 31st August, 1559, writing to James, Lord Mountjoy, to thank him for having stayed and arrested a great number of vagabonds using the manner of the Egyptians. On the 5th September Richard Weston and Richard Harper write to the Council regarding proceedings against the "Egyptians" at the assizes at Dorchester. It is found that they came out of Scotland into England. On the 23rd of the same month Lord Mountjoy writes to the Queen regarding the proposed indictment of these vagabonds, and says that the lawyers are of opinion that they are not chargeable with felony, because they did not come from beyond the seas.

On the 26th of October George Jones, escheator of the county of Gloucester, certifies that he has apprehended certain persons called Egyptians whose names he specifies.

This was followed in the year 1562-3 by a still more severe enactment against the gypsies, the 5 Eliz., c. 20 (1562-3), which is entitled "An Acte for the Punishement of Vagabondes callyng themselfes Egiptians." It recites that under the 1 & 2 Phil. & Mar., c. 4, "there ys a scruple and doubte risen whether suche persons as being borne wthin this Realme of Englande or other the Quenes Highnes Dominions, and are or shall become of the Fellowship or Companie of the said Vagaboundes, by transforming or disguising themselves in their Apparell or in a certaine contrefaite Speache or Behaviour, are punishable by the said Acte in like maner as others of that sort are, being Strangers borne and transported into this Realme of Englande;" and enacts that the "sayd Statute concerning these Vagaboundes shall contynue remayne and bee in full Force Strengthe and Effecte." It also enacts that all persons found disguised in the company of vagabond Egyptians for one month shall be deemed felons, and "suffer Paynes of Deathe Losse of Landes and Gooddes as in cases of Felonye," without benefit of clergy. The Act is not to extend to children under fourteen and prisoners in custody. Persons born in the realm are not compellable to quit it under 1 & 2 Phil. & Mar., c 4, but are only constrained to leave their naughty, idle, and ungodly life and company, and to place themselves in some honest service, or to exercise themselves in some lawful work, trade, or occupation.

A large number of gypsies must have been executed under this Act, as *Harman*, in his "Caveat for Cursetors," writing in the year 1567, says—

"I hope their synne [speaking of English vagabonds] is now at the hyghest; *and that as short and as spedy a redresse wylbe for these, as hath bene of late yeres for the wretched, wily, wandering vagabonds calling and naming themselves Egiptians*, depely dissembling and long hyding and covering their depe, decetfull practises,—feding the rude common people, wholy addicted and geven to novelties, toyes, and new inventions,—delyting them with the strangenes of the attyre of their heades, and practising paulmistrie to such as would know their fortunes: And, to be short, all theves and hores (as I may well wryt),—as some have had true experience, a number can well wytnes, and a great sorte hath well felte it."

The severity with which the gypsies were treated was due not only to their thievish propensities, but also to the hostility of the Church on account of their heathenish practices, and to the popular fears and delusions regarding sorcery and witchcraft.

In 1569 we find Thomas Andrew writing from Winwicke, Northamptonshire, to the Council, explaining the reason of the delay in making a return relative to vagabonds, unlawful beggars, rogues, and Egyptians, and on the 27th April, 1571, we find there is a record of a Bill against "disguised priests," or professors of the Romish religion, being found in England, disguised in the apparel of serving-men, or mariners; and for the punishment of gypsies remaining in England.

The repressive measures against the gypsies appear after a time, however, to have been gradually relaxed, as we find Mr. Edward Hext, a justice of the peace for Somersetshire, writing to the Lord Treasurer in the year 1596 to the following effect :—

"EGYPTIANS.

"Experience teacheth, that the execution of that godly law upon that wicked sect of rogues, the Egyptians, had clean cut them off; but they seeing the liberties of others, do begin to spring up again: and there are in this country of them, but upon the peril of their lives. I avow it, they were never so dangerous as the *wandering soldiers*, or other stout rogues of England: for they went visibly in one company, and were not above thirty or forty of them in a shire. But of this sort of wandering people, there are three or four hundred in a shire: and though they go by two or three in a company, yet all or the most part of a shire do meet, either at fairs or markets, or in some alehouse, once a week. And in a great hay house, in a remote place, there did resort weekly forty, sometimes sixty; where they did roast all kind of good meat. The inhabitants being wonderfully grieved, by their rapines, made complaint at our last Easter sessions, after my lord Chief justice's departure: precepts were made to the tithings adjoining for the apprehension of them. They made answer, they were so strong that they durst not adventure them: whereupon precepts were made to the constables of the shire; but not apprehended, for they have intelligence of all things intended against them. For there be of them that will be present at every assize, sessions, and assembly of justices, and will so clothe themselves for that time, as any should deem him to be an honest husbandman: so as nothing is spoken, done, or intended to be done, but they know it. I know this to be true, by the confession of some.

"And they grow the more dangerous in that they find they have bred that fear in justices, and other inferior officers, that no man dares to call them into question. And at a late sessions, a tall man, a sturdy and ancient traveller, was committed by a justice, and brought to the sessions, and had judgment to be whipped, he, present at the bar, in the face and hearing of the whole bench, swore a great oath, that if he were whipped, it should be the dearest whipping to some that ever was. It strake such a fear in him that committed him, as he prayed he might be deferred until the assizes; where he was delivered without any whipping or other harm, and the justice glad he had so pacified his wrath. And they laugh in themselves at the lenity of the law, and the timorousness of the executioners of it." *

Captain Smith in his "History of Highwaymen" gives the following account of a robbery committed on gypsies by one Tom Waters, a highwayman, about the year 1685. It serves to illustrate the practices of the gypsies at that period:—

* Strype.

"The first Exploit in this kind which he committed was on about twenty or thirty gypsies, whom he seeing to come out of a Barn early one Morning near *Bromley* in *Kent*, he rid up to them; and commanding the strolling Crew to stand, or otherwise he would shoot half a score or dozen of them thro' the Head, they obey'd his Command: But when he next order'd them to undo their Purse-strings, there was as great a Holo-loo set up by them, as among the wild *Irish* for the Loss of a Cock or a Hen; they began to beseech his Pity and Compassion in their shim-sham broken Gibberish, telling him that they would tell him his Fortune without crossing their Hands with a Piece of Silver. Quoth *Tom, a Plague on you for a Parcel of cheating Rogues and Whores, I know it is my Fortune to be hang'd, if I don't mend my Manners: Therefore you must not put your Laradiddles upon me, by telling me my Fortune will be lucky, good, good and prosperous; come, come, down with what you have presently, or else I shall send all your Souls to the Devil this Moment.* When this juggling Tribe found he was resolutely bent to take what they had, they fell to emptying their Purses and Pockets of Silver Spoons, Silver Brandy Tasters, and Gold Rings, which, without doubt, they had stollen from some silly People, whom they drew in up and down the Country to have their Fortunes told them; which Moveables, with what Money he got besides of them, came to above 60 Pounds; but such an Outcry they made for their Loss, that several Rusticks running with Clubs, and Flails, and Pitchforks, to see what was the Occasion of this Sorrowful Lamentation, *Tom* met them, and saying to them, That whilst some of the Gypsies there before them was telling them his Fortune, they had pick'd his Pocket of a very considerable Value, which he could not get again of them, till he had whipt some of them almost within an Inch of their Lives. *Truly* (replied the Country-men) *you did very well, Sir; for there is not such a Pack of Thieves in Hell, as them Gypsies be.* So *Tom* putting Spurs to his Horse, he made the best of his way, before the strolling Jugglers could come up to tell the Country-Fellows their sad and lamentable Story."

Borrow, in his interesting work, "Romano Lavo Lil, or Wordbook of the English Gypsy," gives the following clear and accurate account of their subsequent history :—

"Throughout the reign of Elizabeth there was a terrible persecution of the gypsy race; far less, however, on account of the crimes which were actually committed, than from a suspicion which was entertained that they harboured amidst their companies priests and emissaries of Rome, who had come to England for the purpose of sowing sedition, and inducing the people to embrace again the old discarded superstition. This suspicion, however, was entirely without foundation. The gypsies call each other brother and sister, and are not in the habit of admitting to their fellowship people of a different blood, and with whom they have no sympathy. There was, however, a description of wandering people at that time, even as there is at present, with whom the priests, who are described as going about, sometimes disguised as serving-men, sometimes as broken soldiers, sometimes as ship-wrecked mariners, would experience no difficulty in associating, and with whom, in all probability, they occasionally did associate —the people called in Acts of Parliament, sturdy beggars and vagrants, in the old cant language Abraham men, and in the modern, Pikers. These people have frequently been confounded with the gypsies, but are in reality a distinct race, though they resemble the latter in some points. They roam about like the gypsies, and, like them, have a kind of secret language. But the gypsies are a people of Oriental origin, whilst the Abrahamites are the scurf of the English body corporate. The language of the gypsies is a real language, more like the Sanscrit than any other language in the world; whereas the speech of the Abrahamites is a horrid jargon, composed for the most part of low English words used in an allegorical sense—a jargon in which a stick is called a crack; a hostess, a rum necklace; a barmaid, a dolly-mort; brandy, rum booze; a constable, a horny. But enough of these Pikers, these Abrahamites. Sufficient to observe that if the disguised priests associated with wandering companies, it must have been with these people, who admit anybody to their society, and not with the highly exclusive race the gypsies.

"For nearly a century and a half after the death of Elizabeth, the gypsies seem to have been left tolerably to themselves, for the laws are almost silent respecting them. Chies, no doubt, were occasionally scourged for cauring, that is filching gold and silver coins, and Chals hung for grychoring, that is horse-stealing; but those are little incidents not much regarded in gypsy merripen.*
They probably lived a life during the above period tolerably satis-

* *Merripen* means life, and likewise death.

factory to themselves—they are not an ambitious people, and there is no word for glory in their language—but next to nothing is known respecting them. A people called gypsies are mentioned, and to a certain extent treated of, in two remarkable works—one a production of the seventeenth, the other of the eighteenth century—the one entitled the 'English Rogue, or the Adventures of Meriton Latroon,' the other the 'Life of Bamfylde Moore Carew;' but these works, though clever and entertaining, and written in the raciest English, are to those who seek for information respecting gypsies entirely valueless, the writer having evidently mistaken for gypsies the Pikers, or Abrahamites, as the vocabularies appended to the histories, and which are professedly vocabularies of the gypsy language, are nothing of the kind, but collections of words and phrases belonging to the Abrahamite or Piker jargon. At the commencement of the last century, and for a considerable time afterwards, there was a loud cry raised against the gypsy women for stealing children. This cry, however, was quite as devoid of reason as the suspicion entertained of old against the gypsy communities of harbouring disguised priests. gypsy women, as the writer had occasion to remark many a long year ago, have plenty of children of their own, and have no wish to encumber themselves with those of other people. A yet more extraordinary charge was, likewise, brought against them—that of running away with wenches! Where were they to stow them in the event of running away with them, and what were they to do with them in the event of being able to stow them? Nevertheless, two gypsy women were burnt in the hand in the most cruel and frightful manner, somewhat about the middle of the last century, and two gypsy men, their relations, sentenced to be hanged for running away with a certain horrible wench of the name of Elizabeth Canning, who, to get rid of a disgraceful burden, had left her service and gone into concealment for a month, and on her return, in order to account for her absence, said that she had been run away with by gypsies. The men, however, did not undergo their sentence, for ere the day appointed for their execution arrived, suspicions beginning to be entertained with respect to the truth of the wench's story, they were reprieved, and, after a little time, the atrocious creature who had charged people with doing what they neither did nor dreamt of doing, was tried for perjury, convicted, and sentenced to transportation.

"But though gypsies have occasionally experienced injustice, though Patricos and Sherengroes were hanged by dozens in Elizabeth's time on suspicion of harbouring disguised priests, though gypsy women in the time of the Second George, accused of running away with wenches, were scorched and branded, there can be no doubt that they lived in almost continual violation of the laws intended for the protection of society; and it may be added, that in this illegal way of life, the women have invariably played a more important part than the men. Of them, amongst other things it may be said that they are the most accomplished swindlers in the world, their principal victims being people of their own sex, on whose credulity and superstition they practise.

"But gypsyism is declining, and its days are numbered. There is a force abroad which is doomed to destroy it, a force which never sleepeth either by day or night, and which will not allow the Roman people rest for the soles of their feet. That force is the Rural Police, which had it been established at the commencement instead of towards the middle of the present century would have put down gypsyism long ago. But, recent as its establishment has been, observe what it has produced. Walk from London to Carlisle, but neither by the road's side, nor on heath or common, will you see a single gypsy tent. True gypsyism consists in wandering about, in preying upon the Gentiles, but not living amongst them. But such a life is impossible in these days; the Rural Force will not permit it. "It is a hard thing, brother," said old Agamemnon Caumlo to the writer several years ago, "it is a hard thing, after one has pitched one's little tent, lighted one's little fire, and hung one's kettle by the kettle-iron over it to boil, to have an inspector or constable come up, and say, 'What are you doing here? Take yourself off, you gypsy dog!' A hard thing, indeed, old Agamemnon; but there is no help for it. You must e'en live amongst the Gorgies."

The social condition and habits of the English gypsies is graphically depicted in the following account of them written by a City Missionary in the years 1858-59.

1858.

"Borrow says, 'They everywhere exhibit the same tendencies and hunt for their bread by the same means as if they were not of the human race, but rather of the animal species. In no part of the world are they found engaged in the cultivation of the earth, or in the service of a regular master; but in all lands they are jockeys or thieves or cheats, and if ever they devote themselves to any toil or trade it is assuredly in every material point one and the same.' This is a very true description of them as they have come under my notice. Basket-making, caning chair-seats, skewer, mat, and peg making, is the business they follow about London.

"The homes of this peculiar people are houses, vans, or tents, though but few occupy houses. Those that do, however, either permanently, or only during the winter, generally select the very lowest neighbourhoods for the place of their abode,—often amongst thieves and pickpockets, under wretched roofs, in crowded courts or lanes, where distress and want conceal themselves from the sunlight, and where sorrow in garrets languishes—neglected places, just in contrast with their country residence, which is generally where 'sweet in the summer air is the odour of flowers.'

"In a single little room two, three, and four families of them are often cooped up, with no bed but straw, shavings, or old rags, with no chairs or tables in some cases, and in others just an old table and a broken seat or two. In the midst of filth and discomfort in such abodes they manage to drag out what to lookers-on appears a miserable existence, though long exposure to it in many instances, it would seem, has taken away its keen edge to them.

"The vans and tents occupied by the largest number of them are often found by the road-side, in lanes, fields, and woods, or on a small patch of land, for which they pay a small rent. Families numbering from four to twelve persons are often found in these vans.

"Their tents are little places varying in size, some covering a space about 5 feet by 8 feet, others 6 feet by 10 or 12 feet. Many are not more than half this size, and they are constructed so low that one has to enter them cat-fashion, on all fours. Yet these places compose their bed-room, dressing-room, kitchen, washhouse, and workshop. Here they live in common fellowship with dogs, cats, fowls, birds, and vermin. Many of these hovels are very cesspools of filth; and as they generally have a fire in the middle of the tent, to enter it is to get covered with blacks, as there is no vent for the smoke and dust, save a hole in the top of the fabric. These portable habitations, with their ragged inmates, are moved about to the races and fairs, and wherever wandering tastes may lead.

"Such homes, and the wandering life to which they are adapted, must render their inmates the easy prey of fearful ignorance and frightful immorality. And that such is the case, my visits amongst them during the past year furnish ample illustration.

"Of course the circuit of my district has necessarily been large; taking in Woodford, Loughton, Barkingside, Wanstead, Barking, Forest-gate, Stratford, Barking-road, Bow-common, Hackney-wick, Holloway, Blackheath, Greenwich, Plumstead-common, Streatham, Norwood, Wandsworth, Wimbledon, Putney and Barnes-common, Hammersmith, Chiswick, Kensington Potteries, Paddington, Battersea, Shoreditch, and Borough. All these are regular stations, where I generally meet with gypsies. In addition to these places I visit the hop-gardens in Kent and Surrey during the hop-picking season; also the fairs in the neighbourhood of London, with Epsom races, in quest of gypsies.

"Now for a word respecting the ignorance of the gypsy race. In speaking to an old gypsy woman, about ninety years of age, a short time ago, in reply to the question, 'Can you read?' she replied, 'Read, sir, how's the like of us to learn to read, living under a hedge, or in a bush? We never stopped long enough in a place to larn anything. Our longest stay is when we lay in.' This accounts for so few of them being able to read. As the result of a careful calculation, out of 462 persons, which made up 102 families, only 12 were able to read. In taking these numbers I found one encampment composed of 40 persons, not one of whom could read.

"Their business is duplicity. Frequenting fairs and races for gambling, fortune-telling, and swindling purposes must tend to render them averse and blind to all that is good, and prone to all that is ill.

"By gambling many of them come to ruin. One gypsy man, whom I know well, and who is now just a remove from beggary, told me once he lost 75*l.* in one day gambling at Epsom races. He also told me that several times taking his van to a fair he had come home, having lost his van and money, and pledged some of his clothes. And all this through gambling. He also observed that he had sometimes gained, but that the gold he gained was not worth '5s. a peck,' for somehow or other it never seemed to do him any good.

"Drunkenness again is a frightful vice amongst the gypsy tribe. This, like an unsightly tumour on the human form, absorbs all the real nourishment and comfort from many of their humble homes, and gives them nothing but weakness, poverty, and discontent in return. I have several times gone into an encampment and met men and women with black eyes and scarred faces, the cause of which has been drunkenness. When I have spoken to them about it they have given me to understand that when the beer is in the wit is out. One man told me he had spent many a 5l. at a sitting in beer and spirits. Another spent 3l. for weeks regularly. And another declared that for 5 years he paid regularly 1l. weekly for his beer-score. Several of them have assured me that for months and months they never went to bed sober. This is specially the case with those who go out as musicians to fiddle at low beer-shops. And not only the men, but the women, many of whom are addicted to smoking, are given to the fearful habit of drinking. At fairs they often make good gains in their trade, and then they indulge greatly in drinking. It is often the case that at these places of common meeting, whilst half drunk, they fight with each other and pay off old grudges. Wives will encourage their husbands, and parents their children, in this savage sport. Some of them take delight not only in dog-fighting and cock-fighting, but also in fighting with each other.

"But few gypsies are married. Some of them are living with each other, and have very large families, but do not seem to see any crime in thus living. One man told me, a short time ago, seriously, that he did not see any harm in leaving a woman when you were tired of her and taking up with another. I know some of them who are unmarried appear faithful to those they take as a companion, but I fear many of them are very unfaithful to each other.
"1859.

"The home of the gypsy (if such an apology for a home is entitled to a name so suggestive of sweet associations), which he finds on the desert waste, down the shady lane, or in the open field, is a miserable little van, or more often a tent; that is, a construction of ragged canvas or blankets drawn tightly over a few bent sticks projecting from the earth, and scarcely high enough to admit of a man's standing erect within its enclosure; whilst his stature will measure its width, and often more than half its length. There are small openings in the tops of these tents for the escape of the smoke from the fire enkindled upon the earth inside the chimneyless dwelling. But at times they are so filled with fumes of smoke as to pain the eyes, rendering breathing difficult, cover the person with blacks, and make a visit most disagreeable. The tent beds are composed of straw, dried leaves, or old rags, spread upon the earth, having for a pillow a block of wood; or, like Jacob's pillow when he had his vision of the descending and ascending angels, a stone. Of course such places are on the most intimate terms with filth and vermin. So much is this the case that many times the writer, after rising from a seat on the tent-bed, from the bottom of a tub turned upside down, or from a block cushioned with a gypsy garment, on leaving the tent on all fours, has found himself possessed of a sad cargo of live stock of varied kinds, which have been introduced to his home much to the annoyance of his forbearing wife and all lovers of cleanliness.

"Such homes may be interesting and romantic, as furnishing in the nineteenth century specimens of human beings, isolated from the rest of society, and living in a state of primitive simplicity, and destitution of domestic comforts, which admits of striking comparison with the ancient Britons we read of in our school days, who stained their bodies with a seaweed called woad, and roamed about like Tartars, living in huts formed of boughs of trees in the manner of arbours, &c. To such homes the gypsies are attached. Hence still, when the evening shades draw on, the old people, in company with their young brood, may be seen squatted around a log-fire telling traditional tales about the wild freedom of their forefathers long years agone, and rejoicing in the fact, that though the laws and the rural police are so severe upon the poor gypsy, driving him from place to place, as though he belonged not to the human species, he still holds his home in the tent, pitched in the green field, and midst the music of the woods. I ought to state here that some of the gypsies during the winter months take up their tents and live in houses. But when they do so, they make the place of their abode in the lowest parts of the metropolis. They leave the country and suburban districts of London, as Epping Forest, Woodford, Stratford, Bow Common, Hackney Wick, the Potteries, Hammersmith, Barking-road, Greenwich,

Wandsworth, Barnes, and Putney Common, Wimbledon, Streatham, in all of which places I find them some time during the year, and make their dwelling in some low court in Kent-street, Shoreditch, and Golden Lane, St. Luke's; where two and three families of them will huddle together in one small room, with no chairs, tables, or beds, all, themselves and the missionary who visits them, either having to stand or squat on the floor for a seat. Moreover, they shut these rooms so closely, that the poisoned and heated atmosphere causes them often to exchange the town for the country, wan and wasted, if not ill. But to pass on, whatever of romance belongs to the gypsy home, to the enlightened mind the thought of its moral influence throws a sad gloom over the picture.

"The idea is most repulsive, of large families bundled together in the space above suggested, in common and constant fellowship with dogs, cats, fowls, birds, and vermin; the one room of abode constituting the bedroom, dressing-room, wash-house, kitchen, workshop, &c. It is easy to perceive that such a home must prove the slaughter-house of virtue, and the nursery of vice and licentiousness. And forming my opinion from what I have seen of gypsy life, its general character and pursuits, I am sorry to state that it is just what such a nursery might be expected to yield. Gypsyism has been described as deception, cheating, and flattery, and I must say I am constantly meeting with varied and sad illustrations of the accuracy of such a description.

"There are a few light employments which the more industriously-inclined of the gypsies follow. But I do not know such a thing as a gypsy tailor, carpenter, or stonemason, or following any trade which would tend to locate them. Numbers of the men spend many of their days in idleness, lounging in their tents, or in the neighbourhood of public-houses.

"The children, with heads capless and rough as the back of a dirty Newfoundland dog, their feet shoeless, or slopping about in an old pair of men's boots, and their persons covered with rags and filth of long standing, present themselves before the public as objects for charity, which, when obtained, often only feeds the sloth and vice of their parents.

"The employments at which the men are most active are donkey-racing, cockshying, gambling, and fiddling at races, fairs, and low public-houses. At the latter places their musical talents are called into requisition to lead on the giddy dance and bold song, and to entertain at raffles and suppers. On such occasions their pay is generally 2s. a night, with as much beer and spirits as they like to drink, which sometimes reaches an astonishing quantity. A man, who says he drinks moderately, told me that when playing at a raffle he drank a pint of rum, besides a great quantity of beer, and at another time the same man said he drank twenty-two half-quarterns of rum in about one hour and a half. It is very often the case that they get drunk on such occasions, fall into a disturbance, return home with black eyes and scarred faces, and sometimes to beat their wives.

"But it is the business of the woman to make the principal part of the living. Hence an old gypsy man observed to me a short time ago, 'I should not like my daughter to marry a gypsy man, but I know if my sons marry gypsy women, there is sure to be a living for them, for they will scrat a bread from somewhere, though it would puzzle a lawyer to tell how they get it at times.' Some of the men expect to spend what money they may chance to make for their own private gratification, whilst they leave it to the wife to provide the home support.

"It is well known that the lying practice of fortune-telling is the great source of the gypsy female's gain. During winter she strolls about London duping servant girls and others, whilst the spring, summer, and autumn find her at races and fairs (with the exception of the hop season). During the past year at such places I have often gazed upon the painful picture of silly young women, in some secluded place, behind a tree, bush, or van, with their hands extended, whilst o'er it the brunette sorceress, with silver piece, has traced the line of life with searching view, pretending therefrom, or by the casual turn up of a pack of cards, to tell the colour of their future years, which, of course, is always by such swindlers made to wear a sunny character."

" Fortune-telling.*

"Gypsy women, as long as we have known anything of gypsy history, have been arrant fortune-tellers. They plied fortune-telling about France and Germany as early as 1414, the year when the dusky bands were first observed in Europe, and they

* From Borrow's "Romano Lavo Lil."

have never relinquished the practice. There are two words for fortune-telling in Gypsy, *bocht* and *dukkering*. Bocht is a Persian word, a modification of, or connected with, the Sanscrit *bagya*, which signifies "fate." *Dukkering* is the modification of a Wallaco-Sclavonian word signifying something spiritual or ghostly. In Eastern European Gypsy, the Holy Ghost is called *Swentuno Ducos*. Gypsy fortune-telling is much the same everywhere, much the same in Russia as it is in Spain and in England. Everywhere there are three styles, the lofty, the familiar, and the homely; and every gypsy woman is mistress of all three, and uses each according to the rank of the person whose *vast* she *dukkers*, whose hand she reads, and adapts the luck she promises."

The following extract relates to a past condition of things, though the different species of vagabonds mentioned in it still continue to exist:—

"METROPOLITAN GYPSYRIES—WANDSWORTH, 1864.

"The gypsies are not the sole occupiers of Wandsworth grounds. Strange, wild guests are to be found there who, without being gypsies, have much gypsyism in their habits, and who far exceed the gypsies in number. To pass them by without notice would be unpardonable. They may be divided into three classes: Chorodies, Kora-mengre, and Hindity-mengre. Something about each:—

"The Chorodies are the legitimate descendants of the rogues and outcasts who roamed about England long before its soil was trodden by a gypsy foot. They are a truly detestable set of beings; both men and women being ferocious in their appearance, and in their conversation horrible and disgusting. They have coarse, vulgar features, and hair which puts one wonderfully in mind of refuse flax, or the material of which mops are composed. Their complexions, when not obscured with grime, are rather fair than dark, evidencing that their origin is low, swinish Saxon, and not gentle Romany. Their language is the frowsiest English, interlarded with cant expressions and a few words of bastard Romany. They live in the vilest tents, with the exception of two or three families, who have their abode in broken and filthy caravans. They have none of the comforts and elegancies of the gypsies. They are utterly destitute of civility and good manners, and are generally squalid in their dress, though the women sometimes exhibit not a little dirty tawdriness. The trades of the men are tinkering and basket-making, and some few 'peel the stick.' The women go about with the articles made by their husbands, or rather partners, and sometimes do a little in the fortune-telling line—pretty prophetesses! The fellows will occasionally knock a man down in the dark, and rob him; the women will steal anything they can conveniently lay their hands on. Singular as it may seem to those not deeply acquainted with human nature, these wretches are not without a kind of pride. 'We are no gypsies—not we! no, nor Irish either. We are English, and decent folks—none of your rubbish!' The gypsies hold them, and with reason, in supreme contempt, and it is from them that they got their name of Chorodies, not a little applicable to them. *Choredo* in Gypsy, signifies a poor, miserable person, and differs very little in sound from two words, one Sanscrit and the other Hebrew, both signifying, like the Gypsy term, something low, mean, and contemptible.

"Kora-mengre are the lowest of these hawkers who go about the country villages and the streets of London, with caravans hung about with various common articles, such as mats, brooms, mops, tin pans, and kettles. These low hawkers seem to be of much the same origin as the Chorodies, and are almost equally brutal and repulsive in their manners. The name Kora-mengre is Gypsy, and signifies fellows who cry out and shout, from their practice of shouting out the names of their goods. The word *kora*, or *karra*, is by no means bad Hebrew; *kora*, in the holy language, signifies, he cried out, called, or proclaimed; and a partridge is called in Hebrew *kora*, from its continually crying out to its young, when leading them about to feed. *Koran*, the name of the sacred book of the Mahometans, is of the same root.

"Lastly come the Hindity-mengre, or Filthy People. This term has been bestowed upon the vagrant Irish by the gypsies from the dirty ways attributed to them, though it is a question whether the lowest Irish are a bit more dirty in their ways than the English Chorodies, or indeed so much, and are certainly immeasurably superior to them in many respects. There are not many of them here, seldom more than two families, and sometimes, even during the winter, not a single Irish tent or cart is to be seen. The trade they ostensibly drive is tinkering, repairing old kettles, and making little pots and pans of tin. The one, however, on which they principally depend, is not tinkering, but one far more lucrative, and requiring more cleverness and dexterity; they make false rings, like the gypsy smiths, the *fashiono vangustengre* of old, and whilst speaking Celtic to one whom they deem their countryman, have no hesitation in acknowledging themselves to be ' Cairdean droich oir,' workers of false gold. The rings are principally made out of old brass buttons; those worn by old Chelsea pensioners being considered the very best for the purpose. Many an ancient Corporal Trim, after having spent all his money at the public-house, and only become three-parts boozy, has been induced by the Hindity-mengre to sell his buttons at the rate of three-halfpence a-piece, in order to have wherewithal to make himself thoroughly royal. Each of these Hindity-mengre has his blowpipe, and some of them can execute their work in a style little inferior to that of a first-rate working goldsmith. The rings, after being made, are rubbed with a certain stuff out of a phial, which gives them all the appearance of gold. This appearance, however, does not long endure, for after being worn two or three months, the ring loses its false appearance entirely, and any one can see that it is worthless metal. A good many of these rings are disposed of at good prices by the Hindity women, the wives of these false-gold workers, to servant girls and the wives of small shopkeepers, and not a few, at a lower rate, to certain gentry who get their livelihood by the honourable profession of *ring-dropping*."

The Act of Elizabeth against the gypsies was repealed by the 23 Geo. III., c. 51 (1783), which declares that it is and ought to be considered as a law of excessive severity.

In *Scotland* the Gypsies were several times legislated against. In 1574 and 1579 they were directed to be punished as vagabonds. In 1609 they were ordered to leave the country under pain of death. In 1617 justices of the peace were instructed to enforce the Acts against them. In 1641 constables were ordered to arrest them, and this order appears to have been ineffectual, as a petition was shortly afterwards presented from the Church asking for their repression. In 1647 the Procurators of State were told to report on the overture of the General Assembly relating to gypsies, and in 1661 justices of the peace were again directed to enforce the Acts and constables to arrest them.

In *Ireland*, where they never were very numerous, the gypsies were declared rogues and vagabonds by 10 and 11 Car. I., c. 4 (1634).

The Report of the Commissioners appointed to inquire as to the best means of establishing an efficient Constabulary Force in England and Wales in the year 1839 contains the following evidence regarding the gypsies:—

"The gypsies are the worst of thieves: they live by fortune-telling; they make rings out of brass buttons and pewter, and the wives sell them as gold and silver; they have files and other implements for cutting them out; the metal ones are cast; many of them make bad money. They will coin the money in lanes, or buy of the dealers in towns in the rough and make it up themselves. This is extensively done, most 'up' the country, the south and west of England; more round Sussex, Essex, Kent, Surrey, Northampton. They have no religion; are heavy cursers; go in families; never marry; many of them are sheep-stealers. The two families of the Boslems and Smiths, about sixty in each, are about Nottinghamshire and Derbyshire; hardly an assize or sessions but some of this set are had up; in winter they live in towns, if very severe. They will be in one tent when out; as soon as they are old enough they 'pair,' and if they don't like each other, after a fight the woman will go to her own tribe again, and the man selects another woman. They play cards and drink on Sundays."

CHAPTER XXIII.

SWEDEN, DENMARK, BELGIUM, AND HOLLAND.

SWEDEN.—New poor law of 1871 as to beggars and mendicant children—Definition of vagabonds and vagrants—Nature of their punishment—Number of vagabonds in gaols and houses of correction and employed on public works in 1876.
DENMARK.—Punishment of vagrants—Numbers imprisoned for vagrancy from 1871 to 1880.
BELGIUM, 1808 to 1870.—Law as to vagrants and beggars—Suppression of free admission to the Depôt de Mendicité in 1848—New law of 1866—Population of the Depôts de Mendicité 1840 to 1870.
HOLLAND.—Present penal laws as to beggars and vagrants—Beggars' Institution.

SWEDEN.

THE new poor law enacted in 1871 provides for the mode in which beggars are to be treated.

Every poor union appoints poor inspectors on their own responsibility, whose duty it is to repress mendicity and to arrest beggars.

An arrested beggar, if on investigation he be really destitute, is relieved by the inspector. If he be guilty of imposture and deliberate mendicity, the inspector delivers him over to the nearest Crown bailiff, to be punished as the governor of the province may determine; and if he be taken within his own district of settlement, to the poor law authorities, who will undertake to forward him to the governor.

Children under fifteen years of age found begging outside their district, are removed by the inspector's authority to their own domicile, or to that of their guardian or natural protector, and in case such domicile cannot be ascertained, then temporary relief is afforded by the union in which they are arrested.

Children begging within their own district are relieved by the union if really destitute, and admonished and reprimanded by the poor board if guilty of mendicity. On a repetition of the offence, the police authorities are to see that the child receives proper castigation at the hands of its parents or guardian.

Should it be proved that the child has begged unnecessarily, by order or with the consent of its parents or any other person, these are to be held responsible by the poor board, and the governor will punish them by the infliction of hard labour.

Any beggar convicted of mendicity may be condemned to hard labour by the governor of the province in which he is arrested, or may be sent by prison conveyance to his own domicile, and punished by the governor of his own province.

Hard labour, when inflicted upon beggars, shall not be for less than one month or more than six, and is to be performed in the establishments for the purpose belonging to the district, or if no workhouse exist there, then in the district prison or the Crown jail, or, if the latter be full, then in the house of correction or the labour corps.

Police authorities possess equal rights of arresting beggars as the poor inspectors, and all town bailiffs are required to exert themselves to the utmost to cause beggars to disappear from the country.*

According to the terms of the law, discharged vagabonds and vagrants are persons condemned for crimes involving an ignominious penalty, who after having suffered their punishment lead an idle and vagabond existence, as well as other vagabonds subjected to certain restrictions in the choice of their abode, and obliged to prove that they earn their living honestly. If without authorisation they leave their place of abode, or if after having received a warning they continue to lead an idle and disorderly life they run the risk of losing their liberty and of being sent to the public works in virtue of a decision not of the courts of justice, but of the administrative authority.

Those who have already undergone punishment for a crime or a misdemeanour may be sent to the public works for from two to four years. For such persons there are two working stations, one at Borghamn in Östergötland, and the other on the isle of Tjurkö, in the Blekinge group, ten miles from the town of Karlskrona. In these two places the prisoners are engaged in quarrying and cutting stone : at Borghamn, they win stone on account of the Government ; at Tjurkö, granite for private contractors.

* Report by Nassau Jocelyn, 1872.

On the other hand, vagabonds who have not undergone punishment for a crime involving an ignominious penalty, but who, after having received a warning from the authorities on account of their idleness, their propensity for vagaboudage, and their disorderly life, neglect the work which is assigned to them, may be condemned by the governor to the public works for not less than six months nor more than a year.

This latter class does work for the army at a special station, and is separate from those of persons condemned for crimes or misdemeanours.

For two years, however, in consequence of the absence of work of this kind, a royal decree has authorised the Department to set persons of this class to work in cells, with a reduction of a third on their working time.

Women of the same class are engaged in public work allotted to them in the prison of Norrmalm at Stockholm, but entirely separated from the other prisoners.

In 1845, persons in want of work were permitted to go to work for a certain time in the establishments for the reception of vagabonds. This permission was for several years abused, many persons obtaining subsistence from the State during the autumn and winter seasons, but leaving on the approach of mild weather; it has been sensibly restricted during the last few years, and is no longer accorded except under very exceptional circumstances.

	31st Dec., 1876.		31st Dec., 1877.	
	Males.	Females.	Males.	Females.
In gaols (maîsons centrales), condemned for vagabondage	74	131	55	141
In houses of correction (maîsons secondaires), condemned for vagabondage and mendicity	74	10	165	6
On public works, discharged prisoners, vagabonds and vagrants	777	—	671	—
	*925	141	891	147

DENMARK.

The general rule is that beggars are liable on conviction to fifteen days' imprisonment, with bread and water; vagrants to thirty days of the same punishment. Children under fifteen years of age are not personally punishable; but their parents, if conniving,

* Report of G. F. Almquist, Director-General of Prisons, 1879.

may be held responsible and treated accordingly. Any vagrant person who has no apparent means of subsistence may be sent home to his parish by the police.

The practical temperaments of these rules are not inconsiderable. I am told that in the country and in the smaller towns there is a systematic tolerance of local beggars, but that intrusive beggars are dealt with as the law directs. In Copenhagen the police are strict, and street mendicancy is very seldom seen.*

NUMBER OF PERSONS SENTENCED TO HEAVIER PENALTIES THAN FINES FOR VAGRANCY, MENDICITY, AND MAKING AWAY WITH THE PROPERTY OF INSTITUTIONS FOR THE RELIEF OF THE POOR.

	1871	1872	1873	1874	1875	1876	1877	1878	1879	1880
In Copenhagen	109	89	61	68	72	120	128	136	223	197
Prefectures in the Islands, Copenhagen not included	612	425	359	345	318	399	572	876	763	886
Prefectures in Jutland	367	306	271	214	266	259	514	731	645	689
Total in the whole kingdom	1088	820	691	627	656	778	1214	1743	1631	1772

The apparent progressive increase of late years in vagrancy and mendicity is attributable to the greater vigilance of the police rather than to any real increase of vagrancy.

The total population of Denmark at the last census was 1,000,969.

BELGIUM.

By the decree of 5th July, 1808, begging was prohibited, a dépôt de mendicité was ordered to be created in every department, and every person found begging was to be arrested by the gendarmerie and removed to the dépôt by order of the "local authority," therefore without a judicial sentence. Beggars in a state of vagrancy were to be sent to prison. The penal code of 1810 (Arts. 271, 275) enacts very severe penalties against both offences, and left the culprits at the disposal of the Government after the expiration of their terms of imprisonment, to be detained in the dépôts for any further period. Place was also reserved in the dépôts for homeless paupers who asked for admission. A separation of these different classes and some useful labour was at first attempted, but abandoned as impracticable. Thus the five dépôts de mendicité became great hostelries for supplying board, lodging, and congenial society to all the profligates of the country at the public expense.

* Report by G. Strachey, 1871.

This system was found to be intolerably expensive and perfectly ineffectual as a means of repression. The remedy was thought to lie in the *suppression of free admissions*. Therefore a law was passed in 1848 providing that beggars and vagrants should still be received in the dépôts, but that spontaneous applicants should not be admitted without the sanction of their own communal or other authorities. Paupers thus admitted at their own desire may be forced to remain in the dépôt for thirty days, and if they return within the same year are to be detained for a period of from six to twelve months, at the discretion of the permanent deputation. These restrictions did not produce the desired effect, that of relieving the burden of the communes, but only increased the number of judicial condemnations. For when an applicant was refused admittance, he had only to get himself convicted as a beggar or vagrant, which involved a penalty of one to seven days' imprisonment, and a further sojourn of from six to twelve months in the dépôt, at the discretion of the governor of the province. The law had little effect in keeping down the population of the dépôts, but altered the relative proportions of the free and compulsory inmates.

The main result of the above law has been the toleration of mendicancy, particularly in the rural communes, as a lesser evil than that of supporting beggars in the dépôts for indefinite periods.

The system of dépôts de mendicité was totally transformed by the law of 6th March, 1866, on the principle of bringing ablebodied beggars under severe discipline, while tolerating juvenile and infirm beggars. This law enacts that every able-bodied beggar or vagrant aged more than fourteen years shall be arrested and brought before the *tribunal de simple police*, may be sentenced to prison for from one to seven days, and *may* be placed after that at the disposal of the Government for a term to be fixed by the juge de paix, which term is to be from fifteen days to three months for the first offence, and from three to six months for the second. Culprits under fourteen years old are to be arrested and sent to a reformatory till they attain the age of twenty. Able-bodied culprits over fourteen years of age are to be confined in a penitentiary or a dépôt de mendicité during their term of seclusion. The governor is authorised to suppress all the dépôts and to reorganise them on new principles. If there are extenuating circumstances, the judge is authorised to inflict a penalty of " simple police," *i.e.* seven days' imprisonment without labour or subsequent seclusion.

Additional penalties are awarded by this law to persons who

cause children to beg, or who procure children or cripples to accompany them for the purpose of exciting commiseration. The new penal code of 1867 is very severe upon the offences committed by beggars or vagrants, such as trespass, threats, simulating sores and infirmities, begging in troops or in disguise, carrying arms, bearing false passports or papers, carrying housebreakers' tools, &c. After the expiration of their penalty they may be kept from five to ten years under the surveillance of the police. Vagrants are defined to be those who have no fixed abode or means of subsistence, and who habitually exercise no trade or profession.*

By the law of 1866 vagrants and beggars, infirm, or aged less than fourteen years may be arrested and brought before the tribunal of police. If arrested outside of their own commune, the bourgmestre will, in the first instance, enjoin them to return thereto. They cannot be prosecuted without the sanction of the bourgmestre. This disposition withdraws the repression of mendicity from the exclusive action of the judicial authority when the culprit is infirm or aged less than fourteen. It thus allows the commune to tolerate or put down begging within its own limits as regards these two classes. It is thought probable that each commune will tolerate mendicity exercised by its own inhabitants, and will expel the beggars of neighbouring communes.

Juvenile and infirm beggars when convicted must be placed at the disposal of the government for six months on their first and for two years on their second conviction. They are to be detained in a dépôt, a charitable institution, or a reformatory, according to circumstances, until they are twenty years of age. The reception in the dépôts of voluntary applicants must be previously sanctioned by the college of bourgmestre and aldermen of their " domicile de secours," which is to pay for their maintenance.

DÉPÔTS DE MENDICITÉ.

	Entries.	Average Population.
1840	2,739	2,828
1850	4,508	3,478
1860	3,431	2,448
1862	4,394	2,918
1866	2,851	1,570
1867	4,044	1,659
1869	4,549	1,938
1870	4,836	1,925

* Report by Sir Henry P. T. Barron, 1872.

Although the whole régime of beggars and vagrants is still in a transitional state, the new law has already borne good fruits.

HOLLAND.

In the year 1818 a philanthropic Dutch statesman, General van den Bosch, organised a Society of Beneficence, the programme of which was to purchase wild heathlands in East Holland for the purpose of cultivating them by the labour of the pauper classes. Nearly 10,000 acres of land were acquired at Fredericksoord, near Steenwyk, Ommerschans, near Meppel, and Veenhuizen, near Assen. Beggars and idlers and dissolute vagabonds were by arrangement with the Government sent there, but with insufficient powers of discipline and control. As might naturally be expected, the scheme eventually proved a failure, and in 1859 the Government took the matter in hand, paid off the debts of the Society, and relieved it of the care of the worst classes, who were located at Veenhuizen and Ommerschans, and who were after that time placed under Government control. Even since this change the system is by no means a success, owing to the character of the management. The discipline is imperfect, the association of the inmates being perfectly unchecked at night, and also permitted at intervals during the day. The provision of food is ample if not excessive, the personal accommodation comfortable, the situation of the colonies pleasant, and the amount of work done insufficient. With all these drawbacks to good and firm discipline, which is essential to the reclamation of the vicious or vacillating characters who are the inmates of such establishments, it is not to be wondered at that the recommittals to the colonies amounted in 1875 to 81 per cent. of the total committals, and maintain very much the same proportion in the present day. In fact, in place of being as they should be, places of reclamation, the colonies, like the unreformed casual wards in England, are sources of contamination, and serve to propagate depravity instead of checking it.

REGULATIONS REGARDING BEGGARS.

Beggars are to be confined in a place which has been specially adapted for their reception, and this rule holds good for the whole kingdom. The places appointed for the purpose are Ommerschans and Veenhuizen, where beggars are punished by imprisonment of from fourteen days to six months.

The judge may order that at the end of this punishment the beggar shall be taken to a workhouse (hard labour house). This order is obligatory with reference to such persons as have already been once punished for begging or vagrancy (tramping about the country without means of subsistence).

Convicted beggars who are foreigners may at all times be deported beyond the frontier at the expense of the Government.

Beggars who are not in a healthy condition, who may have used threats or menaces, and have entered premises (whether dwelling house or any building attached to it), or who pretend to have wounds or sores, or who beg in company or in collusion, whether man and wife, or father or mother with young children, or blind people with their guides, are to be punished by imprisonment of from six months to three years.

Any beggar arrested who has in any way disguised himself, or upon whom any weapon is found (although he may not have used it or threatened to use it), or any files, or crow-bars, or other implements which may be used in committing theft or burglary, is punishable by imprisonment for from two to five years. Any beggar upon whom property is found, or money of more than fifty florins value, without being able to give a proper account of it, is punished by imprisonment of from six months to two years.

Any beggar proved to have threatened, or abused, or assaulted any one, is punishable by solitary confinement of from five to ten years, without prejudice to any other heavy punishment, according to the kind of violence used, or the peculiar circumstances under which force may have been employed or the assault committed.

The punishment appointed for such persons as make use of false written characters, false passports, or false travelling orders, is always to be of the maximum degree if committed by vagrants or beggars.

Beggars' Institutions.

These institutions are established at Ommerschans, belonging to the town of Ommer, circle of Ommer, and Overeest, in the province of Overyssel, and at Veenhuizen, in the province of Drentha. The institution at Veenhuizen is divided into three departments:

No. 1 for women, Nos. 2 and 3 for men. These institutions, which are under Government control and are directly subject to the department of Justice, are intended for the reception of beggars and tramps condemned to detention by a judge, and of the children of such persons where they cannot be separated from their parents. The expense of the removal and maintenance of prisoners is borne by Government.

Prisoners are actively employed chiefly as agricultural labourers, wood-cutters, cattle-tenders, and herdsmen; some have to do housework, others are set to do moderate manual labour, such as the making of coffee-bags, knitting stockings, making military gloves, mats, fishing-nets, &c.

On the 1st July, 1883, there were :—

At Ommerschans	891 men.
At Veenhuizen, No. 1	343 women.
,, ,, ,, 2	615 men.
,, ,, ,, 3	794 ,,
Total	2,643 persons.

Amount of live stock in the four divisions :—

Horses	8
Cows, and other horned cattle	468
Sheep and lambs	916

In the grounds there were under cultivation :—

	Acres.
Rye	324
Oats	194
Horsebeans	31
Potatoes	165
Buckwheat	6
Garden Fruit	26
	746

In these establishments are also confined those who have been convicted of repeated public drunkenness and seaweed stealing; they may also be incarcerated for not less than three months nor more than twelve in a Government gaol by sentence of a judge, in virtue of the law of 28th June, 1881. On the 1st July, 1883, the total number under sentence was thirty-two.

In the institutions such of the poor as have not been convicted and are not mentally affected, and who desire a place of refuge, may be received at the cost of their parish.

Future Rules on the Introduction of the New Penal Code. Law Book of 3rd March, 1881, Official Gazette No. 35.

" Whoever begs publicly will be punished with imprisonment for from one to twelve days.

" Three or more persons united for the purpose of begging, if above sixteen years old, will be punished by confinement of from one day up to three months.

" If any of the above-named offenders are again apprehended within a year for the same offence, the judge may increase the penalty by one-third, and if able to work may send them to a Government ' workhouse' for from three months up to three years.

" On the introduction of the new penal code the character of the present Beggar Institutions will be changed; thus Veenhuizen will become a Government ' workhouse ' for the reception of such persons as are able to work, and who will be adjudged to be placed there in accordance with the new Legal Code.

" Veenhuizen I. will then be for females, and II. and III. for males.

" Ommerschans will then be altered to a penal prison as far as it may be available or can be made available for such a purpose, and will thus cease to be a colony or dépôt for beggars."

CHAPTER XXIV.

FRANCE.

570—1885.

Ordinance of the 2nd Council of Tours.—Ordinances of St. Louis.—Edict of John in 1350.—Rôdeurs de filles under Charles VIII.—Measures of repression under François I.—Edict of Henri II.—Description of the various orders of mendicants—Ordinances of Louis XIII.—Suppression of the Cours des Miracles by Louis XIV.—Action of the National Assembly. —Decree of 1809.—Dépôts de Mendicité.—Circulars issued by the Ministry of the Interior to the préfets in 1864, 1872, 1874, and 1881.—Results of the inquiries instituted in consequence of the circular of 1881.—The four classes of vagabonds.—Steps recommended by the préfets for the repression of vagabondage.—Report of a special committee to the National Assembly in 1873.—Census of vagabondage.—Convictions for mendicity and vagabondage.

In the year 570, the second Council of Tours formulated an ordinance, both religious and social, on the assistance to be given to the necessitous and on the prohibition of mendicity. " Let each city, according to its resources, provide for its poor and infirm, and let the expense be divided between the inhabitants and the clergy, so that the poor may no longer wander about." Charlemagne forbid food being given to mendicants who refused to work.

During the Middle Ages the manumission of the serfs, and the incessant wars, famines, and epidemics which occurred, gave mendicity a frightful expansion, which the most rigorous measures could not suppress. The Church in addition, through its swarms of mendicant orders helped to propagate this deplorable state of things, by elevating laziness to the condition of a profession, and, what is worse, by making it under certain circumstances a passport to sanctity.

The number of mendicants became so great, that in order to supervise them with greater ease it was found necessary to open refuges for them, to which they were in some measure confined; it was in this way that the various *Cours des Miracles* were formed, dens into which even justice itself hesitated to penetrate.

The mendicants organised themselves into distinct corporations like government departments; they had their States General, and elected kings. This secret organisation of idleness and theft was a continuous peril to society.

Saint Louis, whose thorough benevolence is beyond question, ordered in his "Institutions" that every idler and vagabond who, owning nothing and earning nothing, frequented taverns, should be arrested and interrogated on his means of existence; if he was discovered in making false statements and convicted of an evil course of life he was to be banished from the town.

In the reign of *John* every kind of scourge ravaged France; war and famine and a fearful epidemic added to the general misery. Troops of peasants and disbanded soldiers, profiting by the universal desolation, overran the town and the country, begging during the day and robbing and murdering at night.

To put a stop to these excesses the King in 1350 issued an edict against able-bodied beggars, which formed the basis of subsequent legislation against mendicity. Able-bodied beggars were forbidden to beg under the penalty of the scourge and the pillory; for a subsequent offence they were to be branded on the forehead with a hot iron and banished. Alms to able-bodied beggars were forbidden; the aid of the pulpit was invoked to prevent assistance from being given to able-bodied idlers and vagabonds; and finally prelates, barons, chevaliers, and burghers were commanded to prohibit their almoners from giving charity to able-bodied beggars. This penal enactment, which erred on the side of excessive severity, was rarely put in force; in every reign it was therefore necessary to endeavour to provide by new ordinances for the inefficiency of former enactments. An ordinance of 1493 condemned beggars and vagabonds to the galleys and their accomplices to the scourge.

Under *Charles VIII.* mention is made of a special order of mendicants, styled in the ordinances prowlers for girls (*rôdeurs de filles*); these wretches carried off young girls, whom they sold after having abused them. By an ordinance of the 6th July, 1495, the King organised a public force entrusted with the superintendence of the security of the roads, and the execution of the regulations against mendicity throughout the kingdom; this was the origin of the *corps de la maréchaussée,* or provost-marshal's force. In the reign of *François I.* a large number of charitable institutions were established, but at the same time very severe measures of repression were enacted against able-bodied mendicants; for instance, on several occasions the magistrates of Paris were ordered to employ the able-bodied poor on the fortifications of Paris, or on other works, and to provide food for those who accepted work; beggars were forbidden to assemble on pain of being whipped and scourged with rods, and in order to ensure the safety of the capital, which was invaded by a great number of vagabonds and idle adventurers, *François I.* instituted a permanent public force composed of a lieutenant and a certain number of archers.

At this period the country was infested with vagabonds and beggars "abandoned to every kind of vice, robbers, murderers, kidnappers, and ravishers of girls, who renounced God, made vice a virtue, and were cruel, inhuman, and wolfish." Miscreants of the worst type, forming themselves into large bands, sacked villages, and sometimes even fortified towns; they subjected the unfortunate peasants to the most cruel tortures. The edicts of 1523 and 1537 ordered these robbers to be pursued and put to death with refinements of cruelty worthy of these barbarous times.

Henri II., by an edict of the 9th July, 1547, again ordered the admission of the able-bodied poor to public works; he completely proscribed mendicity under the penalty of the scourge and banishment for women and the galleys for men.

In these two reigns flourished in all their cynical insolence the associations of beggars known under the name of *bélistres* (rascals). At the top of the tree was the king* of the Bélistres, who bore the title of *Coesre* or Arch-rogue. Then came the *cagous* (master

---

* The "kings," whose reigns were generally of short duration, owing to the demands of the hangman, sometimes took the title of *roi de Thune, Thune* or *Tune* being the old French name for Tunis. Both this epithet and that of *Coesre* were a travesty of the assumption by the leader of the Gypsies of the title of Duke of Egypt. *Coesre* is evidently a brazen-faced appropriation of the name of *Kosru I.,* King of Persia, called by Greek writers *Chosroes,* the glories and happiness of whose reign are frequently extolled by poets as the golden age of the Persian sovereignty. Both titles are no doubt due to smatterings of knowledge obtained from some vagabond student of the *Pierre Gringoire* type.

thieves entrusted with the education of novices) and *archisuppots* (retired leading thieves), governors or intendants of the provinces of the kingdom of rascality; they counterfeited persons of rank ruined or robbed, and crippled soldiers. They were sometimes called the gentry of the *short sword*, on account of the scissors which they used for cutting purses.

Among the inferior ranks were the *orphelins*, the *riffaudés*, the *malingreux*, the *mercandiers*, the *piètres*, the *polissons*, the *francsmitoux*, the *callots*, the *sabouleux*, the *hubins*, the *coquillards*, the *courtauds de boutanche* * (servants or clerks who only took service in a house for the purpose of robbery), the *narquois*, the *capons* (sharpers), &c.

The *orphelins* (orphans) were young boys, who, in troops of three or four, wandered about the streets of Paris almost naked, and inspired pity by the appearance of the most intense misery. The *riffaudés* † (victims of fire), bearing sham testimonials and accompanied by a troop of women and children, passed themselves off as sufferers by fire. The *malingreux* (malingerers or counterfeit cranks) were sham invalids; some counterfeited dropsy, others had their limbs covered with manufactured sores. The *mercandiers* (broken merchants or tradesmen) went from street to street clothed in rags, crying that they were worthy merchants ruined by the wars, the inclemency of the seasons, or by other accidents. The *piètres* ‡ (maimed), walking with crutches, or dragging themselves along by their hands, counterfeited cripples. The *polissons* § (tatterdemalions or "shallow coves") went about almost naked, clad in scanty rags, with a wallet and a bottle at their sides; the winter was their best time, as they then got plenty of clothes, which they sold. The *francs mitoux*, trained to all the practices of the profession, assumed according to choice the appearance of every kind of malady, and even deceived the doctors themselves. The *callots* ‖ (sufferers

* *Courtaud* = shopman, and *boutanche* is a slang adaptation of *boutique*.

† *Riffaudé*, from the Latin *rufus*, red, which is the basis of the verb *rufare*, to redden, to smoke, to smoke out.

‡ *Piètre* is an old French word meaning bad, or in a bad state. According to the Dictionary of the Academy, it means shabby, mean, or of no value.

§ *Polisson* is a derivative of the verb *polir*, and, according to *Littré*, originally signified a *street "polisher"* or scavenger, a street tramp or vagabond. *Scheler*, on the other hand, says that it meant one who was not yet polished, and that the true signification was therefore an ill-bred boy or unlicked cub.

‖ *Callot*, from *Calotte*, the upper half of the skull, where scurvy first shows itself.

BEGGARS

Taken from the Paintings and Tapestries of the City of Rheims, executed in the XVth century.

from scurvy) gave out that they had returned from Alise-Saint
Reine in the Côte d'Or, famous for its mineral waters, where they
had been miraculously cured of the scurvy. The *sabouleux* *
(simulators of epilepsy), with a piece of soap in their mouths,
rolled about in the streets and in the porticoes of churches
simulating the convulsions of an attack of epilepsy. The *hubins*
(devotees of St. Hubert) alleged that they were cured of the bite
of a mad dog through the special protection of Saint Hubert.
The *coquillards* † (pilgrims) covered with shells and a staff in hand,
pretended to have returned from all the known pilgrimages. The
narquois ‡ (archers or " rufflers,") or *drilles* § (soldiers), sometimes
also called *gens de la petite flambe* (men of the short sword) were
mainly recruited from disbanded soldiers, and the *passevolants*, ‖ or
volunteer soldiers, demanded alms in the most insolent manner
with swords at their side. This organisation subsisted up to the
reign of *Louis XIV.*

Nevertheless, in spite of edicts, the beggars refused to take to
work, and continued their vagabond and adventurous life. They
attained such a degree of insolence and boldness, that a public
outcry was raised against them in every part of the kingdom.
The old regulations were consequently renewed in all their
rigour ; persons were forbidden to give alms to mendicants under
a penalty of 10 livres parisis (250 sous) ; finally, the provost
marshal's lieutenants were ordered to go as often as they could
through the town and suburbs, accompanied by sergeants, archers,
and an officer of the high court of justice, for the purpose of whipping *caimands* (male beggars) and *caimandes* (female beggars)
whom they found begging.

All these rigorous measures did not suffice ; it was therefore
found requisite to try other means of action. *Louis XIII.*, by
an order of the 27th of August, 1612, opened asylums where
mendicants were to be confined and fed. Edicts and orders were
issued forbidding vagrancy and mendicity under the penalty for

---

* The *Sabouleux* evidently owe their name to the "*sapo*" or soap they
put in their mouths.
† *Coquillard*, from *coquille*, a shell.
‡ *Narquois* is a slang adaptation of *archer*, a bowman.
§ *Drille*. This word, says *Michel*, undoubtedly springs from *soudard*,
however strange it may appear until one knows that this latter word has
produced *soudrille*, with a similar meaning. The dropping or adding of
syllables to words is a common feature in cant languages.
‖ *Passevolants*, intruders or interlopers.

men of the pillory and the galleys, and for women and girls of the scourge and perpetual banishment; landlords, householders, lodging-house keepers, and sellers of beer or other liquors were specially forbidden to harbour vagabonds under the penalty of exemplary punishment by imprisonment and whipping.

During the early years of the reign of *Louis XIV.* the political troubles favoured the encroachments of the beggars. Some of these assuming the aspect of bullies, in the style of the period, demanded alms with swords by their sides and bands over their ruffs. These wretches lived among themselves in the most promiscuous manner; they brought up and trained their children to mendicity, and sold to recruiting officers adults whom they captured by violence and whom they kept in private confinement in houses which were styled *fours* (ovens). There were then in Paris eleven of the *Cours des Miracles*,* serving as haunts for 40,000 beggars. In this extremity *Louis XIV.* resumed the work almost abandoned by *Louis XIII.*, and founded a hospital in Paris for the detention of the poor. "We will and command," says the edict, "that poor beggars, both able-bodied and infirm of both sexes, shall be confined in a hospital in order to be employed in labour, manufactures, and other forms of work according to their ability." Article 9 of this edict forbids mendicancy under severe penalties. In the year 1656 a veritable army of archers and commissioners invaded the principal *Cour des Miracles* in Paris, since rendered famous by *Victor Hugo.* The inhabitants tried to resist or to fly; they had not time for the one or opportunity for the other. The sovereignty of the *roi de Thune* was broken up, and beggars of all kinds, thieves, and vagabonds were examined and packed off either to prison or to the hospital. Up to the end of the reign of *Louis XIV.* the powers of the State fought energetically against mendicity and vagrancy without accomplishing the repression of these evils. The successors of the *Grand Monarque* did not succeed any better in their difficult task. In 1719 beggars were ordered to be transported to the colonies, but owing to expostulations from the colonies the order was revoked in 1722.

The question of mendicity was thought of such importance by

* The *Cours des Miracles* owed their title to the *miraculous* manner in which the blind, the halt, and the lame who inhabited them recovered from their ailments the moment they reached home.

the National Assembly that it bestowed the name of *Comité pour l'extinction de la mendicité* on the commission entrusted with the organisation of relief.

The present legislation for the suppression of mendicity is founded upon a decree of July 5, 1809. The instruction of the Emperor runs, " Matters ought to be arranged in such a way that it might be said, 'Every beggar will be arrested.' But to arrest him in order to put him in prison would be barbarous or absurd. One or several houses of charity will therefore be necessary in every department." The decree founded upon this instruction declares, "Mendicity is to be forbidden throughout the empire; beggars in each department are to be arrested and taken to the dépôt de mendicité of the department, so soon as this dépôt is established and the following formalities have been complied with : within a fortnight following the establishment and organisation of each dépôt de mendicité, the préfet of the department is to make known by notice that the said dépôt having been established and organised, all persons begging and having no means of subsistence are required to present themselves there; this notice is to be published and repeated in all the communes of the department during three consecutive Sundays; after the third publication, every person who is found begging in the department is to be arrested in accordance with the orders of the local authorities through the medium of the gendarmerie, and immediately taken to the dépôt de mendicité ; vagabond beggars are to be arrested and taken to the Houses of Detention. It was also enacted—each dépôt de mendicité is to be created and organised by a special decree, the expenses of the establishment of the dépôt being concurrently borne by the Treasury, the departments, and the towns; within a month of the publication of this decree the préfets are to address to the Minister of the Interior a report upon the establishment of the dépôt de mendicité of their department."

Article 274 of the Penal Code, modified by the law of April 28, 1832, provides, " Every person who shall be found begging in a locality in which a public establishment exists, organised with a view to preclude mendicity, shall be punished with from three to six months' imprisonment, and shall at the expiration of his punishment be taken to a dépôt de mendicité." Article 275 continues, " In places where such establishments do not yet exist, habitual able-bodied beggars shall be punished with from one to three months' imprisonment, and if they are arrested outside the canton in which they reside they shall be punished with imprisonment from six months to two years."

In accordance with the suggestion of the instruction and the provision of the decree, about forty dépôts de mendicité were established, thirty of which existed in 1872. These were to be "paternal establishments," where benevolence was to temper constraint by gentleness, to maintain discipline by affection, and to revive the feeling of wholesome shame. These philanthropic institutions do not appear to have answered the expectations of the founders. "The expenses," says M. Bechard, "greatly exceeded the calculations, and only served to sustain the laziness of the prisoners and redoubled the audacity of the beggars who could not be admitted." The beggars proved in every sense to be "too many" for the Emperor. "The beggars," says Fodêré, "scoffed at him who scoffed at kings. He has passed away and mendicity has survived." "The dépôt de mendicité," Mr. Hamilton remarks, "which bears some resemblance to the English workhouse, is a departmental establishment intended rather for the punishment of the offence of begging than for the relief of the poor. The dépôt at Saint Denis, near Paris, is practically the only one for the department of the Seine. The management of this dépôt is good, that is, the most refractory class of the population of Paris, when committed for their term of imprisonment, are described as orderly and industrious, earning during the period of their incarceration a sum sufficient to support them for some time after their liberation. But the whole aspect of the place is exceedingly repulsive." "The house of restraint (maîson de répression) at Saint Denis," says M. Maxime Du Camp, "is the foulest sink that can be found." This opinion is a trifle exaggerated, but very near the truth.

The opening phrases of the circulars issued by the Ministry of the Interior* to the various préfets on the subject of vagabondage from the year 1864 downwards, read very like the preambles to old English Acts of Parliament. On the 10th of November, 1864, the Minister writes, "Monsieur de Préfet, the attention of the Government has for a long time been directed to the means of

---

* The archives of the section of the department relating to vagabondage were burnt in the fire of 1871. The following documents are derived direct from the Ministry, and are now published for the first time.

protecting our rural populations from the misdeeds and the depredations of bands of vagabond persons and wanderers known under the name of gypsies (Bohémiens)." The circular then goes on to say that the law is powerless to deal with them by expulsion, as they have neither fixed abode, religion, nor social status, but that if they are placed under the surveillance of the police and assigned a fixed residence, they can if they quit it be transported to Cayenne under a decree of December 8, 1851.

As to those persons who are wanderers by profession, such as acrobats, musicians, street singers, &c., they are subject to police regulations defined by the ministerial circular of January 6, 1863, and the note of the 28th of March following.

The next circular is dated April 4, 1872, and begins, "Monsieur le Préfet, the presence of bands of Gypsies in various parts of the country has been pointed out to me by several of your colleagues, who have sent me on the subject complaints from the inhabitants that the laws and police regulations in force appear to protect them only imperfectly against the incursions and misdeeds of these wandering bands." It then proceeds to say that the decree of December 8, 1851, having been annulled, and the penal code of 1832 revived, by which every one under surveillance is free to choose his own domicile and to change it at will, the surveillance is no longer effective. It then recommends the préfets to take steps for rigidly excluding any persons who present themselves at the frontiers, and who cannot give a satisfactory account of their identity and nationality.

The next is dated May 26, 1874, and opens thus: "Monsieur le Préfet, the attention of the department has been several times directed to the injuries occasioned by the passage of bands of gypsies and vagabonds styled 'fugitive camps' (camps volant) in our towns, and above all in our rural districts. Nevertheless, the measures taken up to this time have only succeeded very imperfectly in repressing the abuses resulting from the incursions of these wanderers, and fresh complaints have been recently further addressed to me on the subject." It then points out that the Préfet of the Saône and Loire has decided that the stationing of the vehicles of the gypsies on the highways or communal lands of his department shall be forbidden, and that individuals of this class who cannot prove that they have a domicile or means of subsistence shall be arrested and brought before the Courts as vagabonds, and recommends the préfet to take steps for suppressing the nuisance.

The last is dated January 5, 1881, and runs thus : " Monsieur le Préfet, the rural inhabitants of several departments complain of the increasing number of beggars and vagabonds who overrun small localities, forcing themselves into isolated houses and farms, demanding meat and drink, and often exacting money. It is important to remedy so far as possible a state of things which indicates a relaxation on the part of the peace officers, of the supervision to which beggars, vagabonds, and foreign wanderers ought to be subject. I beg of you, then, to be good enough to ascertain, in what degree these complaints apply to your department, and in case of need to exert all your authority for providing against, or repressing the abuses which may be reported to you in this respect. In addition to this, as this question is manifestly one of general interest, I shall require every kind of information relating to it. For this purpose, I wish you from the present time to collect particulars so far as they relate to your department in order to forward them to me with a special report. I would draw your special attention to the following points :—

" 1st. Under what forms does vagabondage show itself?

"(Beggars, Gypsies, Bearwards, &c.)

" 2nd. Steps taken up to this time to repress vagabondage?

" 3rd. What measures would be most suitable for repressing vagabondage?

" 4th. Have the Board of Works (Conseil Général) or the Town Councils (Conseils Municipaux) taken up this question?

" 5th. Are there any public institutions for refuge or work provided for beggars, and what are their resources?

" 6th. Are there any private institutions with the same objects?

" 7th. How do the Courts apply the provisions of the criminal law relating to beggars and vagabonds?"

The results of the inquiries set on foot in consequence of this circular are thus given in a report to the Minister of the Interior.

I.

The persons reported as composing the various sub-divisions of vagabondage may be grouped under four classes.

The first comprehends the poor who take to begging. They

may be divided into able-bodied and infirm, habitual beggars and occasional beggars, stationary beggars and wandering beggars. These last, to whom mendicity has become habitual and a sort of profession, have a tendency to blend with vagabonds properly so called. They leave their settlement (commune de leur résidence) for the purpose of roaming about the cantons of the neighbouring departments. Sometimes they quit their settlement (domicile) for ever and pass their life in rambling over the highways, "working" in turn each department, each town, each large village, and returning, at the end of a certain number of years to knock at the same doors at which they were relieved during their previous progresses.

In the second class may be ranked persons styled in the reports of the préfets by the name of "Stagers" (Routiers), "Rounders" (Rouleurs), and other names of the same kind, who have no settled abode or means of subsistence, and who do not habitually exercise any trade or calling. This is a condition of vagabondage such as is to be found defined in Article 270 of the Penal Code. In private houses, workshops, and institutions where they appeal for assistance they commonly describe themselves as workmen out of work. Some of them have fallen out of the ranks of labour destitute of means of livelihood and condemned to live by shifts. The greater number are discharged prisoners whom the difficulty of finding work reduces to the beggar's petition. Some of them are creatures degraded by idleness and vice. All of them are unproductive parasites living on the earnings of the working classes, and this is doubtless the reason why the law regards this mode of life as a misdemeanour, even when it is not accompanied by any aggravating circumstances.

The third class includes wanderers exercising migratory callings, such as acrobats, jugglers, organ-grinders, musicians and street singers, fortune-tellers, conjurors, and public entertainers of every kind. Though leading a wandering and often precarious existence, persons of this class are not vagabonds in the legal sense of the term. They in fact exercise a calling subject to the formality of a double authorisation: the one granted by the préfet, on a special pass bearing a description of the bearer; the other granted by the mayor of the commune in which they wish to exercise their calling. The reports, however, of the departments look upon a great number of these wanderers as being only beggars or vagabonds in disguise.

In the fourth class are included wanderers of foreign origin who are commonly known under the name of Gypsies.

The gypsies are neither beggars nor vagabonds in the judicial sense of these expressions, but they partake at the same time of the character of vagabonds and beggars. It appears, in fact, that the calling they exercise has no other object than to shelter them from the arm of the law, by allowing them to call at houses under colourable pretexts. Sometimes they drag bears or other animals about with them, which they exhibit from door to door at isolated farm-houses. Sometimes they manufacture trifling articles of basket-work or hardware, which they offer at houses. Sometimes they carry on useful callings, such as tinkers, umbrella-menders, &c. But the trade which they profess rarely suffices for their subsistence. Their apparent calling conceals their real calling, which is mendicity. In houses into which they penetrate without the consent of the master or mistress, they begin by offering something for sale and end by soliciting alms. When they find themselves amongst children, women, or old people incapable of defending themselves, they show themselves bold and menacing. They no longer solicit, they demand, and, if necessary, extort. After their passage through a commune it seldom happens that the inhabitants do not complain of depredations or thefts committed to their detriment and for which the authors are vainly to be sought among the inhabitants of the district.

The gypsy does not travel singly. He ordinarily brings with him a numerous family. Sometimes several families unite and form a regular tribe under the management of a head. These wanderers do not lodge in inns. Carriages like waggons and vehicles of all kinds serve as their abodes. When all the members of the tribe cannot find room in these shelters, they live in tents and form a sort of fugitive camp (camp volant).

The fantastic customs of these wanderers, their repulsive appearance, their habitual neglect of attention to cleanliness, the strange character of their language, the menacing tone with which they solicit charity, together with the mystery which hovers over the real cause of their distant peregrinations, contributes to make these strange visitors among the rural inhabitants an object of distrust and fear. In resisting their aggressions the people are afraid of provoking acts of vengeance on their part. In certain departments the inhabitants suspect them of sometimes playing the part of spies.

II.

The steps recommended by the Préfets for the repression of vagabondage may be classified under four heads, corresponding with the classes of persons under consideration.

1st. The first concern beggars.

Begging being ordinarily occasioned by want of work, or incapacity for it, combined with the want of pecuniary means, the first step to be taken in this respect is to provide for the relief of the necessitous (venir en aide aux indigents). Now, in the matter of assistance, it seems that it is less necessary to devise new methods than to methodise those already in practice.

The greater part of the reports propose to multiply the charitable boards (bureaux de bienfaisance) in a certain number of communes which have never been provided with them, to create refuges in the shape of cantonal, district, or departmental almshouses (hospices), asylums for the old and infirm and for all incapable of work, asylums for deserted children, night refuges, and other institutions of a similar character; to encourage by grants societies for the assistance of discharged prisoners, who, rejected by the workshops at which they seek for work, are often obliged to have recourse for a living to public charity. Finally, it would be expedient, according to certain reports, to have recourse to the application of the organic decree of the 5th July, 1808, which compelled every department to have a dépôt de mendicité.

Mendicity rarely begins to be dangerous to the public safety until it becomes vagabond. The greater number of préfets consider that to extinguish this form of mendicity, every commune ought to be compelled in fact, as it is in law, to relieve its own poor. This result might perhaps be attained by an indirect method, if the proper constables (agents) and officers (fonctionnaires) attended to the execution of the provisions of the Penal Code relative to habitual and able-bodied beggars who devote themselves to mendicity outside the canton of their abode.

2nd. With regard to vagabonds of the second class, those only to whom this name properly applies, the préfets consider that the existing law is inadequate.

The penalty for the offence of vagabondage consists in fine, imprisonment in certain cases, the surveillance of the police, and finally, with regard to vagabonds of foreign extraction, expulsion from the State. Now the principal punishment, imprisonment, is not of a nature to repress efficaciously the offence under consideration. The reports of the préfets and those of the judicial magistrates, which in certain departments the préfets have added to their reports, leave no doubt upon this point. The greater number of vagabonds, says one of these reports, come of their own accord in the hard weather to have themselves arrested either by the gendarmerie or the police. Brought to the bar and condemned, they endeavour to prolong the duration of their imprisonment. Set at liberty, they resume their life of adventure until the fall of the thermometer informs them that it is again time to seek an asylum in prison. Other documents say that they almost regard penal repression with indifference. The police reports on them (dossiers) are overladen with convictions. Many beg for their arrest as a favour. Imprisonment of any kind, adds the préfet of one of the northern departments, cannot be regarded as a beneficial form of repression. Vagabonds are not afraid of imprisonment; some, on the contrary, seek it, because through it they obtain rest, subsistence, and an easy and assured existence, though deprived of liberty. Their degeneration or their moral degradation is the explanation of this surprising phenomenon.

For the greater part of old offenders, imprisonment has therefore ceased to be a punishment. As it constitutes the principal punishment, the insufficiency of this means of repression is clearly discernible. The penalty which the major part of the préfets, magistrates, and Boards of Works who have given an opinion on the point call for, is the transportation to one of our colonies of repeatedly convicted vagabonds, after a certain number of convictions.

3rd. The reports show that persons carrying on wandering callings or trades, form a sufficiently important factor in regard to crime in general and to mendicity and vagabondage in particular. This has given rise to the measures proposed with regard to this particular class of persons.

Certain reports ask that greater caution should be exercised than has hitherto been the custom in the delivery of passes to acrobats, and the administrative licences with which these different performers are bound to provide themselves for the exercise of their calling.

Others propose that the prefectoral licences shall only be given to infirm persons, in consequence of their being unable to undertake any other form of work.

Some préfets would like the licences delivered up to this time to be rescinded by a general order, and that the delivery of new licences should be absolutely prohibited.

This would mean the complete prohibition of all these interloping or precarious callings, which permit a multitude of persons to maintain themselves, who are often incapable of undertaking more regular work. In order to get rid of some counterfeit vagabonds, a crowd of mendicants would be created. It appears that the proposed remedy would be worse than the evil.

4th. Finally, with regard to vagabonds of foreign extraction, as well as wanderers exercising suspicious or dangerous callings, and who are known by the name of Gypsies, the reports of the préfets agree with rare exceptions in substantiating the absolute insufficiency of the local police measures.

In consequence, they propose—

A. When these wanderers present themselves at the frontier to forbid their entrance into the territory of the Republic.

B. To apply in a large degree the right of expulsion, resulting from the law of the 3rd December, 1849, when, by eluding the surveillance of the police, they have succeeded in intruding themselves into the interior of the country.

It should be noted that nothing has as yet been resolved upon with regard to the measures proposed by the préfets for the repression of vagabondage, as a consequence of the circular of the 5th January, 1881.

With regard to the nationality of the different hordes of gypsies who have recently made their appearance in France, the Minister of the Interior has furnished the following observations :—

"The gangs of gypsies who roam about France ordinarily, come from the provinces of the Turkish Empire, from the various states which until recently formed part of it, and from the territory of Austria-Hungary. There is further reason to believe that they are not always homogeneous, that is to say, composed of members of the same family or of the same tribe. Individuals may sometimes be noticed, who, while speaking the common language, make use of western idioms, particularly of German, and appear to belong to different nationalities. The heads of certain gangs are furnished with proper passports issued in the different European States and even in England.

"Other gangs appear not to belong to any particular nationality. It is difficult in various instances to ascertain exactly where these people come from."

In a report to the National Assembly presented in 1873 by a committee specially appointed to inquire into the organisation of poor relief in the country, the following recommendations are made for the suppression of mendicity.

1st. The suppression of dépôts de mendicité except for the infirm or for beggars over 50 years of age.

2nd. A new clause 274 of the Penal Code, to run thus: "Every able-bodied person above 50 years of age, habitually devoting himself to the practice of mendicity, shall be sent out to the colonies." This rigorous measure can alone put an end to the shameless speculation which constitutes the sole means of subsistence of a class of the population of the great centres well-known to the public prosecutors of Paris, Lyons, and other large towns. Well-organised poor relief may then easily restrain the practice of mendicity within very narrow limits. Can it completely extinguish it?

TABLE SHOWING THE NUMBER OF PERSONS WITHOUT A CALLING.

	Beggars, Gypsies, and Vagabonds.			Prostitutes.	Persons without a Calling.		
	Males.	Females.	Total.	Females.	Males.	Females.	Total.
Census of 1872	25,461	37,327	62,788	11,875	79,021	143,928	222,949
	Beggars, Vagabonds, and Public Prostitutes.				Callings unknown.		
Census of 1876	27,353	43,970	71,323		90,220	119,997	210,217

In the census of 1881 the classification is of such a heterogeneous character that it is impossible to derive any practically useful information from it.

CONVICTIONS FOR MENDICITY AND VAGABONDAGE.

The accompanying statistical table (see next page) shows that from 1875 to 1884 the number of beggars convicted has increased by 36 per cent. and that of vagabonds by 87 per cent.

The relative proportions of beggars when subdivided into sexes is exactly the same as that obtained when they are aggregated: males 86 per cent. and females 14 per cent.; the same does not hold good with regard to Vagabondage where the females are proportionately less numerous, forming only 9 per cent. With regard to age, there are more vagabonds under 21 years than beggars. In both sexes the latter only constitute one-tenth of the total number, while those apprehended of this age and charged with vagabondage show a proportion for males of 22 per cent. and for females of 29 per cent. The Criminal Courts manifest a little more tenderness towards vagabonds than towards beggars. Of 100 of the former 7 are discharged, while the proportion of the latter is only 4 per cent.

The causes of the increase of vagabondage are both general and special. Amongst the first, there is one which of itself is sufficient to account for the augmentation shown, and that is the agricultural and commercial depression which has reigned on the continent for several years. With regard to individual causes they can only be surmised, such as idleness, poverty, social causes, &c. But to determine in what degree each of them has influenced the result shown, it would be necessary to know the classes of the population which have furnished the most numerous contingent of vagabonds; unfortunately the statistics do not contain any indication of the kind.

MENDICITY AND VAGABONDAGE.

Years.	Number of		Males.			Females.			Number of Prisoners.	
	Causes tried.	Prisoners.	Under 16.	From 16 to 21.	Over 21.	Under 16.	From 16 to 21.	Over 21.	Acquitted or sent to a House of Correction.	Condemned.
Mendicity.										
1875 . .	6,373	7,152	171	362	5,411	62	34	1,112	288	6,864
1876 . .	5,766	6,303	124	323	4,947	56	44	809	214	6,089
1877 . .	6,329	6,981	161	413	5,344	57	38	968	268	6,713
1878 . .	5,891	6,472	164	499	4,829	53	45	882	253	6,219
1879 . .	6,799	7,531	175	562	5,794	57	39	904	237	7,244
1880 . .	7,736	8,471	234	618	6,392	94	64	1,069	324	8,147
1881 . .	7,569	8,370	181	653	6,360	76	57	1,043	336	8,034
1882 . .	7,771	8,425	160	523	6,568	43	63	1,068	272	8,153
1883 . .	8,470	9,276	185	667	7,064	61	34	1,265	331	8,945
1884 . .	8,786	9,719	131	742	7,602	105	59	1,080	263	9,456
Totals . .	71,490	78,700	1,686	5,362	60,311	664	477	10,200	2,836	75,864
Annual average	7,149	7,870	169	536	6,031	66	48	1,020	284	7,586
Percentage .			2	8	90	6	4	90	4	96
			86 %			14 %				
Vagabondage.										
1875 . .	8,429	8,886	400	1,194	6,354	51	245	642	778	8,108
1876 . .	8,270	8,636	345	1,232	6,129	54	229	647	655	7,981
1877 . .	9,667	10,107	314	1,565	7,255	61	237	675	718	9,389
1878 . .	9,910	10,350	343	1,691	7,390	40	225	661	710	9,640
1879 . .	10,639	11,069	421	1,908	7,751	56	264	669	858	10,211
1880 . .	11,513	11,985	392	2,210	8,325	38	287	733	909	11,076
1881 . .	12,452	12,926	331	2,471	9,004	54	287	779	867	12,059
1882 . .	13,583	14,069	290	2,794	9,842	42	263	838	929	13,140
1883 . .	15,076	15,534	255	3,043	11,058	33	282	863	997	14,537
1884 . .	16,110	16,580	254	2,858	12,355	24	258	831	978	15,602
Totals . .	115,649	120,142	3,345	20,966	85,463	453	2,577	7,338	8,399	111,743
Annual average	11,565	12,014	334	2,097	8,546	45	258	734	840	11,174
Percentage .			3	19	78	4	25	71	7	93
			91 %			9 %				

CHAPTER XXV.

GERMAN EMPIRE.

1497—1885.

Historical introduction—Imperial penal code—Societies for the suppression of mendicity—Absence of official statistics—Recent increase of vagrancy —Its probable causes—Abnormal demand for labour in 1871-1874— Large numbers of labourers eventually thrown out of work—Abolition of passes for the interior—Reform of poor laws—Present state of vagrancy not sensibly affected by the state of the labour market—Change for the worse in the present type of vagrants—Reports from country districts— Encouragements to vagabondage—Indiscriminate almsgiving—Alleged negligence of local police—Wayside inns—Statistics from Bavaria, Saxony, and Prussia—Large proportion of juvenile vagrants—Estimate of average number of vagrants in Germany—Proportion of irreclaimable and reclaimable vagabonds—Remedial measures—Vagabondage in Saxe Coburg and Gotha, Leipzig, Bavaria, and Baden—The description of beggars in the *Liber Vagatorum*, edited by Martin Luther in 1528.

So far back as in 1497, 1532, and 1577, laws of the old German Empire prohibited begging and vagrancy, and laid down vague general rules for the relief of persons in distress. These may be considered as the first germs of the system at present in force; but practically, up to the beginning of the last century nothing very definite in the way of legislation had been attempted in any of the states, large or small, which composed the Empire. Under the feudal system, persons in distress were usually maintained either by the lord of the manor, or by the guild to which they had been admitted, or by casual charity. Begging, however, was prohibited, and the communes ("Gemeinden") were, by the law of 1577 above alluded to, bound to support their own poor, send away strangers, and provide accommodation for the sick. Especial care was taken to prevent strangers establishing settlement, a point on which the various states appear to have acted more or less in concert; but as regards the mode of relief, not only each county, but often each district, established a system of its own, entirely regardless of what was done by its neighbour.*

According to the present Imperial Penal Code (s. 361), vagrancy and begging are punished with imprisonment (not exceeding six weeks).

When condemned to imprisonment according to s. 362, the individual may at the same time be sentenced to be delivered over to the police authorities after the termination of the punishment.

The police obtain by this means the authority to confine the condemned person for a period not exceeding two years in a workhouse, or to employ him in useful labour.

At the same time this latter penalty is only admissible when an individual has been three times judicially sentenced in a criminal court in the three preceding years for such offences, or if when begging he has used threatening language or arms.

Besides these penal enactments for the repression of mendicancy, there are in many places voluntary societies (Armen-Vereine), the members of which subscribe to a fund out of which relief is given, especially to poor travellers, in cases which after investigation are found to be deserving.

There are no official statistics showing the exact extent of vagrancy in the German Empire at any given period, but that its rapid increase in late years constitutes a serious social and moral danger calling for energetic treatment, was very generally admitted in the discussions which took place on the subject in the Prussian Parliament on the 28th November, 1882, and again in the Imperial Parliament in February, 1883. On the former occasion the Prussian Minister of the Interior informed the House that a full report on the present state of vagrancy in Prussia had been drawn up for the Government by the Upper President of the kingdom, and was under serious consideration.

Meanwhile the numerous reports published for the use of the society for dealing with vagabondage on principles of self-help, and the proceedings of the central union of this society, supply sufficient material for an approximate estimate of the present extent of vagrancy in Germany.

These reports agree in recording a marked and alarming

* Report by the Hon. F. R. Plunkett, 1872.

increase in the number of vagrants throughout the empire during the last ten years.

This increase was no doubt stimulated in the first instance by the vast displacement of labour which took place between 1871 and 1874, a period marked by an abnormal, and as it eventually turned out purely temporal, demand for labour in all branches of industry, by the construction of a new network of railways, the building mania, and the sudden starting into existence of countless mushroom speculative enterprises, doomed to a speedy collapse, but which lasted long enough to draw away an enormous proportion of labourers from the agricultural districts, who were eventually thrown out of employment, and possibly formed the nucleus of the present flood of vagrancy.

The removal of the old restrictions on free migration by the abolition of obligatory passes for the interior of Germany, and the reform of the poor laws, have also been made in a great measure responsible for the increase above referred to.

Formerly the domicile of birth adhered to the subject of a German State so long as he retained his nationality, and he had to procure a licence or passport to enable him to remove his residence beyond the limits of the poor law union to which he was legally chargeable.

At present, with the exception of Bavaria, which still retains the old rule of native domicile, a German subject, on attaining the age of twenty-seven, loses his poor law domicile if he has been continuously absent from the limits of his union for two years, and the same period of continuous residence is required to qualify him for obtaining a relief domicile in a new union.

These reforms no doubt conferred incalculable benefits on the country at large by encouraging the free circulation of efficient and solid labour, but gave an equal stimulus to pauper vagrancy. The employers found in them a selfish interest in terminating the contract of an inefficient hand, and the landlord for serving notice to quit on a lodger likely to come eventually on the local rates' before the legal period of two years' residence should be completed.

In the States bordering on the Bavarian or foreign frontiers these outcasts were frequently encouraged to cross over the lines, and when returned by the police of the neighbouring State as vagrants after two years' absence, the local unions being relieved of all obligation for their support, they were thrown upon the funds of the State or of the county unions.

This may account for the facts recorded by all the reports that the bulk of present vagrants in Germany are homeless in every sense of the word, having no union to which they are legally chargeable, and that the present tide of vagrancy is not sensibly affected by any briskness or slackness in the labour market.

Employers are naturally shy about enabling a vagrant to acquire a charge upon the local rates by giving him permanent employment.

The reports further record a marked change for the worse in the type of ordinary vagrants.

Pastor Stursberg, of Hanover, an eminent authority on the subject, has been at pains to collect a great amount of information and statistics from all parts of the Empire for the use of the society above referred to, and he shows that the fact of the recent increase of vagabondage has been clearly established both in regard to the towns and country districts. In the former it is kept more out of sight, owing, no doubt, to the greater facilities afforded for dealing with it by measures both of coercion and relief.

The reports from country districts reveal a truly deplorable and alarming state of things. One description is as follows:—

"Outrages, arson, and robberies are multiplying here yearly; the country roads are no longer safe."

"The strolling apprentice in search of employment and experience in his business, once a familiar sight throughout the length and breadth of the land, who was usually clothed with some appearance of comfort, a knapsack on his back, and found ready shelter and a helping hand in every village on his way, has almost entirely disappeared from the roads; in his place you may daily see, singly or in herds, a ragged, vicious tramp, instead of a knapsack a clubbed stick, and a spirit flask invariably concealed somewhere in his rags.

"On a long summer day troops of this description swoop down upon a lonely village, while the able-bodied inhabitants are at work in distant fields, and levy with threats, and often open acts of violence, contributions in kind and money from the defenceless women left in the cottages, the solitary policeman of the village looking on helplessly in the face of superior numbers.

"In some villages the inhabitants are only too willing to pay blackmail in the guise of charity to these troublesome visitors, and pass them on to a neighbouring union, thus avoiding the disagreeable alternative of having their local rates raised by the cost of their detention and punishment by the local police."

Moreover, to use the striking local expression used in this description, many a farmer will readily open his barn door to an ugly customer to avoid seeing the red-cock perch on his thatch,* the local euphemism for having his house set on fire.

The alleged negligence of the local police in these cases is often attributed to want of sufficient accommodation in the workhouses, and a natural fear of harbouring epidemics and contagions which these vagabond-troops not unusually carry in their train.

Tramps of this description are proved to collect as much as from four to six marks a day in this way. These sums they invariably spend in the wayside inns or so-called "Strollers' Homes," chiefly in the consumption of the local spirit, "schnaps." These establishments appear to be in too many cases nothing but hotbeds for the propagation of vagabondage and encouragement of beggars. Here, in addition to the "schnaps," they are often supplied with forged or genuine hawkers' licences to evade the police, in which the innkeepers seem to do a brisk business, also with references and indications of the best line of country and roads to ply their trade of begging with safety.

The police seem to have very little power to put a stop to these malpractices, although it is admitted on all hands that remedial measures will have little prospect of permanent success until the establishments in question can be summarily dealt with or their management reformed.

Pastor Stursberg gives the following statistics, mostly based on official data. In the year 1879, 108,911 persons were punished in Bavaria alone under the vagrancy laws, double the number recorded in 1872. In the kingdom of Saxony in the year 1880 there were punished for the same offence 14,066, and of these

---

* The use of this expression is not confined to Germany :—
"But we'll see if the red cock craw not in his bonnie barn-yard ae morning before day-dawning."
"Hush! Meg, hush! hush! that's not safe talk."
"What does she mean?" said Mannering to Sampson, in an undertone.
"Fire-raising," answered the laconic Dominie.

Guy Mannering, chap. iii.

2,636 were between the ages of fourteen and twenty; 2,461 between those of twenty and twenty-five.

The large proportion of juvenile vagrants is noted in the reports from most of the districts in Germany.

In Prussia the numbers detained in the Houses of Correction were in the following years :—

1874	4,534
1875	5,467
1876	6,974
1877	8,455
1878	10,762
1879	13,160
1880	12,840
1881	15,721

On the basis of these statistics and others collected from numerous smaller local districts, Herr Stursberg makes the rough calculation that at present the average number of vagrants punished in one year in Germany may be set down at 200,000, to which number must be added those who may have succeeded in evading the grasp of the law.

Pastor Bodelschwingh, the indefatigable promoter of the Wilhelmsdorf Labour Colony, and other authorities on the subject, are prepared to admit the general accuracy of this calculation, and also the assumption which follows it, that of this total of 200,000, 100,000 may be set down as inveterate and irreclaimable vagabonds. Dr. Bodelschwingh believes that of the remaining 100,000, 80,000 are probably bonâ-fide seekers of work in some shape or other, requiring only to be removed from the contaminating influence of their associates and directed to a suitable field of labour.

Twenty thousand he considers would represent the maximum number of reclaimable vagabonds, fit subjects for the remedial measures of the society.

Of these measures the most successful and striking in its results has been the founding of the Wilhelmsdorf Labour Colony in Westphalia.

An account of the working of this colony was given in the interesting report drawn up by Mr. Townley, published in Parliamentary Paper, Commercial No. 9, 1883.

The principle on which it is worked is to receive reclaimable vagrants of all creeds on application, to shelter, feed, and clothe them, and then set them to work on the farms attached to the colony, until they have earned by their labour the cost of their clothing and become reaccustomed to working habits ; they are then discharged (as a general rule in three months) and assisted and directed to some more permanent field of employment, where they are left to their own resources.

The principal resolutions passed at a general meeting of the Central Society held at Berlin in February, 1884 were: To persevere in their efforts on the principle of self-help, and in addition to founding new labour colonies, to endeavour to establish all through Germany, at proper intervals, stations for the relief of vagrants by affording them temporary shelter, clothing, and food, but these gifts, wherever possible, to be always made in return for work of some description.

All irreclaimables and disorderly subjects not to be simply discharged, but in every case handed over to the police.

To endeavour to make these stations in time take the place of the wayside inns, or so-called homes for vagrants. No spirits of any kind to be permitted on the premises. The Sunday to be observed as a day of rest, additional hours of labour being imposed on Saturdays and Mondays. Steps, if possible, to be taken to attach to each relief station a registry and inquiry office, with the object of securing employment for vagrants willing to work. To discourage the indiscriminate giving of alms, and to request the existing private charitable societies not to discontinue their efforts in consequence of the exertions of the society, but rather to co-operate with it, and to indicate to such societies, and also to the communal and local relief bodies that the most useful direction in which this assistance could be given would be in trying to provide employment for those out of work.

Without desiring in any way to discourage or underrate the activity of the society for dealing with the vagabondage difficulty by measures of self-help, several authorities of experience have pointed out that private efforts can scarcely be expected to deal successfully with this evil unless supplemented by State assistance; the society has itself shown that it is powerless to deal with the great bulk of the present army of vagrants, "the inveterate and irreclaimable tramps." Of the remainder, at least one per cent. are probably incapable of work from age or infirmity, and few of the able-bodied suited to agricultural labour. Moreover, they believe that the society will find difficulty in establishing sufficiently firm control and discipline in the labour colonies and relief stations to ensure the practical success of its scheme.

The alternative proposed by those who argue thus is a more extended adaptation of the workhouse system to the present exigencies of vagrancy under the control of the central and local authorities, who with the support of permanent and fixed funds will be better enabled to administer relief than a society solely dependent on the fluctuating contributions of private charity.

It has further been pointed out that to meet the cure of irreclaimable vagrants there is no need of fresh legislation, but only of a stricter enforcement of the existing Vagrancy Laws, and common action with renewed energy on the part of the different governments and police forces of the Empire.*

SAXE-COBURG AND GOTHA.—The police punishes all vagabonds and beggars, and if they have no parish in the duchy to which they can be removed, they are immediately escorted out of the duchy.†

HAMBURG.—The isolated condition of Hamburg when surrounded, as was formerly the case, by a wall, and accessible only by gates which were closed at sunset, made it possible to carry out very stringent regulations to prevent the influx of persons who were liable to become destitute. Orders were given to the gatekeepers to prevent "beggars, cripples, Jew pedlars, and other suspicious persons" from entering the town, and the inhabitants were forbidden to receive strange beggars into their houses, or to give them money in the streets, under penalties of ten or five thalers respectively. Although this harsh and unfeeling law has long been obsolete, its spirit was revived in a police regulation issued in the year 1869, forbidding almsgiving in the streets. Owing to these precautions Hamburg has always been much freer from vagrants and beggars than most towns of the same character. When found, beggars and vagrants are punished with one or two days' imprisonment for the first offence, from one to four weeks' imprisonment in subsequent cases, which is increased to imprisonment for two years, with or without hard labour, where it is evident that the individual is determined to pursue a vagrant life.‡

---

* Report of Charles S. Scott, Secretary of the British Embassy, 1884.
† Report by Charles T. Barnard, 1871.
‡ Report by George Annesley, 1871.

LEIPZIG.—Incorrigibly idle and professional beggars are warned that they must work. They are also directed where and how to find work; but money is not given to them. A register is kept in which every applicant and his or her circumstances are minutely noted. Descriptions of beggars are given to the families subscribing to the society, so as they may avoid giving alms to the unworthy.*

BAVARIA.

No published statistics exist specially referring to vagrancy from which it would be possible to state precisely the actual condition of Bavaria in this respect.

The Ministry of the Interior only possesses the statistical information given in the annual reports of the police.

The number of persons charged with this offence was as follows in the undermentioned years:—

1874	14,629
1875	15,017
1876	19,316
1877	26,320
1878	30,129
1879	26,606
1880	27,701
1881	29,458
1882	27,169

BADEN.

The Baden *Police* Penal Code, which was in force up to the end of 1871, contains a number of enactments against vagrancy and mendicancy. Any one begging, causing others under his power or authority to beg, or neglecting to restrain them, was liable to imprisonment for a period not exceeding four weeks.

Able-bodied individuals who had already undergone punishments within a year for vagrancy or mendicancy, who were not supporting themselves in a legitimate way, and refused to engage in any occupation according to their ability, and were unable to prove that they could not obtain work, were liable to a similar penalty.

The *penal code* also contained various statutes directed against vagrancy and mendicancy.

Vagabonds loitering about beyond the limits of their dwelling place with no regular occupation, and without sufficient means for

* Report by J. A. Crowe, 1872.

their support, having been already punished twice by the police in the preceding three years, were liable on a repetition of the offence, and on the demand of the police authorities, to be imprisoned as vagrants with hard labour for a period not exceeding six months. Beggars with false passports, or false testimonials respecting infirmities or accidents, or with passports or testimonials belonging to others and fraudulently used as their own, or using threatening language, were liable to a similar penalty.

Beggars with arms or other instruments of a suspicious nature, were subject to the penalty of being deprived of their freedom, with compulsory labour for a period not exceeding two years, without being previously punished by the police authorities.

Finally, vagrants and beggars, besides being deprived of their freedom, were in all cases liable to be placed under the special supervision of the police, and foreigners to be expelled the country.

An Act passed in 1840 for the repression of mendicancy, authorised the administrative authorities to deliver over persons punished for these offences to the police house of correction (Verwahrungs-Anstalt).

Baden subjects judicially sentenced in a criminal law court for vagrancy or begging, or having been six times punished by the police for these offences, were confined in the house of correction, unless they could show that they could support themselves by some legitimate trade or occupation.

Such persons could obtain their freedom at their own request after two years, or even after one year (but not sooner) if their conduct had been good.

All these penal enactments, as well as the police house of correction, were done away with at the commencement of 1872, upon the introduction of the Imperial Penal Code.*

The following extracts give a picture of the condition of mendicity in Germany at the commencement of the sixteenth century.

The Mendicant Brotherhood.

Here follows a pretty little book, called *Liber Vagatorum*, written by a high and worthy master, *nomine Expertus in Truffis*, to the praise and glory of God, *sibi in refrigerium et solacium*, for all persons' instruction and benefit, and for the correction and conver-

* Report by E. M. Baillie, 1872.

sion of those that practise such knaveries as are shown hereafter; which little book is divided into three parts. Part the first shows the several methods by which mendicants and tramps get their livelihood, and is subdivided into xx chapters, *et paulo plus*,— for there are xx ways, *et ultra*, whereby men are cheated and fooled. Part the second give some *notabilia* which refer to the means of livelihood afore-mentioned. The third part presents a vocabulary of their language or gibberish, commonly called Red Welsh or Beggar lingo.

The beggars are divided into the following classes:—

1. The *Bregers*, or beggars who simply ask an alms for God's or the Holy Virgin's sake.
2. The *Stabülers*, or bread gatherers, who beg bread from the peasants and have their hats and cloaks full of signs of all the saints.
3. The *Lossners*,* or liberated prisoners, who pretend they have been captives among the infidel for several years.
4. The *Klenkners*, or cripples, who sit at the church doors and attend fairs and church gatherings, with real or simulated sore or broken limbs.
5. The *Dobissers or Dopfers*, or church mendicants, carrying about an image of the Virgin or some other saint, passing themselves off as friars, and begging money or contributions of various kinds for a church or chapel.
6. The *Kammesierers*, or learned beggars. Young scholars or young students on the tramp.
7. The *Vagierern* (strollers), clad in yellow garments, who profess to exorcise the devil for hail, for storm, and for witchcraft.
8. The *Grantners*, or knaves with the falling sickness.
9. The *Dutzers*, who pretend to have been ill for a long time, and say that they must obtain a certain sum in alms from each of three pious men each day.
10. The *Schleppers*, or false begging priests.
11. The *Gickisses*, or blind beggars.
12. The *Schwanfelders* or *Blickschlahers*, or naked beggars.
13. The *Voppers*, or demoniacs, for the most part women, who allow themselves to be led in chains as if they were raving mad.
14. The *Dallingers*, or hangmen, who pretend to do penance for having been hangmen.

* Literally prisoners "let loose."

15. The *Dützbetterins*, or lying-in women, who pretend to have been recently confined, or that they have been pregnant with a monster which they must support.

16. The *Süntvegers*, or pretended murderers, who say they have taken a man's life in self-defence, and unless they bring money at the right time they will have their heads cut off.

17. The female *Süntvegers*, who pretend they formerly had led a loose life of which they now repent.

18. The *Bil-wearers* or pretended pregnant women.

19. The *Jungfrauen* (virgins), or pretended lepers.

20. The *Mümsen*, beggars who go about under the pretence of begging.

21. The *Ubern Sönzen Ganger*, or pretended noblemen and knights, who say they have suffered by war, fire, or captivity, or have been driven away and lost all they had.

22. The *Kandierers*, or pretended mercers, who make people believe they had once been merchants over the sea.

23. The *Veranerins*, or baptised Jewesses, who have turned Christians.

24. The *Christianiers Calmierers*, or pretended pilgrims.

25. The *Seffers*, or salvers, who smear themselves all over with salve as if their mouth and face had broken out in sores.

26. The *Schweigers*, or jaundiced, who smear themselves with dung to give themselves the appearance of the yellow sickness, or other dreadful disease.

27. The *Burkhart*, who tie their hands to their throat and say they have St. Anthony's penance or that of any other saint.

28. The *Platschierers*, or blind harpers, who play on the lute in front of churches and tell lies as to the origin of their blindness.[*]

---

[*] "The Book of Vagabonds and Beggars," edited by Martin Luther, 1528. Translated by J. C. Hotten, 1860.

CHAPTER XXVI.

AUSTRIA.

Vagabonds and Beggars in Vienna—Municipal and charitable institutions—Municipal workhouse—Police shelter—Refuge for the homeless—Mendicity Society—Results obtained—Vagrants sent home from Vienna—Vagrants returned to Vienna—Vagrancy in the country—Proposed remedial measures.

VAGABONDS AND BEGGARS IN VIENNA.

ANY practical account of these two categories of the human species I cannot give, they cannot well be separated, so many of the former are beggars and so many of the latter are vagabonds. In such a case I must be excused if I cannot clearly define the difference, and the following information must be deemed the best I can supply from meagre data.

There are various kinds of beggars in Vienna the same as in other large cities. I have personally encountered them, they range from the Society beggar of Dickens to the spectacular beggar of the one-armed or one-legged type. The ordinary Vienna street beggar does not belong to an objectionable race, his toilette is irreproachable, he is very polite, and not annoying or so persistent as the Viennese flower-girls. The pleasantest beggar for an Englishman to meet is the aristocratic beggar (and I am sorry to say that there appear to be many of all ranks, counts, countesses, barons, and baronesses). I have had several personal visits from ruined counts; they send in their card, and on being received, begin immediately in the most impassioned style to assure one that the English are the most noble and generous of all peoples; they express so heartily their opinion of the blessing of being an Englishman, that before the story of their own misfortunes can be narrated the florins are literally flattered out of an Englishman's pocket and into that of the ruined count. I find at the same time that it is a pleasure to open the door myself and bow very politely on their departure. Are they real counts?

The most tormenting class of beggar in Vienna is the midge class, composed of varied sizes of well-fed looking boys and girls, little skirmishers from the queen midges seated on the door-step near by. The members of this annoying class all use the same whining phrases, and, like the insect they represent, are able, through not wearing either shoes or stockings, to pounce silently and suddenly on the unwary, buzzing persistently in their track until threatened with the "polizei," who, however, are wanted when never there, as the places chosen for public torture are off the track of the policeman; the recruiting ground for future vagabonds is thus well chosen. Vagabonds are continually to be seen in Vienna, and I have observed many whose countenances are by no means attractive. Curiously enough they never appear to beg, which leads me to believe that they must be chiefly of the criminal class and under police supervision. It is to be noticed that these observations are entirely personal on my part.

Assistance to the poor is generously afforded by the Vienna municipality and through private charitable institutions with the cordial support of the Imperial family.

In 1879 those receiving relief from municipal funds in the different districts and parishes of Vienna amounted to 44,634, male and female. This was an increase on the two previous years of nearly 3,500 persons.

For the care of those out of work there is a municipal workhouse, where certain conditions are laid down. One, that if a person chooses he can go out and work, but on his return at night he must pay ten kreuzers (about twopence) for his night's lodging; the other, that a person who remains in the workhouse has to work there, for which he gets his meals, shelter, and a small weekly wage. The results of the first condition are shown as follows: in 1877, 6 persons had 897 days' work, paying to the workhouse 89 fl. 70 kr., in 1878, 8 persons with 821 days' work, paying 82 fl. 10 kr.; and in 1879, only 5 persons with 382 days' work, paying 38 fl. 20 kr. Of those under the second condition there were satisfactory symptoms of work being plentiful, as in 1877 those employed in the workhouse amounted to 424 persons, whereas in 1878 there were only 342, and in 1879 they had decreased to 260. The average cost of the institution for the three years was 49,384 florins, or £4,200; the income was only 13,000 florins, or £1,200.

There are lodgings given by the police to honest people who are found without shelter.

There are many beneficent institutions in Vienna besides those of the municipality. One, " the refuge for the homeless," is of immense use to the poor in this city. From 1871 to the end of 1879 the statistics show that 690,000 persons obtained shelter, and that 1,366,000 rations of bread and soup had been given out.

Another admirable institution for helping poverty and distress, the " Verein gegen verarmung und bettelei," is worthy of especial mention. The particular purposes for which it works are as follows :—

1st. For the prevention of threatening distress by furnishing help corresponding to the necessity of the case.

2nd. To assist those in distress but capable of work to gain a living.

3rd. To grant help in urgent cases to those incapable of gaining a living.

4th. To prevent begging. This is done by assisting those capable of work to establish themselves in small trades, and by placing the incapable in the almshouse or by giving them assistance; in the cases of professional beggars means are taken to expose them and render them harmless.

The society was founded in 1879, and since then it has received 24,899 applications for relief from all classes, counts, countesses, barons, baronesses, officers, professors, officials, actors, down to labourers, as well as a large number of professional beggars. Of these 24,899 applicants, however, some applied as many as seventeen times.

All cases of beggars reported by subscribers are looked into by the society, and those who make begging a profession are exposed.

In February, 1884, 600 persons were sent out of Vienna to their homes; 429 to Bohemia, Lower Austria, and Moravia, 72 to other Austrian provinces, 73 to Hungary, and 26 abroad. Of these 352 had no means of support, 11 were prostitutes, 56 were beggars, 100 were sent away with orders never to return, 57 with punishments, and 24 considered dangerous to public order.

Those belonging to Vienna and returned here by the authorities from the provinces and Hungary numbered 264. Of these 110 had no means of subsistence, 8 were vagrants, 35 were beggars, and 111 others with punishments.

From what I am enabled to learn I form the opinion that vagrancy has undoubtedly increased in Austria, and it is a grievance which I notice is attracting attention in the provinces, one which especially concerns the farmers and peasantry, as they suffer much from the numerous vagabonds who infest the country. Both the farmers and peasantry are afraid of them, as they believe if they refuse relief to them that out of revenge the vagabonds would set fire to their barns or houses, or commit other damage.

A landed proprietor in Lower Austria, whose land is distantly removed from the high road, finding so many vagabonds annually called upon him for relief or work, made one year a calculation, which showed that no fewer than 7,200 vagabonds presented themselves. It is also calculated that the peasant's donation to vagabonds in the year (bread, meat, and milk) amounts to more than the taxes he annually pays.

In Salzburg, in 1866, 3,000 vagabonds were counted, and it is calculated that what they received in money and food from the inhabitants amounted to about 600,000 florins, or more than the direct taxes paid by the duchy.

In the towns the authorities are bound to care for vagabonds, they consequently get rid of them as fast as they can. The vagabonds are not loth to be so dealt with, as they are sure of being cared for in the next place they visit; they can thus make the round of the whole country without work. Foreign vagabonds, however, are sent out of the country, if found.

Attention is being given to an excellent system which has met with much success in Germany and Bavaria in diminishing the number of beggars in those districts where it has been carried out. The system is that of making settlements where vagabonds are sent to and employed at agricultural and other useful work.

In 1883 the number of beggars brought under police notice amounted to 5,081. Of this number 1,300 were brought before the courts, and 321 were discharged; 1,551 received an admonition, 1,901 were punished with a term of police arrest, and 321 were imprisoned.

3,894 were men and boys.
1,187 were women and girls.
2,973 were single.

1,306 married.
802 widowed.
1,842 had formerly served in trade.
216 had been in service.
2,987 had been labourers, or without any regular occupation.
1,435 were regular beggars.
44 were cripples.
140 were small children.
1,621 were of the vagabond class.

Laws respecting Beggars and Vagabonds in Austria.

Vagabonds.

Those persons who leave their homes in search of work and finding none, and are known to have no means by which to gain a living, or who do not endeavour to gain an honest living, can be punished as vagabonds, with an arrest of from eight days to one month. If they offend oftener they can be punished with from one to three months' "stringent" arrest (this arrest combines a variety of punishments—imprisonment, fasting, hard labour, hard beds, seclusion, detention in a house of correction, &c., according to the prisoner's offence). The police have authority to require those released after repeated offences to show, during a term of three years, that they are gaining an honest living. If they cannot prove this they can be arrested for from three to fourteen days; again offending they have to undergo one month's stringent arrest.

They can be placed under police supervision, in which case they must remain in the district assigned to them. The police cannot prohibit them from remaining in their native place.

They are obliged to give information of their change of domicile, their means of subsistence, and their intercourse with other persons.

The police can order them to appear on certain days at the police-station; they can prevent their attending meetings, or leaving their lodgings at night-time. Their lodgings and person can be searched. Vagabond youths under eighteen years of age are put into a house of correction, but they are not detained there after they attain the age of twenty.

Beggars.

Beggars are in the first instance warned by the police, and after repeated offences are brought before the tribunals, the punishment varying from eight days to one and even three months' imprisonment. A beggar shamming illness or trying to excite the compassion of the public by pretending bodily defects, is in the first instance punished with one month's imprisonment.

Children under fourteen found begging. In such cases the parents, or those under whose care the children are placed, if it is proved they are aware that the children were begging, can be punished with an arrest of from eight days to one month.

Persons letting out children for begging purposes are similarly punished with from eight days to one month's imprisonment, and for a repetition of the offence with from one to three months' imprisonment.*

* Report of Victor Drummond, 1884.

CHAPTER XXVII.

ITALY.

1586—1872.

Law of 1865 regarding vagrants and beggars—Former attempts at repression—The Company of St. Elizabeth, or Beggars' Guild—" The forty hours"—Description of the orders of beggars by Nobili in 1627—The tricks of the *Bianti* in Sicily—Their punishment by the Duke of Sessa.

By the Public Security Law of March 20th, 1865, as amended by the law of July 6th, 1871, on information laid by the police, or in default thereof, on the ground of public notoriety, the magistrate called Pretone may summon any person charged with being an idler or a vagrant to appear before him within five days. On the appearance of such person, the magistrate, if the charge be admitted or proved, admonishes the idler or vagrant to find regular work, and to show that he has done so within the time prescribed, ordering him not to remove in the meanwhile from the place where he is without previous notice given to the place. When the person summoned denies the charge, and it cannot be immediately established, the case is adjourned for another period of five days, in order to obtain further evidence.

If a person admonished as above-mentioned neglects to comply with the injunctions he has received, such disobedience is punishable with imprisonment for not less than three or more than six months.

Vagrants and idlers under the age of sixteen years may be, according to circumstances, either consigned to the care of their parents or guardians, or placed in a workhouse or reformatory.

At the expiration of his term of imprisonment the vagrant, if a foreigner, is conducted to the frontier and expelled the State; if an Italian citizen, he is directed to the local authority of the commune where he has declared it to be his intention to fix his residence, which he is required not to change without previous notice to that authority.

If he does not keep to the route traced out for him, or if he fails to present himself within the term prescribed to the proper authority, or if he leaves the residence assigned to him without permission, he is liable to imprisonment for a term of not less than one month or more than one year.

A person who has undergone a sentence of imprisonment for vagrancy may be forbidden by the prefect of the province to establish his residence in the place chosen by him, under pain of imprisonment for not less than one month or more than one year.

A place of residence during a period of from six months to two years, or, after conviction for a repeated offence, from one year to five years, may be assigned to such vagrant by the Minister of the Interior.

The law above cited of March 20th, 1865, provides that in communes where there is no mendicity asylum, persons unable to work, and who have neither means of subsistence nor relations bound by law to support them, shall receive from the municipal authorities certificates of poverty and inability to work; which certificates, duly countersigned by the district political authorities, shall be considered as licences to beg within the district.

It is understood, however, that such permission is not to be granted in places where sufficient charitable foundations exist for the relief of the poor. Mendicancy is prohibited in all cases except those above mentioned. Under any circumstance beggars are forbidden to show their sores, injuries, or deformities, to carry heavy sticks or other arms, or to express desperation by words or gestures. Begging by night is always prohibited.

Any person found begging without a licence is taken into custody, and handed over to the judicial authority, to be proceeded against according to law. But in a commune where there exists a mendicity asylum, if the person found begging is unable to work, and without means of subsistence, he is sent to such asylum, and kept there until he has acquired the means of subsistence, or until some one undertakes to maintain him.

Cardinal Morichini records a series of ineffectual endeavours to repress mendicancy in Rome, which were made by several Popes since the middle of the sixteenth century.

Pius V. issued a bull prohibiting begging in churches under the severest penalties. Gregory XIII. charged the arch-confraternity of the Holy Trinity for the care of Pilgrims and Convalescents with the duty of clearing Rome of beggars. Those incapable of working were to be maintained in the monastery of S. Sisto, which he assigned to the society for that purpose, and the able-bodied were to be sent away to earn their livelihood by their own labour. Full power was given to the arch-confraternity to imprison paupers or expel them from the city. In execution of the Pope's brief to this effect, all the beggars in Rome were required to present themselves on a certain day at the hospital of the Holy Trinity. Eight hundred and fifty of them having been so collected were made to march in solemn procession to their destined asylum, which soon, however, had to be abandoned as unsuitable. The measures adopted proved quite inefficacious, as appears from a bull in which, a few years later, Sixtus V. declared that the public places, private houses, and churches were filled with importunate and clamorous beggars, who wandered about the city, without having any fixed abode, without religious instruction, and seeking nothing but food. In order to put an end to such a state of things the Pope established a great asylum or almshouse for the indigent, without distinction of nationality, and he ordered that those who should still persist in begging rather than go into the house should be severely punished, even in some cases with the galleys.

The desired result, however, was far from being obtained. Only twelve years after the death of Sixtus V., according to a contemporary writer, the beggars infesting the streets were so numerous that there was no possibility of walking in the town without being surrounded by them, while, on the other hand, very few indeed remained in the asylum.

Innocent X. ordered all beggars to be shut up in the Apostolical Palace of St. John Lateran; but his intentions do not seem to have been fulfilled, and Pope Innocent XI. came to the conclusion that the design was not realisable. Innocent XII. took up again the plans of Sixtus V. for the extirpation of mendicity, and with that view instituted the "*Ospizio Apostolico.*"

During the greater part of the seventeenth and eighteenth centuries there existed a regularly authorised beggars' society, designated by the name of the Company of S. Elizabeth. It had between 400 and 500 members, each of whom contributed two *bajocchi* and a half (about twopence halfpenny) a month towards the expenses of religious ceremonies, of which there were many. Once a year the blind, led by the lame, went in penitential procession with a military escort to visit four churches. Penalties were inflicted on members of the company who failed to pay their subscriptions, or were wanting in due respect to their superior officers. No one was allowed to beg in the streets who was not a member. Children, able-bodied men and women, and foreigners were excluded. Strangers, however, were sometimes allowed to beg in the winter on payment of the ordinary subscription. All the members of the company were furnished with licences. They practised begging among themselves, certain of the brethren being charged with the duty of soliciting alms from the rest for those who were ill. On Sundays one of the officers of the company, called *Camerlengo*, who was lame, accompanied by two who were blind, called the *Signore* and the *Guardiano*, went about the town with fiddles and a *poet* to collect offerings for the feast of the patroness of the society, S. Elizabeth. The custom was to carry a silver basin for contributions, with ten crowns and a silver snuffbox in it; and every one who put money into the former was asked to take a pinch of snuff from the latter. This grotesque trade union, which was founded in 1613, and lasted until the Revolution at the end of the eighteenth century, was placed under the protection of a cardinal. Its last protector was Cardinal York.

Pius VII. in setting on foot, and Leo XII. in completing, the general system of relief which has already been described, made stringent regulations against mendicity; but their edicts for its suppression seem to have been as fruitless as those of former Popes. Again, in 1837, all beggars were summoned to give an account of themselves. The infirm received a licence to beg and a medal which they were to wear. The able-bodied, if strangers, were sent away, or, if Romans, were required to find work. Non-compliance was punished with imprisonment on bread and water for a first offence, and with heavier penalties for a second offence. A house was subsequently established where unlicensed beggars were temporarily placed.

A singular old custom, still existing when he wrote his book, the second edition of which was published in 1870, is described by Cardinal Morichini. A chosen band of forty beggars received special licence from the Cardinal Vicar to take post outside the doors of churches during the solemnity called *The Forty Hours,* and the devout had to pass on every such occasion between two long rows of vociferous mendicants, whose clamour even disturbed the prayers of the congregation within. Of these privileged beggars, half were blind and the rest cripples. One-third of the whole number were women. The age for admission was not fixed, and the licence was held during good behaviour. The patronage belonged to the Cardinal Vicar, who appointed to vacant places.*

In 1627, *Giacinto Nobili,* a Dominican monk of Viterbo, who wrote under the pseudonym of *Rafaele Frianoro,* published at Venice, under Papal sanction, a work entitled "*Il Vagabondo overo sferza de Bianti e Vagabondi,*" the materials of which he appears to have drawn from some of the arch-vagabonds of the period.

He divides vagabonds into thirty-four classes:—

1. *Bianti,* or Blessed, bearers of false bulls, indulgences, relics, &c.
2. *Felsi,* or Cozeners, or false prophets, who gave out that they were inspired by God and gifted with the spirit of prophecy. They declared that there were concealed treasures in houses guarded by evil spirits, which could only be discovered through the medium of the sacrifices, prayers, and fastings of their confraternity, and that to search for these treasures in any other way would be to risk one's life.
3. *Affrati,* or false monks, who, though they had never been ordained, nevertheless had the hardihood to celebrate mass, saying wherever they went that it was their first mass, in order to obtain more in alms or offerings. The Inquisition made short work of these rascals whenever they fell into its power.
4. *Falsi Bordoni,* or false pilgrims, who sold medals and shells and solicited alms because they said they could not conscientiously live on their own means during their pilgrimage, through fear of breaking their vow.
5. *Acaptosi,* or Redeemed Slaves, who pretended to have escaped from slavery and wanted money to redeem their relations.
6. *Affarfanti,* or Charlatans, who invented miraculous events, stating that they had committed monstrous sins for which they

* Report by Sir A. Paget, 1872.

had been punished by incurable disorders, until they were healed of them through having made a vow to wander through the world, for the purpose of recounting the effects of divine justice and of God's infinite mercy towards miserable sinners.

7. *Accaponi*, or Ulcerated, who made ulcers on their legs with powder, toast, and hare's blood.

8. *Allacrimanti*, or Weepers, who owed their name to the facility with which they shed tears at will, principally in the presence of women. They did not solicit anything, but always had their arms extended to receive offerings.

9. *Ascioni*, or Stupid, who simulated madmen, or deaf and dumb people. They did not ask for anything, but kept their hands extended to receive alms.

10. *Accadenti*, or Epileptics, who pretended to have fits whenever they were in the midst of a number of people from whom it seemed likely they would get alms.

11. *Cagnabaldi*, or Exchangers, who persuaded people to exchange pearls, rings, &c., for pinchbeck.

12. *Mutatori*, or Lenders, who professed to lend money without interest.

13. *Attremanti*, or Tremblers, who shook in every limb, pretending to be impotent or paralytic.

14. *Admiranti*, or Reciters of False Miracles, who pretended that an image of the virgin, or some other saint in a distant locality, had shed tears, or sweated, or inclined its head; they then sold a fac-simile of it, which they declared had worked a miracle.

15. *Acconii*, or Image-bearers of Saints, who carried images of the saints on their breasts to be kissed by the faithful.

16. *Attarantati*, or Bitten, who pretended to be bitten by tarantulas, and to be in consequence smitten with a form of madness. They indulged in the most extravagant capers and did not solicit anything; the companion who conducted them, however, accepted alms.

17. *Appezzenti*, or Bread-eaters, who pretended to eat nothing else. They sold all the whole loaves they collected and eat only the pieces.

18. *Cocchini*, or tattered rogues, answering to our shallow coves or shivering jemmies, who went naked, even in winter, and collected clothes and money, though they pretended to prefer nudity and poverty for the love of God.

AND BEGGARS AND BEGGING.

19. *Spettrini*, or False Priests, resembling the English frater, who pretended to collect for hospitals, and pocketed the money.

20. *Iucchi* or *Ribattezzati*, Christianised or Rebaptised Jews, who pretended to have been rich Jews converted by terrible visions or incredible miracles. In every town they came to they caused themselves to be rebaptised, and by this means drew valuable gifts from their sponsors and others.

21. *Falpatori*, or Masters of Arts, aged or impotent rascals, who taught children the art of cheating.

22. *Affarinati*, or Flourerers, who begged flour to make holy wafers to be used at the celebration of masses for the living and dead.

23. *Allampadati*, or Lampists, who during Passion Week and at the great festivals begged oil for the lamps which are lighted in front of the host, or the images of the virgin.

24. *Reliquiarii*, or Vendors of False Relics.

25. *Pauliani*, or Paulists, who pretended to descend from the Apostle Paul, and drove away snakes and eat and drank venomous things, for which they swallowed antidotes beforehand.

26. *Allacerbanti* or *Protobianti*, or Head Rogues, who often cheated one another.

27. *Calcidiarii*, or Advisers of Pregnant Women, who made pregnant women believe that they would miscarry or meet with other misfortunes unless they made offerings of tapers, wine, bread, and anything in season, which these rascals appropriated.

28. *Lotori*, or Bathers, who pretended to be in possession of miraculous water which would make infants grow to an extraordinary degree, or cause them to die.

29. *Crociarii*, or Saffroners, rogues who sold saffron in places where it did not exist, and cheated people as to its value.

30. *Comparizzanti*, or Searchers for Godfathers, who endeavoured to relieve themselves of the expenses of childbirth and nursing, and at the same time to curry favour with the rich by making them sponsors for their children.

31. *Affamiglioli*, or Fathers of Families who carried about a number of children.

32. *Poveri Vergognosi*, or Respectable Poor ashamed to beg.

33. *Morghigeri*, or Bellringers, who carried a lamp and a bell and asked alms for their prayers.

34. *Testatori,* or Testators, who pretended to be ill and bequeath money to their protectors.

Religious superstition appears to have been the keynote of most of these forms of rascality.

The following will serve as a sample of the modes in which some of these rascals carried on their tricks:—

" *The Bianti.**

" The *Bianti,* or Blessed, are so called because they promise themselves sovereign blessedness in this world through their constant endeavours to enrich themselves by leading a life all the more infamous on account of its apparent misery. . . . . [These impostors are unable to exhibit any example of the efficacy of their prayers, but I will produce one of their roguery.] In the year 1457, at the time Pope *Calixtus III.* admitted S—— the Confessor into the ranks of the Saints a certain *Ser* † named *Gabriele Prato,* having gone to Sicily with several of his companions in rascality, preached the miracles of this great saint, and clothing many persons with the habit of the saint, he sold some prayers he had composed, as if they had been a fruit of the spirit and zeal of the confessor. [This is the way that sinners sometimes made the saints the guarantors for their crimes, and after having abused everything else, finally abused religion itself.]

" One day, being on his way to a town situated at the seaside, and having learned that there was no white cloth there, he left his companions in a neighbouring hamlet, with instructions to disguise themselves as merchants and to come in a short time with a number of pieces of white cloth to a certain spot [on which he would plant his pilgrim's staff]. Then *Gabriele* having entered the place began to propound several miracles of the saint, which no one had ever heard of before, and having preached for two days and exhorted people to assume his habit, he could not find any c'oth suitable for the purpose. Upon this he ordered the people to pray to God for two days and two nights, until it pleased him to favour the zeal of the devotees [of this great Saint and to cause others to believe]. The prayer had scarcely terminated, when a vessel

---

* The portions in brackets were added to a scarce edition of the book published in French in 1644, the author of which is believed to be *Desfontaines,* the dramatist.

† A name given to priests and also to lords and masters.

arrived in port, in charge of the false merchants who generally accompanied Gabriele, and who bringing with them a quantity of white cloth, declared that they were charged to do so by the order and by the revelation of the saint. [Is it to be wondered at after this that Devils sometimes transform themselves into Angels of Light, seeing that the worst men in the world will take the shape of the *Bianti?*]

"The inhabitants of the town and all the neighbouring people attributing this event to an extraordinary Providence, and not to a concerted trick, took the habit of the saint to the number of fifteen thousand persons, and cloth was more wanting than zeal. *Gabriele* by this means acquired so much credit and authority, that though poor on coming into the island, he left it laden with gold and silver amassed by this infamous trade. [Sicily was formerly called the Store house of the Romans but on this occasion it proved that of Beggars and Scoundrels.]

"Finally having returned to *Naples* with his companions, he passed his time in comfort supported by the alms of others, and you would have declared in this case that *Lazarus* had become *Dives.* Instead of wooden utensils he only now used vessels of great value, and those who had known him as a beggar were astonished to see him assuming great state. [A king may give his empire for a glass of water, but the rascal of whom I am speaking, while only drinking water found means if not to become a king, at least to treat himself regally.]

"This change having come to the ears of the Duke of *Sessa*, a man with a subtilty equal to the depth of his judgment, he resolved to trick the trickster, and to avenge the outrage on God and his saints perpetrated by the most contemptible of men. He therefore ordered some of his footmen to station themselves near a pass which leads to the river *Tiano*, and to persuade our *Beati*, who they knew were coming, to present themselves to the Duke, who greatly wanted them, [with the promise that he would give them a handsome reward, which is the magnet for all low natures.]

"The *Beati* having arrived at the pass were entreated to come and absolve the Duke in a reserved case,* according to the very ample and absolute authority they possessed, with which they complied all the more willingly because while they expected a great deal

---

* Sins the absolution of which was reserved for the bishop or even for the Pope.

from such a great lord, they hoped to make the same profits at *Naples* as they did in *Sicily*. They therefore went to *Sessa*. The Duke, having learnt that they had arrived, stationed himself in a room with the windows wholly closed, and having admitted them to an audience, he made his appearance with a melancholy air, his tongue stuttering, his head hanging on one side, and his hands trembling. After pretending to be unable to stand on his feet through weakness, counterfeiting the noodle and the simpleton, though he was sensible and rusé, he told them his wish, in broken words, scarcely audible, as if the shame and the pain which lay heavy on his heart only allowed him to half open his mouth. He asked for absolution for a very great sin, [saying that as great people committed the greatest sins they ought to undergo the greatest penances, if an extraordinary means could not be found to give them dispensation for a part of the penances they deserved.] The *Beati*, looking at one another, began to talk in an unintelligible jargon before the Duke and his attendants, [as rascals make mysteries of what they say quite as much as of what they do not say.]

" Finally they believed they would get a handsome reward, seeing the vacuity of the Duke, whom they credited with being thoroughly stupid and weak. The Duke had beforehand suborned one of his Doctors to ask for and read in his presence the Bulls and Privileges of these *Beati* with a secret instruction to read them aloud, and to say that no Pardoner had ever come from *Rome* with such extensive powers, that they had authority to absolve, not only sins committed but also those which still remained uncommitted.

" The Bull having been drawn up with such authentic approbation, he promised them two hundred crowns, provided they would absolve him from a sin which he had not yet committed. Upon this proposal the *Beati* said they wished to consult amongst themselves as to whether their power extended so far, and if the possibility was within their jurisdiction as well as the act. The Duke appeared satisfied with this, dismissed them for the day, and had them magnificently entertained in his palace with all their followers. Their baggage was even brought in to give them assurance by paying them more respect.

" The following night these Satraps held a meeting, at which it was resolved that the Duke was the greatest fool in the world, and the Doctor who had read their Bulls the greatest donkey and the greatest blockhead that could be found, since he had affirmed that they could absolve future sins by a present remission. So they resolved to take the two hundred crowns and pardon the Duke the monstrous excess which remained still to be committed.

"The following day the Duke sent for them, and asked them what they had decided upon regarding the proposition he had made to them. They informed him they had resolved that their authority was not limited [either by the past, the present, or the future, as God answered in the highest degree by his Eternal Character for all these differences of time, and that Jesus Christ, who is the same to-day as yesterday, must be the same to-morrow.] They therefore prepared the letters patent of absolution for a sin to be committed at whatever time the Duke desired, and having received the two hundred crowns from his own hand, they left Sessa after dinner, I will not say with joy only, but further with a kind of triumph. [The tricksters placed their glory with truth to the account of their infamy. But dupers are sometimes the victims of the dupes.]

"In fact they had hardly arrived at a narrow pass which was not very far from the town, when they found themselves surrounded by the officers of the Duke, who despoiled them of all their money and baggage, and while they took away everything they had, gave them a good cudgelling, [so that they should not go away without taking something with them. They derived this advantage from this treatment, that they went quicker on foot than they did on horseback.]

"Finally, having learnt that this trick had been played by order of the Duke, they went back to Sessa, sad and despoiled as they were, and complained with many tears, that after having granted the Duke such an extraordinary boon, they had received such grievous degradation. The Duke at first pretended to know nothing of the evil design of his Footmen, and having sent for them to his presence, asked them who had given them the order to maltreat these good men? And as they replied that they had received it from his Excellency, the Duke was silent for a little while, and then avowed that the thing was true. Upon this avowal the *Beati* redoubled their complaints, and representing to the Duke his ingratitude towards such indulgent Pardoners, who had absolved him for the whole of his future life, they tried to persuade him to discharge his conscience of such a weighty crime, which added robbery to sacrilege, and to give them back all that had been taken from them.

"Upon this the Duke said to them, 'Come, my friends, this is the sin that I have so long desired to commit. I shall get myself absolved with the powers you have given me, and you will be discharged of such a heavy burden and will return in security to Caretto, without any further fear of being robbed.'"

It does not seem to have occurred to *Nobili* that the Duke in the action he took may not have been animated solely by zeal for religion. Over and above his two hundred crowns which he recovered, the spoil extracted from the *Bianti* must have been considerable, but in the narrative not a word is said of any part of it being devoted to the cause of religion. The conduct of the Duke, in fact, seems to have been based on the policy which guides big fishes to swallow the smaller fry.

"*Of many other Kinds of Vagabonds.*

"There are many other sorts of Vagabonds whom I omit as not worth mentioning or because they are nearly related to others. I shall, however, mention a few. The *Rabunati,* or *Spiritati,* are knaves who wag their heads from time to time, bellowing like bulls, in order to make believe that they are tormented by an evil spirit for having disobeyed their fathers, and incurred their curse.

"The *Ruffiti,* or *Brugiati,* that is to say 'the burnt,' are people who burn all the hair on their heads to make believe that they have been nearly burned to death by a fire which consumed their house, and that they are obliged to beg for fear of thieving.

"The *Sbrici* go nearly naked and try to excite compassion with pitiful appeals, stating that they had been assailed, or taken by the Turks, and that they have at last escaped from their hands, having saved nothing but their lives.

"The *Formigotti* are sham soldiers who state that they have returned from some war against the infidels, and have received a musket shot there which has obliged them to bandage their arms and their feet; they beg to be fed for the love of God, having sacrificed themselves for the faith.

"Others say that they have patent remedies for several maladies which persons have about them, without ever seeing them or reading of them. They sell them at a high price, notwithstanding that all the virtue they have consists in having none at all. They gave the following to a lady who had a quartan fever: *Madonna Giovanna of the* quartan fever, may God give a bad year and a bad week, go to the sea, go on board a vessel, and may a hundred thousand devils take you. A person who had bad eyes also received this charm. *Demon evellat oculos tuos et stercoribus repleat loca vacantia;* 'May the Devil tear out your eyes, and fill the space with dung.' Another woman who made use of objectionable methods to prevent conception received these words from their hand : 'Margarita, Margarita, habbi cura alla tua vita, se l' piede entra nel stivale, questo breve non ti vale.' *

"They sell small iron keys as miraculous remedies, which are in fact useless against the falling sickness. Others give their companions a certain drink which makes them fall into a swoon, and while they are on the ground, the rogues say that it is weakness arising from hunger which causes them to swoon. After this, judge if any one will refuse alms when they believe it will revive a man."

> * " Margaret, Margaret, have a care for your life,
> If in the stirrup your foot you place,
> This remedy will lose its grace."

CHAPTER XXVIII.

RUSSIA, PORTUGAL, BUCHAREST, AND TURKEY.

RUSSIA.—Low standard of comfort of the Russian peasantry—Mendicity among the urban population and its causes—Committee for the relief of beggars in St. Petersburg—Treatment of beggars in Moscow, Odessa, Finland, Revel, and Poland.
PORTUGAL.—General condition of mendicity.
BUCHAREST.—Conditions of mendicity.
TURKEY.—Organisation for the relief of the poor—Professional beggars—Begging dervishes—Incentives to almsgiving—Feigned madmen—Beggars at mosques—Administration of the Imarets and Evcaf—Christian charity in Turkey—Precepts of the Koran regarding charity—Sayings of the Prophet concerning almsgiving and charity.

RUSSIA.

THE actual state of prosperity of the Russian peasantry is still very low. The majority of them save nothing; they live from day to day supplying the wants of their families, and endeavouring to pay the heavy taxes imposed upon them by the produce of their allotments of land, which, in the majority of cases, as already stated, are insufficient for the purpose.

They generally manage to eke out a bare subsistence when the harvest is good, but when that fails, they are thrown into a state of distress, which is still further aggravated by want of work for the able-bodied men.

Under such circumstances the younger men of the villages are sent off to distances in order to find work, and a few become beggars on the high road, and appeal to the charity of the more fortunate inhabitants of villages, where the crops may not have suffered.

The Russian peasant is kind-hearted, and ready to give with an open hand to his distressed brethren, nor is he unmindful of the fact that the charity he bestows on such occasions it may some day be his lot to solicit for himself.

With regard to mendicity amongst the urban population of

VAGRANTS AND VAGRANCY. 567

Russia, it must be repeated that a characteristic feature of the large towns of Russia, and the remark applies particularly to St. Petersburg, consists in the fact that a small proportion only of their inhabitants have a fixed residence in them.

The peasants flock to the towns in search of temporary employment, leaving their families in the country, but rejoining them after a few months' residence in the towns.

Certainly one-half of the population of St. Petersburg is recruited from the adjoining provinces, the amount of the floating population being principally determined by the state of the labour market.

When the harvest is bad and provisions scarce in the provinces, the peasants flock to St. Petersburg, and so great is the demand for hands that employment is generally found for them all.

The insalubrious climate of St. Petersburg, however, seriously affects the health of these country people, who consequently die in considerable numbers.

Widows, also infant children of soldiers, and subordinate employés further add to the list of poor, which is again augmented by that class of confined beggars, found in every country, who embrace mendicity as a lucrative source of living.

All these elements of pauperism, however, are not great when compared to the large population of the city, nor are they difficult to control, thanks to the three classes of institutions that are established in St. Petersburg for the purpose of relieving its poor.

The first class of charitable institution, which is entirely under the Government, consists of a committee formed for the classification and relief of beggars.

The duties of the committee of this institution consist in looking after the persons charged by the police with begging and vagrancy.

The number of such persons averaged during the four years from 1868 to 1871 inclusive from 2,300 to 3,700 annually.

The committee classifies the beggars into three categories, viz. :—

1. Those incapacitated by bodily infirmity from working.
2. Those who, through circumstances over which they exercised no control, may have fallen into distress, but are still capable of working.

3. Those who, through idleness and bad habits, have taken to mendicity as a profession.

4. Those who recently arrived from the provinces have temporarily failed to find employment.

The committee lodge temporarily beggars of the first category in their institutions, and later establish them in the almshouses which exist in St. Petersburg. Persons coming under the second and fourth category are sent back to their native places, frequently at the cost of the committee, or else are recommended for some sort of employment in St. Petersburg. Persons of the third category are sent to justices of the peace.*

In *Moscow*, begging is forbidden by the law, and beggars are prosecuted and punished by being sent to their own communes or to the workhouse; but, notwithstanding this, the streets of Moscow are infested with beggars, many of them professional ones. The police not being very vigilant, and the Russians, especially the old merchant class, being very much addicted to giving money to beggars, these make a good living out of begging.†

At *Odessa*, the law respecting vagrancy and begging is very imperfectly enforced, and, generally speaking, only when the attention of the police is particularly directed to any individual case. Beggars are, or should be, punished by short imprisonment.

Vagrants in poverty, and when strangers and without passports, may be sent back to their respective countries at the charge of the State.‡

In *Finland*, vagrants and beggars are arrested by the police and delivered over to the poor law administration if they belong to the district in which they are apprehended.

Should they, however, belong to another district they are sent there at the expense of the community of that district.§

At *Revel*, tramps and vagabonds, if they belong to a foreign community (parish), are returned to it by means of a compulsory pass. ||

In *Poland*, there are no restrictions on professional mendicancy;

---

* Report by Francis Clare Ford, 1872.
† Report of F. B. Roberts, 1872.
‡ Report by K. E. Abbot, 1871.
§ Report of Wm. Campbell, 1871.
|| Report of Etienne de Soncanton, 1871.

and, owing to the Slav superstition that it is unlucky to refuse the application of a beggar, the professional mendicant makes a prosperous career.*

PORTUGAL.

The Portuguese legislation is not less solicitous with regard to the misfortunes which attend manhood than with those which accompany infancy. The Administrative Code, with the object of repressing mendicity, confers upon the parochial boards the function of committees of charitable relief, and imposes upon them the duty of taking the census of the poor in their respective parishes, and of promoting, in accordance with the laws and regulations and with the instructions of the Government, the extinction of mendicity. In furtherance of these provisions the penal law looks upon mendicants as vagrants, and punishes them with imprisonment not exceeding six months.†

Mr. *Fleetwood Sandeman* says on this subject, " My own impression about beggars and begging in *Portugal* is that the system is encouraged by Portuguese sentiment instead of being grappled with by the law and met by charitable institutions; consequently, a maimed beggar's success in the receipt of alms is, on the whole, proportionate with the influence prevailing upon that sentiment by the nature of the maim. The roadside horrors in the shape of maimed beggars exposed to view throughout *Portugal* form a feature peculiar to that country as compared with any other so-called civilised State. As you are aware, I have travelled in most countries of the world, and I may say that taking the worst of them, say *China* (*Japan* formerly, now much improved), more horrors of the kind may be daily observed in *Portugal* than in the others!"

BUCHAREST.

In Bucharest there are some mendicants, whom the police occasionally drive into the charitable institutions, from which they rapidly escape to renew their professional labours. They are rather favourites with the general public, as in all oriental countries; and although the nationalities on the banks of

* Report by Lt.-Col. Mansfield, 1872.
† Report of A. R. Sampaio, 1872.

the Lower Danube may think they are not Orientals, the frontier of western civilisation, for good or for evil, is Vienna.*

TURKEY.†

In Turkey such organisation as exists for the relief of the poor is left mainly to the mosques and churches. There exist, however, a Dorcas Society and "Sociéties de Bienfaisance," which are managed by foreigners and distribute charity under the personal supervision of English ladies in the first case, and in the latter of sisters belonging to the Roman Catholic orders. In both cases the charity is given without regard to religious belief or race.

Throughout Turkey there are a large number of professional beggars. The begging dervishes with long hair, and usually carrying a battle-axe or a spear as well as a bowl for the collection of alms, are found all over Turkey, and are of course Mussulmans. They bear a bad reputation and are believed to be mendicants or thieves as occasion serves. They are not to be confounded with the ordinary dervishes, who are pietists of industrious lives. Besides these, in all the great cities there are men and women whose profession is mendicancy. They belong to all the nationalities of the empire, and so far as I can judge their numbers compared with the total of beggars correspond to the proportion of their nationality to that of the empire.

They are in many instances well off. For years I was sceptical of the statement made in Constantinople that many of them possess houses of their own and lend out money; but so many instances with names and details have been given that I have now no doubt that the assertion is well founded.

The ideas of the people of Turkey in regard to almsgiving are peculiar. Many, no doubt, give from charitable motives, and rich and poor relieve beggars frequently. But there is a large amount of giving in order to bring good luck. If a speculation is about to be made, a law-suit to be entered on, a new undertaking to be commenced, alms are given freely, and above all are widely spread. Ten paras, or a halfpenny, to four persons is more likely to bring luck than a piastre, or twopence, to one man.

* Report of J. Green, 1871.
† The whole of the account of Turkey is due to the kindness of Dr. Edwin Pears (LL.D.) of Constantinople.

Many Greek merchants give a regular dole to clients, who attend regularly to receive it. Most of the almsgiving is indiscriminate, and the idea appears never to have dawned upon any of the givers that it is desirable to put an end to professional begging. The exercise of the profession of the mendicant is regarded as legitimate as any other, and no efforts are made in any portion of the empire to put an end to it.

In the capital and other large towns numbers of men and women beg everywhere. On the bridge of Constantinople may be seen any day men and women with broken arms or legs, with wounds and sores and deformities, which are wilfully exposed and thrust before passengers as advertisements of their condition. Many of these wounds and deformities are said to be artificially caused. No civilised country would tolerate for a week the horrible exposures which the beggars are allowed to make. Madmen, or people who feign to be mad, form a constant element among the population of the empire. The Moslem notion that they are the favoured of heaven leads to their toleration in all kinds of vagaries. One of these fellows went for years stark-naked about the streets, and, whether mad or not, found out that by going into European shops where ladies were present he generally managed to get a bribe to be off. An English shopkeeper three or four years ago determined not to be fleeced any more, and having arranged that his neighbouring shopkeepers should come at a signal, he and they on his next visit instead of paying him gave him a good thrashing with yard measures. Since then he has not troubled the European quarter of the city. Others, however, who feign madness go about crying aloud, blessing those who give and cursing those who refuse to their heart's content.

In front of every mosque and of every church there are always to be found a number of beggars. The pious Moslem and the pious members of the Eastern Churches agree that beggars are a necessary factor in the community, and the idea appears never to have dawned upon either that mendicancy may be regarded as a crime.

Charity forms one of the five pillars of Mahometanism. Among the Moslems the word is understood to mean almsgiving. Hence throughout Turkey there exists among the Mussulmans a large amount of more or less systematic charity. The construction and endowment of fountains is one of the commonest and least objectionable forms. The scarcity of water in summer and its often very high price makes this form one peculiarly acceptable to the community. Property has been devoted to the distribution of bread among the poor. A rough attempt has been made to organise the latter form of charity in connection with the Imarets. These are offices which are supported by endowments or the gifts of living persons. In the districts where Imarets are established they are entitled to a share of the real property which is forteited for the want of heirs, and this of itself constitutes a considerable item, since while according to Turkish law all persons, Christian or Moslem, native subject or foreigner, can hold land, the same law provides that the unbeliever, that is the non-Moslem, of one nationality cannot succeed to the property of a person belonging to another.

The administration of the Imarets belongs to the department of the Evcaf, which is one of the largest and most important sections of the Turkish Government. The Evcaf collects the revenues of an enormous number of properties in the capital and throughout the country and divides them among the districts of the Imarets. The functions of the Evcaf may be gathered from the fact that in Constantinople it is often spoken of as the department of Pious Foundations.

A poor Turk, in order to get provisions from one of these Imarets, must present to the Evcaf a certificate from the Imam of his quarter declaring that he is destitute, upon which the Evcaf delivers to him a ticket in order that he may obtain relief.

All this sounds better than the facts justify. The Imarets give countenance to or create a large amount of mendicancy. Turkish beggars are everywhere seen, and probably every Turk would believe it to be a sin to forbid a man, woman, or child to beg. The poor are allowed to find shelter in the out-houses of the mosques. There is nothing which corresponds to a workhouse, no provision for the vagrant, and in spite of the Evcaf there exists a terrible amount of unrelieved poverty throughout Turkey.

Individual Turks exist, possibly in considerable numbers, who spend time and money in relieving districts, but very little is done by the Evcaf. It is believed, like other departments in Turkey, to be thoroughly corrupt. Voluntary organisations, either for the establishment of hospitals or for aiding the poor in other ways, are unknown among the Turks.

Among the Christian subjects of the Sultan there is no elaborate organisation like that of the Evcaf, among the rayahs, and of course no assistance from Government for the relief of the poor. But a good deal is done by voluntary and combined efforts. In both the Orthodox and the Armenian Churches this duty, so far as it is organised, centres in the churches.

The churches of each quarter take charge of its destitute people.

Each church makes a special collection every day for the support of the poor. Special donations are made to churches for this object, and endowments have been left which are administered by the church. Each quarter elects members to form a special council for the administration of the funds belonging to its district. According to the decision of this council the poor are supplied with food, fuel, &c., and occasionally with money. Poor children are educated at its expense. Some rich quarters have local hospitals for the sick, and in nearly all the quarters medicine is supplied to the poor at the expense of the council.

Voluntary societies, usually managed by ladies who collect money and superintend its distribution, exist in all the large towns, and undoubtedly prevent a good deal of misery, while this personal supervision is especially valuable in preventing waste and defeating imposture.

The Armenians have a very large hospital at the Seven Towers in Constantinople, together with a lunatic asylum attached to it. Both these institutions are supported by voluntary contributions.

The Greeks, besides these organisations in connection with the Church, have developed a large amount of zeal in the direction of charitable relief. They too have their hospitals and ladies of benevolent societies. But their chief charities are directed towards schools. The amount given for this purpose is remarkable.

A Mr. Zappa, for example, has recently built a girls' school for the middle classes in Constantinople, which cannot have cost him less than £30,000. Poor girls are received gratis and mix with those who pay in a really charitable way. A great number of similar schools, only inferior in size, are found in Turkey, and owe their existence and support to the charity of wealthy Greeks. The late George Zarifi, of Constantinople, expended many thousands on education. Everywhere the Greeks recognise the solidarity of their race and no money is begrudged for educational purposes.

Among the Christians, however, medicancy is quite as prevalent as among the Turks, and at any church door, cripples, women with infants, and other beggars implore aid from the worshippers. I have no doubt that the large amount of almsgiving which they receive is due to the belief that almsgiving is itself a virtue to be duly credited to the donor, independent of all consideration whether the donee is a fit person to be benefited or whether the gift will do harm or good.

The following extracts from the Korân* embody the injunctions regarding almsgiving:—

"To him who is of kin *to thee*, then give his due, and to the poor, and the wayfarer: this is best for those who seek the face of God; and with them it shall be well."—*Sura* xxx. *v.* 38.

"They will ask thee what they shall bestow in alms. SAY: Let the good which ye bestow be for parents, and kindred, and orphans, and the poor, and the wayfarer; and whatever good ye do, of a truth God knoweth it."—*Sura* ii. *v.* 211.

"Fear God then with all your might, and hear and obey: and expend in alms for your soul's weal; for whoso is saved from his own greed, these shall prosper."—*Sura* lxiv. *v.* 16.

"If ye lend God a generous loan, He will double it to you and will forgive you, for God is Grateful, kind."—*Sura* lxiv. *v.* 17.

"O ye who believe! when ye go to confer in private with the Apostle, give alms before your private conference. Better will this be for you, and more pure. But if ye find not *the means*, then truly God is Lenient, Merciful."

"Do ye hesitate to give alms previously to your private conference? Then if ye do it not (and God will excuse it in you), at least observe prayer, and pay the stated impost, and obey God and his Apostle: and God is cognizant of your actions."—*Sura* lviii. *v.* 13, 14.

The following are some of the sayings of Mahomet on the subject of almsgiving, as they occur in the Traditions:—" The upper hand is better than the lower one. The upper hand is the giver of alms, and the lower hand is the poor beggar." "The best of alms are those given by a man of small means, who gives

* Translated by the Rev. J. M. Rodwell. Second Edition. 1876.

of that which he has earned by labour, and gives as much as he is able." "Begin by giving alms to your own relatives." "Doing justice between two people is alms; assisting a man on his beast is alms; good words are alms." "A camel lent out for milk is alms; a cup of milk every morning and evening is alms." "Your smiling in your brother's face is alms; assisting the blind is alms." God says, "Be thou liberal, thou child of Adam, that I may be liberal to thee."

BEGGING.—It is not lawful for any person possessing sufficient food for a day and night to beg, and it is related that the Prophet said: "Acts of begging are scratches and wounds with which a man wounds his own face." "It is better for a man to take a rope and bring in a bundle of sticks to sell than to beg." "A man who continues to beg will appear in the Day of Judgment without any flesh on his face."

CHAPTER XXIX.

EXTRACTS FROM VARIOUS WRITERS ILLUSTRATING THE HABITS AND IMPOSTURES OF THE VAGRANT AND BEGGAR, 1383—1567.

CHAUCER, The Begging Friar and the Pardoner (1383)—FOXE, The Blind Impostor (circa 1433—35)—LYDGATE, The Foolish Penniless Beggar (circa 1430)—SKELTON and the Beggar (circa 1490)—SAMUEL ROWLANDS, The Runnagate Race, a History of Rogues, from 1450 to 1534—ALEXANDER BARCLAY, Of Foolish Beggars and their Vanities (1508)—DUNBAR, The Excess of Beggars (1509)—HENRY WATSON, Of Beggars and their Vanities (1517)—JAMES V. of Scotland, the Gaberlunyie Man (circa 1530—40)—SIR DAVID LYNDSAY, The Pardoner (circa 1539)—A Begging Letter in 1542—HUGH LATYMER, On Valiant Beggars (1552)—The Fraternity of Vagabonds (1561)—THOMAS HARMAN, a Caveat or Warning for Common Cursetors (1567).

THE BEGGING FRIAR AND THE PARDONER.
Circa 1383.

From the "Canterbury Tales," by Geoffrey Chaucer.

A Frere[1] ther was, a wanton and a mery,
A Limitour,[2] a ful solempne man . . .
Therto he strong was as a champioun,
And knew wel the tavernes in every toun,
And every hosteler[3] and gay tapstere,[4]
Better than a lazar[5] or a beggere,
For unto swiche a worthy man as he
Accordeth nought, as by his faculte,
To haven with sike lazars acquaintance.
It is not honest, it may not avance,
As for to delen with no swiche pouraille,[6]
But all with riche, and sellers of vitaille.[7]
And over all, ther as profit shuld arise,
Curteis he was, and lowly of servise.
Ther n'as no man nowher so vertuous.
He was the beste begger[8] in all his hous :
And gave a certaine ferme[9] for the grant,

---

[1] Friar. [2] A friar licensed to beg within a certain district.
[3] Inn-keeper. [4] A *woman* who has the care of a tap in a public-house.
[5] Leper. [6] Poor people. [7] Victuals.
[8] In the *Vision of Peers Ploughman*, Pride confesses that "none was so sturdy a beggar as myself; none so bold in taverns or streets to affirm for truth what was never thought of." [9] Farm.

None of the bretheren came in his haunt.
For though a widewe hadde but a shoo,[1]
(So plesant was his *In principio*)[2]
Yet wold he have a ferthing or he went. . . .
With him[3] ther rode a gentil PARDONERE,
Of Rouncevall,[4] his frend and his compere[5]
That streit was comen from the court of Rome . . .
His wallet lay beforne him in his lappe
Bret-ful[6] of pardon come from Rome al hote . . .
But of his craft, fro Berwike unto Ware,
Ne was ther swiche[7] an other pardonere.
For in his male[8] he hadde a pilwebere,[9]
Which, as he saide, was oure ladies veil :
He saide, he hadde a gobbet[10] of the seyl[11]
Thatte seinte Peter had, whan that he went
Upon the see, till Jesu Crist him hent.[12]
He had a crois of laton[13] ful of stones,
And in a glas he hadde pigges bones.
But with these relikes, whanne that he fond
A poure person dwelling up on lond,
Upon a day he gat him more moneie
Than that the persone gat in monethes tweie.[14]
And thus with fained flattering and japes,[15]
He made the persone,[16] and the peple, his apes.

THE BLIND IMPOSTOR.

Circa 1430—35.

From "the *Actes and Monuments* of matters most speciall and memorable, happenyng in the Church, with an Vniuersall history of the same," by *John Foxe*, 1583 (4th edition), commonly called Fox's Book of Martyrs.

In a "Dialogue concernynge heresyes" *Sir Thomas More* relates having heard his father tell the following story, and it figures in the First part of the *Contention betwixt the two famous houses of Yorke and Lancaster* (1594), which *Shakspere* subsequently converted into the Second part of *King Henry VI.*, and in which the name of *Simpcox* is given to the impostor.

In the yong dayes of this King Henry the sixt, beyng yet under the gouernance of this duke Humfrey, his protector, there came to S. Albones a certayne begger wyth his wife, and was walking there about y⁰ towne, begging fiue or sixe dayes before the Kinges comming thether, saying, yt he was borne blind, and neuer saw in his lyfe, & was warned in hys dreame, that he shuld come out of Barwik, where he sayd he had euer dwelled, to seek S. Albon, and that he had bene at his shrine, and had not bene holpen, and therefore he would go and seek him at some other place : for he had heard some say, since he came, that S. Albones body shoulde be at Colon, and in deede suche a contention hath there bene. But of truth, as I am surely informed, he lyeth here, at S. Albones,

---

[1] Nought but one shoe.
[2] *In principio erat verbum*, the beginning of St. John's Gospel, which the priest was directed to read.
[3] *i.e.* with the Sompnour.
[4] *Roncesvalles* in Spain, celebrated as a sanctuary.   [5] Gossip or near friend.
[6] Brimful.   [7] Such.   [8] A trunk or portmanteau.
[9] A pillow cover.   [10] Morsel.   [11] Sail.   [12] Took.
[13] A kind of mixed metal of the colour of brass.   [14] Two.
[15] Tricks.   [16] Parson.

sauing some Reliques of him, whiche they there shew shryned. But, to tell you foorth, when the King was comen, and the towne full, sodainly this blynde man at S. Albones shrine had hys sight agayne, and a miracle solemnly ronge, and "Te Deum" song, so that nothing was talked of in al the towne, but this miracle. So happened it then, that duke Humfrey of Glocester, a man no les wise, then also well learned, having great ioye to see suche a miracle, called the poore man vnto him, and first, shewing himselfe ioyous of Gods glory, so shewed in the getting of his sight, and exhorting him to meekenes, and to no ascribing of any part of ye worship to himself, nor to be proud of the people's prayse, which would call him a good & godly man therby, at last, he looked well upon his eyne, and asked him whether he could see nothing at al, in his life before. And when as well his wife, as himselfe affirmed fastly no, then hee looked aduisedly upon his eyen againe, and sayd: I beleue you very well, for me thinketh ye cannot see well yet. Yes, syr, quod he, I thanke God and hys holy martyr, I can see now as well as any man Yea can (quod ye duke) what colour is my gowne: Then anon the begger tolde him. What colour (quoth he) is this mans gowne: He told him also, and so forth without any sticking, he told him the names of all ye colours that could be shewed him. And when the duke saw that, he bad him Walke, traytour, and made him to be set openly in the stockes: for though he could haue seene sodenly, by miracle, the difference betwene diuers colours, yet could he not, by the sight, so sodeinly tell the names of al these coulours, except he had known them before, no more then the names of all the men, that he shuld sodaynly see.

The Foolish Penniless Beggar.

Circa 1430.

From the "Order of Fools," "A tale of Threscore Folys and Thre," by Dan John Lydgate.

> Amonge al foolis that foole is most culpable,
> That is cursed and hathe thereof deynté ;[1]
> A poore begger, to be vengeable
> Withe purs penyles, may never the.[2]

The Beggar's Answer to the Poet Skelton.

Circa 1490.

From the Poetical Works of *John Skelton*, edited by the *Rev. Alexander Dyce*.

Tales, and quicke answeres, very mery, and pleasant to rede, printed by Thomas Berthelet, 1567.

Of the beggers answere to M. Skelton, the poete.[3]

A *poure* begger, that was foule, blacke, and lothlye to beholde, cam vpon a tyme vnto mayster Skelton the poete, and asked him his almes. To whom mayster Skelton sayde, I praye the gette the awaye fro me, for thou lokeste as though thou camest out of helle. The poure man, perceyuing he wolde gyue him no thynge, answerd, For soth, syr, ye say trouth ; I came oute of helle.

---

[1] Disdain. [2] Thrive.
[3] This tale is also told in "Pasquil's Iests," mixed with "Mother Bunches Merriments," 1604, as "A poore beggers answer to a rich Citizen," and in "The Pleasant Conceites of old Hobson the Merry Londoner," 1607, as "*A Begers answear to Maister Hobson*."

Why dyddest thou nat tary styl there? quod mayster Skelton. Mary, syr quod the begger, there is no roume for suche poure beggers as I am; all is kepte for suche gentyl men as ye be.

A History of Rogues.

1450—1534.

From "The *Runnagates Race*, or the Originall of the Regiment of Rogues, when they first began to take head, and how they haue succeeded one the other sucessiuely vntill about the sixe and twentieth yeare of King Henry the eight, collected out of the Legend of Lossels."

Contained in *Martin Mark-All*, Beadle of Bridewell, by S(amuel) R(owlands), London, 1610.

Mr. *Edmund Gosse*, in his Memoir of *Samuel Rowlands*, says, "*Martin Mark-All*, his contribution to 1610, . . . professes to be an historical account of the rise and progress of roguery up to the reign of Henry VIII., as stated to the Bellman of London by the Beadle of Bridewell. It has this special interest to modern students, that it contains a very curious dictionary of canting terms, preceding by more than half a century, that in the *English Rogue*. Moreover, buried in a great deal of trash, it includes some valuable biographical notes about famous highwaymen and thieves of the sixteenth century. It is entirely in prose except some queer Gipsy songs."[1]

At what time King *Henry* the sixt of famous memorie bare rule ouer the Britanes, there was one *Iohn Mendal* (alias *Iack Cade*) an Irish man, that named himselfe by the name of *Iohn Mortimer*, cousen to the Duke of Yorke, whereupon hee gathering together a great Company out of Kent, assured and perswaded them, that the enterprise he tooke in hand, was both honourable to God and the King, and profitable to the whole Realme: the Kentish men moued with these perswasions and other faire promises, marched to blacke heath, where they lay for a month pilling the Countrey round about.

At the same time, which was about one thousand foure hundred and fiftie, two vnruly fellowes (the one named *Blewbeard*, the other *Hugh Roberts*) which were lately come ouer from France, who had béen souldiers vnder the Duke of Somerset and the Earle of Shrewsbury in the winning and loosing of Constance, Guysons, Roane and diuers other Cities in France: the which *Blewbeard* in a Commotion, shortly after he came ouer, being made their Captaine, before he had attempted anything at all, was taken and executed: But *Roberts* kéeping in Kent, gathered a great number of Rakehels and Vagabonds together to the number of an hundred in that Countrey, to whom likewise masterlesse men after they had heard of his fame, came cluttering on heapes, so that he had in a short space to the number of fiue hundred followers.

These sturdie Vagabonds ioyning with *Iacke Mendall* in this rebellion, march toward London, and enter Southwarke, and there lodged at the white Harte for a night or two, prohibiting al from Rape, robery and murder, the more to allure the hearts of the people to fauour his enterprise. After, they come into London, and there they play *Rex*, and returne backe into Southwarke againe, where after many conflicts betwéene them and the Citizens, the Kings pardon was proclaimed: at which hearing, the poore people were so glad, and so ready to receiue it, that without bidding farewell to their Captaines, withdrew themselues euery man towards his owne home.

Iack Mendall despairing of succours, and fearing the reward of his lewd dealings, fled away into the woods: But Proclamation made, that whosoeuer

---

[1] This is a mistake, the songs are not in the Gypsy language but in the beggars' cant of the period. See pp. 601-2.

could bring *Iacke* aliue or dead to the King, should haue a thousand markes for his paines, was after slaine by a gentleman in Kent, and so brought to the King.

But *Roberts* kept himselfe in the woods closely a long time after, although not with so great a company as he had before, and there he liued by robbing and spoyling in the night, kéeping themselues close in all the day. And thus by the space of a twelue moneth, they passed their time in villany, robbing and spoyling the Country people of their poultry, pigges, and other sustenance, wherewith they sustained themselues and their families. In which time he set downe lawes and customes to be kept and obserued among them, and to kéepe them in awe and fashion, who are prone of themselues to liue out of all rule and fashion.

1. First he appointed that of euery thing that they got, he had the first taking and leauing of the best thereof at his pleasure.

2. That if any of their fellowes could not purchase any victuals or necessities for foode that night, that then they shold be in cōmons with the rest the day following.

3. That no robbery or violence bee vsed vpon any man within foure miles of the wood, or the place of their aboade.

4. That none be so hardy, as to run to the wood for succor or reléefe, after he hath perpetrated anything, lest that hugh and crie follow, and so discrie the whole company.

Thus after a yeare and vpward was spent by them in this sort, they brake vp their Campe, and Proclamation was made, to méete there in that place euery thrée yeares for a memoriall, if they then liued : In the meane time they spread themselues abroad in the Countrey, some remaining there, others trauelling North-ward, and ioyne themselues with the Duke of Yorke, and generally in all Commotions and rebellions. These in memory of their first acquaintance and loue to their new found Captaine, called themselues by the name of *Roberts-men* [1] as the seruants of *Hugh Roberts* their Commaunder.

This *Roberts* liued rouing vp & down the country for the space of ten years : in which time he kept his Court daies as himselfe listed, and in which time there came to him diuers new followers, and as some decayed and died, some hanged & dead of the poxe (for to that end they all come) so others succéeded in their places.

In the first yeare of *Edward* the fourth, this *Roberts* in the warres against *Henry* the sixt in the North partes (who was deposed) was there slaine, besides 36,776 persons all Englishmen.

Hereupon presently (their late Captaine now dead) all that were left aliue of this company, hye themselues to their wonted place of méeting, where, by the generall assent, they chose one (*Ienkin Cowdiddle*) to bee their ring-leader.

This *Ienkin Cowdiddle* was a man giuen much to swearing, drunkennesse and lechery : he was neuer out of England as souldier or traueller, but from his first beginning he continued a wandring rogue, he was stout of stomacke, audacious and fierce, hee was knowne to all the damned crew for a boone companion, and therefore chosen as fittest for their Captaine : hee first ordained, that none were so hardy as to haue the vndooing of a maid wanderer, or anything to do with her, vnlesse first she were brought to him to be broken vp, or to some of his assignes, that could obtain the same of him by friendship or bribery.

Hee commaunded likewise that all beggers should spend all their gettings,

---

[1] The name is much older, as Roberdesmen are mentioned in the Act 5 Ed. III., c. 14 (1331), which enacts that Roberdesmen and night walkers shall be arrested.

AND BEGGARS AND BEGGING. 581

in the day past, in good Béere or Ale at night, or at the fardest by saterday night: and if any were found or known to haue aboue two pence half-penny in his purse on munday morning, he shold forfeit a dousen of béere, to any whatsoeuer of their company would challenge it. He exercised his commaund about tenne yeares, vntill the time that the great rebellion and vprore was in the Western parts, as Summersetshire, Wilshire, Dorset-shire and Cornewall, about the crowning of Prince *Edw.* son to *K. H.* 6, who had beén all this while in France: and this fell out about the 11. yeare of *Edw.* 4, then this *Ienkin Cowdiddle* accompanied with 300. tottered knaues, ioyned in battell against the K. with the westerne men, in which battell at Teuxbury he was slaine, and buried there with the rest of the dead bodies.

The battel ended, these *Robert-men* (for so they were termed a long time after) hye them to their Randauow, the vsuall and knowne place, and there with the full consent of the whole company, They chose one *Spysing* to be his successour.

And now when as the feast and solemnizing of this new made squire was newly ended, news was brought to this *Spising*, how that one *Thomas Neuell* sonne to *Fankenbridge* (who had béene at Sea as a Pirate, and robbed diuers Merchants) was newly arriued in England, and got a great company of Marriners out of all parts of the land, and many traytors and misgouerned people to follow him, whereunto as fitly for his turne this *Spising* accompanies and enters into league and familiarity, besides diuers also forth of other Countries that delighted in theft and robberies.

And now his strength encreased daily, for hauing bin at Callice, and brought from thence into Kent many euill disposed persons, he began to gather his power in that Country, meaning to attempt some great and wicked enterprise against King *Edward* and his Kingdome, but his quarrell he pretended, was to haue King *Henry* the sixt out of the Towre, and to restore him to his scepter againe. Thus accompanied with seuentéene thousand men, they marched into London by shippes which lay betwéene Black wall and Redriffe: and then came *Spising* with his band at Algate, who behaued themselues so stoutly, that they wan the Bulwarke there, and draue the Citizens backe within the Portcullis, and entred the gate with them to the number of a dousen; but some of them were slaine with the fall of the Port cullis, that was let downe vpon them to kéepe the residue out: but those that were within the wals were suddenly dispatcht.

To be short, at last the Bastard was vanquished and vtterly dispaired; for hearing the King comming with thirtie thousand men, durst stay no longer, but brake vp and despersed themselues some one way, and some another. The Bastard with his Mariners and such rebels, robbers & wicked persons, as sought nothinge but spoile, got them to ship-board as fast as they could. Those that were left behinde, and those of *Spysings* company lurked a day or two about the Countrey secretly in woods, vntill they thought the coastes to be clear, and after met at their wonted place, where they, as merry as pot and canne passe their time in villany and robbery.

This *Spising* was a man giuen to voluptuousnesse, and pleasure, delighting in Bowsing & Venery: He ordered, that euery one that professed himselfe a Wanderer, and taking vpon him the occupation of begging, shal be stauled to the order of rogues; that is, hee shall bee brought to the chiefe Commander then being, and there he shall shew the cause of his going abroad, and what Countrey man he is: which done, he payes a dousen of béere as a fine for his fréedome & Instaulment, and so is permitted to liue and die a rogue: but if he be born a rogue: that is, if his Grandfather were one, & his father one, so yt consequently he must be one also, such a one shal be fréely discharged from such enstaulement, as being made frée by his fathers copie. This *Spysing* about the first yeare of King *Edward* the fift, committed a robbery and murder (neére High-gate in Middlesex) where after he fledde and tooke sanctuary at Westminster, for these places in that time were wonderfully abused by wicked men: rablements of Theéues, Murderers and Traytors would thither flocke when they had atchieued any villany, vnthrifts ryot and runne in debt, vpon boldnesse of these places, rich men runne thither with poore mens goods ; there they build and there they spend, and bid their creditors goe whistle, mens wiues runne thither with their husbands plate, and say they dare not abide with their husbands, for feare of beating : Theeues bring in thither their stolne goods, and there liue upon them vntill al is spent, and when nothing is left, they againe in the night range abroad to séeke other booties : there they deuise new plots to rob and kill, and then to come in again at their pleasure: so those places did not only giue them safegard for their villanies, but a license also to do more. Such a one was this *Spysing* for a yeare or two before he was hanged; for being taken the second time at Womburne in Stafford-shire, for killing a man in a drunken humour, was presently apprehended, and carried to the Goale, and after hanged all saue the head : he Dominéered about eleuen yeares.

Not long after, when certaine newes was blased abroad of their Captaines confusion, they chose a notable swaggering rogue called Puffing *Dicke*, to reuell ouer them, who plaid reuell-rout with them indéede : in this squire there were no villanies left vnattempted, but he was still at the one end.

He first gaue termes to robbers by the high-way, that such as robbe on horsebacke were called high lawyers, and those who robbed on foot he called Padders : the difference of these two sorts of villanes is this.

The first sort are called Gent. Robbers or théeues ; and these ride on horses well appointed, and goe in shew like honest men : the other robbe on foote, and haue no other helpe but a paire of light héeles and a thicke woode. Concerning the first sort, that delight in the credite of a high Lawyer, that with their swords fréeboote abroad in the countrey like Cauileroes on horse-backe, are commonly such men, that eyther are younger brethren, who being brought vp in idlenesse and gaming, when their friends are dead, do fall to this kind of life to maintaine the maine chance: others againe being left well by their friends, having no gouernment of themselues, but banqueting with Whores, and making late suppers, doe greatly impouerish and begger themselues : and when all is spent after this manner, and their money wasted like snow against the Sunne : they for their *Vltimum refugium*, as forced to vndertake this wretched and abhorred profession, robbing honest poore men, and taking all their money from them, yea and often more then is their owne, to the vtter undoing of the poore man, his wife and children for euer, who when they haue it, wast it as vainly as they wickedly purchast it. And others, that hauing béene souldiers when they come from the warres, eyther by breaking vp of the Campe, or by running away from their colours to sée their friends, or what way soueuer, cannot betake themselues to any honest trade of life, but louing to liue in idlenesse, betake themselues to robbing and stealing, vntill they be taken and carried westward there to make their rehersall.

These fellowes first that they may not be knowne, bespeak and get such artificial beards and heads of haire, that although you ride, dine and sup with them from day to day, you shall not be able to discerne them, nor espie their falshood. And in this practice all their villany consists: for I haue heard and partly know a high-way lawyer rob a man in the morning, and hath dined with the martin or honest man so robbed the same day at an Inne being not descried, nor yet once mistrusted or suspected for the robbery.

Their knauery is on this manner ; they haue alwaies good geldings and trusty, which they can make Curtailes when they list, and againe set too large tailes, hanging to the fetlockes at their pleasure, yea and so artificially, that it shall not be perceiued or spied of the Ostler that dresseth them : besides they haue clokes *Tormosant*, as they call them, made with two out-sides, that weare them howsoeuer the right side will bee alwaies outward : now their artificiall beards and heads of haire withall, will make them séeme to dance in a net a long time ere they be espied. Now how easie it is for them to escape all dangers, all Hues and Cries, it may easily be perceiued, for the complexion of the man, and his beard, the garments that he weares, and the making of his horse, thrée things which are the especiall markes whereby notice is taken to make enquiry: which being chaunged and altered, they may escape as safely as they did the robbery.

The other sort of robbers, that hauing no meanes to relieue them, in stead of swift courses to eschue danger, flie away vpon their trustie tenn-toes into woodes and close places, there to continue vntill Hue and Crie bee past: these fellows weare counterfeit beards and heads of haire, as the other sort doe, vsing not many words, but *Stand and deliuer:* some will haue curst and man-kind masties following them, to further and helpe them in this enterprise: some vnder the name of the vpright man or souldier as they goe through townes, begge the charitable deuotion of people, they will goe also strongly with thrée or foure in a company to a farme house, where oftentimes they are relieued more for feare than deuotion: but when they can come in place where they may conueniently take a purse, it shall goe hard but that they will eyther win the horse or loose the saddle, although their hardy aduenture be paid home with a cracke of the best ioynt they haue after.

But to returne againe to *Puffing Dicke;* this diuell incarnate, as he was bold to attempt any wicked enterprise, so he wanted not wit first to lay the plot to atchieue it, and to bring it to passe. He vsed first the cousenage at dice, and to inuent for that purpose false dice, whereby he got much money. But as it was ill got, so was it as ill spent in all manner of vice that could bee named, wherein he excelled all before him: yet this by the way, it is reported of him, that he was frée from murder, and commanded, that whosoeuer vnder his conduct, was so cruell as to murder any man or woman in the attempt of robbing them, should forthwith be discouered to be apprehended: he likewise ordered that all high lawyers, padders, Lifts,[1] Foists,[2] Cheaters or Cony-catchers, shal not presume to purchase any landes or reuenues, nor whord vp their money to the hinderance of good fellowship, maintenance of good natured damsels, and impeachment of the fraternity: but that they shall heartily spend it, among good company and fellowes, such as them selues are, and as they came lightly by it, so lightly to let it flie: he was a man crafty and bolde, yet he died miserably; for after he had commanded now fully eight years, he had the pyning of the Poxe and Neapolitane Scurffe. And here an end of *Puffing Dicke.*

In his place was chosen by the consent of the rablement, one not much inferiour in vice to the former, but in regard of manhood a méere crauant,[3] called *Lawrence Crosbiter,* or long *Lawrence.* This *Lawrence* had béene brought vp all his daies a Seruing-man, and now being about fiftie or thrée score, at what time Seruing men are past the best, and commonly grow lasie, was cast out of seruice, and so was faine to liue among the wicked, sometimes a stander for the padder,[4] sometimes a verser for the cony-cacher,[5] somtimes a stale for a foyst,[6] but most commonly an Apple-squire[7] for a trudging house[8]: he first vsed that art which now is named Crosbiting, and from whose name, this damned art (Crosbiting) tooke her first call, as of *Lawrence Crosbiter* that first inuented the

---

[1] Shoplifters.   [2] Pickpockets.   [3] A coward.
[4] The *Stander* was the Sentinel to the *Padder* or footpad. (A.S. *pœd,* a footpath.)
[5] The *coney,* or rabbit, was the dupe; the *coney catcher,* the sharper who enticed the coney to be fleeced by the *verser,* or card sharper.
[6] The *stall* was the confederate who acted as cover to the *foist,* or pickpocket.
[7] A kept gallant, and also a person who attended on a woman of bad character. (Du. *appel,* an appeal.)
[8] A brothel. (Du. *trouwen,* to marry, to espouse.)

same. The manner in breefe is thus: Some base rogue without the feare of God or man, that kéepeth a whore as a friend, or marries one to be his maintainer, consents or constraines those creatures to yéelde the vse of their bodies to other men, that so taking them together, they may strip the leacher of all the money in his purse or that he can presently make.

He commaunded about sixe yeares, and then as he liued in filthinesse, so was his end, for it was reported that his bowels were eaten out with the poxe, whilst he was yet aliue, so miserable was the end of this wretch.

All these sixe yeares that this *Lawrence* liued in his controulment, he durst neuer be so hardy as once to aide *Perken Warbeck*, in the attempting of the Crowne: so slauish was his mind, and given to cowardize, for all the time that he bare rule among his companions, which was from 1491. until 1497. did *Perkin Warbeck* assay to win the kingdom, fayning himselue to bee the Duke of Yorke, son to *K. Edw.* 4, deceased: to the bringing to passe of which deuise, he assayed many waies, plotted diuers deuises, and attempted mighty matters, and yet all in vaine, for after almost sixe yeares (all which time he was busied about this enterprise) he was taken prisoner, after he had taken Sanctuary at Bewdly not farre from Southampton. . . . . And this is the end of *Perkin Warbecke*: *Lawrence Crosbiter* now dead, and *Perkin Warbecke*, with two of his Councellors *Hearne* and *Asteley*, fledde to Sanctuary: it booted not the company to stay there, but their chiefe leaders fledde, euerie one threw away his armour as people amazed, and betake themselues to their heéles: among the rest *Skelton* a notable knaue, one of *Perkins* Councellors before mentioned, being well knowne among the Rascalitie, was led to the wonted place of méeting, and there solemnely was stawled a rogue, and made their generall.

This *Skelton* was sometimes a Taylor in Taunton in Sommerset shire, who being blowne downe with an vnfortunate blast, was forc't and ready for any Commotion or rebellion: he was of a proude and haughty disposition: he liued in his New Gouernment vntill about the fourth yeare of King *Henry* the eight, which was in the yeare 1501.

This fellow among other decrées and orders confirmed this: That if any one vsing the necessary helpe of his crutches (although indéede hee hath not any néede or vse of them, but onely to deceiue people therewith) shall at any time forsake them for a time, either to runne for a wager with another, or to play at nine-holes, loggets or bowles, or any other game, so that he be séene and marked by some that haue seene him else-where with his crooches halting, and by them so challenged for a counterfeit rogue, he shall forfeite for euery such offence two dousen of béere, as a fine for disgracing so ancient a trade as peregrination.

After him succéeded by the Generall Councell, one *Cocke Lorrell*, the most notorious knaue that euer liued: by trade he was a Tinker, often carrying a panne and a hammer for a shew: but when he came to a good booty, he would cast his profession in a ditch, and play the padder and then would away, and as hee past through the towne, would crie, Ha you any worke for a Tinker. To write of his knaueries, it would aske a long time: I referre you to the old manuscript, remayning on record in maunders hall.

This was he that reduced and brought in forme the Catalogue of Vagabonds or quarterne of knaues called the fiue and twentie orders of knaues: but because it is extant and in euery mans shop, I passe them ouer.

And now about this time, when as warres abroade, and troubles domesticall were ended, swarmed in euery part of the land these Caterpillers, like flies against a plague: in the northerne partes another sort of Vagabonds (at the diuels-arse-a peake in Darbshire) began a new regiment, calling themselues by the name of Egiptians. These were a sort of rogues, that liued and do yet liue by cousening and deceit, practising the arte called legerdemaine, or fast and loose,[1] whereby they got to them selues no small credite among the Countrey

---

[1] For an explanation of this form of cheating see note on p. 346.

people by their déepe dissembling and deceitfull practises, féeding the common people wholly addicted and giuen to nouelties, toyes and new fangles, delighting them with the strangenesse of the attire of their heads, and practising palmistry to such as would know their fortunes.

The first that inuented this new fellowship was one *Giles Hather:* he carried about with him his whore called *(Kyt Calot)* which was termed the Quéene of Egipties: they goe alwaies neuer vnder an hundred men or women, causing their faces to be made blacke, as if they were Egyptians: they wander vp and down the Countrey as it pleaseth them best, with their horses to carry their bastards and baggage after them: and when they come into any countrey towne, they pittifully cousen the poore countrey girles, both of money, siluer and the best linnen onely in hope to heare their good fortunes tould them.

After a certaine time that these vp-start Lossels had got vnto a head; the two chiefe Commaunders of both these regiments met at the Diuels-arse-a-peake, there to parle and intreate of matters that might tend to the establishing of this their new found gouernment: and first of all they thinke it fit to deuise a certaine kinde of language, to the end their cousenings, knaueries and villanies might not be so easily perceiued and knowne, in places where they come: and this their language they spunne out of thrée other tongues, *viz.* Latine, English, and Dutch: these thrée especially, notwithstanding some few words they borrowed of the Spanish and French. They also gaue names to such persons of their company according to the kind of life that he vndertooke: as for example a common begger or rogue, they termed a Clapper-dudgeon, one that counterfeited the falling sicknes, they termed him a counterfeit Cranke, for Cranke in their language is the falling sickenesse, and so Counterfeit Cranke is the false falling sickenesse: and so of the rest.

This *Cocke Lorrell* continued among them longer than any of his predecessours before him, or after him: for he ruled almost two and twentie yeares, vntil the yeare *An. Dom.* 1533. and about the sixe and twenty yeare of K. *Henry* the eight.

1. He made among other, these Statutes among them, that whosoeuer he be, that being borne and bred vp in the trade of maunding, nipping and foisting for the space of tenne years, and hath not the right dexterity in his fingers to picke a pocket, but is faine to cloy his fellowes, and cowarly to demand scrappage; such a one is to be knowne and brought hither to be fined for his faint-hĽartednesse: and if such a one after venter and be taken vpon the first fault, let him know, that he is going the high way to perdition without pitty, as a iust punishment for his folly, that he betooke himselfe so soone to the occupation.

2. *Item,* We thinke it méet that none eat meat, as Pigges, Capons, Géese or such like, vnlesse he purchase it by priuie pilfery and cleanely conueyance, neither shal they be merry in euery Bowsing ken or Alehouse as they list, but in some odde out-house remote from dwellers: a Stawling ken that is knowne of purpose to be trusty, yea and that in the night too, least they be notified and suspected, to be scandalizing of the profession: neither shall they be merry out of measure, least by their extraordinary noyses, the Constable and Watchmen take them, and so carry them to ward, as a iust punishment for their presumptuous and vnordinate procéedings: for which some of late daies haue wofully felt the smart.

Captaine *Giles Hather* first began in *Anno Domini* one thousand fiue hundred twenty and eight: concerning whom, there is nothing made mention of, but of his cousonage and deceit, for these kind of people liued more quietly and out of harme in respect of the other sort, making themselues as strangers, and would never put forth themselues in any tumult or Commotion, as the other sort did: but what vice they exercised not one way, they were not inferiour to them in the like, or rather worse another way; so that what betwéene them

both, they were two pestiferous members in a Common-wealth : but I will
leaue them both, and pray for a prosperous winde to bring my Barke to the
wished port of her desire, which is to be fauoured and well liked if in your
sight : which if good fortune fauour me so much, I shall be bouldened once
more to play the Merchant venturer : at whose second arriuall I will present
you with things more strange, not farre fetcht but déerely bought and wherein,
if license may be permitted, I will procéed and set downe the successours from
Cocke Lorrell vntil this present day, and who at this day beares the greatest
sway amongst them.

OF FOOLISH BEGGARS AND THEIR VANITIES.

1508.

From the " Ship of Fools," by Alexander Barclay.

The original edition of this work is thus entitled—

(This present Boke named the Shyp of folys of the worlde was translated i
the College of saynt mary Otery in the counte of Deuonshyre : out of Laten |
Frenche | and Doche into Englysshe tonge by Alexander Barclay Preste :
and at that tyme Chaplen in the sayde College. traslated the yere of our Lorde
god M.CCCCCVIII. Inprentyd in the Cyte of London in Fletestre at the
signe of Saynt George By Rycharde Pynson to hys Coste and charge : Ended
the yere of our Sauiour M. d. ix. The xiiii. day of December.

OF FOLYSSHE BEGGERS AND OF THEYR VANYTEES.

(Syns I haue taken the charge one me
Mo botis and Barges for Folys to aparayle
And so agayne of newe to take these
I feryd lyst company shulde me fayle
Within my folysshe shyppis to trauayle
But nowe doth beggers them selfe to me present
For fewe of them I fynde of good intent.

A great company of folys may we fynde
Amonge beggers | whiche haue theyr hole delyte
In theyr lewde craft : wherfore I set my mynde
In this Barge theyr maners | brefely for to wryte
For thoughe that nede them greuously do byte
Yet is theyr mynde for all theyr pouerte
To kepe with them of children great plente.

And though that they myght otherwyse well lyue
And get their lyuynge by labour and besynes
Yet fully they theyr myndes set and gyue
To lede this lyfe alway in wretchydnes
The clerke | frere | or monke | whiche hath store of ryches
For all his lyfe, if he it gyde wysely,
Wyll yet the beggers offyce occupy.

Suche oft complayne the charge of pouerte
In garmentis goynge raggyd and to rent
But yet haue they of ryches great plente
Whiche in gode vse can neuer of them be spent
Almys is ordeyned by god omnypotent
And holy churche : for to be gyuyn in dede
Unto good vse | and suche as haue moste nede.

Almes is ordeyned by god our creatour
For men that lyue in nede and wretchydnes

FOOLISH BEGGARS AND THEIR VANITIES (1508)

Therwith their paynfull lyues to socour
And nat for ryche that lyues in viciousnes
But yet suche caytyfs boldly in dare pres
For their lewde lyfe without all maner drede
This almes takynge from them that haue moste nede.

The abbot | the Pryour | and also theyr couent
Ar so blyndyd with vnhappy couetyse
That with theyr owne can they nat be content
But to haue more | they alway mean deuyse
Ye : in so moche that some haue founde a gyse
To fayne theyr bretherne tan in captyuyte
That they may begge so by auctoryte.

They fayne myracles where none were euer done
And all for lucre : some other range about
To gather and begge with some fayned pardon
And at the alehows at nyght all drynkyth out
So ren these beggers in company rowt
By stretis tauernes townes and vyllagys
No place can well be fre of theyr outragys.

Some begge for byldynges | some for relyques newe
Of holy sayntis of countreys farre and strange
And with theyr wordes faynyd and vntrewe
For cause of Lucre | about they ren and range
But in a sympyll vyllage | ferme or grange
Where as these beggers moste sympyll men may fynde
With theyr fals bonys as relykes they them blynde.

Other beynge stronge and full of lustynes
And yonge ynoughe to labour for theyr fode
Gyuyth theyr bodyes fully to slewthfulnes
The beggers craft thynkynge to them moost good
Some ray[1] theyr legges and armys ouer with blood
With leuys & plasters though they be hole and sounde
Some halt as crypls | theyr legge falsly vp bounde.[2]

Some other beggers falsly for the nonys
Disfygure theyr children god wot vnhappely
Manglynge theyr facys | and brekynge theyr bonys
To stere the people to pety that passe by
There stande they beggynge with tedyous shout and cry
There owne bodyes tournynge to a strange fassion
To moue suche as passe to pyte and compassyon.

Suche yonge laddys as lusty ar of age
Myghty and stronge | and wymen in lyke wyse
Wanton and yonge and lusty of cowrage
Gyueth them selfe vtterly to this gyse
The cause is that they labour do despyse
For theyr mynde is in ydylnes to be styll
Or els in vyce to wander at theyr wyll.

---

[1] *Ray*, Fr. *rayer*, to streak, to stripe.
[2] In *Peers Ploughman* we find "Then were idle hypocrites afraid and feigned themselves blind, or laid their legs awry, as such abandoned creatures know how to do."

They paciently theyr prouertye abyde
Nat for deuocion of herte or of mynde
But to the intent that at euery tyde
Other mennys godes sholde them fede and fynde.
But if they a whyle haue ron in the wynde
And in theyr hande the staf some hete hath caught
They neuer after shall leue the beggers craft.

Amonge these beggers also is comonly
Braulynge debate hatered and chydynge
Great othes | mockes | falshode and enuy
And one with other euer more fyghtynge
As for theyr dronkennes and vnsure abydynge
Theyr rebaudry both in dede and cōmunycacion
These ar chefe poyntis of their occupacion.

If the begger haue his staf and his hode
One bagge behynde and another before
Than thynkes he hym in the myddes of his goode
Thoughe that his clothes be raggyd and to tore
His body nere bare he hath no thought therfore
And if some man cloth them well to day
To morrowe it shall agayne be solde away.

And if these caytyfes fortune to begge or cry
For mete or money | on woman or on man
If one to them that | that they aske deny
And so depart : anone these beggers than
Whan he is gone | doth wary curse and ban
And if another gyue them ought of pyte
At the next alestake dronken shall it be.

But if that I sholde gather in my barge
All folysshe beggers | and labour or intende
To note all theyr vyces | to sore sholde be the charge
And as I suppose I neuer sholde make an ende.
Wherfore I counsell them shortly to amende
Or els theyr lewdnes | synne | and enormyte
Shall cause men withdrawe theyr almes of charyte.

(Thenvoy of Barclay the translatour.

(O people vnthrifty gyuen to ydlenes
Spendynge your youth this wyse in vanyte
What ioy haue ye to lyue in wretchydnes
Where ye myht come to better rowme and degre
By worke | and labour : and so auaunsyd be
Yet begge ye styll hauynge your ioy therin
Amende your foly | and lerne ye this of me
That goddes good sholde nat be spent in syn.

The Excess of Beggars.

Circa 1510.

From a "General Satire" by William Dunbar.

Sae mony jacks and brats on beggar's backs
Within this land was never heard nor seen.

OF BEGGARS AND THEIR VANITIES.
1517.
From the "Ship of Fools," by Henry Watson.[1]

The prologue of the translatoure.

.... This booke hathe ben fyrst made in Almayne[2] language | and out of Almayne it was translated in to Latyn | by mayster Jaques Locher | & out of Latyn in to rethoryke Frensshe. I haue consydered that the one delyteth hym in latyn | the other in Frensshe | some in ryme | and the other in prose | for the whiche cause I haue done this. . . . Consyderynge also that the prose is more familiar vnto euery man than ye ryme, I, Henry Watson, ... haue reduced this present boke into our maternall tongue of Englysshe out Frenshe | at ye requeste of my worshypfull mayster wynkyn de worde | thrughe the entysement exhortacyon of the excellent prynces Margarete | cōutesse of Rychemonde and Derby | and grandame vnto our moost naturall souerayne lorde Kynge Henry y^e VIII whome Jhesu preserue from all encombraūce. . . .

¶ By the shyppe we may vnderstande y_e folyes and erroures that the mōdaynes[3] are in | by the se this presente worlde. . . . | Syth that it is so | we must serche in this booke, the whiche may wel be called the doctrynall of fooles. . . .

(Thus endeth the shyppe of fooles of this worlde. Imprynted at Londod in flete strete by wȳkyn de worde. ye yere of our lorde. M. CCCCC. & XVII. (The nynthe yere of ye reygne of our souerayne lorde kynge Henry ye VIII. The. xx. daye of June.

(OF BEGGERS AND OF THEYR VANYTEES. CA. LX.

> (I whiche am a poore almes man
> Haue grete fere to encreace lygnage
> Bycause that I nothynge get can
> To helpe my selfe in myne olde aege
> And my chyldren in theyr domage
> Goynge aboute from doore to doore
> Gyue your good almesse to the poore.

All vacabondes | and myghty beggers | the which gothe beggynge from dore to dore | & ayleth lytell or nought | with lame men and crepylles | come vnto me and I shall gyue you an almesse saluberryme[4] & of grete vertue. The mendycans be in grete nombre | wherfore I wyll declare vnto you some of theyr foolysshe condycyons.

These fooles, the whiche be soūde in theyr corporal bodyes | wyll nouryssh and kepe dyuers chyldren | I byleue fyrmely that they wold not haue theyr lyues in this vale of myserye otherwyse. The mōkes haue this myschefe | and ye clerkes also | the whiche haue theyr coffers ful of grete rychesses | and treasoures. Neuertheles yet they applye themselfe in the offyce of the mendycans | in purchasynge and beggynge on euery syde. They be a grete sorte replenysshed with vnhappynes, saynge that they lede theyr lyues in grete pouerte and calamyte | & therfore they praye eury man to gyue them theyr good almesse | in release of theyr payne and myserye. And yet they haue golde and syluer grete | plentye but they will spende nothynge before the

---

[1] This extract has been kindly collated by Mr. *W. H. Allnutt* of the *Bodleian Library.* This library is the only public institution which contains a copy of this scarce book.
[2] German.   [3] People of the world.
[4] *Saluberrime, Lat.* most beneficial.

comyn people. (Our lord Ihesu cryste hathe ordeyned that almesse sholde be dystrybuted and gyuen vnto ye poore folkes that possedeth nothynge | and that be indygente | to the ende that they lyue here to the laude and praysynge of our lorde Ihesu criste | the whiche thynge is ryght precyous before god. Somtyme the cursed taketh the almesse of the poore indygente. I fynde grete fautes in the abbottes | mōkes | pryours | chanons | and couentes | for all that they haue rentes tenements and possessyons ynough | yet as folkes deuoyde of sence and vnderstondynge | they be neuer satysfyed with goodes. They goo from vyllage to vyllage | and from towne to towne berynge grete bagges vpon theyr neckes | assemblynge so moche goodes | that it is grete meruayle | and whan they be in theyr relygyous cloysters they make theym byleue y^t they haue had lytell gyuen them | or nothynge | for god knoweth they make heuen chere[1] in the countre. And by this occasyon the poore nedy hathe none almesse | or elles it is but small.

There is another sorte of pardoners | the whiche bereth relyques aboute with them, i abusyinge ye pore folkes | for & yf they haue but one poore peny in theyr purses | they must haue it. They gadre togyder golde & syluer in euery place, lyke as yf it grewe. They make ye poore folkes byleue moche gay gere. They sel ye feders of the holy ghoost.[2] They bere the bones of some deed body aboute | the whiche parauenture, is damyned. They shewe the heer of some olde hors | saynge that it is of ye berde of the innocents. Ther is an innumerable syght of suche folkes | and of vacabondes in this realme of englonde, ye whiche be hole of all theyr members | & myghte wynne theyr lyues honestly. Notwithstondẏge they go beggynge from dore to dore | bycause they wyll not werke | and patcheth an olde mauntell | or an olde gowne with an hondred colours | and byndeth foule cloutes about theyr legges | as who say they be sore. And often tymes they be more rycher than they that gyueth them almesse. They breke theyr chyldrens members in theyr youthe | bycause that men sholde haue the more pyte of them.[3] They go wepynge and wryngynge of theyr hands | and counterfettynge ye sorowfull | praynge for goddes sake to gyue them an almesse | and maketh so well ye ypocrytes | that there is no man the whiche seeth them | but that he is abused | and must giue them an almesse. The is some stronge and puysaunt rybaudes the whiche wyll not laboure | but lyue, as these beggers without doynge ony thynge | the whiche be dronke oftentymes. They be well at ease to haue grete legges and bellyes eten to the bonis | for they wyll not put noo medycynes therto for to hele them | but soner enuenymeth them | & dyuers other begylynges of whiche I holde my pease. O poore frantyke fooles | the whiche robbeth them that hathe no brede for to ete | and by aduenture dare not aske none for shame | the auncyent men | poore wedowes | lazars | and blynde men | alas thynke theron | for truely ye shall gyue accomptes byfore hym that created vs.

The Gaberlunyie Man.

Circa 1530—40.

From the "*Gaberlunyie Man*,"[4] supposed to have been written by James V. on one of his intrigues.

---

[1] Dear, *Fr.* cher.

[2] A feather of the Holy Ghost was accounted a relic of the greatest repute.

[3] *Peers Ploughman* says, "These beget bastards, who are beggars by nature, and either break the back, or some other bone of their little ones, and go begging with them on false pretences ever after."

[4] *Gaberlunyie-man*. A *Blue-gown*, or beggar who wears the King's badge ; also a beggar with a wallet. By some of the peasantry in Loth. this term is still used, but confined to a *Bluegown*, or beggar who wears the King's badge,

My dear, quo' he, ye're yet o'er young,
And ha' na learned the beggars tongue,
To follow me frae town to town,
And carry the gaberlunyie on.

Wi' cauk [1] and keel [2] I'll win your bread,
And spindles and whorles [3] for them wha need,
Whilk is a gentle trade indeed,
To carry the gaberlunyie on.

I'll bow my leg, and crook my knee,
And draw a black clout o'er my eye,
A cripple or blind they will ca' me
While we shall be merry and sing.

THE PARDONER.
Circa 1539.

From " *Ane Satyre of the thrie Estaitis,* by Sir David Lyndsay.

My patent Pardouns, ye may se,
Cum fra the Cane of Tartarie,
Weill seald with oster-schellis.
Thocht ye haue na contritioun,
Ye sall have full remissioun,
With help of buiks, and bellis.
Heir is ane relict, lang and braid [4]
Of Fine Macoull the richt chaft blaid
With teith, and al togidder:
Of Colling's cow, heir is ane horne,
For eating of Makconnal's corne,
Was slaine into Baquhidder. [5]
Heir is ane coird, baith great and lang,
Quhilk hangit Johne the Armistrang: [6]

---

and pronounced, according to the erroneous orthography, *Gaberlunzie.* Teut. *loenie, longie,* a loin. Were not *gaberlunyie* so used as apparently to signify something from which the owner is denominated, it might have been supposed that the person had his name *q.* A.S. *gebeor,* hospes, and *lan egenus, i.e.* a poor guest; or as in the song, the *poor man.—Jamieson.*

[1] Chalk.

[2] Ruddle. This alludes to the practice of fortune-tellers, who usually pretend to be dumb, to gain more credit with the vulgar, as being deprived of the ordinary means of knowledge, and therefore have recourse to signs made with chalk or ruddle, in order to make known their meaning. The Gaberlunyie man promises to win his sweetheart's livelihood by telling fortunes.—*Jamieson.*

[3] A round perforated piece of wood put on a spindle.

[4] *Of Fine Macoull the richt chaft blaid.* Of Fyn-Mac-Coul the proper jaw-bone. The allusion is obviously pointed to *Fionn Mac-Cumhail,* the famous Fingal, the son of Cumhail. Fin-Mac-Coull is a personage who, with the other heroes of Ossian, was very familiar to the historians and poets of Scotland, during the age of Lyndsay, and during some centuries before.

[5] *Balquhidder.* " A parish in the west of Perthshire: the MacConnals were a powerful clan in Lyndsay's age; but they lived chiefly in Kintyre."—*Chalmers.*

[6] *Johne the Armistrang.* "Johnny Armstrong, the well-known Border freebooter, who, by a great effort of justice, was hanged, in June, 1529, near Carlenrig, in Teviotdale."—*Chalmers.*

592   VAGRANTS AND VAGRANCY,

> Of gude hemp soft, and sound :
> Gude, halie peopill, I stand for'd
> Quha euer beis hangit with this cord,
> Neids never to be dround.
> The culum[1] of Sanct Bryd's Kow,
> The gruntill [2] of Sanct Antonis sow,
>
> Quhilk buir his haly bell :
> Quha ever he be heiris this bell clinck
> Gif me ane ducat for till drink,
> He sall never gang to hell.

A Begging Letter.
1542.
(From " Notes and Queries.")

The Vicar of Writtle received, as chaplain of a church dependent on the benefice, £6 13s. 4d. from the wardens and fellows of New College. The letter informs us that he has got into debt for buildings, and is under the necessity of meeting a very serious tax on his means. One is glad to see that Warden London, whom Fox paints in very black colours, had compassion on the Rev. William Harse. The date of the letter is Feb. 5, 1542. It may be worth noting here that on April 9 the warden, being on a circuit of visitation, dined at one of his manors on a capon and a "portenans of Lamb," an expression which illustrates Exodus xii. 9.

(In dorso) To my rygth honorabul master Mr. Doctor London warden the New Colegg in Oxforth delyver.

(Refolded and endorsed) To my lovynge frynde M. Pynchym thes be dd. Rygth honorabul my dewty in al pwynts premysyd, I beseche yor masterschepe to be favorabul to me concernynge suche charge as I have leyed owt a ponne my preysts loggynge here. I have sende twyse to M. Coterelle the parcells of ye hole the wych drawyth to iij*li*. ij*s*. ij*d*. A fryday nexte I must pay to the collector for the tenyth & the subsyde of our vycarige here viij*li*. towarde the wych yetto I have scant iiij*li*., urgent necessite compellyth me to masterschepe so desyrynge you to take y^t I have sende you longe lyve with mych ffelycyte yn wrytyn the 5 day of thys ynstant ffebruary.   Yo^r bedman,
                                      Will'm Harse, preyst.

M. Pynchym I pray yow content Mr. Vicar for the repayring of hys prests lodginge thre poundys ijs. ijd. and I w'll alow hit unto yow at y'r audyt.
                                      Yo^r frynd,
                                      John London.

On Valiant Beggars.
1552.

From "the fourth *Sermon made upon the Lordes Prayer* by the Right Reverend father in God Maister *Hugh Latymer* before the right vertuous and honourable lady Katherine, Duchesse of Suffolke." Anno 1552.

Scripture sayth ; *Qui peccat ex diabolo est*, Whosoeuer sinneth is of the deuill, whiche is a very hard worde to bee spoken, of the Holy Ghost, and a fearefull word, able to withdraw us from sinne, if we had any feare of God in our hartes. Amongest these may bee numbred all slouthfull persons, which

---

[1] The fundament, tail.   [2] The snout.

will not trauayle for theyr lyuinges, they doo the will of the deuill. God byddeth us to gette our lyuing with labour ; they will not labour, but go rather about a begging, and spoyle the very poore and needy. Therefore such valiaunt beggers are theeues before God. Some of these valiaunt lubbars, when they came to my house I commoned with them, burthenyng them with the transgression of Gods lawes. Is not this a great labour (say they) to run from one towne to an other to gette our meate ? I thinke we labour as hard as other men doo. In such wise they go about to excuse their vnlawfull beggery and theefery : but such idle lubbars are much deceiued ; For they consider not that such labour is not allowed of God.

The Fraternity of Vagabonds.
1561.

The Fraternitye of Vacabondes. As wel of ruflyng Vacabondes, as of beggerly, of women as of men, of Gyrles as of Boyes, with their proper names and qualities. With a description of the Crafty Company of Cousoners and Shifters. ¶ Wherunto also is adioyned the XXV. Orders of Knaues otherwyse called a Quartern of Knaues. Confirmed for ever by Cocke Lorell. Imprinted at London by Iohn Awdeley, 1575 (originally published about 1561).

¶ An Abraham Man.

An Abraham man is he that walketh bare armed, and bare legged, and fayneth hym selfe mad, and caryeth a packe of wool, or a stycke with baken on it, or such lyke toy, and nameth himselfe poore Tom.

¶ A Ruffeler.

A Ruffeler goeth wyth a weapon to seeke seruice, saying he hath bene a Seruitor in the wars, and beggeth for his reliefe. But his chiefest trade is to robbe poore wayfaring men and market women.

¶ A Prygman.

A Prygman goeth with a stycke in hys hand like an idle person. His propertye is to steale cloathes of the hedge, which they call storing of the Rogeman : or else filtch Poultry, carying them to the Alehouse, whych they call the Bowsyng In, & ther syt playing at cardes and dice, tyl that is spent which they haue so fylched.

¶ A Whipiacke.

A Whypiacke is one, that by coulor of a counterfaite Lisence (which they call a Gybe, and the seales they call Iarckes) doth vse to beg lyke a Maryner. But his chiefest trade is to rob Bowthes in a Faire, or to pilfer ware from staules, which they cal heauing of the Bowth.

¶ A Frater.

A frater goeth wyth a like Lisence to beg for some Spittlehouse or Hospital. Their pray is commonly upon poore women as they go and come to the Markets.

¶ A Quire Bird.

A Quire bird is one that came lately out of prison, & goeth to seeke seruice. He is commonly a stealer of Horses, which they terme a Priggar of Paulfreys.

¶ An Vpright Man.

An Vpright man is one that goeth wyth the trunchion of a staffe, which staffe they cal a Filtchman. This man is of so much authority, that meeting with any of his profession, he may cal them to accompt, & commaund a share or snap vnto him selfe, of al that they haue gained by their trade in one moneth.

And if he doo them wrong, they haue no remedy agaynst him, no though he beate them as he useth commonly to do. He may also commaund any of their women, which they call Doxies, to serue his turne. He hath ye chiefe place at any market walke, & other assembles, & is not of any to be controled.

¶ A Curtall.

A Curtall is much like to the Vpright man, but hys authority is not fully so great. He vseth commonly to go with a short cloke, like to grey Friers, & his woman with him in like liuery, which he calleth his Altham if she be hys wyfe, & if she be his harlot, she is called his Doxy.

¶ A Palliard.

A Palliard is he that goeth in a patched cloke, and hys Doxy goeth in like apparell.

¶ An Irish Toyle.[1]

An Irishe Toyle is he that carieth his ware in hys wallet, as laces, pins, poyntes, and such like. He vseth to shew no wares vntill he haue his almes. And if the good man and wyfe be not in the way, he procureth of the chilldren or seruants a fleece of wool, or the worth of xijd. of some other thing, for a peniworth of his wares.

¶ A Iack Man.

A Iackeman is he that can write and reade, and somtime speake latin. He vseth to make counterfaite licences which they call Gybes, and sets to Seales, in their language called Iarkes.

¶ A Swygman.

A Swygman goeth with a Pedlers pack.

¶ A Washman.

A Washman is called a Palliard, but not of the right making. He vseth to lye in the hye way with lame or sore legs or armes to beg. These men ye right Pilliards wil often times spoile, but they dare not complayn. They be bitten with Spickworts, and somtime with rats bane.

¶ A Tinkard.

A Tinkard leaueth his bag a sweating at the Alehouse, which they terme their Bowsing In, and in the meane season goeth abrode a begging.

¶ A Wylde Roge.

A wilde Roge is he that hath no abiding place but by his coulour of going abrode to beg, is commonly to seeke some Kinsman of his, and all that be of hys corporation be properly called Roges

¶ A Kitchen Co.

A Kitchin Co is called an ydle runagate Boy.

¶ A Kitchen Mortes.

A Kitchin Mortes is a Gyrle, she is brought at her full age to the Vpright man to be broken, and so she is called a Doxy, vntil she come to ye honor of an Altham.

¶ Doxies.

Note especially all which go abroade working laces and shirt stringes, they name them Doxies.

---

[1] Welsh *Teulu*, a family or household.

AND BEGGARS AND BEGGING.

¶ A Patriarke Co.

A Patriarke Co doth make mariages, & that is untill death depart the maried folke, which is after this sort : When they come to a dead Horse or any dead Catell, then they shake hands and so depart euery one of them a seuerall way.

¶ The Company of Cousoners and Shifters.

Under this head are described The CURTESY MAN who with humble salutations and low curtesy begs on behalf of "certaine of us..... which haue come lately from the wars,..... wher as we haue bene welthely brought up." The CHEATOUR or FINGERER. A professional gamester disguised as a countryman who with the aid of a confederate fleeces young men at taverns, and the RING FALLER who drops gilt copper rings in the streets and claims half the estimated value from the finder.

¶ The XXV. Orders of Knaves

otherwise called a quartern of Knaves

deals with the tricks of servants of which the following may serve as specimens—

4 Troll Hazard of Tritrace.

Troll hazard of tritrace, is he that goeth gaping after his Master, looking to and fro tyl he haue lost him. This Knaue goeth gasynge about lyke a foole at euery toy, and then seeketh in euery house lyke a Maisterles dog, and when his Maister nedeth him, he is to seeke.

6 Obloqium.

Obloquium is hee that wyll take a tale out of his Maisters mouth and tell it him selfe. He of right may be called a malapert knaue.

A CAVEAT OR WARNING FOR COMMON CURSETORS.

1567.

From a "Caueat or Warening for Commen Cvrsetors wlgarely called Vagabones, set forth by Thomas Harman, Esquiere, for the vtilitie and proffyt of his naturall cuntrey." 1567.

Thomas Harman was a gentleman and Justice of the Peace of Crayford in Kent, a keen, inquiring social reformer, who during twenty years collected information regarding wandering vagabonds from themselves and exposed their tricks.

He explains in the "Epistle to the Reader" that he calls "these Vagabonds Cursetors in the intytelynge of my booke, as runneres or rangers aboute the countrey, deriued of this Laten word *Curro*."

In the preface to this work, which is dedicated to Elizabeth, Countess of Shrewsbury, who lived at Erith in the next parish, Harman says : " I thought it good, necessary, and my bounden dutye to acquaynte your goodnes with the abhominable, wycked and detestable behauor of all these rousey, ragged, rabblement of rakehelles, that, vnder the pretence of great misery, dyseases, and other innumerable calamites, which they fayne through great hypocrisie, do wyn and gayne great almes in all places where they wyly wander, to the vtter deludinge of the good geuers, deceauinge and impouerishing of all such poore housholders, both sicke and sore, as nether can or maye walke abroad for reliefe and comforte."

He divides Vagabonds into twenty-three varieties.

1. The Ruffler, or discharged soldier or serving man.

2. The Upright Man, or wandering artificer or labouring man addicted to theft.
3. The Hooker or Angler, or stealer of clothes by means of a staff with a hook.
4. The Rogue, feigning to travel in search of a brother or kinsman, &c.
5. The Wild Rogue, or beggar by inheritance.
6. The Prigger of Prancers, or horse stealer.
7. The Palliard, or born beggar who counterfeits sores, &c.
8. The Frater, or fraudulent collector for the poor in Spital houses.
9. The Abraham Man, who feigns madness.
10. The Fresh Water Mariner, or Whipjack.
11. The Counterfeit Crank, who feigns sickness (A.S. *cranc*, near death).
12. The Dommerar, who counterfeits dumbness.
13. The Drunken Tinker.
14. The Swadder or Pedler.
15. The Jarke Man, or counterfeiter of licences and writings ; and the Patrico, or sham priest.
16. The Demander for Glymmar (A.S. *glœm*, brightness), who pretends to have lost his goods by fire.
17. The Bawdy Basket, or woman who goes about with a basket or cap-case on her arm, containing indecent ballads.
18. The Autem Mort : a woman who pretends to be married, and who goes about with children, and pilfers clothes off hedges, &c.
19. The Walking Mort, who sells laces and purses, and pretends to have lost her husband.
20. The Doxy, or Harlot.
21. The Dell, or young wench.
22. The Kynchin Morte, or little girl (*Kindchen*, babe, baby).
23. The Kynchen Co, or little boy.

Most of these varieties exist, with little difference from what they were more than three hundred years ago.

Two of the classes above mentioned, the Pallyards and the Dommerars, Harman says, were mostly constituted of Welshmen ; and towards the conclution of his work he states, " There is above an hundreth Irish men and women that wander about to begge for their lyving, that hath come over within these two yeares. They say they have beene burned and spoyled by the Earle of Desmond."

The inference deducible from this statement is that the vagrants in ancient times were largely recruited from Wales and Ireland, an inference which an analysis of the secret jargon of the Beggar and Vagabond proves to be correct.

¶ A Vpright Man. Ca. 2.

A vpright man, the second in secte of this vnsemely sorte, must be next placed, of these rainginge rablement of rascales ; some be seruing men, artificers, and laboryng men traded vp in husbandry. These not mindinge to get their lyuinge with the swete of their face, but casting of all payne, wyll wander, after their wycked maner, through the most shyres of this realm,—

As Sommerset shyre, Wylshire, Barke shyre, Oxforde shyre, Harfordeshyre, Myddilsex, Essex, Suffolke, Northfolke, Sussex, Surrye and Kent, ar the cheyfe and best shyres of reliefe. Yea, not with out punishment by stockes, whyppinges, and imprisonment, in most of these places aboue sayde. Yet, not with standinge they haue so good lykinge in their lewed, lecherous loyteringe, that full quiclye all their punishmentes is forgotten. And repentaunce is neuer thought vpon vntyll they clyme thrée tres with a ladder. . . .

For you must vnderstand, euery Typplyng ale house wyll neyther receiue them or their wares, but some certayne houses in euery shyre, especially for

that purpose, where they shalbe better welcome to them then honester men.
For by such haue they most gayne, and shalbe conuayde eyther into some loft
out of the waye, or other secret corner not commen to any other ; and thether
repayre, at accustomed tymes, their harlots, whiche they terme Mortes and
Doxes,—not with emty hands ; for they be as skilfull in picking, riffling, *and*
filching as the vpright men, and nothing inferior to them in all kind of wycked-
nes, as in other places hereafter they shalbe touched. At these foresayde
peltinge, peuish places, and vnmannerly meetinges, O! how the pottes walke
about! their talking tounges talke at large. They bowle and bowse one to
another, and for the tyme bousing belly chere. And after there ruysting recreation, yf there be not rome ynough in the house, they haue cleane strawe in
some barne or backehouse near adioyning, where they couch comly to gether,
as it were dogge and byche ; and he that is hardyste maye haue his choyse,
vnlesse for a lytle good maner ; some wyll take there owne that they haue made
promyse unto, untyll they be out of sight, and then, according to the old adage,
" out of minde." Yet these vpright men stand so much vpon their reputation,
as they wyl in no case haue their wemen walke with them, but seperat them
selues for a tyme, a moneth or more. And mete at fayres, or great markets,
where they mete to pylfer and steale from staules, shoppes, or bothes. At these
fayres the vpright men vse commonly to lye and lingar in hye wayes by lanes,
some prety way or distaunce from the place, by which wayes they be assured
that compeny passeth styll two and fro. And ther they wyll demaund, with cap
in hand and comly curtesy, the deuotion and charity of the people. They haue
ben much lately whypped at fayrs. Yf they aske at a stout yemans or farmars
house his charity, they wyll goe strong as thre or foure in a company. Where
for feare more then good wyll, they aften haue reliefe.

¶ A Roge. Cap. 4.

Others therebee that walke sturdely about the countrey, and faineth to seke
a brother or kinsman of his, dwelling within som part of the shire ;—ether that
he hath a letter to deliuer to som honest housholder, dwelling out of an other
Shyre, and will shewe you the same fayre sealed, with the superscription to the
partye he speaketh of, because you shall not thinke him to runne idelly about
the countrey ; either haue they this shyfte, they wyll cary a cirtificate or pas-
port about them from som Iusticer of the peace, with his hand and seale vnto
the same, howe hée hath bene whipped and punished for a vacabonde according
to the lawes of this realme, and that he must return to. T., where he was borne
or last dwelt, by a certayne daye lymited in the same, whiche shalbe a good
longe daye. And all this fayned, bycause without feare they woulde wyckedly
wander, and wyll renue the same where or when it pleasethe them ; for they
haue of their affinity that can wryte and read.

¶ A wylde Roge. Cap 5.

A wilde Roge is he that is borne a Roge : he is more subtil and more geuen
by nature to all kinde of knauery then the other, as beastely begotten in barne
or bushes, and from his infancye traded vp in trechery ; yea, and before ripenes
of yeares doth permyt, wallowinge in lewde lechery, but that is counted
amongest them no sin.
I once rebuking a wyld roge because he went idelly about, he shewed me that
he was a begger by enheritance—his Grandfather was a begger, his father was
one, and he must nedes be one by good reason.

¶ A Pallyard. Cap. 7.

Farther, vnderstand for trouth that the worst and wickedst of all this beastly
generation are scarse comparable to these prating Pallyardes. All for the most
part of these wil either lay to their legs an herb called Sperewort, eyther Arsnicke,

which is called Ratesbane. The nature of this Spereworte wyll rayse a great blister in a night upon the soundest part of his body ; and if the same be taken away, it wyl dry vp againe and no harme. But this Arsnicke will so poyson the same legge or sore, that it will euer after be incurable : this they do for gaine and to be pitied. The most of these that walke about be Walchmen.

¶ A Frater. Cap. 8.

Some of these Fraters wile cary blacke boxes at their gyrdel, wher in they haue a briefe of the Queenes maiesties letters patentes, geuen to such poore spitlehouse for the reliefe of the poore there, whiche briefe is a coppie of the letters patentes, and vtterly fained, if it be in paper or in parchment without the great seale.

¶ A Freshe Water Mariner or Whipiacke. Cap. 10.

These Freshwater Mariners, their shipes were drowned in the playne of Salisbery. These kynde of Caterpillers counterfet great losses on the sea ; these bée some Western men, and most bée Irishe men. These wyll runne about the countrey wyth a counterfet lycence, fayninge either shypwracke, or spoyled by Pyrates, neare the coaste of Cornwall or Deuonshyre, and set a lande at some hauen towne there, hauynge a large and formall wrytinge, as is aboue sayd, with the names and seales of suche men of worshyppe, at the leaste foure or fiue, as dwelleth neare or next to the place where they fayne their landinge. And neare to those shieres wyll they not begge, vntyll they come into Wylshyre, Hamshyre, Barkeshyre. Oxfordshyre, Harfordshyre, Middelsex, and so to London, and downe by the ryver to séeke for their shyppe and goods that they neuer hade : then passe they through Surrey, Sossex, by the sea costes, and so into Kent, demaunding almes to bring them home to their country.

¶ Some tyme they counterfet the seale of the Admiraltie. I have diuers tymes taken a waye from them their lycences, of both sortes, wyth such money as they haue gathered, and haue confiscated the same to the pouerty nigh adioyninge to me. And they wyll not beelonge with out another. For at anye good towne they wyll renewe the same.

¶ A Counterfet Cranke. Cap. 11.

Many of these do go without writinges, and wyll go halfe naked, and looke most pitiously. And if any clothes be geuen them, they immediatly sell the same, for weare it they wyll not, because they would bée the more pitied, and weare fylthy clothes on their heades, and neuer goe without a péece of whyte sope about them, which, if they sée cause or present gaine, they wyll priuely conuey the same into their mouth, and so worke the same there, that they wyll fome as it were a Boore, and maruelously for a tyme torment them selues ; and thus deceiue they the common people, and gayne much. These haue commonly their harlots as the other.

¶ A Dommerar. Cap. 12.

These Dommerars are leud and most subtyll people : the moste part of these are Walch men, and wyll neuer speake, vnlesse they haue extreame punishment, but wyll gape, and with a maruelous force wyll hold downe their toungs doubled, groning for your charyty, and holding vp their handes full pitiously, so that with their deepe dissimulation they get very much.

¶ A Dronken Tinckar. Cap. 13.

These dronken Tynckers, called also Prygges, be beastly people, and these yong knaues be the wurst. These neuer go with out their Doxes, and yf their women haue anye thing about them, as apparell or lynnen, that is worth the selling, they lay the same to gage, or sell it out right, for bene bowse at their bowsing ken. . . . . For besydes money, he looketh for meate and drinke for doing his dame pleasure. For yf she have thrée or foure holes in a pan, hee wyll make as many more for spedy gaine.

¶ A Iarke Man, and a Patrico. Cap. 15.

For as much as these two names, a Iarkeman and a Patrico, bée in the old briefe of vacabonds, and set forth as two kyndes of euil doers, you shall vnderstande that a Iarkeman hathe his name of a Iarke, which is a seale in their Language, as one should make writinges and set seales for lycences and pasporte. And for trouth there is none that goeth aboute the countrey of them that can eyther wryte so good and fayre a hand, either indite so learnedly, as I haue sene *and* handeled a number of them : but haue the same made in good townes where they come, as what can not be hadde for money, as the prouerbe sayth *(" Omnia venalia Rome")* and manye hath confessed the same to me.

Now, also, there is a Patrico, and not a Patriarcho, which in their language is a priest that should make marriages tyll death dyd depart; but they haue none such, I am well assured ; for I put you out of doubt that not one amongest a hundreth of them are maried, for they take lechery for no sinne, but naturall fellowshyp and good lyking loue.

¶ A Demaunder for Glymmar. Cap 16.

These Demaunders for glymmar be for the moste parte wemen; for glymmar in their language, is fyre. These goe with fayned lycences and counterfayted wrytings, hauing the hands and seales of suche gentlemen as dwelleth nere to the place where they fayne them selues to haue been burnt, and their goods consumed with fyre. They wyll most lamentable demaunde your charitie, and wyll quicklye shed salte teares, they be so tender harted. They will neuer begge in that Shiere where their losses (as they say) was. Some of these goe with slates at their backes, which is a shéete to lye in a nightes. The vpright men be very familiare with these kynde of wemen, and one of them helpes an other.

¶ A Bawdy Basket. Cap. 17.

These Bawdy baskets be also wemen, and go with baskets and Capcases on their armes, where in they haue laces, pynnes, nedles, white ynkell, and round sylke gyrdles of al coulours. These wyl bye conneyskins, and steale linen clothes of on hedges. And for their trifles they wil procure of mayden seruants, when their mystres or dame is oute of the waye, either some good peece of béefe, baken, or chéese, that shalbe worth xij. pens, for ii. pens of their toyes.

¶ A Walking Mort. Cap. 19.

These walkinge Mortes bee not maryed : these for their vnhappy yeares doth go as a Autem Morte, and wyll saye their husbandes died eyther at Newhauen, Ireland, or in some seruice of the Prince. These make laces vpon staues, and purses, that they cary in their hands, and whyte vallance for beddes. Manye of these hath hadde and haue chyldren : when these get ought, either with begging, bychery, or brybery, as money or apparell, they are quickly shaken out of all by the vpright men, that they are in a maruelous feare to cary any thinge aboute them that is of any valure.

A Doxe. Cap. 20.

"Then, fyrste tell me," quoth I, " how many vpright men and Roges dost thou knowe or hast thou knowne and byn conuersaunt with, and what their names be ?" She paused a whyle, and sayd, " why do you aske me, or wherefore ? " " For nothinge els," as I sayde, " but that I woulde knowe them when they came to my gate." " Nowe, by my trouth (quoth she) " then, are yea neuer the neare, for all myne acquayntaunce, for the moste parte, are deade." " Dead !"

quoth I, "howe dyed they ; for wante of cherishinge, or of paynefull diseases?" Then she sighed, and sayde they were hanged. "What, all?" quoth I, "and so manye walke abroade, as I dayelye see?" "By my trouth," quoth she, "I knowe not paste six or seuen by their names," and named the same to me. "When were they hanged?" quoth I. "Some seuen yeares a gone, some thrée yeares, and some within this fortnight," and declared the place where they weare executed, which I knewe well to bee true, by the report of others. "Why" (quoth I) " dyd not this sorrowfull and fearefull sight much greue the, and for thy tyme longe and euyll spent?" "I was sory," quoth shée, "by the Masse ; for some of them were good louing men. For I lackt not when they had it, and they wanted not when I had it, and diuers of them I neuer dyd forsake, vntyll the Gallowes departed vs." "O, mercyfull God!" quoth I, and began to blesse me. " Why blesse ye?" quoth she. " Alas ! good gentleman, euery one must haue a lyvinge."

¶ Their Vsage in the Night. Cap. 24.

Now I thinke it not vnnecessary to make the Reader vnderstand how and in what maner they lodge a nights in barnes or backe houses, and of their vsage there, for asmuch as I haue acquaynted them with their order and practises a day times. . . . .

Yet haue we two notable places in Kent, not fare from London : the one is betwene Detforde and Rothered, callen the Kynges barne, standing alone, that they haunt commonly ; the other is Ketbroke, standinge by blacke heath, halfe a myle from anye house. There wyll they boldlye drawe the latche of the doore, and go in when the good man with hys famyly be at supper, and syt downe without leaue, and eate and drinke with them, and either lye in the hall by the fyre all night, or in the barne, if there be no rome in the house for them. If the doore be eyther bolted or lockt, if it be not opened vnto them when they wyl, they wyl breake the same open to his farther cost. And in this barne sometyme do lye xl. vpright men with their Doxes together at one time. And this must the poore Farmer suffer, or els they threaten him to burne him, and all that he hath.

Harman died at May Place, Crayford, June 22, 1569. His Work was afterwards plagiarised and reproduced without acknowledgment in the *Groundworke of Conny-Catching*, 1592 ; The *Belman of London* by Thomas Dekker, 1608 ; and in the Glossary attached to the English Rogue, by Richard Head, 1665.

CHAPTER XXX.

EXTRACTS FROM VARIOUS AUTHORS ILLUSTRATING THE HABITS AND IMPOSTURES OF THE VAGRANT AND BEGGAR.

1610—1700.

SAMUEL ROWLANDS, Slang Beggars' Songs (1610)—SIR THOMAS OVERBURY, A Tinker and a Canting Rogue (1616)—BEN JONSON, The Masque of the Gypsies Metamorphosed (1621)—JOHN FLETCHER, The Beggars' Bush (1622)—The Song of the Beggar (1629)—The Cunning Northern Beggar (1635)—RICHARD BROME, A Jovial Crew, or the Merry Beggars (1641)—The Beggars' Chorus in the Jovial Crew (1641)—The Tinker and the Beggar (1661)—RICHARD HEAD, Meriton Latroon, a Complete History of the most Eminent Cheats of both Sexes (1665)—The Jovial Crew or Beggars' Bush (1671).—Supplementary Verses to the Jovial Crew, styled the Beggar's Song (1700).—DANIEL DEFOE, The Complete Mendicant (1699).

SLANG BEGGARS' SONGS.

1610.

From Martin Mark-all his Apologies to the Bel-man of London, by Samuel Rowlands.

1 *Canyzon.*   *Towre out*[1] *ben morts*[2] *& towre*
                Looke out ben morts & towre
                For all the Rome coues[3] *are budgd a beake*[4]
                And the quire coues[5] *tippe the lowre.*[6]

                 The quire coues are budgd[7] *to the bowsing ken*[8]
                 As Romely[9] *as a ball,*
                 But if we spid[10] *we shall be clyd*[11]
                 And carried to the quirken hall.[12]

                 Out budgd the Coue of the Ken,[13]
                 With a ben filtch[14] *in his quarr 'me*[15]
                 That did the prigg[16] *good that bungd*[17] *in the kisome,*
                 To toure the Coue budge alar'me.

---

[1] Look about.   [2] Good girls.   [3] Good men.   [4] Run away.
[5] Peace officers.   [6] Seize the money.   [7] Run.   [8] Alehouse.
[9] Nimbly.   [10] Spied.   [11] Whipped.   [12] Prison.
[13] Master of the house.   [14] Stolen booty.   [15] Arms.   [16] Thief.   [17] Got.

But now I will shew you what I heard at *Knock-vergos*, drinking there a pot of English Ale, two Maunders borne and bred vp rogues wooing in their natiue language.

2 *Canyzon.* O Ben mort[1] *will thou pad*[2] *with me*
One ben slate[3] *shall serue both thee & me,*
My caster[4] *and Commission*[5] *shall serve us both to maund ;*
My bong,[6] *my lowre,*[7] *& fambling cheates*[8]
Shall be at thy commaund.

O Ben Coue[9] *that may not be,*
For thou hast an Autem mort[10] *who euer that is she,*
If that she were dead & bingd to his long tibb,[11]
Then would I pad[12] *and maund*[13] *with thee,*
And wap and fon the fibb.[13a]

O ben mort Castle out & Towre
Where all the Roome coues slopne that we may tip the loure ;
Whē we haue tipt the lowre[14] *& fenct away the duds*[15]
Then binge we to the bowsing ken,[16]
Thats cut[17] *the Robin Hood.*

But O ben coue what if we be clyd,
Long may we foist[18] *& nip*[19] *at last we shal be spyed,*
If that we be spied, O then begins our woe,
With the Harman beake[20] *out and alas*
To Whittington[21] *we goe.*

Stow[22] *your whids*[23] *& plant,*[24] *and whid*[25] *no more of that,*
Budg a beak[26] *the Crackmās*[27] *& tip lowr with thy prat*[28]
If treyning[29] *thou dost feare, thou ner wilt foist*[30] *a Ian,*[31]
Then mill, and wap and treine for me,
A gere peck[32] *in thy gan.*[33]

As they were thus after a strange maner a wooing, in comes by chance clapper-dudgeon[34] for a pinte of ale, who as soone as he was spied, they left off their roguish poetry, and fell to mocke the poore maunder[35] thus :

The Clapper dugeon lies in the skipper,[36]
He dares not come out for shame,
But when he binges[37] *out he dus budg*[38] *to the Gigger,*[39]
Tipp[40] *in my skew*[41] *good dame.*

---

[1] Good wench. [2] Go on the highway. [3] Sheet. [4] Cloak.
[5] Shirt. [6] Purse. [7] Money. [8] Rings. [9] Good man.
[10] Wife. [11] Gone to her long home. [12] Travel. [13] Beg.
[13a] Take the blow. [14] Seized the money. [15] Stowed away the clothes.
[16] Go we to the alehouse. [17] Called. [18] Pick pockets.
[19] Cut purses. [20] Constable.
[21] Newgate, so-called from the famous Lord Mayor, who left a bequest for rebuilding the gaol. This building existed from 1422 to 1666.
[22] Cease. [23] Words. [24] Hide. [25] Speak.
[26] Run away. [27] Hedge. [28] Buttock. [29] Hanging.
[30] Pick. [31] Purse. [32] Bite or eat. [33] Mouth.
[34] Beggar with a patched cloak. [35] Beggar. [36] Barn.
[37] Gets. [38] Runs. [39] Door. [40] Pour. [41] Cup.

A TINKER AND A CANTING ROGUE.

1616.

From Characters or Witty Descriptions of the Properties of sundry Persons, by Sir Thomas Overbury, Knt.

Overbury claims the distinction of being the earliest writer of characters which this country can boast. Few works have been more popular than the characters of Overbury and Bishop Earle.

A TINKER.

The companion of his travels is some foule sunne-burnt Queane, that since the terrible statute [1] recanted gypsisme, and is termed pedleresse. So marches he all over England with his bag and baggage. . . . . Hee observes truly the statutes, and therefore he can rather steale then begge, in whiche hee is unremoveably constant in spight of whips or imprisonment : and so a strong enemy to idlenesse, that in mending one hole, he had rather make three than want worke, and when hee hath done, hee throwes the wallet of his faults behind him. . . . . To conclude, if he scape Tyburn and Banbury,[2] he dies a begger.

A CANTING ROGUE.

Tis not unlikely but he was begot by some intelligencer under a hedge ; for his mind is wholly given to travell. Hee is not troubled with making of joyntures : he can divorce himselfe without the fee of a proctor, nor feares hee the cruelty of over-seers of his will. Hee leaves his children all the world to cant in, and all the people to their fathers. His language is a constant tongue ; the Northerne speech differs from the South, Welsh from the Cornish : but canting is generall, nor ever could be altered by conquest of the *Saxon, Dane*, or *Norman*. He will not beg out of his limit though hee starve ; nor breake his oath if hee sweare by his *Salomon*,[3] though you hang him : and hee payes his custome as truly to his grand rogue, as tribute is paid to the great Turke. The March sunne breeds agues in others, but hee adores it like the *Indians;* for then begins his progresse after a hard winter. Ostlers [4] cannot indure him, for hee is of the infantry, and serves best on foot. He offends not the statute against the excesse of apparel,[5] for hee will go naked, and counts it a voluntary pennance. Forty of them lye in a barne together, yet are never sued upon the statute of inmates.[6] If hee were learned, no man could make a better description of *England ;* for hee hath travel'd it over and over. Lastly, he brags, that his great houses are repaired to his hands, when churches goe to ruine : and those are prisons.

THE GYPSIES METAMORPHOSED.

1621.

From "a Masque of the Gypsies Metamorphos'd," written by Ben Jonson. First represented at Burleigh on the Hill before King James I., August, 1621. London : Printed for Richard Meighen, 1640.

---

[1] 5 Eliz. c. 20.
[2] From Bishop Corbet's *Iter Boreale*, the town of Banbury appears to have been inhabited chiefly by Puritans. It was also celebrated for its tinkers.
[3] The rogues' inviolable oath. [4] Innkeepers.
[5] Statutes against the excess of apparel were frequently passed. The earliest is the 3 Edw. IV. c. 5.
[6] By 13 Edw. I. St. 2, c. 4, the host was to answer for inmates, but the reference is probably to the *Proclamation* against overcrowding in 1607, see p. 139.

604 VAGRANTS AND VAGRANCY,

Enter a Gypsie, *leading a Horse laden with five little Children bound in a trace of scarffes upon him. A second, leading another Horse laden with stoll'ne Poultrey: The first leading* Gypsie *speaks being the*

JACKMAN.

Roome for the five Princes of *Ægipt*, mounted all upon the Horse like thy foure Sonnes of *Aymon*, to make the miracle the more, by a head, if it mae be : gaze upon them, as on the off-spring of *Ptolomie*, begotten upon several *Cleopatraes*, in their severall Countries ; especially on this brave Sparke strooke out of *Flint-shire*, upon Justice *Jugges* Daughter then Sheriffe of the County ; who running away with a kinsman of our Captaines, and her Father pursuing her to the Marshes, Hee great with Justice, She great with Juggling, they were both for the time turn'd stone upon the sight each of other, in *Chester:*

Till at last (see the Wonder) a Jugge of the Towne Ale, reconciling them ; the memoriall of both their gravities, his in beard and hers in bellie, hath remain'd ever since preserv'd in picture upon the most Stone Jugs of the Kingdome.

The famous impe yet grew a wretchcocke,[1] and though for seven yeares together, he were very carefully carried at his Mother's backe, rock'd in a cradle of Welch-Cheese, like a maggot, and there fed with broken Beere, and blowne Wine o' the best, dayly, yet lookes he, as if he never saw his *Guinquennium*.[2] 'Tis true, he can thread needles o' horse-backe, or draw a yard of inckle[3] through his nose : but what's that to a growne *Gipsie*, one of the bloud, and of his time, if he had thriv'd : Therefore, till with his painefull Progenitors, he be able to beate it on the hard hoofe, or the bene *Bawse*,[4] or the *Starling* Ken, to nip a *Jan*, and *Cly*, the Jack ; 'tis thought fit he march in the Infants' Equipage.

With the Convoy, Cheats, and peckage,[5]
Out of clutch of Harman Beckage,[6]
To the libkins[7] at the Crackmans[8]
Or some skipper of the Black-mans.

THE BEGGARS' BUSH.
1622.

From the "Beggars Bush," written by John Fletcher, gentleman. First represented in 1622. Printed for *Humphrey Robinson* and *Anne Moseley*, 1661.

Actus Secundus. Scæna Prima.

Enter Higgen, Ferret, Prig, Clause, Jaculine, Snap, Gynkes, and other Beggars.

Hig. Come Princes of the ragged regiment,
You o' the blood *Prig* my most upright Lord,
And these (what name or title e're they bear)
Jarkman, or Patrico, Cranke, or Claperdudgeon,
Frater or Abram-man ; I speak to all

---

[1] The smallest of a brood of domestic fowls.
[2] *Quinquennium*, a period of five years.
[3] Inferior tape.
[4] For an explanation of the other Cant terms in this and the following selections, see the extracts from Harman, pp. 468, 596.
[5] Meat.   [6] Beadle.   [7] House or place to sleep.   [8] Hedges.

That stand in fair Election for the title
Of King of Beggars, with the command adjóyning ;
Higgen, your Orator in this Inter-regnum,
That whilome was your Dommerer ; doth beseech you
All to stand fair, and put your selves in rank,
That the first comer may at his first view
Make a free choice, to say up the question.
    Fer. Pr. 'Tis done Lord *Higgen.*
    Hig. Thanks to Prince *Prig,* Prince *Ferret.*
    Fer. Well, pray my Masters all *Ferret* be chosen ;
Y'are like to have a merciful milde Prince of me.
    Prig. A very tyrant, I, an arrant tyrant,
If e're I come to reign ; therefore look to't,
Except you do provide me hum [1] enough,
And Lour to bouze with : I must have my Capons
And Turkeyes brought me in, with my green [2] Geese,
And ducklings i' th' season ; fine fat chickens ;
Or if you chance where an eye [3] of tame Phesants
Or Partridges are kept, see they be mine,
Or straight I seize on all your priviledge,
Places, revenues, offices, as forfeit ;
Call in your crutches, wooden legs, false bellies,
Forc'd eyes and teeth, with your dead arms, not leave you
A durty clout to beg with o' your heads,
Or an old rag with Butter, Frankinsence,
Brimstone and Rozen, birdlime, blood, and cream,
To make you an old sore ; not so much sope
As you may fome with i' th' falling-sickness ;
The very bag you bear, and the brown dish
Shall be escheated. All your daintiest dells too
I will deflow'r, and take your dearest Doxyes
From your warm sides ; and then some one cold night
I'le watch you what old barn you go to roost in,
And there I'le smother you all i' th' musty hay.

    *   *   *   *   *

    Hig. Thou that art chosen, venerable *Clause,*
Our King and Sovereign, Monarch o' th' Maunders.
Thus we throw up our Nab-cheats first for joy,
And then our filches, last we clap our fambles,
Three subject signs, we do it without envy :
For who is he here did not wish thee chosen,
Now thou art chosen ? ask 'em : all will say so,
May swear 't ; 'tis for the King ; but let that pass.
When last in conference at the bouzing ken
This other day, we sate about our dead Prince
Of famous memory, (rest go with his rags :)
And that I saw thee at the tables end
Rise mov'd, and gravely leaning on one Crutch —
Lift the other like a Scepter at my head,
I then presag'd thou shortly wouldst be King,
And now thou art so : but what need presage
To us, that might have read it in thy beard,

---

    [1] Double ale.   [2] Fresh.
            [3] A brood. O.E. *ei,* an egg.

As well as he that chose thee ? by that beard
Thou wert found out, and mark'd for Soveraignty.
  * * * * *
If now the beard be such, what is the Prince
That owes the beard ? a father ; no, a grandfather ;
Nay, the great-grandfather of you his people.
He will not force away your hens, your bacon,
When you have ventur'd hard for 't, nor take from you
The fattest of your puddings ; under him
Each man shall eat his own stoln eggs and butter,
In his own shade, or sun-shine, and enjoy
His own dear Dell, Doxy, or Mort, at night,
In his own straw, with his own shirt, or sheet,
That he hath filtch'd that day, I, and possess
What he can purchase, back or belly cheats
To his own prop ; he will have no purveyors
For Pigs and Poultry.
  * * * * *

Omn. O gracious Prince, 'save, 'save the good King *Clause*.
Hig. A Song to crown him.
Fer. Set a Centinel out first.
Sn. The word ?
Hig. A Cove comes, and fumbumbis to it. *Strike.*

The Song.

Cast our caps and cares away, this is beggars Holy-day ; &c.

   Actus Tertius. Scæna Tertia.
  * * * * *

Ger. Now swear him.
 Hig. I crown thy nab with a gag of ben-bouse,
And stall thee by the salmon into the clowes,[1]
To maund on the pad, and strike all the cheats
To mill from the Ruffmans, Commission and slates,
Twang dells i' th stiromel, and let the Quire Cuffin,
And Hermon Beck strine, and trine to the Ruffin.
 Ger. Now interpret this unto him.
 Hig. I poure on thy pate a pot of good ale,
And by the Rogues oath, a Rogue thee install,
To beg on the way, to rob all thou meets,
To steal from the hedge, both the shirt and the sheets :
And lie with thy wench in the straw till she twang,
Let the Constable, Justice, and Divell go hang.
  * * * * *

   Actus Quintus. Scæna Prima.

 Hig. But what's the action we are for now ? ha ?
Robbing a Ripper[2] of his fish ?
  Prig. Or taking
A poultrer prisoner, without ransome, Bullyes ?

---

[1] Rogues, O. Dutch, *kloet*, a clown or looby.
[2] A person who carried fish from the coast to inland towns.

Hig. Or cutting off a convoy of butter ?
Fer. Or surprising a Boors ken, for granting cheats ?
Prig. Or cackling cheats ?
Hig. Or mergery-praters, Rogers,
And Tibs o'th Buttery ?
Prig. O' I could drive a Regiment
Of geese afore me, such a night as this,
Ten leagues with my hatt, and staffe, and not a hiss
Heard, or a wing of my troops disordered.
Hig. Tell us,
If it be milling of a lag of duds,
The fetching of a back of clothes, or so,
We are horribly out of linnen.

*　　　*　　　*　　　*　　　*

Scæna Secunda.

*　　　*　　　*　　　*　　　*

Hig. Then bear up bravely with your Brute my lads
Higgen hath prig'd the prancers in his dayes,
And sold good peny-worths ; we will have a course.
The spirit of *Bottom* is grown bottomlesse.
Prig. I'le mand no more, nor cant.

The Song of the Begger.
1629.

From " A description of Love. With certaine *Epigrams Elegies* and *Sonnets.* And also Mast. Iohnsons Answere to Master Withers. With the Crie of *Ludgate*, and the Song of the *Begger.* The sixth Edition. London Printed by M.F. for *Francis Coules* at the vpper end of the Old-Baily neere Newgate. 1629.

I am a Rogue and a stout one,
A most couragious drinker,
I doe excell, 'tis knowne full well,
The Ratter, Tom, and Tinker.

> Still doe I cry, good your Worship, good Sir,
> Bestow one Small Denire[1] Sir ;
> And brauely at the bousing Ken
> Ile bouse it all in Beere Sir.

If a Bung[2] be got by the hie Law,[3]
Then straight I doe attend them,
For if Hue and Crie doe follow, I
A wrong way soone doe send them.
Still I doe cry, &c.

Ten miles vnto a Market,
I runne to meet a Miser,
Then in a throng, I nip his Bung,[4]
And the partie ne'er the wiser.
Still doe I cry, &c.

---

[1] A penny ; a deneere ; a small copper coyne valued at the tenth part of an English penny (*Cotgrave*). *Falstaff* says, " I'll not pay a *denier*" (*I. K. Hen. IV.*, III., 3) ; and *Sly* in the *Taming of the Shrew,* answers, " No, not a *denier.*"
[2] A purse.   [3] High lawyers or highwaymen, see p. 582.
[4] Pick his pocket.

My daintie Dals, my Doxis,
  Whene'er they see me lacking,
Without delay, poore wretches they
  Will Set their Duds a packing.
    Still doe I cry, &c.

I pay for what I call for,
  And so perforce it must be,
For as yet I can, not know the man,
  Nor Oastis that will trust me.
    Still I doe cry, &c.

If any giue me lodging,
  A courteous Knaue they find me,
For in their bed, aliue or dead
  I leaue some Lice behind me,
    Still doe I cry, &c.

If a Gentrie Coe be comming,
  Then straight it is our fashion,
My Legge I tie, close to my thigh,
  To moue him to compassion.
    Still doe I cry, &c.

My doublet sleeue hangs emptie,
  And for to begge the bolder,
For meate and drinke, mine arme I shrinke
  Vp close vnto my shoulder.
    Still doe I cry, &c.

If a Coach I heare be rumbling,
  To my Crutches then I hie me.
For being lame, it is a shame,
  Such Gallants should denie me.
    Still doe I cry, &c.

With a seeming bursten belly,
  I looke like one halfe dead Sir,
Or else I beg with a woodden legge,
  And a Night-cap on me head Sir.
    Still doe I cry, &c.

In Winter time starke naked
  I come into some Citie,
Then euery man that spare them can,
  Will giue me clothes for pittie.
    Still doe I cry, &c.

If from out the Low-countrie,
  I heare a Captaines name Sir,
Then Strait I swere I haue bin there ;
  And so in fight came lame Sir.
    Still doe I cry, &c.

My Dogge in a string doth lead me,
  When in the Towne I goe Sir,
For to the blind, all men are kind,
  And will their Almes bestow Sir,
    Still doe I cry, &c.

With Switches sometimes stand I,
In the bottome of a Hill Sir,
There those men which doe want a Switch,
Some monie giue me still Sir.
Still doe I cry, &c.

Come buy, come buy a Horne-booke,
Who buyes my Pins or Needles ?
In Cities I these things doe crie,
Oft times to scape the Beadles.
Still doe I cry, &c.

In *Pauls* Church by a Pillar ;
Sometimes you see me stand Sir,
With a Writ that showes, what care and woes
I past by Sea and Land Sir.
Still doe I cry, &c.

Now blame me not for boasting,
And bragging thus alone Sir,
For my selfe I will be praysing still,
For Neighbours haue I none Sir.

Which makes me cry Good your Worship, good Sir,
Bestow one small Denire, Sir,
And brauely then at the Bousing Ken,
Ile bouse it all in Beere Sir.

THE CUNNING NORTHERN BEGGAR.

CIRCA 1635.

From the Roxburghe Collection of Ballads.

The Roxburghe Collection of Ballads was formed by Robert Harley, subsequently Earl of Oxford, born in 1661. John Bagford the antiquary was one of the buyers he employed. When his printed books were dispersed these ballads were bought by James West, president of the Royal Society. At his death in 1773 they were bought by Major Thomas Pearson, who added to them. At the death of Major Pearson in 1788 they were sold to John, Duke of Roxburghe, who added a few ballads. In 1813 they were sold to Mr. B. H. Bright, who added to them, and in 1843 they were acquired by the British Museum.

The cunning Northerne Begger,
Who all the By-standers doth earnestly pray,
To bestow a penny upon him to-day.
To the Tune of Tom of Bedlam.

I am a lusty begger
And live by others giving,
  I scorne to worke
  But by the highway lurke,
And beg to get my living :
I'le 'ith wind and weather,
And weare all ragged Garments,
  Yet though I'm bare,
  I'm free from care ;

A fig for high preferments.
For still will I cry good your worship good sir,
Bestow one poore denier sir;
    Which when I've got
    At the Pipe and Pot,
I soone will it casheere sir.

I have my shifts about me,
Like Proteus often changing
    My shape when I will,
    I alter still,
About the Country ranging;
As soone as I a Coatch see,
Or Gallants by come riging,
    I take my Crutch
    And rouse from my Couch,
Whereas I lay abiding.
And still doe I cry, &c.

Now like a wandring Souldier
(That has 'ith Warres bin maymed,
    With the shot of a Gunne)
    To Gallants I runne
And begg Sir helpe the lamed,
I am a poore old Souldier,
And better times once viewed,
    Though bare now I goe,
    Yet many a foe,
By me hath bin subdued.
And therefore I cry, &c.

Although I nere was further
Then Kentish Street in Southwarke,
    Nor ere did see
    A Battery
Made against any Bulwarke,
But with my Trulls and Doxes,
Lay in some corner lurking,
    And nere went abroad
    But to beg on the road,
To keepe my selfe from working.
And alwaies to cry, &c.

Anon I'm like a saylor,
And weare old Canvas cloathing,
    And then I say
    The Dunkerks[1] away,
Tooke all and left me nothing:
Sixe ships set all upon us,
'Gainst which wee bravely ventur'd,
    And long withstood,
    Yet could doe no good,
Our ship at length they enter'd.

---

[1] The privateers of Dunkirk were notorious for preying on English merchant ships at this period.

THE CUNNING NORTHERN BEGGAR (CIRCA 1635)

And therefore I cry good your worship good sir
Bestow one poore denier sir :
   Which when I've got,
   At the Pipe and Pot, &c.

     The second part. To the same tune.

Sometime I like a Criple
Upon the ground lye crawling,
   For money I begge,
   As wanting a legge
To beare my corps from falling,
Then seeme I weake of body,
And long t' have been diseased,
   And make complaint,
   As ready to faint,
And of my griefes increased,
And faintly I cry good your worship good sir,
Bestow one poore denier sir,
   Which when I've got,
   At the Pipe and Pot,
I soone will it casheere sir.

My flesh I so can temper,
That it shall seeme to feister,
   And looke all or'e
   Like a raw sore,
Whereon I sticke a plaister.
With blood I daub my face then,
To faigne the falling sicknesse,
   That in every place
   They pitty my case,
As if it came through weakenesse,
And then I doe cry, &c.

Then as if my sight I wanted,
A Boy doth walke beside me,
   Or else I doe
   Grope as I goe
Or have a Dog to guide me :
And when I'm thus accounted,
To th' highway side I hye me
   And there I stand
   With cords in my hand,
And beg of all comes nye me.
And earnestly cry good your worship good sir
Bestow one poore denier, &c.

Next to some country fellow,
I presently am turned,
   And cry alacke
   With a child at my back,
My house and goods were burned :
Then me my Doxes followes,
Who for my wifes believed,

And along wee two
Together goe,
With such mischances grieved.
And still we doe cry good your worship, &c.

What though I cannot labour,
Shall I therefore pine with hunger
  No, rather then I
  Will starve where I lye
I'le beg of the money monger.
No other care shall trouble
My minde, or griefe disease me,
  Though sometimes the slash
  I get, or the lash,
Twill but a while displease me,
And still I will cry good your worship good sir
Bestow one, &c.

No tricks at all shall scape me
But I will by my maunding
  Get some reliefe
  To ease my griefe,
When by the highway standing:
Tis better be a Begger,
And aske of kinde goode fellowes
  And honestly have
  What we doe crave
Then steale and goe to 'th' Gallowes.
Therefore 'Ile cry good your worship good sir,
Bestow one poore denier sir.
  Which when I've got
  At the Pipe and Pot,
I soone will it casheere sir.

      FINIS.

Printed at London for *F. Coules.*

A JOVIAL CREW OR THE MERRY BEGGARS.

1641.

From " A Joviall Crew : or, the Merry Beggars. Presented in a Comedie, at The Cock-pit[1] in Drury-Lane, in the yeer 1641. Written by Richard Brome. London: printed by J. Y. for E. D. and N. E. and are to be sold at the Gun in *Ivy Lane* 1652."

Richard Brome was of mean extraction, and sometime servant to Ben Jonson. At what time he began to write we have no account. "In imitation of his master," says Langbaine, "he studied men and humour more than books ; and his genius affecting comedy, his province was more observation than study ; his plots were his own, and he forg'd all his various characters from the mint of his own experience and judgment."

---

[1] This theatre stood on the site of Pitt Place, properly Cock-pit Place, running out of Drury Lane into Great Wild Street.

AND BEGGARS AND BEGGING. 613

Actus Primus.
Springlove (Steward to Master *Oldrents*), on the stage.

Enter Randal (*a groom*) *and three or fovr servants with a great Kettle, and black Jacks*,[1] *and a Bakers Basket, all empty,* exeunt *with all,* manet *Randal.*
Springlove. Now fellows, what news from whence you came?
Randal. The old wonted news, Sir, from your Guest-house, the old Barn. We have unloaden the Bread-basket, the Beef-Kettle, and the Beer-*Bumbards*[1] there, amongst your Guests the Beggars. And they have all prayed for you and our Master, as their manner is, from the teeth outward, marry from the teeth inwards 'tis enough to swallow your Alms; from whence I think their Prayers seldom come. . . . . It might be better though (if old *Randal*, whom you allow to talk, might counsel) to help to breed up poor mens children, or decayed labourers, past their work, or travel; or towards the setting up of poor young married couples; then to bestow an hundred pound a year (at least you do that, if not all you get) besides our Masters bounty, to maintain in begging such wanderers as these, that never are out of their way; that cannot give account from whence they came, or whither they would; nor of any beginning they ever had, or any end they seek, but still to strowle and beg till their bellies be full, and then sleep till they be hungry.
Spr. Thou art ever repining at those poore people! they take nothing from thee but thy pains: and that I pay thee for too. Why should'st thou grudge?
Ran. Am I not bitten to it every day, by the six-footed blood-hounds that they leave in their Litter, when I throw out the old, to lay fresh straw for the new comers at night. That's one part of my office. And you are sure that though your hospitality be but for a night and a morning for one Rabble, to have a new supply every evening. They take nothing from me indeed, they give too much. . . . .

Scene with the Beggars.

Spr. Thou art a brave fellow, and speak'st like a Commander. Hast thou born arms?
4 *Beggar.* Sir, he has born the name of a *Netherland* Souldier, till he ran away from his Colours, and was taken lame with lying in the Fields by a *Sciatica*: I mean, Sir, the *strapado*.[2] After which, by a second retreat, indeed running away, he scrambled into his Country, and so scap'd the Gallows; and then snap'd up his living in the City by his wit in cheating, pimping, and such like Arts, till the Cart and the Pillory shewed him too publiquely to the world. And so, begging being the last refuge, he enter'd into our society.

Actus Secundus.
Randal *opens the Scene. The Beggars discovered at their Feast. After they have scrambled a while at their Victuals: This Song.*

Here, safe in our Skipper,[3] let's cly [4] off our Peck [5]
And bowse [6] in defiance o' th' Harman-Beck.[7]
Here's Pannum [8] and Lap,[9] and good Poplars [10] of Yarrum,[11]
To fill up the Crib,[12] and to comfort the Quarron.[13]
Now bowse a round health to the Go-well and Com-well
Of Cisley Bumtrincket that lies in the Strummell.[14]

---

[1] A large drinking-can made of leather.
[2] An old form of military punishment, the victim being drawn up to a beam, and then suddenly let fall half way with a jerk, which frequently dislocated his limbs. Ital. *Strappáta*, a violent snatching or pulling away.
[3] Barn. [4] Have. [5] Meat. [6] Drink. [7] Constable. [8] Bread. [9] Butter.
[10] Porridge. [11] Milk. [12] Stomach. [13] Body. [14] Straw.

> *Here's* Ruffpeck[1] *and* Casson,[2] *and all of the best,*
> *And Scraps of the Dainties of* Gentry Cofe's[3] *Feast.*
> *Here's* Grunter[4] *and* Bleater,[5] *with* Tib of the Buttry,[6]
> *And* Margery Prater,[7] *all drest without sluttry.*
> *For all this* bene Cribbing[8] *and* Peck *let us then,*
> Bowse *a health to the* Gentry Cofe *of the* Ken.[9]
> *Now* bouse *a round health to the Go-well and Com-well*
> *Of* Cisley Bumtrincket *that lies in the* Strummel. . . .

Enter Patrico. *Many of the Beggars look out.*

Patrico. Toure cut[10] *with your* Glasiers.[11] I sweare by the *Ruffin*,[12]
That we are assaulted by a *quire Cuffin*.[13]
 Randal. Hold! what d'e mean, my Friends? This is our Master,
The Master of your Feast and feasting House.
 Pat. Is this the *Gentry Cofe?*
 All the Beggars. Lord bless his Worship. His good Worship. Bless his Worship. . . . [*Exit Beggars* manet *Patr.*
 Pat. Sir, I can lay my Function by,
And talk as wilde and wantonly
As *Tom* or *Tib*, or *Jack*, or *Jill*,
When they at *Bowsing Ken*[14] do swill.
Will you therefore daign to hear
My *Autum Mort*,[15] with throat as clear,
As was *Dame Anisses* of the Name;
How sweet in Song her Notes she'll frame,
That when she chides, as lowd is yawning,
As *Chanticlere* wak'd by the dawning.
 Hearty. Yes, pray let's hear her. What is she your wife?
 Pat. Yes Sir, we of our Ministery,
As well as those oth' Presbyterie,
Take wives and defie Dignitie. [*Exit.*
 Hearty. A learned Cleark in veritie.
Enter Patrico *with his old wife, with a wooden Bowle of Drink. She is drunk.*
 Pat. By Salmon,[16] I think my Mort is in drink.
I finde by her stink; and the pretty pretty pink
Of her Neyes, that half wink,
That the tipling Feast, with the *Doxie*[17] in the Neast,
Hath turn'd her brain, to a merry merry vain.
 Mort. Go Fiddle *Patrico*, and let me sing. First set me down here on both my *Prats*.[18] Gently, gently, for cracking of my wind, now I must use it. Hem, hem.

She sings.
> *This is* Bien Bowse,[19] *this is* Bien Bowse
> *Too little is my* Skew[20]
> *I* bowse *no* Lage,[21] *but a whole* Gage[22]
> *Of this I'll* bowse *to you.*
>
> *This* Bowse *is better then* Rom-bowse,[23]
> *It sets the* Gan[24] *a gigling,*

---

[1] Bacon.   [2] Cheese.   [3] Gentleman.   [4] Pork.   [5] Mutton.   [6] Goose.
[7] Fowl.   [8] Good spoil.   [9] House.   [10] Look about.   [11] Eyes.   [12] Devil.
[13] Magistrate.   [14] Ale-house.   [15] Wife.   [16] Sacred oath.   [17] Girl.
[18] Buttocks.   [19] Good ale.   [20] Cup.   [21] Water.   [22] Quart pot.   [23] Wine.
[24] Mouth.

> *The* Autum-Mort *finds better sport*
> *In* bowsing *then in* nigling.
> *This* is Bien-bowse, *&c.*
> [*She tosses off her Bowle, falls back, and is carried out.*

* * * * *

Enter Dauncers.

Pat. See, in their rags, then, dauncing for your sports
Our *Clapper Dugeons* [1] and their *walking Morts.*[2]

Daunce.

Pat. You have done well. Now let each *Tripper*
Make a retreat into the *Skipper;* [3]
And *couch a Hogs-head,*[4] till the *dark man's* [5] past;
Then all with Bag and Baggage *bing awast.*[6] [*Exeunt Beggars.*

Actus Quintus.
Master Sentwell.

Sentwell. But Sir, we have taken with her such *Beggars,* such *Rogues,* such *Vagabonds,* and such *Hedge-birds* (since you call 'em so) as you never knew, or heard of, though now the Countries swarm with 'em under every Hedge, as if an innumerable army of 'em were lately disbanded without Pay. *Hedge-birds* said you? *Hedge Lady-birds, Hedge Cuvaliers, Hedge Souldier, Hedge Lawyer Hedge Fidlers, Hedge Poet, Hedge Players,* and a *Hedge Priest* among 'em. Such we have taken for the *Principals.* But to see how the Multitude scap'd us, was more sport than pitty. How, upon a Watch-word given, they in the instant vanish'd by more severall waies than there were legs among 'em; how the Creeples leap'd over Pales and Hedges; how the Blinde found their way thorow Lakes and Ditches; how a *Doxie* flew with two Children at her back, and two more, perhaps, in her belly—
Justice Clack. A *Hedge Priest* have you taken, say you?
Sen. Yes, Sir, an old *Patrico,* an ancient Prophet, to tell Fortunes, and cozen our poor Country People of their single Money. . . .
Cla. But are there *Players* among the apprehended?
Sen. Yes, Sir. And they were contriving to act a Play among themselves, just as we surpriz'd 'em, and spoil'd their Sport.
Cla. Players! I'll pay them above all the rest.
Sen. You shall do well in that; to put 'hem in stock to set up again.
Cla. Yes, I'll put 'em in Stocks, and set 'em up to the Whipping post. They can act *Justices,* can they? I'll act a *Justice* among 'em; that is to say, I will do justice upon them; that is to say—
Sen. Pray Sir, be not severe, they act *Kings* and *Emperours,* as well as *Justices.* And *Justice* is blinde they say: you may therefore be pleas'd to wink a little. I finde that you have merry old Gentlemen in your House, that are come far to visit you. I'll undertake that these *Players,* with the help of their *Poet;* in a device which they have already studied, and a pack of cloaths which I shall supply 'em with, shall give your Guests much content, and move compassion in you towards the poor *Strowles.*
Cla. But you know my way of *Justice* (and that's a sure way) is to punish 'em first, and be compassionate afterwards, as I finde 'em upon their Examination.

---

[1] Beggars with patched cloaks.
[2] Women who pass for widows.
[3] Barn.
[4] Lie down and sleep.
[5] Night.
[6] Go hence.

The Beggars' Chorus in the "Jovial Crew."

(From the Bagford Collection of Ballads.)

To an excellent New Tune.

" The song belongs to Act IV. sc. 2, and is given at that place in the first edition of Dodsley's *Old Plays* 1744, vol. vi. p. 372. But the words do not appear in the earliest edition of 'A Jovial Crew,' printed in 1652. It is scarcely to be doubted that the song was written either by Richard himself, or by his affectionate namesake Alexander Brome. Although not printed in the 1652 editio princeps of 'A Jovial Crew,' the song was certainly known or popular by or before 1660."

There was a jovial Beggar,
  he had a wooden Leg ;
Lame from his Cradle,
  and forced for to Beg :
And a Begging we will go, we'll go, we'll go,
  And a Begging we will go.

A Bag for my Oat-meal—
  another for my Salt,
A little pair of Crutches,
  to see how I can Halt :
And a Begging, &c.

A Bag for my Bread,
  another for my Cheese,
A little Dog to follow me,
  to gather what I leese : [1]
And a Begging, &c.

A Bag for my Wheat,
  another for my Rye,
A little Bottle by my side,
  to drink when I'm a dry :
And a Begging we will go, we'll go, we'll go,
  And a Begging we will go.

To *Pimlico* [2] we'll go,
  where merry we shall be,
With ev'ry Man, a Can in's Hand,
  and a Wench upon his knee :
And a Begging, &c.

Seven years I served,
  my old Master Wild ;
Seven years I begged
  Whilst I was but a Child :
And a Begging, &c.

---

[1] Lose.

[2] A place of entertainment at Hoxton originally kept by one *Ben Pimlico*. It stood near the junction of the New North Road and Pitfield Street, abutting on Pimlico Walk. It is alluded to by *Ben Jonson* in the *Alchemist*, by *Massinger* in the *City Madam*, and by other writers of the period.

I had the pretty knack
　for to wheedle and to cry ;
By young and by old,
　Much pitied e'er was I.
And a Begging, &c.

Fatherless and Motherless
　still was my Complaint,
And none that ever saw me,
　but took me for a saint :
And a Begging, &c.

I begg'd for my Master,
　and got him store of Pelf ;
But *Jove* now be praised,
　I now beg for my self ;
And a Begging, &c.

Within a hollow Tree
　I live, and pay no Rent ;
Providence provides for me,
　and I am well content,
And a Begging, &c.

Of all Occupations,
　a Beggar lives the best,
For when he is a weary,
　he'll lie him down and rest :
And a Begging, &c.

I fear no Plots against me,
　but live in open Cell ;
Why who wou'd be a King,
　when a Beggar lives so well ?
*And a Begging we will go, we'll go, we'll go,
　And a Begging we will go.*

THE TINKER AND THE BEGGAR.

1661.

From Wit and Drollery, Joviall Poems :

Corrected and much amended, with additions,

By Sir J(ohn) M(ennis) Ja(mes) S(mith) Sir W(illiam) D(avenant) J(ohn) D(onne) and the most refined Wits of the Age.　Edited by E. M.

London Printed for *Nath. Brook*, at the Angel in Cornhil, 1661.

The Preface states that "these Poems reprinted, with additions, are collected from the best Wits, of what above 20 years since, were begun to be preserved, for mirth and friends ; the fear of having some of them imperfectly set forth, hath, though unwillingly made them common."

A Song.

The Tinker.

For he sits all day quaffing and turning ouer the boul,
And goes about from house, to house, to stop the good wifes hole ;

Ting quoth the metal, found quoth the kettle,
He calls to his wife for a hammer,
He goes about from town to town
Most like a Rogue in manner.

Beggar.

And of all occupations Begging is the best,
Whensoever he is weary he may lay him down to rest ;
For howsoe're the world goes they never take any care ;
And whatsoever they beg or get they spend it in good fare.

Up goes the staff, down goes the wallet,
To the alehouse they go with speed ;
They spend many a pot, they care not for the shot,
This is the best occupation indeed.

This hath his doxy, another is almost foxy,
They have still a peny to their need,
They drink many a pot, they care not for the shot :
This is the best trade indeed.

With a hey down derry, they'l be full merry,
Though the marshal stand at the dore ;
When their money is done, they'l have more before noon,
Or drink upon the score.

The English Rogue.

1665.

From the *English Rogue* described in the Life of Meriton Latroon, *a Witty Extravagant*. Being a compleat History of the most Eminent Cheats of both sexes, by Richard Head, 1665. (Corrected by the edition of 1672.)

In the Epistle to the Reader the author says—

"What here I present ye with, is an original in your own mother tongue ; and yet I may not improperly call it a Translation, drawn from the Black Copy of mens wicked actions ; such who spared the Devil the pains of courting them, by listing themselves Volunteers to serve under his Hellish Banners ; with some whereof I have heretofore been unhappily acquainted, and am not ashamed to confess that I have been somewhat soiled by their vitious practices, but now I hope cleansed in a great measure from those impurities."

In a Preface to the Reader subsequently written by Francis Kirkham, the following occurs as to the identity of the author with Meriton Latroon.

"When this piece was first published it was ushered into the World with the usual ceremony of a Preface, and that a large one, whereby the Authour intended and endeavoured to possess the Reader with a belief, that what was written was the Life of a *Witty Extravagant*, the Authours Friend and Acquaintance. This was the intent of the Writer, but the Readers could not be drawn to this belief but in general concurred in this opinion, that it was the Life of the Authour, and notwithstanding all that hath been said to the contrary many still continue in this opinion." . . . .

CHAPTER V.

Wherein he Relates what manner of People they were in whose Society he entered himself ; division of their Tribes, Manners, Customs, and Language.

As soon as I had resolv'd to travel the Country with them, they fitted me for their company, by stripping me, and selling my proper garments, and cloathing me in rags, which they pinn'd about me, giving a stitch here and there, according as necessity required. We used not when we entered our *Libkin*, or Lodging, to pull off our cloaths; which had I been forced to do, I could never have put them on again, nor any, but such who were accustomed to produce *Order* out of a *Babel of Rags*. Being now *ale mode de Tatterdemallion*, to compleat me for their purpose, with green Walnuts they so discoloured my face, that everyone that saw me, would have sworn I was the true son of an *Egyptian*. Before we marcht on, let me give you an account of our Leaders, and the rancks we were disposed in. Our chief Commander was called by the name of *Ruffeler*, the next to him *Vpright-man*, the rest in order thus :

Hookers, (alias) *Anglers.*	*Prigges.*
Priggers of Prancers.	*Swadlers.*
Pallyards.	*Curtals.*
Fraters.	*Irish toyle.*
Swigmen.	*Dommerars.*
Jarkemen.	*Glymmerer.*
Patri-Coes.	*Bawdy-baskets.*
Kitchin-Coes.	*Autem-Morts.*
Abram men.	*Doxies.*
Whip-Jacks.	*Dells.*
Counterfeit-Cranks.	*Kitchin-Morts.*

We muster'd above threescore old and young, and because we were too great a company to march together, we were divided into three Squadrons. The first Squadron that led the Van, was ordered by our Commander, to stick up small boughs all the way they went,[1] that we might know what course they steer'd. For like Wild Fowl we flie one after another, and though we are scattered like the quarters of a Traitor, yet like water when cut with a Sword, we easily came together again. As the *Switzer* hath his Wench and his Cock with him when he goes to Wars: or like a *Scotch Army*, where every soldier almost hath the *Geud Wife* and the *Bearns* following him: so we had every one his *Doxie* or Wench, who carried at her back a *Lullaby-cheat*,[2] and it may be another in her Arms. When they are weary of carrying them, they take their turns to put them in a pair of Panniers, like green Geese going to Market, or like Fish in Dossers[3] coming from *Rye*. Where note, that each division hath a small Horse or two, or else Asses to ease them of their burdens. Some of us were clad Antickly with Bells and other toyes, meerly to allure the Countrey people unto us, which most commonly produced their desired effects. In some places they would flock unto us, in great quantities, and then was our time to make our Markets. We pretended an acquaintance with the Stars (as having an alliance to the *Egyptian Magi*, the founders of Astrologick Art) and that the Ministers of Fate were our Familiars, and so possessing these poor ignorant people with a belief, that we could tell their Fortunes by inspection into either hands or faces; whil'st we were seriously looking thereon, one of our *diving Comrades* pickt their pockets, or with a short sharp knife, and a horn on the thumb *nipt* their *bungs*.[4] . . . .

Thus[5] we rambled up and down the Country; and where the people demean'd themselves not civil to us by voluntary contributions, their Geese, Hens, Pigs, or any such mandible thing we met with, made us satisfaction for their hide-

---

[1] This is evidently founded on the practice of the gypsies who form a trail with three heaps of grass termed "*trooshels.*"
[2] An infant.   [3] Panniers or baskets.
[4] Picked their pockets.   [5] P. 43.

bound injuries. Our revenge most commonly was very bloody, and so merciless, that whatever fell into our hands, never escaped alive, and in our murders so cruel, that nothing would satisfie us but the very hearts-blood of what we killed. The usual sacrifices of our implacable revenge, were innocent Lambs, Sheep, Calves, &c., all of which we handled more severely than Prisoners are by Serjeants, when they are not paid their unjust Demands; Fees, I should have said, but that by experience I have found, they walk not according to the Rules of ancient Constitutions, but are guided by the dictates of their insatiate wills, which is their Law, which poor Prisoners must indulge, (though they rack their slender credits, or pawn their cloaths) or else they must expect less kindness from them, then a Condemned person about to be tyed up by the Hangman, who will stay till he is ready to be turned off. A Goose coming among us, we have a trick to make him so wise, as never to be a Goose again: but let the wisest use what tricks they can, they shall never make some Serjeants honest men. We seize the prey, and leave the Tragical part to our *Morts* or women to act: the *Stage* on which they perform their parts, is either some large *Heath*, or *Firz-bush-Common*, far from any House. This being done and night approaching, we repair to our Dormitories, or Houses of Rest, which are most usually Out-barns of Farmers and Husbandmen, which we make choice of in some poor stragling Village, who dare not deny us, for fear ere the morning they find their Thatcht Houses too hot to hold them. These Barns serve us instead of Cook Rooms, Supping Parlours, and Bed-Chambers: having Supt, (most commonly in a plentiful manner) we cannot *Couch a Hogshead*, that is to say, Sleep, without good store of *Rum-booz*, that is, Drink; and having sufficiently warm'd our brains with humming Liquor, which our *Lower* (Silver) shall procure; if our deceitful *Maunding* (Begging) cannot, we then sing a Catch or two in our own Language, of which we had good store; which for their bawdry[1] I omit: however, give me leave to instance one Canting Song, and I shall wave the rest.

    Bing out bien Morts, and toure and toure,
    Bing out bien Morts, and toure;
    For all your Duds are bing'd awast
    The bien cove hath the loure. . . . .
    And Jybe well jerckt, teck rome confect,
    For back by glymmar to Maund;
    To mill each Ken, let Cove bing then,
    Through-Ruffmans, jague, or Laund,
    Till Crampings quire tip Cove his hire;
    And Quire Ken do them catch,
    A Canniken, mill quire Cuffen,
    So quire to ben Coves watch.
    Bien Darkmans then, Bouse Mort and Ken,
    The bien coves bings awast,
    On Chates to trine by Rome Coves dine,
    For his long lib at last.
    Bing'd out bien Morts and toure and toure,
    Bing out of the Rome vile bine,
    And toure the Cove that cloyd your duds,
    Upon the Chates to trine. . . . .

    Go forth, good girls, and look about and look about,
    Go forth, good girls, and look about;
    For all your clothes are taken away
    The good man hath the money. . . . .
    And pass well sealed, and licence counterfeited,

---

[1] Indecent language.

For back by fire to beg ;
To rob each house, let man go then
Through wood, ditch, or lawn,
Till shackles evil give man his due ;
And prison do them catch,
The Plague take every magistrate,
So wicked as to good men watch.
Good night then, drink girl and house
The good man goes away
On gallows to hang by bad mens command,
For his long sleep at last.
Go forth, good girls, and look about and look about,
Go forth from London lithely,
And look for the man that stole your clothes.
Upon the gallows to hang.

This song originally appeared in English Villanies seven severall times prest to death by the Printers ; But (still reviving again) are now the eighth time, (as at the first) discovered by *Lanthorne and Candle-light ;* and the helpe of a New Cryer, called *O Per se O:* &c., by Thomas Decker, 1637, Chap. xix.

Like most cant songs it is a mere jingle of favourite cant expressions; part of it has been necessarily omitted on account of its indecency.

Having[1] now obtained more than a convenient boldness I travell'd, and begg'd with very good success. But me thought my life was somewhat uncomfortable without a Companion, (all Creatures coveting society, but more especially Man :) at length, according to my desires, I met with one, whose long practice in this Art (besides the Observations of his Predecessours, deriving his Pedegree in a direct line from *Prince Prigg*), indu'd him with so much skill as to furnish me with the knowledge of anything that belonged to the liberal art of Begging. We straight betook ourselves to the *Boozing Ken*[2]; and having *bubb'd rumly*,[3] we concluded an everlasting friendship. Then did he recount to me the most material things observable in our Profession. First he tun'd my voice to that pitch which might most of all raise compassion ; next what form of prayer I was to use upon such an occasion, what upon such, varying according to the humour of those persons that I begged of, gathered from their habit or gesture ; then he told me when he came to *London*, he would acquaint me what places were most fit for our purpose, and what times. That I ought not to be too importunate to some, always wishing well, and loudly praying for the health and safety of Estate and Limbs of such as denied me Alms ; but more especially pronounce a *God bless you Master, and let Heaven reward what you have here done on earth*, if any thing is bestowed upon me. If any should pity my nakedness, and cloath me in garments without holes in them, I should wear them no longer than in the Donors sight, reserving my rags to re-invest myself, and sell the other, as unfit and scandalous to our Occupation. That we should never beg far from one another, and at nights faithfully share the gains. Moreover he inform'd me the way to make all sorts of seeming sores and lameness. That within the tatter'd rags there be places provided for private conveyance. Some of maturer age, if they have no children, rent them of such as have ; but we had no occasion for this fallacy. That if I saw a door open, I should go in boldly ; if I met any in the way, I should then in a very submissive manner implore their help in the assistance of my wants, never desiring any thing but what was of small value, one half-penny, farthing, or some broken crust, (if at a door) pretending the not eating of a bit in two days. If the passage was clear, whip away what was nearest to hand. That the time of rising in the morning

---

[1] Chap. vi. p. 54.   [2] Ale-house   [3] Liquored well.

be very early, shewing myself in the streets : for then will those that pass by, judge I have no other lodging but what a stall affords, that way procuring relief from pitiful-minded persons, and so continue begging till the evening ; when it beginneth to be duskish, if any then walks singly, accost him in a begging form ; coming up so close, as that you may knock him down with a Truncheon, still carried about for that purpose ; which is done securely, and many times with a good booty.

Being full fraught with these, and many more precepts he delivered, we set forth on our progress. We had not gone far, before we were surprized by the Constable, as two sturdy Vagrants, and as *handsail* to my new Trade, we were both soundly whipt out of Town. To avoid this danger for the time to come, we mist all the towns of any considerable note in our way, and only frequented Villages ; nay at last we were forc'd not onely to avoid them but the High-ways too : for Travellers observing our garb, countenances, and weapons, which was a Battoon,[1] suspecting us, would before they came near us, set spurs to their horses and ride as if the Devil drove them.

My course of life appeared so idle (by my lazy stalking and gaping this way and that, sometimes standing still and seriously and viewing what deserved not a minutes observance) that the Beadle [2] took hold on me, telling me it was great pitty that such a lusty young Man should want imployment, and therefore would help me to some : but understanding from him that it must be in *Bridewel*, my leggs failed me, shewing thereby how unwilling they were to be accessary to the punishment which would be inflicted on my back.

Nearly the whole of these experiences of the life of a vagabond, though written more than two hundred years ago, are equally true in the present day.

THE JOVIALL CREW, OR BEGGARS BUSH.

In which a Mad Maunder doth vapour and swagger
With praising the Trade of a bonney bold beggar
To the tune of, From *hunger and cold*, &c.

Circa 1671.

From the Bagford Collection of Ballads.

John Bagford (1651-1716) was a book-collector, agent for noblemen and gentry who desired to win the reputation of possessing valuable libraries. The collection he made was afterwards increased by James West, president of the Royal Society ; next by Major Thomas Pearson, who bought it in 1773. It was acquired in 1788 by the Duke of Roxburghe, who added to it. It passed into the possession of Mr. B. H. Bright in 1813, who made some additions, and was sold to the British Museum in 1845.

A Beggar, a Beggar
A Beggar I'le bee,
There's none lead a Life so jocond as hée ;
A Beggar I was
And a Beggar I am,
A Beggar I'le be, from a Beggar I came :
If (as it begins) our Trading do fall,
I fear (at the last) we shall be Beggers all.
Our Trades-men miscarry in all their Affayrs
And few men grow wealthy, but Courtiers and Players.

A Craver my Father,
A Maunder[3] my Mother,

---

[1] Cudgel.   [2] Chap. xv. p. 157.   [3] A Town Beggar.

A Filer[1] my sister, a Filcher[2] my Brother,
    A Canter[3] my Unckle
    That car'd not for Pelfe ;
A Lifter[4] my Aunt, a Begger my selfe ;
In white wheaten-straw, when their bellies were full,
Then I was begot, between Tinker & Trul.
And therefore a Begger, a Begger I'le be,
For none hath a spirit so jocond as he.

    When Boyes do come to us,
    And that their intent is
To follow our Calling, we here bind them Prentice,
    Soon as they come too't
    We teach them to doo't
And give them a staff and a wallet to boo't,
We teach them their Lingua, to crave and to Cant,
The devil is in them if then they can want.
If any are here, that Beggers will bee,
We without Indentures will make them free.

    We begg for our bread,
    But sometimes it happens
We feast with Pigg, Pullet, Conny and Capons,
    For Churches Affairs
    We are no men slayers
We have no Religion, yet live by our Prayers,
But if when we begg, Men will not draw their purses,
We charge and give fire, with a vally of curses.
The Devil confound your good worship we cry
And such a bold brazen fac'd Begger am I.

London.   Printed for *W. Thackeray, T. Passenger,* and *W. Whitwood.*

This Song was in the year 1700 sung by Mr. Hemskirk at Sadler's Wells with the second part in the following form :—

    We do things in season and have so much Reason
    We raise no Rebellions nor never talk treason
    We billet our Mates at very low Rates
    While some keep their Quarters as high as ye Gates
    With Shinkin ap Morgan[5] with blew Cap[6] or Teague[7]
    We into no Covenants enter nor League
    And therefore a bonny bold Beggar I'll be
    For none leads a life so merry as we.

    For such pretty Pledges as Shirts from ye Hedges
    We are not in fear to be drawn upon Sledges
    But sometimes the Whip does make us to skip
    And then we from Tything to Tything do trip

---

[1] Pickpocket.   [2] Thief.   [3] Tramping beggar.   [4] Shoplifter.
[5] A Welshman. This was one of the names under which the Welsh were satirised by *Ben Jonson* and others in the reign of James I.
[6] A Scotchman.
[7] An Irishman ; from *Tadhg,* a poet or philosopher, a favourite Irish name.

For when at a Poor bousing ken we do bib it
We stand more in fear of ye Stocks than ye Gibbet
And if from ye Stocks we can keep out our Feet
We fear not ye Counter Kings Bench or ye Fleet.

We throw down no Alter nor never do falter
So much as to Change a Gold Chain for a Halter
Tho' some men do flout us and others do doubt us
We commonly bear fourty Guineas about us
But many good fellows are finer and look fiercer
That owe for their Cloaths' to ye Taylor or Mercer
And therefore a merry bold Beggar I'll be
For w^n it is night in ye Barn tumbles he.

Sometimes I feign in my self to be lame
And when a Coach comes I'll hop to my Game
We seldom miscarry or ever do marry
By the brown Common Prayer or Cloke Directory
For Simon and Susan like Birds of a Feather
They kiss and they laugh and so lie together
Like Pigs in the Pease straw entangled they lie
There they beget such a bold Beggar as I.

The Complete Mendicant.

1699.

From the Compleat Mendicant : or, Unhappy Beggar being the Life of an Unfortunate Gentleman by Daniel Defoe, 1699.

When we came at a convenient distance from the Town, I put him in mind of his promise *i.e.* to instruct me in the Secrets, and Mysteries of a Travelling Mendicant, which he readily comply'd with, and withal told me, to prevent being mis-understood, it would be necessary to give me a general Idea and Notion of the business.

As to the Science and Occupation of begging, (for that in strictness of sense is the properest Name I can call it by) 'tis in the main, a kind of *ars vivendi*, a sort of Trade and Profession as well as any of the rest, so that if it be not always nicely conformable to the Rules of Vertue, Justice and Truth, there's as much if not more to be said for it, than for any other Science or Calling. . . . .

To go on therefore, if you intend to be a Proficient in the Science of begging; your first business will be, to consult the Nature and Temper of the Person you are to make your application to, and by what expedient you may best recommend your self to him : our method for this is, commonly to go to some adjacent Alehouse, where for the expence of Six Pence, we may be equipt with the several Characters and Inclinations of all the Gentry and Clergy within four or five Miles round.

When you have hit of the Person, the next thing is, to consult whether it be most proper to attend him your self, or send him the nature of your Case in a letter ; if you do the first, you must be sure to fix upon such a time, when you are morally certain he is not engag'd in business or Company ; if you do the latter, the great difficulty is, to get your Letter handsomly convey'd to him ; my way (and I think 'tis the best) is to carry it my self and walk about the Hall &c. Till I have got my Answer.

CHAPTER XXXI.

EXTRACTS FROM VARIOUS WRITERS ILLUSTRATING THE HABITS AND IMPOSTURES OF THE VAGRANT AND BEGGAR, 1708—1886.

Memoirs of the right villainous JOHN HALL (1708)—The Lazy Beggar (1731)—JAMES CAULFIELD, Earnings of a Beggar (1751)—G. PARKER, Illustrations of Low Life (1781)—ROBERT BURNS, the Jolly Beggars (1785)—FRANCIS GROSE, Beggars and Vagrant Impostors (1796)—J. T. SMITH, Vagabondiana (1817)—PIERCE EGAN, A Cadger's Resort (1821)—WILLIAM HONE, Anty Brignal and the Begging Quaker (1827)—JOHN BADCOCK, Beggars and Tinkers (1828)—W. A. MILES, Poverty, Mendicity, and Crime (1839)—Letters from GEORGE ATKINS BRINE (1848, 1871, 1875)—CHARLES DICKENS, The Begging Letter Writer and Tramps (1850).—HENY MAYHEW, London Labour and the London Poor—The Patterer—The Screever—Beggar Street Sellers (1851)—A Blind Impostor (1865)—J. HORNSBY WRIGHT, Confessions of an Old Almsgiver (1871)—A. H. TOULMIN, Rogues and Vagabonds of the Racecourse (1872)—Pseudo Missionaries (1872)—A Deaf and Dumb Impostor (1874.)—The American Tramp (1878)—What a Beggar Boy buys (1886)—Street begging (1886)—Rich Beggars—Frozenout Beggars—Beggars' Barns—A Christmas Haymaker—Gipsy Anecdote—Begging Letter Impostures (1874).

VAGABOND CHEATS.
1708.

From the "Memoirs of the right Villainous John Hall the late famous and notorious robber," 1708.

John Hall was executed at Tyburn Dec. 17, 1707, for breaking open the house of Captain Guyon near Stepney. He was originally a chimney sweep, and commenced a career of crime about 1675.

SWEETNERS.—Such as drop Money before People,[1] and taking out of Sight, inveigle a Man (after a hot Dispute with some of their Accomplices, who earnestly claim halves of what they find) into a Tavern they use, where they draw him into *Cards, Dice*, or *Buckle* and *Thong*, which they planted in some visible Place, and win all his Money: These sort of Vermine likewise go about the Countrey to cheat People of their Money by the *Legerdemain* Slight of *Cups* and *Ball*,[2] and *Luck in a Bag*;[3] this is a Function too that has not flourished since the late Act for Vagabonds.

---

[1] Generally counterfeit guineas.
[2] A trick performed with three metal cups and four small cork balls, in which the spectator is mystified as to the situation of the balls.
[3] A bag into which the spectator is invited to drop a stipulated coin and draw out a ticket, which entitles him to a prize of greater or less value than his money, according to his luck.

In these memoirs a fearful picture is given of the depraved condition of the prisoners in Newgate.

The Lazy Beggar.
1731.
From the *Gentleman's Magazine*, March, 1731.

Common Beggars, the Author tells us, are, for the most part, idle Counterfeits, Rogues and Profligates ; who, to avoid working, take up this lazy course of Life, and by various Disguises and pretences extort more money from tenderhearted People than can be imagin'd, which they squander away in Drunkenness and Revelling ; and doubts not but many of 'em who beg at our Doors a days, are ready to pick our Pockets, break into our Houses, or assault us in the Streets by Night.

The Evils, he says, are owing to the Weakness of some good People, who give Money to be rid of the miserable Appearances, and dismal Outcries of the vilest Rogues, and worst of Impostors. As a Confirmation of this, tells a Story of a Gentleman crossing *Morefields*, who was followed by a middle-aged shabby Fellow importunately begging for Six Pence. The Gentleman wondered at his odd Demand, and told him he had not for him : But the Fellow walked along, repeating his Intreaties, till finding no likelihood of a Success—Well, Sir, says he, with a melancholy Air, I shall trouble you no more !—but that small Matter would have saved me from doing what I shall now be forc'd to do !— Then fetching a deep Sigh, he shook his Head,—and slowly moved away. The Strangeness of his Words and Behaviour struck the Gentleman ; this poor Creature, thought he, by Want is grown desperate, and shall my Refusal of such a Trifle drive him to Extremities ? With that, calling back the Fellow, Here, Friend, is Sixpence for thee ; but 'pr'ythee tell me the meaning of what you said just now. The Fellow thanked him, and pocketing the Money,—— Why truly, Master, reply'd he, I've been begging here this whole Day to little purpose, and unless your Charity had saved me from it, must have been forced to work, the thoughts of which gave me no small Disquiet.

Earnings of a Common Beggar.
1751.
From "Portraits, Memoirs, and Characters of Remarkable Persons," by James Caulfield (1820).

James Turner, a common beggar, whose silvered locks and flowing beard gave him a patriarchal appearance, raised a considerable sum of money by the veneration generally directed towards aged people in distress. Turner, though an old man, was so well experienced in his profession, that he deemed it no trifling advantage to appear still older than he really was. To form some estimate of how much money this man obtained daily, it is necessary to state that Sir Joshua Reynolds, Mr. Nathaniel Hone, and many other celebrated painters, struck with the singularly reverend character of his aspect, wished to make studies from his head, and solicited him to sit to them. He, however, would not consent, unless paid at the rate of one shilling per hour, which he asserted he always got by his profession of begging. Sir Joshua has often introduced the portrait of Turner into his pictures, particularly in that of Count Ugolino and his Children starved to death.

Hone likewise made Turner the prominent feature in his picture of the Conjuror ; and painted his portrait as he generally appeared in the year 1751, which was engraved by Captain Baillie in the year 1762.

ILLUSTRATIONS OF LOW LIFE.
1781.
From " A view of Society and Manners in High and Low Life, being the Adventures of Mr. G. Parker," 1781.

" A modern Bamfylde Moore Carew, but not like him, who ended his Days comfortably in the country ; this one went about from Race to Race selling Gingerbread nuts, and at last finished his career at the Poor House at Liverpool."

QUEER BIT MAKERS.—A cant word for coiner.

ROYAL SCAMP.—The term appropriated to those highwaymen who rob without using ill.

FOOT SCAMP.—Men not having horses, who are on the *Food-pad Rig*, but whose behaviour is correspondent with that of those who are on the *Royal Scamp*.

KEN[1]-CRACKERS.—A term for house-breakers.

DAISY-KICKERS.—Hostlers belonging to large inns, and are known to each other by this name. You may often hear them ask each other, " When did you sell your Daisy-Kicker or Grogham ?" Daisy-Kicker and Grogham being likewise cant for a horse.

FIDLUM BEN.—These are a kind of general tradesmen, who are likewise called *Peter's Sons*,[2] *with every finger a fish-hook*. They watch all opportunities, rob at all times and all places, from a diamond ring on a lady's toilet down to a dish-clout in the sinkhole.

CHAUNTER CULLS.[3]—A species of pasquinade the most injurious to society. If a man has an enmity to a particular person or family, there is a *House of Call* where a set of men are ready to write on any subject or business., and you hear the song sung in the course of three hours from your time of payment in St. Paul's Churchyard or the Fleet Market.

KIDDY NIPPERS.—Kiddy Nipper is a man out of work among *steel-bar flingers*, which is cant for journeymen tailors. The Kiddy Nipper frequents the *Houses of Call*, especially on Saturday night, when those in work have received their wages. . . . In the course of the evening the *Kiddy Nipper*, who has a pair of scissors about him, sits on the side of the man whom he has destined for his prey, whether he sits on chair or bench, cuts the bottom of his pocket open, and *grabbles* all his *Bit*.[4]

BLUE PIGEON[5] FLYER.—These are journeymen plumbers and glaziers who repair houses, and running dustmen. To *fly the blue pigeon* is cutting off lead from what they call a Prayer Book up to a Bible.

JIBBER THE KIBBER.[6]—Is the watch-word made use of by the people on the coast of Cornwall to point out a wreck.

JIGGER-DUBBER.—Is a term applied to jailors or turnkeys, *jigger* being *flash* or *cant* for door. Dub the jigger is, in other words, *shut the door*.

KNUCKLE.[7]—In the *flash* language signifies those who hang about the lobbies of both Houses of Parliament, the Opera House, and both Play Houses, and in general wherever a great crowd assemble. They steal watches, snuffboxes, &c.

MORNING, EVENING AND UPRIGHT SNEAK.—Names derived from the *sneaking* and mean manner in which they commit their robberies. The other

---

[1] *Ken*, a house. [2] See note on *Peterer*, p. 629.
[3] Gyp. *chal*, lad, boy, son, fellow. [4] Money.
[5] German *Blei*, lead, and *picken*, to pick.
[6] Cornish, *gwybod*, to recognise, and *ceber*, a beam.
[7] O. Dutch, *knevelinge*, robbing or thieving.

part of the epithet is borrowed from the time when their frauds are perpetrated, or as a description of the things they steal.

MORNING SNEAK.—A fellow who watches the maid servants in houses when they open parlour windows, &c., particularly if they carry the shutters backwards or up an entry.

In this interval they sneak their hands into the casement of the windows, and take the first thing they can lay their hands on.

EVENING SNEAKS.—Fellows on the same *lay*.[1]

UPRIGHT SNEAKS.—Those who steel pint and quart pots from out of those people's baskets who have had them to scour, as also from off shelves, staircases, &c.

LUMPERS.—The lowest order and most contemptible species of thieving, for even in thieving there are gradations ; and they look down from a superior upon those in an inferior rank with more contempt than a Peer would on a Porter. They have been expelled from the Society of their brethren for being unable to *scamp*,[2] *prig*,[3] or *dive*,[4] and they then commence Lumpers, which is skulking about ships, lighters, &c., hanging about quays, wharfs, &c., stealing old iron, fruit, sugar, or whatever comes to hand.

THE PINCH.—This *rig* is changing of money.

HOOK[5] *and* SNIVEY, *with* NIX *the* BUFFER.—This practice is executed by three men and a dog: one of the men counterfeits sickness, and has a white handkerchief tied round his head, or wears a night-cap. They go into an alehouse, and are shewn a room: having hid the dog under the table, they ring the bell and call for a pot of beer, and desire to know of the landlord if he has got any cold meat in house, and what two of them must give a-piece to dine, as the third man is very ill? All of them then dine plentifully at the cost of two.

The people who practise this *rig* are dog-stealers. They call the dog a *Buffer*, from a practice among them of killing such dogs as no advertisement or enquiry has been made for, and this they call "*buffing the dog*," whose skin they sell, and feed the remaining dogs with his carcase.

LITTLE SNAKESMAN.—Is a *rig* practised in the following manner: A very small boy is carried by a gang of fellows in the dead of night to a house, the sink-hole of which they have already observed open. When this gang is pretty certain that the family is in bed, they dispatch their ambassador, the boy, or *Little Snakesman*, to obtain their admittance.

SNITCHERS.[6]—Informers against their comrades, who discover their haunts, and lay open their schemes.

Your third rate class of sharpers, when they have won a sum of money, if they should happen to refuse a brother sharper who is *flash* to the *rig*, and has been a by-stander, his whack,[7] are instantly *snitched upon* ; that is, the *Snitcher* follows the loser, and asks him what he will give him (the *Snitcher*) if he puts him in the way of recovering his money?

PRAD[8] BORROWERS.—A term used for Horse-stealers.

RUM SNOOSERS.—If a man who has happened to be out late and fearful of not getting in at home, and desirous of *seeing Life* should stroll into a nighthouse, he ought to be very careful lest he should fall asleep in any of those places ; for if he should, he may be certain of a large piece of paper being fastened to his hat, and set fire to.

Awakened by the cry of fire, he struggles with it, and endeavours to extin-

---

[1] Enterprise or pursuit. [2] Rob on the highway. [3] Thieve. [4] Pick-pockets. [5] Gyp. *Hukni*, ringing the changes. Prov. E. *Snivey*, mean ; G. *nichts*. Dutch, *niets*, nothing. [6] The cant term for share. [7] O. Dutch, *Snicken*, to follow or trace by the scent. [8] Dutch, *Paard*, a horse.

guish the flames that have seized on his wig or hair, which are burned, perhaps destroyed by the fire.

Exasperated by this injury, he offers *half a guinea* if anybody will inform him who has used him thus ; somebody *naps the bit,* and tells him that such a Coachman had done it, that he was just run upstairs, and that his coach had such a number.

He runs up in search of the Coachman, but there is no such person ; and when he returns, the man who had gotten his money has run away, and the Landlord charges the Watch with him for raising a riot in his house ; so the night finishes in a Round-house.

QUEER ROOSTER.—A fellow who gets into a house of rendezvous for thieves, pretends to be asleep, and listens to their conversation in order to discover it to some Justice, or to inform for a reward.

THE RUSH.—Fellows who knock at a street door in a summer's night : if the maid comes with a candle in her hand, they fling some powdered rosin across it, which seems to her to be a flash of lightning ; they then rush past her, leaving, however, one or two behind them to guard her while they rob the house.

PETERERS.[1]—Those who follow coaches and chaises, cutting off the portmanteaus, trunks, &c., from behind.

STAR THE GLAZE.—A term for cracking a Jeweller's show-glass, which when cracked forms a star. *Glaze* is cant for glass.

LIFTERS.—A species of theft executed in the following manner ; A genteel looking woman goes into a large shop, and asks to look at some of the newest-fashion lace ; she has a small fish-hook in her hand, which she fixes in a piece of lace, and then lets it slip down between her and the counter, at the same time covering it with her coats ; this done, she buys a yard of lace, and then in putting her hand into her pocket, pulls a string which is fixed to the hook and communicates with her pocket, into which she lifts the lace by it.

DINING-ROOM POST.—A mode of stealing by a man, who, pretending to be the Postman, goes to lodging-houses under the pretence of having letters for the lodgers. These sham letters being sent up for the postage, which he seems to wait for, as soon as he is left alone, he goes into the first room which he finds open, and whips off with him whatever he can lay hold of, nor once minds the postage of his letter.

READER MERCHANTS.—Reader is cant for a Pocket-book. This business is practised by young Jews who ply only at the Bank and the Royal Exchange, and pick the pockets of those going in and out.

LULLY [2] PRIGGERS.—People who steal linen from hedges, get over walls and take the wet linen from the lines upon which laundresses hang it.

RESURRECTION RIG.—Fellows who live by stealing and selling dead bodies, coffins, shrouds, &c.

TOLLIBAN RIG.[3]—This rig has been exercised in some parts of England with amazing success. A genteel looking woman ties a bit of thread to the end of her tongue, which communicates to a bit of paste that she swallows and draws the tongue back, so as even to make the Faculty believe she was born without one. As soon as she is admitted into a house, she points to her tongue, then puts her fingers to her ears, which she persuades you something has grown over.

Another motion is made to bring her a pen, ink, and paper, when she writes down, that "tho' she has been deprived of her hearing and speech, yet it is sufficiently compensated by a fore-knowledge which the Almighty has given her ;

---

[1] O. Dutch, *Peuteren,* to search thoroughly, or to ransack.
[2] Dutch, *Lul,* the small foresail of a ship.
[3] Gyp. *Tulipen,* grease, fat ; *Rig,* to bear, to carry, to bring.

and as she can look into futurity, she begs leave to cast the figures of their nativity who happen to attend to her." It is not surprising that inferior people should be deceived by these artifices, when very often sensible people give way to their contrivances.

TRAPS.—A term for thief takers.

DOBIN[1] RIG.—Going *upon the dobin*, is done by a woman about seven o'clock on a winter's morning, who is dressed like a servant-maid, with a cream-pot in one hand, and *Betty*[2] in the other; and a number of young *Dubs*[3] hanging by her side; no hat or cloak on as she passes through a street. If she spies an apprentice at a haberdasher's opening the shop windows, she applies for a yard and a half of ribbon, but takes care to stand in the darkest part of the shop. . . . As soon as the ribbon drawer is set before her in order to choose the colour, she begins to *work*. . . . It has been well known, that in a few mornings a woman *has made on the Dobbin Rig* two or three hundred yards of ribbon.

RUM DRAG.[4]—The Rum Dragger generally follows broad-wheel waggons on horseback, and counterfeits drunkenness, tells the waggoner he will give him half-a-crown if he will lead his horse, and let him get half an hour's sleep in his waggon. He then takes off the directions from the trunks and parcels, and puts on others addressed to fictitious personages represented by his confederates who claim them on arrival.

LOW GAGGER.[5]—The professors of this *Rig* are old soldiers, old sailors, gypsies, tinkers, &c. The ways and means which they make use of to excite the pity and compassion of the humane, are innumerable.

An Instance:

An old soldier had *gagged* about London many years. His mode for provoking compassion was to get some sheep's blood and a handful of flour, which he put so artfully upon his knee, as to make the passengers, who saw it, believe it to be a mortification in his leg and thigh.

SHAM LEGGERS.[6] THE DUFF.[7] WHISPERING DUDDERS.—These are divided into several classes: some travel on horseback, and some on foot; some with carts and waggons, &c. They frequent the out-skirts of cities, large towns, markets, villages, and fairs. The goods they have for sale are damaged, which they get from on board ships or out of large manufactories; but tho' damaged, they are generally of the newest fashions and neatest patterns. They endeavour to make you believe that the goods they sell are smuggled, tho' they were really manufactured in Spitalfields and are sold at an enormous profit.

BLEATING RIG.—The stealing of sheep.

CHOSEN PELLS.—Are companions who ride in pairs. They shoe their horses with leather, stop coaches in town, strip ladies, take down their hair, and extract the jewels from their heads, &c., besides taking their purses, &c.

FLYING PORTER.—A fellow dressed like a porter; a pen and ink and sheet of paper set him up. He examines the *Daily Advertiser* for robberies, writes to the victim as from the Landlord of the inn informing him that a suspicious man has been stopped with a sack full of things answering the description and tells him that he has nothing to do but to pay the porter.

THE FAWNEY[8] RIG.—A Ring Dropper; a fellow who has gotten a woman's

---

[1] Dutch, *dobbel*, double dealing.
[2] *Betty*, cant for the key of the street-door.
[3] *Dubs*, cant for a bunch of small keys.
[4] Dutch, *draager*, carrier or bearer.
[5] Dutch, *gagie*, the wages or reward of any service.
[6] Dutch, *legger*, layer, rester, or caster with counters.
[7] Dutch, *duf*, musty or mouldy.
[8] Gyp. *fashono*, false, fashioned, made up; *fashono wangustis*, pretended gold rings; *vangus*, a finger.

pocket, with a pair of scissors, some thread, a thimble, and a housewife with a ring in it, which he drops for some credulous person to pick up. He then *comes* the stale story of " If you will give me eight or nine shillings for my share, you shall have the whole." If you accede to this and swallow his bait, you have the ring and pocket, worth about sixpence.

THE RUNNING SNAVEL.[1]—Men and women who watch little boys of a Monday Morning going to school, with their satchel of books thrown over their shoulders, and the money for their week's schooling in their pockets, and a large piece of bread and butter in their hands.

As soon as the *Snaveller* is *up* to this, he or she coaxes the child up some by-alley, narrow court, or dark passage, and *grabbles* the whole.

LEVANTERS.[2]—These are of the order and number of Black Legs, who live by the *Broads*[3] and the *Turf*.[4]

CROCUSSING RIG.—Is performed by men and women, who travel as Doctor or Doctoresses.

ACADEMY BUZ-NAPPERS.—This *Rig* is generally executed by a young fry of boys, who are first picked up in the purlieus of St. Giles's, and carried to J—y B—s's in —— street, where they are put into a room, in which there are figures dressed up like a man and a woman, with bells in every pocket for the young ones to practice on.

DINGERS.[5]—Is a term for throwing away or hiding : a highwayman will ding his *Upper-Benjamin*,[6] his *Jazey*,[7] his *Sticks*,[8] his *Flogger*,[9] his *Diggers*,[10] his *Beater cases*,[11] &c., and having all these on him when he committed the robbery, is totally transformed by *dinging*.

CLINKING.[12]—Stealing silver tankards, pints, &c.

KID RIG.—Fellows who meet boys coming home with work, pretend that they are sent for the work, and desire the boy to make haste with the rest of it ; or at other times, they propose to a boy who carries a bundle, to give him sixpence if he will deliver a message, and they will hold the parcel.

TICK, BIT AND SACK DIVER. Cant words for watch, purse, and money.

JOLLY BEGGARS.

1785.

From the "Jolly Beggars," by Robert Burns.

When lyart[13] leaves bestrow the yird,[14]
Or wavering like the Bauckie-bird,[15]
 Bedim cauld Boreas' blast ;
When hailstanes drive wi' bitter skyte,[16]
And infant frosts begin to bite,
 In hoary cranreuch[17] drest ;
Ae night at e'en a merry core[18]
O'randie,[19] gangrel[20] bodies,

O. Dutch, *snaphaen*, a robber on the highway.
[2] French, *levant*, a rising up or starting.
[3] *Cant for Cards.* [4] *Horse Racing.* [5] Dutch, *dinger*, a bargainer.
[6] *Great coat.* [7] *Wig.* [8] *Pistols.* [9] *Whip.* [10] *Spurs.*
[11] *Boots.* [12] O. Dutch, *klinckinge*, sounding or tinkling.
[13] Faded, withered. [14] Earth. [15] The Bat. [16] Dash, force.
[17] Hoar frost. [18] Company. [19] Sturdy. [20] Vagrant.

In Poosie-Nansie's[1] held the splore,[2]
  To drink their orra dudies :[3]
Wi' quaffing, and laughing,
  They ranted[4] an' they sang ;
Wi' jumping, an' thumping,
  The vera girdle[5] rang.

First, niest[6] the fire, in auld, red rags,
  Ane sat ; weel brac'd wi' mealy bags,
    And knapsack a' in order ;
His doxy[7] lay within his arm ;
  Wi' *usequebae*[8] an' blankets warm,
    She blinket on her Sodger :
An' ay he gies the tozie drab[9]
  The tither[10] skelpan[11] kiss.
While she held up her greedy gab[12]
  Just like an aumous[13] dish :
Ilk smack still, did crack still,
  Just like a cadger's[14] whip. . . .

Then owre again, the jovial thrang
  The Poet did request
To lowse[15] his Pack an' wale[16] a Sang,
  A ballad o' the best.
    He, rising, rejoicing,
      Between his *twa Deborahs*,
    Looks round him, an' found them
      Impatient for the chorus.

I.

See the smoking bowl before us,
  Mark our jovial, ragged ring !
Round and round take up the Chorus,
  And in raptures let us sing.—

Chorus.

A fig for those by law protected !
Liberty's a glorious feast !
Courts for cowards were erected
Churches built to please the priest.

II.

What is *title*, what is *treasure*,
  What is reputation's care ?
If we lead a life of pleasure,
  'Tis no matter *how* or *where*.
    A fig, &c.

---

[1] A whisky house at Mauchline kept by Agnes Gibson, whose nickname was Poosie (Pussy) Nansie.
[2] Frolic.   [3] Superfluous rags.   [4] Made noisy mirth.
[5] A circular iron plate for baking cakes over the fire.   [6] Next.
[7] Female companion.   [8] Whisky (*uisge-beatha*, water of life).
[9] Tipsy woman.   [10] The other.   [11] Energetic, vigorous.
[12] Mouth.   [13] A plate for receiving alms.
[14] A man who travels the country with his wares on the back of a horse or ass.   [15] Loose.   [16] Choose.

THE SOLDIER AND HIS DOXY

THE POET BETWEEN HIS TWO DEBORAHS

III.

With the ready trick and fable,
Round we wander all the day ;
And at night, in barn or stable,
Hug our doxies on the hay.
A fig, &c.

IV.

Does the train-attended *carriage*
Thro' the country lighter rove ?
Does the sober bed of *marriage*
Witness brighter scenes of love ?
A fig, &c.

V.

Life is all a *variorum,*
We regard not how it goes ;
Let them cant about *decorum*
Who have character to lose.
A fig, &c.

VI.

Here's to *budgets, bags,* and *wallets*
Here's to all the wandering train!
Here's *our ragged Brats and Callets*
One and all cry out, *Amen!*
A fig for those by law protected,
Liberty's *a glorious feast!*
Courts *for cowards were erected,*
Churches *built to please the priest.*

BEGGARS AND VAGRANT IMPOSTORS.

1796.

From "The Olio : Sketches of the Times," by Francis Grose, 1796.

BEGGARS.

There is not a greater reproach to the police of this town, than the number of beggars with which every street swarms. Besides the regular stands, which may, in the military sense, be considered as posts, the streets are patrolled by a variety of irregulars. Many beggars extort charities by practising Faquir-like voluntary austerities and cruelties on themselves; I have seen, during the sharpest frost, one of these wretches lying shivering on the steps of a house, almost naked, his flesh seemingly frost-bitten, and exposed to the open air ; or a woman, with two or three infants hanging about her, apparently dying by the rigour of the season. In these cases, ought not the parish officers to take notice of such objects, and if really in distress, to succour them, or if vagrants and impostors, to bring them to condign punishment ; as those very children, thus educated, serve to carry on the succession of thieves and vagabonds.

It is amazing to observe the industry of rogues to avoid being honest ; I have known an ingenious villain bestow as much time and pains in plating a half-crown, as, if exerted in an honest way, would have earned three shillings.

Besides begging, there are various methods of levying contributions on the public ; a very common one is for two or three sturdy fellows, after a frost, when the streets begin to thaw, to block up the kennel so as to cause an inundation or overflowing near a crossing, over which they lay a board, and with brooms in their hands extort a halfpenny each from every passenger. Here again the police is to blame ; it being the duty of the scavengers to keep the streets and crossings clean and passable.

Sweepers of the crossings in wet weather are another species of beggars whose existence is founded on the non-performance of duty in the scavengers, when the streets are very dirty this is paying for something ; but these sweepers are generally as importunate when the ways are dry and good as in the most dirty and miry state.

The beggars of this metropolis may be divided into cripples, blind men, old men, women, and children, sweepers, match-girls, ballad-singers ; and in winter, sham watermen, fishermen, and gardeners.

Of cripples there are divers sorts, some so from their cradles, such as the man who used to crawl upon all-fours ; another whose lower parts were contained in a kind of porridge-pot.—These people may be said to have very good personal estates, their miserable appearances melting the most obdurate hearts into charity.

Mutilated soldiers or sailors, a wooden leg or a stump hand, holding out the hat, frequently is more persuasive than the most melancholy tone of voice.

Formerly men who pretended their tongues were cut by the Algerines, got a pretty good livelihood ; but this mode of exciting compassion is now out of fashion.

Vagrant Impostors.

Look at those wretched fellows dragging along their fishing-boat, decked with the insignia of mourning : the frost has totally shut up the element by which they earned their scanty maintenance. Those are undoubtedly proper objects of charity particularly in this maritime country, where the fisheries serve as a nursery to our fleets, furnishing them with a number of the hardiest sailors. All this is very good, answered a bye-stander, to one who uttered these sentiments, on seeing a parcel of sturdy vagabonds drawing about a boat hung with mourning, and with a tumultuous cry, demanding and extorting charity from all passengers ; all this is very fine, continued he, but how do you know those fellows are fishermen ? In fact the contrary is the case, and to-morrow they will be begging as gardeners.

Pray observe that poor woman, with those two helpless babes half-naked starving on the steps of that great house. Is she an object of charity, think you ? None at all ; in all likelihood one or both of these children are hired by the day or week, for the purpose of exciting charity—at best the beggar is a professional one.

Vagabondiana.

1817.

From " Vagabondiana," by John Thomas Smith, 1817.

Although a fellow in Holborn was recently so scandalously intoxicated in the middle of the day that it was with the greatest difficulty he could stand, yet many people followed to give him money, because the inscription on his hat declared him to be " Out of employment."

Dublin has ever been famous for a Billy in the Bowl (a cripple in a sledge). A very remarkable fellow of this class, well known in that city, and who thought proper to leave Ireland on the Union, was met in London by a Noble Lord, who observed, " So you are here too ! " " Yes, my Lord," replied the beggar, " the Union has brought us all over."

The celebrated Dr. O'Leary used to entertain his friends with some instances of the ingenuity of beggars. As he was riding to Maynooth College, a beggar accosted him for alms, declaring that he had not received a farthing for three days; the good Doctor gave him some silver, and being accosted on his return, in the evening, with a similar story, he upbraided the petitioner with his falsehood, telling him that he was Dr. O'Leary. "Oh, long life to your reverence," said the beggar, "who would I tell my lies to, except my clargy?"

A Cadger's Resort.

1821.

From "Life in London," by Pierce Egan.

"Indeed, you ought not, JERRY, to return to *Hawthorn Hall* without taking a *peep* at the *Cadgers*,[1] at the *Noah's Ark*, to use the slang of the Oxonian, in the *back slums*,[2] in the *Holy Land*.[3] It is a *rich* view of Human Nature; and a fine page in the Book of Life: but it almost staggers *belief* that mankind can be so debased; that *hypocrisy* should be so successful; and that the fine feelings of the heart should become so *blunted* as to laugh at the charitable and humane persons who have been imposed upon to relieve their assumed wants, and to fatten on their daily crimes, without showing the least remorse. But the Metropolis is so extensive, the population so immense, and the opportunities occur so frequently to impose upon the credulity of the passenger in his hasty walks through the streets of London, who has scarcely time to 'read as he runs,' account, in a great degree, for the *Beggars* escaping without detection. In order to prepare your mind for the scene you are about to experience, be not surprised, my dear JERRY, in observing the *Beggar* who has been writhing to and fro all the day in the public streets in terrific agony, to excite your charity and torture your feelings, here meet his fellows to laugh at the *flats*, count over his gains, and sit down to a rich supper. The wretch who has also pretended to be *blind*, and could not move an inch without being led by his dog, can here *see* and enjoy all the good things of this life, without even *winking*. The poor married woman with twins, who you are led to imagine, from her piteous tale, has been left in distress, in consequence of her husband having been sent to sea, you will find is a single woman, and has only *hired* the children from poor people, who lend them out for the purpose, joins the party, at the *Noah's Ark*, to laugh at the fools who may have relieved her pretended wants in the course of the day. You will, JERRY, likewise witness the *chap* who has been begging upon *crutches* through the streets, the first to propose a dance, after he has carefully deposited his stilts, and to join in a *reel*. The *starved* fellow, who calls his God to witness, as the passengers pass by him, 'that he has not tasted a bit of bread for two days;' and although he has a bag full of broken victuals given to him by the humane and charitable cooks, he would not put a bit in his mouth, his *appetite* being so *nice*, may be seen among this diabolical set of IMPOSTORS blowing up the cook for sending in his rumpsteaks without the garnish of pickles and horseradish, and selling his bag of *grub* to some really poor and industrious persons. The HYPOCRITE who has been singing hymns, in hopes to excite the pity of the passenger on account of his religious conduct, now empties himself by swearing a lot of oaths, and uttering other horrid im-

---

[1] A beggar.   [2] Low, dirty back streets.
[3] A well-know region of St. Giles's in former times also called the "Holy Ground" and the "Rookery." New Oxford Street was formed through the centre of it in 1846-7. An old *fancy* chaunt ends every verse thus—

"For we are the boys of the *Holy Ground*,
And we'll dance upon nothing and turn us round."

precations on account of the bad day's work that he has made. The *pregnant female* is here delivered without the help of an *accoucheur;* while roars of laughter resound from one end of the room to the other, in witnessing her remove the *pillow* from under her stays, drinking success to begging, and singing—

'There's a difference between a beggar and a queen,
And the reason I'll tell you why:
A queen cannot swagger, nor get drunk like a beggar,
Nor be half so happy as I, as I.'

"The *Sweeper of the Crossings*[1] near some of the squares, whose genteel appearance excites the compassion of the ladies, who are often heard to exclaim, 'What a pity it is that such a genteel man can get no employment!' also joins in the laugh, among the begging fraternity, at the credulity of mankind; and is enabled, from his deception, to indulge himself with brandy and water, and much better living than thousands of hard-working journeymen in the Metropolis. In short, my dear Coz., a volume would not contain one-half of the impositions that are daily practised upon the public by the beggars of the Metropolis; notwithstanding the exertions and *exposé* of the Parish Officers, the Police, and the Mendicity Society; or, as our friend Bob emphatically observes, 'every hair of your head will be as thick as a broomstick' on entering this assemblage of *rascality, wickedness,* and *deceit.*" "I am quite impatient for the time to arrive," said JERRY, "and pray let our disguises be got ready."

To the great gratification of JERRY, LOGIC now joined our heroes; and the TRIO started as soon as the darkness of the evening answered their purpose; when it was not long before they entered the *back slums,* and found themselves in the midst of *Cadgers:* but, previous to which, the *Oxonian* observed to HAWTHORN, that, if it was not necessary to cry out "LETHE" among the *Cadgers,* it was essentially requisite for him to mind his P's and Q's, that no detection might take place. The scene was so *rich,* that JERRY whispered to LOGIC, "of all that I have witnessed this must be pronounced as the *climax;*" "P," answered the *Oxonian,* "no more *magging.*[2] Observe and be *silent.*" Although Tom was disguised as a *beggar,* yet he did not lose the traces of a *gentleman;* according to the old adage, that a gentleman in rags does not forget his real character. JERRY did not make his look *beggarly* enough; but LOGIC gammoned[3] to be the *cadger* in fine style, with his *crutch* and *specs;*[4] indeed, if it had not been for the fun, flash,[5] and confidence of the *Oxonian,* they must have completely failed in the expedition. *Peg,* the ballad-singer, all in tatters, and covered with various-coloured rags, yet her pretty face did not escape the roving eye of TOM, upon her winking and leering her ogles[6] at him, and chaunting the ballad, "Poverty's no sin," in hopes to procure a new *fancy-man.*[7] Massa

---

[1] One of the *genteel* impostors, in the summer of 1820, was taken up as a vagabond, and committed to the House of Correction, in Cold-Bath-Fields, for a month, for his saucy behaviour to a lady who had refused to relieve his importunities. On his examination, before the Magistrate, it turned out that he was a journeyman tin-man by trade; and, on his being searched, twenty-five shillings were found in his pockets. For the first two days of his confinement he was *sulky* and refused to eat such wretched refreshment, as he termed the allowance of the House; but, on recovering his temper, he laughed at the *flats,* and asked, "Who would *work hard* for a few shillings per day, when, with only a *broom* in his hand, a *polite bow,* and a *genteel appearance,* at the corner of any of the Squares, the *ladies* could be *gammoned* out of pounds per week; and it was a bad day indeed, that did not produce him from sixteen shillings to a pound."   [2] Chattering.   [3] Pretended.
[4] Spectacles.   [5] Knowingness.   [6] Eyes.
[7] A petticoat retainer; a degraded individual sustained by a prostitute.

A CADGERS' RESORT IN 1821

.Piebald, as they termed him, on account of his *black* mug[1] and *white* mop,[2] was *chaffing* the little *cove*,[3] that, as he had no *pins*[4] to stand upon, he must have a *perch;* and as he was no *starter*,[5] he proposed him for their chairman. The *no-pinn'd*[6] hero, on being elevated, gave, as a toast, "success to FLAT-catching,"[7] which produced roars of laughter and shouts of approbation. The fellow sitting near the stove, whose face seems on the *grin*, from the pleasures he feels on *scratching* himself, offers to lay a quart of *heavy*[8] that he has not *cut his nails* for the last twelve months, he has had such active employment for them. Quarrelsome old *Suke*, who has been hobbling all the day on her *crutches* through the streets, now descends the ladder quickly to join the party, and is *blowing-up* her *ould man* for not taking hold of her crutches, "as he knows she doesn't vant 'em now." Behind the stove, the row has become so great, from the copious draughts of liquor and jollity of the Cadgers, that the gin measure and glasses are thrown at each other; and their crutches and wooden legs are brought in contact to finish the *turn-up*,[9] till they are again wanted to *cadge* with the next day. The black one-legged fiddler is *strumming* away to enliven the party; and the *peck*[10] and *booze*[11] is lying about in such lots, that it would supply numerous poor families, if they had the *office*[12] given them where to apply for it.

ANTY BRIGNAL AND THE BEGGING QUAKER.

1827.

From the "Table Book," by William Hone.

A few years ago a stout old man, with long grey hair, and dressed in the habit of the Society of Friends, was seen begging in the streets of Durham. The inhabitants attracted by the novelty of a "*begging* Quaker," thronged about him, and several questioned him as to his residence, &c. Amongst them was "Anty Brignal," the police-officer, who told him to go about his business, or he would put him in the Kitty[13] "for an *imposteror*." "Who ever heard," said Anthony, "of a begging Quaker?" "But," said the mendicant, while tears flowed down his face, "thou knowest, friend, there be bad Quakers as well as good ones; and, I confess to thee, I have been a bad one. My name is John Taylor; I was in the hosiery business at N——, and through drunkenness have become a bankrupt. The society have turned me out, my friends have deserted me. I have no one in the world to help me but my daughter, who lives in Edinburgh, and I am now on my way thither. Thou seest, friend, why I beg; it is to get a little money to help me on my way: be merciful, as thou hopest for mercy." "Come, come," said the officer, "it won't do, you know; there's not a word of truth in it; 'tis all false. Did not I see you drunk at Nevill's Cross (a public-house of that name) the other night?" "No, friend," said the man of unsteady habits, "thou didst not see *me* drunk there, but I was there, and saw *thee* drunk; and thou knowest when a man is drunk he thinks everybody else so!" This was a poser for the police officer. The crowd laughed, and "Anty Brignal" slunk away from their derision, while money fell plentifully into the extended hat of the disowned quaker.

---

[1] Face. [2] Hair. [3] Man. [4] Legs.
[5] One who leaves a drinking party, a milksop. [6] Legless.
[7] Imposing on the simple. [8] Beer.
[9] Hasty fight. [10] Food. [11] Drink. [12] Information.
[13] A house of correction is so called in Durham. Su. Got. *Kœtta*, to confine.

BEGGARS AND TINKERS.
1828.

From a "Living Picture of London for 1828," by Jon Bee (John Badcock).

Beggars and *tinkers* are, properly enough, suspected of contributing to burglaries; but then those people *work* for themselves, and seldom carry off great amounts.

JUVENILE VAGABONDS AND BEGGARS.
1839.

From "Poverty, Mendicity, and Crime," by W. A. Miles.

It is among these children that the youngest in years may be found to be the most reckless and the most hardened in crime. A boy only 10 years of age was sentenced to death, together with his father, for housebreaking, and on his return from the court to his cell, preceded by the clergyman and his father, he said in an under-tone to the prisoners, who were anxious to know the result of the trial, "I'm bless'd, if they havn't stuck it[1] into our old chap at last!" pointing with his thumb to his doomed parent.

At certain periods the beggars and idle persons, including women and girls, leave St. Giles's in order to make their country circuits. Many hundreds emigrate into Kent to pick hops, and to steal what they can. The beggars follow on the heels of the fashionable world, and when fashion rusticates, the mendicant leaves London. Some travel the round of the races; some go systematically begging at every door in each town, and at every house in the rural districts. They exchange routes in St. Giles's before they start, and give each other written memoranda of various gentlemen's seats, and what tale of deception is best calculated to awaken the owners' sympathies. These vagabonds return as periodically as they start, and none of them ever starve upon the road.

A poor ragged sweep, about 16 years of age, without shoes or stockings, and his red legs cracked with the cold, was brought to prison for some trifling offence. The warm bath into which he was put much delighted him, but nothing could exceed his astonishment on being told to put on shoes and stockings. "And am I to *wear* them, and this, and this too?" he said, as each article of dress was given to him. His joy was complete when they took him to his cell; he turned down the bed-clothes with great delight, and, half doubting his good fortune, hesitatingly asked if he was really to sleep in the bed! On the following morning the governor, who had observed the lad's surprise, asked him what he thought of his situation? "Think of it, master! why I'm damned if ever I do another stroke of work!" The boy kept his word, and was ultimately transported.

Beggars never wear any clothes that may be given to them—some go about without shoes, stockings, or shirt, only a pair of trowsers and a knit jacket, to excite compassion; and yet clothes daily given to them, which yield them 4s. and 5s. a day.

LETTERS FROM GEORGE ATKINS BRINE.
1848.

Communicated by William Tucker, Esq., Chairman of the Guardians of the Axminster Union to the Poor Law Board, *February* 26, 1848.

George Atkins Brine, of the Parish of Sherborne, in the Sherborne Union, County Dorset. I have added this case of vagrancy, which came before the Dorset justices at the last sessions, as one, perhaps, of the most extraordinary which has ever been heard before a bench of justices. George Atkins Brine is

---

[1] *Stick it into*, to victimise, to overreach.

about 40 years of age, and was educated in the charity school of Sherborne, and formerly apprenticed to a butcher in that town. This man, for many years past, has made mendicancy his entire mode of living, and has made it his boast that he could go to his town house, Dorchester gaol, whenever he wanted a home. He is a man of considerable attainment, as the subjoined letter, written by him, in most excellent handwriting, during his imprisonment in Dorchester gaol, to one of his comrades, will show. I have attached the copy of the list of his offences, as laid before the justices at the last sessions, together with his present sentence, certified by Mr. Duke, the governor of the gaol.

List of GEORGE BRINE'S OFFENCES, laid before the Justices at the Epiphany Sessions, 1848.

When convicted.	Before whom.	Crime.	Event of Trial.
29 Aug., 1831.	Rev. John Parsons.[1]	Misbehaviour in service.	Hard labour 2 cal. months.
29 Feb., 1832.	Ditto.	Leaving service.	Hard labour 3 cal. months.
10 July, 1835.	S. Pretor, Esq., Rev. J. Parsons.	Profane swearing.	Hard labour, 16 days.
25 Jan., 1837.	Rev. John Parsons.	Vagrancy.	Hard labour 2 cal. months.
14 May, 1841.	Ditto.	Ditto.	Hard labour 3 cal. months.
Midsummer Sessions, 1842.	George Bankes, Esq.	Stealing a sod iron.	Acquitted.
30 Sept., 1842.	Rev. John Parsons.	Breach of peace.	Imprisonment 3 cal. months.
7 Aug., 1843.	Ditto.	Breaking windows.	Hard labour 2 cal. months.
8 Aug., 1844.	Samuel Pretor, Esq.	Ditto.	Ditto.
26 Oct., 1844.	Rev. John Parsons.	Breaking a bottle containing wine.	Ditto.
29 May, 1845.	Rev. J. Parsons, W. J. Goodden, Esq.	Breach of peace.	Imprisonment, 1 year.
Epiphany Sessions, 1847.	George Bankes, Esq., &c.	For want of sureties to keep the peace, &c.	No prosecution.
22 Jan., 1847.	John Gawler Bridge, Esq.	Breaking windows.	Hard labour 2 cal. months.
16 June, 1847.	Rev. John Parsons.	Vagrancy.	Hard labour 3 cal. months.

Remarks.—He is now under sentence of six calendar months' imprisonment with hard labour, and to be once whipped, having at the last sessions been convicted of being an incorrigible rogue and vagabond.—C. DUKE.

Copy of GEORGE ATKINS BRINE'S LETTER, directed to Mr. George Vincent, King's Arms Inn, Thornford, Sherborne, Dorsetshire.

Dorset County Gaol, December 27, 1847.

MY DEAR FRIEND,
You will remember my promise of writing to you, which I will now endeavour to fulfil. You are, no doubt, aware that I am committed for trial at

[1] The Rev. John Parsons was Vicar of Sherborne from 1830 till his death in 1854.

the sessions on a charge of vagrancy, for being found sleeping in a stall belonging to Mark Sherrin, the butcher. I do not know what the issue of that trial may be, but I expect a term of imprisonment, and a corporal punishment by flagellation.[1] The magistrate who committed me told me no effort on his part should be wanting to serve me, of which I have no manner of doubt. It seems a pleasure to him to have an opportunity of vomiting his waspish and dyspeptic spleen at me, but I am invulnerably proof against it. The dastardly pitiful schemes he has recourse to only serve to add to his disgrace, and to protract the immortality of his shame. I suppose Mark Sherrin means to carry on the crusade which his deceased brother so long and so unsuccessfully waged against me. He had declared eternal war, but was cut off in a moment, "and sent to his last account, with all his imperfections on his head." And who knows the destiny of the immortal spirit ? It may be, for aught we know, imprisoned in all the hellish perpetuity of confinement, in those doleful regions where Ixion for ever turns his wheel; and where Tantalus in vain endeavours to slake his everlasting thirst with the water which eludes his lips ; where Sisyphus, with unavailing labour, rolls up the stone which eternally falls back ; and where Tityus feels the vulture incessantly preying on his heart, which as fast as it is devoured is again renewed. But methinks I have indulged in an unwarrantable and uncharitable strain. The pertinent remarks of the poet rush across my mind, who says—

> "There is a spell by nature thrown
> Around the voiceless dead,
> Which seems to soften censure's tone,
> And guard the dreamless bed
> Of those, who whatsoe'er they were,
> Wait heaven's conclusive audit there."—*Quarles.*

My dear friend, please to give my respects to the indomitable Mr. Aldous,[2] and to Master Robert England, to Charles Edmunds, and his copper-coloured majesty, James King of Thornford, likewise to your brother John, and most especially to your father and mother—I owe them the debt immense of endless gratitude ; never can I forget their generous kindness to me when I worked for them on the railway. I omitted to tell you that I had been in Yeovil for two days previous to my apprehension. Davis, the man I went to London with, called upon me at Sherborne, and wished me to accompany him to Plymouth, but to this I could not consent; I promised to go as far as Exeter, but did not intend fulfilling my engagement; we staid together two days in Yeovil, when I gave him the slip; he would not stay an hour in Sherborne—the reason of this is obvious ; so you see, in striving to escape the whirlpool of Charybdis, I struck upon the rocks of Scylla. And now I must close my epistle : farewell, my valued friend, for the present, and believe me to remain, with the most sincere regard and respect,

Yours faithfully,
GEORGE ATKINS BRINE.

P.S.—Davis is become an itinerant quack doctor, and has a hopeful shoot with him (a son of the Emerald Isle), apparently about 16 or 17.

---

[1] Brine's prophetic instincts of a flagellation were subsequently fully realised.
[2] Mr. Aldous and the father of Master Robert England were sub-contractors on the Great Western Railway, then in course of construction near Thornford. Charles Edmunds was a miller there. "His copper-coloured majesty" was some time afterwards an inmate of the Union with Brine. While there they indulged in a fight in which they made scarecrows of one another, and were as a consequence brought before the Board for punishment.

GEORGE ATKINS BRINE (1874)

WALTER SCOTT (1874)

AND BEGGARS AND BEGGING.

SHERBORNE: *July* 3, 1871.

Honoured Sir,—Apologising for not having replied to your courteous note earlier, I beg to answer some of Mr. Ribton-Turner's inquiries respecting me. In the first place, Mr. Ribton-Turner desires to know what induced me to adopt such a mode of livelihood ; 2ndly, how I have supported myself in my wanderings ; 3rdly, the casual wards I have visited and my opinion of them ; and, 4thly, the gaols in which I have been incarcerated, with the cause of these incarcerations. Now, in reply to the first question, I left Sherborne to seek employment at my trade (that of a butcher), and not succeeding for a time, I soon discovered that more money could be got without work than with it. What knowledge I lacked was soon instilled into my mind by professional vagrants.

2ndly. How I have supported myself during my wanderings ? Now, I mean to make a clean breast of it ; I will candidly declare that I have stuck at nothing. I have worked (but very little) at my trade ; I have been a cattle drover ; I have been salesman with three different cheap-Jacks ; I have been a pot hawker ; I have been a vendor of pens, paper, razors (Peter Pindar's), spectacles, laces, &c. ; I have been a distributor of religious tracts ; I have been in the employ (for two years together) of manslaughtering quack doctors— four different ones (I am more ashamed of this than of any other of my follies, for the majority of them are not robbers only, but homicides). I have sold cards at all the principal races in England. I also attended for many years all the principal prize-fights. I have been a "shallow cove" (*i.e.* a member of the land navy ; also a "highflyer" (*i.e.* a begging-letter impostor) ; a "lurker" (one who is forty different trades, and master of none). My favourite "lurk" was butcher, tallow chandler, or currier, and to crown all, I have been a preacher ! This game pays well in remote village streets on Sunday evenings, provided you are well stocked with tracts ; but I was not fit for it ; my risibility is too easily tickled, and once, when I was invited to "hold forth" in a small chapel, I was in no little danger of grinning in the pulpit at my own roguery. This was at Rothbury, Northumberland. I must also tell you, in short, I have been a rogue, impostor, and vagabond of each and every denomination. I say this because it is true, and because I am now heartily ashamed of it.

3rdly. Mr. Ribton-Turner wants to know my opinion of the casual wards I have visited. Now I have visited but very few—I think I could swear that I never was in twenty different ones during the twenty-two years I was rambling—but I am fully convinced that they all tend to foster vagrancy. Even such places as Oxford, Cambridge, Bath, Rochester, Norwich, and Hastings, do more harm than good ; for out of every ten tramps there are nine impostors, or professional tramps. You may think this is saying too much, but I am sure this is the truth. If there was no relief to be had, there would be no vagrants. The difficulty lies in distinguishing between the honest working man and the rogue. Now the distributors of Watts's Charity in Rochester seem to pride themselves upon their own sagacity on this point. I have been a recipient of Watts's no less than eight times, so I leave you to guess whether they relieved a deserving customer in me, or otherwise. In Norwich, at St. Andrew's Hall, it is the same. I once gave my ticket, which I had obtained there, to a poor blacksmith who had been refused one. The reason he had been refused was because he was not so consummate a liar as I was. This is truth. If he had been a trading liar he would have gotten his bread, cheese, beer, and bed, valued at 8d.

Again, Mr. Ribton-Turner and his colleagues will never deal effectually with vagrancy unless they begin at the right end. Let them, or the Legislature, suppress two-thirds of the common "padding-kens," or low lodging-houses. These are the great receptacles of vice in its most repulsive aspect. It is there the supply of vagrants is manufactured, aye, in the very womb; it is there they dispose of their ill-gotten gains, for great numbers of them are regular "fencing cribs," and great numbers of them will not lodge a working man at all, if they know it, lest he should divulge their secrets. And all lodging-houses ought to be under stricter police surveillance. Again, sir, you know, or ought to know, that the greater the villain the more plausible is his tale, and the more assured invincible impudence he possesses the likelier he is to attain his ends, at least with people who are little acquainted with these mysteries, for rogues don't care to deal with rogues—in truth, they will never trust each other, and I assure you, sir, the gullibility of the British public is so great, and their hearts so finely susceptible to what they believe to be a tale of genuine distress, that their generous benevolence is unbounded. They don't like to be imposed upon; but, as I said before, the rogue, liar, and impostor, practised as he is, soon convinces them, that he, at least, does not belong to the cadging fraternity. And now, fourthly, how many gaols? This is a poser. Well, here goes. I have been in gaol more than one hundred different times! There are but two counties in England that I have escaped "limbo." I have also been in several in Scotland and Wales. In the great majority of cases drunkenness has been the cause; I have never been convicted of felony or larceny, but I have for obtaining money under false pretences, and several times for hawking without a licence; many times for vagrancy, smashing windows, and other offences, for the whole of which I richly deserve hanging. To this, I presume, sir, you will say "Amen."

I am, honoured Sir, your unworthy servant,

To S. JELFS, Esq. G. A. BRINE.

SHERBORNE WORKHOUSE: *April* 12, 1875.

Honoured Sir,—In compliance with your request, I will now endeavour to describe to you some forms of "lurk," in which I myself have been an actor. I have found that the "bereavement lurk" is a lucrative one—(*i.e.*) the pretended loss of a wife, leaving me with a young and helpless family to support. I practised the following scheme for the first time in Manchester:—I obtained three children, two girls and a boy, between the ages of five and ten years, of their parents, at a common "padding-ken" in Blakeley Street (now Charter Street) for three shillings, to "stand pad" with me, from seven o'clock until twelve p.m. on a Saturday. I agreed to give the children plenty to eat before starting, and some pence for themselves when we returned; so after the children had been well washed and clean pinafores put on them, and had been plentifully regaled with bread and butter and tea; and I had taught them their lesson (which was a very short one); and I had provided a placard to place on each of their breasts, with the word "Motherless" written in large letters upon it, we sallied forth on our expedition, and took up our position at one of the entrances to Shudehill Market, and there "stood pad"—(*i.e.*) stood with the children by me, and did not speak unless I was spoken to. I had frequently to answer questions as to how long the wife had been dead, &c., but was not otherwise interfered with. In five hours I had more than 30s. given me in silver and copper. I should think I drank at least a shilling's worth of rum during the time; besides buying some cakes, &c. for the children, and giving them fourpence each for themselves, I had £1 8s. odd for myself.

At another time I tried the same game at Sunderland, with two children (girls), but one of them was too old for me. I should think she was between eleven and twelve, and in the midst of my performance she became refractory, when I gave her a slight slap on the shoulders as a correction, but this inflamed her Irish blood to fury. She called me "rogue, rascal, impostor," &c. (she told the truth). She said her father was dead, and that I was not her father; that I had paid her mother half-a-crown for herself and sister for the evening, and that her mother was getting drunk with the money. This was about nine o'clock, when I was taking money fast; and I was compelled to "pitch the crack" (discontinue the game) and to "make tracks" the same evening towards Durham, with only seven or eight shillings, which I fully expected to have doubled, and perhaps trebled.

"Another lurk I tried was the cripples," at Holywell, Flintshire, N.W., where is a famous spring called St. Winifred's Well. Tradition says that the Saint was beheaded on a hill above the spring, where St. Winifred's Church now stands; and that the head, after decapitation, rolled to the bottom of the hill, and where it stopped the well sprung up. Be this as it may, many people —it is said—have derived great benefit from the water, by drinking it, and from bathing in it. It is said to be infallible in relief of rheumatics, neuralgia, sciatica, &c. So I took it into my head to simulate rheumatism for a time; so one day I said to the woman who was with me, "Let us go and see what we can do at Holywell." At this time we were at Rhyl. She consented, and after maturing our plans, the next day we started to Holywell, where we took a small furnished room upstairs, in a back room at a cobbler's, for 3s. a week. We told them we were come from the West of England for the benefit of the celebrated waters, as we were both suffering from rheumatic pains, and had been advised to try whether the spring would do us any good. So having paid a week's rent in advance, the next day we commenced operations. We soon found out the names and residences of the most benevolent persons, and succeeded beyond our expectations.

The following morning we bathed at the spring. A man is kept there to attend males, and a female attends females. I went there, supported on two sticks, but I subsequently got a crutch. I pretended to be much worse than my wife (?) She was afflicted in the arms; I in the legs. We continued this game for a few days, and then ladies came to see us at our lodgings, and never leaving without a donation. Some days we got as much as 10s. a day, besides wine, porter, mutton, cakes, &c., and books to read. I carried on this game for five weeks, living on the fat of the land, till one unfortunate day I sent my wife for a half-pint of rum, which so exhilarated us that we got another; after which I insisted on having a dance together in the room, which through our operations and jumps brought down part of the plaster of the ceiling underneath us, on the table where the cobbler and his wife were at tea. It was an old rickety house, and the man told me afterwards that, hearing the rumpus overhead, he and his wife had gone upstairs and seen us dancing together for a quarter of an hour before the ceiling fell. When I got down stairs I found the room half full of the neighbours, to whom the cobbler and his wife had given the intelligence about the dancing cripples. This, together with the row about the damaged ceiling (it was a large piece of plaster; I should think it was 16 or 20 feet in circumference), made me resolve to "hook" it at once, for the news had spread like wildfire.

I then hastily told my wife she would meet me at a certain place in Benjonson Street, Liverpool, and having given her some money, I started at once for Chester (17 miles), which place I reached within four hours, and the next day I reached Liverpool, where the woman found me two days after.

There are many "lurks" which I have not now the time or space to dwell upon; neither have I time or opportunity just now to say much about pseudo-doctors; but another week, sir, if you please to forward me (*per* Mr. Jelfs) another stamped envelope, I will do my best for your information.

I remain, honoured Sir, with the greatest respect,
Your unworthy servant,
GEORGE ATKINS BRINE.

To C. J. RIBTON-TURNER, Esq.

P.S.—There are many remarks I should like to make respecting vagrancy.

Imprimis, the motive-power must be stopped before the machinery can be brought to a stand-still. People who indiscriminately give alms are far more to blame than the recipients. Until this truth be widely known and acted upon, mendicity will flourish. This, and this alone, is the greatest obstacle that impedes your progress, although, I should say, not an insurmountable one.
G. A. B.

The events chronicled in this letter happened about twenty years before the date of it, and though there may be here and there embellishments of the truth, inquiry seems to show that the account given is substantially accurate.

SHERBORNE UNION WORKHOUSE : *April* 19, 1875.

Honoured Sir,—I duly received your note of the 15th inst., to which I now reply. I commence with the quack doctors. In the first place, I must tell you that I never engaged in the dirty business on my own account. I have been a tool in the hands of others. The first time it was in Yarmouth. A quack who was lodging at the same "ken" with me asked me if I was willing to earn a couple of shillings easily. I replied in the affirmative. This was to come into the market-place in the afternoon, while he himself was expatiating on the virtues of his infallible medicines, and purchase half-a-dozen boxes of the pills, saying that myself and others had derived immense benefit from their use, and that, for the future, I was resolved never to be without them, the money to pay for them having been given me beforehand by the "doctor" (save the mark). Well, I carried out my instructions to the letter, and so well pleased the modern Æsculapius, that in the evening he employed me to work for him at a salary of £1 per week, besides travelling expenses. I was now to be initiated in the sublime mystery of compounding the "medicines," almost invariably "pills." My duty was to collect the ingredients, and I now solemnly declare that I got them ready-made from the sheepfold or the rabbit-warren. Those from the sheepfold had to be considerably reduced in size, after which they were coated with finely pulverized sugar and flour, and, after being dried to a proper consistency, were placed in pill-boxes, which are easily obtained, and then held forth to the dolts who were silly enough to listen to him as " American sugar-coated pills," purely vegetable, and warranted not to contain one particle of mercury, colocynth, or other deleterious poison, so extensively used by regular doctors. These pills are a sovereign remedy for bilious disorders, liver complaints, dyspepsia, or indigestion, the symptoms of which are learnedly described by the " orator " (which was generally myself), learnt by heart from a medical work by Dr. Buchanan.

When we were travelling in country villages there was no " ill which flesh is heir to " but what my master (blatant ignoramus as he was) would not undertake to cure—worms, piles, tusky or itch, gout, rheumatism, ulcers, fits, &c. ; but the naked truth is that he was a greater fool than I ; he could not read a paragraph in a newspaper, and could scarcely write his own name. He knew no more about the maladies he professed to cure than a hog ; but he possessed in an eminent degree that grand, indispensable qualification, any amount of cheek, and his takings on an average were £10 a week.

I travelled with this man for about four months, chiefly in the eastern counties, when I expressed a desire to leave him, when he immediately offered to raise my wages by giving me 25s. a week, but I would not accept it and left him. I have travelled with three others, all of the same kidney, since that time : suffice it to say that a set of more unprincipled, ignorant rascals never disgraced earth.

Perhaps, sir, you may think that by turning " Queen's evidence " I am worse than the ones I impeach ; but I don't wish to exonerate myself, for I confess that I am about the most worthless of beings, but the truth ought to be known; poor people ought not to be systematically robbed by quack doctors or any other description of rogue; for rogues, rascals, and liars are the whole fraternity, myself included.

* * * * * *

To C. J. RIBTON-TURNER, Esq.

Yours unworthily,
G. A. BRINE.

P.S.—I was born October 29, 1812.

Brine died April 12, 1881. He was up to the last an irreclaimable rascal. One of the ex-officio guardians endeavoured to reform him, but without avail. A short time before Brine's death he furnished him with a good suit of black clothes. Brine immediately left the workhouse, for the last time as it turned out, and commenced drinking, the result being that by the evening the clothes were completely spoiled and Brine had to be conveyed to the police-station on a truck. A life of him appeared in 1883, under the title of "The King of the Beggars."

BEGGING-LETTER WRITERS AND TRAMPS.

1850.

From "Household Words" and "All the Year Round," by Charles Dickens.

In the year 1850, *Mr. Charles Dickens* published in "Household Words" and "All the Year Round" two pungent and graphic descriptions of the Begging-letter Writer and the Tramp, from which the following extracts are taken. In consequence of the exposures contained in them, *Mr. Henry Mayhew* tells us "that from being a favourite author amongst the patterers, *Dickens* went down sadly in the scale on account of 'coming it so strong' against the begging-letter department."

THE BEGGING-LETTER WRITER.

I ought to know something of the Begging-letter Writer. He has besieged my door at all hours of the day and night; he has fought my servant; he has lain in ambush for me, going out and coming in; he has followed me out of town into the country; he has appeared at provincial hotels, where I have been staying only for a few hours; he has written to me from immense distances, when I have been out of England. He has fallen sick; he has died and been buried; he has come to life again, and again departed from this transitory scene: he has been his own son, his own mother, his own baby, his idiot brother, his uncle, his aunt, his aged grandfather. He has wanted a greatcoat, to go to India in; a pound to set him up in life for ever; a pair of boots to take him to the coast of China; a hat to get him into a permanent situation under Government. He has frequently been exactly seven and sixpence short of independence. He has had such openings at Liverpool—posts of great trust and confidence in merchants' houses, which nothing but seven and sixpence was wanting to him to secure—that I wonder he is not Mayor of that flourishing town at the present moment.

The natural phenomena of which he has been the victim are of a most astounding nature. He has had two children who have never grown up; who have never had anything to cover them at night; who have been continually driving him mad, by asking in vain for food; who have never come out of fevers and measles (which I suppose has accounted for his fuming his letters with tobacco smoke as a disinfectant); who have never changed in the least degree through fourteen long revolving years. As to his wife, what that suffering woman has undergone, nobody knows. She has always been in an interesting situation through the same long period, and has never been confined yet. His devotion to her has been unceasing. He has never cared for himself: *he* could have perished, he would rather, in short—but was it not his Christian duty as a man, a husband, and a father, to write begging-letters when he looked at her? (He has usually remarked that he would call in the evening for an answer to this question.)

He has been the sport of the strangest misfortunes. What his brother has done to him would have broken anybody else's heart. His brother went into business with him, and ran away with the money; his brother got him to be security for an immense sum and left him to pay it; his brother would have given him employment to the tune of hundreds a-year, if he would have consented to write letters on a Sunday; his brother enunciated principles incompatible with his religious views, and he could not (in consequence) permit his brother to provide for him. His landlord has never shown a spark of human feeling. When he put in that execution I don't know, but he has never taken it out. The brokers' man has grown grey in possession. They will have to bury him some day.

He has been attached to every conceivable pursuit. He has been in the army, in the navy, in the Church, in the law; connected with the press, the fine arts, public institutions, every description and grade of business. He has been brought up as a gentleman; he has been at every college in Oxford and Cambridge; he can quote Latin in his letters (but generally mis-spells some minor English word); he can tell you what Shakspeare says about begging, better than you know it. It is to be observed, that in the midst of his afflictions he always reads the newspapers; and rounds off his appeal with some allusion, that may be supposed to be in my way, to the popular subject of the hour....

Once he wrote me rather a special letter, proposing relief in kind. He had got into a little trouble by leaving parcels of mud done up in brown paper, at people's houses, on pretence of being a Railway-Porter, in which character he received carriage money. This sportive fancy he expiated in the House of Correction. Not long after his release, and on a Sunday morning, he called with a letter (having first dusted himself all over), in which he gave me to understand that, being resolved to earn an honest livelihood, he had been travelling about the country with a cart of crockery. That he had been doing pretty well until the day before, when his horse had dropped down dead near Chatham, in Kent. That this had reduced him to the unpleasant necessity of getting into the shafts himself, and drawing the cart of crockery to London—a somewhat exhausting pull of thirty miles. That he did not venture to ask again for money; but that if I would have the goodness *to leave him out a donkey*, he would call for the animal before breakfast!—*Household Words, May* 18, 1850.

TRAMPS.

Another class of tramp is a man, the most valuable part of whose stock-in-trade is a highly perplexed demeanour. He is got up like a countryman, and you will often come upon the poor fellow, while he is endeavouring to decipher the inscription on a milestone—quite a fruitless endeavour, for he cannot read. He asks your pardon, he truly does (he is very slow of speech, this tramp, and he looks in a bewildered way all round the prospect while he talks to you), but all of us shold do as we wold be done by, and he'll take it kind, if you'll put a power man in the right road fur to jine his eldest son as has broke his leg bad in the masoning, and is in this heere Orspit'l as is wrote down by Squire Pouncerby's own hand as wold not tell a lie fur no man. He then produces from under his dark frock (being always very slow and perplexed) a neat but worn old leather purse, from which he takes a scrap of paper. On this scrap of paper is written, by Squire Pouncerby, of the Grove, "Please to direct the

Bearer, a poor but very worthy man, to the Sussex County Hospital, near Brighton "—a matter of some difficulty at the moment, seeing that the request comes suddenly upon you in the depths of Hertfordshire. The more you endeavour to indicate where Brighton is—when you have with the greatest difficulty remembered—the less the devoted father can be made to comprehend, and the more obtusely he stares at the prospect ; whereby, being reduced to extremity, you recommend the faithful parent to begin by going to St. Albans, and present him with half-a-crown. It does him good, no doubt, but scarcely helps him forward, since you find him lying drunk that same evening in the wheelwright's sawpit under the shed where the felled trees are, opposite the sign of the Three Jolly Hedgers.[1]

The young fellows who trudge along barefoot, five or six together, their boots slung over their shoulders, their shabby bundles under their arms, their sticks newly-cut from some roadside wood, are not eminently prepossessing, but are much less objectionable. There is a tramp fellowship among them. They always go at a fast swing—though they generally limp too—and there is invariably one of the company who has much ado to keep up with the rest. They generally talk about horses, and any other means of locomotion than walking : or, one of the company relates some recent experiences of the road— which are always disputes and difficulties. As for example. "So as I'm a standing at the pump in the market, blest if there don't come up a Beadle, and he ses, 'Mustn't stand here,' he ses. 'Why not ?' I ses. 'No beggars allowed in this town,' he ses. 'Who's a beggar?' I ses. 'You are,' he ses. 'Who ever see *me* beg ? Did *you* ?' I ses. 'Then you're a tramp,' he ses. 'I'd rather be that than a Beadle,' I ses." (The company express great approval.) "'Would you ?' he ses to me. 'Yes, I would,' I ses to him. 'Well,' he ses, 'anyhow, get out of this town.' 'Why, blow your little town !' I ses, 'who wants to be in it? Wot does your dirty little town mean by comin' and stickin' itself in the road to anywhere ? Why don't you get a shovel and a barrer, and clear your town out o' people's way ?'" (The company expressing the highest approval and laughing aloud, they all go down the hill.)—*All the Year Round,* June 16, 1850.

THE PATTERER. THE SCREEVER. BEGGAR STREET SELLERS.
1851.
From " London Labour and the London Poor," by Henry Mayhew.

Mr. Henry Mayhew in his *Magnum opus, London Labour and the London Poor,* published in 1851, gives amongst a multitude of other illustrations of the dodges of the vagrant class the following characteristic instances :—

It is to be supposed that, in country districts, where there are no streets, the patterer (street orator) is obliged to call at the houses. As they are mostly without the hawker's licence, and sometimes find wet linen before it is lost, the rural districts are not fond of their visits ; and there are generally two or three persons in a village reported to be " gammy," that is (unfavourable). If a patterer has been " crabbed," that is (offended at) any of the " cribbs " (houses) he mostly chalks a signal on or near the door. I give one or two instances.

◇ " Bone," meaning good.
▽ " Cooper'd," spoiled by the imprudence of some other patterer.
☐ " Gammy," likely to have you taken up.
⊙ " Flummut," sure of a month in quod.

In most lodging-houses there is an old man who is the guide to every " walk " in the vicinity, and who can tell every house, on every round, that is " good for

---

[1] This genus of tramp agrees with Harman's description of the Rogue in 1567. See p. 597.

a cold 'tater." In many cases there is over the kitchen mantle-piece a map of the district, dotted here and there with memorandums of failure or success. . . .

Two hawkers (pals) go together, but separate when they enter a village, one taking each side of the road, and selling different things ; and, so as to inform each other as to the character of the people at whose houses they call, they chalk certain marks on their door-posts :

⌒ means "Go on. *I* have called here ; don't *you* call—it's no go."

⌒+ means "Stop—you may call here ; they want" (for instance) "what *you* sell, though not what *I* sell ;" or else, "They had no change when I was there, but may have it now ;" or, "If they don't buy, at least they'll treat you civilly."

⊃- on a corner house or a sign-post means, "I went this way ;" or "Go on in this direction.

⊃+ on a corner-house or sign-post means, "Stop—don't go any further in this direction."

⊙ as before explained, means "danger."

OF THE DIFFERENT GRADES OF PATTERERS.

I will endeavour to sketch a few of the most renowned "performers" on this theatre of action. By far the most illustrious is "Nicholas A——," a name well known to the whole cadging fraternity as a *real* descendant from Bamfylde Moore Carew, and the "prince of lurkers" and patterers for thirty years past. . . . Scarcely was he out of his teens, when he honoured the sister country with his visits and his depredations.

This man's ingenuity was then taxed as to the next move, so he thought it expedient to *tax* somebody else. He went with his "pal" to a miscellaneous repository, where they bought a couple of old ledgers—useful only as wastepaper—a bag to hold money, two ink-bottles, &c. Thus equipped, they waited on the farmers of the district, and exhibited a "fakement" (forged document) setting forth parliamentary authority for imposing a tax upon the geese ! They succeeded to admiration, and weeks elapsed before the hoax was discovered. The coolness of thus assuming legislatorial functions, and being at the same time the executive power, has rarely been equalled. . . . .

I will give an account of the pretended missionary proceedings of a man, well known to the vagrant fraternity as "Chelsea George." . . . .

After a career of incessant "lurking" and deceit, Chelsea George left England, and remained abroad, writes my informant, four or five years. . . . .

Some time after his return to England, and while pursuing the course of a "high-flyer" (genteel beggar), he met with an interruption to his pursuits which induced him to alter his plan without altering his behaviour. The newspapers of the district, where he was then located, had raised before the eye and mind of the public, what the "patterers" of his class proverbially call a "stink,"— that is, had opened the eyes of the unwary to the movements of 'Chelsea George ;' and although he ceased to renew his appeals from the moment he heard of the notice of him, his appearance was so accurately described that he was captured and committed to Winchester jail as a rogue and vagabond. The silent system was not then in vogue, consequently there existed no barrier to mutual intercourse between prisoners, with all its train of conscience-hardening tendencies. . . . .

Chelsea George had by this time scraped acquaintance with two fellowprisoners—Jew Jem and Russian Bob. The former in "quod" (prison) for "pattering" (holding forth) as a "converted Jew," the latter for obtaining money under equally false, though less theological, pretences.

Liberated about one time, this trio laid their heads together,—and the result was a plan to evangelize, or rather victimize, the inhabitants of the collier villages in Staffordshire and the adjoining counties. To accomplish this purpose, some novel and imposing representation must be made, both to lull suspicion and give the air of piety to the plan, and disinterestedness to the agents by whom it was carried out.

George and his two fellow-labourers were "square-rigged"—that is, well-dressed. Something, however, must be done to colour up the scene, and make the appeal for money touching, unsuspected, and successful. Just before the time to which I allude, a missionary from Sierra Leone had visited the larger towns of the district in question, while the inhabitants of the surrounding hamlets had been left in ignorance of the "progress of missions in Africa and the East." George and his comrades thought it would be no great harm at once to enlighten and fleece this scattered and anxious population. The plan was laid in a town of some size and facility. They "raised the wind" to an extent adequate to some alteration of their appearances, and got bills printed to set forth the merits of the cause. The principal actor was Jew Jem, a converted Israelite, with "reverend" before his name, and half the letters of the alphabet behind it. He had been in all the islands of the South Sea, on the coast of Africa, all over Hindostan, and half over the universe; and after assuring the villagers of Torryburn that he had carried the Gospel to various dark and *uninhabited* parts of the earth, he introduced Russian Bob (an Irishman who had, however, been in Russia) as his worthy and self-denying colleague, and Chelsea George as the first-fruits of their ministry—as one who had left houses and land, wife and children, and taken a long and hazardous voyage to show Christians in England that their sable brethren, children of one common Parent, were beginning to cast their idols to the moles and to the bats. Earnest was the gaze and breathless the expectation with which the poor deluded colliers of Torryburn listened to this harangue; and as argument always gains by illustration, the orator pulled out a tremendous black doll, bought for a "flag" (fourpence) of a retired rag-merchant, and dressed up in Oriental style. This, Jew Jem assured the audience, was an idol brought from Murat in Hindostan. He presented it to Chelsea George for his worship and embraces. The convert indignantly repelled the insinuation, pushed the idol from him, spat in its face, and cut as many capers as a dancing-bear. The trio at this stage of the performances began "puckering" (talking privately) to each other in murdered French, dashed with a little Irish; after which the missionaries said that their convert (who had only a few words of English) would now profess his faith. All was attention as Chelsea George came forward. He stroked his beard, put his hand in his breast to keep down his dickey (false shirt front), and turning his eyes upwards, said : "I believe in Desus Tist—dlory to 'is 'oly Name!"

This elicited some loud "amens" from an assemblage of nearly 1,000 persons, and catching the favourable opportunity, a "school of pals," appointed for the purpose, went round and made the collection. Out of the abundance of their credulity and piety the populace contributed sixteen pounds! The mission-party and their "pals" took the train to Manchester, and as none of them were teetotallers, the proceeds of their imposition did not last long.

OF THE "SCREEVERS," OR WRITERS OF BEGGING-LETTERS AND PETITIONS.

It is not uncommon in extensive districts—say for instance, a section of a county taking in ten or a dozen townships—for a school of lurkers to keep a secretary and remit his work and his pay at the same time. In London this functionary is generally paid by commission, and sometimes partly in food, beer, and tobacco. The following is a fair estimate of the scale of charges :—

	s.	d.
Friendly letter	0	6
Long ditto	0	9
Petition	1	0

		s.	d.
Ditto, with ream monekurs (genuine signatures)	. .	1	6
Ditto, with gammy monekurs (forged names)	. .	2	6
Very "heavy" (dangerous)	.	3	0
Manuscript for a broken-down author .	. . .	10	0
Part of a play for ditto	.	7	6

To this I may add the prices of other articles in the begging line :—

		s.	d.
Loan of one child, without grub	.	0	9
Two ditto	.	1	0
Ditto, with grub and Godfrey's Cordial .	. . .	0	9
If out after twelve at night, for each child, extra .	.	0	2
For a school of children, say half a dozen	. . .	2	6
Loan of any garment, per day	.	0	2
Going as a pal to vindicate any statement	. . .	1	0

Such is an outline, open to circumstantial variation, of the pay received for the sort of accommodation required.

There is a very important species of "lurking" or "screeving" which has not yet been alluded to.

It is well known that in the colliery districts an explosion of fire-damp frequently takes place, when many lives are lost, and the men who escape are often so wounded as to render amputation of a leg or arm the only probable means of saving them from the grave. Of course the accident, with every particular as to date and locality, goes the round of the newspapers. Such an event is a sort of God-send to the begging-letter writer. If he is anything of a draughtsman so much the better. He then procures a sheet of vellum, and heads it with a picture of an explosion, and exhibiting men, boys, and horses up in the air, and a few nearer the ground, minus a head, a leg, or an arm; with a back-ground of women tearing their hair, and a few little girls crying. Such a "fakement," professionally filled up and put into the hands of a professional lurker, will bring the "amanuensis," or "screever," two guineas at least, and the proceeds of such an expedition have in many cases averaged £60 per week.

Of the Beggar Street-Sellers.

In a few instances the street-sellers of small articles of utility are also the manufacturers. . . . . Some few profess to be the makers of their commodities, solely with the view of enlisting sympathy, and thus either selling the trifles they carry at an enormous profit, or else of obtaining alms.

An inmate of one of the low lodging-houses has supplied me with the following statement:—"Within my recollection," says my informant, "the great branch of trade among these worthies was the sale of sewing-cotton, either in skeins or on reels. In the former case, the article cost the 'lurkers' about 8d. per pound; one pound would produce thirty skeins, which, sold at one penny each, or two for three-halfpence, produced a heavy profit. The lurkers could mostly dispose of three pounds per day; the article was of course damaged, rotten, and worthless."

The mode of sale consisted in the "lurkers" calling at the several houses in a particular district, and representing themselves as Manchester cotton-spinners out of employ. Long tales, of course, were told of the distresses of the operatives, and of the oppression of their employers; these tales had for the most part been taught them at the padding ken (lodging-house) by some old and experienced dodger of "the school;" and if the spokesman could patter (talk) well, a much larger sum was frequently obtained in direct alms than was reaped by the sale.

Cotton on reels was—except to the purchaser—a still better speculation;

the reels were large, handsomely mounted, and displayed in bold relief such inscriptions as the following :—

PIKE'S
PATENT COTTON.
120 YARDS.

The reader, however, must divide the "120 yards," here mentioned, by 12, and then he will arrive at something like the true secret as to the quantity ; for the surface only was covered by the thread.

The cotton lurk is now "cooper'd" (worn out) ; a more common dodge—and, of course, only an excuse for begging—is to envelope a packet of "warranted" needles, or a few inches of "real Honiton lace" in an envelope, with a few lines to the "Lady of the House," or a printed bill, setting forth the misery of the manufacturers, and the intention of the parties leaving the "fakement" to presume to call for an answer in a few hours.

STATEMENT OF A BEGGAR.

"Fits" are now bad, and "paralytics" are no better. The *lucifer lurk* seems getting up though. I don't mean the selling, but the dropping them in the street as if by accident. It's a great thing with the children ; but no go with the old 'uns. I'll tell you of another lurk : a woman I know sends out her child with a quarter of an ounce of tea and half a quarter of sugar, and the child sits on a door-step crying, and saying, if questioned, that she was sent out for tea and sugar, and a boy snatched the change from her, and threw the tea and sugar in the gutter. The mother is there, like a stranger, and says to the child :—"And was that your poor mother's last shilling, and daren't you go home, poor thing ?" Then there is a gathering—sometimes 18d. in a morning.

A BLIND IMPOSTOR.
1866.
(From *The Times*, 1866.)

There is a middle-aged woman who makes a handsome livelihood by simulating blindness, perambulating the thoroughfares with eyes shut and hands extended, solicitive of alms. Notwithstanding that the face of this woman was positively unctuous with comfortableness and good-feeding, many a copper I at times deposited in her fat hands. Indeed, I should no doubt have gone on contributing to this hour, had I not happened accidentally, when walking one day in a back street, to meet her with her eyes open, and evidently seeing perfectly. The next time I found her begging I could not restrain my indignation. "You old humbug !" I said ; "you know you are no more blind than I am !" Her answer was perfect (with a sardonic grin) : "Well, sir, and ain't that a blessing to be very thankful for !" I was speechless. The argument and the audacity were alike confounding.

CONFESSIONS OF AN OLD ALMSGIVER.
1871.

From the "Confessions of an Old Almsgiver," by J. Hornsby Wright.

The late Mr. Hornsby Wright was a gentleman of fortune, whose name was a synonym for high-minded, sympathetic, and self-denying benevolence.

"On one occasion, returning from my rounds, I found the basement of my establishment boiling over with beatific excitement. A quietly-dressed and modest-mannered female, pale of face and with a seeming cough, had been found sitting in the sweep. She begged not, but rather apologized for the liberty she had taken in staggering in and sinking down on the ground when seized with sudden faintness. They had placed her in a chair just within the side-door, and brought a whole fraternity of smelling-bottles into requisition. Invited to take a little brandy, she respectfully declined, asking for a little water instead. She accepted with thanks a small piece of bread, of which, however, she seemed too ill to eat much. To myself the apparent invalid stated that she had come from some place on the North' Kent line to see a married sister at Kilburn, who she had little doubted would have helped her in a sudden emergency; but on reaching her sister's late home found they had gone away, the people in the house not knowing whither; and that she had spent her last sixpence on an omnibus to these parts, being too ill to walk.

I directed some bread to be given her, adding that the gardener (old enough to be her grandfather) should, she being so weak, accompany her to London Bridge, pay for a ticket for her, and see her safe into the train, so that she might promptly reach home and be able to bring her case before those who knew her personally.

She entreated me to put myself to no such trouble on her account, but, I persisting, off she went with her aged escort. In a very short space he returned out of breath with astonishment, and exclaiming, "Well, sir, this is a rum start. We got into a Atlas 'bus, and when half way down the Wellington Road she sings out to the conductor, 'Here, you sir: you let me out! This old fool's to pay for me.' And with that she bolted out and ran off to a couple of young chaps waiting at the corner of Circus Road." . . .

An affecting case of the hunger and thirst after charity which unorganised almsgiving begets was brought to my notice many years ago, in fact on my first settling in my present neighbourhood, by a deceased City Missionary. His statement in substance was this :—

"In a small court in his missionary district there once lived several hard-working and, on the whole, sober families. A room in it at length fell vacant, which was let to a dissolute couple who lived on the charitable, chiefly by means of begging-letters. They, of course, lived far better than the rest of the court, indeed, as the phrase goes, like 'fighting cocks.' Two maiden ladies, supposed sisters, visited them, and often relieved them. By degrees one after another of the remaining families got discontented with their condition, and thought they might as well try and get a slice of these ladies' bounty. The usual dodges were adopted, including pledging their things and cultivating rags and wretchedness. They succeeded but too well. In vain the City Missionary tried to waylay these ladies, in order to give them a private caution. If he attempted to address them, off they shot, as if they thought he had small-pox. Their movements, indeed, were wholly eccentric. They came and vanished like shadows,—no, they did not vanish like them, for shadows leave nothing behind them : they left moral desolation in their wake. No band of locusts could have done their work more effectually; for the fruit of their labours was that not an undemoralized household remained in that luckless court. Idleness, drink, vice in various forms, with rejection of missionary visitation once welcomed, or at least accepted, at length took the place of the opposite habits previously cherished. Once more had that kind, self-denying, conscientious evil-doer, unorganized Charity, been sowing by mistake a curse for a blessing."

THE THREE-CARD MAN.
1872.

From "Rogues and Vagabonds of the Racecourse," by Alfred H. Toulmin.

Next, perhaps, to the roulette man, though considerably lower in the social scale of racecourse rogues and vagabonds, comes the three-card man. Not that he does less harm; truly he may only gather to his pockets, ever yawning to receive his dupes' all, but a very small percentage of the gains accrued by his more fortunate and more aristocratic brother swindler, yet, for all that, the class on which, as a rule, he levies his black-mail can less afford to lose their shillings and half-crowns than can the victims sacrificed on the altar of roulette their sovereigns or five-pound notes.

It would be doing the three-card man a gross injustice not to allow that, as a scoundrel, he has not his match, more especially in the versatility of his genius ; and just as great minds are apt to grow weary when concentrated on one single object, so will he of the lowest order of card-sharper while away an hour or so before the races begin by playfully knocking children down, and abstracting the coppers that should have been spent in gingerbread, or invested in independent file-firing for nuts. Then, whilst more ordinary beings are engaged in such commonplace pursuits as the consumption of lobster salad and champagne, he will, in his errant fancy, help himself to coats and race-glasses : but it is during a well-contested race, or an exciting finish, that he is most dreaded amongst the carriages.

He also finds an agreeable change in the purse-trick. Watch how indefatigably he rushes frantically about with his stool, on which he stands irresistibly reminding one of a naughty boy at school, conjuring the bystanders to accept his " *solemn word*, the *word of a gentleman*, that there are two 'arf-crowns and a sixpence in the purse, and all for a shilling," concluding his eloquent harangue somewhat in this style : " If they ain't all in, give me in charge—take me before the magistrate—put me into prison—brand-me-as-an-impostor-for-obtaining-money-under-false-pretences-from-the-working-classes,"—all this in a breath.

Pseudo-Missionaries.
1872.
A Personal Experience.

An individual, who, following the example of the Reverend Giles Jowls, the illuminated cobbler, had dubbed himself Reverend,[1] and who had also appointed himself to the dual office of President and Secretary of a pseudo-charity, called the " National Bible and Clothing Society," was summoned to the Marlborough Street Police Court in July, 1872, for collecting money under false pretences. He had received about £1,000 in subscriptions, and was able to prove that he had expended about £10 in Bibles and £2 in clothing—the charge therefore fell to the ground, as the embezzlement of charitable funds is unfortunately not an offence against the law. This man, who was a journeyman tailor, alleged that he took the title of " Reverend " " because he was a member of the Baptist community," though he confessed that it was not a common practice on the part of the members of that community. Having suddenly dropped the title he was asked why he did so, to which his reply was, " that he had come to the conclusion that no one was Reverend but the Lord." Two years afterwards this man was convicted on another charge.

A Deaf and Dumb Impostor.
1874.
A Personal Experience.

In January, 1874, a man named *Walter Scott* was brought before the Mayor of Hertford charged with begging under the pretence of being deaf and dumb. He had circulated a written appeal, in which he set forth that he was a hairdresser by trade, and had lost his hearing and the sight of one eye by lightning, and had not been able to speak since. Evidence was given to shew that he had obtained a good deal of money in the town, and it transpired in the course of the inquiry that on presenting his letter at one house, the occupier after looking at it, said to the prisoner, " What's this you say ? " Upon which the prisoner put his hand to his head and exclaimed, " I'm dumb, ma'am." This, it need hardly be said, sufficed to convict him.

---

[1] This species of impostor is a lineal descendant of the *Frater* described on pp. 593, 598.

The American Tramp.
1878.
From " The Tramp : his Tricks, Tallies, and Tell-Tales, by an Ex-tramp."
(New York, 1878.)

We soon found ourselves, under the guidance of Coal-tar George, in the middle of a large camp, surrounded by trees. Here, on all sides, were rude shanties or tents made out of the limbs of trees, leaves, grass and rags, some little more than kennels, others large enough to enable a man to stand upright ; and one, a tent twelve feet square, furnished with a table, a chair and a leather valise, I learned was the quarters of the Perfessor, or the Fillofficer, as he was sometimes called.

" We better 'nitiate them right away," suggested Coal-tar George. The word was passed round, producing immediately a considerable flutter throughout the camp. Much to my relief, I found they had selected Chivvy as the first to go through the ordeal. Chivvy looked *pert* and *sassy*, and seemed to enjoy the prospect of a *lark*, as he called it, hugely.

The whole gang having formed a ring around the enclosure, Coal-tar George led Chivvy into the centre, and placed before him three stools. On one stool he laid a motley collection of ugly looking knives, on another a handful of ropes with slip nooses at the end, and on the third a bundle of rough clubs. Now about a dozen of the gang, whose faces were striped with black, red and white paint, stepped forward, and Chivvy, under the direction of Coal-tar George, handed each of them a club. On receiving this, every one in turn uttered a short grunt, struck an attitude like the stage assassin, and commenced flourishing it over Chivvy's head. When the whole were supplied with sticks, they struck another attitude, with the clubs held aloft, and so remained as rigid as statues, while the little cockney, now beginning to look rather pale, repeated after Coal-tar George, sentence for sentence, the initiatory oath as follows : " I solemnly swear, by my bones, my blood and vitals, in the presence of these brothers now around me assembled, that I will never betray the brotherhood ; that I will never tell anything that may occur in this or any other camp of the brotherhood ; that I will never betray a brother ; that I will never lie to a brother ; that I will never rob a brother, but that I will always aid, counsel and cheer a brother ; that I will share with him when he is in need ; I will comfort him when he is sick ; I will aid him when he is in trouble, and will fight for him when he is in danger. If I fail in this my solemn oath, I hope the blood may dry in my veins, and my bones rot in my flesh ; that I may tramp bare-footed through New Jersey till I am a hundred years old ; that every man's promise made to me may be broken ; that everything I love may learn to hate me ; that my food and drink may turn to muck in my mouth ; that all children may curse me, and that I may die alone. I also swear that if any brother turns traitor, I will aid, to the utmost of my ability, in bringing him to punishment, and carry out, without shirking, all orders of the duly elected officers of the brotherhood, to that end, whether by fire or water, club, knife or halter."

Here the twelve painted Tramps gave a grunt, a long groan changing into a roar, flung their clubs in a heap on the ground, and resumed their places in the circle.

After a few moments' pause, the twelve men, who were called " Executioners," again stepped forward, and Chivvy was instructed to hand them each a knife, when the same ceremony was performed as with the clubs, varied only by placing the knives across the novitiate's throat, instead of over his head. Then the halters were placed around his neck, and the ceremony repeated for a third time. After this, Coal-tar George placed a black bag over the novitiate's head, and tied it round his neck, while the twelve executioners

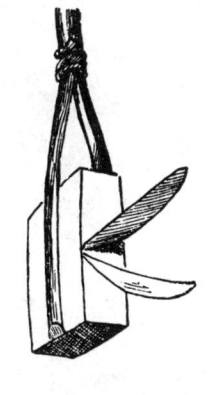

INSTRUMENT FOR REMOVING CLOTHES-PINS

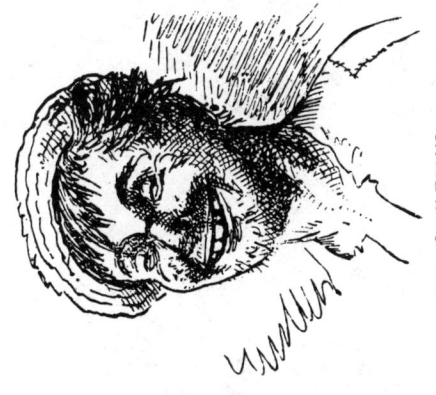

THE JOLLY TRAMP

THE POTATO HOOK

THE BULLY TRAMP

marched round him, each muttering in his right ear as he passed, first the words, " Remember the club ! " then, on the second round, " Remember the knife ! " and on the third round, " Remember the rope ! "

The bag was now removed, and Chivvy escorted in solemn procession to the tent of the " Perfessor," where he was instructed in the different grips, signs and passwords of the brotherhood.

Here I must hold up a moment to describe this singular character. The " Perfessor " was a man of no little importance in the gang. He was about five feet ten in height, had a large, well-developed head, wore his gray hair and beard long, and a patch over his right eye. His rusty black coat hung down below his knees, his pantaloons were tucked into his boots, and he carried a hooked stick under his arm. If you add to this picture a long-limbed, vicious-looking dog, which always slouched at his heels, you will have a good general idea of the " Perfessor."

The grip consisted in pressing the nail of the thumb in the back of the other person's hand, and was answered by the other person taking your middle and fore-fingers in his hand and squeezing them firmly. The sign consisted in scratching the chin with the right hand, and then holding the lobe of the right ear between the finger and thumb of the same hand ; the recognition of this sign was performed by placing the clenched fist of either hand, right or left, over the heart. The signal of danger, such as the presence or approach of some suspicious person, was made by pressing the back of the head with either hand, and putting the lips to the back of the same hand. The general password was as follows :

QUESTION : " What might you be ? "
ANSWER : " A Rover."
QUESTION : " What kind of a Rover ? "
ANSWER : " A Ragged Rover."
QUESTION : " Any color ? "
ANSWER : " Red."

Our gang was called The Ragged Red Rovers, or The Rovers for short. There are numerous other gangs all over the country, such as The Alligators, The Bang Woos, Billy Dubb's Guard, The Good Time Comings, The Help Yourselves, and numerous others.

Each gang has a certain set of signs, or hieroglyphics, which they mark up, with chalk, on houses, fences, trees, &c., as a guide to others of their gang who may come the same road. Our signs, of which the " Perfessor" handed us each a copy, were as represented in the annexed engravings.

The "Perfessor" explained to us the different punishments inflicted by the brotherhood, ranging from death, in aggravated cases of treachery, down to a severe reprimand. Some of the tortures were very curious, and not unfrequently invented for the occasion by the executioners, or the Tycoon or Tyke. One consisted in sewing the culprit up in a sack, with or without thorns ; another, in stripping him naked, and chasing him through the woods with rods ; another was to hook the victim by the nose, after binding him hand and foot, and to make him stand on tip-toe for a certain length of time. Again, another was to bind a man's hands and feet together, seat him on thorns, and set all the women to work to tell him unpleasant things about his personal appearance, his previous life, his future fate, his moral and intellectual faculties, his friends and relatives, &c., &c. Still another was to dress a man in woman's attire, and put him in Coventry.

Two of their punishments we had an opportunity of witnessing on the very day of our initiation, they being expedited, I fancy, for our especial benefit and admonition.

As soon as my initiation was over, which occurred immediately after poor little Chivvy was put through his particular course of sprouts, the " Perfessor " took us kindly by the hands, and said : " And so, gentlemen, you have joined our ragamuffin band? Well, you will find us a pretty amiable lot of vagabonds, with a good deal more kindness and charity among us (so long as you are true to the order) than exists in most church congregations; not, perhaps, quite so much of the *suaviter in modo*, but a good deal more of the *fortiter in re*. I can hardly say that we are an industrial organization, though many of us would work if we could get work to do. I am not one of the number, however. I am constitutionally tired. Nothing pleases me more than to see industry in others. I can sit and contemplate such a spectacle for days together; but as for myself—well, my tastes are different. Do you gentlemen like to work?"

We told him we had no objection to it, provided we could thereby make a living.

"Ah! well then," he continued, " we shall have to classify you under the head of Bees. We have two orders among us, you must know—Butterflies and Bees: the Bees work when they can; the idle vagabonds call themselves Butterflies—a little bit of a misnomer, by the way, for the butterfly is a harmless, beautiful object, flitting about from flower to flower, delighting the eyes of all beholders—whilst our poor fellows, I fear, do not attract any very general admiration by their loveliness, and play the devil's own mischief too, sometimes, with the farmers' chicken-roosts and potato patches; however, they encourage the raising of a very fine breed of watch dogs, and, so far, do some good in the world. But excuse me, I think I have not explained to you our form of government, which I will now proceed to do. It is very simple, and will detain you only a few minutes. The brotherhood is governed by an autocrat called the Tyke, or Tycoon, who is at present, as he has been for the last year and a half, Coal-tar George. He is the executive, and his word is absolute, subject only to the veto of the non-executive Judge, which latter position I now fill myself. Both these officers are elected by popular vote, and can be deposed at any moment by a majority vote. The brotherhood may call for an election, or the twelve executioners may at any time order one to be held; but we have very little trouble or grumbling, and not much punishment, although this evening we have one case—a rather aggravated one, I am sorry to say. A brother refused aid to the famished wife and child of a member of the order, and was afterwards detected in a saloon spending money for beer. I have talked to him, and I do not think, at the time, he fully realised the necessity of the case, and he is now quite penitent; still, his punishment will be severe.

I found the "Perfessor" to be the organizer, the systematizer, the recorder—in fact, the brains of the brotherhood. In his valise he had a nice collection of books, some legal, and others books of reference; he had also maps, mathematical instruments, and writing materials. He had a large map of one whole neighbourhood, enlarged from a county map, whereon was marked every house for miles round, with numerous comments, derived chiefly from information given him by members of the order, who all reported to him on their return to camp. The comments would run something like the following, each house being distinguished by a combination of numbers or letters, thus:—

X2.—Family lost a son in the war. Females feel kindly towards old soldiers, particularly those who marched with Sherman to the sea; all the better if wounded, as old man likes to set them to work.

VV.—Old woman has a son out West; good thing to say you are making your way to Indiana.

P6.—Ugly bull-dog. Family pious. Ask for reading matter; say your father was a minister. Don't ask, and you may get something.

BB.—Old man has been swindled out of a lot of money by relatives. Tell some kind of story. Good stock of poultry. Chicken-house in rear easily got at. Dog fat and lazy.

DD8.—Shiftless; leave things round loose. Can't work on their feelings.
189.—Always can get a job of work here, and a square meal. No good for Butterflies.
SS.—Old man and wife; old man goes to the tavern about seven; blazing drunk by ten; old woman deaf.
VL.—Man and wife quarrel. Abuse husband to wife; abuse wife to husband.
TTT.—Don't like long faces; be jolly.
YO.—Down on men who are cheerful.
T31.—Safe with children; baby if possible.
222.—Old chap subject to biles; bile him.

The "Perfessor" would mark out routes on this map for different Tramps, and often give them rough copies of the line they were to follow. He had several maps, extending over a large section of the country, and containing thousands of homes. His memory was wonderful, and his knowledge of the peculiarities of hundreds of families something marvellous. He was in correspondence with a grand central lodge somewhere out West; but the name of the place I could never ascertain, for that secret was guarded with jealous care. I learned, however, that the Tramp organization was something immense, and that their organization is political and revolutionary. They have nothing in common with the Socialists, whose chief object is to organize and stimulate labor, and who are bitterly opposed to all loafers, tramping or stationary; but the tramp's object is, when any trouble takes place, to aid the revolutionary party, strikers or what not, and reap a large harvest of plunder.

I must here draw attention to one fact which very few people seem to understand—or won't understand—and that is, that every poor fellow who is ragged and hungry, and looking for work, is by no means necessarily a Tramp in the invidious sense of the word. Thousands of them are good honest fellows, who would rejoice at obtaining employment. I suppose, of course, the most of well-to-do people know this; but they prefer to lump them all together, and by howling at them bad names—Tramp, loafer, thief, &c.—salve their own conscience for not striving to better their condition, as they ought to do, and as they will bitterly rue not doing at no very distant day. For the Tramps are a fearful power in this country at present, under a most perfect system of organization, and ready at any moment, when the opportunity occurs, to hurl their power at the throat of organized authority. If the supine and prosperous citizen could only hear, as I have done, from thousands of lips, the glorious pictures of riot and anarchy, painted in the rudest of rude word-colours, they would not sleep quite so calmly in their beds as they now do.

But to proceed with the "Perfessor's" functions. One of his offices was to devise numerous disguises and make-ups, like a property man or costumer in a theatre. In these duties he was assisted by a subordinate called "the Artist." This artist had paints, and patches, and odds and ends of various kinds, with which he could get you up a very fair imitation of a man recovering from the small-pox or yellow fever. Men got up in this style would be sent to families known to be nervous on the subject of infectious disease, who would pay liberally to induce so dangerous a visitor to leave their threshold. With the aid of a huckle-berry, or a currant, and a little collodion, he could counterfeit the most venomous looking boil, with which he would ornament Tramps wishing to excite commiseration and avoid work. With the same materials he could imitate scars and wounds for sham soldiers. He had a wardrobe of a few old soldier and sailor clothes, and rags of the most picturesque description. Also some fine suits, with the full black rig of a minister; these were used on special occasions for special purposes, and were the property of the brotherhood. He had, too, various implements useful in picking and stealing. One, a belt with hooks, for poultry, to be worn round the waist, and under the dress of a female tramp.

Another little instrument made out of a cork, or piece of wood, in one side of which was fastened a barbed nail, in the other a feather and a long string. A Tramp, concealed on one side of a fence, would dart this at a heap of potatoes on the other side, harpoon a potato, and drag it within reach with the string. This, of course, could be used on apples, turnips, and various other small game.

The Ragsooker was an instrument attached to the end of a long pole for removing clothes-pins from the lines, and afterwards dragging the released clothes over the fence; this will be better understood by a glance at the annexed diagram.

He had a kind of armour made of strips of wood, covered with padding, to protect the arms and legs against dogs; these were generally charged with cayenne pepper and snuff to choke the animals. When attacked in front by a fierce dog, the Tramp would present his left arm, covered with this armour, which the creature would seize in his teeth, whereupon the Tramp would at once pound him over the head with a short club, or piece of iron. This practice was found very effective on night excursions for chickens or harness, when the foragers were apt to be disturbed by the watch-dog. Whenever they could, however, they tried to make away with the dog beforehand, by means of medicated meat balls, of which the "Perfessor" had several kinds. The difficulty in this case was that the poison often did not act quickly enough, and it would not answer to poison a dog before the owner went to bed, as the discovery that such a thing had been done would naturally excite suspicion,

They had an instrument for muzzling pigs, to prevent their squealing, and various others, which my space will not permit me to describe.

Each Tramp had a peculiar character to perform; he was cast, like an actor, for a particular part best suited to his appearance and ability. There was:—

> The meek Tramp, with children,
> The bully Tramp,
> The ragged Tramp,
> The respectable Tramp,
> The Tramp who asks for work,
> The unwholesome Tramp,
> The lubberly Tramp,
> The abject Tramp,
> The jolly Tramp,
> Mrs. Tramp,
> And many others,

I do not mean to say that these men all *played* parts as actors do—not at all. The "Perfessor" seeing the natural character of each man in the brotherhood, only coached him artistically how to make the most of his natural disadvantages. Here, for example, was Sam Discoll, the jolly Tramp. The "Perfessor" put him through a regular course of training; taught him many pert sayings, jokes and complimentary speeches for farmers' wives and daughters, such, " Ah, mum, I had a wife once, and a good wife, too, and nearly as handsome as you, though you'd hardly think it of a poor Tramp like me;" or, "Ah, well! a smile from you'd be as good as a square meal for a man any day;" or, "I caught a bad cold last night, ma'am, sleeping in a feld with the gate open and the grass not aired," and such like stuff. Sam had been a deck-hand on a North River barge, and once thought he might become President of the United States; he now hopes he may have a clam-cart of his own some day. There was Bill Gouch; the "Perfessor" saw he had the natural talent for a bully, and gently trained his mind to distinguish the right objects for bullying; but still he would make mistakes now and then, and come home with a black eye in consequence.

THE UNWHOLESOME TRAMP

MRS. TRAMP

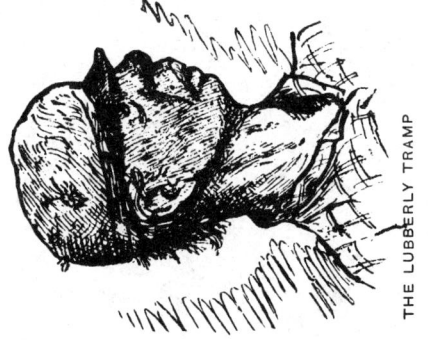

THE LUBBERLY TRAMP

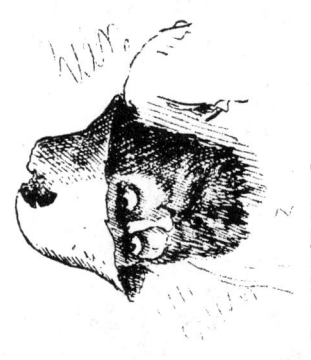

THE ABJECT TRAMP

Sharkey, the lubberly Tramp, was taught to whine; but he was a difficult subject to make much of, having no special gift for anything, honest or dishonest, except robbing small children, which the "Perfessor" would never tolerate.

George Shime, the unwholesome Tramp, was very effective in the smallpox and yellow fever line of business, and the "Perfessor" instructed him how to counterfeit all the systems of various disorders, including a hacking cough and Saint Vitus's dance. He had once been assistant to an onion and potato butcher, and had no idea where he was drifting, either here or hereafter.

Abner Howe, the abject Tramp, was taught a tale of suffering and misfortune, dates and places all complete, that would have melted the heart of a fashionable lady.

Then there was Sarah Rook, Mrs. Tramp, the deserted wife, whose husband had run away and left her with four children, three of whom had died in her arms, while the fourth had done worse, and married a journeyman hatter with tight pantaloons and an incurable taste for drink, a thing Mrs. Tramp could not overlook in any man—though she didn't mind taking three times as much of her share of whisky in camp when she could get it. . . .

The "Perfessor" often told me that there were half a million of tramps all over the country belonging to their organization, who could be concentrated at various points in less than a week.

1886.

What a Beggar Boy Buys.

From the *Echo*, February 15, 1886.

A bright-faced child, giving the name of William Archer, ten years of age, and living at Notting Hill, was charged at Marylebone Police-court on Saturday with begging of foot-passengers at Porchester Road, Bayswater. A constable proved the charge, and informed the Magistrate that the boy had told him that if he did not take home three or four shillings each day he got a good whacking from his parents. The boy, whose head just reached the height of the solicitor's table, made a statement to the officer to the effect that he rarely received less than four shillings as the result of a day's begging, and that he sometimes got as much as ten shillings on a Sunday, his most liberal patrons being foreigners. When asked what he did with the money he said that when he got about four shillings he always "went in" for sausages, vegetables, bread and butter, cake, coffee, and finished up by smoking tobacco. The rest of the money he took home.

Street Begging.

From the *Standard*, March 20, 1886.

For the last four or five years, between eleven and half-past eleven p.m., a woman—pale and, apparently, destitute—has taken her seat on the south steps of St. Martin's Church, and occasionally on a door-step in Pall Mall East. She does not solicit alms, but she nurses a baby about six to twelve months of age, in all weathers. The baby also, apparently, never gets any older. It is not a dummy, but a real baby.

Between the same spot and the south-east corner of the churchyard another woman perambulates at the same hour, pestering everyone to give her something, and as an inducement she thrusts a bunch of dirty artificial flowers under one's nose. This woman is hale and hearty.

The flowers are never renewed. I suppose they stand the east wind better than the baby.

I have spoken to various constables, without result, and I have given the matter up.

When these two women come on duty and when they go off I have no knowledge. I speak of the hour only when I see them.   M.

RICH BEGGARS.

There are multitudes of instances of beggars who, amid squalor, rags and dirt utterly miserable, contrive to amass considerable sums of money. For obvious reasons, they generally conceal their wealth during life, and it is only when the breath is out of their body that the golden hypocrisy is discovered. Usually, the hoarded coins are found sewn up in rags or straw-beds, or otherwise hidden in holes and corners; it is only in a few instances that the beggar ventures to invest his money in a bank. Among the many recorded examples of rich beggars, have been Daniel Eagle, who begged for thirty years in London, and lived in a room which was never entered by any one but himself, and never cleaned during the whole period; after his death, coins to the value of £25 were found there.—Margaret Coles, who died in wretched filth in St. Giles's at the age of 101, and in whose hovel was found £30 in gold and silver, and £10 in copper.—Margaret Everett, an equally squalid beggar, who left £150 behind her.—Esther Davies, who died in London at the advanced age of 103, and who for thirty years had the double chances of a street-beggar and a parish pauper; she left £160 — Mary Wilkinson, beggar and bone-grubber, whose rags of clothing concealed £300 in money.—Alice Bond, who had risen to the dignity of £300 in the funds, besides £50 in guineas, half-guineas, and seven-shilling pieces, and £23 in silver.—Frances Beet, whose bed and rickety furniture yielded a booty of no less than £800. And "Poor Joe all alone," a famous character about a century ago, who wore a long beard, and had not lain in a bed for fifty years; he left £3,000, and with it a will, by which he bequeathed all the money to certain widows and orphans. Foreign countries are not without instances of like kind. Witness the case of Dandon, of Berlin, who died in 1812; he was competent to teach as a professor of languages during the day, and went out begging at night. After his death, 20,000 crowns were found secreted under the floor of his room. He had refused to see a brother for thirty-seven years, because he once sent him a letter without prepaying the postage. This Dandon, however, was an exampler rather of the miser than of the beggar, popularly so considered.

Some beggars have been remarkable quite as much for their eccentricity, as for the amount of money they left behind them. Such was the case with William Stevenson, who died at Kilmarnock on the 17th of July, 1817. Although bred a mason, the greater part of his life was spent as a beggar. About the year 1787, he and his wife separated, making this strange agreement—that whichever of them was the first to propose a reunion, should forfeit £100 to the other. According to the statements in the Scotch newspapers, there is no evidence that they ever saw each other again. In 1815, when about 85 years old, Stevenson was seized with an incurable disease, and was confined to his bed. A few days before his death, feeling his end to be near, he sent for a baker, and ordered twelve dozen burial-cakes, a large quantity of sugared biscuit, and a good supply of wine and spirits. He next sent for a joiner, and instructed him to make a good sound, dry, roomy, "comfortable" coffin. Next he summoned a grave-digger, whom he requested to select a favourable spot in the church-yard of Riccarton, and there dig a roomy and comfortable grave. This done, he ordered an old woman who attended him, to go to a certain nook, and bring him out £9 to pay all these preliminary expenses: assuring her that she was remembered in his will. Shortly after this he died. A neighbour came in to search for his wealth, which had been shrouded in much mystery. In one bag was found large silver pieces, such as dollars and half-dollars, crowns and half-crowns; in a musty heap of rags, was found a collection of guineas and seven-shilling pieces, and in a box were found bonds of various amounts, including one for £300—giving altogether a sum of about £900. A will was also found, bequeathing £20 to the old woman, and most of the remainder to distant relations, setting aside sufficient to give a feast to all the beggars who chose to come and see his body "lie in state." The influx was immense; and after the funeral, all retired to a barn which had been fitted up for the occasion; and there they indulged in revelries but little in accordance with the solemn season of death.—*The Book of Days*, edited by R. Chambers.

A Beggar in Moorfields used daily to have a penny given him by a merchant on his way to the Exchange. The penny was withheld, and the appearance of the merchant manifested his embarrassment and distress. The beggar at length spoke to him, offered him a loan of £500, and another of the same sum if it were required. It re-established his affairs.—*Panorama*, vol. x.

Obituary, 1784. April 23. Was found dead, in his house at Frome, William Thatcher, an old man, who for many years past had subsisted on the charitable benefactions of his neighbours. His success in the begging trade was considerable, as may be perceived by the following inventory of property found in his house at his death: 22*l.* in silver, 2 guineas in gold, 5*l.* in copper, 12 old hats, 14 pair of shoes, 14 pair of stockings, 35 cakes, 2 bushels of morsels of bread, cheese, flesh, &c., &c.—The above has not been long accumulating; for but two years since his house was robbed of the valuables it then contained, which were much more considerable than the above.—*The Gentleman's Magazine*.

Obituary, 1811, March. Aged 90, Edmund Mashiter, alias *Old Honey*, of Bolton, near Lancaster. He had been a beggar 70 years; and was justly entitled to the appellation of *King of the Beggars*. His father was a schoolmaster at Halstead, in Yorkshire, who gave him a good education; but, after his father's death, he preferred the wandering life of a mendicant, and pertinaciously persisted in it; nor could threats or entreaties make him desist, till within the last four years, during which time he had been bed-ridden.—*The Gentleman's Magazine*.

BLANDFORD. *Mendicancy not always Poverty.*—On Tuesday a coroner's inquest was held at the King's Arms Inn, in this town, on the body of an old man named John Collins, a mendicant, who died suddenly at a lodging-house in Back Lane on Thursday afternoon. It appears from the evidence, that the deceased came to the house on Tuesday night, having obtained an order from the Relieving Officer for a bed. He was rather unwell at the time, but seemed better the next day, and slept there again on Wednesday night. He refused to have a medical man, and died very quietly while sitting before the fire. The jury returned a verdict of "Died by the Visitation of God." He is supposed to be between 60 and 70 years of age. This case excited some attention from the fact that, on the deceased's clothes being searched, a Blandford Savings' Bank book was found on him, by which it appears that he had no less a sum than £365 invested in the savings bank. On the 29th of January he drew out £10, but only a few shillings were found on him. It has since been ascertained that he was a native of East Orchard, near this town. His sister has identified him.—*Sherborne, Dorchester, and Taunton Journal*, March 30, 1848.

An Opulent Vagrant.

At the Town Hall, Nottingham, yesterday, James Carrigan was charged with begging the previous night. Prisoner denied that he was begging, and said that he was simply trying to find a person "of the name of Smith." Police-constable Stafford said that the prisoner had three-halfpence in his possession and a Post Office Savings Bank book, showing that the prisoner had £20 10s. in the bank. In reply to the Bench, prisoner said he lodged at 94, Parliament Street, Nottingham, and his money was in the Post Office Savings Bank. He was remanded.—*Echo*, March 13, 1886.

A Wealthy Crossing-sweeper.

John Sullivan, 56, and Kate Sullivan, 50, both Irish, were accused of being concerned together in stealing £32 in gold and 20s. in silver, the money of Mary Blake, a crossing-sweeper, lodging at 19, Paul Street, Lisson Grove. The prosecutrix, a very old woman and very feeble, when asked how old she was said she knew she was over sixty. She swept a crossing by Hyde Park, and near the house of Lord Coleridge. She met with an accident on New Year's Eve and broke her arm, and she was taken to St. Mary's Hospital. When she left home she left thirty yellow sovereigns— (laughter)—in a purse in a drawer, which she locked. She also locked her room-door. At the hospital she gave her clothes, with the keys, to a Mrs. Mahoney, with directions that she was to keep the key of the drawers and to give the room-door key to Mrs. Sullivan, who was her landlady. The prosecutrix, who was most difficult to understand, owing to her broad Irish dialect, and her running on from one point to another, continuing, said she met Mr. Sullivan on reaching home, and he gave her the keys. She at once looked into the drawer and found every farthing gone. She called his attention to the loss of the money, and he said, "Oh dear, oh dear! I don't know anything about it. I knew she" (his wife) "was not up to anything good, because she has been out drinking. Don't make a hurrah * about it. I am sorry for you, but I can't help it." Mrs. Sullivan had left home, and when she returned on the following Friday she (prosecutrix) said nothing to her, as the matter had then been communicated to the police. After that the male prisoner came to her and gave her £2, and told her she must be quiet about the matter. He was an honest man.—Mr. Frith: What's that? Do you say Sullivan is honest?—Prosecutrix: Yes, he is a honest hard-working man—(laughter)—and wouldn't do any one harm. It's not his fault, he said so. (Renewed laughter.) Besides that, he's a teetotaller. He promised to find out who robbed me. Mary Mahoney spoke to receiving the keys from the prosecutrix and handing them to the male prisoner. Detective-sergeant Recard, D Division, said he arrested the defendants on Saturday night. The man said he could not have taken the money as he did not have the keys, but the prosecutrix said she received them from him on returning from the hospital. Witness asked Sullivan if he had any money, and he replied that he had 9s., being the balance of 19s. which he had received as wages. That was all he had. When witness, however, searched the prisoners' room he found concealed in a purse between two beds £6 in gold and 8s. 6d. in silver. In cross-examination, the witness said the man had been in respectable employment for some years, and was an abstainer. Mr. de Rutzen then remanded the defendants.—*Daily Telegraph*, January, 25, 1887.

"Frozen-out" Beggars.

A protracted frost necessarily deranges the lower class of employments in such a city as London, and throws many poor persons into destitution. Just

---

* Erse, *ura, urach,* contention.

as sure as this is the fact, so sure is it that a vast horde of the class who systematically avoid regular work, preferring to live by their wits, simulate the characteristic appearances of distressed labourers, and try to excite the charity of the better class of citizens. Investing themselves in aprons, clutching an old spade, and hoisting, as their signal of distress, a turnip on the top of a pole or rake, they will wend their way through the West-end streets, proclaiming themselves in sepulchral tones as *Frozen-out Gardeners*, or simply calling, "Hall frozen out!" or chanting "We've got no work to do!" The faces of the corps are duly dolorous; but one can nevertheless observe a sharp eye kept on the doers and windows they are passing, in order that if possible they may arrest some female gaze on which to practice their spell of pity. It is alleged on good grounds that the generality of these victims of the frost are impostors, and that their daily gatherings will often amount to double a skilled workman's wages. Nor do they usually discontinue the trade till long after the return of milder airs has liquidated even real claims upon the public sympathy.—*The Book of Days*, edited by R. Chambers.

Beggars' Barns.

From the *Times*, February 23, 1874.

"Sir,—Sixty years ago there was in this small parish (and in most others) a "Beggars' Barn," where travellers were entitled to a night's lodging and a meal gratis. The farmer who happened to live nearest the church was bound to furnish this measure of hospitality to all wayfarers claiming it. When I inquired of the old people still living, who remember the Beggars' Barn here, what a traveller would have done if the farmer had refused him lodging &c., I was informed that he had a right to sleep in the church porch, and that if he did so the farmer would be both censured and fined by his fellow-parishioners in Vestry. A country magistrate, on hearing this statement from an old inhabitant of this village, said he recollected hearing, when he was a boy, his aunt speaking of a woman in their parish, who threatened to bring her bed and place it in the church porch to shame the people, unless certain relief was given her. This, as he said, was an evidence of the prevalence of the idea of a right to lodge in the church porch, and of other curious points in the old system of relieving the poor.

I have a lithograph, or rather an engraving, published by R. Ackermann, 101, Strand, in 1815, of the Beggars' Barn of this parish.

I remain, your obedient servant,
G. H. BILLINGTON.
Chalbury Rectory, Wimborne, Feb. 20.

A Christmas Haymaker.

A repartee, which never loses its reward of applause, is recorded as having been made to old Master Barnard, a shoemaker. A sturdy vagrant was begging at his door one Christmas time, and Master Barnard, thinking that the man was able-bodied enough to work, said, rather indignantly, "No, I've got nothing to give you; a strong, able-bodied man like you ought to get a trade and work at it, as I'm forced to do." "I do work at my trade when I can get work," said the man, "but there's nothing much doing in my trade just now." "Your trade!" said old Barnard. "I wonder what sort of a trade yours is." "I'm a haymaker by trade," said the man, "and my trade's very slack this Christmas time."

The Gypsies.

From "Romano Lavo-lil: word-book of the Romany," by George Borrow, 1874.

Something like the following little anecdote is related by the Gypsies in every part of Continental Europe:—

Beg On, Brother.

A Gypsy brat was once pestering a gentleman to give him a halfpenny. The mother, who was sitting nigh, cried in English, "Leave off, you dog, and come here! Don't trouble the gentleman with your noise!" and then added in Romany, "*Mang, Prala, mang!*"[1] And so the brat did till the gentleman flung him a sixpence.

Begging Letter Impostures.

From the *Times* of November 10, 1874.

Sir,—In consequence of the large extent to which frauds by begging-letter impostors are now carried on, I have prepared a statement regarding them, as over three thousand names of persons residing in London and its suburbs have been found marked in the directories—thirty-four in number—which were used by one of the chiefs of a London gang of begging-letter impostors, and have recently come into my possession.

The following are the marks, with their meanings:—

— means "doubtful," or not called on before.
× ,, "good," or likely to give.
* ,, "very good," or very likely to give.
O ,, "has given something recently."
⊖ ,, "has given something recently and will give again if called on."

The gang consists of over fifty persons, who are believed on an average to make at least £5 a week each by their proceedings.

Personal descriptions of fifty-two of them are kept at my office for purposes of identification.

The letters and petitions sent or presented in each case are skilful fabrications and forgeries; sometimes they are sent by post, but more frequently they are presented in person.

The petitions often profess to be signed by the vestry clerk of the parish, and have attached to them excellent imitations of the signatures of a number of influential people who are stated to have contributed to the case. Sometimes the case is that of a laundress whose horse has taken fright and dashed her van to pieces, injuring her only son and causing her great loss. At other times the case is represented as that of a widow in distress, whose husband has died under afflicting circumstances and left her unprovided for—the circumstances varying with the supposed social position of the husband. Or a widow is represented as being in danger of ruin in consequence of her shop having been robbed by burglars, or of her having an execution in her house, or of her cows having died from pleuro-pneumonia.

In other instances sad cases of losses at sea are put forward, apparently vouched by the consul at some foreign port, by the captain of the ship, or by the city authorities, written on paper prepared for the purpose, headed with the Royal or city arms and the place or office from which they profess to issue.

---

[1] Beg on, brother!

	£	s.	d.
Rent	35	12	6
Levy		3	6
Man per day		2	6
£			

Mr. *S. Ann Clarke* or whom else it may concern.

By Virtue of an Authority to me, given by your Landlord Mr *George Robinson* TAKE NOTICE, that I have this day distrained the Goods, Chattels, and Things, mentioned in the Inventory hereunder written, for the sum of *Thirty five* Pounds, *Twelve* Shillings, and *Six* Pence, being for *Rent* Arrears of Rent due to the said above-mentioned Mr *George Robinson* on the *21st* day of *May* 1872, for the use and occupation of *House and Premises*, situate and being No. *7 Earl Street Kensington* in the Parish of *Kensington* in the County of *Middlesex* And unless you pay the said Rent, together with the said Expenses attending this Distress, or Replevy the said Goods, within five days from the date hereof, they will be Appraised and Sold to satisfy the Rent and Expenses, pursuant to the statute in that case made and provided.

Dated this *12th* day of *June* 1872.

Yours, &c. *George Preever*
Sworn Broker &c

The Inventory to which the above Notice refers, viz.—

On the Premises

And any other Goods and Effects that may be found in or about the said premises, to pay the said Rent and Expenses of this Distress.

Removing any Goods off the Premises to avoid a Distress, or any person Aiding, Assisting, or Concealing the same, will subject themselves to double the value of such Effects so removed or concealed, or suffer imprisonment in the House of Correction, there to be kept to hard labour, without Bail or Mainprise, for six months, pursuant to Act 11th. Geo. II.

Sold by W. Davis, Stationer, Printer, and Bookbinder, 46, Rochester Row, S.W.

"Parish of Kensington
Middlesex

"This is to certify that Mrs Ann Clarke (widow of the late Jos. Clarke) carried on business as Cow Keeper & Dairywoman in this parish for several years, & has hitherto supported a large family in respectability. Owing to the disease (Pleuro Pneumonia) so prevalent amongst cattle she has lost five valuable Milch Cows estimated at £75. which has reduced herself and family from a sphere of comfort to great distress.

"I have been solicited by the Parochial Authorities to draw up this statement of her loss, with a view to realizing by voluntary contributions a sum sufficient to enable Mrs Clarke to follow her occupation as heretofore, and pay her Landlord for arrears of rent, and for which her effects are under Execution for, And beg to recommend her case to public notice as deserving of Commiseration and assistance.

"Having a family of five Children depending on her for support.

"Dated at the Vestry Hall "Kensington" _____ 20/-
this 12. day of June 1872.

"Vestry Clerk"

	£ s d	
Revd. D. Hepey	2 2 0	Lady Holland, Holland Ho.
St. Barnabas Parsonage		Mr. Richd. Hepey £2-0-0
John H. Yeoman		
Ch. Warden		J. D. High — 1 1 0
(?) Arthur J. Sinclair	2 0 0	Henry Lumsden 2
Vicarage		Meaple Castle 2
Henry A. Brassey	£	
Lady Geo. Pratt	1 0	
Kitchen Garden		
Chas. Thos. Fissell	1 0 0	
Mrs. J. Fiske	£	
Ld. Strathmore	2 0 0	
W. Ct. Fordyce	1 1 0	
Lord Saltoun	£2	

Applications sent by post usually ask for an answer to be sent to some place not easy of access in the suburbs of London, or to some address in England, Scotland, or Ireland, whence the letters are re-transmitted to London. These letters advance an infinitude of pleas for assistance, all of which are without foundation. Sometimes also appeals are sent from some foreign country on behalf of some non-existent person in distress, who is alleged to be a distant relation of the person written to.

In the cases of travellers newly arrived from India, or persons having relations in India, an impostor introduces himself to them by carefully got-up references to persons and incidents connected with Indian life, and then winds up by soliciting a subscription towards opening a college in the Himalayas or towards supporting some other pseudo-Indian institution.

Last year female members of the gang called on benevolent persons, representing that they were the daughters of people in the country slightly known to the person on whom they called—that it was essential on various grounds that they should immediately send £8 to their father, but that the post-office being closed they were unable to do so, the visits being, of course, made in the evening. They therefore in each case begged for a cheque for £8 in return for eight sovereigns. The cheques, being obtained, were afterwards altered to cheques for £80 and presented and paid.

Frequently the members of the gang assume a variety of characters and call upon people without letters or petitions and recommend one another for assistance on every kind of plea—an invalid child requiring to be placed in an asylum, a distressed tradesman or foreigner, a singer of celebrity who has fallen into poverty, or a sufferer by shipwreck or fire. Sometimes the members of the gang call singly; at other times they work in parties of four or six, two going into the house while the others keep watch in the neighbourhood to give warning of danger.

The names of the neighbouring clergy are freely used either as writers of recommendatory letters accompanying petitions, or as contributors or references; or the visiting cards of people of position are employed as introductions, these cards having been taken from the card-baskets lying in the halls of other people.

The leaders of the gang take in the *Morning Post*, by which they know the movements of the fashionable world; they are also well supplied with directories and every kind of work of reference likely to be useful to them.

I am, Sir, your obedient servant,
C. J. RIBTON-TURNER.

CHAPTER XXXII.

L'ENVOYÉ.

"My name is Nicolas Genings, and I came from Lecester to séeke worke, and I am a hat-maker by my occupation, and all my money is spent, and if I coulde get money to paye for my lodging this night, I would seke work tomorowe amongst the hatters."—*Story told by Nicolas Genings, a begging impostor, on New Year's Day*, 1567.

THE history of vagrancy is in earlier times frequently a history of social oppression by which the labourer is driven to lead a wandering life; the history of begging is from first to last a history of craft on the part of the beggar, and of credulity on the part of his supporters.

The beggars of England, France, and Germany, in the sixteenth century, exhibit a strong family resemblance; there are slight variations in their external characteristics, but none in their governing principle, which is simply to utilise human suffering in its most harrowing phases as the keynote of their deceptions. In Italy, on the other hand, superstitious credence appears to have been the lever used by both beggar and rogue. Though the forms prevalent in that country, in the seventeenth century, were nearly all non-existent in England at the same time, there seems good cause to suppose that they flourished here at an earlier period, and that the reason why a detailed chronicle of them has not reached us, is probably owing to the fact that the Reformation, with its iconoclastic consequences, followed very closely on the era of the introduction of printing. The revelations made in connection with the Holy Maid of Kent show that such knavish pranks existed, indeed religious credulity in any country could hardly go further than a full belief in the efficacy of such relics as the beard of the innocents, and the feathers of the Holy Ghost, which are chronicled in Watson's *Ship of Fools*.*

* See p. 590.

    These two pictures lyuely set out,
One body and soule, God send him more grace:
    This monstrous dissembler, a Cranke all about.
Uncomly coueting of eche to imbrace,
    Money or wares, as he made his race.
And somtyme a mariner, and a seruing man:
    Or els an artificer, as he would fayne than.
Such shiftes he vsed, being well tryed,
    Abandoning labour till he was espyed:
Conding punishment for his dissimulation,
    He surely receyved with much exclamation.

NICOLAS GENINGS, THE BEGGING IMPOSTOR (1567)

VAGRANTS AND VAGRANCY. 667

With regard to mendicity in the present day, a careful study of the whole of the evidence must create astonishment, that in a highly civilised country, a horde of profligate men and women should not only be permitted, but actually be encouraged, to wander about our streets and highways in a state of idleness, and that the modern imitators of Nicolas Genings should be able to obtain money by means of the same false story quite as easily now as he did more than three hundred years ago. The practice of the beggar is founded upon a total and cruel disregard of every person, and every consideration, which does not further his aims in preying upon the public.*

It is pitiable to have to realise that men and women of the most abandoned lives are still permitted both daily and nightly to prowl about our streets polluting some of the most beautiful devotional songs by the base uses to which they apply them, and dragging about with them children of whose health they are utterly regardless, and whom they educate in the worst forms of depravity.

* An additional incident or two from personal experience may possibly be of some service to the indiscriminate almsgiver.

A little time ago a woman, leading a child by the hand, was obtaining alms in the streets. Seeing that she from time to time applied a rag to the eyes of the child, a lady went up to her to ascertain the cause. The woman said that the child was afflicted with "blight." It was, in fact, apparent that the poor little creature was suffering from some terrible form of ophthalmia, and ought, as the lady forcibly told the woman, to have been taken to some hospital or dispensary, where she would have been properly attended to. No policeman, however, being near, the woman persisted in making a market out of the child's sufferings.

Blind beggars are, unhappily, among the most profligate of the mendicant fraternity. Their infirmity brings them in such a profitable return, that all their worst tastes are pandered to and encouraged by the parasites with whom they are associated.

A few years ago, there used to be stationed in Portman Square a man commonly known as *Blind Jack*, who used to indulge his patrons with the pleasant fiction—derived, no doubt, from some older beggar—that he had lost his sight while serving with the British army in Egypt at the beginning of this century, calmly ignoring the fact, that if he was in arms at the period in question it must have been in those of his mother. A personal friend was in the habit of giving him a small weekly sum. One summer's night this friend was returning on foot from a theatre when a smart shower overtook him in the neighbourhood of Portman Square. He ran into a public-house for shelter, and there found *Blind Jack* considerably advanced in his cups. Accosting him, he told him that he had hitherto been in the habit of assisting him regularly, believing him to be a deserving character, and that he was sorry to be undeceived by finding him in such a condition. "You've been in the habit of assisting me regularly!" said *Blind Jack* with a hiccough, and producing a handful of small silver. "Then you're a jolly good fellow. What'll you take to drink?"

Crime of every class is within the scope and practice of the vagrant, ranging from the robbery of the infant of the cherished halfpenny which is to buy him sweets, to the murder of the unoffending working man whose little savings the tramp covets.* The receiver of stolen goods is rightly held to be a greater criminal than the thief, and similarly, the indiscriminate almsgiver must be deemed to be more blameworthy than the beggar. If there were no indiscriminate almsgivers, there would be no beggars.

To meet a tale of distress by a small gift of money, is the merest mockery, and no more contributes to rescue the recipient from pauperism, than does the casting of chips of wood to a drowning man. So long as the inducements to vagrancy and mendicity are superior to the punishments inflicted for indulging in them, the vagrant and mendicant will continue to exist, and will continue to give uncontrolled licence to inclinations which, however bad they may be, are encouraged and subsidised by their supporters.

While attesting the fact, that all legislation hitherto directed to the repression of vagrancy and mendicity has failed in its effect, I have ventured to express an opinion, that a remedy yet remains to be tested. Penal legislation has been tried, but reformatory legislation, which has been applied with good results to the juvenile vagrant, has not yet been extended to the adult. The duration of the reformatory process would have to depend upon the degree of curability of the patient. The powers of detention would therefore have to be elastic enough to admit of the speedy return to social life of those whose cases appeared to justify it, and the equally speedy re-incarceration of those who abused the confidence placed in them. While in the majority of cases I believe a cure would sooner or later be effected, I should be quite prepared to find that a residuum existed which no effort of philanthropy could permanently improve. In this case I can only say that it is manifestly better that such moral lepers should be under a restraint, tempered only by the safeguards which they themselves

* The instances of murder by tramps are numerous. The following are two of the most cruel examples in recent years. In May, 1870, Emmanuel Marshall, an industrious blacksmith, his wife, sister, mother, and three children were murdered, for the sake of plunder, at Denham, near Uxbridge, by a tramp named John Owen. In July, 1878, William Watkins, a farm labourer, his wife, and three children were murdered at Llangibby, near Usk, by a tramp named Joseph Garcia.

proved to be indispensable rather than that they should be suffered to roam about the world, not only to do mischief on their own account, but also to propagate their evil influences.

It would nevertheless be a mistake for the State to undertake a greater responsibility in dealing with the question than it now does in the case of Industrial Schools, because if the plan will bear the test of experiment, it will in all probability receive the support of philanthropic people on principles similar to Industrial Schools, and it must be evident that to interest the public in the solution of the matter is essential to the plan, in order to limit the temptations to which the beggar is now exposed by the unthinking almsgiver.

From a financial point of view, the saving would be very great. The vagrant and beggar now cost the community a large sum annually in the provision which has to be made for them in workhouses and gaols, and the value of their depredations amounts to a considerable yearly sum. This is wholly irrespective of the contributions in money of which they are the recipients, the amount of which in England and Wales was long ago estimated at £3,000,000* yearly, and which is without doubt not an excessive computation in the present day.

If this large sum or the greater part of it, were devoted to promoting a system of co-operation amongst the toilers at the East-end of London, and in many other localities, we should no longer hear of women earning one penny per thousand for making paper bags, and twopence farthing per gross for making matchboxes, while the middlemen over them are amassing large fortunes.

To save these people, who are numbered by thousands, from the cruel life and lingering death to which they are condemned by the "sweating" system would be a noble work of philanthropy. The vicarious penny or shilling improvidently bestowed on such poor people would be worse than useless, it would simply make them hunger for more without lifting them out of their wretchedness.

By amassing all the idle pennies which now go to support the worthless beggar, an East-end institute might, however, be raised, not by hands, but by intelligent and energetic personal exertion to improve the condition of its inhabitants, which would transcend in usefulness and beneficence any which has yet been devised.

* See p. 232.

Pending the necessary legislation on the subject of vagrancy, something may, however, yet be done to ameliorate the present condition of things. Supporters of missions to the heathen may learn from the evidence quoted in these pages that it is not necessary to send to Africa to meet with the object of their benevolent zeal. He exists in rank luxuriance at their own doors. No foreign heathen can compare with him in his utter disregard of religion, in his obscenity of language, and in his utter brutality and filthiness of life and action. He is now daily discharged both from the workhouse and from the foul dens in which he lodges,* utterly friendless, utterly uncared for, and left to pursue the broad path to evil, without being offered the slightest encouragement to a contrary course. Surely here is a fine field for missionary effort. To reclaim such savages would be a work of mercy to them and of kindness to society.

It may seem to some people that the opinion I have expressed in the opening of the fourteenth chapter that the deserving and really necessitous poor never beg is a matter which may admit of debate. All I can say in support of it is, that in the course of my experience, which extends to several thousands of cases, I have never yet met with a beggar who was driven to beg by sheer want or misfortune, nor have I encountered any one who after investigation had ever found one in such a case. Amongst the numerous friends I have tested on the subject was the late Mr. Hornsby Wright, whose genuine philanthropy was of the widest extent.

A still stronger testimony of the fallacy of popular judgment in matters of destitution was furnished me by the late Dr. Hardwicke, the Coroner for Central Middlesex, who told me, in answer to inquiries occasioned by the suspicious aspect of certain cases, in which verdicts of death from starvation had been recorded, that in his official experience he had never met with a case of starvation arising from an inability to obtain the necessaries of life, but from an inability to utilise them, brought about by debauchery or by disease engendered by debauchery. This by no means implies that there are not people who die by slow starvation, but inquests are never held on them, because they have died a linger-

---

* Under the Common Lodging Houses Acts, 1851 and 1853 (14 and 15 Vic., cap. 28, and 16 and 17 Vic., cap. 41), the metropolitan police have full power to inspect such houses, and to cause them to be kept in good sanitary condition; but, judged by recent revelations, it seems very doubtful if these powers are adequately exercised.

ing death in the course of nature. Too proud to obtrude their misfortunes on strangers, they go silently down to the grave. But the indiscriminate almsgiver is powerless to rescue them, for they would not for one moment adopt the methods which stimulate him to action. As a working man in his hour of need once almost fiercely said to Mr. Hornsby Wright, "Considering who gets the lion's share, I'd die on a doorstep before I'd accept 'dirty' charity."*

Luther in his preface to the *Liber Vagatorum* admirably sums up the whole matter when he says, "Everybody should be prudent and cautious in dealing with beggars, and learn that, whereas people will not give and help honest paupers and needy neighbours, as ordained by God, they give, by the persuasion of the devil, and contrary to God's judgment, ten times as much to vagabonds and desperate rogues."

The opinion of the *Reverend James Hervey*, who in the last century was remarkable for his gentleness, fervent piety, and self-denying benevolence, is even more emphatic on the subject.

"Towards the distressed but industrious poor I would cultivate a tender and ever-yearning compassion; I would anticipate their complaints; and, as a sacred writer directs, would even seek to do them good. But as to common beggars, I frankly own that I look upon it as my duty to discourage such cumberers of the ground. They are, generally speaking, lusty drones, and their habitual *begging* is no better than a specious *robbing* of the public hive. For such *sturdy* supplicants, who are able to undergo the fatigue of travelling; able to endure the inclemencies of the weather; and consequently much more able, were they equally willing, to exercise themselves in some species of laudable industry; for these the *house* of *correction* would be a far more salutary provision than any supply from our table; and *confinement to labour* a much more beneficial charity than the liberality of the purse. We should remember and *they* should be taught that the law ordained by the court of heaven is, *If a man will not work, neither shall he eat.*† If then we contribute to support them in idleness, do we not counteract and frustrate this wise regulation established by the great Sovereign of the universe? Is it not also a *wrong* to the deserving poor if we suffer these wens on the body politic to draw off the nourishment which ought to circulate amongst the valuable

---

* "Confessions of an Old Almsgiver," p. 99.　　† 2 Thess. iii., 10.

and useful members? Money or victuals bestowed on these worthless wretches is not real beneficence, but the *earnest-penny* of sloth. It hires them to be good for nothing, and pays them for being public nuisances.

"Let us then unanimously join to shake off these *dead weights* from our wheels, and dislodge these *swarms* of *vermin* from our state. Let us be deaf to their most importunate clamours, and assure ourselves that by this determined inflexibility we do God, we do our community, we do them the most substantial service."*

* "Theron and Aspasio," Dialogue XVII. (1755).

AND BEGGARS AND BEGGING.

RETURN OF THE NUMBER OF PERSONS CHARGED WITH ACTS OF VAGRANCY AT THE SEVERAL POLICE OFFICES IN THE METROPOLIS.

From June 21, 1823, to June 21, 1824 3,103
From June 21, 1824, to March 31, 1825 . . . 2,092
Ordered by the House of Commons to be printed 26th April, 1825.

RETURN SHOWING THE NUMBER OF VAGRANTS APPREHENDED, CONVICTED, AND DISCHARGED DURING THE YEARS 1831 TO 1885 INCLUSIVE.

Year.	Apprehended.			Tried and Convicted.		Tried and Acquitted.		Summarily Convicted.		Discharged.		Remarks.
	Total of Males and Females.	Males.	Females.	Males.	Females.	Males.	Females.	Males.	Females.	Males.	Females.	
1831	6,293	4,177	2,116	—	—	—	—	2,294	963	1,883	1,153	
1832	9,325	5,957	3,368	—	—	—	—	3,951	1,908	2,006	1,460	
1833	6,757	4,652	2,105	—	—	—	—	2,443	906	2,209	1,199	
1834	5,494	3,686	1,808	—	1	—	—	1,815	740	1,871	1,067	
1835	3,867	2,487	1,380	—	—	—	—	1,331	632	1,156	748	
1836	3,081	2,280	801	—	—	—	—	1,164	426	1,116	375	
1837	4,287	2,805	1,482	—	—	—	—	1,229	550	1,576	932	
1838	3,997	2,669	1,328	—	—	—	—	1,354	547	1,315	781	
1839	3,780	2,432	1,348	—	—	—	—	1,203	524	1,229	824	
1840	4,428	2,923	1,505	1	—	—	—	1,256	460	1,666	1,045	
1841	4,841	3,220	1,621	1	—	—	2	1,613	689	1,606	930	
1842	5,526	4,155	1,371	—	—	—	—	2,469	618	1,686	753	
1843	4,403	3,411	992	1	1	—	—	2,072	419	1,338	572	
1844	4,841	3,668	1,173	—	—	—	—	2,064	508	1,604	665	
1845	3,937	2,868	1,069	—	—	—	—	1,717	522	1,151	547	
1846	3,758	2,647	1,111	—	—	—	—	1,588	480	1,059	631	
1847	4,450	3,058	1,392	—	—	—	—	1,928	679	1,130	713	
1848	5,598	3,768	1,830	—	—	—	—	2,330	1,025	1,438	805	
1849	6,515	4,450	2,065	—	—	—	—	2,810	1,217	1,640	848	
1850	3,810	2,790	1,020	—	—	—	—	1,798	608	992	412	
1851	4,316	2,876	1,440	—	—	—	—	1,708	821	1,168	619	
1852	3,708	2,418	1,290	—	—	—	—	1,441	727	977	563	
1853	3,214	1,921	1,293	—	—	—	—	1,141	722	780	571	
1854	3,511	2,175	1,336	—	—	—	—	1,302	763	873	573	
1855	2,866	1,586	1,280	1	1	—	—	899	729	686	550	
1856	3,259	1,856	1,403	—	—	—	—	1,127	829	729	574	
1857	4,162	2,512	1,650	1	1	—	—	1,511	974	1,000	675	
1858	3,420	1,951	1,469	—	2	—	—	1,094	914	857	553	
1859	2,576	1,491	1,085	2	—	—	—	859	638	630	447	
1860	2,753	1,449	1,304	1	—	—	—	781	689	667	615	
1861	2,760	1,700	1,060	3	1	—	—	1,046	612	651	447	
1862	3,331	2,135	1,196	3	4	—	—	1,306	749	826	443	
1863	3,081	1,915	1,166	1	1	—	—	1,335	800	579	365	
1864	3,440	2,051	1,389	1	2	—	—	1,437	1,029	613	358	
1865	4,971	3,387	1,584	1	1	—	—	2,234	986	1,152	597	
1866	4,315	3,042	1,273	6	1	—	—	1,860	690	1,176	582	
1867	5,766	4,312	1,454	7	—	—	—	2,498	792	1,807	662	
1868	5,434	4,107	1,327	11	1	—	—	2,585	755	1,511	571	

674   VAGRANTS AND VAGRANCY.

RETURN showing the Number of Vagrants Apprehended, Convicted, and Discharged during the Years 1831 to 1885 inclusive (*continued*).

Year	Apprehended. Total of Males and Females.	Apprehended. Males.	Apprehended. Females.	Tried and Convicted. Males.	Tried and Convicted. Females.	Tried and Acquitted. Males.	Tried and Acquitted. Females.	Summarily Convicted. Males	Summarily Convicted. Females.	Discharged. Males.	Discharged. Females.	Remarks.
1869	7,054	5,443	1,611	13	2	—	—	3,698	888	1,732	721	
1870	6,340	5,015	1,325	18	7	—	—	3,596	801	1,401	517	
1871	5,911	4,570	1,341	18	5	2	1	3,150	854	1,400	481	
1872	5,163	3,857	1,306	26	8	2	1	2,598	811	1,231	486	
1873	4,555	3,535	1,020	37	7	—	2	2,439	634	1,059	377	
1874	3,858	2,999	859	30	8	—	—	2,133	549	836	302	
1875	3,549	2,728	821	17	7	1	1	1,914	481	796	332	
1876	3,830	2,926	904	17	5	—	—	2,009	543	900	356	
1877	4,101	3,273	828	16	5	—	—	2,369	512	888	311	
1878	3,960	3,095	865	16	6	—	—	1,972	508	1,107	351	
1879	4,188	3,340	848	27	6	—	—	2,167	475	1,146	367	
1880	4,213	3,421	792	31	11	1	—	2,111	425	1,278	356	
1881	4,018	3,238	780	51	10	—	—	1,928	412	1,259	358	
1882	4,392	3,536	856	49	9	—	—	2,199	456	1,288	391	
1883	5,492	4,575	917	53	7	1	—	3,016	503	1,505	407	
1884	4,799	3,984	815	39	9	—	—	2,506	422	1,439	384	
1885	4,573	3,773	800	62	8	—	1	2,128	392	1,583	399	

C. H. CUTBUSH, *Chief Inspector.*

Metropolitan Police Office,
  4, Whitehall Place,
    10*th February*, 1887.

INDEX OF STATUTES.

ENGLAND.

	PAGE
HLOTHÆRE (673-685) and EADRIC (685-686).—C. 15. A man to be responsible for a stranger whom he entertains three nights	5
WIHTRÆD (690-725).—C. 7. A shorn man wandering to be entertained once only	7
INE (688-725).—C. 24. An English "wīte-theow" who steals himself away to be hanged	7
C. 25. Chapmen to traffic before witnesses	6
C. 30. A ceorlish man harbouring a fugitive to pay for him according to his wēr	7
C. 39. A man going from his lord without leave, to return and pay 60 shillings	7
C. 48. A "wīte-theow" committing theft before he becomes a "wīte-theow" may be scourged by his accuser	7
ALFRED (870-901).—C. 34. Chapmen to bring men whom they take with them before the King's reeve	6
EDWARD THE ELDER (901-924).—C. 10. No man to receive another man's man without leave	9
ÆTHELSTAN (924-940).—I., c. 2. Lordless men to be domiciled by their kindred to folk-right	10
I., c. 8. Landless men becoming followers in another shire and again seeking their kinsfolk, may be harboured on condition of being presented to folk-right	10
I., c. 22. No man to receive another man's man without his leave .	11
II., c. 4. No man to harbour another man's man without his leave .	11
III., c. 4. Whoever harbours another man's man, and on his ill-doing has let him depart and is unable to punish him, to pay one hundred and twenty shillings to the King, and the man to return to his master	11
IV., c. 1. Whoever receives another man's man whom he, for his evil conduct, turns away from him, to pay for him to his former master, and also to pay the King one hundred and twenty shillings .	11
EDMUND (940-946).—C. 3. No one to harbour another man's man before he is quit in all respect of every authority that may claim right from him	12
CNUT (1017-1035).—C. 21. Every man above twelve to make oath that he will neither be a thief nor cognizant of theft	14
C. 28. No one to receive any man longer than three nights unless he is recommended	13
C. 35. A friendless man without "borh" to go to prison . .	13
EDWARD THE CONFESSOR (1042-1066).—C. 23. Any one entertained for two nights may be kept as a sojourner, and if the man do wrong, the host shall suffer no loss, provided the wrong was not done by his counsel,	

676   INDEX OF STATUTES.

                                                                            PAGE
        but if he entertains him a third night, the host shall be responsible
            for him as one of his own household . . . . , .   .   14
    Libertas Civitatum.—C. 2. A citizen of London may kill a guest who
            makes a forcible sojourn in his house   15
WILLIAM THE CONQUEROR (1066-1087).—C. 15. Of the method of manumit-
            ting slaves   19
        C. 16. Slaves remaining unclaimed for a year and a day in cities,
            boroughs, walled towns, or castles, to be free   33
        C. 30. Bondmen not to quit their lands   19
        C. 48. No one to harbour a guest beyond three nights unless bidden so
            to do by his previous entertainer   19
HENRY I. (1101).—C. 8, s. 5. No one shall retain an unknown or a wandering
            man beyond three nights, and shall not harbour another man's man
            without a recommendation or a pledge   20
        C. 43, s. 2. A man leaving his lord without licence to be fined and com-
            pelled to return   20
        C. 58. A vagabond to be brought before the judge of the place to be dealt
            with   21
        C. 65, s. 5. A friendless man or a foreigner on his first accusation to be
            committed to prison and sustained by his accuser until he is tried .   21
        C. 82, s. 2. A vagabond who does wrong to be brought to trial in the
            place where he is found to be   21
        C. 83, s. 5. Any one despoiling a grave to be accounted a "wargus," or
            outcast   22
HENRY II. (1166).—*Assize of Clarendon.* No vagabond or unknown man to
            be entertained in any place except a borough, and only there for a
            single night, unless he be detained by sickness   26
        (1176).—*Assize of Northampton.* No one, either in a borough or vill, to
            entertain for more than one night any stranger for whose forthcoming
            he shall be unwilling to give security   26
        (1180).—C. 23. A person may entertain a friend or a stranger for
            two nights as a guest, without incurring a penalty, but if he enter-
            tain him a third night, he is to be responsible for him as one of his
            own household   27

                        ENGLAND AND WALES.

12 EDWARD I. (1284).—C 1. Wales. To inquire of them that give lodging
        unto persons unknown more than two nights. (Repealed 6 Geo. IV.
        c. 50, s. 62)   34
13 EDWARD I. (1285).—C. 4. The gates of walled towns to be closed from
        sunset to sunrise. Persons harbouring suspicious lodgers in the
        suburbs to be liable to the bailiffs. Strangers to be arrested by the
        watch. (Repealed Stat. Law Rev. Act, 1863) . . .   36, 603
13 EDWARD I. (1285).—*Stat. Civ. Lond.* No one to wander about the streets
        of the city after curfew, with arms for doing mischief, nor in any
        other manner unless he be a lawful person of good repute. (Repealed
        Stat. Law Rev. Act, 1863) 38, 58
2 EDWARD III. (1328).—C. 2. In what cases only pardons of felony shall be
        granted. (Repealed 44 & 45 Vict. c. 59, s. 3)   41
    C. 3. No man to come before the justices, or to go, or ride armed. (Re-
        pealed 44 & 45 Vict. c. 59, s. 3)   41
4 EDWARD III. (1330).—C. 13. Confirming 2 Edward III. c. 2, touching
        granting of pardons. (Repealed 44 & 45 Vict. c. 59, s. 3) .   41
5 EDWARD III. (1331).—C. 14. Robberdesmen, Wastours, and Drawlatches to
        be arrested. Confirmed by 7 Richard II. c. 5. (Repealed 19 &
        20 Vict. c. 64) 42, 58, 388, 469, 580
23 EDWARD III. (1349).—St. 1, c. 7. No person to give anything to beggars
        able to labour, upon pain of imprisonment. (Repealed 21 James I.
        c. 28, s. 11) 43, 59

INDEX OF STATUTES.

PAGE

25 EDWARD III. (1350).—St. 1, c. 7. Proceedings in respect of servants, labourers, or artificers flying from one county to another. (Repealed 21 James I. c. 28, s. 11) 43, 46, 59, 64

34 EDWARD III. (1360-1).—C. 1. To appoint justices of the peace with jurisdiction over offenders, rioters, barrators, and vagabonds . . . 49, 50
C. 10, 11. Fugitive labourers to be outlawed, imprisoned, and burned in the forehead. Mayors and bailiffs to deliver them up. (Repealed Stat. Law Rev. Act, 1863) 50

1 RICHARD II. (1377).—C. 6. Commissions to be awarded to inquire of and punish the misbehaviour of villeins and land tenants to their lords. (As to England, repealed Stat. Law Rev. Act, 1863; as to Ireland, repealed Stat. Law Rev. Act. 1872) 56

2 RICHARD II. (1378).—C. 8. To confirm the statute 23 Edward III., and all other statutes of labourers. (Repealed 5 Eliz. c. 4) . . . 43

7 RICHARD II. (1383).—C. 5. For the punishment of vagabonds. Confirms 5 Edward III. c. 14. (Repealed as to vagabonds 39 Eliz. c. 4; altogether repealed 21 James I. c. 28, s. 11) 58

12 RICHARD II. (1388).—C. 3, 7, 8. For the regulation of servants, labourers, beggars, and vagrants. (Repealed 21 James I. c. 28, s. 11) . 59, 64, 66

13 RICHARD II. (1389-90).—C. 8. The rates of labourers' wages to be assessed and proclaimed by the justices of peace. (Repealed 44 & 45 Vict. c. 59, s. 3) 63, 66

15 RICHARD II. (1392).—C. 6. In appropriation of benefices, provision to be made for the poor and the vicar. (As to England, repealed Stat. Law Rev. Act, 1863; as to Ireland, repealed Stat. Law Rev. Act, 1872) 63

4 HENRY IV. (1402).—C. 27. No westours, rhymers, minstrels, or vagabonds to be sustained in Wales. (Repealed 19 & 20 Vict. c. 64) . . 63

7 HENRY IV. (1405).—C. 17. No man to put his son or daughter to be an apprentice unless he have twenty shillings in land or rent. (Repealed Stat. Law Rev. Act, 1863) 64

1 HENRY V. (1413).—C. 8. Irishmen and Irish clerks mendicant to depart the realm. (Repealed Stat. Law Rev. Act, 1863) 64

2 HENRY V. (1414).—C. 4. Justices empowered to send their writs for fugitive servants or labourers to every sheriff of England. (Repealed Stat. Law Rev. Act, 1863) 65

1 HENRY VI. (1422).—C. 3. Irishmen to depart the realm. (Repealed Stat. Law Rev. Act, 1863) 65

6 HENRY VI. (1427).—C. 3. Justices to assign the wages of artificers and workmen by proclamation. (Repealed Stat. Law Rev. Act, 1863) . 66

23 HENRY VI. (1444).—C. 12. To assess the wages of servants, labourers, and artificers, and to provide for the punishment of those who refuse to serve. (Repealed Stat. Law Rev. Act, 1863) 66

25 HENRY VI. (1446-7).—All statutes against Welchmen confirmed. (Repealed 21 James I. c. 28, s. 11) 66

11 HENRY VII. (1495).*—C 2. Against vagabonds and beggars. (Repealed as to vagabonds 39 Eliz. c. 4; altogether repealed 21 James I. c. 28, s. 11) 67, 68
C. 22. To fix the wages of servants and artificers. (Repealed 12 Henry VII. c. 3, 5 Eliz. c. 4, and Stat. Law Rev. Act, 1863) 68

19 HENRY VII. (1503-4).—C. 12. To fix the wages of servants and artificers. (Repealed 21 James I. c. 28, s. 11) 68

3 HENRY VIII. (1511-12).—C 9. Mummers or disguised persons, to be arrested as suspects or vagabonds, and committed to gaol. (Repealed Stat. Law Rev. Act, 1863) 70

6 HENRY VIII. (1514-15).—C. 3. Concerning the wages of artificers and labourers. (Repealed Stat. Law Rev. Act, 1863) . . . 71

22 HENRY VIII. (1530-1).—C. 10. Concerning Egyptians. (Repealed 19 & 20 Vict. c. 64) 72, 486

---

* By the 10 Henry VII. cap. 22 (1495) of the *Parliament of Ireland*, all English statutes enacted up to this time concerning the public weal are to be deemed good and effectual, and to be accepted, used, and executed in *Ireland*.

INDEX OF STATUTES.

	PAGE
22 HENRY VIII. (1530-1).—C. 12. Punishment of beggars and vagabonds. (Explained and amended 27 Hen. VIII., continued as therein mentioned by 28 Hen. VIII. c. 6, 31 Hen. VIII. c. 7, 33 Hen. VIII. c. 17; repealed 1 Edw. VI. c. 3; revived and amended 3 & 4 Edw. VI. c. 16. That Act and this confirmed 5 & 6 Edw. VI. c. 2 and 5 Eliz. c. 3. This Act and Statutes 3 & 4 Edw. VI., 5 Eliz., repealed by 14 Eliz. c. 5. See also 35 Eliz. c. 7, ss. 6, 7; and this Act finally repealed by 21 James I. c. 28, s. 11) . 72, 81, 82, 95, 98, 100, 106, 121, 391, 393, 411	
25 HENRY VIII. (1533-4).—C. 13. To limit the number of sheep kept by any one man. (Repealed 19 & 20 Vict. c. 64)	78
26 HENRY VIII. (1534).—C. 6. No person to levy or gather any commorthe. (Repealed 19 & 20 Vict. c. 64) 79, 431, 439	
27 HENRY VIII. (1535-6).—C. 25. Punishment of sturdy vagabonds and beggars, to continue to the end of next Parliament. (Repealed Stat. Law Rev. Act, 1863)	81
27 HENRY VIII. (1535-6).—C. 28. To dissolve all religious houses under the yearly revenue of two hundred pounds. (Repealed in part 21 James I. c. 28, s. 11)	83
28 HENRY VIII. (1536-7).—C. 6. Continuing 22 Hen. VIII. c. 12. (Repealed Stat. Law Rev. Act, 1863)	
31 HENRY VIII. (1539).—C. 7. Continuing 22 Hen. VIII. c. 12, and 27 Hen. VIII. c. 25, until the end of next Parliament. (Repealed Stat. Law Rev. Act, 1863)	72, 81
31 HENRY VIII. (1539).—C. 13. To dissolve monasteries and abbeys .	83
33 HENRY VIII. (1541-2).—C. 8. Persons using invocations, or other practices of sorcery, to discover treasure, &c., or to destroy or injure any one, or to provoke unlawful love, declared felons without clergy, &c. (Repealed Stat. Law Rev. Act, 1863)	134
33 HENRY VIII. (1541-2).—C. 14. Persons pretending to make prophecies as to what shall become of those who bear arms, cognizances, or badges derived from their arms, badges, &c., declared guilty of felony. (Repealed Stat. Law Rev. Act, 1863)	135
33 HENRY VIII. (1541-2).—C. 17. Continuing 22 Hen. VIII. c. 12, until the end of next Parliament. (Repealed Stat. Law Rev. Act, 1863)	72
34 & 35 HENRY VIII. (1543).—C. 1. Penalty on persons printing or selling prohibited books, or playing or singing, or rhyming any matter contrary to 31 Hen. VIII. c. 14. (Repealed 1 Edw. VI. c. 12, s. 2)	87
1 EDWARD VI. (1547.)—C. 3. For the punishment of vagabonds, and for the relief of the poor, and impotent persons, to continue to the end of the next Parliament. Repeals 22 Hen. VIII. c. 12. (Repealed Stat. Law Rev. Act, 1863)	89
1 EDWARD VI. (1547).—C. 12, s. 2. Repeals 34 & 35 Hen. VIII. c. 1. .	87
2 & 3 EDWARD VI. (1548-9).—C. 15, s. 1. To impose penalties on butchers, bakers, &c., conspiring to sell victuals only at certain prices; and on artificers conspiring as to the prices or times of work. 1st offence £10 or imprisonment for twenty days; 2nd offence £20 or pillory; 3rd offence £40 or pillory, loss of an ear and infamy. (Repealed 6 Geo. IV. c. 129, s. 2)	102
3 & 4 EDWARD VI. (1549-50).—C. 15. Against false prophecies founded on arms, badges, relating to the King, for the purpose of raising insurrections. (Repealed Stat. Law Rev. Act, 1863)	135
3 & 4 EDWARD VI. (1549-50).—C. 16. For the punishment of vagabonds and other idle persons. Revives and amends 22 Hen. VIII. c. 12. (Repealed 21 James I. c. 28, s. 11) . . . 94, 95, 98, 100, 106	
3 & 4 EDWARD VI. (1549-50).—C. 22, s. 5. Journeymen clothiers, weavers, tailors, and shoemakers, not to be hired for less than a quarter of a year; penalty one month's imprisonment and fine of forty shillings. (Repealed Stat. Law Rev. Act, 1863)	102
5 & 6 EDWARD VI. (1551-52).—C. 2. To confirm 22 Hen. VIII. c. 12, and 3 & 4 Edw. VI. c. 16, and to appoint collectors of alms. (Repealed Stat. Law Rev. Act, 1863)	95

INDEX OF STATUTES. 679

	PAGE
5 & 6 EDWARD VI. (1551-2).—C. 21. Against tinkers, pedlars, and such-like vagrant persons. (Repealed 1 James I. c. 25, s. 7)	95
7 EDWARD VI. (1552-3).—C. 11. To continue the 3 & 4 Edw. VI. c. 15, till the next session of Parliament. (Repealed Stat. Law Rev. Act, 1863)	135
1 MARY (1553).—Stat. 2, c. 13. To continue 5 & 6 Edw. VI. c. 2, until the end of next Parliament. (Repealed Stat. Law Rev. Act, 1863)	97
1 & 2 PHILIP & MARY (1554).—C. 4. For the punishment of certain persons calling themselves Egyptians. (Repealed 19 & 20 Vict. c. 64)	97, 489
2 & 3 PHILIP & MARY (1555).—C. 5. To confirm and amend 22 Hen. VIII. c. 12, and 3 & 4 Edw. VI. c. 16. To continue until the end of the first session of the next Parliament. (Repealed Stat. Law Rev. Act, 1863)	98, 99, 100, 175
4 & 5 PHILIP & MARY (1557).—C. 9. To continue 2 & 3 Phil. & Mar. c. 5. (Repealed Stat. Law Rev. Act, 1863)	99
5 ELIZABETH (1562-3).—C. 3. To confirm and amend 22 Hen. VIII. c. 12, and 3 & 4 Edw. VI. c. 16. To continue until the end of the first session of the next Parliament. (Repealed 14 Eliz. c. 5, s. 1)	100, 106, 176
5 ELIZABETH (1562-3).—C. 4. Wages of servants, labourers, and ar ificers to be assessed by the Justices, servants taking more than is taxed to be punished. Repeals 2 Rich. II. c. 8. (Repealed 38 & 39 Vict. c. 86, s. 17)	101
5 ELIZABETH (1562-3).—C. 15. Against false prophecies founded on arms, badges, &c., relating to the Queen, for the purpose of raising insurrections. (Repealed Stat. Law Rev. Act, 1863)	135
5 ELIZABETH (1562-3).—C. 16. Against persons practising witchcraft. (Repealed 1 James I. c. 12)	134
5 ELIZABETH (1562-3).—C. 20. For the punishment of vagabonds calling themselves Egyptians. (Repealed 23 Geo. III. c. 51)	102, 490, 505, 603
14 ELIZABETH (1572).—C. 5. For the punishment of vagabonds and for the relief of the poor and impotent. To continue for seven years and thence to the end of the next Parliament. Repeals 22 Hen. VIII. c. 12; 3 & 4 Edw. VI.; 5 Eliz. c. 3. (So much of this Act as concerns the gaoling, boring through the ear, and death (in the second degree) of vagabonds, repealed, 35 Eliz. c. 7, s. 6; as concerns the punishment of vagabonds, 39 Eliz. c. 4)	106, 116, 121, 147, 344, 471
18 ELIZABETH (1575-6).—C. 3. For the setting of the poor on work and for the avoiding of idleness. To continue for seven years and thence to the end of the next Parliament. (Gaoling, boring through the ear, and death (in the second degree) of vagabonds, repealed by 35 Eliz. c. 7, and the remainder by Stat. Law Rev. Act, 1863)	115, 148
35 ELIZABETH (1593-4).—C. 7, ss. 6 & 7. Penalties of imprisonment, &c., of vagabonds under statutes 14 Eliz. c. 5, 18 Eliz. c. 3, repealed. Punishment of vagabonds by whipping, under Stat. 22 Hen. VIII. c. 12, s. 2, &c., revived. To continue to the end of next Parliament. (Repealed Stat. Law Rev. Act, 1863)	121
39 ELIZABETH (1597-8).—C. 3. Of the office and duty of overseers of the poor. (Repealed Stat. Law Rev. Act, 1863.)	128
39 ELIZABETH (1597-8).—C. 4. For the punishment of rogues, vagabonds, and sturdy beggars. To continue to the end of the first session of the next Parliament. Repeals 7 Rich. II. c. 5, as to vagabonds; 11 Hen. VII. c. 2, as to vagabonds. (Continued by several Acts, and last by 16 Charles I. c. 5, but repealed by Stat. 13 Anne c. 26)	128, 133, 165, 180, 182
39 ELIZABETH (1597-8).—C. 12, ss. 2, 3. Justices empowered to rate wages in sessions for divisions of shires. Proclamation of the rates to be made by the sheriffs. (Repealed Stat. Law Rev. Act, 1863.)	
39 ELIZABETH (1597-8).—C. 17. Against lewd and wandering persons pretending themselves to be soldiers and mariners. To continue until the end of next Parliament. (Continued by several Acts, and last by 16 Charles I. c. 5; but repealed by 52 Geo. III. c. 31, and by 6 Geo. IV. c. 50, s. 62)	130, 148, 216

INDEX OF STATUTES.

43 ELIZABETH (1601).—C. 2. For the relief of the poor. To continue until the end of next Parliament 131
43 ELIZABETH (1601).—C. 3. Soldiers and mariners taken begging to be punished as rogues and vagabonds. (Repealed Stat. Law Rev. Act, 1863) 130, 213
1 JAMES I. (1603-4).—C. 6. s. 2. To make more effectual 5 Eliz. c. 4. Labourers, weavers, spinners, and workmen's wages to be rated by the justices. Proclamations to be made by the sheriff of the rates of wages. (Repealed 19 & 20 Vict. c. 64) 154
1 JAMES I. (1603-4).—C. 7. For the continuance and explanation of 39 Eliz. c. 4. (Continued by 3 Charles I. c. 4, s. 22 ; 16 Charles I. c. 5 ; but repealed by 13 Anne, c. 26) 131, 148, 165, 166, 182
1 JAMES I. (1603-4).—C. 12. Against conjuration, witchcraft, and dealing with evil and wicked spirits. Repeals 5 Eliz. c. 16. (Repealed 9 Geo. II. c. 5, s. 1) 135
1 JAMES I. (1603-4).—C. 25. To continue 39 Eliz. c. 17, and explain 39 Eliz. c. 4, s. 10. To continue to the end of the first session of the next Parliament. Repeals 5 & 6 Edw. VI. c. 21. (Repealed Stat. Law Rev. Act, 1863) 95, 128, 130
1 JAMES I. (1603-4).—C. 31. Persons infected with the plague and commanded to keep house, going abroad, to be punished. (Repealed 7 Will. IV. and 1 Vict. c. 91, s. 4) 135
3 JAMES I. (1605-6).—C. 21. To restrain the abuses of players. (Repealed 6 & 7 Vict. c. 68, s. 1) 134
7 JAMES I. (1609-10).—C. 4. For the due execution of divers laws and statutes heretofore made against rogues, vagabonds, and sturdy beggars, and other lewd and idle persons. To continue for seven years, and from thence to the end of the next session of Parliament. (Continued by 3 Charles I. c. 5, s. 22 ; 16 Charles I. c. 4 ; in part repealed by 13 Anne, c. 26, s. 8, and 4 Geo. IV. c. 64 ; altogether repealed by Stat. Law Rev. Act, 1863) 140, 182
21 JAMES I. (1623-4).—C. 28, s. 11. Repeals 23 Edw. III. Stat. 1, c. 7; 25 Edw. III. Stat. 1, c. 7 ; 7 Rich. II. c. 5 ; 12 Rich. II. cc. 3, 7, 8 ; 25 Hen. VI.; 11 Hen. VII. c. 2 ; 19 Hen. VII. c. 12; 27 Hen. VIII. c. 28, in part ; 3 & 4 Edw. IV. c. 16.
1 CHARLES I. (1625).—C. 1. For punishing divers abuses committed on Sunday. (Repealed in part Stat. Law Rev. Act, 1863) 147
3 CHARLES I. (1628).—C. 5. To continue 39 Eliz. c. 4 (as amended by 1 James I. c. 25, and 7 James I. c. 4), and 1 James I. c. 6, until the end of the first session of next Parliament. (Repealed Stat. Law Rev. Act, 1863) 147,148
16 CHARLES I. (1641).—C. 4. To continue all Acts continued by 3 Charles I. c. 5, until some other Act be made touching the Statutes so continued. (Repealed Stat. Law Rev. Act, 1863.) 148
22 CHARLES I. (1647).—C. 97. Common players to be punished as rogues . 155
22 CHARLES I. (1647). For the relief and employment of the poor, and the punishment of vagrants and other disorderly persons . . . 158
23 CHARLES I. (1648).—C. 106. Common players to be punished as rogues, whether they are wanderers or not 155
COMMONWEALTH (1656).—C. 21. Against vagrants and wandering, idle, dissolute persons 161, 356
13 & 14 CHARLES II. (1662).—C. 12. ss. 16, 17, 18, 23. To procure due execution of 39 Eliz. c. 4, and 1 James I. c. 7. Orders a reward of two shillings for the apprehension of each beggar. To continue until May 29, 1665, and thence to the end of the first session of the next Parliament. (Repealed Stat. Law Rev. Act, 1863) 164, 172, 189, 215, 447
15 CHARLES II. (1663).—C. 2. Persons cutting, stealing, or spoiling wood or underwood, for a first offence to pay a penalty of ten shillings; for a second to be sent to hard labour for a month ; and for a third to be deemed incorrigible rogues. (Repealed 7 & 8 Geo. IV. c. 27, s. 1) 167

INDEX OF STATUTES. 681

	PAGE
1 JAMES II. (1685).—C. 17. To continue 13 & 14 Charles II. c. 12 for seven years. (Repealed in part by Stat. Law Rev. Act, 1863)	172
3 WILLIAM & MARY (1691).—C. 11. For supplying defects of the former laws for the settlement of the poor. (Repealed in part by Stat. Law Rev. Act, 1867)	173
4 WILLIAM & MARY (1692).—C. 8. To encourage the apprehending of highwaymen. (Repealed 7 Geo. IV. c. 64, s. 32)	173
8 & 9 WILLIAM III. (1696-97).—C. 30. Persons receiving alms to wear a badge. (Repealed in part 50 Geo. III. c. 52; 7 & 8 Vict. c. 101, s. 13; finally repealed Stat. Law Rev. Act, 1867)	173, 215
11 & 12 WILLIAM III. (1698-9).—C. 18. For the more effectual punishment of vagrants, and sending them whither by law they ought to be sent. To continue for three years and thence to the end of the next session of Parliament. (Persons deemed rogues and vagabonds to be dealt with as directed by this Act. See 2 & 3 Anne c. 6, s. 16; continued for seven years by 6 Anne c. 32; repealed Stat. Law Rev. Act, 1867)	176. 178, 180
1 ANNE (1702).—St. 2, c. 13. To make more effectual the Statute 11 Will. III. c. 18. To continue for three years and thence to the end of the next session of Parliament. (Repealed 6 Geo. IV. c. 50, s. 62)	178
2 & 3 ANNE (1703).—C. 6, s. 16. Persons adjudged rogues and vagabonds by 39 Eliz. c. 4, to be taken up for the sea service, according to Stat. 11 Will. III. c. 18. (Repealed 5 & 6 Will. IV. c. 19, s. 1)	179
6 ANNE (1706).—C. 32. For the continuance of the laws for the punishment of vagrants, and for making such laws more effectual. To continue for seven years and thence to the end of the next session of Parliament. (Repealed Stat. Law Rev. Act, 1867)	625
13 ANNE (1713).—C. 26. For reducing the laws relating to rogues, vagabonds, sturdy beggars, and vagrants into one Act of Parliament, and for the more effectual punishing such rogues, vagabonds, sturdy beggars, and vagrants, and sending them whither they ought to be sent. Repeals 39 Eliz. c. 4; 1 James I. c. 7; 7 James I. c. 4, in part. (Repealed 13 Geo. II. c. 24, s. 36. Publicly whipping female offenders abolished by 1 Geo. IV.)	180, 195
4 GEORGE I. (1716).—C. 11, s. 5. Merchants or others may contract with persons of the age of fifteen, and under twenty-one, to serve them in America for eight years. (Repealed 7 & 8 Geo. IV. c. 27, s. 1)	185
5 GEORGE I. (1717).—C. 8. For the more effectual relief of wives and children deserted by husbands or parents	185
6 GEORGE I. (1718).—C. 19, s. 2. Justices may commit vagrants, &c., to the common gaol or house of correction. (Repealed Stat. Law Rev. Act, 1867.)	
7 GEORGE I. (1719).—C. 7. For preserving and encouraging the woollen and silk manufactures. (Repealed Stat. Law Rev. Act, 1867)	186
13 GEORGE I. (1726-7).—C. 23. End gatherers buying and receiving ends of yarn, wefts, thrums, and other refuse cloth, &c., on conviction to be deemed incorrigible rogues. (Repealed 3 & 4 Will. IV. c. 28)	186
7 GEORGE II.) 1734).—C. 21. For the more effectual punishment of assaults with intent to commit robbery. (Repealed 4 Geo. IV. c. 54, s. 5)	192
9 GEORGE II. (1736).—C. 5, s. 1. Repeals 9 James I. c. 12.	
10 GEORGE II. (1736-7).—C. 19, s. 1. Stage players acting within five miles of the Universities of Oxford or Cambridge, to be deemed rogues and vagabonds. (Repealed 6 & 7 Vict. c. 68, s. 1)	192
10 GEORGE II. (1736-7).—C. 28. Stage players who perform for gain in a place where they have no settlement, without letters patent or licence from the Lord Chamberlain, to be deemed rogues and vagabonds. (Repealed 6 & 7 Vict. c. 68, s. 1)	195, 236
12 GEORGE II. (1738-9).—C. 29. To authorise the charges for maintaining and conveying vagrants to be paid out of the general county rate. (Repealed in part 53 Geo. III. c. 113, s. 1; 55 Geo. III. c. 51, s. 17; 15 & 16 Vict. c. 81, s. 1; Stat. Law Rev. Act, 1867)	197

INDEX OF STATUTES.

	PAGE
12 GEORGE II. (1738-9).—C. 31. Persons loitering about the city of Bath, after being discharged from the hospital, to be deemed vagabonds, and all beggars resorting to the city to be liable to be sent to the house of correction for not more than twelve months . . .	197
13 GEORGE II. (1739-40).—C. 24. To amend and enforce the laws relating to rogues, vagabonds, and other idle and disorderly persons, and to reduce the same into one Act of Parliament, also to amend the laws relating to houses of correction. Repeals 13 Anne c. 26. (Repealed 17 Geo. II. c. 5, s. 34)	199
17 GEORGE II. (1743-4).—C. 5. To repeal 13 Geo. II. c. 24, and to amend and make more effectual the laws relating to rogues, vagabonds, and other idle and disorderly persons, and to houses of correction. (Repealed in part Stat. Law Rev. Act, 1867) 110, 202, 209, 212, 214, 215, 227, 228	
25 GEORGE II. (1751-2).—C. 36, s. 12. To empower Justices to examine upon oath, persons apprehended as rogues and vagabonds, as to their place of settlement and means of livelihood. To continue for three years. (Repealed Stat. Law Rev. Act, 1867)	203
26 GEORGE II. (1753).—C. 34, s. 2. To amend 17 Geo. II. by authorising county treasurers, instead of high constables, to pay the cost of passing vagrants from one county to another. (Repealed Stat. Law Rev. Act, 1867)	203
28 GEORGE II. (1755).—C. 19. To make perpetual 25 Geo. II. c. 36. (Repealed Stat. Law Rev. Act, 1867)	203, 229
6 GEORGE III. (1766).—C. 48. For the punishment of persons convicted of damaging or taking away wood or underwood. (Repealed Stat. Law Rev. Act, 1867)	204, 229
9 GEORGE III. (1768).—C. 41. For the punishment of persons convicted of destroying or carrying away hollies, thorns, or quicksets. (Repealed Stat. Law Rev. Act, 1867)	205, 229
22 GEORGE III. (1782).—C. 83, s. 31. For the prosecution of idle persons who neglect to provide for their families. (Repealed Stat. Law. Rev. Act, 1871)	208, 229
23 GEORGE III. (1782-3).—C. 51. To repeal 5 Eliz. c. 20 against gypsies .	505
23 GEORGE III. (1782-3).—C. 88. To extend the provisions of 17 Geo. II. c. 5 to persons apprehended with implements of house-breaking. (Repealed Stat. Law Rev. Act, 1861)	208
27 GEORGE III. (1787).—C. 1, s. 3. To extend the provisions of 17 Geo. II. c. 5 to persons who deal in lottery tickets without taking out a licence. (Repealed 46 Geo. III. c. 148, s. 64)	210
27 GEORGE III. (1787).—C. 11. To authorise the commitment of vagrants either to the common gaol or the house of correction, as shall seem most proper. (Repealed Stat. Law Rev. Act, 1871) . .	210
32 GEORGE III. (1792).—C. 45. To amend 17 Geo. II. c. 5 by ordering rogues and vagabonds to be whipped or sent to the house of correction before being passed; rewards for apprehension not to be paid before punishment; female vagabonds not to be whipped; soldiers and mariners found begging to be deemed vagabonds; persons neglecting their families to be deemed idle and disorderly. (Amended 43 Geo. III. c. 61. Repealed Stat. Law Rev. Act, 1861) .	212, 214
35 GEORGE III. (1795).—C. 101. To prevent the removal of poor persons until they become chargeable, and to authorise the suspension of the removal of sick persons. (Repealed in part by Stat. Law Rev. Act, 1871)	215, 216, 229
39 & 40 GEORGE III. (1800).—C. 50. Persons to the number of two or more found poaching in the night, to be deemed rogues and vagabonds. (Repealed 57 Geo. III. c. 90, s. 5)	209
39 & 40 GEORGE III. (1800).—C. 87, s. 12. Suspected persons and reputed thieves frequenting the River Thames, and the quays, warehouses, &c., adjoining, with felonious intent, to be deemed rogues and vagabonds. (Repealed Stat. Law Rev. Act, 1871) . . .	210

INDEX OF STATUTES.

	PAGE
42 GEORGE III. (1802).—C. 76, s. 18. To extend the provisions of 17 Geo. II. c. 5 to ill-disposed and suspected persons, and reputed thieves, frequenting public places with intent to commit felony. To continue till 1807. (Repealed Stat. Law Rev. Act, 1861)	210
42 GEORGE III. (1802).—C. 119. Persons setting up mischievous games or lotteries to be deemed rogues and vagabonds	210, 229
43 GEORGE III. (1803).—C. 61. To amend 32 Geo. III. c. 45, and to allow soldiers, marines, and sailors, and their wives, carrying certificates, to ask relief on their route home. (Repealed Stat. Law Rev. Act, 1872)	212, 236, 237
45 GEORGE III. (1805).—C. 66, s. 3. For the punishment of persons who take away bark from woods or wood grounds. (Repealed Stat. Law Rev. Act, 1872)	205
46 GEORGE III. (1806).—Cap. 148, s. 64. Repeals 27 Geo. III. c. 1, s. 3.	
49 GEORGE III. (1809).—C. 124. To empower justices to suspend the removal by pass of sick or infirm vagrants, and of other persons nearly connected with them or related to them, living together as one family at the time of the order of removal. (Repealed Stat. Law Rev. Act, 1872)	216
50 GEORGE III. (1810).—C. 52. Repeals 8 & 9 Will. III. c. 30, s. 2, regarding badges. (Wholly repealed Stat. Law Rev. Act, 1872, No. 2)	216
51 GEORGE III. (1811).—C. 119, s. 18. To repeat provisions of 42 Geo. III. c. 76, s. 18; to continue till 1813. (Repealed 54 Geo. III. c. 37)	210
52 GEORGE III. (1812).—C. 31. To repeal 39 Eliz. c. 17, against lewd and wandering persons pretending themselves to be soldiers or mariners. (Repealed Stat. Law Rev. Act, 1861)	216
54 GEORGE III. (1813).—C. 37, s. 18. To repeat provisions of 51 Geo. III. c. 119, s. 18. To continue till 1820 ; repeals 51 Geo. III. c. 119, s. 18. (Repealed 1 & 2 Geo. IV. c. 118, s. 1)	210
57 GEORGE III. (1817).—C. 90, s. 5. Repeals 39 & 40 Geo. III. c. 50.	
59 GEORGE III. (1819).—C. 12, s. 33. To empower the removal by pass of chargeable poor born in Ireland, Scotland, the Isle of Man, or Channel Islands, although they have not committed any act of vagrancy and without being first whipped or imprisoned. (Repealed 31 & 32 Vict. c. 122, s. 36)	227
1 & 2 GEORGE IV. (1820).—C. 118, s. 1. Repeals 54 Geo. III. c. 37, s. 18.	
3 GEORGE IV. (1822).—C. 40. To consolidate into one Act and amend the laws relating to idle and disorderly persons, rogues and vagabonds, incorrigible rogues, and other vagrants in England. Repeals all former provisions relating to such persons, except the 10 Geo. II. c. 28, or any Act relating to players. To continue to September 1, 1824. (Repealed 5 Geo. IV. c. 83, s. 1)	110, 234, 236
4 GEORGE IV. (1823).—C. 54, s. 5. Repeals 7 Geo. II. c. 21.	
4 GEORGE IV. (1823).—C. 64. Repeals 7 James I. c. 4, in part.	
5 GEORGE IV. (1824).—C. 83. For the punishment of idle and disorderly persons, and rogues and vagabonds in England. Repeals all former provisions relating to such persons. (3 Geo. IV. c. 40.) (Amended 1 & 2 Vict. c. 38 ; 7 & 8 Vict. c. 101 ; 11 & 12 Vict. c. 110 ; 12 & 13 Vict. c. 103 ; 28 & 29 Vict. c. 79 ; 29 & 30 Vict. c. 113 ; 31 & 32 Vict. c. 52 (which is repealed by 36 & 37 Vict. c. 38); 34 & 35 Vict. c. 112 ; 39 & 40 Vict. c. 61)	236, 251, 303
6 GEORGE IV. (1825).—C. 50, s. 62. Repeals 12 Edw. I. c. 1; remainder of 39 Eliz. c. 17 ; 1 Anne, St. 2, c. 13, ss. 2 & 3.	
6 GEORGE IV. (1825).—C. 129, s. 2. Repeals 2 & 3 Edw. VI. c. 15, s. 1.	
7 GEORGE IV. (1826).—C. 64, s. 32. Repeals 4 Will. & Mary, c. 8.	
7 & 8 GEORGE IV. (1826-7).—C. 27, s. 1. Repeals 15 Car. II. c. 2 ; 4 Geo. I. c. 11.	
3 & 4 WILLIAM IV. (1833).—C. 28. Repeals 13 Geo. I. c. 23.	
4 & 5 WILLIAM IV. (1834).—C. 76. For the amendment and better administration of the laws relating to the poor in England and Wales	241
5 & 6 WILLIAM IV. (1835).—C. 19, s. 1. Repeals 2 & 3 Anne, c. 6, s. 16.	

INDEX OF STATUTES.

7 WILLIAM IV. & 1 VICTORIA (1837).—C. 91, s. 4. Repeals 1 James I. c. 31.

1 & 2 VICTORIA (1838).—C. 38. Persons exposing obscene prints in shop windows to be liable to punishment as rogues and vagabonds . . 238

5 & 6 VICTORIA (1842).—C. 57, s. 5. To empower guardians to set the occasional poor to work. (Repealed in part 10 & 11 Vict. c. 109, s. 22. Repealed Stat. Law Rev. Act, 1874, No. 2) . . . 238, 250, 273

6 & 7 VICTORIA (1843).—C. 68, s. 1. Repeals 3 James I. c. 21, & 10 Geo. II. c. 19, s. 1.

7 & 8 VICTORIA (1844).—C. 101, ss. 6, 41, 53. Women able to maintain their bastard children and neglecting to do so to be deemed idle and disorderly persons. To provide for the establishment of asylums for the temporary relief of the houseless poor in London, Liverpool, Manchester, Bristol, Leeds, and Birmingham, and to enact that any person received into such an asylum giving a false name, or making a false statement, or giving different names on different occasions. is to be deemed a rogue and vagabond. (Repeals 8 & 9 Will. III. c. 30) 238, 250, 291

8 & 9 VICTORIA (1845).—C. 83, s. 77. To authorise the removal of English, Irish, and Manx paupers in Scotland. (Repealed in part 24 & 25 Vict. c. 37; 25 & 26 Vict. c. 113, s. 8; Stat. Law Rev. Act, 1875) .

8 & 9 VICTORIA (1845).— C. 117. To amend the laws relating to the removal of poor persons born in Scotland, Ireland, the Islands of Man, Scilly, Jersey, or Guernsey, and chargeable in England. (Repealed in part 24 & 25 Vict. c. 76, s. 7; 26 & 27 Vict. c. 89, s. 3, and *see* s. 6; Stat. Law Rev. Act, 1875.)

10 and 11 VICTORIA (1847).—C. 109, s. 22. Repeals in part 5 & 6 Vict. c. 57, s. 5.

11 & 12 VICTORIA (1848).—C. 110, s. 10. Persons in possession of means applying for relief to a relieving officer or at a workhouse, and not making a correct disclosure of their means, to be punishable as idle and disorderly persons 238, 277

12 & 13 VICTORIA (1849).—C. 103, s. 3. Persons chargeable to the common fund of a union, to be in respect of proceedings to be taken under 5 Geo. IV. c. 83, regarded as persons chargeable to a parish . 238, 278

14 & 15 VICTORIA (1851).—C. 28. Power to local authority to make regulations respecting common lodging-houses. (Repealed and re-enacted as to E. *except as to the Metropolitan Police District*, 38 & 39 Vict. c. 55, s. 343) 670

16 & 17 VICTORIA (1852-53).—C. 41, s. 8. Power to local authority to order reports from keepers of common lodging-houses kept for beggars and vagrants. (Repealed and re-enacted as to E. *except as to the Metropolitan Police District*, 38 & 39 Vict. c. 55, s. 343) . . . 670

19 & 20 VICTORIA (1856).—C. 64. Repeals 5 Edw. III. c 14; 4 Hen. IV. c. 27; 22 Hen. VIII. c. 10; 25 Hen. VIII. c. 13; 26 Hen. VIII. c. 6; 1 & 2 Phil. & Mar. c. 4; 1 James I. c. 6.

20 & 21 VICTORIA (1857).—C. 48. To authorise the committal of vagrant children to an Industrial School up to the age of fifteen. (Repealed 24 & 25 Vict. c. 113) 286, 287

23 & 24 VICTORIA (1860).—C. 108. To transfer the powers of the Committee of Council on Education under 20 & 21 Vict. c. 48, to a Secretary of State. (Repealed 24 & 25 Vict. c. 113, s. 27) . . . 286, 287

24 & 25 VICTORIA (1861).—C. 113. To authorise the committal of children under fourteen found begging or wandering in a state of destitution to an Industrial School. To continue until January 1, 1864. Repeals 20 & 21 Vict. c. 48. (Repealed 29 & 30 Vict. c. 118) . 286, 288

Statute Law Revision Act, 1861.—Repeals 23 Geo. III. c. 88; 32 Geo. III. c. 45; 42 Geo. III. c. 76, s. 18; 52 Geo. III. c. 31.

25 & 26 VICTORIA (1862).—C. 10. To continue the 24 & 25 Vict. c. 113 till January 1, 1867. (Repealed 29 & 30 Vict. c. 118, s. 3) . . 287, 288

Statute Law Revision Act, 1863.—Repeals 13 Edw. I. c. 4, and Stat. Civ.

INDEX OF STATUTES.

685

PAGE

Lond.; 34 Edw. III. c. 10, 11; 1 Rich. II. c. 6 (England); 15 Rich.
II. c. 6; 7 Hen. IV. c. 17; 1 Hen. V. c. 8; 2 Hen. V. c. 4; 1
Hen. VI. c. 3; 6 Hen. VI. c. 3; 23 Hen. VI. c. 13; 11 Hen. VII.
c. 22; 13 Hen. VIII. c. 9; 6 Hen. VIII. c. 3; 27 Hen. VIII.
c. 25; 31 Hen. VIII. c. 7; 33 Hen. VIII. c. 8; 33 Hen. VIII.
c. 14; 33 Hen. VIII. c. 17; 1 Edw. VI. c. 3; 3 & 4 Edw. VI.
c. 15; 3 & 4 Edw. VI. c. 22; 5 & 6 Edw. VI. c. 2; 7 Edw. VI.
c. 11; 1 Mary, St. 2, c. 13; 2 & 3 Phil. & Mary, c. 5; 4 & 5 Phil.
& Mary, c. 9; 5 Eliz. c. 15; 5 Eliz. c. 16; remainder of 18 Eliz.
c. 3; 35 Eliz. c. 7, ss. 6 and 7; 39 Eliz. c. 3; 43 Eliz. c. 3; 1 James
I. c. 25; 7 James I. c. 4; 1 Charles I. c. 1, in part; 3 Charles I.
c. 5; 16 Charles I. c. 4; 14 Charles II. c. 12, ss. 16, 17, 18, 23; 1
James II. c. 17, in part.

27 & 28 VICTORIA (1864).—C. 116. To empower guardians to provide proper
wards for the reception of destitute wayfarers, and to relieve them
at the cost of the Metropolitan Board of Works. (Repealed in part
28 & 29 Vict. c. 34, s. 1; 30 & 31 Vict. c. 6, s. 60) . . 291, 331

28 VICTORIA (1865).—C. 34. To repeal in part and make perpetual 27 & 28
Vict. c. 116. (Repealed in part Stat. Law Rev. Act, 1875) . . 291

28 & 29 VICTORIA (1865).—C. 79, s. 7. Paupers returning within twelve
months after removal to be deemed idle and disorderly persons . 238

29 & 30 VICTORIA (1866).—C. 113, s. 15. Persons relieved out of the workhouse refusing to perform a task of work to be punishable as idle
and disorderly persons 239

29 & 30 VICTORIA (1866).—C. 118. To authorise the committal to an Industrial School of children under fourteen found begging or wandering
in a state of destitution. Repeals 24 & 25 Vict. c. 113; 25 & 26
Vict. c. 10 287

30 VICTORIA (1867).—C. 6. To authorise the payment out of the Metropolitan
Common Poor Fund of the expenses of providing for the reception
and relief of casual paupers in any union or parish in the metropolis.
Repeals in part 27 & 28 Vict. c. 116. (Repealed 31 & 32 Vict. c. 122,
s. 9; 32 & 33 Vict. c. 63, ss. 9, 20; Stat. Law Rev. Act, 1875; 42
& 43 Vict. c. 6, s. 11) 301

Statute Law Revision Act, 1867.—Repeals 3 Will. & Mary, c. 11, in part; 8
& 9 Will. III. c. 30; 11 Will. III. c. 18; 6 Anne, c. 32; 6 Geo. I.
c. 19; 7 Geo. I. c. 7; 17 Geo. II. c. 5, in part; 25 Geo. II. c. 36,
s. 12; 26 Geo. II. c. 34, s. 2; 28 Geo. II. c. 19; 6 Geo. III. c. 48;
9 Geo. III. c. 41.

31 & 32 VICTORIA (1867-8).—C. 52. To extend the provisions of 5 Geo. IV.
c. 83 to gaming in public with any coin, card, token, or other means
of wagering or gaming in public. (Repealed 36 & 37 Vict. c. 38,
s. 5) 238

31 & 32 VICTORIA (1867-8).—C. 122, s. 36. Repeals 59 Geo. III. c. 12, s. 33.

33 & 34 VICTORIA (1870).—C. 75, ss. 27, 28, 36. To authorise board schools
to contribute to, or to establish Industrial Schools . . . 289

34 & 35 VICTORIA (1871).—C. 108. To provide for the regulation, control,
and discharge of paupers from workhouses and wards provided for
the casual poor. (Repealed in part 45 & 46 Vict. c. 36, s. 4) . 239, 302,
310, 318, 319, 331

34 & 35 VICTORIA (1871).—C. 112, s. 14. To authorise the children of women
convicted of crime for a second time to be sent to Industrial Schools.
(Repealed in part 39 & 40 Vict. c. 20, s. 5; Stat. Law Rev. Act,
1883) 238, 288
   S. 15. To extend the provisions of 5 Geo. IV. c. 83 to suspected
persons or reputed thieves frequenting any highway or place adjacent to a street or highway 238

Statute Law Revision Act, 1871.—Repeals 22 Geo. III. c. 83; 27 Geo. III.
c. 11; 35 Geo. III. c. 101, in part; 39 & 40 Geo. III. c. 87, s. 12 .

Statute Law Revision Act, 1872.—Repeals 1 Rich. II. c. 6 (Ireland); 15
Rich. II. c. 6 (Ireland); 43 Geo. III. c. 61; 45 Geo. III. c. 66,
s. 3; 49 Geo. III. c. 124.

INDEX OF STATUTES.

	PAGE
Statute Law Revision Act, 1872 (No. 2).—Repeals 50 Geo. III. c. 52.	
35 & 36 VICTORIA (1872).—C. 21. To empower the prison authority to contribute towards the expenses of Industrial Schools	288
36 & 37 VICTORIA (1873).—C. 38. To repeal 31 & 32 Vict. c. 52, and allow a fine to be imposed in lieu of imprisonment at the discretion of the magistrate	238
Statute Law Revision Act, 1874 (No. 2).—Repeals 5 & 6 Vict. c. 57, s. 5.	
Statute Law Revision Act, 1875.—Repeals 8 & 9 Vict. c. 83, and 8 & 9 Vict. c. 117.	
38 & 39 VICTORIA (1875).—C. 86, s. 17. Repeals 5 Eliz. c. 4.	
39 & 40 VICTORIA (1876).—C. 61, s. 44. The word "pauper" in the Poor Law Amendment Act, to include any person who obtains relief by wilfully giving a false name, or making a false statement, and such person to be punishable as an idle and disorderly person	239
39 & 40 VICTORIA (1876).—C. 79, ss. 11, 12, 13, 14, 15, 16. To authorise children habitually neglected by parents or habitually wandering to be sent to a certified efficient school, and in case of non-compliance, to a Day Industrial School. To permit the establishment of day Industrial Schools	289
44 & 45 VICTORIA (1881).—C. 59, s. 3. Repeals 2 Edw. III. c. 2; 4 Edw. III. c. 13; 13 Rich. II. c. 8; 7 Hen. IV. c. 17; 2 Hen. V. c. 4; 6 Hen. VI. c. 3; 23 Hen. VI. c. 13.	
45 & 46 VICTORIA (1882).—C. 36. To extend the time of detention of casual paupers authorised by 34 & 35 Vict. c. 112. Repeals in part 34 & 35 Vict. c. 108	239, 319, 331

SCOTLAND.

ROBERT II. (1385).—Caterans and vagrants destroying and taking goods by violence to be arrested.	337
Ordo Justiciare.—Sorning to be a point of dittay at the justice ayre	337
JAMES I. (1424).—C. 7. Sorners to be punished as breakers of the King's peace	337
(1424).—C. 21. No one between the ages of fourteen and seventy to beg, unless provided with a token from the sheriff or bailies	337, 342
(1425).—C. 20. The sheriff to arrest and imprison idle men unless they find a master	338
(1426).—C. 3, 4. The aldermen and town councils to fix the wages of craftsmen	362
(1427).—C. 4. The chamberlain at his ayre yearly to enforce the acts against beggars	338
JAMES II. (1449).—C. 9. Masterful beggars with horses and hounds, as also feigned fools and bards, to be punished	339
(1455).—C. 8. Sorners to be punished by the sheriff as thieves or reivers	340
(1455).—C. 13. The king, on going to any head burgh, to inquire whether there be any sorners or oppressors of the poor, and to punish them	340
(1457).—C. 26. The justiciar at his ayres to punish sorners, bards, masterful beggars, and feigned fools. Repeats provisions of James I. (1424), c. 21	337, 340
JAMES III. (1478).—C. 10, 11. The Acts of James I. against masterful beggars and sorners to be rigorously enforced at justice-ayres	340
JAMES IV. (1493).—C. 14. Craftsmen making rules for payment of wages on holidays to be indicted as common oppressors	362
(1493).—C. 20. Idle able-bodied men to be compelled to serve for wages as sailors	362
(1496).—C. 5. Craftsmen taking exorbitant prices to be punished	362

INDEX OF STATUTES. 687

JAMES IV. (1503).—C. 14. The Act of James I. against "stark beggars" to be enforced; the crooked, blind, impotent, and weak alone allowed to beg 341, 342
JAMES V. (1535).—C. 29. The former Acts against masterful beggars to be rigorously enforced; no one to beg except in the parish where he was born, and with a token from the headsman of the parish . 342, 343
JAMES V. (1540).—C. 21. The meal market at Edinburgh to be removed, because a multitude of vile, unhonest, and miserable creatures frequent it daily for sustentation 343
MARY (1551).—C. 16. Repeals provisions of James V. c. 9 (1535) . . . 343
(1551).—C. 18. All provosts and bailies to ordain reasonable prices for craftsmen 362
(1555).—C. 38. Repeats provisions of James V. c. 29 (1535) . . . 343
JAMES VI. (1567).—C. 17. Vagabonds having no goods, and shooting with culverin, crossbow, or handbow at doe, roe, hart, hind, hare, rabbit, dove, heron, or fowl of the river, to be punished 343
(1574).—Vagabonds and strong and idle beggars between the ages of fourteen and seventy to be apprehended and tried . . . 344, 505
(1579).—C. 12. Repeats Act of 1574. (Referred to in the Scotch Poor Law Act, 8 & 9 Vict., c. 83, ss. 79, 80) 344, 505
(1579).—C. 21. Actions for servants' wages to prescribe in three years 362
(1581).—Ratifies James VI. c. 12 (1579) 344
(1587).—C. 59, s. 7. Vagabonds and "unanswerable" men in the borders, highlands, and isles to find security to underlie the law . . 348
(1592).—C. 28. Judges to inquire, search, and apprehend sorners, strong vagabonds, and beggars wandering about the realm . . . 348
(1592).—C. 28. The lieges to inform against traitors and unknown vagabonds 348
(1592).—C. 28 ratified; the ministers and elders in every parish empowered to appoint two or three persons to enforce the Act . . 348
(1593).—Vagabonds and masterless men to find security to underlie the law 348
(1593).—The Acts of 1579 and 1581 against vagabonds and beggars to be enforced by the ordinary judges or justices 348
(1594).—C. 33. Students wandering with swords, pistolets, or other weapons to have them confiscated 349
(1594).—C. 37. For punishing theft, reiff, oppression, and sorning on the part of several Highland clans 349
(1594).—C. 58. The magistrates of Canongate to remove common and idle beggars from the High gate and street 350
(1597).—C. 39. The Acts against strong and idle beggars, vagabonds, and Egyptians ratified, with this addition, that strong beggars and their bairns are to be employed in common works, and their service mentioned in the Acts of 1579 to be prorogated during their lifetime 350, 505
(1600).—C. 28. A penalty of £20 to be exacted from Kirk-sessions in case of neglect to carry out the Act of 1597 350
(1606).—C. 10. Masters of coalheughs and saltpans may apprehend and put to labour all vagabonds and sturdy beggars . . . 351
(1609).—C. 20. Vagabonds, sorners, and common thieves, commonly called Egyptians, to quit the kingdom by the 1st August . 352, 505
(1617).—C. 7, s. 7. Justices of peace to put in execution the Acts against wilful beggars and vagabonds, solitary and idle men, and women without calling or trade 354, 355, 356
(1617).—C. 8, s. 11. Hostlers not to receive masterless men, rebels at the horn, vagabonds, or other persons guilty of known crimes . 354
(1617).—C. 8, s. 5. Constables to arrest all vagabonds, sturdy beggars, and Egyptians 354, 505
(1617).—C. 8, ss. 14, 18. Justices of the peace to appoint at their quarter sessions the ordinary hire and wages of labourers, workmen, and servants. A price to be set on craftsmen's work 362

INDEX OF STATUTES.

	PAGE
JAMES VI. (1621).—C. 21. Servants not to leave their masters at Whitsuntide, unless able to prove that they are hired by another master from Whitsuntide to Martinmas	363
CHARLES I. (1625).—Missive from the king, stating that he understands that the laws against beggars are not properly enforced. He commands the former Acts to be put in execution	354
(1630).—Complaint that the Acts against beggars are not enforced, and enjoining that penalties for the non-execution of the Acts are to be enforced	355
(1630).—Estimate of the wages to be paid to herring-fishers	363
(1639, 7th September).—Petition by the General Assembly anent idle beggars remitted to a committee, who are to meet and peruse all Acts of Parliament and Council anent idle beggars, idle persons, servants and servants' fees, and the instruction given to justices of the peace,	355, 364
(1639, 13th September).—The committee anent sturdy beggars to give in their overtures	355
(1639, 1st October).—The Act that all vagabond knaves without passes be apprehended, delayed	355
(1640).—Commissioners for manufactories to set masterless beggars to work at reasonable rates	355
(1641).—C. 100. The Commissioners for Manufactories to appoint correction houses for the restraint of idle and masterless beggars	355, 364
(1641).—C. 124. The maximum wages of colliers to be 20 merks	355
(1641).—C. 124. Petition of the Commissioners of the Kirk that order may be taken with sturdy beggars, Egyptians, and vagabonds	355, 505
(1646).—C. 290. Manufactories to be erected and encouraged as the best ways and means of restraining idle and sturdy beggars, and masterless vagabonds	355
(1647).—C. 341. The Procurator of State to consider all the Acts of Parliament relating to idle and sturdy beggars and gypsies, and to report to the next session	355, 505
CHARLES II. (1649).—C. 161. Able-bodied beggars to be compelled to work. Begging to be punished, as directed in former Acts	355
ACTS AND ORDINANCES OF THE GOVERNMENT, 9 (1655).—The Commissioners of the peace to put the laws in execution against the classes described in 1617, c. 7, s. 7	355, 364
ACTS AND ORDINANCES OF THE GOVERNMENT, 13 (1655).—Innkeepers or hoastlers receiving masterless men or vagabonds to be fined	355, 356
Constables to arrest vagabonds, sturdy beggars, and Egyptians	356
Each parish to maintain its own poor	356
Masterless idle vagabonds, and robbers to be apprehended and transported	356
Lists of idle masterless vagabonds and robbers, to be given in from time to time, to the governors of Inverlochy and Inverness, and to the commander-in-chief on the south side of the Forth	356
ACTS AND ORDINANCES OF THE GOVERNMENT, 16 (1655).—The Commissioners of the Peace to appoint at their Quarter Sessions, to be kept in February and August, the ordinary hire and wages of labourers, workmen, and servants	356
(1656).—All idle, loose, and dissolute persons found wandering after the 1st of July declared to be rogues, vagabonds, and sturdy beggars, and punishable as such under 39 Eliz. c. 4	161, 356
CHARLES II. (1661).—C. 275. Persons to be appointed in each parish to instruct poor children, vagabonds, and other idlers	356
(1661).—C. 338. The Commissioners of the Peace to put the laws in execution against the classes described in 1617, c. 7, s. 7	356
(1661).—C. 238. Hostlers not to receive masterless men, rebels at the horn, vagabonds, or other persons guilty of known crimes, under the penalties set forth in 1655, c. 13	356
(1661).—C. 238. Constables to arrest vagabonds, sturdy beggars, and Egyptians	356, 505
(1661).—C. 333. Coalmasters not to give more than 20 merks a year as wages. Coalhewers and workmen to work six days a week	364

INDEX OF STATUTES.

	PAGE
CHARLES II. (1663).—C. 52. Recites and ratifies c. 74 of the 6th Parliament of James VI., c. 268 of the 15th Parliament of James VI., and c. 10 of the 22nd Parliament of James VI., and ordains that persons or societies who have set up manufactories may seize vagabonds found begging, and employ them in their service	356, 364
CHARLES II. (1672).—C. 42. An Act for establishing correction houses for idle beggars and vagabonds	357
JAMES VII. (1686).—C. 22. The magistrates of Edinburgh to lay down effectual ways for freeing and purging the streets, wynds, and closes of the numerous beggars which repair in and about them	357
WILLIAM (1695).—C. 64. Idle, loose, and vagabond persons, without wives or children, to be compelled to serve as soldiers	358
(1695).—(C. 74. All Acts of Parliament, and Acts and proclamations of Council, for maintaining the poor and repressing beggars, ratified, approved, and revived, and ordained to be put in immediate execution	357
(1696).—C. 23. Sheriffs to cause vagabonds to be seized for service in the army	358
(1696).—C. 29. Acts, &c., for maintaining the poor and repressing beggars ratified; supervisors to be appointed to enforce them	357
(1698).—C. 40 Acts again ratified	357
1700. Overtures for providing the poor and repressing beggars, remitted to the Committee for security to bring in an Act	358
1700. Petition from Roxburgh that the laws already made be put in execution for maintaining the poor in ilk shire, and restraining idle and vagrant persons	358
1701. Acts, &c., for maintaining the poor and repressing beggars, &c., ratified. Heritors to provide and lay down rules for the maintenance of the poor *	358
8 & 9 VICTORIA (1845).—C. 83, s. 70. Destitute persons to be relieved although having no settlement in the parish to which they apply	364
17 & 18 VICTORIA (1854).—C. 74. To render Reformatory and Industrial Schools in Scotland more available for the benefit of vagrant children. (Repealed 24 & 25 Vict. c. 132, s. 9)	284, 372
17 & 18 VICTORIA (1854).—C. 86. For the better care and reformation of youthful offenders in Great Britain. (Repealed 29 & 30 Vict. c. 117, s. 37)	372
18 & 19 VICTORIA (1855).—C. 87. To amend the Act for the better care and reformation of youthful offenders, and the Act to render Reformatory and Industrial Schools in Scotland more available for the benefit of vagrant children. (Repealed 29 & 30 Vict. c. 117, s. 37)	372
19 & 20 VICTORIA (1856).—C. 28. To make further provisions for rendering Reformatories and Industrial Schools in Scotland more available for the benefit of vagrant children. (Repealed 24 & 25 Vict. c. 132, s. 29)	372
19 & 20 VICTORIA (1856).—C. 109. To amend the mode of committing criminal and vagrant children to Reformatory and Industrial Schools. (Repealed 29 & 30 Vict. c. 117, s. 37)	372
24 & 25 VICTORIA (1861).—C. 117, s. 37. Repeals 17 & 18 Vict. c. 86 ; 18 & 19 Vict. c. 87 ; 19 & 20 Vict. c. 109.	
24 & 25 VICTORIA (1861).—C. 132. To consolidate and amend the law relating to Industrial Schools in Scotland. Repeals 17 & 18 Vict. c. 74 ; 19 & 20 Vict. c. 28. (Repealed 29 & 30 Vict. c. 118, s. 3)	288
25 & 26 VICTORIA (1862).—C. 10. To continue 24 & 25 Vict. c. 132, until January 1, 1867. (Repealed 29 & 30 Vict. c. 118, s. 3)	287
25 & 26 VICTORIA (1862).—C. 101, s. 331. Vagrants, beggars, &c., in towns, under the Act, to be apprehended and, upon conviction, imprisoned.	365
28 & 29 VICTORIA (1865).—C. 56. Persons lodging in any premises, or encamping or lighting a fire on or near any enclosed land without the	

* One peculiarity distinguishes the old Scotch statutes prior to the Union, which is this, that those statutes lost their force by desuetude, that is, by mere lapse of time, coupled with neglect or non-observance, or at least with a contrary usage.—*Chambers*.

INDEX OF STATUTES.

	PAGE
consent of the owner or occupier, liable to a penalty of 20s. or fourteen days' imprisonment for a first offence, and 40s. or twenty-one days' imprisonment for a subsequent offence	366
29 & 30 VICTORIA (1866).—C. 118. To consolidate and amend the Acts relating to Industrial Schools in Great Britain. Repeals 24 & 25 Vict. c. 132; 25 & 25 Vict. c. 10	287
34 & 35 VICTORIA (1871).—C. 112, s. 14. To authorise the children of women convicted of crime for a second time to be sent to Industrial Schools. (Repealed in part 39 & 40 Vict. c. 20, s 5)	288
39 & 40 VICTORIA (1876).—C. 79, ss. 11-16. To authorise children habitually neglected by parents, or habitually wandering, to be sent to a certified efficient school, and in case of non-compliance to a Day Industrial School. To permit the establishment of Day Industrial Schools	289

IRELAND.

SENCHUS MOR (*Great Law Compilation*), (438-441).—Alms prevent the period of a plague, the suspension of amity between a king and his country, and the occurrence of a general war 374

No labourer, fuidhir, imbecile vagrant, shepherd, cowherd, or cart-boy, to be distrained in a decision about debts 375

Notice of one day to be served on a vagrant before removing him . 375

CORUS BESCNA (*Customary Law*).—Regulations regarding refections connected with charity and duty 375

Penalty on persons who entertain fugitives 376

BOOK OF AICILL (*Ancient Irish Criminal Law*), (circa 650).—Regulations relating to compulsory hospitality 377

Penalties against those who feed proclaimed persons . . . 378

Responsibility for sheltering a violator of the King's laws . . 379

CRITH GABHLACH (circa 1300-1325).—Rights of chiefs as regards compulsory hospitality 379

3 EDWARD II. (1310).—C. 1. To restrain great lords from taking prises, lodging, or sojourning against the will of the owner. (Repealed 9 Geo. IV. c. 53, s. 1) 383

3 EDWARD II. (1310).—C. 2. Against idle men and kearns being kept in times of peace to live upon the poor of the country. (Repealed Stat. Law. Rev. (I.) Act, 1878) 382

18 HENRY VI. (1440).—C. 3. No lord or other to charge the King's subjects with horses, horsemen, or footmen, without their good wills. (Repealed 9 Geo. IV. c. 53, s. 1) 384

25 HENRY VI. (1447).—C. 7. The sons of labourers and travailers of the ground to labour as their fathers and parents have done. (Repealed Stat. Law Rev. (1) Act, 1878) 384

28 HENRY VI. (1450).—C. 1. No marcheour or other man to keep more horsemen or footmen than they shall answer for and maintain upon their own charges. (Repealed 10 & 11 Charles I. c. 6) . . . 385

28 HENRY VI. (1450).—C. 3. To make it lawful for every liege man to kill or take notorious thieves. (Repealed 10 Geo. IV. c. 34, s. 1) . 386

5 EDWARD IV. (1465).—C. 2. To make it lawful to take, kill, and decapitate thieves. (Repealed 10 & 11 Charles I. c. 6) 387

10 HENRY VII. (1495).—C. 4. No Parliament to be held in Ireland till the Lieutenant and Council certify the King's licence in affirmation thereof and to summon the said Parliament. (Repealed 28 Hen. VIII. c. 4 & 20. Explained 3 & 4 Ph. & M. c. 4. Repealed 11 Eliz. 1 & 8. Finally repealed Stat. Law Rev. Act (I.), 1878) 387

10 HENRY VII. (1495).—C. 22. All English statutes concerning the public weal enacted up to this time to be deemed good and effectual in law, and to be accepted, used, and executed in Ireland. (Extended by 21 & 22 Geo. III. c. 48 (Ir.) Repealed so far as it extended certain enactments as to Parliamentary elections by 35 & 36 Vict. c. 33, sch. 6 . 387

INDEX OF STATUTES. 691

33 HENRY VIII. (1542).—C. 15. Against vagabonds. (Repealed 11 & 12 Geo. III. c. 30) 391, 393, 395, 411
33 HENRY VIII. (1542).—C. 9. Wages by the day of artificers and labourers, to be proclaimed by the justices at every Easter, and Michaelmas sessions. (Repealed 5 Geo. IV. c. 95, s. 1, and 6 Geo. IV. c. 129, s. 2.) 390
11 ELIZABETH (1569).—C. 4. Five persons of the best and eldest of every nation amongst the Irishrie to bring in all the idle persons of their surname. (Repealed 10 & 11 Charles I. c. 6, s. 1) 391
11 ELIZABETH (1569).—C. 5, Sess. 1. To make perpetual 33 Hen. VIII. c. 9. (Repealed Stat. Law Rev. Act, 1878) 391
10 & 11 CHARLES I. (1634-35).—C. 4. For erecting houses of correction and for the punishment of rogues, vagabonds, sturdy beggars, Egyptians, and other lewd and idle persons. (Repealed 11 & 12 Geo. III. c. 30) 392, 395, 411, 506
10 & 11 CHARLES I. (1634-35).—C. 6. Repeals 28 Hen. VI. c. 1; 33 Hen. VI. c. 3; 5 Edw. IV. c. 2; and 11 Eliz. c. 4. (Repealed Stat. Law Rev. (I.) Act, 1878) 393, 400
10 & 11 CHARLES I. (1634-35).—C. 16. For suppressing cosherers and idle wanderers. (Repealed Stat. Law Rev. (I.) Act, 1878) . . 340, 393
7 WILLIAM III. (1695).—C. 21. For the better suppressing tories, robbers, and rapparees. (Repealed Stat. Law Rev. (Ireland) Act, 1878) . 396
9 WILLIAM III. (1697).—C. 9. To amend 7 Will. III. c. 21. (Repealed Stat. Law Rev. (Ireland) Act, 1878). 396
2 ANNE (1703).—C. 19. To erect a workhouse in the city of Dublin for employing and maintaining the poor, and to relieve, regulate, and set to work all vagabonds and beggars. (The corporation hereby created dissolved by 1 Geo. II. c. 27; repealed 11 & 12 Geo. III. c. 11, s. 1) 397, 412
6 ANNE (1707).—C. 11. Against vagrants and pretenders to be Irish gentlemen wandering about. (Repealed 28 Vict. c. 33) . . 399, 405
2 GEORGE I. (1715).—C. 17. To empower justices to determine disputes about wages. Ministers and churchwardens of a parish empowered to bind out any child begging, or any poor child to a Protestant housekeeper or tradesman. (Repealed in part 54 Geo. III. c. 116, s. 1; 9 Geo. IV. c. 53, s. 1; 5 & 6 Vict. c. 97, s. 2; 16 & 17 Vict. c. 113, s. 69, in general terms and leaving parts of ss. 2, 3, 4, 5, 6, 7, 9, 10, 15, 16, 17 Stat. Law Rev. (I.) Act, 1878-79) 400
6 GEORGE I. (1719).—C. 12. To continue and amend the Acts for suppressing tories, robbers, and rapparees. (Repealed Stat. Law Rev. (I.) Act, 1878) 396, 401
8 GEORGE I (1721).—C. 9. To continue and amend the Acts for suppressing tories, robbers, and rapparees. (Repealed 11 & 12 Geo. III. c. 9) . 401
10 GEORGE I. (1723).—C. 3, s. 17. The Lord Mayor of Dublin may make rules for the beadles to clear the city, &c., of beggars, and inflict a fine of 10s. for each breach. (Repealed Stat. Law Rev. (I.) Act, 1878) 402
1 GEORGE II. (1727).—C. 27, s. 30. Workhouse authorities, or any five of them, empowered to cause beggars and vagrants to be seized; and any fifteen of them may sentence them to confinement in the workhouse for not longer than four years. Corporation created by 2 Anne, c. 19, dissolved. (Repealed 11 & 12 Geo. III. c. 29) . . 402
3 GEORGE II. (1729).—C. 14. All contracts or bye-laws in unlawful clubs of tradesmen for advancing wages to be void. (Repealed in part 54 Geo. III. c. 116, s. 1; 6 Geo. IV. c. 129, s. 2; and 9 Geo. IV. c. 53, s. 1; residue by Stat. Law Rev. (I.) Act, 1878) . . . 405
3 GEORGE II. (1729).—C. 17, s. 4. One member of the workhouse board empowered to exercise the powers delegated to five by 1. Geo. II. c. 27, and beadles, bell-hours, and constables neglecting to apprehend beggars liable to fine of 20s. (Repealed 11 & 12 Geo. III. c. 29) 402, 407
5 GEORGE II. (1731).—C. 14, s. 12. Vagrants and beggars committing disorders in the workhouse to be committed to Bridewell. (Repealed 11 & 12 Geo. III. c. 29) 403

INDEX OF STATUTES.

	PAGE
9 GEORGE II. (1735).—C. 6, ss. 2, 3, 4. Loose, idle vagrants, and all loose persons of infamous lives and characters, on presentment or on warrant, may be committed to the county gaol till they can be sent on board the fleet or to the plantations in America. Continues 7 Will. III. c. 21; 9 Will. III. c. 9; 6 Anne, c. 11; part of 11 Geo. II. c. 9. (Repealed Stat. Law Rev. (I.) Act, 1878.)	405
9 GEORGE II. (1735).—C. 25, s. 15. Enacts provisions similar to 3 Geo. II. c. 17, s. 4, for the city of Cork. (Spent. Local.)	403
19 GEORGE II. (1745).—C. 21, s. 11. Repeats provisions of 3 Geo. II. c. 17, s. 4. (Repealed 11 & 12 Geo. III. c. 11.)	402
23 GEORGE II. (1749).—C. 11, s. 10. Beggars and vagrants labouring under offensive disorders, rendering them offensive to the sight, and dangerous to health, to be sent to the workhouse. (Repealed Stat. Law Rev. (I.) Act, 1879)	406
3 GEORGE III. (1763).—C. 34, ss. 23, 24. Combinations to raise wages or the price of labour or workmanship in linen, cotton, or any other manufacture to be punished. (Repealed 6 Geo. IV. c. 122, s. 1, and Stat. Law Rev. (I.) Act, 1879)	407
11 & 12 GEORGE III. (1771-2).—C. 9. Repeals 8 Geo. I. c. 9.	
11 & 12 GEORGE III. (1771-2).—C. 11, ss. 13, 14, 15. No vagabond or strolling beggar to be sent to the workhouse. Beadles, bellowers, and constables to arrest vagrants under a penalty of 20s. (Repealed Stat. Law Rev. (I.) Act, 1879)	407, 412
11 & 12 GEORGE III. (1771-2).—C. 18, s. 40. Combinations to raise wages or price of labour in the city of Cork to be punished. Wages to be settled every Easter sessions. (Repealed 15 & 16 Vict. c. 142, s. 1).	408
11 & 12 GEORGE III. (1771-2).—C. 29. Repeals 1 Geo. II. c. 27; 3 Geo. II. c. 17; 5 Geo. II. c. 14; 2 Anne, c. 19; 19 Geo. II. c. 21. (Repealed Stat. Law Rev. (I.) Act, 1879).	
11 & 12 GEORGE III. (1771-2).—C. 30, ss. 4, 5, 6, 7, 8, 10. Corporations for the relief of the poor to grant badges to the helpless poor who have resided one year in their district, and to grant them a licence to beg. Workhouses to be established for the relief of the poor. Repeals 33 Hen. VIII. c. 15; 10 & 11 Charles I. c. 4	409, 410, 411, 418, 420
11 & 12 GEORGE III. (1771-2).—C. 33. Combinations of journeymen tailors and shipwrights to raise wages in the city of Dublin to be punished. (Repealed Stat. Law Rev. (I.) Act, 1879).	408
13 & 14 GEORGE III. (1773-4).—C. 46, ss. 3, 4, 5, 6, 8, 21. Beggars in Dublin may be sent to the House of Industry. News-cryers, shoe-cleaners, basket-carriers from market, and vendors of small wares in Dublin without licence may be committed as vagabonds. (Repealed Stat. Law Rev. (I.) Act, 1879)	410, 411
15 & 16 GEORGE III. (1775-6).—C. 25. Poor children above one year old not to be received into the Foundling Hospital. (Repealed Stat. Law Rev. (I.) Act, 1879)	412
19 & 20 GEORGE III. (1779-80).—C. 19, s. 2. Making bye-laws or orders for regulating or advancing the price of labour to be evidence of unlawful combination. (Repealed Stat. Law Rev. (I.) Act, 1878)	408
19 & 20 GEORGE III. (1779-80).—C. 27. Journeymen in the city of Cork only to be whipped after conviction by a jury. Amends 11 & 12 Geo. III. c. 18. (Never repealed, but no longer in force because the Act which it amends is repealed)	408
19 & 20 GEORGE III. (1779-80).—C. 36. Combinations to fix the price of labour amongst those concerned in the provision trade in Dublin to be punished. (Repealed Stat. Law Rev. (I.) Act, 1879)	408
21 & 22 GEORGE III. (1781-2).—C. 22. To amend 19 & 20 Geo. III. c. 36. (Repealed Stat. Law Rev. (I.) Act, 1879)	409
21 & 22 GEORGE III. (1781-2).—C. 45. Sums raised for providing for the impotent poor and beggars under 11 & 12 Geo. III. c. 30, and which have not been applied to the purposes of the Act, to be applied to the purposes of the county. (Repealed Stat. Law Rev. (I.) Act, 1879)	410

INDEX OF STATUTES.

	PAGE
23 & 24 GEORGE III. (1783-4).—C. 54. To continue 21 & 22 Geo. III. c. 22, to the year 1786. (Repealed Stat. Law Rev. (I.) Act, 1878) . 409
23 & 24 GEORGE III. (1783-4).—C. 58. Subscribers to the charitable purposes mentioned in 11 & 12 Geo. III. c. 30, declared to be members of the Corporation erected by the Act. (Repealed Stat. Law Rev. (I.) Act, 1879) 410
27 GEORGE III. (1787).—C. 57. To enable the Corporation of the Poor in Dublin to acquire and take lands within two miles of the Castle for the purposes of the House of Industry. (Repealed Stat. Law Rev. (I.) Act, 1879) 410
30 GEORGE III. (1790).—C. 32. To render the transportation of felons and vagabonds more easy. (Repealed Stat. Law Rev. (I.) Act, 1879) . 413
31 GEORGE III. (1791).—C. 44. Continues 6 Anne, c. 11. (Repealed Stat. Law Rev. (I.) Act, 1879) 413
35 GEORGE III. (1795).—C. 36, ss. 27, 28, 35. Any person harbouring a rogue or vagabond to be liable to a fine of £50 for a first offence, and £100 for every subsequent offence. Superintendent magistrates or constables, &c., may enter ale-houses, &c., and apprehend journeymen, apprentices, servants, or labourers drinking or gaming at unseasonable hours. (Repealed 48 Geo. III. c. 140, the marginal reference in which Act is wrong) 413
36 GEORGE III. (1796).—C. 20, ss. 15, 18, 19, 20, 22, 30, 31, 32, 34. Strangers may be arrested and examined on oath as to their place of abode, &c. Persons found out of their place of abode one hour after sunset to sunrise, if not out for a lawful purpose may be sent on board the navy as recruits. (Repealed 47 Geo. III. sess. 2, c. 13) . . 414, 415
37 GEORGE III. (1797).—C. 34. To empower the Corporation of the House of Industry to choose seven governors until May 1, 1798, any three or more of whom are to have the sole management. (Amended by 40 Geo. III. c. 40) 410
37 GEORGE III. (1797).—C. 38, s. 5. Persons taking unlawful oaths liable to be sent to serve in the army or navy. (Repealed 47 Geo. III. Sess. 2, c. 13) 415
38 GEORGE III. (1798).—C. 21, s. 4. Persons found in possession of arms, or offensive weapons, to be deemed disorderly persons. (Repealed 47 Geo. III. Sess. 2, c. 13) 415
38 GEORGE III. (1798).—C. 34. To continue the seven governors of the house of industry in office until May 1, 1799. No beggar to be discharged without the consent of three governors. (Continued and amended by 39 Geo. III. c. 38; 40 Geo. III. c. 33; 50 Geo. III. c. 192. Obsolete, left unrepealed by Stat. Law Rev. Act (I.), 1879, as being local) 410, 416
38 GEORGE III. (1798).—C. 35. Nine persons named in the Act to be appointed as governors of the house of industry with power to elect officers at salaries not exceeding £990 in the aggregate. (Continued by 39 Geo. III. c. 38. Repealed Stat. Law Rev. (I.) Act, 1879) . . . 410
39 GEORGE III. (1799).—C. 38. To continue 38 Geo. III. c. 34, and 38 Geo. III. c. 35, until May 1, 1800, and thence to the end of the next session of parliament. (Repealed Stat. Law Rev. (I.) Act, 1879) 410
40 GEORGE III. (1800).—C. 33. To continue and amend 38 Geo. III. c. 34., aggregate salaries may be increased to £1,190. (Amended by 50 Geo. III. c. 192. Repealed in part Stat. Law Rev. (I.) Act, 1879; residue local) 410
40 GEORGE III. (1800).—C. 40. To amend 37 Geo. III. c. 34, by empowering the Lord Lieutenant to appoint not more than five governors of the House of Industry instead of seven. (Amended by 41 Geo. III. c. 50, and 1 Geo. IV. c. 49. Local) 410
41 GEORGE III. (1801).—C. 50. To amend 40 Geo. III. c. 40, by empowering the five governors to elect three others. (Repealed 50 Geo. III. c. 192) 410
46 GEORGE III. (1806).—C. 95. Where any member of a Corporation for the

INDEX OF STATUTES.

	PAGE
Poor shall make it appear to any judge of assize that a greater sum should be levied than the sums mentioned in 11 & 12 Geo. III. c. 30, and 23 & 24 Geo. III. c. 58, the grand jury shall present such sums up to not less than £400 nor more than £500 for any town, nor less than £500 nor more than £700 for a county. (Repealed Stat. Law Rev. Act, 1872)	410
47 GEORGE III. (1807).—Sess. 2, c. 13. Repeals 36 Geo. III. c. 20; 37 Geo. III. c. 38; 38 Geo. III. c. 21.	
48 GEORGE III. (1808).—C. 140. Night-walkers to be treated as vagrants, and if children to be apprenticed. Repeals 35 Geo. III. c. 36. (Repealed in part 5 Geo. IV. c. 102, ss. 6, 15, 20, 23; Stat. Law Rev. Acts, 1872 (No. 2.), 1873)	416
50 GEORGE III. (1810).—C. 192. To amend and continue 38 Geo. III. c. 34, and 40 Geo. III. c. 33. Repeals 41 Geo. III. c. 50. . . .	410
54 GEORGE III. (1814).—C. 116, s. 1. Repeals in part 2 Geo. I. c. 17; 3 Geo. II. c. 14.	
54 GEORGE III. (1814).—C. 128. To amend the several Acts for regulating the Foundling Hospital in Dublin, and to empower the governors to suspend the admission of infants for six months in the year. .	412
1 GEORGE IV. (1820).—C. 49. To amend the laws relating to the House of Industry in Dublin, and to empower the Lord Lieutenant to appoint one governor only with a salary not exceeding £500 per annum, in whom all the powers of former governors are to be vested. The Lord Lieutenant may appoint visitors to meet quarterly and report to him.	410
5 GEORGE IV. (1825).—C. 95, s. 1. Repeals 33 Hen. VIII. c. 9.	
5 GEORGE IV. (1825).—C. 102, ss. 6, 15, 20, 23. Repeals 48 Geo. III. c. 140, in part.	
6 GEORGE IV. (1826).—C. 122. Repeals 3 Geo. III. c. 34.	
6 GEORGE IV. (1826).—C. 129, s. 2. Repeals 33 Hen. VIII. c. 9; 3 Geo. II. c. 14, in part.	
9 GEORGE IV. (1829).—C. 53, s. 1. Repeals 3 Edw. II. c. 1; 18 Hen. VI. c. 3; 28 Hen. VI. c. 3; 3 Geo. I. c. 17 in part; 3 Geo. II. c. 14 in part.	
10 GEORGE IV. (1830).—C. 34, s. 1. Repeals 28 Hen. VI. c. 3.	
1 & 2 VICTORIA (1837).—C. 56, ss. 3, 59. Houses of Industry and Foundling Hospitals to be under the direction and control of the Poor Law Commissioners. Persons deserting their wives or children to be liable to three months' hard labour. (Repealed 2 & 3 Vict. c. 1, s. 10; 6 & 7 Vict. c. 92, ss. 9, 10; 10 & 11 Vict. c. 31, ss. 16, 17; 10 & 11 Vict. c. 84, s. 1; 10 & 11 Vict. c. 90, ss. 9, 13; 12 & 13 Vict. c. 104, ss. 2, 12; 25 & 26 Vict. c. 83, s. 13; 31 & 32 Vict. c. 49, s. 15; Stat. Law Rev. Act, 1874, No 2.) . . .	410, 419, 421
2 & 3 VICTORIA (1838).—C. 1, s. 10. Repeals 1 & 2 Vict. c. 56, in part.	
5 & 6 VICTORIA (1842).—C. 97, ss. 2, 9, 10. Repeals 2 Geo. I. c. 17, in part.	
6 & 7 VICTORIA (1843).—C. 92, ss. 9, 10. Repeals 1 & 2 Vict. c. 56, in part	
10 & 11 VICTORIA (1847).—C. 31, ss. 16, 17. Repeals 1 & 2 Vict. c. 56, in part.	
10 & 11 VICTORIA (1847).—C. 84. For the punishment of vagrants and persons offending against the laws in force for the relief of the destitute poor in Ireland. (The first 8 sections of this Act are still law. The last section (9) is repealed by Stat. Law Rev. Act, 1875) . .	421
10 & 11 VICTORIA (1847).—C. 90, ss. 9, 13. Repeals 1 & 2 Vict. c. 56, in part.	
12 & 13 VICTORIA (1849).—C. 104, ss. 2, 12. Repeals 1 & 2 Vict. c. 56, in part.	
15 & 16 VICTORIA (1852).—C. 142, s. 1. Repeals 11 & 12 Geo. III c. 18.	
16 & 17 VICTORIA (1853).—C. 113 s. 69. Repeals 2 Geo. I. c. 17, in general terms.	
25 & 26 VICTORIA (1862).—C. 83, s. 13. Repeals 1 & 2 Vict. c. 56, in part.	
28 VICTORIA (1865).—C. 33. Repeals 6 Anne, c. 11.	

INDEX OF STATUTES. 695

                                                                                                        PAGE

31 & 32 VICTORIA (1868).—C. 25. To extend the Industrial Schools Act (29 & 30 Vict. c. 118) to Ireland 426
31 & 32 VICTORIA (1867-8).—C. 49, s. 15. Repeals 1 & 2 Vict. c. 56, in part.
Stat. Law Rev. Act (1872). Repeals 46 Geo. III. c. 95.
Stat. Law Rev. Act (1872), (No. 2), (1875). Repeals 48 Geo. III. c. 140, in part.
Stat. Law Rev. Act (1874) (No. 2). Repeals 1 & 2 Vict. c. 56, in part.
Stat. Law Rev. Act (1875). Repeals s. 9 of 10 & 11 Vict. c. 84.
Stat. Law Rev. (I.) Act (1878). Repeals 3 Edw. II. c. 2 ; 25 Hen. VI. c. 7 ; 11 Eliz. c. 5, sess. 1 ; 10 & 11 Car. I. c. 6 ; 10 & 11. Car I. c. 16 ; 7 Will. III. c. 21 ; 9 Will. III. c. 29 ; 2 Geo. I. c 17 ; 6 Geo. I. c. 9 ; 6 Geo. I. c. 12 ; 10 Geo. I. c. 3 ; residue of 3 Geo. II. c. 14 ; 9 Geo. II. c. 6 ; 19 & 20 Geo. III. c. 19 ; 19 & 20 Geo. III. c. 36 ; 21 & 22 Geo. III. c. 22 ; 23 & 24 Geo. III. c. 54.
Stat. Law Rev. (I.) Act (1879). Repeals 23 Geo. II. c. 11 ; 3 Geo. III. c. 34 ; 11 & 12 Geo. III. c. 11 ; 11 & 12 Geo. III. c. 30 ; 11 & 12 Geo. III. c. 33 ; 13 & 14 Geo. III. c. 46 ; 15 & 16 Geo. III. c. 25 ; 21 & 22 Geo. III. c. 45 ; 23 & 24 Geo. III. c. 58 ; 27 Geo. III. c. 57 ; 30 Geo. III. c. 32 ; 31 Geo. III. c. 44 ; 38 Geo. III. c. 35 ; 39 Geo. III. c. 38 ; 40 Geo. III. c. 33, in part.

WALES.

VENEDOTIAN CODE (circa 1080).—Book I. c. 34, s. 11. Gwestva dues of the land-maer 434
    Book II. c. 2, ss. 12, 14. The men of Arvon privileged as to payments for guests. The privileges of Arvon 434
DIMETIAN CODE (circa 1180).—Book II. c. 8, s. 13. Harbouring of a guest . 430
    Book II., c. 17, s. 49. Caption fee for a fugitive bondman . . . 432
    Book III. c. 3, s. 8. The bondman to be valued as a beast . . . 433
GWENTIAN CODE (circa 943).—Book I. c. 4. Of the king's retinue . . 434
    Book II. c. 39, s. 46. Fine for an offence against a homeless beggar . 432
SUNDRY OR ANOMALOUS LAWS.—Book V. c. 2, s 111. Description and worth of an adventitious and a domestic bondman 433
    Book VI. c. 1, s. 72. Description of a serving bondman . . . 433
    Book IX. c. 35, s. 1. Guardians required for custody of guests . . 431
    Book X. c. 8, s. 8. The nine nights of the guest house a nine of law . 431
    Book X. c. 13, s. 1. Uchelwrs permitted to rule their bondmen according to conditional bondage in South Wales, and perpetual bondage in Gwynedd 433
    Book XI. c. 1, s. 12. Punishment for feeding a food-forbidden man . 434
    Book XI. c. 2, s. 2. Conventional bondmen may be sold or given by their lords 433
    Book XIV. c. 2, s. 3. As to exonerating a guest 431
    Book XIV. c. 3, s. 31. The king's Gwestva cow 434
    Book XIV. c. 10, s. 6. The lord's Gwestva dues from his man . . 434
    Book XIV. c. 12, s. 7. As to exonerating a guest 431
    Book XIV. c. 12, s. 11. As to exonerating a guest 431
    Book XIV. c. 15, s. 6. As to exonerating a guest 431
    Book XIV. c. 15, s. 22. As to exonerating a guest 431
    Book XIV. c. 16, s. 9. Guardians appropriate for lawful guests . . 431
    Book XIV. c. 21, s. 3. As to an arddelw of custody of guests . . 432
    Book XIV. c. 21, s. 14. As to an arddelw of custody of guests . . 432
    Book XIV. c. 30, ss. 1, 2, 3, 4. Of theft absent, for which an arddelw is not had, and against which guardians are to be had . . . 432

BORDER LAWS BETWEEN ENGLAND AND SCOTLAND.

HENRY III. of England and ALEXANDER II. of Scotland (1249).—C. 3. Methods of recovering fugitive vassals or bondmen . . . 32
EDWARD VI. of England and MARY of Scotland (1549).—C. 7. Murderers,

thieves, robbers, runaways, rebels, or other evil-doers whatsoever flying from one country to the other to be delivered up within ten days after the presentation of a letter of requisition 97
ELIZABETH of England and JAMES VI. of Scotland (1586).—None of the broken borderers to keep in their company any idle persons not employed in any honest service or trade; no idle persons to be suffered to remain in the border villages or ale-houses 130

ISLE OF MAN.

9 HENRY V. (1422).—No man of whatever condition to go out of the island without licence of the lord or his lieutenant 441
Chapmen and shipmen to have licence to go to England 442
Tenants or servants not to be taken out of the island without licence of the lieutenant on pain of forfeiture of the vessel in which they are conveyed, &c. All Scots to avoid the land. No man to bring beggars or vagabonds into the island on pain of forfeiture of his boat . . 442
3 ELIZABETH (1561).—No alien coming into any haven with merchandise or otherwise to pass further without licence on pain of forfeiture of his goods and imprisonment. Irish women loitering and not working commanded forth of the isle, and no boat hereafter to bring any such persons into the isle on pain of forfeiture 442
7 JAMES I (1609).—To fix the wages of ploughmen, drivers, horsemen, tailors, woollen and linen weavers, fullers, masons, carpenters, shipwrights, hoopers, slaters, thatchers, and blacksmiths 443
4 CHARLES II. (1664).—Persons conveying natives out of the island without special licence to be fined, and servants leaving without licence to be proceeded against. Refractory servants to be punished by imprisonment and spare diet. Vagrant servants to be punished. Male servants not to be compelled to serve unless engaged in winter time, and female servants within a reasonable time of summer . 445, 446
5 CHARLES II. (1665).—The poor not to beg out of their own parish, if they do they are to be warned back; if they neglect or refuse they are to be compelled and whipped, and if they continue disobedient they are to be taken to gaol until they declare themselves conformable. None but blind, lame, maimed, decrepid, or other infirm persons are to be relieved. Young and sound persons are to labour or otherwise made to serve as servants, or else be committed until they submit . . 446
Apprentices to enter into surety to serve for five years, and when out of time not to take apprentices themselves for one year, nor to marry for one year without special licence 447
7 CHARLES II. (1667).—To fix the wages of ploughmen, drivers, horsemen, household fishermen, men servants, and shepherds. Refractory servants to be imprisoned and dieted. Persons not to have the benefit of choice children except with the approbation of the jury of servants 449
10 VICTORIA (1846).—C. 40. Masters of vessels bringing over paupers or vagrants to be imprisoned until they enter into sureties to maintain the pauper or vagrant while in the island, and to convey him back to the port from whence he was brought. (Repealed 1870) . . 451
47 & 48 VICTORIA (1884).—C. 40. To enable Manx children to be sent to Reformatory or Industrial Schools in Great Britain.

INDEX OF STATUTES.

CHANNEL ISLANDS.

JERSEY.

	PAGE
CHARLES II. (1669).—Letters Patent of Charles II. providing for the setting to work of poor and idle people	454
GEORGE III. (Code of 1771).—Provision to be made in each parish for the maintenance of the poor	455
As to Mendicants. Infirm poor people may be licensed to beg in their own parish only. Those who beg outside their parishes may be punished	455
Persons giving alms to those forbidden to beg may be fined	456
Strangers may not take children chargeable to the parishes out of the island under a penalty of £50	456
The able-bodied poor over thirteen years of age may be let out	456
As to Strangers. No inhabitant to receive a stranger for more than one night without giving notice to the constable	456
Constables to report the arrival of strangers to the Governor	456
Strangers not to be allowed to remain in the island or to marry the women of the country without permission of the Governor	456
As to Tavern-keepers. Tavern-keepers to reserve at least two beds for strangers, and not to tolerate drunkards, blasphemers, vagabonds, idlers, and persons of bad repute. Nor to harbour young men or servants, or to permit the poor to drink beyond their means	457

GUERNSEY.

HENRY VIII. (1534).—No one to harbour a stranger under a penalty of sixty sols	458
1537. Poor strangers who cannot live without begging to quit the country under pain of scourging. All native beggars to beg in their own parish	458
1537. The sheriff to note the names of all passengers who arrive in vessels, and see that they return whence they came	458
1542. All young men and women living by themselves, to take service by next All Saints' day	459
ELIZABETH (1566).—Orphans or destitute children of poor persons to be apprenticed or sent to England	459
1566-7. Strange servants not to be received into service without a licence	459
1566-7. No masters of vessels to put on shore passengers without permission	460
1583. Banished criminals to quit the island under pain of capital punishment	460
1588-9. Vagabonds, idlers, &c., who are strangers to quit the island within forty days after being ordered	461
1588-9. No strangers to let lodgings, keep a tavern, &c.	461
1588-9. No strangers to be permitted to marry and settle.	462
1588-9. No strangers to be permitted to live in the island without giving sureties from inhabitants	462
1588-9. No young children or others of more mature age to go begging; their relations are to support them. If they have none, or if they are too poor, the constable is to take charge of them	462
1597. Persons who languish in their homes without the means of soliciting charity to be supported at the common cost	463
JAMES I. (1611).—No person to beg without a licence	463
1611. Constables, &c. to make a rate for the relief of the poor	463
CHARLES II. (1684-5).—Ordinances relating to the poor and mendicants re-enacted	464

LAW TEXTS CITED.

ENGLAND.—Ancient Laws and Institutes of England. In 1 vol. fol. Printed by Command. 1840.
 The Statutes of the Realm to the end of the reign of Queen Anne, from original Records and authentic Manuscripts. In 11 vols. fol. Printed by Command. 1810—1822.
 The Public General Acts to the present time. Published by Authority.
SCOTLAND.—The Acts of the Parliaments of Scotland from 1124 to 1707. In 12 vols. fol. Printed by Command. 1844—1875.
IRELAND.—Ancient Laws of Ireland. In 4 vols. 8vo. Published under direction of the Commissioners. 1865—1879.
 The Statutes at large passed in the Parliaments held in Ireland from 1310 to 1801. In 20 vols. fol. Published by Authority. 1786—1801.
WALES.—Ancient Laws and Institutes of Wales. In 1 vol. fol. Printed by Command. 1841.
THE BORDERS.—Leges Marchiarum, or Border Laws. In 1 vol. 8vo. By W. Nicolson. 1705.
ISLE OF MAN.—The Ancient Ordinances and Statute Laws of the Isle of Man. In 1 vol. 8vo. By M. A. Mills. 1832.
 Statute Laws of the Isle of Man promulgated since the year 1836. In 1 vol. 8vo. By J. Gell. 1848.
JERSEY.—A Codex of Law for the Island of Jersey. In 1 vol. 8vo. 1771.
GUERNSEY.—Approbation des lois, coutumes et usages de l'ile de Guernesey. In 1 vol. 8vo. 1822.

INDEX

OF THE PRINCIPAL VARIETIES OF BEGGARS AND ROGUES DEPICTED IN THE HISTORY.

I.—BEGGARS.

(1) *Afflicted Classes.*

Accident, sufferers from, 311
Blind, 45, 55, 72, 223, 233, 361, 371, 556, 577, 590, 591, 608, 611, 634, 651, 667. (*Gickisses*) 545
Blind harpers (*Platschierers*), 546
Cripples, 45, 72, 81, 178, 184, 234, 361, 371, 542, 557, 584, 587, 589, 591, 605, 608, 610, 611, 616, 621, 634, 637, 643. (*Billies-in-the-Bowl*) 634; (*Klenkners*) 545; (*Piètres*) 520
Deaf and dumb, 179, 312, 361, 653. (*Ascioni*) 558; (*Dummerers*) 596, 598, 605, 619
Demoniacs or madmen, 56, 172. (*Abraham men*) 340, 593, 596, 604, 619; (*Spiritati*) 564; (*Voppers*) 545
Fits, sufferers from, 81, 221, 605, 651. (*Accadenti*) 558; (*Counterfeit Cranks*) 587, 596, 598, 604, 619; (*Grantners*) 545; (*Sabouleux*) 521
Invalids, 55. (*Dutzers*) 545
Jaundice, sufferers from (*Schweigers*), 546
Lame beggars, 556, 589
Lepers, 46, 51, 81, 83, 338, 344, 576, 590. Female lepers (*Jungfrauen*) 546
Lying-in women, 223. (*Dutzbetterins*) 546
Maimed persons, 55, 179, 188, 371, 569, 571, 587. (*Piètres*) 520
Malingerers (*Malingreux*), 520
Pregnant women, 220. (*Bil-wearers*) 546
Scurvy, sufferers from (*Callots*), 520
Sores, bites, &c., sufferers from, 81, 188, 220, 406, 571, 590, 611, 621. (*Accaponi*) 558; (*Attarantati*) 558; (*Clapper dudgeons*) 473, 585, 602, 615; (*Flowches*) 81; (*Francs mitoux*) 520; (*Low gaggers*) 630; (*Palliards*) 476, 477, 594, 597, 619; (*Seffers*) 546; (*Washmen*) 594
Weepers (*Allacrimanti*) 558

(2) *Distressed Classes.*

Apprentices, 262, 294
Beggars, ordinary, (*Bregers*) 545; (*Caimands and Caimandes*) 521; (*Crumb-foxes*) 382; (*Shoulers*) 425; (*Stocachs*) 394; (*Truands*) 80; (*Westours*) 35, 42, 63, 64, 439

INDEX OF BEGGARS AND ROGUES

Beggars, naked or in rags, 264, 312, 571, 586, 588, 608, 609. (*Blichschlahers*) 545; (*Cocchini*) 558; (*Polissons*) 520; (*Schwanfelders*) 545.
Bluegowns, 99, 361, 590
Bread and butter lurkers, 312
Calenderers, 312
Captives, prisoners, or slaves released, 81, 587, 634. (*Acaptosi*) 557; (*Lossners*) 545; (*Sbrici*) 564
Children, 45, 221, 322, 323, 548, 587, 590, 616, 623, 635, 638, 642, 650, 659, 667; (*Kinchen or Kitchen Coes and Mortes*) 594, 596, 619; (*Lullaby Cheats*) 619
Colliers, 312, 323, 650
Cotton spinners, 312, 650
Countrymen, 258
Family men, 312, 642. (*Affamiglioli*) 559
Fire, victims of, 311, 361, 611. (*Demanders for Glimmer or Glimmerers*) 596, 599, 619; (*Brugiati*) 564; (*Riffaudés*) 520; (*Ruffiti*) 564
Foreigners, 312
Frozen-out gardeners or watermen, 312, 634, 662
Merchants or tradesmen broken down, 641, 646. (*Kandierers*) 546; (*Mercandiers*) 520
Negroes, 221, 247, 637
Noblemen or knights or gentlemen broken down. (*Highflyers*) 312, 641, 648; (*Ubern Sönzen Ganger*) 546, 547, 549
Orphans, 642. (*Orphelins*) 520
Sailors shipwrecked or distressed, 127, 220, 224, 249, 250, 311, 322, 323, 610, 634, 641, 664. (*Nightingales of Newgate*) 81; (*Whipjacks*) 593, 596, 598, 619
Scholars or students, 60, 61, 62, 73, 81, 107. (*Kammesierers*) 545
Servants out of place, 258, 312
Soldiers discharged, 126, 216, 308, 309, 371, 595, 608, 610, 613, 634. (*Drilles, Narquois, Passevolants*) 521; (*Formigotti*) 564; (*Katherans*) 337; (*Kearns*) 383; (*Rufflers*) 82, 593

(3) *Religious Classes.*

APPURTENANCES OF RELIGION:
    Church mendicants, 219. (*Dobissers*) 545
    Flour for the Host, seekers for (*Affarinati*), 559
    Exorcisers (*Vagiereren*), 545
    Godfathers, seekers for (*Comparizzanti*), 559
    Miracle mongers (*Admiranti*), 558
    Miraculous water vendors (*Lotori*), 559
    Oil for church lamps, seekers for (*Allampadati*), 559
    Pardoners, 74, 562, 577, 587, 590, 591
    Pregnant women, advisers of (*Calcidiarii*), 559
    Relic vendors (*Reliquiarii*), 559
CONVERTS:
    Jews, 649. (*Iucchi*) 559
    Jewesses (*Veranerin*), 546
PENITENTS:
    St. Anthony's (*Burkhart*), 546
    Bread eaters (*Appezzenti*), 558. (*Stabulers*) 545
    For enormities (*Affarfanti*), 557
    Hangmen (*Dallingers*), 545
    Manslayers (*Suntvegers*), 546
PILGRIMS:
    Devotees of St. Hubert (*Hubins*), 521
    Image bearers of saints (*Acconii*), 558
    Pilgrims proper (*Christianiers Calmierers*), 546. (*Coquillards*) 521; (*Falsi Bordoni*) 557
PROFESSORS OF RELIGION:
    Bedesmen with a bell (*Morghigeri*), 559

False monks (*Affrati*), 557. (*Curtalls*) 582, 594, 619
  (*Fraters*) 593, 596, 598, 604, 619, 653
False prophets (*Felsi*), 557
False descendants of the Apostle Paul (*Pauliani*), 559
False priests, 87. (*Patriarcos*), 474, 476, 496, 595, 596, 599, 604, 615, 619.
  (*Spettrini*) 559

II.—ROGUES AND VAGABONDS.

CHEATS OR SHARPERS:
  Barrators, 49, 336
  At buckle and thong, 625
  Coney catchers, 583
  Versers to the coney catcher, 583
  At cups and ball, 625
  At fast and loose, 346, 584
  Fawney riggers, ring droppers or fallers, 248, 505, 595, 630
  At hook and snivey, 628
  Levanters, 631
  At luck in a bag, 625
  Money lenders (*Mutatori*), 558
  Pinchers, 628. (*Cagnabaldi*) 558
  Purse tricksters, 653
  Snitchers, 628
  Sweetners, 625
  Testators (*Testatori*), 560
  Thimble riggers, 275
  Three-card men, 312, 652
SHAM OR VAGABOND EMPLOYMENTS:
  Air balloon carriers, 312
  Bawdy baskets, 596, 599, 619
  Ballad singers, 249, 295, 323, 361, 525, 634, 636. (*Bards*) 35, 339 ; (*Chaunter Culls*) 627
  Bearwards, 107, 111, 128, 180, 199, 202, 235, 237, 324, 392, 528
  Cab touters, 312
  China menders, 295, 323
  Crossing sweepers, 267, 634, 636, 662
  Fencers, 39, 107, 112, 115, 121, 128, 180, 199, 202, 392
  Fiddlers, 162, 499, 501, 615, 637
  Flower sellers, 220, 547, 659
  Irish toyle, 594, 619
  Jockies or strolling minstrels, 346, 359
  Jugglers, 107, 180, 199, 202, 346, 392, 484, 527
  Petty hawkers, 126, 128, 245, 295, 323, 364, 369, 370, 371, 542, 650. (*Coneyskin dealers*) 154, 599 ; (*Glassmen*) 126, 154 ; (*Muggers*) 370 ; (*Potmen*) 154 ; (*Swadlers or Swigmen*) 594, 596, 619
  Match carriers, 312, 651
  Minstrels, 35, 64, 87, 107, 128, 162, 180, 199, 202, 323, 346, 359, 361, 525, 527
  Picture carriers, 312
  Flying porters, 630
  Quack doctors, 248, 312, 324, 479, 631, 641, 644
  Rag sellers, 248, 323
  Saffron sellers (*Crociarii*), 559
  Sham leggers, 630
  Staff-strikers or cudgel-players, 53
  Soap vendors, 249
  Tale-tellers, 96, 346 ; (*Skelaghes*) 390
  Tinkers, 95, 126, 295, 323, 371, 504, 528, 584, 594, 596, 598, 603, 617, 638
  Umbrella repairers, 249, 295, 323, 528
  Walking morts, 596, 599

FORTUNE TELLERS:
  Gypsies, 498, 502
  Sham gypsies, 247, 249, 312, 527, 619. (*Tolliban rig*) 629
PROFESSORS OF PALMISTRY AND PHYSIOGNOMY, 74, 75, 128, 180, 199, 202, 235, 236, 392
PROSTITUTES: 253, 263, 271, 293, 294, 295, 297, 298, 324. (*Dells*) 596, 606, 608, 619; (*Doxies*) 594, 596, 597, 599, 605, 606, 608, 610, 611, 614, 615, 619, 632; (*Fylloks*) 80; (*Gyllots*) 469; (*Autem morts*) 594, 596, 602, 606, 614, 619; (*Walking morts*) 596, 599, 615
PROWLERS FOR GIRLS:
  (*Apple squires*) 583; (*Rôdeurs de filles*) 518
RAPPAREES AND TORIES, 396, 399, 403
THIEVES:
  Highwaymen, 39, 579, 580. (*Chosen pells*) 630; (*Dingers*) 631; (*High lawyers*) 582, 607; (*Padders*) 582; (*Prigmen or Prigs*) 593, 619; (*Roberdesmen*) 42, 52, 58, 580; (*Royal scamps*) 627; (*Rufflers*) 82, 593
  Housebreakers, 265, 275, 298. (*Drawlatches*) 42, 55, 58; (*Ken crackers*) 627; (*Little snakesmen*) 628
  Makers and utterers of false coin, 506, 633. (*Queer bit makers*), 627; (*Smashers*) 295, 479
  Pickpockets, 607, 619. (*Filers*) 623; (*Foists*) 583, 585; (*Stall to a foist*) 583; (*Kiddy nippers*) 627; (*Reader merchants*) 629
  Reivers, 340, 349
  Rogues, 579, 596, 597, 606, 647. (*Bianti*) 560; (*Capons*) 521; (*Sack divers*) 631; (*Wild rogues*) 594
  Servants or shopmen with false characters (*Courtauds de boutanche*), 520
  Thieves in general, 80, 87, 249, 276, 293, 294, 295, 296, 300, 583. (*Academy buz nappers*) 631; (*Bleating rig*) 630; (*Blue pigeon flyers*) 627; (*Clinking*) 631; (*Dining-room post*) 629; (*Dobin rig*) 630; (*Fidlum Ben*) 627; (*Fowl stealers*) 275, 580, 605, 606, 607, 619, 656, 657, 658; (*Hedge creepers*) 80; (*Hookers or anglers*) 596, 619; (*Kibbers*) 627; (*Kid rig*) 631; (*Lifters*) 583, 623; (*Limmers*) 350; (*Long gang*) 296; (*Losels*) 80; (*Lumpers*) 628; (*Lusks*) 80; (*Michers*) 80; (*Peterers*) 629; (*Poachers*) 263, 275; (*Prad borrowers*) 628; (*Priggers of palfreys or prancers*) 593, 607, 619; (*Rum draggers*) 630; (*Running snavellers*) 631; (*Rushmen*) 629; (*Sneaks*) 628; (*Starrers of the glaze*) 629
INSTRUCTORS OF THIEVES:
  (*Cagous*) 519; (*Falpatori*) 559
RETIRED THIEVES:
  (*Archisuppots*) 520
  Upright men, 583, 593, 619
  Writers of begging letters or petitions, 649. (*Jack or jarkmen*) 594, 596, 599, 604, 619

GENERAL INDEX.

A. B., an anonymous vagrant, evidence of, 257
Abbeys, suppression of, 83
A'Becket, Thomas, edict against his Welsh sympathisers, 27
Aberdeen, scholars of the University of, forbidden to beg without licence, 346
idle persons in, 348
vagrancy in the county of, 366
Abraham men, 340, 593, 596, 604, 619
Academy Buz-nappers, description of, 631
Acaptosi, or pretended redeemed slaves, 557
Accadenti, or sham epileptics, 558
Accaponi, or Italian palliards, 558
Acconii, or image-bearers of saints, 558
Actors. *See* Players
Admiranti, or reciters of false miracles, 558
Æromancy, prediction by, 77
Æthelstan, reign of, 9
Affamiglioli, or family man, 559
Affarfanti, or feigned penitents, 557
Affrati, or false monks, 557
Affarinati, or beggars for flour, 559
Aged poor, relief of, 108, 462
Ages of vagrants, average of, 298
Agricultural labourer, 43, 47, 51, 53, 54, 57, 59, 63, 64, 66, 71, 101, 107, 150, 154, 164, 173, 177, 243, 252, 263, 317, 360, 384, 385, 390
nomadic habits of, 329, 330
Agriculture in Scotland, former state of, 360
Aicill, book of, regulations of, 377, 378
Aill of Reneurling, court held upon, 441
Albans, St., blind impostor at, 557
Algerine beggars, 634
Allacerbanti, or Italian "upright men," 559
Allacrimanti, or weepers, 558
Allampadati, or beggars for oil, 559

Alectromancy, prediction by, 77
Alehouses, 38, 98, 126, 130, 152, 153, 162, 184, 188, 212, 217, 219, 247, 293, 457, 539, 576, 585, 587, 588, 593, 596, 601, 602, 605, 609, 614, 618, 621, 624, 632, 637
punishment of vagrants lodging in, 235
excess of, in Ireland, 395
Alexander II. of Scotland (1214—1249), border law in the reign of, 32
Alfred, King, law of, 6
almsgiving by, 9
Alfric, or Ælfric, Archbishop of York (circa 965-1051), homily of, 12
Aliens without a licence forbidden in Guernsey, 461
in the Isle of Man, 442
in Jersey, 457
Alms for the poor, collection of, 95, 98, 99, 100, 128
preventing the period of a plague, 374
Almsgiving, evils of indiscriminate, 652
prohibition of, 67, 68
American tramp, 654
Ammianus Marcellinus on the Attacotti, 3
Andrew's, St., scholars of the university of, forbidden to beg without a licence, 346
Anglers or hookers, 596, 619
Anglo-Saxon laws, 5—16
Anne, Queen, 178, 397
Anty Brignal and the begging Quaker, 637
Appezzenti, or bread-eaters, 558
Apprentice, the idle, 262
Apprentices in Dublin, regulation of the wages of, 409
in Guernsey, 459
in the Isle of Man, 447, 448
Apprenticing children of labourers forbidden, 64

Archisuppots, or retired leading thieves, 520
Armstrong, Johnnie, the freebooter, 342, 591
Army, compulsory service in, 146, 358
Arson, crime of, 13, 191, 298, 313
Artificers absenting themselves from service, punishment of, 48, 50, 51, 59
regulation of wages of, 70
Ascioni, or Italian dummerers or idiots, 558
Asser (*d.* 910), on King Alfred, 9
Attacotti, or Aitheach-Tuatha, 3
Attarantati, or persons who pretend to be bitten, 558
Attremanti, or tremblers, or shivering Jemmies, 558
Augury, prediction by, 74
Austria-Hungary, beggars and vagabonds in, 547
Autem mort, the, 594, 596, 602, 606, 614, 619
Auvergne, thieves from, 22

BADEN, mendicity and vagrancy in, 543
Badges to be worn by beggars in England, 99, 101, 174, 175
in Ireland, 410
in Scotland, 330
" Bagford Ballads," extracts from, 616, 622
Bán-apadh, or white proclamation, meaning of, 376 *n.*
Bang beggar, nature of the, 419
Banishment of English vagabonds, 106, 129, 133, 141, 143, 165, 180, 182, 185
Guernsey, 461
Irish, 400, 401, 402, 403, 406, 413
Scotch, 336, 338, 340, 356
Gypsies, 488
Banquets, ancient Irish, connected with charity and religion, 375, 376
Barclay, Alexander (1475—1552), extract from the " Ship of Fools," 586
Bards in Ireland, 394
in Scotland, 339, 340, 344, 347, 348
in Wales, 35, 63, 64, 439
Bark, stealers of, deemed rogues, 205
Barns frequented by beggars, 71, 153, 597, 600, 603, 613, 620, 624, 663
Barrators, punishment of, 49, 336
Basset, Ralph, thieves hanged by, 23
Bastard children, penalty for deserting, 141, 238, 250
Bath, beggars at, 109, 112, 129, 197, 263
Bawdy basket, the, 596, 599, 619
Bavaria, mendicity and vagrancy in, 543

Beadles, 52, 104, 105, 170, 184, 226, 273, 402, 407, 604, 622, 647
abuses by, 184
Bearbaiting, 111, 147, 193, 237
Beard of the Innocents, sale of the hair of, 590
Bearwards in England, 107, 111, 128, 180, 199, 202, 235, 237, 324 *n.*
France, 528
Ireland, 392
Bede, the Venerable (672—735), on charity, 12
on English slavery, 6
Bee, Jon (John Badcock), extract from " A Living Picture of London," 638
Beg, licence to, in England, 74, 83, 92, 95, 99, 100, 108
Scotland, 341
Beggars abroad. *See* Austria-Hungary, Baden, Bavaria, Belgium, Bucharest, Denmark, France, Finland, Germany, Hamburg, Holland, Italy, Poland, Portugal, Revel, Russia, Saxe-Coburg and Gotha, Sweden, Turkey
banishment of. *See* Banishment
Beggar boy, what a, buys, 659
Beggars at Bristol, 176
Bush, 604
carried home in triumph, 421
Beggar catcher in Peeblesshire, 361
Beggars' Chorus, 616
infesting the court, 72, 78
Beggar, the Cunning Northern, 609
derivation of the word, 470
Beggars, description of, in "Peers Ploughman," 55, 405, 576, 587
preferring to be diseased, 98, 187
in Edinburgh, 353, 357
gains, 177 216—225, 233, 324
in general, 214, 576, 578, 580, 585, 616 618, 626
in Guernsey, 458, 462, 463, 464, 465
Mr. Joshua Gee on, 186
Sir Matthew Hale on, 168
Beggars, harbouring of, forbidden in the Border counties, 130
in England, 68, 74, 153
in France, 522
in Guernsey, 458
in Ireland, 391
in the Isle of Man, 448
in Jersey, 456
in Scotland, 347
Beggars, Italian, in England, 303
in the Isle of Man, 451—455
in Jersey, 457
in London. *See* London.
proclamations against, 78, 95, 97, 121

GENERAL INDEX. 705

Beggars, punishment of, in England, 60, 67, 68, 73, 81, 89, 90, 94, 99, 100, 106, 109, 117, 119, 121, 128, 133, 135, 136, 148, 153, 158, 159, 160, 161, 162, 164, 165, 166, 167, 174, 179, 180, 190, 197, 199, 202, 235, 236, 238, 602, 615, 622, 623, 636, 639, 642, 648, 651
  punishment of, in Guernsey, 458, 461, 462, 463, 464
  in Ireland, 391, 392, 398, 399, 401, 427
  in the Isle of Man, 446
  in Jersey, 455
  in Scotland, 337
Beggars, rich, 660
Beggar, the song of the, 607
Beggars' songs, 601, 604, 607, 609, 611, 613, 616, 618, 620, 622, 631
  Stanley's remedy for, 136
  stark, in Scotland, 341
Beggar, statement of a, 651
  street sellers, 650
Beggars, sturdy, 53, 82, 93, 104, 106, 108, 117, 121, 129, 137, 161, 165, 172, 174, 179, 180, 187, 190, 201, 471, 576, 587, 589, 593, 597, 609, 622, 633, 671
  the Supplication for, 72
  and Vagrant Impostors, 633
  and their Vanities, 586, 589
  to be sent to Virginia, 141, 143, 144
  in Wales, protection of homeless, 432, 438
  whipping of. *See* Whipping
Begging, 71
  friars, 480, 576, 587, 590
  letter in 1542, 592
  letters, charges for, 649
  letter impostors, 663
  letter writer, the, by Dickens, 645
Béghards, 470
Béguines, 470
Bell-hour, or bellower, signification of, 402
Belgium, beggars and vagrants in, 510
Bélistre, signification of, 519
Bethlehem Hospital, a sham collector for, pilloried, 65
  warning issued by, against sham lunatics, 172
Berkshire system of repressing vagrancy, 319
Betting men to be punished as rogues and vagabonds, 235, 236, 238
Bianti, the tricks of, in Italy, 560
Bibblesworth, Walter de, directions by, for laying the table, 45
Bidale prohibited, 79, 439
Billy in the bowl, the, 634
Bil-wearers, or pretended pregnant women, 546

Bishop to remonstrate with persons neglecting to give alms, 98, 100
Black death, ravages of the, 42
Blackmen beggars, 221, 247
Bleating rig, description of, 630
Blome, John, indicted as a vagabond, 39
Blickschlahers, or naked beggars, or shallow coves, 545
Blind beggars, 45, 51, 108, 182, 223, 233, 361, 371, 590, 667
Blind impostors 182, 577, 591, 611, 634, 651
Bluebeard, a captain of rogues, 579
Blue pigeon flyer, description of, 627
Bo-aire, chief privileges of, 378
Bonaght, an Irish exaction, 388
Bondmen, English, 3, 4, 5, 7, 9, 11, 12, 17, 18, 19, 20, 21, 32, 43, 47, 50, 51, 52, 53, 56, 57, 58, 88, 113
  sale of, out of the country forbidden, 19
  manumission of, 88, 113
  Scottish, 334, 335
  Welsh, 432, 433
Border laws, 32, 97, 130
Borh, signification of 13, *n.*
Bōt, signification of, 9, *n.*
Bradford (Yorkshire), stocks at, 48
Branding, punishment of, in England, 51, 90, 125, 133, 138
  in France, 518
  in Scotland, 338
Breakfast, or edraugh, an Irish exaction, 393
Bregers, or beggars, in Germany, 545
Brehon laws, the, 373
Brignal, Anty, and the begging Quaker, 637
Brine, George Atkins (1812—1881), a noted vagrant, letters from, 639—645.
Brislington, prohibition of the relief of vagrants at, 198
Bristol, complaint from, regarding Irish vagrants, 148
  treatment of beggars at, 176, 187, 240
Britain, origin of the name, 1 *n.*
Brittany, extract from the ancient customary of, 381 *n.*
Brome, R. (*d.* 1652), extracts from "A Jovial Crew," 612
Brugiati, or burnt (Italian demanders for glimmer), 564
Bucharest, mendicity at, 569
Bull-baiting, 147, 193
Burkhart, or St. Anthony's penance, 546
Burning through the ear, punishment of, 106, 121, 344, 345
Burns, Robert (1759—1796), extract from the "Jolly Beggars," 631

GENERAL INDEX.

Bury St. Edmunds, distribution of alms at, 84
Butchers in Dublin, regulation of the wages of, 409
Burton-on-Trent, treatment of the poor at, 174, 202
Buxton, diseased poor forbidden to resort to, without licence, 109, 112, 129

CADE, JACK, rebellion of, 66
Cadgers' resort, a, by Pierce Egan, 635
Cagnabaldi, or exchangers, in Italy, 558
Cagous, or master thieves, in France, 519
Calcidiarii, or advisers of pregnant women, 559
Callots, or sufferers from scurvy, 520
Calot, Kyt, mistress of Giles Hather, 585
Cambrensis, Giraldus (circa 1146—1219), extracts from, relating to Ireland (A.D. 1185). 28, 115, 379
    relating to Wales (A.D. 1188), 435
Cambridge, scholars of, begging without licence to be punished, 73, 107
    plays at, 193
    vagabonds at, in 1555, 99
Cant language, 245, 466—479, 623
    origin of, 466
    first specimen of, 467
Capons, or sharpers, in France, 520
Captives, redeemed, 545, 557, 564, 587
Cardinals robbed, 39
Cary, John, on the treatment of beggars, 176
Casual wards, 250. 253, 255, 256, 269, 274, 276, 277, 291, 295, 296, 301
    robberies planned in, 258
Catherans deemed rebels, 337
Cattle, importation of Irish, into England forbidden, 396
Caulfield, James, extract from, 626
Censerie, an oppressive tax, 24
Ceorl, condition of the, 18
    the fugitive, 7
Certificate, false begging, 127
Channel Islands, vagrants from, in England, 278, 281
    penalty on masters of vessels bringing vagrants or beggars from, 182
Chapman, the, in Anglo-Saxon times, 5, 6
Chapmen, petty punishment of, 107, 128, 154, 200, 202, 235, 236
Charitable contributions, punishment of collectors of, under false pretences, 235, 236
Charity Organization Society, 303, 327
Charles I., reign of, in England, 147
    in Ireland, 392
    in Scotland, 354

Charles II., reign of, in England, 163
    remarks on the poor, 166
    in Ireland, 395
    in Scotland, 355
Charles VIII. of France, 518
Chaucer, Geoffrey (1345—1402), extracts from, 576, 577
Cheke, Sir John (1514—1557), as a Member of Parliament, 89
    extract from the "Hurt of Sedicion," 92
Chelsea, George, imposture of, 648
Children of beggars in England, 83, 91, 95, 108, 159, 168, 169, 176, 178, 185, 190, 191, 208, 213, 214, 216, 217, 218, 221, 223, 224, 225, 236, 246, 284—290, 296, 303, 312, 314, 322, 323, 587, 590, 594, 611, 615, 616, 619, 621, 623, 628, 633, 634, 635, 638, 642, 650, 651, 659, 664, 667
    Ireland, 398, 401, 404, 407, 410, 416, 423, 426, 427
    Scotland, 344, 347, 350, 354, 365
Children to be apprenticed to the sea, 179
    begging, their tricks, 178, 221, 246, 659, 664
    desertion of, 180, 185, 199, 202, 235, 236, 250
    in industrial schools, 284—290
    Italian, in England, 303, 304
Chosen Pells, description of, 630
Christallomancy, prediction by, 74
Christianiers Calmierers, or pretended pilgrims, 546
Christmas haymaker, a, 663
Churchwardens to collect alms for the relief of the infirm poor, 82
Clack dish, the beggar's, 46
Clans, certain Scottish, denounced as thieves, 349
Clapper dudgeon, the, 473, 585, 602, 615
Clarendon, the assize of, 25
Clidomancy, prediction by, 74
Clinking, description of, 631
Clothing of vagrants, 241, 262
Cnut, King, reign of, 13
Coal heughs, vagrants employed in, 351, 356, 357, 364
Cocchini, or tattered rogues, 558
Cock Lorrell, a captain of rogues, 584
    extracts from, 593
Coesre, signification of, 519
Coigny in Ireland, 383, 385, 388
    in Scotland, 335
Coinage of small money established, 145
Collection of alms for the impotent poor, 82, 95
Collectors for gaols, hospitals, punishment of fraudulent, 128, 199, 202
Colquhoun, P. (1745—1820), on begging, 213, 214

GENERAL INDEX. 707

Comedians. *See* Players
Commission of Elizabeth for the enfranchisement of villeins, 113
of Charles I. for putting into execution the laws for the relief of the poor, 151
Commitments for vagrancy in England, number of, 206, 241, 246, 673
in Scotland, number of, 370
Commons, House of, committees on vagrancy and poor removal, 183, 198, 206, 216, 228, 251, 278, 306.
Commortha. *See* Cymmortha.
Comparizzanti, or searchers for godfathers, 559
"Complete Mendicant," extract from the, 624
Concealment of property by vagrants, 275
Coney-catching, explanation of, 583
"Confessions of an Old Almsgiver," extracts from, 651
Conjurations, enchantment, and witchcraft, punishment of, 134, 135
Constables, 42, 44, 47, 48, 49, 54, 58, 73, 81, 91, 96, 101, 108, 115, 116, 117, 129, 133, 137 n., 141, 143, 149, 153, 159, 161, 165, 166, 172, 177, 178, 181, 182, 186, 187, 188, 197, 198, 203, 230, 237, 244, 250, 253, 255, 258, 275, 279, 280, 285, 291, 292, 294, 295, 296, 297, 298, 299, 318, 320, 321, 327, 328, 331, 354, 355, 356, 363, 365, 367, 402, 407, 413, 414, 446, 447, 453, 455, 456, 458, 459, 463, 469, 488, 489, 496, 500, 601, 602, 606, 613, 622, 633, 637, 662
Constabulary Commissioners report on vagrancy, 244
Conveyance of beggars and vagrants, 178, 180, 207, 215, 216, 224, 229, 241
Coopers in Dublin, regulation of the wages of, 409
Copland, Robert, author of "The Hyeway to the Spyttelhouse," 79, 467
Coquillards, or pretended pilgrims, 521
Corilomancy, prediction by, 77
Cornish language, the, 2
Cornish place, or Llan Cerniw, 2
Correction, houses of. *See* Houses of Correction
Corus Bescna, or customary law, regulations of, in Ireland, 374, 375
Coscinomancy, prediction by, 77
Coshering an Irish exaction, 16, 379, 390, 393, 394, 400
Council, the Privy, action and orders of, 97, 102, 103, 112, 119, 122, 124, 133, 141, 142, 143, 144, 148, 149, 155, 460, 490

Court, the, infested by vagabonds, 72, 78
Courtauds de Bouianche, or servants or shopmen with false characters, 520
Cowdiddle Jenkin, a captain of rogues, 580
Cozeners and shifters, the company of, 595
Crank the Counterfeit, 596, 598
Cripples, begging, 45, 51, 182, 184
sham, 584, 587, 589, 605, 608, 610, 611, 616, 621, 634. 637, 643
Crith Gabhlach, extracts from, 379, 380, 381
Crociarii, or fraudulent saffron-sellers, 559
Crocus. *See* Quack Doctor
Crocussing rig, description of, 631
Cromwell, Thomas (1490—1540), letter regarding the gypsies, 487
Crosbiter, Lawrence, a captain of rogues, 583
Cross, begging like a cripple at a, 45, 46
Crumb fox, signification of, 382
Cuddy, an Irish exaction, 385
Cumberland, system of repressing mendicity in, 321
Cumhal, explanation of, 377
Cunning northern beggar, the, 609
Curtall, the, 582, 594, 619
Cymmortha, a Welsh exaction, 35, 63, 79, 439
Cymry, or Welsh, the, 2
Cyprus, King of, robbed, 53

Dacre, Lord, payment of Scottish outlaws by, 342
Dactilomancy, prediction by, 77
Daggers or dirks, persons in possession of, in Ireland, deemed vagabonds, 415
Daisy Kicker, description of, 627
Dallingers, or pretended hangmen, 545
David II. of Scotland, reign o', 337
Davis, Sir John (1569—1626), on Ireland, 383, 388
Deaf and dumb impostors, 178, 312, 653
Death, punishment of, for vagabondage in England, 91, 94, 107, 121, 129, 130, 133, 135, 145
in Scotland, 340, 344, 345, 348
in Guernsey, 461
Defoe, Daniel (1661—1731), extracts from works of, 190, 624
Dekker, Thomas (d. 1641), works of, 144, 467, 600, 621
Dell, the, 596, 606, 608, 619
Demander for glimmer, description of, 596, 599
Demon feasts in Ireland, nature of, 375
Denier, signification of, 607
Denmark, beggars and vagabonds in, 509
Denville, Sir Gosseline, his robberies, 39

708   GENERAL INDEX.

Depôts de Mendicité in France, 523, 524, 532
Derby, household order against vagrants, 121
Earls of, as kings of Man, 441, 442, 445, 447
Derg-apadh, or red proclamation, meaning of, 376
Desertion of wives or children in England, 180, 185, 199, 202, 235, 236, 238, 250
  in Ireland, 419, 421
Desmond, Earl of, beheaded, 387
  devastation caused by, 596
Devil, the, would not be refused relief at Kirk Michael, 451
Dickens, Charles (1812—1870), on the begging letter writer and tramps, 645
Dimetian Code, laws of the, 430, 432
Dingers, description of, 631
Dining-room post, description of, 629
Disease voluntarily preferred by beggars, 98
Dobin-rig, description of, 630
Dobissers, or church mendicants, or image-bearers of saints, 545
Doctors, quack, or crocuses. *See* Quack Doctors
Dogs, vagabonds with, in Scotland, 339
  in Ireland, 393
Dommerer, the, 596, 598, 605, 619
Dopfers, or church mendicants, or image-bearers of saints, 545
Dorset system of repressing vagrancy, 318
Douglas, house of, excesses of, 342
  Isle of Man, beggars in, 452
Doxies, 594, 596, 597, 599, 605, 606, 608, 610, 611, 614, 615, 619, 632
Drawlatches, vagabonds so called, 42, 55, 58
Dreams, prediction by, 78
Drilles, or disbanded soldiers, 521
Drink, evil of, in Guernsey, 464
Drinking among beggars and vagabonds, 71, 82, 187, 219, 220, 233, 234, 247, 257, 258, 262, 295, 296, 297, 326, 580, 581, 582, 588, 590, 592, 597, 605, 609, 610, 614, 618, 620, 621, 631, 634, 637, 643
Dublin, beggars in, 397, 398, 399, 402, 403, 406, 407, 411, 412, 413, 414, 416, 420
  workhouse in, 397, 398, 402, 410, 411, 414, 420
  picture of, in 1818, 416
Duffe, King, reign of (968—972), 336
Dunbar, William (1460—1520), extract from a general satire, 588
Dunstan, St. (*d.* 988), influence of, 12
Dunkirk privateers, 610

Dutton, John, exemption in favour o the heirs of, 109, 129, 133, 148, 182, 201, 202
  origin of the privileges granted to the heirs of, 109 *n.*
Dutzbetterins, or lying-in women, 546
Dutzers, or pretended invalids, 545
Dwellings, overcrowding in, forbidden, 122, 139

Eadric, King of Kent, laws of, 5
Earnings of the working classes, 316, 317
Ears of vagabonds to be burnt through, 106, 121, 344, 345
  to be cut off, 74, 82, 339
  to be nailed to the trone and cut off, 339
Eaught and Edraugh, Irish exactions, 393
Ecclesiastical institutes on almsgiving, 12
Ecgbert, Archbishop of York, ordinances of, 8, 21
Edinburgh, vagrants in, 343, 353, 357
Edgar, King, laws of, 12
Edmund, King, laws of, 11
Edward the Confessor, laws of, 14, 15, 27
Edward I., reign of, 34
  II., reign of, 39
  II., robbed by Sir Gosseline Denville, 40
  II., poem on the evil times of, 84
  III., reign of, 40
  III., impecuniosity of, 53
  III., introduces the practice of feeding and clothing the poor on Maunday Thursday, 52
  IV., reign of, 67, 387
  VI., reign of, 89
Egan, Pierce (1772—1849), extract from " Life in London," 635
Eglintoun, beggars at the funeral of the Earl of, 360
Elizabeth, reign of, 100, 391, 490
  annoyed by beggars, 119
Elizabeth, St., beggars, company of, 555
End gatherers to be deemed rogues, 186
Entertainment of guests in Wales, 430, 435, 436, 437, 438
Epilepsy, simulation of, 81, 221, 521, 545, 558, 587, 596, 598, 604, 605, 619, 651
Erasmus (1467-1536) on astrology, 77
Ere the ground, labourers in Ireland ceasing to, 384
Erse, derivation of cant words from the, 473
Essex justices' letter to the Council regarding Irish beggars, 148
Evcaf, department of the, in Turkey, 572

Fairs frequented by vagrants, 251, 268, 275, 498, 499, 597

GENERAL INDEX.

Falpatori, or instructors of young thieves, 559
Falsi Bordoni, or pretended pilgrims, 557
Families, punishment of persons neglecting to support their, in England, 180, 185, 200, 202, 212, 235, 236, 238, 250
   in Ireland, 419, 421
Famine, the Irish, 259, 266, 422
Farms, union of, forbidden, 78
Fast and loose, a cheating game amongst vagrants, 346 *n.*, 584
Fawney rig, description of the, 630
Feathers of the Holy Ghost, sale of, 590
Feigned fools in Scotland, 339, 340
Feitors, punishment of, 58
Felsi, or false prophets, 557
Female slaves, traffic in, 14
Fencers in England, 39, 107, 112, 115, 121, 128, 180, 199, 202
   in Ireland, 392
Fiddlers, punishment of, 162
Fidlum Ben, description of, 627
Fielding, Henry (1707—1754), on beggars, 203
Finland, beggars in, 568
Fire, punishment of persons pretending losses by, 129, 235
Fish, Simon (*d.* 1531), the "Supplication for beggars," 72
Fish, order for the consumption of, on certain days, 112, 124
Fits, imposition by means of feigned. *See* Epilepsy
FitzStephen (*d.* 1191), description of London, 33
Fletcher, Andrew, of Saltoun (1653—1716), on Scottish vagabonds, 359
Fletcher, John (1576—1625), extract from the "Beggars' Bush," 604
Flying porter, description of, 630
Flyma, signification of, 10 *n.*
Folk-right, signification of, 10.*n.*
Food collected by vagrants, 220, 247, 249, 250, 262, 264, 276, 293, 294, 453, 545, 558, 590, 605, 613, 616, 621, 623, 632, 635, 637, 643, 648, 649, 661
Foolish beggars and their vanities, 586, 589
Foot scamp, description of, 627
Forest laws, the, 30
Formigotti, or pretended soldiers, 564
Fortune-tellers, punishment of, in England, 199, 202, 235, 236
   in Scotland, 346
Fortune-telling, 134, 135, 247, 249, 498, 502, 619
Forty hours, begging in Italy during the, 557
Foundling hospital in Dublin, 398, 410, 412

Foxe, John (1517-1587), extract from acts and monuments, 577
France, beggars and vagabonds in, 517
   thieves from, 22
François I., reign of, 519
Francs mitoux, 520
Frater, 593, 596, 598, 619, 653
Fraternity of vagabonds, extract from the, 593
Free borgh or frith borg, signification of, 10 *n.*
Freshwater mariner, description of, 250
Froissart, Jean (1337-1410), on the reign of Richard II., 63
Frozen-out beggars, 662
Frum-tihtle, signification of, 13 *n.*
Fugitives forbidden to be harboured in England, 9, 10, 11, 13, 19, 20, 26, 29, 68
   in Ireland, 376
   in Scotland, 347
Fuller, Thomas (1608—1661), rendering by, of Gower's verses on the rebellion of Wat Tiler, 57
   on the hospitality of abbeys, 85

Gaberlunyie man, the, 590
Gaels, arrival of the, in England, 1
Gaelic, derivation of cant words from the, 473
Gallowglass, the, in Ireland, 382
Game, persons in pursuit of, in England deemed vagabonds, 209
   persons shooting at, in Scotland deemed vagabonds, 343
Gay, John (1688—1732), extracts from "Trivia," 184
Gee, Joshua, on the treatment of beggars and vagrants, 186
Gemōt, signification of, 6 *n.*
"Gentleman's Magazine," extracts from, 191, 213, 215, 360, 661
Geomancy, prediction by, 77
George I., reign of, 183, 400
   II.,   ,,   192, 402
   III.,   ,,   204, 407
   IV.,   ,,   228, 409
Germany, vagrancy and mendicity in, 535
Gervase of Canterbury (*fl.* 12th cent.), extract from, 27
Gesithman, signification of, 7 *n*
Gickisses, or blind beggars, 545
Gilbert's Act for the better relief and employment of the poor, 208
Giles's, St., beggars in, 218, 635, 638
Glasgow, scholars of the University of, forbidden to beg without licence, 346
Glassmen classed as rogues, 133, 154
Glaze, starring the, description of, 629

GENERAL INDEX.

Glimmer, the demander for (or Glimmerer), 596, 599, 619
Gloucester system of repressing vagrancy, 321
Gloucestershire, bands of outlaws in, 42
Godly banquets in Ireland, nature of, 375
Gower, John (1325—1403), verses on the rebellion of Wat Tiler, 57
Grantners, or knaves with the falling sickness, 545
Grand jury of Middlesex, presentment of, against beggars, 201
Gray, Lord, complaints of the soldiery in Ireland, 388
Gregory, St., and English slaves. 6, 115
Gringoire Pierre, the ragged, starveling poet of *Notre-Dame de Paris*, 519
Grogham, description of, 627
Grose, Francis (1731—1791), on beggars and vagrant impostors, 633
Guernsey, laws of, 457
poor, removal of, from England, 227, 237
Guests, custody and entertainment of, in Wales, 430
Gwentian Code, laws of, 432, 434
Gwestva, nature of, 16, 434, 439
Gwestwr or Westour, the, 35, 63, 64, 439
Gwilym, Dafydd ab, the "Welsh Petrarch" (1340 — 1400), extract from, 471
Gypsies, Acts against, in England, 72, 97, 102, 486, 489, 490, 603
in Ireland, 393
in Scotland, 344, 346, 352, 355, 356
Gypsies, first appearance in England, 485
Gypsies, arrest of, ordered, 103, 490
counterfeit, 247, 249, 312, 495, 584
counterfeit, punishment of, 129, 180, 199, 202, 235
deportation of, to Norway, 488
description of, in 1858-59, 496—502
fortune-telling by, 498, 502
in France, 525, 528, 531
language of, 245
language of, derivation of cant words from, 475, 479
letter from Thomas Cromwell regarding, 487
malpractices of, 491, 492, 493, 494, 498, 499, 501, 502, 505, 506
masque of the metamorphosed, 603
names by which they are known, 483
origin of, 483
punishment of, in England, 488, 490, 491, 492
punishment of, in Ireland, 393
punishment of, in Scotland, 344, 352, 354, 355

Gypsies in Scotland, 371
Gypsyries at Wandsworth, 503

HACKBALL, a notorious Dublin beggar, 412
Hale, Sir Matthew (1609—1676), on thieves and beggars, 168
Hallam, Henry, on monastic charity, 85
Hamburg, beggars and vagabonds in, 542
Hants, system of repressing vagrancy, 326
Harbouring of vagrants forbidden in England, 53, 68, 94, 108, 153, 201, 202
in Scotland, 347
in Ireland, 393
Harbouring of fugitives in Ireland, penalty for, 376, 379
in Wales, 434
Harman, Thomas (d. 1569). Extracts from the "Caveat for Cursetors," 71, 466, 468, 477, 595
Harrington, a cant name for a farthing, 146
Harrison, William (d. 1594), extracts from his "Description of Britain," 88. 119, 129, 336, 466
Harse, William, begging letter from, in 1542, 592
Harvesting, certain labourers allowed to leave their homes for that purpose, 47, 49, 200
Hawick, a great centre of crime, 343
Hawkers. *See* Pedlars
Head Act, the, in Ireland, 387
Head, Richard, extract from the "English Rogue," 618
Hempen manufacture in Ireland, regulation of wages in the, 407
Hedge pulling, punishment for, 205
Heidelberg, ordinance at, forbidding students to carry arms, 349
Henri II., reign of, in France, 519
Henry I., laws of, 20
II., reign of, 25
III. ,, 31
IV. ,, 63
V. ,, 65
VI. ,, 65, 384
VII. ,, 67, 387
VIII. ,, 70, 390, 486
Hervey, James (1714—1758), extract from, 671
Hext, Edward, letters of, regarding vagabonds and gypsies, 125, 491
Highlands of Scotland, vagabonds in, 344, 348, 349, 359
Highwaymen in England, 39, 53, 173, 192
"Histrio Mastix," by William Prynne, extract from, 156

GENERAL INDEX. 711

Hlothære, King of Kent, laws of, 5
Hoblors in Ireland forbidden to be quartered on the inhabitants, 384
Hohnstein in Saxony, house of correction at, 331 *n*.
Holland, beggars and vagrants in, 513
Holy Ghost, sale of the feathers of, 590, 666
Holy ground, the, in St. Giles's, 635
Hone, William (1779—1842), extract from the "Table Book," 637
Hooded men in Ireland forbidden to be quartered on the inhabitants, 384
Hook and Snivey, with Nix the buffer, description of, 628
Hooker or angler, the, 596, 619
Horn, rebels at the, 352, 354, 356
Horse races frequented by vagrants, 251, 268, 292, 297, 498, 501
Horses and hounds, vagabonds with, in Ireland, 393
Scotland, 339
Hospitals, abuses in the administration of, 65
attracting poor country people to London, 256
Hospitality, Anglo-Saxon, 9, 15
Irish, 377, 379
Scotch, 335, 360
Welsh, 435, 436
Hostlers in Scotland forbidden to receive vagabonds, 354, 356
Hounds, vagabonds with, in Ireland, 393
in Scotland, 339
House of Correction, 116, 125, 129, 136, 140, 153, 158, 165, 167, 174, 177, 181, 193, 197, 198, 199, 206, 207, 208, 211, 227, 231, 235, 393, 636, 671
management of, temp. Elizabeth, 116
Housebreaking implements, punishment of persons in possession of, in England, 209, 235, 236
in Scotland, 365
Houseless Poor Acts, 291, 301, 302, 310
Houseless person, penalty for feeding, in Ireland, 378
Hoveden Roger de (*fl.* 1204), extracts from, 27, 28, 30
Howel dda (*d.* 948), laws of, 429
Hubert, Archbishop of Canterbury (1193 —1205), oath of peace of, 29, 341
Hubins or devotees of St. Hubert, 521
Human banquets, Irish nature of, 375
Humfrey, Duke of Gloucester (1391—1447), and the blind impostor, 577
Huncothoe, thieves hanged at, 23
Hydromancy, prediction by, 77
"Hyeway to the Spyttelhouse," extracts from, 79, 467

IDLE and disorderly persons, punishment of, 182, 199, 202, 235, 236
Imarets, administration of the, in Turkey, 572
Impotent poor, provision for, 63, 73, 82, 92, 108
regulations for, 60, 67, 69, 73, 108, 116
In-borg, signification of, 21 *n*.
Incorrigible rogues, punishment of, 181, 199, 202, 235, 236
Industrial schools in England, 284—290
in Ireland, 426
in Scotland, 284, 372
Industry, House of, in Dublin, 397, 402, 403, 406, 407, 410, 411, 413, 416, 420
Ine, King of Wessex, laws of, 6, 7
Innkeepers in Scotland forbidden to receive vagabonds, 354, 356
Innocents, sale of the hair of the beard of, 590
Intercommunication of vagrants, 273, 299
Inverness, beggars in, 360
Ireland, slave trade with, 28
Irish beggars and vagrants in England, 64, 109, 129, 148, 149, 150, 182, 201, 202, 214, 216, 220, 225, 226, 227, 230, 232, 234, 239, 240, 245, 253, 258, 259, 260, 263, 266, 267, 269, 270, 271, 272, 273, 276, 278, 279, 281, 282, 283, 292, 305, 306, 504, 596, 534, 640, 642
in Ireland, 392, 393, 398, 399, 401—427
in the Isle of Man, 442, 454
in Guernsey, 465
in Scotland, 280, 281, 307, 372
Irish, condition of, in the twelfth century, 379
fourteenth century, 380
Irish kings, their body guards, 380
Irish men and Irish clerks, mendicant, to quit England, 64
Irishmen, Act against, 65
Irish surnames taken by the English, 384
Irish toyle, the, 594, 619
Islip, Archbishop (1349—1366), on the impecuniosity of Edward III., 53
Italian children begging in England, 303, 304
Italy, beggars and vagabonds in, 553
Iucchi, or Christianised Jews, 559

JACKMAN. *See* Jarkeman.
James I. of England, reign of, 132
II.   „   „   172
James I. of Scotland, reign of, 337
II.   „   „   339
III. „   „   340
IV.   „   „   341

GENERAL INDEX.

James V. of Scotland, reign of, 342; supposed author of the Gaberlunyie Man, 590
VI. of Scotland, reign of, 343
Jarkeman, or Jackman, the, 594, 596, 599, 604, 619
Jargon of the mendicant and vagrant, description of, 466
Jersey, laws of, 454
Jibber the kibber, signification of, 627
Jigger dubber, signification of, 627
Jingo, derivation of, 479
Jockies or strolling minstrels in Scotland, 359
John of England, reign of, 31
John of France, reign of, 518
"Jolly Beggars," the, extract from, 631
Jonson, Ben (1573—1637), extracts from the "Gypsies Metamorphosed," 603
"Jovial Crew, the, or the Merry Beggars," 612, 616, 622
Jowls, the Reverend Giles, the illuminated cobbler, 653
Jugglers, punishment of, in England, 107, 180, 199, 202
in Ireland, 392
in Scotland, 346
Jungfrauen, or pretended female lepers, 546
Justices empowered to regulate wages, 63, 66, 390

KAMMESIERERS, or begging students, 545
Kandierers, or broken-down merchants, 546
Katherans. See Catherans.
Kearns forbidden to be kept in Ireland in time of peace, 383
Keighley, Yorkshire, last use of the stocks at, 48 n.
Ken cracker, description of, 627
Kenilworth, the award of, 32
Kenneth III., reign of, 336
Kent system of repressing vagrancy, 326
Kernety, an Irish exaction, 390
Kid rig, description of the, 631
Kiddy nipper, description of the, 627
Kilmallock union beggars carried home with rejoicing, 421
Kinchin or kitchen co, 594, 596, 619
Kinchin or kitchen morte, 594, 596, 619
King's laws, penalty for sheltering the violator of, in Ireland, 379
Kitty, a name for a lock-up in Durham, 637
Klenkners, or cripples, 545
Knocker beggars, description of, 218
Knuckle, description of, 627
Korân, extracts from, 574

LABOURERS, statute of, 43, 46
apprenticing the children of, forbidden, 64
and artificers punishment of, for absenting themselves from service, 44, 48, 50, 51, 56, 59, 64, 66, 71, 102, 107, 363, 400
flocking to London, proclamation against, 51
in Ireland forbidden to become kearns, 384
statutes against, confirmed, 64, 65, 66
Lambard, William (1536—1601), on the origin of the word rogue, 471
Laneham, Robert, his letter from Kenilworth, 111
Langland, William (1332—1402), extracts from "Peers Ploughman," 54, 405, 470, 576, 587, 590
Latymer, Hugh (1485—1555), on valiant beggars, 592
Lauderdale, beggars at the funeral of the Duke of, 357
Lazar houses, 46
Lazy beggar, the, 626
Leipzig, beggars and vagabonds at, 543
Leper's alms basket and window, 46
Leprous and bedridden creatures in England, 51, 81, 83, 94, 108
Lepers in Scotland, 338, 344
Levanters, description of, 631
Licences to beg, 74, 83, 92, 95, 99, 100, 108
"Life in London," extract from, 635
Lifters, description of, 629
Lincoln's Inn, beggars in, 185, 219, 221
Linen manufacture in Ireland, regulation of wages in the, 407
Little go lotteries, setters up of, deemed rogues, 211
Liverpool, vagrancy in, 232, 240, 259, 281, 282, 283, 305
Livery, an Irish exaction, 383, 388
Livre Tournois, value of, in Guernsey, 458
Llan Cerniw, or the Cornish place, 2
Lodging houses for vagrants, 217, 226, 233, 247, 249, 276, 298, 300, 302, 313, 322, 323, 325, 331, 641, 647, 650, 661, 670
London, beggars and vagrants in, 52, 79, 97, 104, 105, 106, 115, 119, 120, 122, 125, 141, 142, 143, 144, 146, 149, 150, 155, 158, 159, 160, 167, 171, 178, 184, 187, 188, 189, 190, 191, 203, 207, 213, 214, 216—227, 253—259, 268, 275, 291, 292, 312, 313, 327, 328, 596, 598, 600, 602, 609, 610, 616, 625, 626, 627, 628, 629, 630, 631, 633, 634, 635, 636, 638, 646, 650, 651, 652, 653, 659, 664, 667

GENERAL INDEX. 713

London, Irish beggars in, 149, 214, 216, 220, 225, 226, 230, 253, 258, 292, 427, 594, 634, 662
  proclamation in 1359 against labourers flocking to, 51
  ordinances against beggars, 52, 104, 122
  punishment of beggars in, 119, 122, 155, 190, 224, 602, 636
  Statutes of, 15, 38
"London Labour and the London Poor," extracts from, 647
Long gang, description of a, 296 n.
Lord's Day, Act for the better observance of the, 147
Lossners, or liberated prisoners, 545
Lotori, or vendors of miraculous water, 559
Lottery tickets, unlicensed dealers in, deemed rogues, 211
Louis IX. (Saint Louis), reign of, 518
  XII., 521
  XIV., 521
  XV., 521
Low gaggers, description of, 630
Lowland Scotch, derivation of cant words from the, 473
Luggage, excessive, of vagrants, 242
Lulley priggers, description of, 629
Lumpers, description of, 628
Lunatics, wandering, 56
  sham, 172
Lurks of vagrants, 246, 311, 641, 648, 650, 651
Luther, Martin, on vagrants and beggars, 544, 671
Lydgate, Dan John (1373—1460), extract from the "Order of Fools," 578

"MABINOGION," or "Juvenile Amusements" (Welsh prose romances of the fourteenth century), extracts from the, 436, 438
Macaulay, Lord, on Oliver Cromwell's soldiers, 163
Magna Charta, protection afforded to the villein by, 31
Mahomet the Prophet, sayings of, 574
Malingreux, or malingerers, 520
Malmesbury, William of (1095—1143), extracts from, 9, 14, 17
Malvern system of repressing vagrancy, 327
Man, Isle of, vagrancy in, 440
  tenants and servants not to leave without licence, 442, 445
Mansfeldt, Count, levy of vagrants for his army, 146
Manufactories in Scotland, vagrants to work in, 354, 356

Manx vagrants in England, 109, 129, 182, 201, 202. 227, 278, 281
Marchers in Ireland, exactions of, 385
Margaret, sister of Edgar Atheling, charity of, 33
Mariners, freshwater. *See* Sailors, sham.
Martin's, St., in the Fields, vagrancy in, 183, 268
Mary, Queen of England, reign of, 97
Mary of Guise, regency of, in Scotland, 343
Mary, Queen of Scots, reign of. 343
Marylebone, St., vagrancy and pauperism in, 257, 292
Massalian heretics, practices of the, 483
Masterful beggars in Scotland, 339, 340, 341
Masterless men, proclamation against, 96, 97, 105
  punshment of, 106, 115
  relief to, forbidden in the Derby household, 121
Masterless vagabonds in Scotland, 355
Maundy Thursday, introduction of the custom of feeding and clothing the poor on, 52
Mayhew, Henry (b. 1812), extracts from "London Labour and the London Poor," 647
Meed money, signification of, 11 n.
Mendall, Jack, *alias* Cade, 579
Mendicant or begging friars, 82, 576, 587, 589
Mendicants in Jersey, regulations for, 455
Mendicity Society in London, 253, 327
  in Dublin, 420
Mercandiers, or broken-down tradesmen, 520
"Merry Beggars, the, or a Jovial Crew," 612
Metoposcopy, prediction by, 77
Metropolitan gypsyries, description of, 503
Minstrels in England, punishment of, 87, 107, 128, 162, 180, 199, 202
  in Scotland, 346, 359, 361
  in Wales, 35, 64
Missionaries, pseudo, 653
Moles on the body, prediction by, 78
Monasteries, suppression of, 83
  their charity, 84
Money, Scottish value of, 347 n.
Monks, wandering, 8
Monmouth, order for the apprehension of vagabonds in, 113
More, Sir Thomas (1480—1535), extracts from his "Dialogues," 110, 111, 577
Morghigeri, or bedesmen with a bell, 559

GENERAL INDEX.

Morichini, Cardinal, on mendicity, 557
Mort, the Autem, description of, 596
Mort, the Walking, 596, 599, 615
Mortimer, Sir Hugh de, charity of, 33
Morton, Earl of, Regent of Scotland, 344, 348
Mountebank, reason for being dishonoured in Ireland. 376, 381
Mummers in England deemed vagabonds, 70
   in Ireland, 381
Mümsen, or beggars in Germany, 546
Murders by vagrants, 668
Mutatori or pretended money-lenders, 558
Myddle, parish of, removal of poor in, 175

Narquois, or rufflers, 521
Nativus, or bondman, in England, 19
Navy, vagabonds in Ireland to be sent to serve in, 400, 414, 415
Napoleon I., reign of, 523, 524
National Assembly on mendicity, 523, 532
Necromancy, prediction by, 77
News-tellers in England, 96
   in Ireland, 389
"Nigelli Speculum Stultorum," extract from, 60
Night refuges for vagrants, 253, 255, 256, 258, 267, 313, 641
   profitable character of, 256
Night suppers an Irish exaction, 385
Night, usage of vagrants in the, 71, 600, 603, 613, 620, 641, 663
Night-walkers in England, punishment of, 235
   Ireland, 416
Norfolk justices, punishment of vagabonds by the, 119
Northampton, the assize of, 26
   the statute of, 41
Northbrook, John, on beggars, vagabonds, and players, 120, 134
North Wales system of repressing vagrancy, 319
Norwich, treatment of musicians at, 201
Notices of vagrants to one another, 299, 300, 313, 619, 647, 648

Oath of peace sent out by Hubert, Archbishop of Canterbury, 29
   in Scotland, 341
Obloquium, description of, 595
O'Brien's Bridge, destruction of, 388
Obscene language. *See* under Vagrants.
Obscene prints, punishment of those who exhibit, 236
Oferhyrnes, signification of, 9 *n.*
"Olio," the, by Francis Grose, extracts from, 633

Omens, signification of, 78
Ommerschans, beggars and vagabonds at, 513, 514, 515, 516
Oneirocracy, prediction by, 78
Onychomancy, prediction by, 78
Ordericus Vitalis (1075—1150), extract from, 25
Orphelins, or pretended orphans, 520
Oswald, King of Northumberland (634 —642), charity of, 12
Overseers of the poor, 128, 141
Overliers in Scotland, description of, 339 *n.*
Oxford scholars begging without licence to be punished, 73, 107
   plays at, forbidden, 192

Palatine war, levy of vagrants for the, 146
Pale, limits of the English, in Ireland, 373
Palliard, the, 476, 477, 594, 596, 597, 619
Palmistry, prediction by, 75
   punishment in England of professors of, 74, 128, 180, 199, 202, 235, 236
   in Ireland, 392
Pardoners, their practices, 562, 577, 587, 590, 591
   their punishment, 74
Pardons for felony forbidden, 41
Parker, G., extracts from "A View of Society," 627
Patent gatherers, punishment of, 128, 199, 202
Passevolants, or volunteer soldiers, 521
Patrico, patriarch co, or pattering cove, 474, 476, 595, 596, 599, 604, 615, 619
Patterers' signs, 647, 648
Pauliani, or pretended descendants of the Apostle Paul, 559
Peasant, description of, in "Peers Ploughman," 54
   by Taylor, the water poet, 150
Pedlars, their practices, 126, 128, 312, 323, 364, 369, 370, 371, 594, 619, 650
   punishment of, 95, 107, 154, 200, 202, 235, 236
Peeblesshire, beggars in, 361
Peel, Isle of Man, beggars in, 452
Pembroke, justices of, on Irish beggars, 148, 150
Peterers, description of, 629
Petty, Sir William (1623—1687), on the state of Ireland, 396
Philip and Mary, reign of, 97, 489
Physiognomy, prediction by, 75
   punishment in England of professors of, 74, 128, 180, 199, 202
   in Ireland, 392

GENERAL INDEX. 715

Piètres, or maimed beggars, 520
Picarde, nature of a, 109 n.
Pikes and pike-heads, persons found in possession of, in Ireland deemed vagabonds, 415
Pillory, the, as a punishment, 74, 522, 613
Pimlico, locality so called, 616
Pinch, description of the, 628
Pinghim, explanation of, 377 n.
Plague, the, 42, 135
Platschierers, or blind harpers, 546
Players, motives of the legislation against, 110, 134, 156, 157, 194, 196, 381 n., 615
    legislation against, in England, 70, 87, 107, 128, 134, 147, 155, 156, 157, 180, 192, 195, 199, 202, 235
    legislation against, in Ireland, 376, 381, 392
    proclamations against, 95, 97, 102
Plays forbidden on Sundays, 147
Plough alms, nature of, 14 n.
"Ploughman, Peers," extracts from. *See* Langland, William
Poachers deemed rogues and vagabonds, 209
Poland, beggars in, 568
Police. *See* Constables.
Polissons or tatterdemalions, 520
Poor Law Amendment Act, 241
Population of England, estimate of, in 1688, 177
Portugal, beggars in, 569
"Poverty, Mendicity, and Crime," extracts from, 638
Prad borrowers, description of, 628
Prigger of prancers, the, 596, 607, 619
Prigmen, or Prigs, 593, 619
Prises, Act against taking, in Ireland, 382
Proclaimed person, penalty for feeding, in Ireland, 378
Proclamation against Irish beggars in England, 149
    against beggars and vagabonds in England, 78, 95, 97, 132, 139, 160, 171
    in Scotland, 358
Proclamation against pretended soldiers, 125
Proctors, punishment of, 74, 128
Procurors, punishment of, 128
Prophecies, legislation against, 135
Prostitutes, punishment of, 115, 235, 236
    vagrant, 262, 271, 272, 295, 297
Provost marshals, 121, 125, 142, 143, 224, 618
Prynne, William (1600—1669), extract from the "Histrio-Mastix," 156
Puffing Dick, a captain of rogues, 582

Purse trick, description of the, 653
Purveyance, Acts against taking, in Ireland, 382
Pyromancy, prediction by, 78

QUACK doctors, 248, 312
Quaker, the begging, 637
Queer bird, description of, 593
Queer bit-makers, description of, 627
Queer rooster, description of, 629

RACECOURSE, rogues and vagabonds of the, 652
Races frequented by vagrants, 251, 268, 292, 297, 498, 501
Rag-sellers, the tricks of, 248
Rapparees in Ireland, 396
Read William (b. 1816), a vagrant examined by a parliamentary committee, 257
Reader merchants, description of, 629
Red cock perching on the thatch, meaning of, 539
Redesdale, description of, in 1542, 85
Refuges. *See* Night Refuges.
Regality, signification of, 341 n.
Reivers, punishment of, 340, 341
Relief of the poor, measures for the, 81, 95, 98, 99, 100, 128, 142, 147, 158
Reliquarii, or vendors of false relics, 559
Remigius, Bishop of Lincoln, on slavery, 28
Removal orders, suspension of, 215, 216
Reneurling, Aill of, meeting upon the, 441
Reports on vagrancy by Poor Law Inspectors, 261, 292
Resurrection rig, description of, 629
Revel, beggars in, 568
Rewards for the apprehension of vagrants, 166, 181, 200, 202, 230, 231, 235
Rhonabwy, the dream of, 436
Rialte, signification of, 341 n.
Ribalds, the banishment of, 52
Richard I., reign of, 29
    II.,   "   56
    III.,   "   67
Rich beggars, 660
Riffaudés, or sufferers by fire (French demanders for glimmer), 520
Ring-faller or dropper, the, 248, 505, 595, 630
Ripper of fish, signification of, 606 n.
Robert II., reign of, 337
Roberdesmen, 42, 52, 58, 580
Roberts, Hugh, a captain of rogues, 580
Robbery in Anglo-Saxon times, 14
Robbery by organised bands, 32, 37

716 GENERAL INDEX.

Rochester, wreck of the, 260
Rôdeurs de filles, or prowlers for girls, 518
Roger de Hoveden, extracts from, 27, 28, 30
Roger le Skirmisour indicted, 39
Rogue, the description of, 581, 596, 597, 603
   the wild description of, 594, 596, 597
   derivation of the word, 471
Rogues, captains of; Bluebeard, 579; Hugh Roberts, 580; Jenkin Cowdiddle, 580; Spising, 581; Puffing Dick, 582; Lawrence Crosbiter, 583: Skelton, 584; Cock Lorrell, 584; Giles Hather, 585
   march, the, 331
   punishment of, 53, 103, 109, 115, 117, 119, 129, 133, 136, 137, 140, 148, 153, 154, 155, 158, 160, 161, 162, 164, 165, 166, 167, 179, 186, 199, 202, 203, 205, 209, 210, 211, 212, 235, 236, 238, 392
Rolle, Richard (d. 1349), on charity, 44
Romany, derivation of cant words from the, 475, 479
Rowlands, Samuel (1570—1625), extracts from the works of, 466, 485, 489, 579, 601, 602
"Roxburghe Ballads," extract from the, 609
Royal scamp, description of the, 627
Ruffeler, description of the, 593
Ruffelers, punishment of, 82
Ruffiti, or sufferers by fire (Italian demanders for glimmer), 564
Rum-drag, description of the, 630
   snoozer, description of the, 628
Runnagates' race, the, by Samuel Rowlands, 579
Running snavel, description of the, 631
Rush, description of the, 629
Rushton, Mr., evidence on vagrancy, 259, 281
Russia, beggars and vagrants in, 566

SACHENTEGES, torture by, 24
Sailors begging in England to carry certificate, 131, 180, 200, 202, 212, 235, 236
   Scotland, 346
   forbidden to beg, 130, 131
   sham, 127, 220, 246, 248, 250, 311, 593, 596, 598, 610, 619, 634, 641, 664
Salt, consumption of, by Irish vagrants, 272
Salters in Dublin, regulation of the wages of, 409

Salt-pans, beggars and vagabonds in Scotland to work in, 351, 357, 364
Saunders, Richard, extract from "Palmistry," 75
Savages, vagrants described as living as, 154, 350, 359
Saxe-Coburg and Gotha, mendicity in, 542
Sbrici, or fugitive captives, 564
Scholars of the universities in England not to beg without a licence, 60, 67, 68, 73, 107
   in Scotland, 346
Scotland, English slaves in, 28
   native slaves in, 351
   beggars and vagrants in, 334
   former state of agriculture in, 360
Scotch, incursions of the, into England, 25, 28, 33
   Lowland, derivation of cant words from the, 473
   scholars begging in England, 62
Scothala, or Scotteshale, a forest exaction, 31, 184
Scott, John (1730—1783), on workhouses, 208
   Walter, a deaf and dumb impostor, 653
Scottish beggars and vagrants in England, 129, 227, 239, 242, 258, 278
   beggars and vagrants in the Isle of Man, 442
   bondmen, 334, 335
   border, condition of, in 1542, 85
   money, value of, 347 n.
Screpall, explanation of, 377 n.
Schwanfelders, or naked beggars, or shallow coves, 545
Schweigers, or jaundiced persons, 546
Screevers, or writers of begging letters and petitions, 649
Sea, children to be apprenticed to the, 179
   vagabonds to be sent to, 180, 400, 414, 415
Seffers, or persons afflicted with sores, 546
Senchus Mor, the, or Great Law of Ireland, 374
Servants quitting service before the time agreed on to be imprisoned, 44, 48, 50, 51, 56, 59, 64, 66, 102, 107, 363, 401, 445, 450
   regulation of the wages of, 43, 44, 47, 48, 50, 51, 56, 59, 63, 65, 66, 71, 101, 102, 154, 362, 363, 364, 390, 405, 408, 409, 443, 444, 445, 446, 447, 449, 450
   jury of, in the Isle of Man, 445, 449
   not to quit the Isle of Man without licence, 442, 445

GENERAL INDEX. 717

Sessings, an Irish exaction, 390
Settlement, laws of, 164, 172, 173, 215, 306
Shakspere (1564—1616), extracts from, 120 n., 341, 475, 476, 577, 607
 use of the name of God by, 134
Sham leggers, description of, 630
Sheep, Act limiting the number to be kept, 79
Sheep-stealers, 126, 630
Shipmen pretending losses at sea to be punished, 74, 107, 129
Shipwrecked mariners begging in England to carry certificates, 67, 68
 Scotland, 346, 347
Shipwrights in Dublin, regulation of the wages of, 408
Shoulers, or wandering beggars in Ireland, 425
Signs of patterers and tramps, 619, 647, 648
Silures, origin of the, 1
Simpcox, the blind impostor at St. Alban's, 577
Skelaghes, or news-tellers, in Ireland, 389
Skelton, John, the poet (1460—1529), cant words in the works of, 477
 and the beggar, 578
 a captain of rogues, 584
Slaves, manumission of, in England, 17, 33, 88, 113
 beggars and vagabonds in England, to serve as, 90
 in Scotland, 344, 345, 347, 350, 351, 354, 355
Snakesman, the little, description of, 628
Sneaks, morning, evening, and upright, description of, 628
Snitchers, description of, 628
Soke, right nature of, 11 n.
Soldiers begging to carry certificates, 67, 130, 180, 200, 202, 212, 235, 236
 discharged, becoming vagrants, 308, 309, 310
 English plundering their countrymen, 67
 forbidden to beg, 130, 131
 levy of vagrants as, 146
 proclamation against pretended, 125
 sham, 81, 246, 595, 608, 610, 613, 615, 634, 656
 vagabonds in Scotland to serve as, 358
Song of the beggar, the, 607
Songs, beggars', 601, 602, 604, 606, 607, 608, 609, 610, 611, 612, 613, 614, 616, 618, 620, 622, 623
Sorners in Scotland, 337, 339, 340, 341, 346, 352
Sorning, nature of, 16, 337

Soup kitchens promoters of vagrancy 313
Spenser, Edmund (1553—1599), extract from the "View of the State of Ireland," 394
Spettrini, or false priests, or fraters, 559
Spiritati, or demoniacs, 564
Spising, a captain of rogues, 581
Stabulers, or bread gatherers, 545
Staf-strikers, or cudgel-players, 53
Stage-players. See Players.
Stanley's remedy for beggars, thieves, pickpockets, &c., 136
Star Chamber, proceedings in, 122
Star the glaze, to, meaning of, 629
Statistics of vagrancy and mendicity in England, 178, 206, 213, 216, 225, 231, 232, 239, 240, 241, 252, 253, 259, 260, 263, 265, 280, 281, 282, 290, 302, 318, 320, 325, 673
 Ireland, 413, 417, 427
 Scotland, 367—371
Stephen, reign of, 23
Stirpes or families in Ireland to justify all idle persons of their surname, 391
Stocach, signification of, 394
Stocks, punishment of the, 48, 51, 52, 59, 64, 67, 68, 73, 82, 108, 150, 176, 401, 463, 488, 615, 624
Strabo on British slaves, 3, 115
Strafford, Earl of (1593—1641), Lord Deputy of Ireland, 392
Strangers in Jersey, treatment of, 456
 Guernsey, 458, 461, 462
Street sellers, beggar, 650
Students, wandering, forbidden to carry arms, 349
Sturdy beggars. See Beggars.
Suntvegers, or pretended man-slayers, 546
Suppers, a form of Irish exaction, 385, 393
Supplication for the beggars by Simon Fish, 72
Surnames, Irish, taken by the English, 384
Swadder, or pedlar, the, 596, 619
Swearing and cursing, Act against, 434
Sweden, beggars and vagabonds in, 507
Sweep, delight of a poor, on going to prison, 638
Sweetners, description of, 625
Swigman, the, 594, 619

TAILORS, journeymen, in Dublin, regulation of the wages of, 408
Tallages in Ireland, nature of, 390
Tanist, meaning of the term, 390
Taylor, John, the water poet (1580—1654), description of the ploughman in 1630, 150

GENERAL INDEX.

Tale letters forbidden in Ireland, 390
Scotland, 346
Tavern-keepers in Jersey, regulations for, 457
Tenant ale forbidden, 79
Tenants and servants not to be taken out of the Isle of Man without licence, 442, 445
Tenements, small, forbidden in the city, 122, 139
Terrible statute, the. 102, 490, 603
Testatori, or pretended testators, 560
Thames, ill disposed frequenters of the, deemed rogues, 210
Theodore, Archbishop of Canterbury, ordinances of, 8, 9, 21
Theow, the, 4, 19
Thieves, foreign, in England, 22
Thieves hanged at Huncothoe, 23
in Ireland, to be killed by any liege man, 387
Thimble rig, description of, 275 n.
Three-card man, description of the, 652
Tick bit and sack diver, meaning of, 631
Tiler, Wat, the rebellion of, 57
Tinker, description of a drunken, 594, 596, 598, 603
Tinkers, 95, 126, 323, 371, 504, 528, 584, 594, 617, 638
in Scotland, 371
punishment of, 95, 107, 154
Tokens issued by James I., 145
Tolliban rig, description of, 629
Tories in Ireland, 396, 399
Toulmin, A. H., extract from "Rogues and Vagabonds of the Racecourse," 652
Tours, second council of, 517
Towns, precautions for preventing robbery in, 36, 38
Trades unions, their allowance to travelling members, 314
Tramps. *See* Vagabonds.
Tramps, by Charles Dickens, 646
Transportation of vagrants in England, 132, 141, 143, 182, 185
in Ireland, 395, 399
in Scotland, 356
Traps, signification of, 630
Trencher, signification of, 45
Troll Hazard of Tritrace, description of, 595
Trone, ears of vagabonds in Scotland to be nailed to the, 339
Trudging or trugging house, 583
Turner, James, a common beggar, 626
Turner, William (1515—1568), extracts from his new booke of spirituall physick, 98
Twopenny-post beggars, description of, 218

Ubern Sönzer ganger, or pretended noblemen and knights, 546
Umbrella menders, 249, 295, 323, 528
University scholars in England not to beg without licence, 60, 67, 68, 73, 107
in Scotland, 346
Universities, plays at the, forbidden, 192
Uprightman, description of, 583, 593, 596

"Vagabondiana," by J. T. Smith, extracts from, 634
Vagabonds in England, 164, 165, 166, 179, 186, 190, 197, 199, 202, 203, 235, 236, 238, 579
Vagabonds in England, apprehension of, 112
banishment of, 133
conveyance of, 178, 180, 207, 209, 210, 211, 212, 215, 216, 224, 225, 229, 230, 231, 241
conduct of, in casual wards, 256, 257, 269, 274, 295, 296
female, 262, 263, 271, 295, 297
harbourage of, 53
letter of Mr. Hext regarding, in 1596, 125, 491
in London. *See* London.
punishment of, 59, 67, 68, 73, 81, 90, 94, 99, 100, 101, 106, 117, 119, 120, 121, 128, 133, 135, 140, 148, 153, 158, 159, 160, 161, 162
proclamations against. *See* Proclamations.
relief to, forbidden in the Derby household, 121
to be sent to Virginia, 141, 143, 144
Vagabonds in foreign countries. *See* Beggars Abroad.
in Guernsey, 461, 464
in Ireland, 375, 379, 381, 384, 385—390, 391—395, 398
in the Isle of Man, 442, 448
in Jersey, 457
in Scotland, 336—361, 364—372
the fraternity of, extracts from, 593
Vagiereren, or exorcisers, 545
Vagrancy, county systems for the repression of, 318—327
discussion on, in the House of Commons, 307
increase of, at various periods, 144, 241, 251, 266, 268, 308
"Vagrant impostors," by Francis Grose, 633
lurks. *See* Lurks.
removal of the, in Ireland, 375
Vagrants, average ages of, 298
their conduct at night, 71, 80, 217, 247, 257, 263, 294, 295, 296, 600, 620

GENERAL INDEX. 719

Vagrants, frequently thieves, 245, 257, 258, 265, 276, 293, 318, 580, 593, 596, 602, 605, 607, 614, 619, 620, 623, 626, 627, 630, 639, 658
   intercommunication of, 273, 299, 300, 313
   obscene language of, 223, 258, 263, 269, 294, 295, 296, 635
   proportion who are habitual, 264, 265, 296
   statistics of. *See* Statistics.
Veenhuizen, beggars and vagabonds at, 513, 514, 515
Venedotian code, laws of the, 434
Veranerins, or Christianised Jewesses, 546
Vergognosi, or persons ashamed to beg, 559
Viage, signification of, 109 *n*.
Victoria, Queen, reign of, 243
Vienna, beggars and vagabonds in, 547
Villanus, or bondman, 19
Villeins under Richard II., 56
   manumission of, 88, 113
Violator of the king's laws, penalty for sheltering, in Ireland, 379
Virginia, poor to be sent to, 141, 143, 144
Visors, persons wearing, punishable as vagabonds, 70
Vocabulary of cant, 468
Voppers, or demoniacs, 545

WAGES in the reign of Edward III., 48
   regulation of, in England, 48, 63, 66, 68, 71, 101
   Ireland, 390
   Isle of Man, 447, 448, 449, 450
   Scotland, 362, 363, 364
Wainage of the villein, 31
Wales, arrival of the Cymry in, 2
   extortion and oppression of the people of, 66
   condition of the Welsh border in the time of Edward I., 36
   Irish vagrants in, 148, 150, 270, 271
   laws and institutes of, 429
   North, system of repressing vagrancy in, 319
   the statute of, 34
Walsingham, Thomas (*b*. 1410), extract from "Historia brevis," 53
Wargus, the, or outcast, 22
Washman, description of the, 594
Wastours. *See* Westours.
Waters, Tom, his robbery of gypsies, 493
Watson, Henry, extract from the "Ship of Fools," 589

Watson, sheriff, on vagrancy in Scotland, 366
Waytingas, Scottish, 335
Welsh, Acts to repress the forays of, 64
   bards and idlers, 35, 63, 64, 439
   derivation of cant words from the, 473
   expulsion of, from England, 27
   incursions of, in England, 19, 25
Wem, removal of poor in, 175
Wendover, Roger of (*d*. 1237), extract from, 25
Wentworth, Earl of Strafford, Lord Deputy of Ireland, 392
Wēr, signification of, 7 *n*.
West Indies, banishment of vagabonds to the, 133, 401
Westour, or Gwestwr, the, 35, 42, 63, 64, 439
Wheedle, origin of the word, 13
Whipjack, the, 593, 596, 598, 619
Whipping of beggars and vagabonds in England, 57, 73, 78, 82, 83, 101, 106, 108, 116, 117, 118, 119, 120, 121, 129, 137, 140, 150, 170, 176, 181, 200, 202, 205, 227, 597, 613, 623, 639
   in Ireland, 401, 408
Whipping-posts, 150, 176, 205
Wickliffe, John, (1324 — 1384), on begging friars, 481
Wihtræd, King of Kent, reign of, 7
William the Conqueror, reign of, 18
   II., reign of, 20
   III., reign of, 173, 396; and remarks on the poor, 178
   IV., reign of, 240
Wilts, system of repressing vagrancy in, 327
Winchester, statute of, 36
   William, Bishop of, council held by, 25
Witchcraft, legislation against, 134, 135
Wite, signification of, 6 *n*.
Wite-theow, the, 7
Wives, punishment for desertion of, in England, 180, 185, 199, 202, 235, 236
   in Ireland, 419, 421
Wodsworth, W. D., on Irish vagabonds, 398
Wogan, Sir John, Lord Justice of Ireland, 382
Wolves, rewards for the destruction of, in Ireland, 395
Wood, spoilers of, punishable as rogues, 167, 204, 205
Workhouses, advantages of, 168, 176, 188, 189
   bad state of, 191, 208

Working classes, earnings of the, 307, 317
Workmen quitting service before time agreed upon to be imprisoned, *See* Labourers.
Wounds or deformities, punishment for the exposure of, in England, 235, 236
  in Scotland, 365
Wretchcock, signification of, 604

Wright, J. Hornsby (1817—1885), extract from the "Confessions of an old Almsgiver," 651
Wulfstan, Bishop of Worcester, on the foreign slave trade, 28

YARDING, nature of, in the Isle of Man, 445
York, Richard, Duke of, Lieutenant of Ireland, 385

PATTERSON SMITH REPRINT SERIES IN CRIMINOLOGY, LAW ENFORCEMENT, AND SOCIAL PROBLEMS

1. *Lewis: *The Development of American Prisons and Prison Customs, 1776–1845*
2. Carpenter: *Reformatory Prison Discipline*
3. Brace: *The Dangerous Classes of New York*
4. *Dix: *Remarks on Prisons and Prison Discipline in the United States*
5. Bruce et al.: *The Workings of the Indeterminate-Sentence Law and the Parole System in Illinois*
6. *Wickersham Commission: *Complete Reports, Including the Mooney-Billings Report.* 14 vols.
7. Livingston: *Complete Works on Criminal Jurisprudence.* 2 vols.
8. Cleveland Foundation: *Criminal Justice in Cleveland*
9. Illinois Association for Criminal Justice: *The Illinois Crime Survey*
10. Missouri Association for Criminal Justice: *The Missouri Crime Survey*
11. Aschaffenburg: *Crime and Its Repression*
12. Garofalo: *Criminology*
13. Gross: *Criminal Psychology*
14. Lombroso: *Crime, Its Causes and Remedies*
15. Saleilles: *The Individualization of Punishment*
16. Tarde: *Penal Philosophy*
17. McKelvey: *American Prisons*
18. Sanders: *Negro Child Welfare in North Carolina*
19. Pike: *A History of Crime in England.* 2 vols.
20. Herring: *Welfare Work in Mill Villages*
21. Barnes: *The Evolution of Penology in Pennsylvania*
22. Puckett: *Folk Beliefs of the Southern Negro*
23. Fernald et al.: *A Study of Women Delinquents in New York State*
24. Wines: *The State of Prisons and of Child-Saving Institutions*
25. *Raper: *The Tragedy of Lynching*
26. Thomas: *The Unadjusted Girl*
27. Jorns: *The Quakers as Pioneers in Social Work*
28. Owings: *Women Police*
29. Woolston: *Prostitution in the United States*
30. Flexner: *Prostitution in Europe*
31. Kelso: *The History of Public Poor Relief in Massachusetts, 1820–1920*
32. Spivak: *Georgia Nigger*
33. Earle: *Curious Punishments of Bygone Days*
34. Bonger: *Race and Crime*
35. Fishman: *Crucibles of Crime*
36. Brearley: *Homicide in the United States*
37. *Graper: *American Police Administration*
38. Hichborn: *"The System"*
39. Steiner & Brown: *The North Carolina Chain Gang*
40. Cherrington: *The Evolution of Prohibition in the United States of America*
41. Colquhoun: *A Treatise on the Commerce and Police of the River Thames*
42. Colquhoun: *A Treatise on the Police of the Metropolis*
43. Abrahamsen: *Crime and the Human Mind*
44. Schneider: *The History of Public Welfare in New York State, 1609–1866*
45. Schneider & Deutsch: *The History of Public Welfare in New York State, 1867–1940*
46. Crapsey: *The Nether Side of New York*
47. Young: *Social Treatment in Probation and Delinquency*
48. Quinn: *Gambling and Gambling Devices*
49. McCord & McCord: *Origins of Crime*
50. Worthington & Topping: *Specialized Courts Dealing with Sex Delinquency*
51. Asbury: *Sucker's Progress*
52. Kneeland: *Commercialized Prostitution in New York City*

* new material added

PATTERSON SMITH REPRINT SERIES IN
CRIMINOLOGY, LAW ENFORCEMENT, AND SOCIAL PROBLEMS

53. *Fosdick: *American Police Systems*
54. *Fosdick: *European Police Systems*
55. *Shay: *Judge Lynch: His First Hundred Years*
56. Barnes: *The Repression of Crime*
57. †Cable: *The Silent South*
58. Kammerer: *The Unmarried Mother*
59. Doshay: *The Boy Sex Offender and His Later Career*
60. Spaulding: *An Experimental Study of Psychopathic Delinquent Women*
61. Brockway: *Fifty Years of Prison Service*
62. Lawes: *Man's Judgment of Death*
63. Healy & Healy: *Pathological Lying, Accusation, and Swindling*
64. Smith: *The State Police*
65. Adams: *Interracial Marriage in Hawaii*
66. *Halpern: *A Decade of Probation*
67. Tappan: *Delinquent Girls in Court*
68. Alexander & Healy: *Roots of Crime*
69. *Healy & Bronner: *Delinquents and Criminals*
70. Cutler: *Lynch-Law*
71. Gillin: *Taming the Criminal*
72. Osborne: *Within Prison Walls*
73. Ashton: *The History of Gambling in England*
74. Whitlock: *On the Enforcement of Law in Cities*
75. Goldberg: *Child Offenders*
76. *Cressey: *The Taxi-Dance Hall*
77. Riis: *The Battle with the Slum*
78. Larson: *Lying and Its Detection*
79. Comstock: *Frauds Exposed*
80. Carpenter: *Our Convicts.* 2 vols. in one
81. †Horn: *Invisible Empire: The Story of the Ku Klux Klan, 1866–1871*
82. Faris et al.: *Intelligent Philanthropy*
83. Robinson: *History and Organization of Criminal Statistics in the U. S.*
84. Reckless: *Vice in Chicago*
85. Healy: *The Individual Delinquent*
86. *Bogen: *Jewish Philanthropy*
87. *Clinard: *The Black Market: A Study of White Collar Crime*
88. Healy: *Mental Conflicts and Misconduct*
89. Citizens' Police Committee: *Chicago Police Problems*
90. *Clay: *The Prison Chaplain*
91. *Peirce: *A Half Century with Juvenile Delinquents*
92. *Richmond: *Friendly Visiting Among the Poor*
93. Brasol: *Elements of Crime*
94. Strong: *Public Welfare Administration in Canada*
95. Beard: *Juvenile Probation*
96. Steinmetz: *The Gaming Table.* 2 vols.
97. *Crawford: *Report on the Penitentiaries of the United States*
98. *Kuhlman: *A Guide to Material on Crime and Criminal Justice*
99. Culver: *Bibliography of Crime and Criminal Justice, 1927–1931*
100. Culver: *Bibliography of Crime and Criminal Justice, 1932–1937*
101. Tompkins: *Administration of Criminal Justice, 1938–1948*
102. Tompkins: *Administration of Criminal Justice, 1949–1956*
103. Cumming: *Bibliography Dealing with Crime and Cognate Subjects*
104. *Addams et al.: *Philanthropy and Social Progress*
105. *Powell: *The American Siberia*
106. *Carpenter: *Reformatory Schools*
107. *Carpenter: *Juvenile Delinquents*
108. *Montague: *Sixty Years in Waifdom*

* new material added   † new edition, revised or enlarged

PATTERSON SMITH REPRINT SERIES IN CRIMINOLOGY, LAW ENFORCEMENT, AND SOCIAL PROBLEMS

109. *Mannheim: *Juvenile Delinquency in an English Middletown*
110. Semmes: *Crime and Punishment in Early Maryland*
111. *National Conference of Charities & Correction: *History of Child Saving in the United States*
112. †Barnes: *The Story of Punishment*
113. Phillipson: *Three Criminal Law Reformers*
114. *Drähms: *The Criminal*
115. *Terry & Pellens: *The Opium Problem*
116. *Ewing: *The Morality of Punishment*
117. †Mannheim: *Group Problems in Crime and Punishment*
118. *Michael & Adler: *Crime, Law and Social Science*
119. *Lee: *A History of Police in England*
120. †Schafer: *Compensation and Restitution to Victims of Crime*
121. †Mannheim: *Pioneers in Criminology*
122. Goebel & Naughton: *Law Enforcement in Colonial New York*
123. *Savage: *Police Records and Recollections*
124. Ives: *A History of Penal Methods*
125. *Bernard (ed.): *Americanization Studies*. 10 vols.:
    Thompson: *Schooling of the Immigrant*
    Daniels: *America via the Neighborhood*
    Thomas: *Old World Traits Transplanted*
    Speek: *A Stake in the Land*
    Davis: *Immigrant Health and the Community*
    Breckinridge: *New Homes for Old*
    Park: *The Immigrant Press and Its Control*
    Gavit: *Americans by Choice*
    Claghorn: *The Immigrant's Day in Court*
    Leiserson: *Adjusting Immigrant and Industry*
126. *Dai: *Opium Addiction in Chicago*
127. *Costello: *Our Police Protectors*
128. *Wade: *A Treatise on the Police and Crimes of the Metropolis*
129. *Robison: *Can Delinquency Be Measured?*
130. *Augustus: *John Augustus, First Probation Officer*
131. *Vollmer: *The Police and Modern Society*
132. Jessel & Horr: *Bibliographies of Works on Playing Cards and Gaming*
133. *Walling: *Recollections of a New York Chief of Police;* & Kaufmann: *Supplement on the Denver Police*
134. *Lombroso-Ferrero: *Criminal Man*
135. *Howard: *Prisons and Lazarettos*. 2 vols.:
    The State of the Prisons in England and Wales
    An Account of the Principal Lazarettos in Europe
136. *Fitzgerald: *Chronicles of Bow Street Police-Office*. 2 vols. in one
137. *Goring: *The English Convict*
138. Ribton-Turner: *A History of Vagrants and Vagrancy*
139. *Smith: *Justice and the Poor*
140. *Willard: *Tramping with Tramps*
141. *Fuld: *Police Administration*
142. *Booth: *In Darkest England and the Way Out*
143. *Darrow: *Crime, Its Cause and Treatment*
144. *Henderson (ed.): *Correction and Prevention*. 4 vols.:
    Henderson (ed.): *Prison Reform;* & Smith: *Criminal Law in the U. S.*
    Henderson (ed.): *Penal and Reformatory Institutions*
    Henderson: *Preventive Agencies and Methods*
    Hart: *Preventive Treatment of Neglected Children*
145. *Carpenter: *The Life and Work of Mary Carpenter*
146. *Proal: *Political Crime*

* new material added   † new edition, revised or enlarged

PATTERSON SMITH REPRINT SERIES IN CRIMINOLOGY, LAW ENFORCEMENT, AND SOCIAL PROBLEMS

147. *von Hentig: *Punishment*
148. *Darrow: *Resist Not Evil*
149. Grünhut: *Penal Reform*
150. *Guthrie: *Seed-Time and Harvest of Ragged Schools*
151. *Sprogle: *The Philadelphia Police*
152. †Blumer & Hauser: *Movies, Delinquency, and Crime*
153. *Calvert: *Capital Punishment in the Twentieth Century* & *The Death Penalty Enquiry*
154. *Pinkerton: *Thirty Years a Detective*
155. *Prison Discipline Society [Boston] Reports 1826–1854.* 4 vols.
156. *Woods (ed.): *The City Wilderness*
157. *Woods (ed.): *Americans in Process*
158. *Woods: *The Neighborhood in Nation-Building*
159. Powers & Witmer: *An Experiment in the Prevention of Delinquency*
160. *Andrews: *Bygone Punishments*
161. *Debs: *Walls and Bars*
162. *Hill: *Children of the State*
163. Stewart: *The Philanthropic Work of Josephine Shaw Lowell*
164. *Flinn: *History of the Chicago Police*
165. *Constabulary Force Commissioners: *First Report*
166. *Eldridge & Watts: *Our Rival the Rascal*
167. *Oppenheimer: *The Rationale of Punishment*
168. *Fenner: *Raising the Veil*
169. *Hill: *Suggestions for the Repression of Crime*
170. *Bleackley: *The Hangmen of England*
171. *Altgeld: *Complete Works*
172. *Watson: *The Charity Organization Movement in the United States*
173. *Woods et al.: *The Poor in Great Cities*
174. *Sampson: *Rationale of Crime*
175. *Folsom: *Our Police [Baltimore]*
176. Schmidt: *A Hangman's Diary*
177. *Osborne: *Society and Prisons*
178. *Sutton: *The New York Tombs*
179. *Morrison: *Juvenile Offenders*
180. *Parry: *The History of Torture in England*
181. Henderson: *Modern Methods of Charity*
182. Larned: *The Life and Work of William Pryor Letchworth*
183. *Coleman: *Humane Society Leaders in America*
184. *Duke: *Celebrated Criminal Cases of America*
185. *George: *The Junior Republic*
186. *Hackwood: *The Good Old Times*
187. *Fry & Cresswell: *Memoir of the Life of Elizabeth Fry.* 2 vols. in one
188. *McAdoo: *Guarding a Great City*
189. *Gray: *Prison Discipline in America*
190. *Robinson: *Should Prisoners Work?*
191. *Mayo: *Justice to All*
192. *Winter: *The New York State Reformatory in Elmira*
193. *Green: *Gambling Exposed*
194. *Woods: *Policeman and Public*
195. *Johnson: *Adventures in Social Welfare*
196. *Wines & Dwight: *Report on the Prisons and Reformatories of the United States and Canada*
197. *Salt: *The Flogging Craze*
198. *MacDonald: *Abnormal Man*
199. *Shalloo: *Private Police*
200. *Ellis: *The Criminal*

* new material added † new edition, revised or enlarged

WAYNESBURG COLLEGE LIBRARY,
WAYNESBURG, PA.